United States
Presidential Elections,
1788–1860

United States Presidential Elections, 1788–1860

The Official Results by County and State

M<small>ICHAEL</small> J. D<small>UBIN</small>

McFarland & Company, Inc., Publishers
Jefferson, North Carolina, and London

Library of Congress Cataloguing-in-Publication Data

Dubin, Michael J.
United States presidential elections, 1788–1860 : the official
results by county and state / Michael J. Dubin.
p.   cm.
Includes bibliographical references and indexes.
ISBN 0-7864-1017-5 (library binding : 50# alkaline paper) ∞
1. Presidents — United States — Election — Statistics.
2. United States — Politics and government —1789–1815.
3. United States — Politics and government —1815–1861.   I. Title.
JK524 .D778   2002   324.973 — dc21   2001054442

British Library cataloguing data are available

Manufactured in the United States of America

*McFarland & Company, Inc., Publishers
Box 611, Jefferson, North Carolina 28640
www.mcfarlandpub.com*

To Joe, Nancy, Jay and Jeffrey

TABLE OF CONTENTS

INTRODUCTION

Generally accepted compilations of the popular vote for presidential elections date back to 1824. Curiously little is known about the election returns before then.

The idea of compiling such data both on a state and county level was the initial purpose of this volume. However, in doing the research I found that no definitive set of returns by county exists for the elections from 1824 through 1832 either. So the research was extended to cover those elections.

Even though W. Dean Burnham published a nearly complete set of presidential returns by state and county from 1836 through 1892 (*Presidential Ballots 1836–1892*, Baltimore: Johns Hopkins University Press, 1955), I decided to extend my efforts through the historic election of 1860 to end the volume at a significant point in our history and encompass the first two-party systems and the emergence of the present system.

Unfortunately, finding all returns, even at the statewide level not to mention on a county level, for every election, particularly prior to 1824, has been impossible. Nevertheless, I offer the reader what I believe to be the most comprehensive and accurate set of returns for the presidential election for the period from 1788, the first, through 1860.

I am particularly indebted to Philip Lampi of Gilbertville, Massachusetts, who graciously let me use his definitive collection of pre–1824 election returns. The use of these materials has greatly enhanced both the scope of the information presented and the accuracy of the data. Without his generosity this volume would be substantially less complete.

To the librarians of many state archives, historical societies, and other libraries who facilitated my search for returns and also aided me in obtaining material via interlibrary loan, which reduced the need for what would have been endless trips to out-of-state institutions, I offer great thanks. My gratitude goes especially to the interlibrary loan departments of the Glendale and Phoenix public libraries in Arizona, who filled my myriad requests for material promptly and efficiently.

THE CHOOSING OF
PRESIDENTIAL ELECTORS

Originally the individuals chosen to serve as presidential electors were to exercise independent judgment in determining who were to be the president and vice president. The emergence of political parties soon put an end to that practice. By the third presidential election, in 1796, electors had become agents of the parties, selected by them and pledged in advance to vote for their nominees. Electors became the constitutional surrogates of the candidate.

As the phenomenon of the direct or popular election of electors grew,* the idea that the people elected the president gained prominence; campaigns were organized around the party's candidate and the electors became merely instruments of the voter. Yet, constitutionally, nothing had changed: the electors still elected the president and vice president.

In 1800, the parties further institutionalized the ceremonial role of electors by holding a national party caucus and formally selecting candidates.† It was the role of the parties in the election of 1800 that produced the tie between Jefferson and Burr that led to the 12th Amendment to the Constitution, providing for separate votes for president and vice president. By 1836, all the states but one provided for the popular election of electors by statewide vote.

A voter could and occasionally did vote for electors representing different candidates. In very close elections this resulted in electors being chosen who were pledged to different candidates, thus splitting a state's electoral vote; Pennsylvania in 1796 and both New Jersey and Virginia in 1860 were examples.

The vote had to be compiled individually for each prospective elector, producing a different total for each in most cases. Newspapers, however, usually reported the total for only one electoral candidate per slate.

Until now the vote for electors (the "popular vote" or, as it is often but erroneously called, the vote for president) in elections prior to 1824 has been a mystery, or at least never

the subject of any systematic compilation. Several factors no doubt have contributed to this. To begin with, many states did not provide for the popular election of electors, and even in those states that did, either returns were not always complete or documentary records of them have not survived in their entirety, even at the state level. Additionally some of the elections of this era were at best nominally contested (1816, 1820) or void of partisan competition (1788/9, 1792). Notwithstanding these problems, the returns presented do offer insight into the politics of the early period of the Republic and serve a historical purpose.

In 1824, three-quarters of the states (18 of 24) provided for the popular election of electors, the highest percentage up to that time. This coincided with the first truly contested election in 12 years. No doubt the combination of these events produced the first full compilation nationally of the popular vote for president.

Along with the growth of the popular election of electors came the eventual adoption of a uniform method for such voting. Until 1836, one or more states divided their territory into districts, often like Congressional districts, and the voter chose usually one elector, instead of the current almost universal method of a statewide election of all electors. (See "Methods of Choosing Presidential Electors," next page.)

The reader will note that from time to time there have been some unusual electoral arrangements; fusion tickets, different vice presidential candidates, different candidates of the same party running in different states. One should keep in mind that the candidates for electors are chosen at the state, not the national, level and the national nominee was subject to the approval of individual state parties. Perhaps the best example of state parties' pursuing separate policies regarding electoral slates happened in the election of 1860. That election saw three states with fusion electoral

---

*The number and percentage of states that provided for the popular election of electors changed with every election. In 1800, only five states provided for this type of election of electors, representing the smallest number and lowest percentage in history. Not until 1820 did the trend move in an upward direction with 15 states providing for popular election; 18 did in 1824; and by 1828, all but two chose electors by popular vote. The high point prior to 1824 was in 1804 when 11 of 16 states provided for the popular election of electors; this was also the first time that a majority of the states did.

†Neither Adams nor Jefferson were formally nominated in 1796. However, electoral slates pledged to one or the other candidates were well advertised in the states that provided for the direct election of electors. In 1800, both parties inaugurated the Congressional caucus that served as the national nomination vehicle during the remainder of the Democratic-Republican and Federalist era.

slates, two of them involving three candidates and the other, two candidates. Even as recently as 1960, we have examples of where electors were not pledged to support the national nominee.*

Methods of Choosing Presidential Electors (1788–1832)

State	1788/9	1792	1796	1800	1804	1808	1812	1816	1820	1824	1828	1832
Connecticut	L	L	L	L	L	L	L	L	PV-S	PV-S	PV-S	PV-S
Delaware	PV-D	L	L	L	L	L	L	L	L	L	L	PV-S
Georgia	L	L	PV-S	L	L	L	L	L	L	L	PV-S	PV-S
Maryland	PV-S	PV-S	PV-D	PV-D	PV-D	PV-D	PV-D	PV-D	PV-D	PV-D	PV-D	PV-D
Massachusetts	L-PV-d	PV-d-L	PV-d-L+	L	PV-S	L	PV-D	L	PV-S	PV-S	PV-S	PV-S
New Hampshire	PV-s-L	PV-S	PV-s-L	L	PV-S	PV-S	PV-S	PV-S	PV-S	PV-S	PV-S	PV-S
New Jersey	L	L	L	L	PV-S	PV-S	L	PV-S	PV-S	PV-S	PV-S	PV-S
Pennsylvania	PV-S	PV-S	PV-S	L	PV-S	PV-S	PV-S	PV-S	PV-S	PV-S	PV-S	PV-S
South Carolina	L	L	L	L	L	L	L	L	L	L	L	L
Virginia	PV-D	PV-D	PV-D	PV-S	PV-S	PV-S	PV-S	PV-S	PV-S	PV-S	PV-S	PV-S
New York		L	L	L	L	L	L	L	L	L	PV-CD+	PV-S
North Carolina		L	PV-D	PV-D	PV-D	PV-D	L	PV-S	PV-S	PV-S	PV-S	PV-S
Rhode Island		L	L	PV-S	PV-S	PV-S	PV-S	PV-S	PV-S	PV-S	PV-S	PV-S
Vermont		L	L	L	L	L	L	L	L	L	PV-S	PV-S
Kentucky		PV-D	PV-D	PV-D	PV-D	PV-D	PV-D	PV-D	PV-D	PV-D	PV-S	PV-S
Tennessee			L	L-e	PV-D	PV-D	PV-D	PV-D	PV-D	PV-D	PV-D	PV-S
Ohio					PV-S	PV-S	PV-S	PV-S	PV-S	PV-S	PV-S	PV-S
Louisiana							L	L	L	L	PV-S	PV-S
Indiana								L	L	PV-S	PV-S	PV-S
Alabama									L	PV-S	PV-S	PV-S
Illinois									PV-D	PV-D	PV-S	PV-S
Maine									PV-D,S	PV-D,S	PV-D,S	PV-D
Mississippi									PV-S	PV-S	PV-S	PV-S
Missouri									L	PV-D	PV-S	PV-S
Popular election	5	6	8	5	11	10	9	10	15	18	22	23
Legislative selection	5	9	9	11	6	7	9	9	9	6	2	1

By 1836 and for the remainder of the elections through 1860, all states chose electors by statewide vote except South Carolina where the legislature chose the electors.

L	electors chosen by the Legislature.
L-e	legislature appointed individuals who then chose electors.
L-PV-d	electors chosen first by voters by district; legislature made final choice from top two.
PV-D	popular vote by district.
PV-D,S	popular vote by district plus two elected statewide.
PV-D+	popular vote by Congressional district; these electors then chose two remaining electors.
PV-d-L+	popular vote by district, but legislature chose where there was no majority and also chose two additional electors.
PV-S	popular vote, all electors chosen statewide.
PV-s-L	popular vote statewide, but legislature made choice where there was no majority.

*In 1960, six of Alabama's Democratic candidates for electors ran as unpledged electors as did all of Mississippi's. They were all elected and did not vote for John F. Kennedy; instead they voted for Senator Byrd of Virginia. In 1948, the Democratic electors in four states were not pledged to the party's nominee, President Truman, but to Governor Strom Thurmond of South Carolina.

SOURCES

The primary goal in collecting the returns was to obtain the results from official sources, either from the manuscript returns or newspapers that printed these data. While this has not been universally possible, the majority of the returns used here were obtained from one or the other source. When a source was not considered official, it is noted accordingly. Sources are listed below the county returns for each state in each election.

In addition to official returns, two other sources were consulted on several occasions: W. Dean Burnham, *Presidential Ballots 1836–1892,* Arno Press, New York, 1976 (reprint edition), and various editions of the *Whig/Tribune Almanac.* When using the former, I usually indicated its source. The *Almanac* was on some occasions the only known source of county returns and it often listed its returns as official.

Two other historical sources were checked for statewide totals: Svend Petersen, *A Statistical History of the American Presidential Elections*, Frederick Ungar Publishing Co., New York, 1963, and *Guide to U.S. Elections,* 1st edition, Congressional Quarterly, Washington, 1975.

Although the election of the president is considered a national election, the compilation of returns was and to a large degree still is a state matter. While the electoral college vote of the states has long been fully and accurately compiled by federal officials, the popular vote has not been. The National Archives has a definitive collection of electoral vote results, but compilations of popular vote returns, particularly at the county level, are largely attainable only through research carried out in each of the states.

The necessity for local research was even more significant for the elections through 1832, because of the availability for the later period of state and county returns in *Presidential Ballots* and the annual editions of the *Whig/Tribune Almanac.* Neither title was, however, used as an initial source because of the desire to obtain, whenever possible, the official returns. As the reader will note these two sources were indeed used on occasion, either because official returns were not found or because they were discovered to be incomplete. Almost all returns were found either in the original manuscripts, usually located at a state archive, or in newspapers. Listed below is a summary of the material found in each state. See individual elections for specific information.

ALABAMA

A manuscript compiled by Philip Loveman at the state archives is the main source of returns.

ARKANSAS

There are no known manuscript returns. Even the newspapers fail to provide a complete run of the appropriate data.

CALIFORNIA

The state archives provided copies of the original manuscript returns for all elections.

CONNECTICUT

Manuscript returns found at the state archives were used for almost all elections, as well as editions of the *Manual.*

DELAWARE

A combination of newspapers and the *Governor's Register* (published for the elections of 1832 through 1848) provided all the returns.

FLORIDA

The first election was compiled from manuscript returns while all the others were found in editions of the (Tallahassee) *Floridian.*

GEORGIA

Most of the returns were found in the *Executive Minutes*; when they were lacking in this source, newspapers were used.

ILLINOIS

All returns from the manuscripts have been published: in Theodore Pease, *Illinois Election Returns 1818–1848*, and then in *Illinois Election Returns 1818–1990* by Howard and Lacey. In addition, I obtained copies of the manuscript returns from the state archives.

INDIANA

The returns through 1848 were published in Riker and Thorbrough, *Indiana Election Returns 1816–1851*. The remainder came from the (Indianapolis) *Indiana Sentinel* or *Journal*.

IOWA

Except for the 1848 election, which was found detailed in the (Iowa City) *Iowa Capitol Reporter*, the returns were from the manuscript returns supplied by the state archives.

KENTUCKY

Newspapers were virtually the sole source for returns. There is a published volume by McQuown and Shannon, *Presidential Politics in Kentucky 1824–1948,* which was of some value.

LOUISIANA

Newspapers from Baton Rouge and New Orleans generally were the sources used.

MAINE

Returns since statehood plus some official documents were found in a variety of newspapers located at the state archives, the Maine Historical Society, and the Portland Public Library.

MARYLAND

All research was done at the Hall of Records in Annapolis, which has a complete run of returns. In addition, John T. Willis has published the material in *Presidential Elections in Maryland*.

MASSACHUSETTS

All returns were obtained from the manuscript collection at the state archives in Boston.

MICHIGAN

Both manuscript returns and editions of the *Michigan Manual* were used to compile these returns.

MINNESOTA

For the state's one election we used *Minnesota Votes* by Bruce M. White.

MISSISSIPPI

Manuscript returns at the state archives in Jackson, and newspapers in that city when the former source could not be located, were used.

MISSOURI

Returns were found in St. Louis and Jefferson City newspapers; manuscript returns at the state archives were also consulted.

NEW HAMPSHIRE

For elections prior to 1808, newspapers were the sole source of data; for elections after that date, the manuscript returns at the state archives in Concord, and the 1889 edition of the *Manual* for the last three elections, were consulted.

NEW JERSEY

In the absence of manuscript returns (except for the election of 1860), newspapers from Trenton and Newark located at the state archives and library were used.

NEW YORK

Primarily, the sources were the manuscript returns at the state archives in Albany and issues of the *Albany Argus*. New York was one of the few states that required the official returns to be published as a matter of law in one or more newspapers of the state.

NORTH CAROLINA

Manuscript returns at the state archives and, for returns prior to 1812 (when electors were chosen by districts), newspapers from the collection of the same institution were used.

OHIO

The 1985–6 edition of *Ohio Election Statistics* contains the statewide returns through 1820; the (Columbus) *Ohio State Journal* was used through 1848, and *Ohio Executive Documents, 1865* thereafter.

OREGON

For the 1860 election, *Oregon Votes 1858–1972* by Burton W. Onstine was consulted.

PENNSYLVANIA

Newspapers were the most frequently used source. There are few manuscript entries.

RHODE ISLAND

Most of the returns were located in either the manuscript collection or Providence newspapers.

TENNESSEE

All returns were obtained from Nashville newspapers.

TEXAS

All returns were found in the *Governor's Register*.

VERMONT

The manuscript returns at the state archives were used.

VIRGINIA

Mostly the manuscript returns at the state archives were used, while the *Richmond Enquirer* was consulted in the absence of those documents.

WISCONSIN

James Donoghue, *How Wisconsin Voted 1848–1872*, and the manuscript returns at the state archives were used.

PARTY ABBREVIATIONS

A	American	IR	Independent Republican
Ab	Abolitionist	J	Jacksonian
a-f	Anti-Federal	Lty	Liberty
AM	Anti-Mason	ND	Northern Democrat
CU	Constitutional Union	NR	National Republican
D	Democratic	R	Republican
D Fus	Democratic-Fusion	SD	Southern Democrat
D-R	Democratic-Republican	SoR	Southern Rights
f	federalist	StrA	"Straight out Fillmore [American Party] ticket"
F	Federalist (Party)		
FS	Free Soil	U	Union
Fus	Fusion	UW	Union Whig
ID	Independent Democrat	W	Whig

ELECTION DATES

Until the election of 1848, the states were free to schedule the popular vote for electors as they wished. In practice, however, the election was held during a two week period, as illustrated by the following table of dates for the 1840 presidential election. Beginning with the 1848 election, all presidential electors chosen by popular vote were uniformly selected on the first Tuesday after the first Monday in November. This has been the case ever since.

State	Date
Ohio	October 30
Pennsylvania	
Arkansas	November 2
Connecticut	
Georgia	
Illinois	
Indiana	
Kentucky	
Maine	
* Michigan	

State	Date
Missouri	
New Hampshire	
† New York	
Rhode Island	
Virginia	
Louisiana	November 3
* Mississippi	
* New Jersey	
Tennessee	
Alabama	November 9
Maryland	
Massachusetts	
Delaware	November 10
Vermont	
North Carolina	November 12
§ South Carolina	November 23

*first of two days
†first of three days
§date legislature chose electors

xvi

COUNTY NAMES

Each state's counties at the time of its first popular election of electors (or in some cases, as noted below, at the first election for which returns have been found) are shown in the returns for that year. Listed below are the counties created later, in chronological order by date of establishment.

ALABAMA

County	Created from	Year
Walker	Marion, Tuscaloosa	1823
Dale	Covington, Henry	1824
Fayette	Marion, Pickens, Tuscaloosa	1824
Lowndes	Butler, Dallas, Montgomery	1830
Barbour	Indian Lands	1832
Benton	Indian Lands	1832
Chambers	Indian Lands	1832
Coosa	Indian Lands	1832
Macon	Indian Lands	1832
Randolph	Indian Lands	1832
Russell	Indian Lands	1832
Sumter	Indian Lands	1832
Talladega	Indian Lands	1832
Tallapoosa	Indian Lands	1832
Cherokee	Indian Lands	1836
De Kalb	Indian Lands	1836
Marshall	Blount, Indian Lands	1836
Coffee	Dale	1841
Choctaw	Sumter, Washington	1847
Hancock	Walker	1850

ARKANSAS

County	Created from	Year
Benton	Washington	1836
Marion	Izard	1836
Franklin	Crawford	1837
Desha	Arkansas, Chicot	1838
Poinsett	Greene, Saint Francis	1838
Searcy	Marion	1838
Bradley	Union	1840
Perry	Conway	1840
Yell	Pope, Scott	1840
Fulton	Izard	1842
Montgomery	Hot Springs	1842
Newton	Carroll	1842
Ouachita	Union	1842
Polk	Sevier	1844
Dallas	Bradley, Clark	1845
Drew	Arkansas, Bradley	1846
Prairie	Pulaski	1846
Ashley	Chicot, Drew, Union	1848
Calhoun	Dallas, Ouachita	1850
Sebastian	Crawford, Polk, Scott	1851
Columbia	Lafayette, Hempstead, Ouachita	1852
Craighead	Greene, Mississippi, Poinsett	1859

CALIFORNIA

County	Created from	Year
Alameda	Contra Costa, Santa Clara	1853
Humboldt	Trinity	1853
San Bernardino	Los Angeles	1853
Amador	Calaveras	1854
Plumas	Butte	1854
Stanislaus	Tuolumne	1854
Merced	Mariposa	1855
Fresno	Mariposa, Merced	1856
San Mateo	San Francisco	1856
Tehama	Butte, Colusa, Shasta	1856
De Norte	Klamath	1857

FLORIDA

County	Created from	Year
Putnam	Alachua, Marion, Orange, St. Johns	1849
Sumter	Marion	1853
Hernando	Alachua, Benton	1850
Volusia	St. Lucas	1854
Liberty	Franklin, Gadsden	1855
Manatee	Hillsboro	1855
Lafayette	Madison	1856
Taylor	Madison	1856
New River	Columbia	1858
Clay	Duval	1858
Suwannee	Columbia	1858

GEORGIA

Compilation starts following the election of 1836, the first where complete county returns were found other than 1796.

County	Created from	Year
Dade	Walker	1837
Macon	Houston, Marion	1837
Chattooga	Floyd, Walker	1838
Clinch	Lowndes, Ware	1850

County	Created from	Year
Gordon	Cass, Floyd	1850
Polk	Floyd, Paulding	1851
Spalding	Fayette, Henry, Pike	1851
Whitfield	Murray	1851
Taylor	Macon, Marion, Talbot	1852
Catoosa	Walker, Whitfield	1853
Dougherty	Baker	1853
Fulton	DeKalb	1853
Hart	Elbert, Franklin	1853
Pickens	Cherokee, Gilmer	1853
Webster	Kinchafoonee	1853
Worth	Dooly, Irwin	1853
Calhoun	Baker, Early	1854
Charlton	Camden	1854
Chattahoochee	Marion, Muscogee	1854
Clay	Early, Randolph	1854
Coffee	Clinch, Irwin, Telfair, Ware	1854
Fannin	Gilmer, Union	1854
Berrien	Coffee, Irwin, Lowndes	1856
Colquitt	Lowndes, Thomas	1856
Haralson	Carroll, Polk	1856
Miller	Baker, Early	1856
Terrell	Lee, Randolph	1856
Towns	Rabun, Upson	1856
Dawson	Gilmer, Lumpkin	1857
Glasscock	Warren	1857
Mitchell	Baker	1857
Pierce	Appling, Ware	1857
Schley	Marion, Sumter	1857
White	Habersham	1857
Wilcox	Dooly, Irwin, Pulaski	1857
Banks	Franklin, Habersham	1858
Brooks	Lowndes, Thomas	1858
Clayton	Fayette, Henry	1858
Echols	Clinch, Lowndes	1858
Johnson	Emanuel, Laurens, Washington	1858
Quitman	Randolph, Stewart	1858

ILLINOIS

County	Created from	Year
Greene	Madison	1821
Hamilton	White	1821
Lawrence	Crawford, Edwards	1821
Montgomery	Bond, Madison	1821
Pike	Bond, Clark, Madison	1821
Sangamon	Bond, Madison	1821
Johnson	Randolph	1822
Edgar	Clark	1823
Fulton	Pike	1823
Marion	Fayette, Jefferson	1823
Morgan	Sangamon	1823
Clay	Fayette, Lawrence, Wayne	1824
Clinton	Bond, Crawford, Fayette, Washington	1824
Wabash	Edwards	1824
Adams	Pike	1825

County	Created from	Year
Calhoun	Pike	1825
Hancock	Pike	1825
Henry	Fulton	1825
Knox	Fulton	1825
Mercer	Pike	1825
Peoria	Fulton	1825
Putnam	Fulton	1825
Schuyler	Fulton, Pike	1825
Warren	Pike	1825
McDonough	Schuyler	1826
Vermilion	Edgar	1826
Jo Daviess	Henry, Mercer, Putnam	1827
Perry	Jackson, Randolph	1827
Shelby	Fayette	1827
Tazewell	Sangamon	1827
Macon	Shelby	1829
Macoupin	Greene, Madison	1829
Coles	Clark, Edgar	1830
McLean	Tazewell	1830
Cook	Putnam	1831
Effingham	Crawford, Fayette	1831
Jasper	Clay, Crawford	1831
LaSalle	Putnam, Vermilion	1831
Rock Island	Jo Daviess	1831
Champaign	Vermilion	1833
Iroquois	Vermilion	1833
Kane	La Salle	1836
McHenry	Cook	1836
Ogle	Jo Daviess	1836
Whiteside	Henry, Jo Daviess	1836
Winnebago	Jo Daviess	1836
Will	Cook, Iroquois	1836
Boone	Winnebago	1837
Bureau	Putnam	1837
Cass	Morgan	1837
DeKalb	Kane	1837
Marshall	Putnam	1837
Stephenson	Jo Daviess, Winnebago	1837
Brown	Schuyler	1839
Carroll	Jo Daviess	1839
Christian	Sangamon, Shelby	1839
DeWitt	Macon, McLean	1839
Hardin	Pope	1839
Jersey	Greene	1839
Lake	McHenry	1839
Lee	Ogle	1839
Logan	Sangamon	1839
Marshall	Putnam	1839
Menard	Sangamon	1839
Scott	Morgan	1839
Stark	Knox, Putnam	1839
Williamson	Franklin	1839
Grundy	LaSalle	1841
Henderson	Warren	1841
Kendall	Kane, LaSalle	1841
Mason	Tazewell	1841

Piatt	DeWitt, Macon	1841
Richland	Clay, Lawrence	1841
Woodford	McKean, Tazewell	1841
Cumberland	Coles	1843
Massac	Jefferson, Pope	1843
Pulaski	Johnson	1843
Saline	Gallatin	1847
Kankakee	Iroquois, Will	1853
Douglas	Coles	1859
Ford	Clark	1859

INDIANA

County	Created from	Year
Clay	Owen, Putnam, Sullivan, Vigo	1825
Fountain	Montgomery, Parke	1826
Tippecanoe	Parke	1826
Delaware	Randolph	1827
Warren	Fountain	1827
Carroll	Unorganized Territory	1828
Hancock	Madison	1828
Cass	Carroll	1829
Boone	Hendricks, Marion	1830
Clinton	Tippecanoe	1830
Elkhart	Allen, Cass	1830
Saint Joseph	Cass	1830
Grant	Cass, Delaware, Madison	1831
Huntington	Allen, Grant	1832
Lagrange	Allen, Elkhart	1832
LaPorte	Saint Joseph	1832
Miami	Cass	1832
White	Carroll	1834
Adams	Allen, Randolph	1835
De Kalb	Allen, Lagrange	1835
Fulton	Allen, Cass, Saint Joseph	1835
Jasper	Warren, White	1835
Jay	Delaware, Randolph	1835
Kosciusko	Cass, Elkhart	1835
Marshall	Elkhart, Saint Joseph	1835
Noble	Allen, Elkhart, Lagrange	1835
Porter	Saint Joseph	1835
Pulaski	Cass, Saint Joseph	1835
Steuben	Lagrange	1835
Wabash	Cass, Grant	1835
Wells	Allen, Delaware, Randolph	1835
Whitley	Allen, Elkhart	1835
Brown	Bartholomew, Jackson, Monroe	1836
Lake	Newton, Porter	1836
Blackford	Jay	1838
Benton	Jasper	1840
Richardville	Carroll, Cass, Grant, Hamilton, Miami	1844
Ohio	Dearborn	1844
Tipton	Cass, Hamilton, Miami	1844
Starke	Saint Joseph	1850
Newton	Jasper	1859

IOWA

The year indicated is the year the county was organized.

County	Created from	Year
Allamakee	Clayton	1849
Boone	Polk	1849
Lucas	Monroe	1849
Madison	Mahaska	1849
Marshall	Benton, Jasper	1849
Warren	Mahaska	1849
Decatur	Appanoose	1850
Fremont	Pottawattamie	1850
Clarke	Lucas	1851
Fayette	Clayton	1851
Guthrie	Jackson	1851
Mills	Pottawattamie	1851
Page	Pottawattamie	1851
Taylor	Pottawattamie	1851
Wayne	Appanoose	1851
Winneshiek	Clayton	1851
Tama	Linn	1852
Adams	Taylor	1853
Black Hawk	Benton, Buchanan	1853
Bremer	Winnebago, Indian Lands	1853
Cass	Pottawattamie	1853
Chicksasaw	Fayette	1853
Hardin	Black Hawk	1853
Harrison	Pottawattamie	1853
Mitchell	Chickasaw	1853
Montgomery	Polk	1853
Shelby	Cass	1853
Story	Benton	1853
Union	Clarke	1853
Woodbury	Indian Lands	1853
Butler	Black Hawk, Buchanan	1854
Floyd	Chickasaw	1854
Greene	Dallas	1854
Mitchell	Chickasaw	1854
Monona	Harrison	1854
Adair	Cass	1855
Audubon	Black Hawk, Cass	1855
Carroll	Guthrie	1855
Cerro Gordo	Floyd	1855
Crawford	Shelby	1855
Franklin	Chickasaw	1855
Howard	Chickasaw, Floyd	1855
Ida	Cherokee	1855
Kossuth	Webster	1855
Ringgold	Mahaska, Taylor	1855
Grundy	Black Hawk	1856
Sac	Greene	1856
Cherokee	Crawford	1857
Hamilton	Webster	1857
Humboldt	Webster	1857
Webster	Hamilton	1857
Winnebago	Kossuth	1857

Clay	Indian Lands	1858
Dickinson	Kossuth	1858
Hancock	Wright	1858
Palo Alto	Kossuth	1858
Plymouth	Woodbury	1858
Worth	Mitchell	1858
Buena Vista	Clay, Sac	1859
Emmet	Dickinson, Kossuth	1859
Pocahontas	Greene, Humboldt	1859
O'Brien	Cherokee	1860
Sioux	Plymouth	1860

KENTUCKY

Compilation begins after the election of 1824, the first election where county returns are listed.

County	Created from	Year
McCracken	Hickman	1824
Spencer	Bullitt, Nelson, Shelby	1824
Edmonson	Grayson, Hart, Warren	1825
Laurel	Clay, Knox, Rockcastle, Whitley	1825
Russell	Adair, Cumberland, Pulaski, Wayne	1825
Anderson	Franklin, Mercer, Washington	1827
Hancock	Breckinridge, Daviess, Ohio	1829
Marion	Callaway	1834
Clinton	Cumberland, Wayne	1836
Trimble	Gallatin, Henry, Oldham	1837
Carroll	Gallatin, Henry, Trimble	1838
Carter	Greenup, Lawrence	1838
Breathitt	Clay, Estill, Perry	1839
Kenton	Campbell	1840
Ballard	Hickman, McCracken	1842
Boyle	Lincoln, Mercer	1842
Crittenden	Livingston	1842
Letcher	Harlan, Perry	1842
Marshall	Callaway	1842
Johnson	Floyd, Lawrence, Morgan	1843
Larue	Hardin	1843
Owsley	Breathitt, Clay, Estill	1843
Fulton	Hickman	1845
Taylor	Green	1848
Powell	Clark, Estill, Montgomery	1852
Lyon	Caldwell	1854
McLean	Daviess, Muhlenberg, Ohio	1854
Rowan	Fleming, Morgan	1856
Jackson	Clay, Estill, Laurel, Madison, Owsley, Rockcastle	1858
Boyd	Carter, Greenup, Lawrence	1860
Magoffin	Floyd, Johnson, Morgan	1860
Metcalfe	Adair, Barren, Cumberland, Green, Monroe	1860
Webster	Henderson, Hopkins, Webster	1860
Wolfe	Breathitt, Morgan, Owsley, Powell	1860

LOUISIANA

Parish	Created from	Year
Livingston	Saint Helena	1832
Caddo	Natchitoches	1838
Caldwell	Catahoula, Ouachita	1838
Madison	Concordia	1838
Union	Ouachita	1839
Calcasieu	Saint Landry	1840
Bossier	Claiborne	1843
De Soto	Caddo, Natchitoches	1843
Franklin	Catahoula, Madison, Ouachita	1843
Sabine	Natchitoches	1843
Tensas	Concordia	1843
Morehouse	Ouachita	1844
Vermilion	Lafayette	1844
Jackson	Claiborne, Ouachita, Union	1845
Bienville	Claiborne	1848
Winn	Catahoula, Natchitoches, Rapides	1852

MAINE

Compilation begins after the election of 1804.

County	Created from	Year
Oxford	Cumberland, York	1805
Somerset	Kennebec	1809
Penobscot	Hancock	1816
Waldo	Hancock, Kennebec, Lincoln	1827
Franklin	Cumberland	1838
Piscataquis	Penobscot, Somerset	1838
Aroostook	Washington	1839
Androscoggin	Cumberland, Kennebec, Oxford	1854
Sagadahoc	Lincoln	1854
Knox	Lincoln, Waldo	1860

MARYLAND

County	Created from	Year
Allegany	Washington	1789
Carroll	Baltimore, Frederick	1837
Howard	Anne Arundel, Baltimore	1851

MASSACHUSETTS

Compilation begins after the election of 1804.

County	Created from	Year
Franklin	Hampshire	1811
Hampden	Hampshire	1812

MICHIGAN

The year indicated is the year the county was organized.

County	Created from	Year
Eaton	Calhoun, Kalamazoo, St.Joseph	1837
Ionia	Kent	1837
Ottawa	Kent	1837
Shiawassee	Genesee, Oakland	1837

County	Created from	Year
Van Buren	Cass	1837
Ingham	Eaton, Jackson, Washtemaw	1838
Clinton	Kent, Shiawassee	1839
Chippewa	Mackinac	1843
Houghton	Chippewa	1848
Marquette	Chippewa, Houghton	1848
Sanilac	Lapeer, Oakland, St. Clair	1848
Midland	Saginaw	1850
Montcalm	Ionia	1850
Tuscola	Saginaw	1850
Newaygo	Kent, Muskegon, Ottawa	1851
Cheboygan	Mackinac	1853
Emmet	Mackinac	1853
Ontonagon	Chippewa, Houghton	1853
Gratiot	Clinton, Saginaw	1855
Manistee	Grand Traverse, Mackinac, Oceana, Ottawa	1855
Manitou	Emmet	1855
Mason	Oceana, Ottawa	1855
Oceana	Ottawa	1855
Alpena	Cheboygan	1857
Bay	Midland, Saginaw	1857
Iosco	Cheboygan, Saginaw	1857
Huron	St. Clair, Sanilac, Saginaw	1859
Isabella	Midland, Saginaw	1859
Mecosta	Kent, Newaygo	1859
Muskegon	Ottawa	1859

MISSISSIPPI

County	Created from	Year
Hinds	Choctaw Cession	1821
Monroe	Chickasaw Cession	1821
Copiah	Hinds	1823
Simpson	Choctaw Cession	1824
Yazoo	Hinds	1824
Jones	Covington, Wayne	1826
Washington	Warren, Yazoo	1827
Madison	Yazoo	1828
Rankin	Hinds	1828
Lowndes	Monroe	1830
Attala	Choctaw Cession	1833
Carroll	Choctaw Cession	1833
Choctaw	Choctaw Cession	1833
Holmes	Yazoo	1833
Jasper	Indian Lands	1833
Kemper	Choctaw Cession	1833
Lauderdale	Choctaw Cession	1833
Leake	Neshoba	1833
Noxubee	Choctaw Cession	1833
Oktbbeha	Choctaw Cession	1833
Scott	Choctaw Cession	1833
Smith	Choctaw Cession	1833
Tallahatchie	Choctaw Cession	1833
Winston	Choctaw Cession	1833
Yalobusha	Choctaw Cession	1833
Bolivar	Choctaw Cession	1836
Chickasaw	Choctaw Cession	1836
Coahoma	Choctaw Cession	1836
De Soto	Indian Lands	1836
Itawamba	Chickasaw Cession	1836
Lafayette	Chickasaw Cession	1836
Marshall	Chickasaw Cession	1836
Newton	Neshoba	1836
Panola	Neshoba	1836
Pontotoc	Neshoba	1836
Tippah	Neshoba	1836
Tishomingo	Neshoba	1836
Harrison	Hancock, Jackson	1841
Issaquena	Washington	1844
Sunflower	Bolivar	1844
Calhoun	Lafayette, Yalobusha	1852

MISSOURI

County	Created from	Year
Jackson	Lafayette	1826
Marion	Ralls	1826
Crawford	Gasconade	1829
Carroll	Oregon, Reynolds, Ripley, Shannon	1833
Clinton	Clay	1833
Lewis	Marion	1833
Greene	Crawford, Wayne	1833
Ripley	Wayne	1833
Warren	Montgomery	1833
Henry	Lafayette	1834
Johnson	Lafayette	1834
Barry	Greene	1835
Benton	Greene, Pettis	1835
Shelby	Marion	1835
Stoddard	New Madrid	1835
Audrain*	Callaway, Monroe, Ralls	1836
Caldwell*	Ray	1836
Clark*	Lewis	1836
Daviess*	Ray	1836
Livingston	Carroll	1837
Macon	Chariton, Randolph	1837
Miller	Cole, Pulaski	1837
Taney	Greene	1837
Buchanan	Platte Purchase	1838
Adair	Macon	1841
Andrew	Platte Purchase	1841
Bates	Van Buren	1841
Camden	Benton, Morgan, Pulaski	1841
Dade	Barry, Polk	1841
Dallas	Polk	1841
Grundy	Livingston	1841
Jasper	Barry	1841
Osage	Gasconade	1841
Ozark	Taney	1841
Shannon	Ripley	1841
Wright	Pulaski	1841

Atchison	Holt	1845
Cedar	Dade, Saint Clair	1845
De Kalb	Clinton	1845
Dunklin	Stoddard	1845
Gentry	Clinton	1845
Harrison	Daviess	1845
Hickory	Benton, Polk	1845
Lafayette	Cooper	1845
Lawrence	Barry, Dade	1845
Mercer	Grundy	1845
Nodaway	Andrew	1845
Oregon	Ripley	1845
Schuyler	Adair	1845
Sullivan	Linn	1845
Texas	Shannon, Wright	1845
McDonald	Newton	1849
Pemiscot	New Madrid	1849
Butler	Wayne	1849
Bollinger	Cape Girardeau, Madison, Stoddard, Wayne	1851
Dent	Crawford, Shannon	1851
Stone	Taney	1851
Barton	Jasper	1855
Maries	Osage, Pulaski	1855
Vernon	Bates	1855
Webster	Greene	1855
Douglas	Ozark	1857
Howell	Oregon	1857
Iron	Madison, Reynolds, St. Francois, Washington, Wayne	1857
Christian	Greene, Taney, Webster	1859

*Created after the 1836 election.

NEW HAMPSHIRE
Compilation begins after the election of 1808.

County	Created from	Year
Merrimack	Hillsborough, Rockingham	1823
Sullivan	Cheshire	1827
Belknap	Merrimack, Strafford	1840
Carroll	Strafford	1840

NEW JERSEY

County	Created from	Year
Warren	Sussex	1824
Atlantic	Gloucester	1837
Passaic	Bergen, Essex	1837
Mercer	Burlington, Hunterdon, Middlesex, Sussex	1838
Hudson	Bergen	1840
Camden	Gloucester	1844
Ocean	Monmouth	1850
Union	Essex	1857

NEW YORK

County	Created from	Year
Chemung	Tioga	1836
Fulton	Montgomery	1838
Schuyler	Chemung, Steuben, Tompkins	1854

NORTH CAROLINA
Compilation begins after the election of 1800.

County	Created from	Year
Columbus	Bladen, Brunswick	1808
Haywood	Buncombe	1808
Davidson	Rowan	1822
Macon	Haywood	1828
Yancey	Buncombe, Burke	1833
Davie	Rowan	1836
Henderson	Buncombe	1838
Cherokee	Macon	1839
Caldwell	Burke, Wilkes	1841
Cleveland	Lincoln, Rutherford	1841
Stanly	Montgomery	1841
Catawba	Lincoln	1842
McDowell	Burke, Rutherford	1842
Union	Anson, Mecklenburg	1842
Gaston	Lincoln	1846
Alexander	Caldwell, Iredell, Wilkes	1847
Alamance	Orange	1849
Forsyth	Stokes	1849
Watauga	Ashe, Caldwell, Wilkes, Yancey	1849
Yadkin	Surry	1850
Jackson	Haywood, Macon	1851
Madison	Buncombe, Yancey	1851
Harnett	Cumberland	1855
Polk	Henderson, Rutherford	1855
Wilson	Edgecombe, Johnston, Nash, Wayne	1855
Alleghany	Ashe	1859

OHIO
Compilation begins after the election of 1824.

County	Created from	Year
Carroll	Columbiana, Harrison, Jefferson, Stark, Tuscarawas	1833
Lucas	Henry, Sandusky, Wood	1835
Erie	Huron, Sandusky	1838
Lake	Cuyahoga, Geauga	1840
Ottawa	Erie, Lucas, Sandusky	1840
Summit	Medina, Stark, Summit	1840
Defiance	Henry, Paulding, Williams	1845
Wyandot	Crawford, Hancock, Hardin, Marion	1845
Ashland	Huron, Lorain, Richland, Wayne	1846
Mahoning	Columbiana, Trumbull	1846
Auglaize	Allen, Mercer	1848
Morrow	Delaware, Knox, Marion, Richland	1848

Fulton	Henry, Lucas, Williams	1850
Vinton	Athens, Gallia, Hocking, Jackson, Ross	1850
Noble	Guernsey, Monroe, Morgan	1851

PENNSYLVANIA

County	Created from	Year
Mifflin	Cumberland, Northumberland	1789
Somerset	Bedford	1795
Greene	Washington	1796
Wayne	Northampton	1798
Adams	York	1800
Armstrong	Allegheny, Butler, Clarion, Indiana, Jefferson, Westmoreland	1800
Beaver	Allegheny, Washington	1800
Butler	Allegheny	1800
Centre	Huntingdon, Lycoming, Mifflin, Northumberland	1800
Cambria	Bedford, Huntingdon, Somerset	1800
Erie	Allegheny	1800
Mercer	Allegheny	1800
Venango	Allegheny, Lycoming	1800
Warren	Allegheny, Lycoming	1800
Indiana	Lycoming, Westmoreland	1803
Crawford	Allegheny	1804
Clearfield	Lycoming, Huntingdon	1804
McKean	Lycoming	1804
Potter	Lycoming	1804
Tioga	Lycoming	1804
Susquehanna	Luzerne	1810
Schuylkill	Berks, Northampton	1811
Bradford	Luzerne, Lycoming	1812
Lehigh	Northampton	1812
Columbia	Northumberland	1813
Lebanon	Dauphin, Lancaster	1813
Union	Northumberland	1813
Pike	Northampton	1814
Perry	Cumberland	1820
Juniata	Mifflin	1831
Clarion	Armstrong, Venango	1839
Clinton	Centre, Lycoming	1839
Wyoming	Luzerne	1842
Carbon	Monroe, Northampton	1843
Elk	Clearfield, Jefferson, McKean	1843
Blair	Bedford, Huntingdon	1846
Sullivan	Lycoming	1847
Forest	Jefferson, Venango	1848
Lawrence	Beaver, Mercer	1849
Fulton	Bedford	1850
Montour	Columbia	1850
Snyder	Union	1855
Cameron	Clinton, Elk, McKean, Potter	1860

TENNESSEE

Compilation begins after the election of 1824. Counties continued to vote with the parent counties until the first election after the next decade.

County	Created from	Year
Benton	Henry, Humphreys	1835
Lauderdale	Dyer, Tipton	1835
Bradley	Indian Lands	1836
Cannon	Coffee, Warren, Wilson	1836
Coffee	Bedford, Franklin, Warren	1836
Johnson	Carter	1836
Marshall	Bedford, Giles, Lincoln, Maury	1836
Meigs	Hamilton, McMinn, Rhea	1836
DeKalb	Cannon, Warren, White	1837
Polk	Bradley, McMinn	1839
Van Buren	Bledsoe, Warren, White	1840
Macon	Smith, Sumner	1842
Putnam	DeKalb, Jackson, Overton, White	1842
Lewis	Hickman, Lawrence, Maury, Wayne	1843
Grundy	Coffee, Warren	1844
Hancock	Claiborne, Hawkins	1844
Crockett	Dyer, Gibson, Haywood, Madison	1845
Decatur	Perry	1845
Scott	Anderson, Fentress, Morgan	1849
Union	Anderson, Campbell, Claiborne, Grainger, Knox	1850
Cheatham	Davidson, Dickson, Montgomery	1856
Cumberland	Bledsoe, Morgan, Roane	
Sequatchie	Hamilton	1857

TEXAS

The year indicated is the year the county was organized.

County	Created from	Year
Bell	Milam	1850
Ellis	Navarro	1850
El Paso	Bexar	1850
Falls	Limestone, Milam	1850
Freestone	Limestone	1850
McLennan	Milam	1850
Tarrant	Navarro	1850
Trinity	Houston	1850
Wood	Van Zandt	1850
Hidalgo	Cameron	1850
Orange	Jefferson	1850
Hill	Navarro	1853
Burnet	Bell, Travis, Williamson	1854
Bosque	McLennan	1854
Coryell	Bell	1854
Johnson	Ellis, Hill, Navarro	1854
Karnes	Bexar	1854
Parker	Bosque, Navarro	1855
Atascosa	Bexar	1856
Bandera	Bexar, Uvalde	1856
Comanche	Bosque, Coryell	1856

Erath	Bosque, Coryell	1856
Kerr	Bexar	1856
Lampasas	Bell, Travis	1856
Live Oak	Nueces, San Patricio	1856
Llano	Bexar	1856
San Saba	Bexar	1856
Uvalde	Bexar	1856
Wise	Cooke	1856
Young	Bosque, Fannin	1856
Bee	Goliard, Live Oak, Refugio, San Patricio	1857
Brown	Comanche, Travis	1857
Clay	Cooke	1857
Jack	Cooke	1857
Montague	Cooke	1857
Palo Pinto	Bosque, Navarro	1857
Blanco	Burnet, Comal, Gillespie, Hays	1858
Chambers	Jefferson, Liberty	1858
Hardin	Jefferson, Liberty	1858
Mason	Gillespie	1858
Zapata	Starr, Webb	1858
Marion	Cass	1860
Wilson	Bexar, Karnes	1860

VIRGINIA

County	Created from	Year
Bath	Augusta, Botetourt, Greenbrier	1790
Patrick	Henry	1790
Madison	Culpeper	1792
Brooke	Ohio	1796
Wood	Harrison	1798
Monroe	Greenbrier	1799
Tazewell	Russell, Wythe	1799
Jefferson	Berkeley	1801
Mason	Kanawha	1804
Giles	Craig, Mercer, Monroe, Montgomery, Tazewell, Wythe	1806
Nelson	Amherst	1807
Cabell	Kanawha	1809
Scott	Lee, Russell, Washington	1814
Tyler	Ohio	1814
Lewis	Harrison	1816
Nicholas	Greenbrier, Kanawha	1818
Preston	Monongalia	1818
Morgan	Berkeley, Hampshire	1820
Pocahontas	Bath, Pendleton, Randolph	1821
Alleghany	Bath, Botetourt, Monroe	1822
Logan	Cabell, Giles, Kanawha	1824
Fayette	Greenbrier, Kanawha, Logan	1831
Floyd	Franklin, Montgomery	1831
Jackson	Kanawha, Mason, Wood	1831
Page	Rockingham, Shenandoah	1831
Smyth	Washington, Wythe	1832
Rappahannock	Culpeper	1833
Marshall	Ohio	1835

Braxton	Kanawha, Lewis, Nicholas	1836
Clarke	Frederick	1836
Warren	Frederick, Shenandoah	1836
Mercer	Giles, Tazewell	1837
Greene	Orange	1838
Roanoke	Botetourt, Montgomery	1838
Pulaski	Montgomery, Wythe	1839
Appomattox	Buckingham, Campbell, Charlotte,	1839
Carroll	Grayson, Patrick	1842
Marion	Harrison, Monongalia	1842
Wayne	Cabell	1842
Barbour	Harrison, Lewis, Randolph	1843
Taylor	Barbour, Harrison, Marion, Preston	1844
Ritchie	Harrison, Lewis, Wood, Prince Edward	1845
Doddridge	Harrison, Lewis, Ritchie, Taylor	1845
Gilmer	Kanawha, Lewis	1845
Wetzel	Tyler	1846
Arlington	Fairfax	1847
Highland	Bath, Pendleton	1847
Boone	Cabell, Kanawha, Logan	1847
Hancock	Brooke	1848
Putnam	Cabell, Kanawha, Mason	1848
Wirt	Jackson, Wood	1848
Raleigh	Fayette	1850
Wyoming	Logan	1850
Craig	Allegheny, Botetourt, Giles, Monroe, Montgomery, Roanoke	1851
Pleasants	Ritchie, Tyler, Wood	1851
Upshur	Barbour, Lewis, Randolph	1851
Calhoun	Gilmer	1856
Roane	Gilmer, Jackson, Kanawha	1856
Tucker	Randolph	1856
Wise	Lee, Russell, Scott	1856
Buchanan	Russell, Tazewell	1858
Clay	Braxton, Nicholas	1858
McDowell	Tazewell	1858
Webster	Braxton, Nicholas	1860

WISCONSIN

County	Created from	Year
Kenosha	Racine	1850
Marathon	Portage	1850
Door	Brown	1851
La Crosse	Crawford	1851
Oconto	Brown and unorganized area	1851
Outgamie	Milwaukee	1851
Vernon	Bad Ax, Richland	1851
Waupaca	Brown, Winnebago	1851
Waushara	Marquette	1851
Kewaunee	Manitowoc	1852
Buffalo	Trempealeau	1853
Clark	Crawford	1853
Jackson	La Crosse	1853
Ozaukee	Milwaukee	1853

Pierce	Saint Croix	1853	Eau Claire	Chippewa	1856
Polk	Saint Croix	1853	Wood	Portage	1856
Shawano	Oconto	1853	Juneau	Adams	1856
Douglas	La Pointe	1854	Green Lake	Marquette	1858
Dunn	Chippewa	1854	Pepin	Dunn	1858
Monroe	La Crosse	1854	Ashland	La Pointe	1860
Trempealeau	Crawford, La Crosse	1854			
Burnett	Polk	1856*	*Organized in 1865.		

Defunct County Names

The county names used in the returns and on the maps are those in existence at that time. Listed below are the counties whose names have been changed or abolished.

State	Name on Map/Returns	Present Name (Year Changed)
Alabama	Benton	Calhoun (1858)
	Decatur	abolished in 1825
	Hancock	Winston (1858)
California	Buena Vista	abolished*
	Klamath	abolished in 1874
Florida	Benton	Hernando (1850)
	New River	Bradford (1861)
	Saint Lucas	Brevard (1855)
Georgia	Campbell	became part of Fulton in 1930
	Cass	Bartow (1861)
	Kinchafoonee	Webster (1856)
	Milton	became part of Fulton in 1930
Indiana	Richardville	Howard (1847)
Michigan	Michilmackinac	Mackinac (1849)
Missouri	Lillard	Lafayette (1825)
	Decatur	Ozark (1845)
	Dodge	abolished in 1853
	Niangua	Dallas (1844)
	Rives	Henry (1842)
North Carolina	Glasgow	abolished in 1799
Wisconsin	Bad Ax	Vernon (1862)
	La Pointe	Bayfield (1866)

*It is not clear if the county was ever organized. It is mentioned only in conjunction with the election of 1856.

PRESIDENTIAL ELECTION RETURNS

The vote by county is provided for each election. Beginning with the election of 1800, a national summary by state precedes the vote by county.

In determining the state totals the county returns were added; where the sum differed from totals reported by the state, both are listed. Only the county totals are used in the national summary.

The reader will note that in several instances, county returns were found that had not been included in the official returns. These returns are listed separately following the rest of the returns, with an explanation. They are not included in the state totals.* Throughout the book, incomplete returns are enclosed in parentheses.

Where county returns were missing from the official returns, the names of these counties are listed in two different ways: when they follow the rest of the county returns, it is assumed that no valid returns were made or sent to state officials; when they are in the alphabetical list of counties it is because no returns were located.

1788/9

Electoral Vote[1][†]

State	George Washington	John Adams	John Jay	Robert H. Harrison	John Rutledge	others
Connecticut	7	5				2[2]
Delaware	3		3			
Georgia	5					5[3]
Maryland	6			6		
Massachusetts	10	10				
New Hampshire	5	5				
New Jersey	6	1	5			
Pennsylvania	10	8				2[4]
South Carolina	7				6	1[5]
Virginia	10	5	1			4[6]
Total	**69**	**34**	**9**	**6**	**6**	**14**

Connecticut

Electors chosen by the legislature

Delaware[7]

One elector chosen in each county

Kent	John Banning	no vote given
New Castle	Gunning Bedford Sr.	163
Sussex	George Mitchell	522

Source—*Delaware History*, April, 1970; Merrill Jensen and Robert A. Becker, eds., *Documentary History of the First Federal Elections 1788–1790*, Vol. 1, Madison: University of Wisconsin Press, 1976, pp. 82–83.

---

*Returns were omitted from the official tally most frequently because they were received by the state after the deadline for counting the vote but were otherwise correct. In some cases, however, the reason for their omission remains unknown.

†Numbered superscript notes are given at the conclusion of each quadrennial section.

Georgia

Electors chosen by the legislature

Maryland

County	(f)	(a-f)
Anne Arundel	678 (55.2%)	551 (44.8%)
Baltimore	745 (54.9%)	613 (45.1%)
Baltimore (City)	843 (69.0%)	379 (31.0%)
Calvert	254 (72.0%)	99 (28.0%)
Caroline	129 (100%)	0
Cecil	519 (100%)	0
Charles	190 (98.4%)	3 (1.6%)
Dorchester	111 (100%)	0
Frederick	790 (99.6%)	3 (0.4%)
Harford	444 (85.0%)	239 (15.0%)
Kent	178 (81.3%)	41 (18.7%)
Montgomery	320 (98.5%)	5 (1.5%)
Prince George's	510 (69.1%)	228 (30.9%)
Queen Anne's	55 (73.3%)	20 (26.7%)
St. Mary's	116 (90.6%)	12 (9.4%)
Somerset	212 (99.1%)	2 (0.9%)
Talbot	254 (100%)	0
Washington	1,164 (100%)	0
Worcester	153 (64.3%)	85 (35.7%)
Total	**7,665 (77.1%)**	**2,280 (22.9%)**

SOURCE—Manuscript returns, Hall of Records, Annapolis.

Massachusetts

Legislature made final selection of electors from each district, choosing one of the top two as well as two additional electors

Essex
George Cabot	955
Samuel Phillips	676
John Titcomb	323
Arzoi Orne	184
Samuel Holten	155
Benjamin Goodhue	100

Suffolk
Jabez Foster	801
Caleb Davis	585
Thomas Davies	132
scattering	278

Middlesex
Francis Dana	572
John Brroks	338
Nathaniel Goodhue	333
Eleazur Brooks	267
Oliver Prescott	259
Joseph B. Varnum	182
scattering	429

Worcester
Moses Gill	340
Abel Wolver	335
John Sprague	281
Artemas Ward	176
Samuel Baker	163
Amos Singletary	154
Jonathan Warner	144

Martin Kinstry	135
Peter Penssiman	123
Timothy Fuller	104
Timothy Paine	101

Hampshire & Berkshire
Samuel Henshaw	614
Elijah Dwight	509
Samuel Lyman	473
Thompson Skinner	455
Samuel Fowler	200
John Hastings	160

Plymouth & Barnstable
Samuel Savage	373
William Lever	319
Nathaniel Cushing	92

Bristol, Dukes & Nantucket
Ekisha May	437
Walter Spooner	357
Samuel Tobey	332
Holden Slocum	300
Phanuel Bishop	295
David Colb	162

District of Maine
David Sewall	231
Daniel Coney	213
Josiah Thacher	196
William Sittgow	168
William Widgerery	157

New Hampshire[8]

A majority vote being necessary for election, the legislature chose all the electors

Benjamin Gilman	1,759
John Pickering	1,364
Ebenezer Thompson	1,063
John Sullivan	872
John Parker	851
John Dudley	718
Joshua Wentworth	667
Nathaniel Folsom	589
Ebenezer Smith	543
Joseph Cilley	528

SOURCE—*First Federal Elections*, Vol. 1, pp. 814–816.

New Jersey

Electors chosen by the legislature

New York

Because the legislature could not agree on electors, the state did not participate in this election

Pennsylvania

County	Federal[9]	Anti-Federal[10]
Allegheny	no returns[11]	
Bedford	62 (100%)	0

Berks	157	(100%)	0
Bucks	443	(100%)	0
Chester	501	(57.0%)	378 (43.0%)
Cumberland	155	(100%)	0
Dauphin	369	(73.2%)	135 (26.8%)
Fayette		no returns[12]	
Franklin	349	(91.1%)	34 (8.9%)
Huntingdon	90	(78.9%)	24 (21.1%)
Lancaster	549	(98.4%)	9 (1.6%)
Luzerne	36	(100%)	0
Montgomery	343	(95.5%)	16 (4.5%)
Northampton	324	(99.7%)	1 (0.3%)
Northumberland	157	(100%)	0
Philadelphia	2,192	(99.4%)	14 (0.6%)
Washington	21	(100%)	0
Westmoreland	105	(63.6%)	60 (36.4%)
York	858	(99.9%)	1 (0.1%)
Total	**6,711**	**(90.9%)**	**672 (9.1%)**

SOURCE—*First Federal Elections*, Vol. 1, pp. 390–392. This volume cites the original manuscript on file at the National Archives.

South Carolina

Electors chosen by the legislature

Virginia[13]

1st District

John Pride	(301)
Edward Carrington	(155)
Theodorick Bland	(52)
scattering	(1)

2nd District

John Harvie No returns located

3rd District

Zachariah Johnston	(1,082)
Thomas Madison	(120)

4th District

John Roane	(145)
Meriwether Smith	(28)
Robert Gilchrist	(26)
scattering (8)	

5th District

David Stuart	(218)
Thomas Blackburn	(16)

6th District

William Fitzhugh	(115)
John Rowe	(9)

7th District

James Wood	419	(50.1%)
William Darke	275	(32.9%)
Robert Rutherford	113	(13.5%)
scattering	29	(3.5%)

8th District

Anthony Walke	(280)
Isaac Avery	(194)
Henry Guy	(117)
scattering	(33)

9th District[14]

Samuel Kello	(776)
Joseph Jones	(356)

10th District

Patrick Henry   No returns located

11th District

Edward Stevens	1,042 (63.3%)
William Cabell	604 (36.7%)

12th District

Warner Lewis   No returns located

SOURCE—*First Federal Elections*, Vol. 2, pp. 306–309.

NOTES

1. New York did not participate, having failed to agree on electors. North Carolina and Rhode Island had not ratified the Constitution. Two electors in Maryland and Virginia were not present.

2. Samuel Huntington.

3. John Milton 2; James Armstrong, Benjamin Lincoln, and Edward Telfair 1 each.

4. John Hancock.

5. John Hancock.

6. John Hancock 1, George Clinton 3.

7. Banning was unopposed. Only the winner's vote was reported. Henry Latimer may have been a candidate in New Castle.

8. In the incomplete returns found in *First Federal Elections*, dozens of other candidates received votes throughout the state. The total number of votes cast was 20,142.

9. Federal or Lewisburg ticket.

10. Harrisburg or Anti-Federal ticket. High elector is used for each group.

11. Although Allegheny County was created the previous year, there is no record of any returns for this or the congressional elections held in 1788.

12. According to the original manuscript no election was held as not enough people showed up to conduct one.

13. Returns are incomplete in all but the 7th and 11th districts. The missing counties are as follows: **1st.** Amelia, Chesterfield, Lunenberg, Mecklenberg and Powhatan. **2nd.** Charles City, Goochland, Henrico, James City, Louisa and New Kent. **3rd.** Bourbon, Fayette, Jefferson, Lincoln, Madison, Mercer, Nelson and Rockingham. **4th.** Caroline, Hanover, King & Queen and King William. **5th.** Fauquier, Loudoun and Prince William. **6th.** King George, Lancaster, Northumberland, Richmond and Stafford. **8th.** Nansemond and Norfolk. **9th.** Dinwiddie. **10th.** Bedford, Campbell, Charlotte, Franklin, Halifax, Henry, Pittsylvania and Prince Edward. **12th.** Elizabeth City, Gloucester, Middlesex, Warwick and York.

14. No winner was certified in the 9th District.

1792

Electoral Vote[1]

State	George Washington	John Adams	George Clinton	Thomas Jefferson	Aaron Burr
Connecticut	9	9			
Delaware	3	3			
Georgia	4		4		
Kentucky	4			4	
Maryland	8	8			
Massachusetts	16	16			
New Hampshire	6	6			
New Jersey	7	7			
New York	12		12		
North Carolina	12		12		
Pennsylvania	15	14	1		
Rhode Island	4	4			
South Carolina	8	7			1
Vermont	3	3			
Virginia	21		21		
Total[2]	**132**	**77**	**50**	**4**	**1**

Connecticut

Electors chosen by the legislature

Delaware

Electors chosen by the legislature

Georgia

Electors chosen by the legislature

Kentucky

Two electors elected from each of two districts;
no returns located

Maryland

County	Federalist
Allegany	38
Anne Arundel	36
Baltimore	8
Baltimore (city)	179
Calvert	11
Caroline	26
Cecil	128
Charles	66
Dorchester	15
Frederick	45
Harford	50
Kent	54
Montgomery	28
Prince George's	14
Queen Anne's	35
St. Mary's	13
Somerset	51
Talbot	68
Washington	33
Worcester	0
Total	**898**

Source—Manuscript returns.

Massachusetts

The legislature made the choice when there was no majority.[3]
Those elected as a result of the popular vote are indicated by a +.
Numbers in parentheses indicate number of electors chosen per district.

Suffolk-Essex-Middlesex (5)
+Azor Orne	2,022
+Frances Dana	1,339
+Thomas Davies	1,301
Thomas Davies	1,086
Samuel Phillips	1,012
Samuel Holten	809
Charles Jarvis	645
Eleazur Brooks	623
Theophilus Tansens	459
Richard Devins	375
Thomas Russell	343

Hampshire-Berkshire-Worcester (5)
William Shepard	979
Moses Gill	787
Elijah Dwight	742
Dwight Foster	740
Thompson Skinner	739
Levi Lincoln	403
Samuel Henshawing	393
Simeon Strang	388
Ebenezer Mattoon	354
Martin Kinsley	345

(Nine other candidates received from 112 to 277 votes)

Barnstable-Bristol-Dukes-Nantucket (3)

+Walter Spooner	713
+William Seaver	582
Solomon Freeman	467
Samuel Savage	154
Phanuel Bishop	145
James Warren	132
George Partridge	126
Hodder Slocum	120

District of Maine (3)

Thomas Rice	409
Nathaniel Wells	359
Daniel Cony	263
Edward Cutts	247
Peleg Wadsworth	168
Kilby Smith	160

(14 other candidates received from 6 to 150 votes.)

SOURCE—Manuscript returns.

New Hampshire

Six elected

Josiah Bartlett	1,782
John T. Gilman	1,754
Jonathan Freeman	1,607
Benjamin Bellows	1,489
John Pickering	1,298
Ebenezer Thompson	994
Timothy Farrar	980
Ebenezer Smith	678
Daniel Rindge	437
Joseph Cilley	376
Thomas Cogswell	324
Timothy Walker	235

SOURCE—*New Hampshire Manual, 1917*; Nathaniel Bouton et al., *Documents and Records Relating to New Hampshire*, Vol. 21.

New Jersey

Electors chosen by the legislature

New York

Electors chosen by the legislature

North Carolina

Electors chosen by the legislature

Pennsylvania[4]

County	William Henry[5]	Charles Broole
Allegheny	0	0
Bedford	no returns	
Berks	103 (53.9%)	88 (46.1%)
Bucks	397 (85.4%)	68 (14.6%)
Chester	160 (69.9%)	197 (30.1%)
Cumberland	161 (48.2%)	173 (51.8%)
Dauphin	161 (59.0%)	112 (41.0%)
Delaware	54 (91.5%)	5 (8.5%)
Fayette	49 (50.0%)	50 (50.0%)
Franklin	no returns	
Huntingdon	no returns	
Lancaster	201 (100%)	0
Luzerne	47 (100%)	0
Mifflin	no returns	
Montgomery	131 (56.0%)	103 (44.0%)
Northampton	181 (61.6%)	113 (38.4%)
Northumberland	52 (61.2%)	33 (38.8%)
Philadelphia	1,022 (77.1%)	303 (22.9%)
Washington	no returns	
Westmoreland	no returns	
York	639 (97.6%)	16 (2.4%)
Total	**3,358 (72.7%)**	**1,261 (27.3%)**

SOURCE—Manuscript returns, state archives, dated November 21, 1792.

Rhode Island

Electors chosen by the legislature

South Carolina

Electors chosen by the legislature

Vermont

Electors chosen by the legislature

Virginia

One elector chosen from each of 21 districts; no returns located

---

NOTES

1. Three electors were absent, two in Maryland and one in Vermont.

2. Although Washington was the choice of every elector, the vote for Adams and Clinton has been considered by some as the first indication of partisan politics at the national level. Clinton was a leading Anti-Federalist, the Governor of New York, and had led the fight at the New York state convention to oppose the ratification of the Constitution. Adams had long since been considered a supporter of a strong federal government and had vigorously supported a broad (Federalist) interpretation of the Constitution. While it would be folly to argue that this was a formalized partisan effort at this time, nevertheless it clearly represented a vote for men with two very different views of government.

3. The minimum number of votes needed for election in each district was as follows: Suffolk-Essex-Middlesex 1,218; Hampshire-Berkshire-Worcester 1,122; Barnstable-Bristol-Dukes-Nantucket 559; District of Maine 543.

4. Earlier editions of the (Pennsylvania) *Manual* support some of these results. However their totals are slightly different for the high candidate. In addition they list William Todd as the highest of the unsuccessful candidates. Their totals, no county returns given, was Henry—3,479 and Todd—1,097, with four counties missing.

Newspaper returns for this election are virtually nonexistent. The (Philadelphia) *Aurora* indicates that literally dozens of individuals received votes but the manuscript lists only 26 people.

5. Henry was one of a slate generally considered pledged to President Washington who received the greatest number of votes. Broole finished highest among the unsuccessful candidates. The

manuscript lists 13 such individuals. See Harry M. Tinkcom, *The Republicans and Federalists in Pennsylvania,* Pennsylvania Historical and Museum Commission, Harrisburg, 1950, p. 66, for a brief discussion of a second slate.

1796

Electoral Vote[1]

State	John Adams	Thomas Jefferson*	Thomas Pinckney	Aaron Burr*	Samuel Adams*	Oliver Ellsworth	George Clinton*	others
Connecticut	9		4					5[2]
Delaware	3		3					
Georgia		4					4	
Kentucky		4		4				
Maryland	7	4	4	3				2[3]
Massachusetts	16		13			1		2[4]
New Hampshire	6					6		
New Jersey	7		7					
New York	12		12					
North Carolina	1	11	1	6				5[5]
Pennsylvania	1	14	2	13				
Rhode Island	4					4		
South Carolina		8	8					
Tennessee		3		3				
Vermont	4		4					
Virginia	1	20	1		15		3	1[6]
Total	**71**	**68**	**59**	**30**	**15**	**11**	**7**	**15**

Connecticut

Electors chosen by the legislature

Delaware

Electors chosen by the legislature

Georgia

County	*Jefferson (D-R)		*Adams (F)	
Bullock	13	(100%)	0	
Burke	606	(94.7%)	34	(5.3%)
Chatham	347	(72.4%)	132	(27.6%)
Columbia	418	(66.6%)	210	(33.4%)
Effingham	129	(84.3%)	24	(15.7%)
Elbert	460	(79.4%)	119	(20.6%)
Franklin	392	(62.6%)	234	(37.4%)
Greene	270	(52.7%)	242	(47.3%)
Hancock	739	(91.8%)	66	(8.2%)
Jackson	161	(80.9%)	38	(19.1%)
Jefferson	509	(67.2%)	248	(32.8%)
Liberty	85	(96.6%)	3	(3.4%)
Lincoln	166	(59.3%)	114	(40.2%)
Montgomery	0		17	(100%)
Oglethorpe	454	(93.0%)	34	(7.0%)
Richmond	209	(37.9%)	343	(62.1%)
Scriven	108	(92.3%)	9	(7.7%)
Warren	337	(80.4%)	82	(19.6%)

Washington	214	(82.9%)	44	(17.1%)
Wilkes	583	(46.5%)	651	(53.5%)
Total[7]	**6,200**	**(70.1%)**	**2,644**	**(29.9%)**

SOURCE—Executive Council Minutes, *Augusta Chronicle,* December 17, 1796.

Kentucky

One elector chosen from each of four districts;
no returns located

Maryland

Electors were chosen by district, as indicated below the county returns. Each county's district is indicated by the number in parentheses next to the county.

County	Adams (F)		Jefferson (D-R)	
(4) Allegany	646	(99.5%)	3	(0.5%)
(5) Anne Arundel	86	(22.1%)	304	(77.9%)
(6) Baltimore	504	(68.9%)	227	(31.1%)
(5) Baltimore (city)	236	(30.8%)	530	(69.2%)
(1) Calvert	224	(100%)	0	
(9) Caroline	69	(42.6%)	93	(57.4%)
(7) Cecil	48	(12.2%)	344	(87.8%)
(1) Charles	0		121	(100%)
(9) Dorchester	582	(99.8%)	1	(0.2%)
(3) Frederick	1,121	(58.5%)	796	(41.5%)
(6) Harford	47	(7.6%)	571	(92.4%)

(7) Kent	232 (30.0%)	542	(70.0%)
(2) Montgomery	943 (72.0%)	367	(28.0%)
(2) Prince George's	469 (38.3%)	757	(61.7%)
(8) Queen Anne's	183 (34.0%)	355	(66.0%)
(1) St. Mary's	295 (100%)	0	
(10) Somerset	24 (100%)	0	
(8) Talbot	489 (84.2%)	92	(15.8%)
(4) Washington	698 (34.3%)	1,337	(65.7%)
(10) Worcester	133 (100%)	0	
Total	**7,029 (52.2%)**	**6,440**	**(47.8%)**
1st District[8]	519 (81.1%)	121	(18.9%)
2nd District	1,412 (55.7%)	1,124	(44.3%)
3rd District	1,121 (58.5%)	796	(41.5%)
4th District	1,344 (50.1%)	1,340	(49.9%)
5th District	322 (27.9%)	834	(72.1%)
6th District	551 (40.8%)	798	(59.2%)
7th District	280 (24.0%)	886	(76.0%)
8th District	672 (60.1%)	447	(39.9%)
9th District	651 (87.4%)	94	(12.6%)
10th District	157 (100%)	0	

SOURCE—Manuscript returns; John T. Willis, *Presidential Elections in Maryland*, Mt. Airy, MD: Lomond Publications, 1984, p 161.

Massachusetts

The legislature made the final choice in districts where no candidate received a majority of the vote. They also chose two additional electors. Those chosen by popular vote are marked with an asterisk (*). The districts were the same as those used to elect the state's representatives to Congress.

1st Western
*Simon Larned	748
–– Roseten	499
Truman Wheeler	426
scattering	493

2nd Western
Ebenezer Hunt	539
Caleb Strong	412
William Shephard	287
Justin Ely	157
scattering	100

3rd Western
*Ebenezer Mattoon	685
Daniel Bigelow (D-R)	394
scattering	

4th Western
*Joseph Allen	963
Moses Gill	138
Artemas Ward	127
scattering	

1st Middle
*Thomas Davies	1,712
Samuel Adams	1,377

2nd Middle
James Winthrop	529
Elbridge Gerry (D-R)	527
Eleazer Brooks	496
scattering	

3rd Middle
Samuel Walter	235
James Norris	235

Benjamin Hall	162
Loammi Baldwin (F)	124

4th Middle
*Samuel Phillips	365
Bailey Bartlett (F)	265

1st Southern
*Ebenezer Bacon	547
Solomon Freeman	260
Walter Spooner	130

2nd Southern
William Seaver	398
Edward H. Robbins (F)	253
scattering	190

3rd Southern
Elisha May (F)	245
Seth Paddleford	220
Zephaniah Leonard	206
James Williams	142

1st Eastern (District of Maine)
Thomas Rice	325
Amos Stoddard	157
David Coney	130
scattering	161

2nd Eastern (District of Maine)
*Stephen Longfellow	418
Lemuel Wells	123

3rd Eastern (District of Maine)
*Nathaniel Wells	390
Ichabod Goodwin	92

SOURCE—Manuscript returns.

New Hampshire

*The legislature chose Walker over Woodward as there was no majority for the last elector.

Oliver Peadbody (F)	3,719
John T. Gilman (F)	3,408
Benjamin Bellows (F)	3,176
Timothy Farrar (F)	3,027
Ebenezer Thompson (F)	2,867
*Timothy Walker (F)	980
*Bazaleel Woodward (F)	2,077
Joseph Badger	681
Simeon Olcott	481
Robert Wallace	444
Thomas Bellows	443
Peter Wingate	310

SOURCE—*New Hampshire Manual, 1917*, p. 221.

New Jersey

Electors chosen by the legislauture

New York

Electors chosen by the legislature

North Carolina

One elector chosen from each of 12 districts; no returns located

Pennsylvania

County	Jefferson (D-R)	Adams (F)
Allegheny	392 (83.6%)	77 (26.4%)
Bedford	190 (95.0%)	10 (5.0%)
Berks	710 (55.2%)	576 (44.8%)
Bucks	359 (26.4%)	1,001 (73.6%)
Chester	122 (18.7%)	530 (81.3%)
Cumberland	853 (78.9%)	238 (21.1%)
Dauphin	233 (34.9%)	435 (65.1%)
Delaware	127 (28.9%)	312 (71.1%)
Fayette	407 (85.9%)	67 (14.1%)
Franklin	344 (58.3%)	246 (41.7%)
Huntingdon	22 (6.6%)	313 (93.4%)
Lancaster	619 (23.1%)	2,061 (76.9%)
Luzerne	8 (1.9%)	407 (98.1%)
Mifflin	469 (94.6%)	27 (5.4%)
Montgomery	332 (38.4%)	532 (61.6%)
Northampton	460 (55.4%)	371 (44.6%)
Northumberland & Lycoming	796 (84.2%)	149 (15.8%)
Philadelphia	3,565 (70.5%)	1,490 (29.5%)
Somerset	26 (35.1%)	48 (64.9%)
Washington	1,259 (98.4%)	21 (1.6%)
Westmoreland	872 (94.4%)	52 (5.6%)
York	141 (4.2%)	3,222 (95.8%)
*Total	**12,306 (50.3%)**	**12,185 (49.7%)**
Greene[9]	210 (82.7%)	44 (17.3%)

Rhode Island

Electors chosen by the legislature

South Carolina

Electors chosen by the legislature

Tennessee

Electors chosen by the legislature

Vermont

Electors chosen by the legislature

Virginia

One elector chosen from each of 21 districts;
no returns located

NOTES

1. This was the first presidential election in which the role of parties was the paramount factor. While there was no formal nomination process, it was generally accepted that Adams and Jefferson were the presidential candidates of their respective parties. Electoral candidates were pledged in advance on behalf of these two individuals and their running mates. Several Federalist electors who voted for Adams did not vote for his running mate Pinckney, apparently out of fear there was a move on by other Federalists to deprive Adams of the presidency by voting for Pinckney and not Adams. Electors of this time cast two votes for president, with the person with the second highest total becoming the vice president. The result of this was to allow Jefferson to become vice president. Burr's vote as Jefferson's apparent running mate seems less clear cut as more than half the Democratic-Republican electors voted for someone other than Burr.

2. John Jay.

3. Patrick Henry.

4. Samuel Johnston.

5. James Iredell 3, George Washington 1, Charles Pinckney 1.

6. George Washington 1.

7. This represents the vote for the highest candidate of each party. However, there was a substantial difference between these totals and those for other Democratic-Republican as well as Federalist electors. In addition, a total of 51 candidates received votes, although 34 received fewer than 20 votes. The statewide vote for the other candidates receiving 100 or more votes; Edward Telfair (D-R) 4,610, Charles Abercrombie (D-R) 4,357, William Barnett (D-R) 3,965, George Walton (F) 2,357, John Milton (F) 1,042, Burwell Pope (F) 910, George Mathews (F) 710, Benjamin Taliaferro (F) 249, -- Marshall (F) 163, -- Madlock (F) 127, John Berrien (?) 126, Joseph Clay (?) 104.

8. In the 1st District, there were actually two Federalist candidates: John Plater, who received the most votes in the district, received no votes in Charles County. His vote is used in all of the above figures. John Campbell received 271 votes in Charles County and 431 in the district.

9. The returns from Greene County were received after Governor Thomas Mifflin's proclamation of the returns and not included in the official tally. Had they been included all 15 Democratic-Republican electors would have been chosen; as it was 13 were elected along with two Federalists.

For a discussion of the controversy surrounding the delayed returns and Mifflin's role in the matter see Harry M. Tinckom, *The Republicans and Federalists in Pennsylvania 1790–1801*, Pennsylvania Historical And Museum Commission, Harrisburg, 1950. pp. 168–174.

1 8 0 0

National Summary

State	Thomas Jefferson (D-R)	John Adams (F)
Connecticut	electors chosen by the legislature	
Delaware	electors chosen by the legislature	

State	Thomas Jefferson (D-R)		John Adams (F)	
Georgia	electors chosen by the legislature			
Kentucky	no returns located			
Maryland	10,629	(51.48%)	10,018	(48.52%)
Massachusetts	electors chosen by the legislature			
New Hampshire	electors chosen by the legislature			
New Jersey	electors chosen by the legislature			
New York	electors chosen by the legislature			
North Carolina	(7,540)		(7,403)	
Pennsylvania	electors chosen by the legislature			
Rhode Island	2,345	(52.18%)	2,149	(47.82%)
South Carolina	electors chosen by the legislature			
Tennessee	electors chosen by the legislature			
Vermont	electors chosen by the legislature			
Virginia	21,002	(77.27%)	6,178	(22.73%)
Total	**(41,516)**		**(25,748)**	

Electoral Vote[1]

State	Thomas Jefferson & Aaron Burr	John Adams & Charles C. Pinckney
Connecticut		9
Delaware		3
Georgia	4	
Kentucky	4	
Maryland	5	5
Massachusetts		16
New Hampshire		6
New Jersey		7
New York	12	
North Carolina	8	4
Pennsylvania	8	7
Rhode Island		4
South Carolina	8	
Tennessee	3	
Vermont		4
Virginia	21	
Total	**73**	**65**

Connecticut

Electors chosen by the legislature

Delaware

Electors chosen by the legislature

Georgia

Electors chosen by the legislature

Kentucky

One elector chosen from each of four districts;
no returns located

Maryland

Electors were chosen by district, and these returns are below the county returns. The number in parentheses next to each county indicates the electoral district the county was in.

County	Democratic-Republican		Federalist	
(4) Allegany	207	(36.3%)	364	(63.7%)
(5) Anne Arundel	882	(72.4%)	336	(27.6%)
(6) Baltimore	843	(78.3%)	234	(21.7%)
(5) Baltimore (city)	1,497	(77.4%)	438	(22.6%)
(1) Calvert	57	(25.9%)	163	(74.1%)
(9) Caroline	438	(78.2%)	122	(21.8%)
(7) Cecil	600	(59.1%)	415	(40.9%)
(1) Charles	10	(1.6%)	611	(98.4%)
(9) Dorchester	191	(22.5%)	659	(77.5%)
(3) Frederick	1,724	(45.3%)	2,084	(54.7%)
(6) Harford	797	(98.6%)	11	(1.4%)
(7) Kent	431	(56.9%)	327	(43.1%)
(2) Montgomery	327	(26.0%)	931	(74.0%)
(2) Prince George's	454	(38.1%)	738	(61.9%)

	Democratic-Republican		Federalist	
(8) Queen Anne's	597	(72.5%)	227	(27.5%)
(1) St. Mary's	0		340	(100%)
(10) Somerset	1	(0.3%)	301	(99.7%)
(8) Talbot	425	(61.7%)	264	(28.3%)
(4) Washington	1,144	(55.2%)	928	(44.8%)
(10) Worcester	4	(0.8%)	525	(99.2%)
Total	**10,629**	**(51.5%)**	**10,018**	**(48.5%)**
1st District	67	(5.7%)	1,114	(94.3%)
2nd District	781	(31.9%)	1,669	(68.1%)
3rd District	1,724	(45.3%)	2,084	(54.7%)
4th District	1,351	(51.1%)	1,292	(48.9%)
5th District	2,379	(75.5%)	774	(24.5%)
6th District	1,640	(87.0%)	245	(13.0%)
7th District	1,031	(58.2%)	742	(41.8%)
8th District	1,022	(67.5%)	491	(32.5%)
9th District	629	(44.6%)	781	(55.4%)
10th District	5	(0.6%)	826	(99.4%)

SOURCES—Manuscript returns; John T. Willis, *Presidential Elections in Maryland*, Mt. Airy, MD: Lomond Publications, 1984, p. 162.

Massachusetts

Electors chosen by the legislature

New Hampshire

Electors chosen by the legislature

New Jersey

Electors chosen by the legislature

New York

Electors chosen by the legislature

North Carolina

Electors were chosen by district. The number in parentheses next to each county indicates the electoral district it was in. *No returns located.

County	Democratic-Republican		Federalist	
(8) Anson	24	(69.6%)	321	(30.4%)
(1) Ashe	62	(100%)	0	
(10) Beaufort	25	(80.5%)	16	(19.5%)
*(11) Bertie				
(7) Bladen	6	(1.7%)	341	(98.3%)
*(7) Brunswick				
(1) Buncombe	156	(86.0%)	26	(14.0%)
(1) Burke	427	(77.8%)	122	(22.2%)
(4) Cabarrus	101	(42.1%)	139	(57.9%)
*(12) Camden				
(9) Carteret	14	(8.7%)	147	(91.3%)
(3) Caswell	139	(57.2%)	104	(42.8%)
(5) Chatham	397	(63.2%)	231	(36.8%)
*(12) Chowan				
(9) Craven	301	(47.8%)	331	(52.2%)
(8) Cumberland	136	(20.5%)	528	(79.5%)
*(12) Currituck				
*(7) Duplin				
(10) Edgecombe	323	(61.4%)	203	(38.6%)
(6) Franklin	224	(76.7%)	68	(23.3%)
*(12) Gates				
(5) Granville	379	(67.0%)	187	(33.0%)
(10) Greene	45	(15.5%)	245	(84.5%)
(3) Guilford	23	(9.5%)	219	(90.5%)
(6) Halifax	466	(69.0%)	209	(31.0%)
*(11) Hertford				
(10) Hyde	44	(64.7%)	214	(35.3%)
*(2) Iredell				
(9) Johnston	92	(35.4%)	168	(64.6%)
(9) Jones	87	(38.0%)	142	(62.0%)
(9) Lenoir	227	(65.0%)	122	(35.0%)
(1) Lincoln	11	(4.4%)	240	(95.6%)
*(11) Martin				
(4) Mecklenburg	292	(51.6%)	274	(48.4%)
(4) Montgomery	54	(16.3%)	277	(83.7%)
(8) Moore	5	(0.9%)	525	(91.1%)
(6) Nash	101	(68.2%)	47	(31.8%)
*(7) New Hanover				
*(11) Northampton				
*(7) Onslow				
(3) Orange	149	(52.1%)	137	(47.9%)
*(12) Pasquotank				
*(12) Perquimans				
(5) Person	241	(79.5%)	62	(20.5%)
(10) Pitt	209	(35.0%)	388	(65.0%)
(3) Randolph	137	(91.5%)	25	(8.5%)
(8) Richmond	38	(10.6%)	322	(89.4%)
(8) Robeson	60	(25.9%)	172	(74.1%)
*(2) Rockingham				
(4) Rowan	563	(46.7%)	643	(53.3%)
(1) Rutherford	361	(85.7%)	60	(14.3%)
*(8) Sampson				
*(2) Stokes				
*(12) Tyrrell				
(5) Wake	302	(53.2%)	266	(46.8%)
(6) Warren	549	(97.5%)	14	(2.5%)
*(12) Washington				
(9) Wayne	413	(94.9%)	22	(5.1%)
(1) Wilkes	357	(90.8%)	36	(9.2%)
Total	**(7,540)**		**(7,403)**	
1st District	1,374	(74.0%)	484	(26.0%)
2nd District				
3rd District	448	(48.1%)	485	(51.9%)
4th District	1,010	(43.1%)	1,333	(56.9%)
5th District	1,319	(63.9%)	746	(36.1%)
6th District	1,340	(79.9%)	338	(20.1%)
7th District	(6)		(341)	
8th District	(263)		(1,868)	
9th District	1,134	(54.9%)	932	(45.1%)
10th District	(646)		(876)	
11th District				
12th District				

SOURCES—Manuscript returns; *Raleigh Register*, November 11 and 18, 1800.

Pennsylvania

Electors chosen by the legislature

Rhode Island

County	Federalist		Democratic-Republican	
Bristol	213	(75.3%)	70	(24.7%)
Kent	359	(63.2%)	209	(36.8%)
Newport	454	(45.8%)	537	(54.2%)
Providence	1,008	(56.5%)	775	(43.5%)
Washington	311	(35.8%)	558	(64.2%)
Total	**2,345**	**(52.2%)**	**2,149**	**(47.8%)**

SOURCE—*Newport Mercury*, November 18 and 25, 1800; (Providence) *Impartial Observer*, December 1, 1800; *Acts and Resolves of the General Assembly, 1801–1804*, p.4.

South Carolina

Electors chosen by the legislature

Tennessee

The legislature chose three electors from each county in the state who in turn picked one elector from each of three districts in the state.

Vermont

Electors chosen by the legislature

Virginia

County	Democratic-Republicans		Federalists	
Accomack	22	(7.2%)	284	(92.8%)
Albemarle	561	(94.4%)	33	(5.6%)
Amelia	243	(100%)	0	
Amherst	303	(94.1%)	19	(5.9%)
Augusta	237	(33.9%)	462	(66.1%)
Bath	112	(67.1%)	55	(42.9%)
Bedford	269	(62.1%)	164	(37.9%)
Berkeley	417	(52.9%)	371	(47.1%)
Botetourt	144	(60.0%)	96	(40.0%)
Brooke	220	(87.3%)	32	(12.7%)
Brunswick	385	(93.9%)	25	(6.1%)
Buckingham	501	(100%)	0	
Campbell	211	(75.4%)	69	(24.6%)
Caroline	369	(98.4%)	6	(1.6%)
Charles City	111	(68.5%)	51	(31.5%)
Charlotte	342	(92.9%)	26	(7.1%)
Chesterfield	460	(98.7%)	6	(1.3%)
Culpeper	372	(78.8%)	100	(21.2%)
Cumberland	289	(96.3%)	11	(3.7%)
Dinwiddie	318	(97.0%)	10	(3.0%)
Elizabeth City	82	(80.4%)	20	(19.6%)
Essex	209	(82.0%)	46	(18.0%)
Fairfax	240	(52.4%)	218	(47.6%)
Fauquier	308	(70.2%)	131	(29.8%)
Fluvanna	246	(96.5%)	9	(3.5%)
Franklin	531	(94.8%)	29	(5.2%)
Frederick	527	(71.4%)	211	(28.6%)
Gloucester	203	(79.0%)	54	(21.0%)
Goochland	298	(95.8%)	13	(4.2%)
Grayson	117	(100%)	0	
Greenbrier	28	(9.1%)	279	(90.9%)
Greensville	194	(97.0%)	6	(3.0%)
Halifax	764	(98.1%)	15	(1.9%)
Hampshire	180	(47.4%)	200	(52.6%)
Hanover	201	(81.7%)	45	(18.3%)
Hardy	90	(39.1%)	140	(60.9%)
Harrison	163	(71.5%)	65	(28.5%)
Henrico	211	(83.1%)	43	(16.9%)
Henry	184	(85.6%)	31	(14.4%)
Isle of Wight	254	(90.7%)	26	(9.3%)
James City	72	(67.3%)	35	(32.7%)
Kanawha	no returns located			
King & Queen	237	(83.5%)	47	(16.5%)
King George	91	(65.5%)	48	(44.5%)
King William	128	(59.8%)	86	(40.2%)
Lancaster	139	(72.0%)	54	(28.0%)
Lee	33	(94.3%)	2	(5.7%)
Loudoun	132	(39.2%)	205	(60.8%)
Louisa	440	(94.2%)	27	(5.8%)
Lunenburg	243	(90.3%)	26	(9.7%)
Madison	238	(90.5%)	25	(9.5%)
Mathews	171	(85.5%)	29	(14.5%)
Mecklenburg	292	(72.8%)	109	(27.2%)
Middlesex	118	(78.7%)	32	(21.3%)
Monongalia	254	(57.9%)	185	(42.1%)
Monroe	42	(21.3%)	155	(78.7%)
Montgomery	212	(92.6%)	17	(7.4%)
Nansemond	181	(87.4%)	26	(12.6%)
New Kent	105	(54.7%)	87	(45.3%)
Norfolk	241	(88.9%)	30	(11.1%)
Northampton	28	(16.4%)	143	(83.6%)
Northumberland	220	(89.1%)	27	(10.9%)
Nottoway	190	(100%)	0	
Ohio	164	(72.9%)	61	(27.1%)
Orange	337	(98.0%)	7	(2.0%)
Patrick	130	(100%)	0	
Pendleton	111	(51.2%)	106	(48.8%)
Pittsylvania	584	(92.7%)	46	(7.3%)
Powhatan	183	(89.3%)	22	(10.7%)
Prince Edward	344	(99.1%)	3	(0.9%)
Prince George	197	(95.6%)	9	(4.4%)
Prince William	168	(80.0%)	42	(20.0%)
Princess Anne	204	(53.7%)	176	(46.3%)
Randolph	31	(59.6%)	21	(40.4%)
Richmond	123	(81.5%)	28	(18.5%)
Rockbridge	219	(57.2%)	164	(42.8%)
Rockingham	584	(88.2%)	78	(11.8%)
Russell	31	(100%)	0	
Shenandoah	710	(94.5%)	41	(5.5%)
Southampton	214	(69.5%)	94	(30.5%)
Spotsylvania	277	(95.8%)	13	(4.5%)
Stafford	151	(62.4%)	91	(37.6%)
Surry	184	(96.8%)	6	(3.2%)
Sussex	379	(98.7%)	5	(1.3%)
Tazewell	82	(93.2%)	6	(6.8%)
Warick	53	(89.8%)	6	(10.2%)
Washington	290	(98.0%)	9	(2.0%)
Westmoreland	73	(45.1%)	89	(54.9%)
Wood	54	(87.1%)	8	(12.9%)
Wythe	113	(89.7%)	13	(10.3%)
York	74	(75.5%)	24	(24.5%)
Norfolk (boro)	111	(48.5%)	118	(51.5%)
Richmond (town)	79	(52.3%)	72	(47.7%)
Williamsburg (town)	25	(51.0%)	24	(49.0%)
Total	**21,002**	**(77.3%)**	**6,178**	**(22.7%)**

SOURCE—*Richmond Examiner*, November 21, 1800.

NOTES

1. All the Republican electors cast votes for Jefferson and Burr creating a tie and throwing the election into the House of Representatives. On the 36th ballot Jefferson was elected ten states to four, and two evenly divided. All Federalist electors voted for Adams and Pinckney, except one in Rhode island who voted for Adams and cast his other vote for John Jay.

As a result of this election and the realization that electors were now universally chosen based on party affiliation, Congress passed and the states ratified the 12th Amendment before the next presidential election, designating separate voting for president and vice president.

Only five of the 16 states provided for the popular election of electors, the lowest percentage in history. In fact four states switched from popular election in the previous election to legislative choice — Georgia, Massachusetts, New Hampshire and Pennsylvania — while Virginia changed from district election to statewide choice of electors.

1 8 0 4

National Summary[1]
(electoral vote in parentheses)

State	Thomas Jefferson (D-R)			Charles C. Pinckney (F)		
*Connecticut						(9)
*Delaware						(3)
*Georgia			(6)			
Kentucky	5,080		(8)	?		
Maryland	7,301	(74.79%)	(9)	2,461	(25.21%)	(2)
Massachusetts	29,514	(53.33%)	(19)	25,832	(46.67%)	
New Hampshire	9,088	(52.08%)	(7)	8,364	(47.92%)	
New Jersey	13,119	(100%)	(8)			
*New York			(19)			
North Carolina	(1,068)		(14)	(464)		
Ohio	2,502	(87.30%)	(3)	364	(12.70%)	
Pennsylvania	22,081	(94.69%)	(20)	1,238	(5.31%)	
Rhode Island	1,311	(100%)	(4)			
*South Carolina			(10)			
**Tennessee			(5)			
*Vermont			(6)			
Virginia	12,879	(100%)	(24)			
Total	**(103,943)**		**(162)**	**(38,723)**		**(14)**

Electors chosen by the legislature.
**No returns located.*

Connecticut

Electors chosen by the legislature

Delaware

Electors chosen by the legislature

Georgia

Electors chosen by the legislature

Kentucky

The figures in parentheses are for Hardin, Nelson, Shelby and Washington counties. Complete returns for these candidates could not be found.

Northern District (four elected)
Charles Scott (D-R)	2,827
John Coburn (D-R)	1,806
Hubbard Taylor (D-R)	1,592
William Irvine (D-R)	1,267
Thomas Bodley	1,185
James Garrard	777
Robert Sanders	695
Duval Payne	386
Roberr Todd	385
John Hall	317
George S. Smith	263
John Price	226
Thomas Irwin	52

Southern District (four elected)
Isaac Shelby (D-R)	2,253

Ninian Edwards (D-R)	1,585
Joseph Lewis (D-R)	1,310
William Roberts (D-R)	1,207
Joseph Winlock	(402)
Stephen Ormsby	(337)
Thomas Roberts	(337)
James Allen	(222)
Samuel Wells	(187)
Richard Bibb	(82)
Henry Davidge	(74)
Fortunatus Cosby	(69)
Robert Mosby	(57)
Robert Ewing	(22)
John W. Sample	(13)

SOURCES—Northern—(Lexington) *Kentucky Gazette*, November 27, 1804. Southern—(Bardstown) *Western American*, November 23, 1804; (Frankfort) *Palladium*, November 17, 1804; and *Western American*, November 16, 1804.

Maryland

Electors were chosen by district, and these returns are below the county returns.

County	Jefferson (D-R)		Pinckney (F)	
(4) Allegany	236	(97.5%)	6	(2.5%)
(3) Anne Arundel	248	(99.2%)	2	(0.8%)
(5) Baltimore	276	(99.3%)	2	(0.7%)
(3) Baltimore (city)	758	(99.7%)	2	(0.3%)
(2) Calvert	221	(99.5%)	1	(0.5%)
(8) Caroline	287	(100%)	0	
(6) Cecil	238	(100%)	0	
(1) Charles	118	(24.3%)	368	(75.7%)
(8,9) Dorchester	181	(43.1%)	239	(56.9%)
(4) Frederick	1,523	(100%)	0	

(6) Harford	430	(100%)	0	
(7) Kent	189	(60.0%)	126	(40.0%)
(2,3) Montgomery	82	(97.6%)	2	(2.4%)
(1,2) Prince George's	242	(87.4%)	35	(12.6%)
(7) Queen Anne's	235	(82.7%)	49	(17.3%)
(1) Saint Mary's	106	(32.8)%)	217	(67.2%)
(9) Somerset	259	(32.8%)	573	(67.2%)
(8) Talbot	374	(77.6%)	108	(22.4%)
(4) Washington	611	(100%)	0	
(9) Worcester	687	(48.4%)	731	(51.6%)
Total	**7,301**	**(74.8%)**	**2,461**	**(25.2%)**
1st District	239	(28.0%)	616	(72.0%)
2nd District	498	(98.6%)	7	(1.4%)
*3rd District (2 elected)	1,038	(99.6%)	4	(0.4%)
*4th District (2 elected)	2,370	(99.7%)	6	(0.3%)
5th District	276	(99.3%)	2	(0.7%)
6th District	668	(100%)	0	
7th District	424	(70.8%)	175	(29.2%)
8th District	793	(85.1%)	139	(14.9%)
9th District	995	(39.7%)	1,512	(60.3%)

The number in parentheses next to each county indicates the electoral district the county was in. The votes in the 3rd and 4th Districts are for the candidate receiving the highest vote.

SOURCES—Manuscript returns; John T. Willis, *Presidential Elections in Maryland*, Mt. Airy, MD: Lomond Publications, 1984, p. 163.

Massachusetts

County	Jefferson (D-R)		Pinckney (F)	
Barnstable	724	(64.24%)	403	(35.76%)
Berkshire	2,146	(58.54%)	1,520	(41.46%)
Bristol	1,729	(60.33%)	1,137	(39.67%)
Dukes	60	(37.27%)	101	(62.73%)
Essex	3,194	(51.07%)	3,060	(48.93%)
Hampden	2,545	(33.16%)	5,129	(66.84%)
Middlesex	3,636	(68.82%)	1,647	(31.18%)
Nantucket	176	(79.64%)	45	(20.36%)
Norfolk	1,070	(52.20%)	980	(47.80%)
Plymouth	2,034	(63.15%)	1,187	(36.85%)
Suffolk	1,585	(40.82%)	2,298	(59.18%)
Worcester	2,943	(43.79%)	3,773	(56.21%)
Massachusetts	*21,842*	*(50.65%)*	*21,280*	*(49.35%)*
Cumberland	1,171	(47.12%)	1,314	(52.88%)
Lincoln	2,031	(67.43%)	981	(32.57%)
Hancock	731	(60.87%)	470	(39.13%)
Kennebec	1,812	(66.06%)	931	(33.94%)
York	1,927	(69.24%)	856	(30.76%)
District of Maine	*7,672*	*(62.76%)*	*4,552*	*(37.24%)*
Total	**29,514**	**(53.33%)**	**25,832**	**(46.67%)**

SOURCE—Manuscript returns.

New Hampshire

No county returns have been located for this election

Jefferson (D-R)	Pinckney (F)
9,088 (52.1%)	**8,364 (47.9%)**

SOURCES—(Concord) *Courier of New Hampshire*, November 28, *Portsmouth Phoenix*, December 8, 1804.

New Jersey

No county returns have been located for this election

Jefferson (D-R)
13,119   (100%)

SOURCE—(Trenton) *True-American*, November 26, 1804.

New York

Electors chosen by the legislature

North Carolina

No other returns have been located for this election

County	Jefferson (D-R)		Pinckney (F)	
Anson	2	294	0	282
Cumberland	375	56	142	7
Richmond	2	96	91	80
Robeson	113	15	217	11
8th district	**480**	**461**	**450**	**380**
*Montgomery	12	22	158	155
Bertie	195	1		
Hertford	158	1		
Northampton	128	1		
10th district	**481**	**3**		
*Martin	8	510		
Franklin (14th District)	**95**	**1**	**6**	**1**

*In these counties the sheriff failed to report the returns and therefore they were not part of the official returns.

SOURCE—Manuscript returns; *Raleigh Register*, November 12 and 22, 1804.

Ohio

No county returns have been located for this election

Jefferson (D-R)	Pinckney (F)
2,502 (87.3%)	**364 (12.7%)**

Source—*Ohio Election Statistics 1985–86*, p. 171.

Pennsylvania

County	Jefferson (D-R)		Pinckney (F)	
Adams	208	(45.4%)	250	(54.6%)
Allegheny	526	(100%)	0	
Beaver	202	(100%)	0	
Bedford	174	(90.6%)	18	(9.4%)
Berks	2,779	(97.2%)	80	(2.8%)
Bucks	1,129	(96.4%)	42	(3.6%)
Butler	86	(100%)	0	
Centre	378	(93.1%)	28	(6.9%)
Chester	1,402	(94.7%)	78	(5.3%)
Crawford	208	(100%)	0	
Cumberland	668	(88.7%)	85	(11.3%)
Dauphin	569	(95.9%)	24	(4.1%)
Delaware	244	(85.3%)	42	(14.7%)
Erie	112	(100%)	0	
Fayette	173	(100%)	0	
Franklin	509	(72.1%)	197	(27.9%)
Greene	105	(84.0%)	20	(16.0%)
Huntingdon	409	(77.2%)	161	(22.8%)
Lancaster	1,262	(97.6%)	31	(2.4%)
Luzerne	276	(97.2%)	8	(2.8%)
Lycoming	259	(100%)	0	
Mercer	74	(100%)	0	

Mifflin	429	(92.1%)	37	(7.9%)
Montgomery	1,197	(100%)	0	
Northampton	1,670	(98.2%)	31	(1.8%)
Northumberland	1,138	(99.6%)	5	(0.4%)
Philadelphia	3,333	(99.97%)	1	(0.03%)
Somerset	247	(88.2%)	33	(11.8%)
Washington	881	(100%)	0	
Wayne	18	(100%)	0	
Westmoreland	474	(98.5%)	7	(1.5%)
York	942	(94.0%)	60	(6.0%)
Total	**22,081**	**(94.7%)**	**1,239**	**(5.3%)**

SOURCE—*Lancaster Intelligencer*, November 27, 1804.

Rhode Island

County	Jefferson (D-R)
Bristol	38
Kent	138
Newport	345
Providence	574
Washington	216
Total	**1,311**

SOURCE—Manuscript returns.

South Carolina

Electors chosen by the legislature

Tennessee

One elector chosen from five districts; no returns located

Vermont

Electors chosen by the legislature

Virginia

County	Jefferson (D-R)
Accomack	23
Albemarle	416
Amelia	93
Amherset	67
Augusta	289
Bath	33
Bedford	53
Berkeley	134
Botetourt	81
Brooke	147
Brunswick	83
Breckinridge	262
Campbell	84
Caroline	166
Charles City	73
Charlotte	313
Chesterfield	126
Culpeper	177
Cumberland	109
Dinwiddie	81
Elizabeth City	57
Essex	138
Fairfax	171
Fauquier	91
Fluvanna	183
Franklin	171
Frederick	316
Gloucester	226
Goochland	160
Grayson	49
Greenbrier	94
Greensville	94
Halifax	398
Hampshire	90
Hanover	171
Hardy	32
Harrison	317
Henrico	163
Henry	78
Ise of Wight	239
James City	63
Jefferson	98
Kanawha	no returns
King & Queen	270
King George	87
King William	85
Lancaster	182
Lee	62
Loudoun	57
Louisa	130
Lunenburg	68
Madison	160
Mathews	103
Mecklenburg	144
Middlesex	137
Monongalia	272
Monroe	72
Montgomery	61
Nansemond	23
New Kent	47
Norfolk	157
Northampton	8
Northumberland	219
Nottoway	84
Ohio	144
Orange	124
Patrick	40
Pendleton	119
Pittsylvania	358
Powhatan	111
Prince Edward	188
Prince George	57
Prince William	123
Princess Anne	153
Randolph	55
Richmond	132
Rockbridge	240
Rockingham	421
Russell	31
Shenandoah	360
Southampton	133
Spottsylvania	102
Stafford	63
Surry	93
Sussex	203
Tazewell	49
Warick	51
Washington	409
Westmoreland	68
Wood	65
Wythe	33
York	68

Norfolk (boro)	148
Richmond (town)	67
Williamsburg (town)	34
Total	**12,879**

SOURCE—*Richmond Enquirer*, November 1804.

NOTES

1. This was the first presidential election conducted under the 12th Amendment. Each elector still had two votes but one was for president and the other separately for vice president. The electoral vote for vice president was 162 for George Clinton (D-R) and Rufus King (F) 14.

1 8 0 8

National Summary[1]
(electoral vote in parentheses)

State	James Madison (D-R)		Charles C. Pinckney (F)			others	
*Connecticut				(9)			
*Delaware				(4)			
*Georgia		(6)					
Kentucky	(2,679)	(7)	(54)				
Maryland	15,346 63.36%)	(9)	8,873 (36.64%)		(2)		
*Massachusetts				(19)			
New Hampshire	12,744 (47.64%)		14,006 (52.36%)	(7)			
New Jersey	18,488 (55.73%)	(8)	14,684 (44.27%)				
*New York		(13)				(6) George Clinton	
North Carolina	(9,932)	(11)	(7,969)		(3)	(933)†	
Ohio	3,645 (75.64%)	(3)	1,174 (24.36%)				
Pennsylvania	42,508 (78.37%)	(20)	11,735 (21.63%)				
Rhode Island	2,692 (45.91%)		3,172 (54.09%)		(4)		
*South Carolina		(10)					
**Tennessee		(5)					
*Vermont		(6)					
Virginia	15,682 (78.63%)	(24)	758 (3.80%)			3,504 (17.57%)†	
Total	**(123,716)**	**(122)**	**(62,425)**	**(47)**		**(6)**	**(4,437)**

*Electors chosen by the legislature.
**No returns located.
†Republican slate pledged to James Monroe.

Connecticut

Electors chosen by the legislature

Delaware

Electors chosen by the legislature

Georgia

Electors chosen by the legislature

Kentucky

Northern District (four elected)

Charles Scott (D-R)	2,679
Robert Trimble (D-R)	2,064
Hubbard Taylor (D-R)	1,936
Christopher Greenup (D-R)	1,860
William Irvine	1,394
Thomas Bodley	841
Duval Payne	751
John Simpson	729
John Payne	579
Walter Carr	579
Thomas Wilson	564

Robert H. Grayson	411
Thomas Clay	299
–– Spencer	270
John Hall	224
John Rogers	164
–– Overton	104

Southern District (four elected)

Samuel Hopkins (D-R)	no returns located
William Logan (D-R)	no returns located
Robert Ewing (D-R)	no returns located
Mathew Walton (D-R)	no returns located
Charles F. Wing	no returns located
Richard Taylor	no returns located
William Wallace	no returns located
James Crutcher	no returns located
David Caldwell	no returns located
Joseph H. Daviess (F)	54

SOURCES—Northern—(Lancaster) *Political Theatre*, November 18 and 25, 1808. Southern—(Lexington) *Kentucky Gazette*, December 5, 1808.

Maryland

Electors were chosen by district, and these returns are below the county returns. The number in parentheses next to each county indicates the electoral district the county was in.

County	Madison (D-R)		Pinckney (F)	
(4) Allegany	359	(42.6%)	484	(57.4%)
(3) Anne Arundel	618	(98.1%)	12	(1.9%)
(5) Baltimore	1,673	(94.0%)	107	(6.0%)
(3) Baltimore (city)	2,847	(99.6%)	11	(0.4%)
(2) Calvert	339	(46.6%)	389	(53.4%)
(8) Caroline	559	(62.2%)	339	(37.8%)
(6) Cecil	682	(77.4%)	199	(22.6%)
(1) Charles	10	(2.5%)	383	(97.5%)
(8,9) Dorchester	272	(42.0%)	375	(58.0%)
(4) Frederick	2,471	(51.4%)	2,341	(48.6%)
(6) Harford	996	(86.0%)	162	(14.0%)
(7) Kent	459	(98.5%)	7	(1.5%)
(2,3) Montgomery	483	(49.8%)	486	(50.2%)
(1,2) Prince George's	627	(54.4%)	526	(45.6%)
(7) Queen Anne's	431	(100%)	0	
(1) Saint Mary's	0		321	(100%)
(9) Somerset	167	(22.5%)	574	(77.5%)
(8) Talbot	536	(50.9%)	521	(49.1%)
(4) Washington	1,525	(58.9%)	1,064	(41.1%)
(9) Worcester	292	(33.8%)	572	(66.2%)
Total	**15,346**	**(63.4%)**	**8,873**	**(36.6%)**
1st District	25	(31.0%)	781	(69.0%)
2nd District	1,268	(51.6%)	1,189	(48.4%)
*3rd District (2 elected)	3,631	(95.8%)	158	(4.2%)
*4th District (2 elected)	4,355	(51.6%)	3,889	(48.4%)
5th District	1,673	(94.0%)	107	(6.0%)
6th District	1,678	(82.3%)	361	(17.7%)
7th District	890	(99.2%)	7	(0.8%)
8th District	1,287	(57.6%)	948	(42.4%)
9th District	539	(27.3%)	1,433	(72.7%)

*The vote in the 3rd and 4th Districts are for the higher of the two electoral candidates in each district.

SOURCES—Manuscript returns; John T. Willis, *Presidential Elections in Maryland*, Mt. Airy, MD: Lomond Publications, 1984, p. 164.

Massachusetts

Electors chosen by the legislature

New Hampshire

County	Pinckney (F)		Madison (D-R)	
Cheshire	3,402	(63.0%)	1,994	(37.0%)
Coos	208	(47.4%)	231	(52.6%)
Grafton	2,511	(67.8%)	1,193	(31.2%)
Hillsborough	2,401	(45.5%)	2,877	(54.5%)
Rockingham	3,173	(43.9%)	4,052	(56.1%)
Strafford	2,311	(49.1%)	2,397	(50.9%)
Total	**14,006**	**(52.4%)**	**12,744**	**(47.6%)**

SOURCE—Manuscript returns, State Archives, Concord.

New Jersey

County	Madison (D-R)		Pinckney (F)	
Bergen	891	(48.7%)	939	(51.3%)
Burlington	1,053	(31.7%)	2,264	(68.3%)
Cape May	115	(27.2%)	308	(72.8%)
Cumberland	906	(59.7%)	612	(40.3%)
Essex	3,220	(84.5%)	589	(5.5%)
Gloucester	1,349	(49.1%)	1,398	(50.9%)
Hunterdon	2,077	(52.4%)	1,885	(47.6%)
Mercer	2,417	(83.1%)	493	(16.9%)
Middlesex	1,216	(44.4%)	1,523	(55.6%)
Monmouth	1,357	(45.6%)	1,618	(54.4%)
Salem	1,059	(63.4%)	612	(36.6%)
Somerset	848	(39.6%)	1,293	(60.4%)
Sussex	1,980	(61.5%)	1,240	(38.5%)
Total	**18,488**	**(55.7%)**	**14,714**	**(44.3%)**
			(14,684)*	

*Stated total.

SOURCE—*Newark Centinel*, November 22, 1808.

New York

Electors chosen by the legislature

North Carolina

County	Madison (D-R)		Pinckney (F)		Monroe (D-R)	
(8) Anson	77	(10.2%)	191	(25.3%)	488	(64.6%)
*(3) Ashe						
(11) Beaufort	350	(80.5%)	85	(19.5%)		
*(10) Bertie						
(13) Bladen	256	(44.1%)	325	(55.9%)		
(13) Brunswick	149	(62.3%)	90	(37.7%)		
(1) Buncombe	741	(99.6%)			3	(0.4%)
(1) Burke	59	(57.8%)	1	(1.0%)	42	(41.2%)
(4) Cabarrus	114	(39.9%)	172	(60.1%)		
*(9) Camden						
(12) Carteret	96	(33.4%)	191	(66.6%)		
*(5) Caswell						
(7) Chatham	(394 majority)					
*(9) Chowan						
(12) Craven	406	(49.4%)	416	(50.6%)		
(8) Cumberland	34	(4.6%)	704	(95.1%)	2	(0.3%)
*(9) Currituck						
(13) Duplin	604	(91.9%)	53	(8.1%)		
(11) Edgecombe	611	(4.0%)	215	(26.0%)		
(14) Franklin	433	(94.3%)	18	(3.9%)	8	(1.7%)

*(9) Gates				
(6) Granville	657	(69.5%)	288	(30.5%)
(12) Greene	80	(23.7%)	258	(76.3%)
*(5) Guilford				
*(14) Halifax				
*(10) Hertford				
(11) Hyde	245	(98.4%)	4	(1.6%)
(2) Iredell	151	(25.9%)	433	(74.1%)
(6) Johnston	254	(54.9%)	209	(45.1%)
(12) Jones	76	(34.9%)	142	(65.1%)
(12) Lenoir	282	(75.4%)	92	(24.6%)
*(2) Lincoln				
*(10) Martin				
(2) Mecklenburg				

(8) Montgomery 6 (1.6%) 224 (53.7%) 187 (44.8%)
(7) Moore (600 majority)
*(14) Nash
(13) New Hanover 425 (67.6%) 204 (32.4%)
*(10) Northampton
(13) Onslow 183 (46.4%) 211 (53.6%)
(7) Orange (311 majority)
*(9) Pasquotank
*(9) Perquimans
*(5) Person
(11) Pitt 29 (4.3%) 649 (95.7%)
(4) Randolph 446 (85.9%) 73 (14.1%)
(8) Richmond 20 (3.7%) 389 (72.0%) 131 (24.3%)
(8) Robeson 181 (36.8%) 309 (62.8%) 2 (0.4%)
*(5) Rockingham
(4) Rowan 808 (49.1%) 836 (50.9%)
(1) Rutherford 130 (26.5%) 291 (59.3%) 70 (14.3%)
(13) Sampson 333 (70.0%) 143 (30.0%)
*(3) Stokes
*(3) Surry
(11) Tyrrell 13 (100%) 0
(6) Wake 492 (59.3%) 338 (40.7%)
(14) Warren 519 (99.8%) 1 (0.2%)
(11) Washington 98 (85.2%) 17 (14.8%)
(12) Wayne 375 (48.6%) 397 (51.4%)
*(3) Wilkes

Total   **(9,932)**   **(7,969)**   **(933)**

1st District   930 (69.6%)   292 (21.8%)   115   (8.6%)
2nd District   (151)   (433)
*3rd District
4th District   1,368 (55.9%) 1,081 (44.1%)
*5th District
6th District   1,403 (62.1%)   835 (37.9%)
*7th District
8th District   318 (10.8%) 1,817 (61.7%)   810 (27.5%)
*9th District
*10th District
11th District   1,546 (61.4%)   970 (38.6%)
12th District   1,315 (46.8%) 1,496 (53.2%)
13th District   1,949 (65.5%) 1,026 (34.5%)
14 District   (952)   (19)   (8)

*No returns have been located for these counties and districts for this election

Sources—Manuscript citing: (New Bern) *Morning Herald,* November 18, 1808; *Raleigh Register,* December 8, 1808; (Raleigh) *Minerva,* November 17 and 24, 1808; (Washington) *Washington Gazette & Weekly Advertiser,* November 22 and 29, 1808.

Ohio

No county returns have been located for this election

Madison (D-R)	Pinckney (F)
3,645 (76.3%)	1,174 (23.7%)

Source—*Ohio Election Statistics 1985–6.*

Pennsylvania

County	Madison (D-R)	Pinckney (F)
Adams	414 (53.1%)	366 (46.9%)
Allegheny	982 (75.5%)	319 (24.5%)
Armstrong	178 (100%)	0
Beaver	243 (100%)	0
Bedford	668 (71.1%)	271 (28.9%)
Berks	3,206 (87.9%)	240 (12.1%)
Bucks	1,660 (60.0%)	1,106 (40.0%)
Butler	294 (85.2%)	51 (14.8%)
Cambria	62 (89.9%)	7 (10.1%)
Centre & Clearfield	858 (95.5%)	40 (4.5%)
Chester	2,545 (66.6%)	1,278 (33.4%)
Crawford	269 (64.5%)	148 (35.5%)
Cumberland & McKean	1,772 (79.2%)	464 (20.8%)
Dauphin	2,120 (90.1%)	232 (9.9%)
Delaware	703 (45.1%)	855 (54.9%)
Erie	200 (69.9%)	86 (30.1%)
Fayette	892 (88.8%)	113 (11.2%)
Franklin	1,419 (81.5%)	323 (18.5%)
Greene	353 (98.1%)	7 (1.9%)
Huntingdon	355 (63.4%)	205 (36.6%)
Indiana & Jefferson	132 (94.3%)	8 (5.7%)
Lancaster	2,560 (98.9%)	29 (1.1%)
Luzerne	456 (52.8%)	407 (47.2%)
Lycoming, Potter & Tioga	598 (74.3%)	207 (25.7%)
Mercer	288 (100%)	0
Mifflin	789 (96.3%)	30 (3.7%)
Montgomery	2,444 (78.6%)	665 (21.4%)
Northampton	2,273 (79.7%)	580 (20.3%)
Northumberland	2,688 (93.6%)	183 (6.4%)
Philadelphia	6,238 (68.8%)	2,956 (31.2%)
Somerset	384 (88.1%)	52 (11.9%)
Venango & Warren	88 (83.0%)	18 (17.0%)
Washington	1,794 (96.9%)	157 (3.1%)
Wayne	178 (88.6%)	23 (11.4%)
Westmoreland	595 (80.7%)	142 (19.3%)
York	1,810 (91.6%)	167 (8.4%)
Total	**42,508 (78.4%)**	**11,735 (21.6%)**

Sources—(Philadelphia) *Aurora, General Advertiser,* December 16, 1808; *History of Erie County, Pennsylvania,* Chicago, IL: Warner Beers & Co., 1884, p. 343.

Rhode Island

County	Pinckney (F)	Madison (D-R)
Bristol	179 (42.7%)	240 (57.3%)
Kent	612 (67.9%)	289 (32.1%)
Newport	605 (52.6%)	545 (47.4%)
Providence	1,222 (49.8%)	1,234 (50.2%)
Washington	554 (59.1%)	384 (40.9%)
Total	**3,172 (54.1%)**	**2,692 (45.9%)**
	(3,072)	

Source—(Providence) *Columbian Phoenix,* November 26, 1808.

South Carolina

Electors chosen by the legislature

Tennessee

One elector chosen from five districts; no returns located

Vermont

Electors chosen by the legislature

Virginia

County	Madison (D-R)	Pinckney (F)	Monroe (D-R)
Accomack	30 (7.0%)	0	397 (93.0%)
Albemarle		no returns	
Amelia	187 (97.4%)	0	5 (2.6%)
Amherst	202 (95.3%)	0	10 (4.7%)
Augusta	334 (50.5%)	326 (49.3%)	1 (0.2%)
Bath	51 (67.1%)	25 (32.9%)	0
Bedford	160 (87.9%)	7 (3.8%)	15 (8.2%)
Berkeley	131 (45.6%)	2 (0.7%)	154 (53.7%)
Botetourt	97 (77.0%)	0	29 (23.0%)
Brooke	112 (67.9%)	0	66 (32.1%)
Brunswick	291 (100%)	0	0
Buckingham	305 (93.8%)	0	20 (6.2%)
Campbell	167 (76.6%)	42 (19.3%)	9 (4.1%)
Caroline	209 (82.6%)	0	44 (17.4%)
Charles City	93 (90.3%)	3 (2.9%)	7 (6.8%)
Charlotte	298 (80.3%)	1 (0.3%)	72 (19.4%)
Chesterfield	327 (94.0%)	0	21 (6.0%)
Culpeper	271 (83.9%)	0	52 (16.1%)
Cumberland	210 (90.5%)	4 (1.7%)	18 (7.8%)
Dinwiddie	303 (98.4%)	0	5 (1.6%)
Elizabeth City	69 (71.9%)	0	27 (28.1%)
Essex	134 (76.1%)	0	42 (23.9%)
Fairfax	136 (69.0%)	58 (29.4%)	3 (1.5%)
Fauquier	177 (84.7%)	24 (11.4%)	8 (3.8%)
Fluvanna	161 (87.0%)	0	24 (13.0%)
Franklin	359 (100%)	0	0
Frederick	297 (71.2%)	4 (1.0%)	116 (27.8%)
Giles	40 (93.0%)	0	3 (7.0%)
Gloucester	180 (82.6%)	1 (0.5%)	37 (17.0%)
Goochland	192 (82.1%)	0	42 (17.9%)
Grayson	134 (100%)	0	0
Greenbrier	54 (62.1%)	0	34 (37.9%)
Greensville	127 (97.7%)	0	3 (2.3%)
Halifax	382 (83.4%)	0	76 (16.6%)
Hampshire	124 (69.1%)	1 (0.6%)	53 (29.8%)
Hanover	206 (91.9%)	0	19 (8.1%)
Hardy	31 (29.2%)	0	75 (70.8%)
Harrison	98 (41.7%)	0	137 (58.3%)
Henrico	238 (89.1%)	0	29 (10.9%)
Henry	161 (100%)	0	0
Isle of Wight	218 (86.1%)	0	35 (13.9%)
James City	65 (56.5%)	8 (7.0%)	42 (36.5%)
Jefferson		no returns	
Kanawha		no returns	
King & Queen	303 (93.2%)	0	22 (6.8%)
King George	87 (75.7%)	28 (24.3%)	0
King William	123 (83.7%)	0	24 (16.3%)
Lancaster	154 (87.5%)	0	22 (12.5%)
Lee	52 (100%)	0	0
Loudoun	87 (41.2%)	0	124 (58.8%)
Louisa	302 (98.7%)	0	4 (1.3%)
Lunenburg	119 (99.2%)	0	1 (0.8%)
Madison	188 (98.9%)	2 (1.1%)	0
Mason	51 (100%)	0	0
Mathews	81 (98.8%)	0	1 (1.2%)
Mecklenburg	245 (92.5%)	0	20 (7.5%)
Middlesex	121 (95.3%)	0	6 (4.7%)
Monongalia	169 (100%)	0	0
Monroe	60 (69.0%)	0	27 (31.0%)
Montgomery	83 (89.2%)	0	10 (10.8%)
Nansemond	123 (83.1%)	0	25 (16.9%)
Nelson	157 (84.0%)	0	30 (16.0%)
New Kent	60 (53.6%)	0	52 (46.4%)
Norfolk	148 (60.4%)	0	97 (39.6%)
Northampton	9 (6.9%)	0	121 (93.1%)
Northumberland	233 (88.3%)	0	31 (11.7%)
Nottoway	121 (90.3%)	0	13 (9.7%)
Ohio	182 (99.5%)	0	1 (0.5%)
Orange	293 (99.3%)	0	2 (0.7%)
Patrick	104 (100%)	0	0
Pendleton	85 (66.9%)	3 (2.4%)	39 (30.7%)
Pittsylvania	245 (97.2%)	0	7 (2.8%)
Powhatan	152 (83.5%)	0	30 (16.5%)
Prince Edward	200 (83.0%)	0	41 (17.0%)
Prince George	162 (95.3%)	0	5 (4.7%)
Prince William	137 (82.0%)	6 (3.6%)	24 (14.4%)
Princess Anne	80 (35.1%)	0	148 (64.9%)
Randolph	56 (100%)	0	0
Richmond	127 (66.8%)	0	63 (33.2%)
Rockbridge	173 (54.0%)	77 (24.1%)	70 (21.9%)
Rockingham	331 (95.4%)	0	16 (4.6%)
Russell	43 (100%)	0	0
Shenandoah	527 (98.7%)	0	7 (1.3%)
Southampton	78 (59.5%)	0	53 (40.5%)
Spotsylvania	211 (83.7%)	0	41 (16.3%)
Stafford	118 (95.9%)	0	5 (4.1%)
Surry	124 (84.4%)	0	23 (15.6%)
Sussex	143 (81.7%)	0	32 (18.3%)
Tazewell	26 (100%)	0	0
Warick	17 (30.4%)	0	39 (69.6%)
Washington	354 (98.1%)	0	7 (1.9%)
Westmoreland	48 (34.8%)	0	90 (65.2%)
Wood	49 (40.8%)	0	71 (59.2%)
Wythe	240 (100%)	0	0
York	68 (82.9%)	0	14 (17.1%)
Norfolk (boro)	202 (65.6%)	82 (26.6%)	24 (7.8%)
Richmond (town)	110 (60.8%)	1 (0.6%)	70 (38.7%)
Williamsburg	19 (48.7%)	3 (7.7%)	17 (43.6%)
Total	**15,682 (78.6%)**	**758 (3.8%)**	**3,504 (17.6%)**

Source—Manuscript returns.

Notes

1. The electoral vote for vice president was George Clinton (D-R) 113, Rufus King (F) 47, John Langdon (D-R) 9, James Madison (D-R) 3, and James Monroe (D-R) 3.

1 8 1 2

National Summary[1]
(electoral vote in parentheses)

State	James Madison (D-R)		De Witt Clinton[2] (F)	
*Connecticut				(9)
*Delaware				(4)
*Georgia		(8)		
Kentucky	(8,501)	(12)	(144)	
*Louisiana		(3)		
Maryland	14,751 (50.81%)	(6)	14,280 (49.19%)	
Massachusetts	27,272 (34.85%)		50,978 (65.15%)	(22)
New Hampshire	15,792 (43.12%)		20,248 (56.18%)	(8)
*New Jersey				(8)
*New York				(29)
*North Carolina		(15)		
Ohio	7,420 (69.21%)	(7)	3,301 (30.79%)	
Pennsylvania	49,397 (62.60%)	(25)	29,509 (37.40%)	
Rhode Island	2,084 (34.07%)		4,032 (65.93%)	(4)
*South Carolina		(11)		
**Tennessee		(8)		
*Vermont		(8)		
Virginia	14,980 (72.88%)	(25)	5,573 (27.12%)	
Total	**(140,197)**	**(128)**	**(128,065)**	**(89)**

*Electors chosen by the legislature.
**No returns located.

Connecticut

Electors chosen by the legislature

Delaware

Electors chosen by the legislature

Georgia

Electors chosen by the legislature

Louisiana

Electors chosen by the legislature

Kentucky

1st District (four elected)
no returns located

2nd District (four elected)

Richard Taylor (D-R)	3,314
William Logan (D-R)	3,009
William Irvine (D-R)	3,009
Robert Mosby (D-R)	2,293
Willis Green (F)	144
Joshua Newell (F)	129

3rd District (four elected)

Thomas D. Owings (D-R)	5,187
Duval Payne (D-R)	5,056
Walker Baylor (D-R)	5,050
Hubbard Taylor (D-R)	4,942
David Lodge (F)	289
Rhodes Thompson (F)	289
George M. Bedinger (F)	281
William E. Boswell (F)	268

SOURCES—Second—(Lexington) *Kentucky Gazette,* November 24, 1812. Third—(Lancaster) *Intelligencer & Weekly Advertiser,* December 12, 1812.

Maryland

Electors were chosen by district,
and these returns are below the county returns.
The number in parentheses next to each county
indicates the electoral district the county was in.

County	Madison (D-R)	Clinton (F)
(4) Allegany	436 (45.9%)	514 (54.1%)
(3) Anne Arundel	733 (58.0%)	531 (42.0%)
(5) Baltimore	1,668 (69.7%)	726 (30.3%)
(3) Baltimore (city)	2,622 (75.6%)	845 (24.4%)
(2) Calvert	242 (40.4%)	357 (59.6%)
(8) Caroline	502 (45.2%)	609 (54.8%)
(6) Cecil	768 (49.6%)	781 (50.4%)
(1) Charles	34 (7.6%)	415 (92.4%)
(8,9) Dorchester	322 (29.0%)	788 (71.0%)
(4) Frederick	2,126 (45.1%)	2,590 (54.9%)
(6) Harford	1,072 (81.8%)	338 (18.2%)
(7) Kent	467 (47.5%)	517 (52.5%)
(2,3) Montgomery	314 (28.1%)	805 (71.9%)

	Clinton (F)	Madison (D-R)
(1,2) Prince George's	489 (44.1%)	620 (55.9%)
(7) Queen Anne's	771 (68.5%)	355 (31.5%)
(1) St. Mary's	58 (18.6%)	253 (81.4%)
(9) Somerset	49 (64.1%)	716 (35.9%)
(8) Talbot	670 (48.1%)	722 (51.9%)
(4) Washington	1,354 (59.0%)	940 (41.0%)
(9) Worcester	54 (5.9%)	858 (94.1%)
Total	**14,751 (50.8%)**	**14,280 (49.2%)**
1st District	107 (12.4%)	757 (87.6%)
2nd District	959 (44.3%)	1,206 (55.7%)
*3rd District (two elected)	3,426 (64.8%)	1,863 (35.2%)
*4th District (two elected)	3,915 (49.2%)	4,044 (50.8%)
5th District	1,668 (69.7%)	726 (30.3%)
6th District	1,840 (62.2%)	1,119 (37.8%)
7th District	1,238 (58.7%)	872 (41.3%)
8th District	1,484 (50.5%)	1,455 (49.5%)
9th District	113 (4.8%)	2,238 (95.2%)

The votes in the 3rd and 4th Districts are for the higher of the two electoral candidates in each district.

SOURCES—Manuscript returns; John T. Willis, *Presidential Elections in Maryland*, Mt. Airy, MD; Lomond Publications, 1984, p. 165.

Massachusetts

Electors chosen by districts as indicated. All votes listed represent the high vote for each electoral slate. The numbers in parentheses represent the number of electors chosen in each district.

County	Clinton (F)	Madison (D-R)
Barnstable	1,282 (71.6%)	509 (28.4%)
Berkshire	2,223 (58.6%)	1,569 (41.4%)
Bristol	3,189 (69.7%)	1,384 (30.3%)
Dukes	213 (61.7%)	132 (38.3%)
Essex	5,439 (78.3%)	1,508 (21.7%)
Franklin	2,379 (79.0%)	622 (21.0%)
Hampden	1,654 (66.4%)	837 (33.6%)
Hampshire	2,648 (89.5%)	311 (10.5%)
Middlesex	3,264 (52.0%)	3,016 (48.0%)
Nantucket	349 (62.7%)	208 (37.3%)
Norfolk	2,058 (51.7%)	1,919 (48.3%)
Plymouth	2,917 (64.3%)	1,619 (35.7%)
Suffolk	3,164 (78.4%)	873 (21.6%)
Worcester	6,422 (74.1%)	2,250 (25.9%)
Massachusetts	*37,201 (68.9%)*	*16,757 (31.1%)*
Cumberland	3,033 (63.6%)	1,738 (36.4%)
Hancock	1,449 (58.6%)	1,023 (41.4%)
Kennecbec	1,932 (52.3%)	1,761 (47.7%)
Lincoln	2,578 (61.1%)	1,643 (38.9%)
Oxford	1,084 (46.5%)	1,248 (53.5%)
Somerset	739 (55.1%)	603 (44.9%)
Washington	370 (74.9%)	124 (25.1%)
York	2,592 (52.2%)	2,375 (47.8%)
District of Maine	*13,777 (56.7%)*	*10,515 (43.3%)*
Total	**50,978 (65.2%)**	**27,272 (34.8%)**
Essex-Middlesex-Suffolk (5)	11,867 (68.7%)	5,397 (31.3%)
Berkshire-Franklin-Hampden-Hampshire-Worcester (6)	15,326 (69.9%)	5,589 (30.1%)
Barnstable-Bristol-Dukes-Nantucket-Norfolk-Plymouth (4)	10,008 (63.4%)	5,771 (36.6%)
Cumberland-York-Oxford (3)	6,709 (55.6%)	5,361 (44.4%)
Kennebec-Lincoln-Somerset (3)	5,249 (56.7%)	4,007 (43.3%)
Hancock-Washington (1)	1,819 (61.3%)	1,147 (38.7%)

SOURCE—Manuscript returns.

New Hampshire

County	Clinton (F)	Madison (D-R)
Cheshire	5,518 (67.1%)	2,708 (32.9%)
Coos	215 (42.8%)	287 (57.2%)
Grafton	3,036 (63.5%)	1,742 (36.5%)
Hillsborough	3,259 (42.3%)	4,448 (57.7%)
Rockingham	4,708 (55.3%)	3,800 (44.7%)
Strafford	3,512 (55.6%)	2,807 (44.4%)
Total	**20,248 (56.2%)**	**15,792 (43.8%)**
	(20,386)	

SOURCE—Manuscript returns.

New Jersey

Electors chosen by the legislature

New York

Electors chosen by the legislature

North Carolina

Electors chosen by the legislature

Ohio

No county returns have been located for this election

Madison (D-R)	Clinton (F)
7,420 (69.2%)	**3,301 (30.8%)**

SOURCE—*Ohio Election Statistics 1985–6.*

Pennsylvania

County	Madison (D-R)	Clinton (F)
Adams	410 (34.6%)	746 (60.0%)
Allegheny	966 (60.0%)	645 (40.0%)
Armstrong	121 (70.3%)	51 (29.7%)
Beaver	(152 majority)	
Bedford	721 (56.2%)	562 (43.8%)
Berks	3,025 (81.2%)	693 (18.8%)
Bucks	2,184 (49.0%)	2,270 (51.0%)
Butler	375 (80.0%)	94 (20.0%)
Cambria	89 (64.0%)	50 (36.0%)
Centre, Clearfield & McKean	1,241 (85.2%)	216 (14.8%)
Chester	2,790 (47.3%)	3,109 (52.7%)
Crawford	269 (63.3%)	156 (36.7%)
Cumberland	2,455 (74.6%)	834 (25.4%)
Dauphin	1,842 (77.1%)	547 (22.9%)
Delaware	592 (32.6%)	1,225 (67.4%)
Erie	152 (54.1%)	129 (45.9%)
Fayette	999 (83.6%)	196 (16.4%)
Franklin	1,513 (66.9%)	749 (33.1%)
Greene	425 (65.0%)	229 (35.0%)
Huntingdon	712 (51.1%)	681 (48.9%)
Indiana & Jefferson	(54 majority)	
Lancaster	2,439 (39.3%)	3,762 (60.7%)
Lehigh	1,039 (82.5%)	220 (17.5%)
Luzerne	713 (36.4%)	1,245 (63.6%)
Lycoming, Potter & Tioga	933 (72.4%)	356 (27.6%)
Mercer	368 (79.1%)	97 (20.9%)
Mifflin	1,053 (89.5%)	123 (10.5%)
Montgomery	2,623 (59.1%)	1,814 (40.9%)
Northampton	1,550 (80.1%)	386 (19.9%)

Northumberland	3,416 (85.1%)	596	(14.9%)
Philadelphia	6,987 (60.1%)	4,637	(39.9%)
Schuylkill	535 (90.1%)	59	(9.9%)
Somerset	422 (71.9%)	165	(28.1%)
Susquehanna	190 (67.4%)	92	(32.6%)
Venango & Warren	131 (78.4%)	36	(21.6%)
Wayne	297 (74.4%)	102	(25.6%)
Washington	2,334 (84.6%)	426	(15.4%)
Westmoreland	818 (64.0%)	461	(36.0%)
York	2,090 (59.8%)	1,407	(40.2%)
Total[3]	**49,397 (62.6%)**	**29,509**	**(37.4%)**
	(48,819)	**(29,166)**	

SOURCES—Manuscript returns; (Uniontown) *Genius of Liberty*, November 5, 1812; *Lancaster Journal*, November 13, 1812; Henry W. Storey, *History of Cambria County*, Volume 1, p.104.

Rhode Island

County	Clinton (F)	Madison (D-R)
Bristol	298 (68.0%)	140 (32.0%)
Kent	663 (75.4%)	216 (24.6%)
Newport	752 (62.7%)	448 (37.3%)
Providence	1,603 (60.3%)	1,056 (39.7%)
Washington	716 (76.2%)	224 (23.8%)
Total	**4,032 (65.9%)**	**2,084 (14.1%)**
		*(2,086)

*Stated total.

SOURCE—(Providence) *Columbian Phoenix*, November 28, 1812.

South Carolina

Electors chosen by the legislature

Tennessee

One elector chosen from eight districts; no returns have been located

Vermont

Electors chosen by the legislature

Virginia

County	Madison (D-R)	Clinton (F)
Accomack	62 (21.8%)	322 (78.2%)
Albemarle	353 (83.8%)	68 (16.2%)
Amelia	113 (100%)	0
Amherst	176 (100%)	0
Augusta	244 (38.1%)	396 (61.9%)
Bath	119 (63.6%)	68 (36.4%)
Bedford	222 (82.8%)	46 (17.2%)
Berkeley	186 (44.0%)	237 (56.0%)
Botetourt	128 (49.2%)	132 (51.0%)
Brooke	155 (72.1%)	60 (27.9%)
Brunswick	168 (100%)	0
Buckingham	250 (100%)	0
Cabell	44 (100%)	0
Campbell	159 (90.3%)	17 (9.7%)
Caroline	142 (86.1%)	23 (13.9%)
Charles City	60 (76.9%)	18 (23.1%)
Charlotte	185 (61.7%)	115 (38.3%)
Chesterfield	233 (98.7%)	3 (0.3%)

County	Madison (D-R)	Clinton (F)
Culpeper	260 (85.8%)	43 (14.2%)
Cumberland	121 (91.7%)	11 (8.3%)
Dinwiddie	217 (100%)	0
Elizabeth City	93 (98.9%)	1 (1.1%)
Essex	108 (97.3%)	3 (2.7%)
Fairfax	154 (60.2%)	102 (39.8%)
Fauquier	219 (45.9%)	258 (54.1%)
Fluvanna	140 (100%)	0
Franklin	329 (100%)	0
Frederick	457 (58.1%)	329 (41.9%)
Giles	60 (93.8%)	4 (6.2%)
Gloucester	226 (96.6%)	8 (3.4%)
Goochland	148 (94.3%)	9 (5.7%)
Grayson	73 (61.5%)	45 (38.5%)
Greenbrier	85 (32.6%)	176 (67.4%)
Greensville	116 (96.7%)	4 (3.3%)
Halifax	214 (93.0%)	16 (7.0%)
Hampshire	180 (42.4%)	245 (57.6%)
Hanover	224 (84.2%)	42 (15.8%)
Hardy	50 (17.2%)	240 (82.8%)
Harrison	no returns	
Henrico	209 (90.1%)	23 (9.9%)
Henry	111 (100%)	0
Isle of Wight	167 (96.5%)	6 (3.5%)
James City	101 (93.5%)	7 (6.5%)
Jefferson	157 (43.7%)	202 (56.3%)
Kanawha	23 (65.7%)	12 (34.3%)
King & Queen	183 (97.9%)	4 (2.1%)
King George	84 (71.8%)	33 (28.2%)
King William	119 (90.8%)	1 (9.2%)
Lancaster	130 (91.5%)	12 (8.5%)
Lee	67 (100%)	0
Loudoun	132 (26.6%)	364 (73.4%)
Louisa	232 (97.9%)	5 (2.1%)
Lunenburg	155 (100%)	0
Madison	190 (99.5%)	1 (0.5%)
Mason	40 (85.1%)	7 (14.9%)
Mathews	67 (100%)	0
Mecklenburg	112 (96.8%)	5 (3.2%)
Monongalia	84 (55.6%)	67 (44.4%)
Monroe	67 (19.4%)	279 (80.6%)
Montgomery	181 (75.7%)	58 (24.3%)
Nansemond	152 (99.3%)	1 (0.7%)
Nelson	111 (66.1%)	57 (33.9%)
New Kent	64 (53.8%)	55 (46.2%)
Norfolk	217 (90.0%)	24 (10.0%)
Northampton	7 (5.8%)	114 (94.2%)
Northumberland	243 (94.9%)	13 (5.1%)
Nottoway	159 (100%)	0
Ohio	229 (62.6%)	137 (37.4%)
Orange	206 (99.5%)	1 (0.5%)
Patrick	140 (100%)	0
Pendleton	105 (42.3%)	143 (57.7%)
Pittsylvania	153 (92.7%)	12 (7.3%)
Powhatan	133 (100%)	0
Prince Edward	104 (77.6%)	30 (22.4%)
Prince George	176 (100%)	0
Prince William	153 (80.7%)	37 (19.3%)
Princess Anne	184 (79.7%)	47 (20.3%)
Randolph	28 (28.3%)	71 (71.7%)
Richmond	111 (87.4%)	16 (12.6%)
Rockbridge	289 (58.9%)	202 (41.1%)
Rockingham	456 (87.9%)	63 (12.1%)
Russell	126 (100%)	0
Shenandoah	548 (97.9%)	12 (2.1%)
Southampton	108 (79.4%)	28 (20.6%)
Spotsylvania	205 (97.6%)	5 (2.4%)
Stafford	92 (69.2%)	39 (30.8%)
Surry	84 (95.5%)	4 (4.5%)
Sussex	116 (100%)	0
Tazewell	66 (97.1%)	2 (2.9%)

Warick	61 (100%)	0
Washington	355 (81.6%)	80 (18.4%)
Westmoreland	29 (41.4%)	41 (58.6%)
Wood	122 (68.5%)	56 (31.5%)
Wythe	129 (87.1%)	19 (12.9%)
York	52 (69.3%)	23 (30.7%)
Norfolk (boro)	235 (77.6%)	68 (22.4%)
Richmond (town)	113 (73.4%)	41 (26.6%)
Williamsburg (town)	35 (87.5%)	5 (12.5%)
Total	**14,980 (72.9%)**	**5,573 (27.1%)**
	(15,126)	

Stated total.

SOURCE—Manuscript returns.

NOTES

1. The vote for vice president was Elbridge Gerry (D-R) 131 and Jared Ingersoll (F) 86.

2. The Federalists did not formally nominate Clinton, who in fact was a Democratic-Republican. He has often been considered the so-called "peace" candidate as much as a Federalist candidate. At a Federalist convention held in New York City, September 15–17, 1812, the following resolution was passed relative to a national nominee: "the delegates decided that it was impracticable and inexpedient to nominate a candidate of their own; that the party should support candidates likely to follow a policy different from that of the Madison administration." Clinton who had already had support amongst dissatisfied Democratic-Republicans was considered the subject of the resolution according to Sanford W. Higginbotham, *The Keystone in the Democratic Arch: Pennsylvania Politics 1800–1816*, Harrisburg, PA: Pennsylvania Historical and Museum Commission, 1952, p. 261; and James T. Havel *U.S. Presidential Candidates and the Elections*, Vol. 2, New York, NY: Prentice Hall International, 1996, p. 9.

3. The totals are for the high elector on each slate as published in the (Philadelphia) *Democratic-Press*, November 20, 1812, but without the county vote. The totals in parentheses are the added total of the county returns. The county returns are the official returns at the state archives, but the figures for two counties are missing.

1 8 1 6

National Summary[1]

(electoral vote in parentheses)

State	James Monroe (D-R)		Federalists[2]		others
*Connecticut				(9)	
*Delaware				(3)	
*Georgia		(8)			
*Indiana		(3)			
**Kentucky	(1,864)	(12)			†(803)
*Louisiana		(3)			
Maryland	7,435 (70.92%)	(8)	3,048 (29.08%)		
*Massachusetts				(22)	
New Hampshire	15,197 (53.27%)	(8)	13,330 (46.73%)		
New Jersey	5,441 (100%)	(8)	0		
*New York		(29)			
North Carolina	9,549 (93.72%)	(15)	640 (6.28%)		
Ohio	3,326 (84.93%)	(8)	593 (15.07%)		
Pennsylvania	25,653 (59.32%)	(25)	0		‡17,589 (40.68%)
Rhode Island	1,236 (100%)	(4)	0		
*South Carolina		(11)			
**Tennessee		(8)			
*Vermont		(8)			
Virginia	6,859 (100%)	(25)	0		
Total[3]	**(76,560)**	**(183)**	**(17,611)**	**(34)**	**(18,392)**

Electors chosen by the legislature.
**No returns located.*
†*Other Republicans.*
‡*Independent Republicans.*

Connecticut

Electors chosen by the legislature

Delaware

Electors chosen by the legislature

Georgia

Electors chosen by the legislature

Indiana

Electors chosen by the legislature

Kentucky

*1st District (four elected)
Robert Ewing (D-R)
Samuel Caldwell (D-R)   no
Alexander Adair (D-R)   returns
Samuel Murrell (D-R)   located

2nd District (four elected)

William Lee (D-R)	1,508
Willis A. Logan (D-R)	1,454
Richard Taylor (D-R)	1,344
William Irvine (D-R)	1,139
Robert B. McAfee (D-R)	803
Joseph Pollard (D-R)	444
David Oliver (D-R)	409

3rd District (four elected)

Thomas Bodley	(356)
Hubbard Taylor	(234)
Robert Trimble	(200)
Thomas D. Owings	(142)
Duval Payne	(140)
Walker Baylor	(100)
John Jouitt	(42)
William Moore	(12)

*It appears that in the 1st District, many other candidates ran, all pledged to Monroe.

SOURCES—(Lexington) *Kentucky Gazette*, November 18, 1816, and *Reporter*, November 20, 1816; (Frankfort) *Western Argus*, November 29, 1816.

Louisiana

Electors chosen by the legislature

Maryland

Electors were chosen by district,
and these returns are below the county returns.
The numbers in parentheses next to each county
indicate the electoral district the county was in.

County	Monroe (D-R)	Federalist
*(4) Allegany	216 (86.1%)	0
(3) Anne Arundel	475 (100%)	0
(5) Baltimore	693 (100%)	0
(3) Baltimore (city)	944 (100%)	0
(2) Calvert	138 (100%)	0
(8) Caroline	446 (43.2%)	587 (56.8%)
(6) Cecil	448 (52.1%)	412 (47.9%)
(1) Charles	0	117 (100%)
(8,9) Dorchester	275 (44.5%)	343 (55.5%)
*(4) Frederick	922 (95.8%)	0
(6) Harford	490 (95.5%)	23 (4.5%)
(7) Kent	308 (100%)	0
(2,3) Montgomery	95 (92.2%)	8 (7.8%)
(1,2) Prince George's	308 (65.1%)	165 (34.9%)
(7) Queen Anne's	372 (100%)	0
(1) Saint Mary's	0	99 (100%)
(9) Somerset	12 (3.6%)	318 (96.4%)
(8) Talbot	561 (46.3%)	650 (53.7%)
*(4) Washington	717 (100%)	0
(9) Worcester	15 (4.4%)	326 (95.1%)
Total	**7,435 (70.7%)**	**3,048 (29.0%)**
1st District	0	270 (100%)
2nd District	520 (82.4%)	111 (17.6%)

†3rd District (two elected)	1,440 (99.4%)	8 (0.6%)
†*4th District (two elected)	1,855 (95.7%)	0
5th District	693 (100%)	0
6th District	938 (68.3%)	435 (31.7%)
7th District	680 (100%)	0
8th District	1,282 (48.9%)	1,338 (51.1%)
9th District	27 (2.9%)	886 (97.1%)

*Scattering of 83 votes in each of three counties that made up the 4th District as follows: Allegany (35), Frederick (40) and Washington (8).
†The votes in the 3rd and 4th Districts are for the higher of the two electoral candidates in each district.

SOURCES—Hall of Records; John T. Willis, *Presidential Elections in Maryland*, Mt. Airy, MD: Lomond Publications, 1984, p. 166.

Massachusetts

Electors chosen by the legislature

New Hampshire

County	Monroe (D-R)	Federalist
Cheshire	2,724 (43.5%)	3,536 (56.5%)
Coos	254 (62.7%)	151 (37.3%)
Grafton	1,539 (43.8%)	1,977 (56.2%)
Hillsborough	4,364 (64.3%)	2,428 (35.7%)
Rockingham	3,578 (53.1%)	3,154 (46.9%)
Strafford	2,738 (56.8%)	2,084 (46.2%)
Total	**15,197 (53.3%)**	**13,330 (46.7%)**

SOURCE—State archives.

New Jersey

No county returns have been located for this election

Democratic-Republican
5,441 (100%)

SOURCE—(Newark) *Sentinel of Freedom*, December 3, 1816.

New York

Electors chosen by the legislature

North Carolina

No county returns have been located for this election

Monroe (D-R)[4]
9,549 (93.7%)

SOURCE—Manuscript returns, state archives.

Ohio

No county returns have been located for this election

Monroe (D-R)	Federalist
3,326 (84.9%)	593 (15.1%)

SOURCE—*Ohio Election Statistics 1985–6.*

Pennsylvania

County	Monroe (D-R)	Independent Republican[5]
Adams	205 (31.4%)	448 (68.6%)
Allegheny	218 (34.2%)	419 (65.8%)
Armstrong	71 (45.2%)	86 (54.8%)
Beaver	180 (70.0%)	77 (30.0%)
Bedford	423 (66.2%)	216 (33.8%)
Berks	1,563 (65.6%)	821 (34.4%)
Bradford	395 (82.8%)	82 (17.2%)
Bucks	1,789 (47.8%)	1,950 (52.2%)
Butler	154 (84.2%)	29 (15.8%)
Cambria	75 (76.5%)	23 (23.5%)
Centre, Clearfield & McKean	479 (66.4%)	242 (33.6%)
Chester	1,999 (55.0%)	1,634 (45.0%)
Columbia	544 (89.5%)	64 (10.5%)
Crawford	95 (52.5%)	86 (47.5%)
Cumberland	1,262 (70.6%)	525 (29.4%)
Dauphin	510 (66.8%)	253 (33.2%)
Delaware	348 (42.5%)	471 (57.5%)
Erie	85 (39.5%)	130 (60.5%)
Fayette	271 (63.2%)	158 (36.8%)
Franklin	934 (88.0%)	127 (12.0%)
Greene	140 (89.7%)	16 (10.3%)
Huntingdon	474 (87.1%)	70 (12.9%)
Indiana & Jefferson	76 (39.8%)	115 (60.2%)
Lancaster	1,223 (46.0%)	1,438 (54.0%)
Lebanon	516 (72.3%)	198 (27.7%)
Lehigh	596 (70.7%)	247 (29.3%)
Luzerne	378 (54.1%)	313 (45.9%)
Lycoming & Potter	267 (94.0%)	17 (6.0%)
Mercer	131 (68.2%)	61 (31.8%)
Mifflin	525 (82.5%)	111 (17.5%)
Montgomery	1,885 (60.7%)	1,219 (39.3%)
Northampton	860 (61.6%)	536 (38.4%)
Northumberland	506 (76.3%)	157 (23.7%)
Philadelphia	2,846 (40.9%)	4,110 (59.1%)
Pike	124 (78.0%)	35 (22.0%)
Schuylkill	340 (83.3%)	68 (16.7%)
Somerset	251 (82.0%)	55 (18.0%)
Susquehanna	242 (71.6%)	96 (28.4%)
Tioga	86 (78.9%)	23 (21.1%)
Union	522 (86.6%)	81 (13.4%)
Venango & Warren	100 (89.3%)	12 (10.7%)
Washington	489 (78.7%)	132 (21.3%)
Wayne	82 (87.2%)	12 (12.8%)
Westmoreland	414 (57.4%)	307 (42.6%)
York	980 (75.5%)	318 (24.5%)
Total	**25,653 (59.3%)**	**17,588 (40.7%)**

SOURCE—*Lancaster Intelligencer*, November 23, 1816.

Rhode Island

No county returns have been located for this election

Monroe (D-R)
1,236 (100%)

SOURCE—*Newport Mercury*, November 30, 1816.

South Carolina

Electors chosen by the legislature

Tennessee

One elector chosen from eight districts; no returns located

Vermont

Electors chosen by the legislature

Virginia

County	Monroe (D-R)
Accomack	5
Albemarle	259
Amelia	39
Amherst	72
Augusta	53
Bath	29
Bedford	84
Berkeley	66
Botetourt	74
Brooke	90
Brunswick	45
Breckinridge	105
Cabell	no returns
Campbell	87
Caroline	58
Charles City	23
Charlotte	112
Chesterfield	143
Culpeper	75
Cumberland	46
Dinwiddie	30
Elizabeth City	65
Essex	61
Fairfax	93
Fauquier	65
Fluvanna	45
Franklin	106
Frederick	146
Giles	25
Gloucester	144
Goochland	51
Grayson	49
Greenbrier	17
Greensville	74
Halifax	83
Hampshire	6
Hanover	39
Hardy	8
Harrison	96
Henrico	221
Henry	24
Isle of Wight	160
James City	67
Jefferson	30
Kanawha	no returns
King & Queen	79
King George	63
King William	36
Lancaster	96
Lee	no returns
Loudoun	66
Louisa	102
Lunenburg	47
Madison	98
Mason	68
Mathews	27
Mecklenburg	69

Middlesex	105	Tazewell	32
Monongalia	no returns	Tyler	63
Monroe	55	Warrick	49
Montgomery	no returns	Washington	97
Nansemond	39	Westmoreland	38
Nelson	49	Wood	169
New Kent	26	Wythe	25
Nicholas	no returns	York	42
Norfolk	57	Norfolk (boro)	156
Northampton	no returns	Petersburg (town)	114
Northumberland	139	Richmond (town)	21
Nottoway	49	Williamsburg (town)	29
Ohio	38		
Orange	74	**Total**	**6,859**
Patrick	59		
Pendleton	94		
Pittsylvania	104		
Powhatan	no returns		
Prince Edward	52		
Prince George	31		
Prince William	63		
Princess Anne	84		
Randolph	no returns		
Richmond	74		
Rockbridge	127		
Rockingham	107		
Russell	13		
Scott	no returns		
Shenandoah	260		
Southampton	91		
Spotsylvania	111		
Stafford	62		
Surry	52		
Sussex	88		

SOURCE—Manuscript returns

NOTES

1. The electoral vote for vice president was Daniel D. Tompkins (D-R) 183, John E. Howard (F) 22, James Ross (F) 5, John Marshall (F) 4, and Robert G. Harper (F) 3.

2. The Federalists made no nomination. Rufus King (F) received the votes of all the Federalist electors, but they were all cast in states where the electors were chosen by the legislature.

3. Three electors from Maryland and one from Delaware, all Federalists, did not attend the official casting of ballots.

4. The high vote for an unsuccessful elector was 640 for Andrew Read.

5. Not pledged to any individual. See Sanford W. Higginbotham, *The Keystone in the Democratic Arch: Pennsylania Politics 1800–1816,* Harrisburg, PA: Pennsylvania Historical and Museum Commission, 1952, pp. 321–322.

1 8 2 0

National Summary[1]

State	James Monroe (D-R)[2]		Federalists[3]		others[4]	
*Alabama						
Connecticut	3,889	(100%)				
*Delaware						
*Georgia						
Illinois	938	(65.59%)			492	(34.41%)
*Indiana						
Kentucky	(3,169)		**			
*Louisiana						
Maine	4,867	(89.24%)			587	(10.76%)
Maryland	4,544	(89.01%)	386	(7.56%)	175	(3.43%)
Massachusetts	7,689	(32.00%)	16,341	(68.00%)		
Mississippi	490	(60.12%)			325	(39.88%)
*Missouri[5]						
New Hampshire	9,448	(100%)				
New Jersey	4,321	(100%)				
*New York						
North Carolina	3,300	(100%)				
Ohio	7,164	(100%)				
Pennsylvania	30,313	(94.12%)			1,893	(5.88%)
Rhode Island	724	(100%)				
*South Carolina						
Tennessee	(1,080)				(821)	

State	James Monroe (D-R)	Federalists	others
*Vermont			
Virginia	5,247 (100%)		
Total[6]	(87,183)	(16,727)	(4,293)

*Electors chosen by the legislature.
**No returns located.

Alabama

Electors chosen by the legislature

Connecticut

County	Monroe (D-R)
Fairfield	511
Hartford	416
Litchfield	657
Middlesex	215
New Haven	602
New London	703
Tolland	215
Windham	570
Total	**3,889**

SOURCE—Manuscript returns, state archives.

Delaware

Electors chosen by the legislature

Georgia

Electors chosen by the legislature

Illinois

1st District

County	James Moore (D-R)	William Kinney	John Y. Sawyer	Abraham Prewitt
Bond	39 (45.9%)	39 (45.9%)	0	1 (1.4%)
Madison	27 (18.0%)	20 (13.3%)	82 (54.7%)	14 (14.0%)
Monroe	121 (80.7%)	29 (19.3%)	0	0
St. Clair	72 (39.6%)	103 (56.6%)	7 (3.8%)	0
Total	**259 (45.7%)**	**191 (33.7%)**	**89 (15.7%)**	**15 (3.9%)**

2nd District

County	Michael Jones (D-R)	Peter Kimmel	John Edgar	Elisha Mills
Alexander	10 (52.6%)	9 (47.4%)	0	0
Franklin	6 (42.9%)	8 (57.1%)	0	0
Jackson	47 (49.0%)	44 (45.8%)	5 (5.2%)	0
Johnson	6 (20.0%)	22 (73.3%)	0	2 (6.7%)
Pope	75 (100%)	0	0	0
Randolph	170 (79.8%)	1 (0.5%)	42 (19.7%)	0
Union	127 (94.1%)	6 (4.4%)	1 (0.7%)	1 (0.7%)
Washington		no returns		
Total	**441 (75.8%)**	**90 (15.5%)**	**48 (8.2%)**	**3 (0.5%)**

3rd District

County	Adolphus F. Hubbard (D-R)	Charles Campbell	William Campbell
Clark		no returns	
Crawford	93 (91.2%)	0	9 (8.8%)
Edwards	10 (100%)	0	0
Gallatin	67 (70.5%)	28 (29.5%)	0
Jefferson	30 (88.2%)	4 (11.8%)	0
Wayne	38 (76.4%)	15 (28.4%)	0
White		no returns	
Total	**238 (81.0%)**	**47 (16.0%)**	**9 (3.1%)**

SOURCE—Theodore C. Pease (ed.), *Illinois Election Returns 1818–1848*, Springfield, IL: Illinois State Historical Library, 1923, pp. 7–10.

Indiana

Electors chosen by the legislature

Kentucky

1st District (four elected)
David Caldwell (D-R)
Ephraim M. Ewing   no
John E. King (D-R)   returns
Samuel Murrrell   located

2nd District (four elected)
John Pope (D-R)   1,911
Willis A. Lee (D-R)   1,471
Richard Taylor   1,432
Martin D. Hardin   1,346
Joseph Winlock   1,158
William Williams   1,096
Abner Baker   985
Abraham Chapline   791
Dabney C. Crosby   680
William Smith   672
John Pollard   639
Henry Speed   418
James Alexander   296
Richard N. Coffey   137

3rd District (four elected)
James Johnson (D-R)   1,258
Jesse Bledsoe (D-R)   1,159
Thomas Bodley (D-R)   1,069
Hubbard Taylor (D-R)   1,051
William Russell   928
James Chambers   806

Adam Beatty   711
James Morrison   500
Elijah Stapp   499
Gilson Payne   490
William Moore   489
Michael Dougherty   410
William C. Prewitt   408
Benjamin W. Leathers   220
Barker C. Nicholson   167
Josiah Berryman   59

SOURCES—First and Second District—(Frankfort) *Argus of Western America*, November 30, 1820. Third District—(Lexington) *The Western Monitor*, November 28, 1820.

Louisiana

Electors chosen by the legislature

Maine[7]

No county returns have been located for this election

Congressional District	Monroe (D-R)		scattering	
1	793	(92.1%)	68	(7.9%)
2	622	(97.3%)	17	(2.7%)
3	927	(91.8%)	83	(8.2%)
4	500	(57.7%)	366	(42.3%)
5	1,046	(100%)	0	
6	524	(93.7%)	35	(6.3%)
7	455	(96.2%)	18	(3.8%)
Total	**4,867**	**(89.2%)**	**587**	**(10.8%)**

SOURCE—(Portland) *Eastern Argus*, December 19, 1820.

Maryland[8]

Electors were chosen by district, and the returns are below the county returns.
The number in parentheses next to each county indicates the electoral district the county was in.

County	Monroe (D-R)		Federalist		scattering	
(4) Allegany	140	(100%)	0		0	
(3) Anne Arundel	175	(100%)	0		0	
(5) Baltimore	283	(100%)	0		0	
(3) Baltimore (city)	568	(100%)	0		0	
(2) Calvert	105	(93.4%)	0		7	(6.6%)
(8) Caroline	163	(100%)	0		0	
(6) Cecil	191	(97.9%)	0		4	(2.1%)
(1) Charles	138	(75.0%)	46	(25.0%)	0	
(8,9) Dorchester	193	(58.5%)	109	(33.0%)	28	(8.5%)
(4) Frederick	444	(100%)	0		0	
(6) Harford	297	(99.3%)	0		2	(0.7%)
(7) Kent	181	(100%)	0		0	
(2,3) Montgomery	89	(89.0%)	9	(9.0%)	2	(2.0%)
(1,2) Prince George's	300	(81.7%)	53	(14.4%)	14	(3.8%)
(7) Queen Anne's	259	(100%)	0		0	
(1) Saint Mary's	378	(90.2%)	41	(9.8%)		
(9) Somerset	89	(64.1%)	49	(31.4%)	18	(11.5%)
(8) Talbot	232	(85.6%)	29	(10.7%)	10	(3.7%)
(4) Washington	218	(98.2%)	0		4	(1.8%)
(9) Worcester	101	(42.6%)	50	(21.1%)	86	(36.3%)
Total	**4,544**	**(89.0%)**	**386**	**(7.6%)**	**175**	**(3.4%)**
1st District	541	(79.4%)	0		0	
2nd District	469	(94.9%)	0		25	(5.1%)
3rd District (two elected)	769	(98.8%)	9	(1.1%)	0	
4th District (two elected)	802	(99.8%)	0		2	(0.2%)

5th District	283	(100%)	0		0
6th District	488	(98.8%)	0		6 (1.2%)
7th District	440	(100%)	0		0
8th District	552	(92.9%)	29	(4.9%)	13 (2.2%)
9th District	226	(40.1%)	208	(36.9%)	129 (22.9%)

In the 3rd and 4th Districts, the vote represents the total for the high elector.

SOURCES—Hall of Records; John T. Willis, *Presidential Elections in Maryland*, Mt. Airy, MD: Lomond Publications, 1984, p. 167.

Massachusetts

County	Federalist	Monroe (D-R)
Barnstable	648 (76.7%)	197 (23.3%)
Berkshire	1,208 (51.3%)	1,147 (48.7%)
Bristol	2,394 (69.5%)	1,050 (30.5%)
Dukes	23 (50.0%)	23 (50.0%)
Essex	1,621 (81.7%)	362 (18.3%)
Franklin	677 (92.7%)	53 (7.3%)
Hampden	612 (63.4%)	353 (36.6%)
Hampshire	649 (99.2%)	5 (0.8%)
Middlesex	1,042 (90.8%)	1,513 (9.2%)
Nantucket	170 (96.6%)	6 (3.4%)
Norfolk	930 (49.9%)	933 (50.1%)
Plymouth	1,515 (58.2%)	1,087 (41.8%)
Suffolk	3,483 (94.9%)	186 (5.1%)
Worcester	1,369 (63.9%)	774 (36.1%)
Total	**16,341 (68.0%)**	**7,689 (32.0%)**

SOURCE—State archives.

Mississippi

County	*Republican	*Republican
Adams	45 (63.4)	26 (36.6)
Amite	48 (66.7)	24 (33.3)
Claiborne	95 (97.9)	2 (2.1)
Covington	0	22 (100)
Franklin	26 (100)	0
Greene	0	16 (100)
Hancock	9 (50.0)	9 (50.0)
Jackson	no election held	
Jefferson	84 (86.6)	13 (13.4)
Lawrence	0	21 (100)
Marion	43 (48.9)	45 (51.1)
Pike	46 (58.2)	33 (41.8)
**Perry	no returns	
Warren	5 (100)	0
Wayne	18 (19.4)	75 (80.6)
Wilkinson	71 (76.3)	22 (23.7)
Total	**490 (60.1)**	**325 (39.9)**

There was no organized opposition to the Democratic-Republicans and the party affiliation of all the electoral candidates was probably Democratic-Republican. The vote used here is for the highest electoral candidate, Duncan Stewart, and the highest of the unsuccessful candidates, John H. Norton. In all, 22 individuals received votes but 12 of these received 16 or fewer.

**Created in 1820 from Greene County*

SOURCE—Manuscript returns.

Missouri

Electors chosen by the legislature

New Hampshire

County	Monroe (D-R)
Cheshire	2,119
Coos	252
Grafton	1,499
Hillsborough	2,085
Rockingham	1,969
Strafford	1,524
Total	**9,448**

SOURCE—State archives.

New Jersey

No county returns have been located for this election

Monroe (D-R)
4,321 (100%)

SOURCE—(Newark) *Sentinel of Freedom*, November 21, 1820.

New York

Electors chosen by the legislature

North Carolina

County	Monroe (D-R)
Anson	no returns
Ashe	34
Beaufort	55
Bertie	148
Bladen	no returns
Brunswick	10
Buncombe	64
Burke	72
Cabarrus	44
Camden	84
Carteret	no returns
Caswell	202
Chatham	64
Chowan	24
Columbus	no returns
Craven	51
Cumberland	74
Currituck	140
Duplin	149
Edgecombe	13
Franklin	no returns
Gates	24
Granville	171
Greene	19
Guilford	24
Halifax	96
Haywood	112
Hertford	95
Hyde	27

Iredell	31
Johnston	0
Jones	0
Lenoir	22
Lincoln	80
Martin	0
Mecklenburg	55
Montgomery	no returns
Moore	0
Nash	10
New Hanover	103
Northampton	66
Onslow	61
Orange	131
Pasquotank	34
Perquimans	16
Person	75
Pitt	no returns
Randolph	130
Richmond	53
Robeson	12
Rockingham	no returns
Rowan	55
Rutherford	20
Sampson	no returns
Stokes	13
Surry	223
Tyrrell	65
Wake	40
Warren	130
Washington	43
Wayne	26
Wilkes	10
Total	**3,300**

SOURCE—Manuscript returns, state archives.

Ohio

No county returns have been located for this election

Monroe (D-R)
7,164 (100%)[9]

SOURCE—*Ohio Election Statistics 1985–6.*

Pennsylvania

Complete county returns have not been found.
The *Manual* gives statewide totals without any county returns.
These are: Monroe 30,313 and Ind. Rep. 1,893.
The totals below, from 25 of the state's 53 counties,
are Monroe 21,388 and Ind. Rep. 1,783.

County	Monroe (D-R)		Independent Republican[10]	
Adams	330	(100%)	0	
Bedford	549	(100%)	0	
Bucks	1,128	(98.8%)	14	(1.2%)
Cambria	47	(100%)	0	
Centre & Clearfield	865	(100%)	0	
Chester	1,480	(98.7%)	20	(1.3%)
Cumberland	1,062	(100%)	0	
Dauphin	716	(100%)	0	
Fayette	360	(87.8%)	50	(12.2%)
Franklin	969	(100%)	0	
Huntingdon	476	(100%)	0	
Lancaster	1,508	(91.1%)	147	(8.9%)
Luzerne	377	(96.9%)	12	(3.1%)
Mifflin	594	(100%)	0	
Montgomery	2,199	(97.7%)	52	(2.3%)
Northampton	1,740	(98.8%)	22	(1.2%)
Northumberland	638	(100%)	0	
Perry	402	(100%)	0	
Philadelphia	3,333	(70.6%)	1,389	(29.4%)
Somerset	287	(94.4%)	17	(5.6%)
Venango	74	(100%)	0	
Washington	640	(100%)	0	
Westmoreland	650	(100%)	0	
York	964	(94.1%)	60	(5.9%)

SOURCES—(Philadelphia) *Democratic Press*; (Lancaster) *Intelligencer & Weekly*; (Harrisburg) *Pennsylvania Republican, Manual, 1917.*

Rhode Island

County	Monroe (D-R)
Bristol	52
Kent	128
Newport	100
Providence	300
Washington	144
Total	**724**

South Carolina

Electors chosen by the legislature

Tennessee[11]

5th District

County	John J. White (D-R)		Lee Sullivan (D-R)	
Smith	83	(20.6%)	319	(79.4%)
Sumner	201	(99.0%)	2	(1.0%)
White	264	(97.8%)	6	(2.2%)
Total	**548**	**(62.6%)**	**327**	**(37.4%)**

6th District

	Joseph Dickson (D-R)		William B. Lewis (D-R)		C. Shaw (D-R)	
Davidson	73	(17.5%)	329	(79.1%)	14	(3.4%)

No returns for the other three counties: Bedford, Lincoln and Rutherford

8th District

	Henry Small (D-R)	Steve Thomas (D-R)	Joseph Williams (D-R)
	(459)	(165)	(140)

Returns from Dickson, Humphrey, Montgomery, Robertson and Stewart counties

Total	(1,080)	(821)	(154)

SOURCES—*Nashville Gazette*, November 4 and December 16, 1820; *Nashville Whig*, December 22, 1820; *Clarksville Gazette*, July 22, August 12 and 26, and October 14 and 21, 1820.

Vermont

Electors chosen by the legislature

Virginia

County	Monroe (D-R)
Accomack	no returns
Albemarle	212

Amelia	12
Amherst	26
Augusta	78
Bath	no returns
Bedford	52
Berkeley	66
Botetourt	74
Brooke	90
Brunswick	45
Buckingham	105
Cabell	no returns
Campbell	87
Caroline	58
Charles City	23
Charlotte	112
Chesterfield	143
Culpeper	75
Cumberland	46
Dinwiddie	30
Elizabeth City	65
Essex	61
Fairfax	93
Fauquier	65
Fluvanna	45
Franklin	106
Frederick	146
Giles	25
Gloucester	144
Goochland	16
Grayson	no returns
Greenbrier	7
Greensville	15
Halifax	16
Hampshire	16
Hanover	19
Hardy	20
Harrison	70
Henrico	66
Henry	19
Isle of Wight	87
James City	36
Jefferson	21
Kanawha	no returns
King & Queen	14
King George	39
King William	7
Lancaster	57
Lee	no returns
Lewis	36
Loudoun	36
Louisa	102
Lunenburg	47
Madison	98
Mason	68
Mathews	27
Mecklenburg	69
Middlesex	105
Monongalia	10
Monroe	no returns
Montgomery	71
Morgan	60
Nansemond	52
Nelson	51
New Kent	no returns
Nicholas	81
Norfolk	41
Northampton	13
Northumberland	36
Nottoway	35
Ohio	121

Orange	46
Patrick	22
Pendleton	48
Pittsylvania	103
Powhatan	23
Preston	no returns
Prince Edward	24
Prince George	11
Prince William	50
Princess Anne	91
Randolph	no returns
Richmond	76
Rockbridge	102
Rockingham	37
Russell	67
Scott	10
Shenandoah	152
Southampton	25
Spotsylvania	41
Stafford	33
Surry	29
Sussex	21
Tazewell	32
Tyler	42
Warrick	12
Washington	122
Westmoreland	11
Wood	67
Wythe	26
York	12
Norfolk (boro)	72
Richmond (town)	17
Williamsburg (town)	14
Petersburg (town)	41
Total	**5,247**
	(4,320)*

*Stated totals.

SOURCE—Manuscript returns.

NOTES

1. The electoral vice-presidential vote was Daniel D. Tompkins (D-R) 218, Richard Tompkins (F) 8, Daniel Rodney (F) 4, Robert G. Harper (F) 1, and Richard Rush (F) 1.

2. Monroe was unopposed. Even in Massachusetts where the Federalists' slate was victorious, their votes were cast for Monroe.

3. The Federalists put up no candidate in this election.

4. For an explanation of the votes listed in this category, see the individual state returns.

5. The Missouri returns were challenged in Congress on the grounds that Missouri had not been admitted as a state. The President of the Senate read the final tally both with and without Missouri's vote, thus the issue was never resolved.

6. The electoral vote is not listed as Monroe received all the votes but one in New Hampshire which was cast for John Quincy Adams. One elector was absent in Mississippi, Pennsylvania and Tennessee. Monroe's total was 231.

7. In addition to electors chosen by congressional district, two electors were chosen statewide. The vote was William Moody (D-R) 4,364 and Joshua Wingate (D-R) 3,493. In the 5th District, all of the scattering vote was cast for William Prince. In all the other districts this vote was not broken down by individual.

8. In the 3rd District and Montgomery County, I have included in Monroe's total 26 votes cast for John S. Smith. In the other counties of the district the high Monroe elector was listed as John Stephens, who received no votes in Montgomery. The same was true of the other electoral candidate Alexander McKim who also received no votes in Montgomery, while Isaac McKim received 26 votes. In

Worcester County it appears that Federalist support was split between Charles Goldsborough, who received votes in each county of the district, and Littleton Dennis who received 37 votes in Worcester only. Also S. Doves got 49 votes only in Worcester.

9. There is some evidence that additional unsuccessful candidates also ran who were pledged to Monroe. See explanation in *Ohio Election Statistics 1985–86*, p. 184.

10. The opposition slate was little publicized and was organized relatively late in the campaign. The slate was pledged to De Witt Clinton.

11. One elector was chosen from each of eight districts. For the most part, the returns are missing. All candidates were Democratic-Republicans. The names of the winning candidates appeared in the *Nashville Gazette*, December 16, 1820, except in the 4th district where no elector was present. In computing the total vote, the numbers for the high elector were used in each district.

1 8 2 4

National Summary[1, 2]

State	Andrew Jackson	John Quincy Adams	William H. Crawford	Henry Clay	others
Alabama	9,461 (69.35%)	2,422 (17.75%)	1,663 (12.19%)	96 (0.70%)	
Connecticut	0	7,556 (79.25%)	1,978 (20.75%)	0	
*Delaware					
*Georgia					
Illinois	1,143 (24.28%)	1,540 (32.72%)	847 (17.99%)	1,012 (21.50%)	**165 (3.51%)
Indiana	7,444 (46.94%)	3,093 (19.50%)	0	5,321 (33.55%)	
Kentucky	6,433 (27.50%)	120 (0.51%)	3 (0.01)	16,837 (71.97%)	
*Louisiana					
Maine		10,289 (77.32%)	3,018 (22.68%)	0	
Maryland	14,470 (44.22%)	14,189 (43.36%)	3,371 (10.30%)	695 (2.12%)	
Massachusetts	0	31,851 (82.28%)	6,860 (17.74%)	0	
Mississippi	3,307 (65.56%)	1,738 (34.44%)	0	0	
Missouri	1,167 (34.32%)	191 (5.62%)	0	2,042 (60.06%)	
New Hampshire	0	9,454 (100%)		0	
New Jersey	10,342 (51.76%)	8,406 (42.07%)	1,233 (6.17%)	0	
*New York					
North Carolina	20,417 (56.65%)	0	15,622 (43.35%)	0	
Ohio	18,373 (36.74%)	12,315 (24.63%)	0	19,318 (38.63%)	
Pennsylvania	35,893 (76.07%)	5,403 (11.45%)	4,184 (8.87%)	1,706 (3.62%)	
Rhode Island	0	2,142 (91.46%)	0	0	200 (8.54%)
*South Carolina					
Tennessee	19,947 (96.19%)	224 (1.08%)	316 (1.52%)	250 (1.21%)	
*Vermont					
Virginia	2,890 (18.11%)	4,071 (25.51%)	8,565 (53.68%)	430 (2.69%)	
Total	**151,287 (42.22%)**	**111,811 (31.23%)**	**47,417 (13.23%)**	**47,707 (13.33%)**	**365 (0.11%)**

*Electors chosen by the legislature.
**See Illinois returns for explanation of this vote.

Electoral Vote

State	Andrew Jackson	John Quincy Adams	William H. Crawford	Henry Clay
Alabama	(3)			
Connecticut		(8)		
Delaware		(1)	(2)	
Georgia			(9)	
Illinois	(2)	(1)		
Indiana	(5)			
Kentucky				(14)
Louisiana	(3)	(2)		
Maine		(9)		
Maryland	(7)	(3)	(1)	
Massachusetts		(15)		
Mississippi	(3)			
Missouri				(3)

State	Andrew Jackson	John Quincy Adams	William H. Crawford	Henry Clay
New Hampshire		(8)		
New Jersey	(8)			
New York	(1)	(26)	(5)	(4)
North Carolina	(15)			
Ohio				(16)
Pennsylvania	(28)			
Rhode Island		(4)		
South Carolina	(11)			
Tennessee	(11)			
Vermont		(7)		
Virginia			(24)	
Total[3]	**(99)**	**(84)**	**(41)**	**(37)**

Alabama

County	Jackson	Crawford	Clay	Adams
Autauga	274 (51.0%)	195 (36.3%)	0	68 (12.7%)
Baldwin	87 (70.2%)	10 (8.1%)	0	27 (21.8%)
Bibb	170 (57.8%)	71 (24.1%)	0	53 (18.0%)
Blount	167 (6.0%)	3 (1.7%)	1 (0.6%)	3 (1.7%)
Butler	96 (39.0%)	48 (19.5%)	0	102 (41.5%)
Clarke	253 (76.7%)	33 (10.0%)	3 (0.9%)	40 (12.1%)
Conecuh	200 (67.1%)	13 (4.4%)	2 (0.7%)	83 (27.9%)
Covington	13 (76.7%)	4 (23.5%)	0	0
Dallas	411 (51.8%)	148 (18.6%)	0	235 (29.6%)
Decatur	161 (94.1%)	0	10 (5.9%)	0
Franklin	409 (84.2%)	6 (1.2%)	14 (2.9%)	57 (11.7%)
Greene	343 (48.1%)	86 (12.1%)	1 (1.4%)	283 (39.7%)
Henry	151 (77.5%)	31 (15.9%)	0	13 (6.7%)
Jackson	141 (94.0%)	0	3 (2.0%)	6 (4.0%)
Jefferson	340 (74.6%)	24 (5.3%)	0	92 (20.2%)
Lauderdale	530 (77.2%)	4 (0.6%)	10 (1.5%)	142 (20.7%)
Lawrence	617 (80.3%)	71 (9.2%)	9 (1.2%)	71 (9.2%)
Limestone	418 (83.6%)	53 (10.6%)	9 (1.8%)	20 (4.0%)
Madison	1,294 (77.8%)	155 (9.3%)	21 (1.3%)	194 (11.7%)
Marengo	150 (80.6%)	8 (4.3%)	3 (1.6%)	25 (13.4%)
Marion	120 (85.7%)	12 (8.6%)	0	8 (5.7%)
Mobile	205 (50.4%)	47 (11.5%)	0	155 (38.1%)
Monroe	420 (72.9%)	35 (6.1%)	1 (0.2%)	120 (8.8%)
Montgomery	452 (47.6%)	334 (35.2%)	1 (0.1%)	163 (17.2%)
Morgan	430 (90.9%)	8 (1.7%)	4 (0.8%)	31 (6.6%)
Perry	252 (68.1%)	60 (16.2%)	0	58 (15.7%)
Pickens	221 (78.1%)	29 (10.2%)	0	33 (11.7%)
Pike	74 (74.0%)	12 (12.0%)	0	14 (14.0%)
St. Clair	163 (87.6%)	9 (4.8%)	0	14 (7.5%)
Shelby	248 (80.8%)	24 (7.8%)	0	25 (8.1%)
Tuscaloosa	382 (55.7%)	114 (16.6%)	4 (0.6%)	186 (27.1%)
Washington	77 (66.4%)	16 (13.8%)	0	23 (19.8%)
Wilcox	192 (71.1%)	0	0	78 (28.9%)
Total	**9,461 (69.4%)**	**1,663 (12.2%)**	**96 (0.7%)**	**2,422 (17.8%)**

SOURCES—Manuscript compiled by Louis V. Loveman, state archives.

Connecticut

County	Adams	Crawford
Fairfield	1,180 (92.0%)	103 (8.0%)
Hartford	1,089 (60.4%)	714 (39.6%)
Litchfield	1,019 (87.4%)	147 (12.6%)
Middlesex	643 (83.2%)	130 (16.8%)
New Haven	1,086 (92.6%)	87 (7.4%)
New London	1,151 (73.9%)	407 (26.1%)
Tolland	497 (75.8%)	159 (24.2%)
Windham	891 (79.4%)	231 (20.6%)
Total	**7,556 (79.3%)**	**1,978 (20.7%)**

SOURCE—Manuscript returns.

Delaware

Electors chosen by the legislature

Georgia

Electors chosen by the legislature

Illinois

1st District

County	Adams	Jackson	Crawford	Clay	scattering
Bond	74 (63.8%)	10 (8.6%)	13 (11.2%)	6 (5.2%)	*13 (11.2%)
Fayette	38 (33.0%)	0	65 (56.5%)	12 (10.4%)	0
Fulton	27 (62.7%)	0	4 (9.3%)	4 (9.3%)	8 (18.6%)
Greene	85 (27.6%)	0	214 69.5%	8 (2.6%)	1 (0.3%)
Madison	243 (49.0%)	5 (1.0%)	198 (39.9%)	49 (1.0%)	1 (0.2%)
Montgomery	21 (53.8%)	0	0	11 (28.2%)	*7 (17.9%)
Morgan	86 (64.7%)	12 (9.0%)	21 (15.8%)	11 (8.3%)	*3 (2.3%)
Pike	193 (96.5%)	6 (3.0%)	1 (0.5%)	0	
St. Clair	170 (42.5%)	0	104 26.0%	119 (29.8%)	*7 (1.8%)
Sangamon	125 (42.5%)	17 (5.8%)	9 (3.1%)	123 (41.8%)	*20 (6.8%)
Total	*1,062 (49.5%)*	*50 (2.3%)*	*629 (29.3%)*	*343 (16.0%)*	*60 (2.8%)*

2nd District

County	Adams	Jackson	Crawford	Clay	scattering
Clark	13 (68.4%)	1 (5.3%)	0	5 (26.3%)	
Crawford	43 (25.0%)	64 (37.2%)	0	64 (37.2%)	1 (0.6%)
Edgar	34 (35.1%)	37 (38.1%)	0	26 (26.8%)	
Edwards	29 (15.1%)	55 (28.6%)	0	103 (53.6%)	5 (2.6%)
Gallatin	47 (14.9%)	199 (63.0%)	0	41 (13.0%)	29 (9.2%)
Hamilton	4 (5.6%)	36 (50.7%)	0	25 (35.0%)	6 (8.5%)
Lawrence	16 (14.3%)	31 (27.7%)	0	65 (58.0%)	
Wayne	6 (7.0%)	62 (72.1%)	0	18 (20.9%)	
White	33 (10.9%)	111 (36.6%)	0	129 (42.6%)	30 (9.9%)
Total	*225 (16.4%)*	*596 (43.6%)*	*0*	*476 (34.8%)*	*71 (5.2%)*

3rd District

County	Adams	Jackson	Crawford	Clay	scattering
Alexander	3 (9.4%)	28 (87.5%)	0	1 (3.1%)	
Franklin	1 (1.6%)	49 (76.6%)	5 (7.8%)	9 (14.1%)	
Jackson	6 (6.1%)	46 (46.9%)	7 (7.1%)	39 (39.8%)	
Jefferson	1 (1.4%)	62 (84.9%)	1 (1.4%)	9 (12.3%)	
Johnson	2 (4.3%)	40 (87.0%)	0	4 (8.7%)	
Monroe	35 (44.9%)	2 (2.6%)	11 (14.1%)	30 (38.5%)	
Pope	11 (13.1%)	41 (48.8%)	0	0	**32 (38.1%)
Randolph	149 (38.5%)	47 (12.1%)	177 (45.7%)	12 (3.1%)	**2 (0.5%)
Union	15 (8.3%)	153 (84.5%)	3 (1.7%)	10 (5.5%)	
Washington	30 (19.7%)	29 (19.1%)	14 (9.2%)	79 (52.0%)	
Total	*253 (21.1%)*	*497 (41.6%)*	*218 (18.2%)*	*193 (16.2%)*	*34 (2.8%)*
Total	**1,540 (32.7%)**	**1,143 (24.3%)**	**847 (18.0%)**	**1,012 (21.5%)**	**165 (3.5%)**

*There were two Jackson electoral candidates in the district. John W. Scott is listed under the Jackson column by virtue of having polled one more vote than Jonathan Berry whose votes appear in the "scattering" column.

**There were two Clay candidates in this district. Humphrey B. Jones (Clay), received all but two of his votes in Pope County; the other two were in Randolph. In Pope the regular Clay candidate did not get any votes. Jones' vote is tallied in the "scattering" column.

SOURCE—Theodore Pease (ed.), *Illinois Election Returns 1818–1848*, Springfield, IL: Illinois State Historical Society Library, 1923, pp. 30–35.

Indiana

County	Jackson	Clay	Adams
Allen	11 (15.9%)	44 (65.4%)	14 (20.3%)
Bartholomew	96 (44.7%)	99 (46.0%)	20 (9.3%)
Clark	589 (60.2%)	156 (16.0%)	233 (23.8%)
Crawford	34 (27.9%)	45 (35.2%)	43 (36.9%)
Daviess	114 (50.7%)	92 (40.9%)	19 (8.4%)
Dearborn	668 (57.7%)	122 (10.5%)	367 (31.7%)
Decatur	55 (38.1%)	72 (50.0%)	17 (11.8%)
Dubois	32 (54.2%)	18 (30.5%)	9 (15.3%)
Fayette	355 (49.0%)	277 (38.3%)	92 (12.7%)
Floyd	216 (56.3%)	50 (13.0%)	118 (30.7%)
Franklin	471 (50.4%)	244 (26.1%)	219 (23.4%)
Gibson	133 (42.0%)	169 (53.3%)	15 (4.7%)
Greene	28 (56.0%)	10 (20.0%)	12 (24.0%)
Hamilton	4 (8.9%)	31 (6.9%)	10 (2.2%)
Harrison	185 (41.5%)	129 (28.9%)	132 (29.6%)
Hendricks	6 (16.2%)	30 (85.8%)	1 (2.7%)
Henry	42 (26.3%)	96 (60.0%)	22 (13.8%)
Jackson	176 (68.8%)	23 (9.0%)	57 (22.3%)
Jefferson	298 (40.8%)	371 (50.8%)	61 (8.4%)
Jennings	131 (44.0%)	76 (25.5%)	91 (30.5%)
Johnson	28 (35.0%)	38 (47.5%)	14 (17.5%)
Knox	171 (35.3%)	280 (57.7%)	34 (7.0%)
Lawrence	228 (76.0%)	44 (14.7%)	28 (9.3%)
Madison	6 (9.4%)	54 (84.4%)	4 (6.3%)
Marion	99 (30.2%)	213 (64.9%)	16 (4.9%)
Martin	44 (39.3%)	30 (26.8%)	38 (33.9%)
Monroe	149 (55.0%)	71 (26.2%)	51 (18.0%)
Montgomery	40 (35.1%)	57 (50.0%)	17 (14.9%)
Morgan	71 (43.2%)	83 (50.6%)	10 (6.1%)
Orange	213 (50.8%)	145 (34.6%)	61 (14.6%)
Owen	33 (27.0%)	77 (63.1%)	12 (9.8%)
Parke	45 (27.6%)	111 (68.1%)	7 (4.3%)

Perry	5	(19.2%)	12	(46.2%)	9	(34.6%)
Pike	62	(44.9%)	73	(52.9%)	3	(2.2%)
Posey	173	(41.8%)	228	(55.1%)	13	(3.1%)
Putnam	27	(32.5%)	31	(37.3%)	25	(30.1%)
Randolph	62	(44.0%)	7	(5.0%)	72	(51.1%)
Ripley	119	(46.9%)	102	(40.2%)	33	(13.0%)
Rush	118	(49.0%)	108	(44.8%)	15	(6.2%)
Scott	123	(53.0%)	83	(35.8%)	26	(11.2%)
Shelby	144	(56.0%)	104	(40.5%)	9	(3.5%)
Spencer	10	(20.8%)	33	(10.4%)	5	(10.4%)
Sullivan	104	(34.7%)	175	(58.3%)	21	(7.0%)
Switzerland	161	(54.2%)	108	(36.4%)	28	(9.4%)
Union	254	(53.6%)	135	(28.5%)	85	(17.9%)
Vanderburgh	32	(26.4%)	56	(46.3%)	33	(27.3%)
Vermillion	2	(2.4%)	79	(92.9%)	4	(4.7%)
Vigo	54	(16.7%)	225	(69.7%)	44	(13.6%)
Warrick	54	(49.5%)	44	(40.4%)	11	(10.1%)
Washington	668	(67.1%)	55	(5.5%)	272	(27.3%)
Wayne	501	(37.2%)	306	(22.7%)	541	(40.1%)
Total	**7,444**	**(46.9%)**	**5,321**	**(33.6%)**	**3,093**	**(19.5%)**

SOURCE—Dorothy F. Riker and Gayle Thornbrough (eds.), *Indiana Election Returns 1816–1851*, Indianapolis, IN: Indiana Historical Bureau, 1960, pp. 4–9.

Kentucky

Electors were chosen by district: four from District One and five each from Districts Two and Three.
The district returns are below the county returns.
The number in parentheses next to each county indicates the electoral district the county was in.

County		Clay		Jackson
(1) Adair	292	(54.0%)	249	(46.0%)
(1) Allen	106	(73.1%)	39	(26.9%)
(1) Barren	388	(95.1%)	20	(4.9%)
(3) Bath	352	(86.3%)	56	(13.7%)
(3) Boone	205	(67.9%)	97	(32.1%)
(3) Bourbon	591	(80.5%)	143	(19.5%)
(3) Bracken	187	(89.9%)	21	(10.1%)
(2) Breckinridge	215	(97.3%)	6	(2.7%)
(2) Bullitt	176	(58.3%)	126	(41.7%)
(1) Butler	93	(98.9%)	1	(1.1%)
(1) Caldwell	272	(60.0%)	181	(40.0%)
(1) Calloway	41	(23.4%)	134	(76.6%)
(3) Campbell	199	(46.9%)	225	(53.1%)
(1) Casey	45	(100%)	0	
(1) Christian	283	(88.7%)	36	(11.3%)
(3) Clarke	271	(77.4%)	79	(22.6%)
(2) Clay	37	(75.5%)	12	(24.5%)
(1) Cumberland	205	(100%)	0	
(2) Daviess	101	(90.2%)	11	(9.8%)
(3) Estill		no returns		
(3) Fayette	846	(77.0%)	252	(23.0%)
(3) Fleming	246	(87.9%)	34	(12.1%)
(3) Floyd	57	(66.3%)	29	(33.7%)
(3) Franklin	568	(80.7%)	136	(19.3%)
(3) Gallatin	208	(73.8%)	74	(26.2%)
(2) Garrard	316	(92.7%)	25	(7.3%)
(1) Graves	16	(41.0%)	23	(59.0%)
(2) Grayson	129	(89.0%)	16	(11.0%)
(2) Green	313	(51.7%)	293	(48.3%)
(3) Greenup	79	(42.0%)	109	(58.0%)
(2) Hardin	232	(51.7%)	217	(48.3%)
(2) Harlan	8	(14.3%)	48	(85.7%)
(3) Harrison	449	(64.6%)	246	(35.4%)
(2) Hart	103	(73.0%)	38	(27.0%)
(1) Henderson	111	(71.2%)	45	(28.8%)
(2) Henry	402	(91.8%)	36	(8.2%)
(1) Hickman	31	(31.6%)	67	(68.4%)

(1) Hopkins	135	(91.2%)	13	(8.8%)
(2) Jefferson	573	(38.7%)	906	(61.3%)
(3) Jessamine	291	(75.2%)	96	(24.8%)
(2) Knox	81	(85.3%)	14	(14.7%)
(3) Lawrence	59	(52.2%)	54	(47.8%)
(3) Lewis	194	(90.7%)	20	(9.3%)
(2) Lincoln	274	(88.4%)	36	(11.6%)
(1) Livingston	191	(62.6%)	114	(37.4%)
(1) Logan	328	(73.1%)	121	(26.9%)
(2) Madison	453	(96.2%)	18	(3.8%)
(3) Mason	647	(92.0%)	56	(8.0%)
(2) Meade	66	(93.0%)	5	(7.0%)
(2) Mercer	671	(87.4%)	97	(12.6%)
(1) Monroe	85	(58.6%)	60	(41.4%)
(3) Morgan	23	(34.3%)	44	(65.7%)
(1) Muhlenberg	136	(97.1%)	4	(2.9%)
(2) Nelson	363	(81.6%)	82	(18.4%)
(3) Nicholas	262	(83.4%)	52	(16.6%)
(2) Ohio	136	(96.5%)	5	(3.5%)
(2) Oldham	127	(82.5%)	27	(17.5%)
(3) Owen	143	(84.6%)	26	(15.4%)
(3) Pendleton	112	(91.8%)	10	(8.2%)
(2) Perry	52	(42.3%)	71	(57.7%)
(3) Pike	3	(8.3%)	33	(91.7%)
(2) Pulaski	111	(82.8%)	23	(17.2%)
(2) Rockcastle	38	(69.1%)	17	(30.9%)
(3) Scott	456	(64.8%)	248	(35.2%)
(2) Shelby	705	(58.9%)	493	(41.1%)
(1) Simpson	211	(61.5%)	132	(38.5%)
(1) Todd	237	(81.7%)	53	(18.3%)
(1) Trigg	124	(89.9%)	14	(10.1%)
(1) Union	105	(0.5%)	11	(9.5%)
(1) Warren	341	(74.1%)	119	(25.9%)
(2) Washington	448	(86.5%)	70	(13.5%)
(1) Wayne	85	(69.7%)	37	(30.3%)
(3) Whitley	40	(67.8%)	19	(32.2%)
(3) Woodford	363	(82.1%)	79	(17.9%)
Total[4]	**16,837**	**(72.4%)**	**6,433**	**(27.6%)**
	†(16,793)		†(6,403)	
1st District	3,861	(72.4%) †(3,817)	1,473	(27.6%)
2nd District	6,165	(69.5%)	2,711	(30.5%)
3rd District	6,811	(75.2%)	2,249	(24.8%)†(2,219)
*(3)Grant	151	(71.9%)	59	(28.1%)
*(3)Montgomery	390	(64.8%)	212	(35.2%)

*These counties apparently were not included in the official returns.
†Stated totals.

SOURCES—(Lexington) *Kentucky Gazette,* and *Reporter,* November 29, 1824; (Frankfort) *Western Argus,* November 24, 1824, and *Commentator,* December 4, 1824.

Louisiana

Electors chosen by the legislature

Maine[5]

Congressional District		Adams		Crawford
1	1,642	(78.1%)	461	(21.9%)
2	1,526	(52.7%)	1,370	(47.3%)
3	1,511	(87.4%)	217	(12.6%)
4	1,357	(88.3%)	180	(11.7%)
5	1,093	(91.1%)	107	(8.9%)
6	1,396	(78.2%)	389	(21.8%)
7	1,764	(85.7%)	294	(14.3%)
Total	**10,289**	**(77.3%)**	**3,018**	**(22.7%)**

SOURCE—(Portland) *Eastern Argus,* November, 1824 and June 15, 1844.

Maryland

Electors were chosen by district, and the returns are below the county returns.
The number in parentheses next to each county indicates the electoral district the county was in.

County	Jackson	Adams	Crawford	Clay
(4) Allegany	364 (63.7%)	69 (12.1%)	7 (1.2%)	131 (22.9%)
(3) Anne Arundel	790 (52.2%)	867 (47.6%)	3 (0.2%)	0
(5) Baltimore	1,936 (66.5%)	976 (33.5%)	0	0
(3) Baltimore (city)	3,903 (56.5%)	3,004 (43.5%)	0	0
(2) Calvert	83 (24.2%)	231 (67.3%)	29 (8.5%)	0
(8) Caroline	0	317 (31.5%)	689 (68.5%)	0
(6) Cecil	703 (54.2%)	594 (45.8%)	0	0
(1) Charles	299 (36.4%)	403 (49.1%)	119 (14.5%)	0
(8,9) Dorchester	315 (30.8%)	410 (40.1%)	297 (29.1%)	0
(4) Frederick	2,002 (46.8%)	1,882 (44.0%)	0	391 (9.1%)
(6) Harford	657 (49.7%)	665 (50.3%)	0	0
(7) Kent	298 (37.8%)	469 (59.5%)	21 (2.7%)	0
(2,3) Montgomery	325 (30.5%)	632 (59.3%)	108 (10.1%)	0
(1,2) Prince George's	411 (41.3%)	243 (24.4%)	341 (35.3%)	0
(7) Queen Anne's	455 (49.9%)	427 (46.8%)	30 (3.3%)	0
(1) Saint Mary's	135 (18.4%)	414 (56.4%)	185 (25.2%)	
(9) Somerset	191 (17.4%)	619 (56.4%)	288 (26.2%)	0
(8) Talbot	2 (0.2%)	747 (59.9%)	496 (39.8%)	0
(4) Washington	1,358 (58.2%)	800 (34.3%)	4 (0.2%)	173 (7.4%)
(9) Worcester	243 (17.1%)	420 (29.6%)	754 (53.2%)	0
Total	**14,470 (44.2%)**	**14,189 (43.3%)**	**3,371 (10.3%)**	**695 (2.1%)**
1st District	482 (27.5%)	878 (50.2%)	390 (22.3%)	0
2nd District	628 (41.0%)	518 (33.8%)	386 (25.2%)	0
*3rd District (2 elected)	4,836 (52.3%)	4,398 (47.6%)	9 (0.1%)	0
*4th District (2 elected)	3,724 (51.9%)	2,751 (38.3%)	11 (0.2%)	695 (9.7%)
5th District	1,936 (66.5%)	976 (33.5%)	0	0
6th District	1,360 (51.9%)	1,259 (48.1%)	0	0
7th District	753 (44.3%)	896 (52.7%)	51 (3.0%)	0
8th District	72 (2.7%)	1,215 (45.1%)	1,407 (52.2%)	0
9th District	679 (21.9%)	1,298 (42.0%)	1,117 (36.1%)	0

*In the 3rd and 4th Districts, the vote represents the total for the higher elector.

SOURCES—Manuscript returns; John T. Willis, *Presidential Elections in Maryland*, Mt. Airy, MD: Lomond Publications, p. 168.

Massachusetts[6]

County	Adams	Crawford
Barnstable	769 (83.2%)	155 (16.8%)
Berkshire	2,381 (78.7%)	645 (21.3%)
Bristol	2,065 (86.7%)	316 (13.3%)
Dukes	80 (90.9%)	8 (9.1%)
Essex	3,448 (71.0%)	1,411 (29.0%)
Franklin	1,619 (76.4%)	500 (23.6%)
Hampden	1,616 (83.6%)	316 (16.4%)
Hampshire	2,006 (88.1%)	271 (11.9%)
Middlesex	4,303 (89.6%)	498 (10.5%)
Nantucket	261 (82.9%)	54 (17.1%)
Norfolk	2,428 (84.3%)	451 (15.7%)
Plymouth	2,169 (87.6%)	306 (12.4%)
Suffolk	3,146 (73.4%)	1,140 (26.6%)
Worcester	5,560 (87.7%)	780 (12.3%)
*Total	**31,851 (82.3%)**	**6,860 (17.7%)**

*In addition returns have been found for 14 towns not included in the official returns: The numbers are 1,164 for Adams and 214 for Crawford.

SOURCES—Manuscript returns; (Boston) *Columbian Sentinel*, November 3 and 6, 1824; (Newburyport) *Newburyport Herald*, November 5, 1824; (Northampton) *Hampshire Gazette*, November 10, 1824; (Salem) *Salem Gazette*, November 2, 5 and 9, 1824, and *Essex Register*, November 4 and 8, 1824.

Mississippi

County	Jackson	Adams
Adams	322 (57.4%)	239 (42.6%)
Amite	221 (72.0%)	86 (28.0%)
Claiborne	316 (55.4%)	254 (44.6%)
Copiah	53 (82.8%)	11 (17.2%)
Covington	56 (73.7%)	20 (26.3%)
Franklin	133 (71.5%)	53 (28.5%)
Greene	81 (58.7%)	57 (41.3%)
Hancock	52 (89.7%)	6 (10.3%)
Hinds	52 (80.0%)	13 (20.0%)
Jackson	no returns	
Jefferson	318 (58.9%)	222 (41.1%)
Lawrence	248 (82.7%)	52 (17.3%)
Marion	122 (55.7%)	97 (44.3%)
Monroe	323 (80.5%)	78 (19.5%)
Perry	60 (71.4%)	24 (28.6%)
Pike	242 (81.5%)	25 (18.5%)
Simpson	58 (75.3%)	19 (24.7%)
Warren	238 (53.8%)	204 (46.2%)
Wayne	46 (52.9%)	41 (47.1%)
Wilkinson	321 (58.6%)	227 (41.4%)
Yazoo	45 (81.8%)	10 (18.2%)
Total	**3,307 (65.6%)**	**1,738 (34.4%)**

SOURCE—Manuscript returns, state archives.

Missouri

Electors were chosen by district,
and the returns are below the county returns.
The number in parentheses next to each county indicates
the electoral district the county was in.

County	Clay		Jackson		Adams	
(1) Boone	267	(74.0%)	94	(26.0%)	0	
(1) Callaway	109	(63.7%)	62	(36.3%)	0	
(3) Cape Girardeau	102	(34.8%)	180	(61.4%)	11	(3.8%)
(1) Chariton	67	(38.1%)	109	(61.9%)	0	
(1) Clay	74	(65.5%)	39	(34.5%)	0	
(1) Cole	20	(64.5%)	11	(35.5%)	0	
(1) Cooper	136	(72.0%)	53	(28.0%)	0	
(2) Franklin			no returns			
(2) Gasconade			no returns			
(1) Howard	377	(80.4%)	92	(19.6%)	0	
(3) Jefferson	23	(37.1%)	22	(35.5%)	17	(27.4%)
(1) Lillard	38	(28.8%)	94	(71.2%)	0	
(2) Lincoln	83	(89.2%)	6	(6.5%)	4	(4.3%)
(3) Madison			no returns			
(2) Montgomery	62	(88.6%)	6	(8.6%)	2	(2.9%)
(3) New Madrid	10	(83.3%)	1	(8.3%)	1	(8.3%)
(3) Perry			no returns			
(2) Pike	81	(64.3%)	33	(26.2%)	12	(9.5%)
(2) Ralls	78	(55.3%)	62	(44.0%)	1	(0.7%)
(1) Ray	13	(27.1%)	35	(72.9%)	0	
(2) St. Charles	61	(41.2%)	47	(31.8%)	40	(27.0%)
(3) St. Francois	22	(38.6%)	35	(61.4%)	0	
(2) St. Louis	239	(56.2%)	86	(20.2%)	100	(23.5%)
(3) Ste. Genevieve	50	(82.0%)	10	(16.4%)	1	(6.6%)
(1) Saline	10	(32.3%)	21	(67.7%)	0	
(3) Scott	12	(52.2%)	11	(47.8%)	0	
(3) Washington	107	(69.9%)	44	(28.8%)	2	(1.3%)
(3) Wayne	1	(6.7%)	14	(93.3%)	0	
Total	**2,042**	**(60.1%)**	**1,167**	**(34.3%)**	**191**	**(5.6%)**
1st District	1,111	(64.6%)	610	(35.4%)	0	
2nd District	604	(60.2%)	240	(21.9%)	159	(15.9%)
3rd District	327	(48.4%)	317	(46.9%)	32	(4.7%)

New Hampshire

County	Adams
Cheshire	1,966
Coos	122
Grafton	1,654
Hillsborough	2,624
Rockingham	1,562
Strafford	1,526
Total	**9,454**

SOURCE—Manuscript returns.

New Jersey

County	Jackson		Adams		Crawford	
Bergen	449	(60.4%)	167	(22.5%)	127	(17.1%)
Burlington	799	(43.3%)	770	(41.8%)	275	(14.9%)
Cape May	54	(20.8%)	171	(65.8%)	35	(13.5%)
Cumberland	863	(52.8%)	764	(46.7%)	8	(4.9%)
Essex	1,426	(41.0%)	1,734	(49.8%)	319	(9.2%)
Gloucester	550	(53.7%)	455	(44.4%)	20	(2.0%)
Hunterdon	1,124	(60.6%)	725	(39.1%)	7	(3.8%)
Mercer	824	(45.1%)	752	(41.1%)	253	(13.8%)
Middlesex	665	(47.6%)	730	(53.8%)	2	(1.4%)
Monmouth	839	(62.5%)	499	(37.2%)	5	(3.7%)
Salem	666	(44.3%)	784	(52.1%)	54	(3.6%)
Somerset	638	(62.9%)	375	(37.0%)	1	(1.0%)
Sussex	1,445	(70.4%)	480	(23.4%)	127	(6.2%)
Total	**10,342**	**(51.8%)**	**8,406**	**(42.1%)**	**1,233**	**(6.2%)**

SOURCE—(Trenton) *True American*, November 27, 1824.

New York

Electors chosen by the legislature

North Carolina

County	Jackson		Adams	
Anson	456	(65.9%)	236	(34.1%)
Ashe	169	(38.9%)	265	(61.1%)
Beaufort	296	(50.4%)	291	(49.6%)
Bertie	269	(43.2%)	353	(56.8%)
Bladen	57	(12.9%)	386	(87.1%)
Brunswick	56	(36.6%)	97	(63.4%)
Buncombe	405	(95.7%)	18	(4.3%)
Burke	508	(85.5%)	86	(14.5%)
Cabarrus	322	(86.3%)	51	(13.7%)
Camden	66	(45.8%)	78	(54.2%)
Carteret	271	(96.1%)	11	(3.9%)
Caswell	90	(8.0%)	1,036	(92.0%)
Chatham	178	(20.6%)	688	(79.4%)
Chowan	151	(52.6%)	136	(47.4%)
Columbus	102	(52.0%)	94	(48.0%)
Craven	400	(65.5%)	211	(34.5%)
Cumberland	568	(72.5%)	165	(27.5%)
Currituck	127	(83.0%)	26	(17.0%)
Davidson	422	(77.7%)	121	(22.3%)
Duplin	284	(47.1%)	319	(52.9%)
Edgecombe	406	(45.8%)	481	(54.2%)
Franklin	440	(59.9%)	295	(40.1%)
Gates	201	(87.8%)	28	(12.2%)
Granville	187	(17.4%)	889	(82.6%)
Greene	222	(44.5%)	13	(55.5%)
Guilford	250	(30.0%)	584	(70.0%)
Halifax	347	(38.0%)	567	(62.0%)
Haywood	592	(100%)	0	
Hertford	275	(77.5%)	80	(22.5%)
Hyde	148	(85.1%)	26	(14.9%)
Iredell	273	(44.2%)	345	(55.8%)
Johnston	257	(55.5%)	206	(44.5%)
Jones	196	(76.0%)	62	(24.0%)
Lenoir	172	(53.4%)	149	(46.6%)
Lincoln	636	(65.6%)	334	(34.4%)
Martin	187	(41.7%)	261	(58.3%)
Mecklenburg	661	(73.9%)	234	(26.1%)
Montgomery	453	(85.1%)	76	(14.9%)
Moore	198	(44.4%)	248	(55.5%)
Nash	170	(32.7%)	350	(67.3%)
New Hanover	236	(40.5%)	347	(59.5%)
Northampton	154	(31.5%)	335	(68.5%)
Onslow	295	(56.7%)	225	(43.3%)
Orange	638	(57.9%)	591	(42.1%)
Pasquotank	330	(95.4%)	13	(4.6%)
Perquimans	94	(59.1%)	65	(40.9%)
Person	56	(19.8%)	283	(80.2%)
Pitt	361	(65.3%)	192	(34.7%)
Randolph	141	(26.4%)	394	(73.6%)
Richmond	441	(82.7%)	92	(17.3%)
Robeson	235	(74.1%)	82	(25.9%)
Rockingham	561	(62.2%)	341	(37.8%)
Rowan	979	(90.6%)	101	(9.4%)
Rutherford	654	(78.7%)	177	(21.3%)
Sampson	431	(73.4%)	156	(26.6%)

County			
Stokes	709	(71.3%)	286	(28.7%)
Surry	810	(66.3%)	411	(33.7%)
Tyrrell	144	(98.6%)	2	(1.4%)
Wake	700	(60.0%)	466	(40.0%)
Warren	152	(23.5%)	496	(76.5%)
Washington	125	(53.2%)	110	(46.8%)
Wayne	264	(62.1%)	161	(37.9%)
Wilkes	436	(52.2%)	400	(47.8%)
Total	**20,417**	**(56.7%)**	**15,622**	**(43.3%)**

SOURCE—Thad Eure (Secretary of State) *North Carolina Government, 1585–1979*, Raleigh, NC: 1979, pp. 1329–1330.

Ohio

County	Clay		Jackson		Adams	
Adams	240	(21.6%)	808	(72.7%)	63	(5.7%)
Athens	176	(41.2%)	29	(6.8%)	222	(52.0%)
Ashtabula	193	(28.8%)	12	(1.8%)	466	(69.4%)
Belmont	879	(71.5%)	166	(13.5%)	185	(15.0%)
Brown	210	(18.1%)	787	(67.8%)	164	(14.1%)
Butler	536	(23.1%)	1,602	(69.1%)	182	(7.8%)
Champaign	401	(60.7%)	100	(15.1%)	160	(24.2%)
Clark	543	(60.0%)	210	(23.2%)	152	(16.8%)
Clermont	317	(20.4%)	914	(58.8%)	324	(20.8%)
Clinton	199	(34.5%)	197	(34.2%)	180	(31.3%)
Columbiana	178	(19.6%)	539	(59.4%)	190	(20.9%)
Coshocton	220	(47.1%)	235	(50.3%)	12	(2.6%)
Cuyahoga	494	(61.7%)	25	(3.1%)	282	(35.2%)
Darke	97	(28.8%)	231	(68.5%)	9	(2.7%)
Delaware	55	(10.3%)	71	(13.3%)	409	(76.4%)
Fairfield	486	(48.4%)	397	(39.5%)	122	(12.1%)
Fayette	198	(58.8%)	104	(30.9%)	35	(10.4%)
Franklin	465	(43.5%)	241	(22.5%)	364	(34.0%)
Gallia	208	(56.4%)	83	(22.5%)	78	(21.1%)
Geauga	349	(42.8%)	3	(0.4%)	464	(56.9%)
Greene	160	(15.9%)	347	(34.4%)	502	(49.8%)
Guernsey	347	(56.1%)	256	(41.4%)	15	(2.4%)
Hamilton	697	(15.2%)	2,667	(58.2%)	1,217	(26.6%)
Harrison	81	(9.7%)	456	(54.7%)	297	(35.6%)
Highland	336	(48.3%)	234	(33.7%)	125	(18.0%)
Hocking	83	(73.5%)	29	(25.7%)	1	(0.9%)
Huron	134	(21.1%)	59	(9.3%)	442	(69.6%)
Jackson	197	(60.1%)	126	(38.4%)	5	(1.5%)
Jefferson	605	(35.8%)	907	(53.7%)	177	(10.5%)
Knox	289	(44.0%)	270	(41.1%)	98	(14.9%)
Lawrence	82	(84.5%)	10	(10.3%)	5	(5.2%)
Licking	482	(46.6%)	121	(11.7%)	432	(41.7%)
Logan	300	(64.0%)	31	(7.1%)	9	(3.5%)
Lorain	142	(61.2%)	8	(3.4%)	82	(35.3%)
Madison	169	(52.5%)	83	(25.8%)	70	(21.7%)
Marion	54	(35.6%)	13	(8.4%)	87	(56.5%)
Medina	244	(61.9%)	1	(2.5%)	149	(32.8%)
Meigs	108	(37.1%)	19	(6.5%)	164	(56.4%)
Mercer	45	(68.1%)	9	(13.6%)	12	(18.2%)
Miami	427	(57.8%)	197	(26.7%)	115	(15.6%)
Monroe	95	(56.5%)	34	(20.2%)	39	(23.2%)
Montgomery	653	(41.6%)	711	(45.3%)	207	(13.2%)
Morgan	176	(60.1%)	53	(18.1%)	64	(21.8%)
Muskingum	1,102	(80.7%)	177	(13.0%)	86	(6.3%)
Perry	221	(28.6%)	506	(65.5%)	46	(6.0%)
Pickaway	557	(52.3%)	451	(42.3%)	57	(5.4%)
Pike	459	(70.9%)	164	(25.3%)	24	(3.7%)
Portage	277	(29.7%)	161	(17.3%)	494	(53.0%)
Preble	723	(73.3%)	204	(20.7%)	60	(6.1%)
Richland	296	(43.9%)	273	(40.5%)	105	(15.6%)
Ross	1,401	(75.4%)	301	(16.2%)	155	(8.3%)
Sandusky	7	(5.1%)	5	(3.7%)	124	(91.2%)
Scioto	316	(70.9%)	107	(24.0%)	23	(5.2%)
Seneca	37	(21.1%)	26	(14.9%)	112	(64.0%)
Shelby	87	(48.3%)	71	(39.4%)	22	(12.2%)
Stark	308	(48.2%)	293	(45.9%)	38	(5.9%)
Trumbull	108	(5.3%)	501	(24.8%)	1,409	(69.8%)
Tuscarawas	255	(60.0%)	149	(35.1%)	21	(4.9%)
Union	33	(26.0%)	1	(0.8%)	93	(73.2%)
Warren	312	(19.9%)	750	(48.0%)	502	(32.1%)
Washington	89	(11.3%)	236	(30.1%)	460	(58.6%)
Wayne	315	(31.4%)	599	(59.7%)	89	(8.9%)
Williams	41	(89.1%)	3	(6.5%)	2	(4.3%)
Wood	24	(60.0%)	0		16	(40.0%)
Total	**19,318**	**(38.6%)**	**18,373**	**(36.7%)**	**12,315**	**(24.6%)**

SOURCE—(Sandusky) *Clarion*, November 26, 1824.

Pennsylvania

County	Jackson		Adams		Crawford		Clay	
Adams	390	(52.2%)	348	(46.6%)	0		9	(1.2%)
Allegheny	1,384	(76.1%)	18	(1.0%)	398	(21.9%)	18	(1.0%)
Armstrong	286	(92.6%)	16	(5.2%)	6	(1.9%)	1	(1.3%)
Beaver	465	(73.5%)	1	(0.2%)	165	(26.0%)	2	(0.3%)
Bedford	664	(85.8%)	102	(13.2%)	2	(0.3%)	6	(0.8%)
Berks	1,685	(90.4%)	53	(2.8%)	76	(4.1%)	49	(2.6%)
Bradford	639	(94.9%)	18	(2.7%)	16	(2.4%)	0	
Bucks	1,280	(77.4%)	180	(10.9%)	117	(7.1%)	76	(4.6%)
Butler	506	(67.9%)	2	(0.3%)	234	(31.4%)	3	(0.4%)
Cambria	87	(91.6%)	5	(0.5%)	3	(0.3%)	0	
Centre	603	(84.7%)	89	(12.5%)	19	(2.7%)	1	(0.1%)
Chester	1,471	(71.4%)	164	(8.0%)	80	(3.9%)	344	(16.7%)
Clearfield	116	(87.9%)	16	(12.1%)	0		0	
Columbia	507	(89.1%)	8	(1.4%)	54	(9.5%)	0	
Crawford	312	(86.7%)	40	(11.1%)	8	(2.2%)	0	
Cumberland	730	(78.4%)	180	(19.3%)	5	(0.5%)	16	(1.7%)
Dauphin	770	(83.7%)	123	(13.4%)	22	(2.4%)	5	(0.5%)
Delaware	329	(51.1%)	118	(18.4%)	61	(9.5%)	135	(21.0%)
Erie	302	(80.5%)	55	(14.7%)	10	(2.7%)	8	(2.1%)
Fayette	850	(71.1%)	16	(1.3%)	52	(4.3%)	278	(23.2%)
Franklin	952	(59.1%)	614	(38.1%)	12	(0.7%)	34	(2.1%)
Greene	374	(89.3%)	6	(1.4%)	9	(2.1%)	30	(7.2%)
Huntingdon	473	(68.7%)	54	(7.8%)	70	(10.1%)	92	(13.4%)

Indiana & Jefferson	258 (89.9%)	27 (9.4%)	2 (0.7%)	0
Lancaster	1,667 (81.4%)	202 (9.9%)	147 (7.2%)	32 (1.6%)
Lebanon	536 (85.6%)	2 (0.3%)	85 (13.6%)	3 (0.5%)
Lehigh	753 (98.7%)	5 (0.7%)	5 (0.7%)	0
Luzerne	631 (78.4%)	31 (3.9%)	125 (15.5%)	18 (2.2%)
Lycoming, McKean & Potter	560 (86.8%)	40 (6.2%)	44 (6.8%)	1 (0.2%)
Mercer	438 (75.5%)	0	142 (24.5%)	0
Mifflin	662 (88.3%)	78 (10.4%)	6 (0.3%)	4 (0.2%)
Montgomery	1,479 (73.3%)	48 (2.4%)	445 (22.0%)	47 (2.3%)
Northampton	1,157 (91.6%)	44 (3.5%)	29 (2.3%)	33 (2.6%)
Northumberland	643 (87.4%)	6 (0.8%)	87 (11.8%)	0
Perry	292 (92.1%)	24 (7.6%)	0	1
Philadelphia	5,894 (63.0%)	2,072 (22.2%)	1,188 (12.7%)	196 (2.1%)
Pike	116 (92.1%)	0	10 (7.9%)	0
Schuylkill	346 (94.1%)	0	18 (4.9%)	6 (1.6%)
Somerset	615 (91.4%)	50 (7.4%)	3 (0.5%)	5 (0.7%)
Susquehanna	319 (63.3%)	31 (6.2%)	126 (25.0%)	28 (5.6%)
Tioga	281 (98.6%)	3 (1.1%)	1 (0.4%)	0
Union	700 (96.2%)	0	26 (3.6%)	2 (0.3%)
Venango	265 (94.0%)	1 (0.4%)	15 (5.3%)	1 (0.4%)
Warren	153 (93.9%)	7 (4.3%)	3 (1.8%)	0
Washington	970 (65.5%)	120 (8.1%)	184 (12.4%)	208 (14.0%)
Wayne	175 (81.4%)	25 (11.6%)	15 (7.0%)	0
Westmoreland	963 (95.7%)	34 (3.4%)	6 (0.6%)	3 (0.3%)
York	844 (68.3%)	327 (26.5%)	53 (4.3%)	11 (0.9%)
Total	**35,893 (76.1%)**	**5,403 (11.5%)**	**4,184 (8.9%)**	**1,706 (3.6%)**
		*(5,405)	*(4,186)	*(1,701)

*Stated totals.

SOURCE—(Harrisburg) *Intelligencer*, November 16, 1824.

Rhode Island

County	Adams	Opposition
Bristol	170 (73.0%)	63 (27.0%)
Kent	242 (99.6%)	1 (0.4%)
Newport	448 (83.4%)	89 (16.6%)
Providence	982 (98.6%)	14 (1.4%)
Washington	300 (90.1%)	33 (9.9%)
Total	**2,142 (91.5%)**	**200 (8.5%)**

SOURCE—(Newport) *Rhode Island Republican*, December 2, 1824.

South Carolina

Electors chosen by the legislature

Tennessee[7]

Electors were chosen by electoral district,
with one elector being chosen from each of 11 districts

2nd Electoral District

County	Jackson	*Jackson
Campbell	159 (97.0%)	5 (3.0%)
Claiborne	248 (92.9%)	19 (7.1%)
Cocke	377 (87.1%)	56 (12.9%)
Grainger	243 (79.2%)	64 (20.8%)
Jefferson	282 (53.1%)	249 (46.9%)
Sevier	121 (100%)	0
	1,430 (78.4%)	*393 (21.6%)*

3rd Electoral District

County	Jackson	
Anderson	112 (100%)	
Blount	129 (100%)	
Knox	403 (100%)	
Morgan	61 (100%)	
Roane	208 (100%)	
	913 (100%)	
	(914)	

4th Electoral District

	Jackson
	1,525 (100%)

No county returns located

*5th Electoral District

County	Jackson	Jackson
Fentress	17 (12.3%)	121 (87.9%)
Franklin	396 (100%)	0
Jackson	177 (97.3%)	5 (2.7%)
Overton	43 (44.3%)	54 (55.7%)
Warren	444 (100%)	0
White	312 (100%)	0
	1,389 (89.0%)	*180 (11.0%)*

7th Electoral District

County	Jackson	Crawford	Adams
Davidson	1,015 (90.0%)	81 (7.2%)	32 (2.8%)
Rutherford	891 (79.0%)	72 (6.4%)	165 (14.6%)
Williamson	663 (79.8%)	163 (19.6%)	5 (0.6%)
	2,569 (83.2%)	*316 (10.2%)*	*202 (6.5%)*

8th Electoral District

"In Bedford County, Mr. Clay received a very respectable support, and in the upper end of the county had a considerable majority, but in the District Col. Brown is elected." *Nashville Whig*, November 15, 1824.

9th Electoral District

County	Jackson	Jackson
Giles		
Lawrence		
Lincoln	771 (96.3%)	30 (3.7%)

11th Electoral District

County	Jackson	Jackson	Clay	Clay	Adams
Carroll	125 (55.6%)	70 (31.1%)	29 (12.9%)	1 (0.4%)	0
Dyer	43 (71.7%)	0	5 (8.3%)	12 (20.0%)	0
Gibson	17 (100%)	0	0	0	0
Hardeman	85 (97.7%)	0	0	1 (1.1%)	1 (1.1%)
Hardin	95 (89.6%)	7 (6.6%)	3 (2.8%)	0	1 (0.9%)
Haywood	32 (65.3%)	0	17 (34.7%)	0	0
Henderson	218 (85.5%)	7 (2.6%)	6 (2.4%)	14 (5.5%)	10 (3.9%)
Henry	168 (82.8%)	0	35 (17.2%)	0	0
Madison	443 (83.7%)	7 (1.3%)	77 (14.6%)	1 (0.2%)	1 (0.2%)
McNairy	125 (97.7%)	0	3 (2.3%)	0	0
Obion	41 (89.1%)	0	5 (10.9%)	0	0
Perry	89 (40.8%)	106 (48.6%)	7 (3.2%)	7 (3.2%)	9 (4.1%)
Shelby	no returns				
Tipton	25 (54.3%)	0	21 (45.7%)	0	0
Wayne	156 (84.8%)	27 (14.7%)	1 (0.5%)	0	0
Weakley	199 (97.5%)	0	5 (2.5%)	0	0
	(1,861)	(224)	(214)	(36)	(22)

Total[8]   20,197   0   Crawford

actual vote[9]   (10,458 + 827)   (214+36)   216   312

224   316

Two electoral candidates ran, both pledged to Jackson.
**Two electors pledged to Jackson and two pledged to Clay.*

SOURCES—(Jackson) *Jackson Gazette,* October 23 and November 13, 1824; (Knoxville) *Knoxville Register,* November 12, 19 and 26 and December 3, 1824, and *Knoxville Enquirer,* November 10, 17 and 24, 1824; (Sparta) *Review,* November 17, 1824; (Nashville) *Nashville Whig,* November 15, 1824, and *Nashville Republican,* November 13, 1824; (Fayetteville) *Village Messenger,* November 10 and 17, 1824.

The electoral candidates by district were:

District	Jackson	Adams	Clay	Crawford
1	John Rhea			
2	Tighman A. Howard / Baldwin Harle			
3	William E. Anderson			
4	Benjamin C. Stout / Solomon Riggle / John Rice			
5	William Mitrchell / Richard C. Brown			
6	Samuel Hogg			
7	William A. Sublett	James Wade		William V. Shelton
8	Joseph Brown / Tilman Dixon		Giles Burdett	
9	Joel Pinson / Spencer Clark			
10	Willie Blount / Stephen Thomas / Mortimer A. Martin			
11	Robert H. Dyer / John Graham	Josiah Hall	Jesse Benton / John A. Newland[10]	

Vermont

Electors chosen by the legislature

Virginia

County	Crawford	Adams	Jackson	Clay
Accomack	4 (22.2%)	7 (38.9%)	7 (38.9%)	0
Albemarle	304 (89.9%)	25 (7.4%)	9 (2.7%)	0
Alleghany	28 (77.8%)	3 (8.3%)	3 (8.3%)	2 (5.5%)
Amelia	103 (97.2%)	3 (2.8%)	0	0
Amherst	110 (57.6%)	71 (37.1%)	10 (5.2%)	0
Augusta	124 (47.7%)	88 (33.8%)	48 (18.5%)	0
Bath	25 (58.1%)	7 (16.3%)	11 (25.6%)	0
Bedford	116 (30.9%)	220 (58.5%)	40 (10.6%)	0

County	Crawford	Adams	Jackson	Clay
Berkeley	30 (16.9%)	57 (28.3%)	50 (24.9%)	64 (31.8%)
Botetourt	62 (44.9%)	4 (2.9%)	69 (50.0%)	3 (2.2%)
Brooke	42 (39.1%)	0	68 (55.3%)	13 (10.6%)
Brunswick	128 (70.8%)	20 (12.1%)	20 (12.1%)	0
Buckingham	179 (100%)	0	0	0
Cabell	42 (82.4%)	9 (17.6%)	0	0
Campbell	102 (36.0%)	145 (51.2%)	36 (12.7%)	0
Caroline	114 (82.6%)	14 (10.1%)	10 (7.2%)	0
Charles City	34 (81.0%)	7 (16.7%)	1 (2.4%)	0
Charlotte	222 (81.1%)	29 (11.5%)	1 (0.4%)	0
Chesterfield	179 (82.1%)	39 (17.9%)	0	0
Culpeper	203 (70.4%)	10 (3.5%)	75 (26.0%)	0
Cumberland	104 (80.0%)	21 (18.5%)	2 (0.5%)	0
Dinwiddie	70 (39.8%)	56 (31.8%)	50 (28.4%)	0
Elizabeth City	36 (45.6%)	41 (51.8%)	2 (2.5%)	0
Essex	66 (50.4%)	13 (9.9%)	52 (39.7%)	0
Fairfax	79 (74.5%)	0	27 (25.5%)	0
Fauquier	114 (57.9%)	22 (11.1%)	60 (30.5%)	1 (0.5%)
Fluvanna	113 (98.3%)	0	2 (1.7%)	0
Franklin	206 (46.4%)	182 (41.0%)	56 (12.6%)	0
Frederick	128 (25.9%)	84 (17.0%)	279 (56.5%)	3 (0.6%)
Giles	18 (2.8%)	615 (97.2%)	0	0
Gloucester	162 (73.3%)	47 (21.2%)	12 (5.4%)	0
Goochland	80 (90.9%)	3 (3.4%)	5 (5.7%)	0
Grayson		no returns		
Greenbrier	56 (39.4%)	75 (52.8%)	8 (5.6%)	3 (2.1%)
Greensville	102 (89.5%)	11 (9.6%)	1 (0.9%)	0
Halifax	295 (94.2%)	5 (1.6%)	13 (4.2%)	0
Hampshire	43 (47.8%)	47 (51.3%)	0	0
Hanover	83 (85.6%)	14 (14.4%)	0	0
Hardy	3 (7.0%)	34 (79.1%)	6 (14.0%)	0
Harrison	4 (3.4%)	15 (12.8%)	53 (45.3%)	45 (38.3%)
Henrico	144 (87.3%)	19 (11.5%)	2 (1.2%)	0
Henry	84 (42.0%)	37 (18.5%)	79 (39.5%)	0
Isle of Wight	121 (85.2%)	21 (14.8%)	0	0
James City	59 (98.3%)	1 (1.7%)	0	0
Jefferson	33 (28.0%)	30 (25.4%)	48 (40.7%)	7 (6.0%)
Kanawha	47 (48.0%)	26 (26.5%)	25 (25.5%)	0
King & Queen	45 (50.6%)	42 (47.2%)	2 (2.2%)	0
King George	68 (76.4%)	13 (14.6%)	8 (9.0%)	0
King William	44 (84.6%)	6 (11.5%)	2 (3.9%)	0
Lancaster	46 (47.9%)	49 (55.0%)	1 (1.0%)	0
Lee	3 (3.4%)	29 (33.3%)	55 (62.2%)	0
Lewis	8 (16.7%)	19 (39.6%)	21 (43.8%)	0
Logan	65 (84.7%)	0	11 (15.3%)	0
Loudoun	68 (29.3%)	102 (44.0%)	62 (26.7%)	0
Louisa	205 (92.3%)	6 (2.7%)	11 (5.0%)	0
Lunenburg	76 (66.7%)	10 (8.8%)	28 (24.1%)	0
Madison	124 (89.2%)	4 (2.9%)	11 (7.9%)	0
Mason	43 (65.2%)	18 (27.3%)	5 (7.6%)	0
Mathews	50 (64.1%)	22 (28.2%)	6 (7.7%)	0
Mecklenburg	100 (92.6%)	2 (1.9%)	6 (5.6%)	0
Middlesex	77 (86.5%)	9 (10.1%)	3 (3.4%)	0
Monongalia	14 (10.1%)	28 (20.3%)	79 (57.2%)	17 (12.3%)
Monroe	43 (84.3%)	8 (15.7%)	0	0
Montgomery	71 (45.8%)	15 (9.7%)	69 (44.5%)	0
Morgan	65 (68.4%)	0	18 (18.9%)	12 (12.6%)
Nansemond	112 (71.8%)	41 (26.3%)	3 (1.9%)	0
Nelson	72 (54.1%)	58 (43.6%)	3 (2.3%)	0
New Kent	24 (77.4%)	4 (12.9%)	3 (9.7%)	0
Nicholas	29 (61.7%)	12 (25.0%)	3 (6.4%)	3 (6.4%)
Norfolk	35 (23.9%)	81 (55.5%)	30 (20.5%)	0
Northampton	60 (80.0%)	11 (14.7%)	4 (5.3%)	0
Northumberland	63 (66.3%)	23 (24.2%)	9 (9.5%)	0
Nottoway	68 (87.2%)	6 (7.7%)	4 (5.1%)	0
Ohio	6 (2.0%)	28 (9.5%)	14 (4.7%)	248 (83.8%)
Orange	102 (68.0%)	22 (14.7%)	26 (17.3%)	0
Patrick	28 (17.9%)	42 (26.9%)	86 (55.1%)	0
Pendleton	40 (37.4%)	62 (57.9%)	4 (3.7%)	1 (0.3%)

County	Crawford		Adams		Jackson		Clay	
Pittsylvania	188	(54.5%)	67	(19.4%)	90	(26.1%)	0	
Pocahontas	0		26	(72.2%)	10	(27.8%)	0	
Powhatan	87	(91.6%)	8	(8.4%)	0		0	
Preston	12	(66.7%)	2	(11.1%)	3	(16.7%)	1	(5.6%)
Prince Edward	117	(7.5%)	3	(2.5%)	0		0	
Prince George	42	(70.0%)	6	(10.0%)	12	(20.0%)	0	
Prince William	108	(88.5%)	7	(5.7%)	7	(5.7%)	0	
Princess Anne	41	(21.2%)	148	(76.7%)	4	(2.1%)	0	
Randolph	23	(33.3%)	43	(62.3%)	1	(1.5%)	2	(2.9%)
Richmond	78	(69.6%)	18	(16.1%)	16	(14.3%)	0	
Rockbridge	146	(36.6%)	156	(39.1%)	97	(24.3%)	0	
Rockingham	115	(38.3%)	0		184	(61.3%)	1	(0.3%)
Russell	24	(22.2%)	6	(5.6%)	78	(72.2%)	0	
Scott	18	(32.1%)	4	(7.1%)	34	(60.7%)	0	
Shenandoah	132	(50.0%)	28	(10.6%)	104	(39.4%)	0	
Southampton	134	(77.0%)	38	(21.8%)	2	(1.1%)	0	
Spotsylvania	171	(56.8%)	40	(13.3%)	90	(29.9%)	0	
Stafford	73	(58.4%)	27	(21.6%)	25	(20.0%)	0	
Surry	72	(69.9%)	31	(30.1%)	0		0	
Sussex	88	(87.1%)	10	(9.9%)	3	(3.0%)	0	
Tazewell	17	(34.0%)	1	(2.0%)	32	(64.0%)	0	
Tyler	3	(13.6%)	11	(50.0%)	4	(18.2%)	4	(18.2%)
Warick	32	(100%)	0		0		0	
Washington	112	(45.3%)	33	(13.4%)	102	(41.3%)	0	
Westmoreland	26	(37.1%)	18	(25.7%)	16	(22.9%)	0	
Wood	86	(46.0%)	86	(46.0%)	15	(8.0%)	0	
Wythe	57	(60.0%)	11	(11.6%)	27	(28.4%)	0	
York	47	(100%)	0		0		0	
Norfolk (boro)	58	(20.6%)	159	(56.6%)	64	(22.8%)	0	
Petersburg (town)	60	(38.5%)	53	(34.0%)	43	(27.6%)	0	
Richmond (town)	110	(58.2%)	79	(41.8%)	0	0		
Williamsburg (town)	33	(91.7%)	3	(8.3%)	0	0		
Total	**8,565**	**(53.7%)**	**4,071**	**(25.5%)**	**2,890**	**(18.1%)**	**430**	**(2.7%)**
	*(8,558)		*(3,419)		*(2,975)		*(419)	

*Stated totals.

SOURCE—Manuscript returns.

NOTES

1. The electoral vote for vice president was John C. Calhoun 182, Nathan Sanford 30, Nathaniel Mason 24, Martin Van Buren 9, Henry Clay 2, and one absent.

2. Except for Crawford who was nominated by the last congressional caucus, all the candidates were nominated by individual state legislatures. There was no party distinction; all were considered to be Democratic-Republicans, as the Federalists had already passed from the scene.

3. No candidate having received a majority of the electoral vote the election was decided by the House of Representatives. On the first ballot Adams was elected: 13 states for Adams, 7 for Jackson and 4 for Crawford.

4. A small number of votes in Districts One and Three were recorded for Adams and Crawford, but were not broken down by county; they are listed in the national summary. It is not clear whether either or both candidates received votes in the Second District.

5. The vote represents the vote for the district electors. No county vote has been found for either of the at-large electoral candidates.

6. William Walker was on both tickets and polled 38,243 votes. The returns here are for the high elector on each ticket. The Crawford, or as it was also referred to the "unpledged" slate, was originally made up of eight Federalists and seven Democratic-Republicans. But in several towns a slate solely made of Federalists was substituted. This ticket included the original group of Federalists and seven others.

7. Most of the analysis on Tennessee electoral candidates was done by Phil Lampi who researched papers in each of the Electoral districts to obtain the names and affiliation of the electoral candidates. Jackson had little opposition in his home state and was unopposed in eight of the 11 districts. There are no surviving official returns for the state. The returns used by Svend Petersen in *A Statistical History of the American Presidential Elections*, New York, NY: 1963, apparently were from an edition of the *Tribune Almanac* but the *Almanac* was first published in 1838, so it obviously relied on some older source. In the files of the Tennessee archives (RG #87, Presidential Election of 1824) is a copy of a document that cited election returns published in the (Harrisburg) *Pennsylvania Intelligencer*, no date. The document itself was published in Knoxville in 1828. This is the oldest known reference to these returns but where the *Intelligencer* obtained these returns from is unknown. Thus the origin of these oft quoted totals is unclear and of questionable accuracy. But given the returns that have been found, the state totals are probably reasonably close to correct. Indeed the totals for Adams and Crawford as actually reported are complete and vary only slightly from the published totals. However, Clay is credited with at least 250 votes as opposed to none in the published returns. The big difference is in the Jackson totals, but this is no doubt due to the fact that no returns have been located in four districts and all but one county in another. Jackson was unopposed in four of these districts. I have used the published totals in the state summary with modifications; I have deducted the Clay vote from the Jackson total on the assumption that he (Jackson) was credited with votes that should have gone to Clay. See the *Jackson Gazette*, October 23, 1824, and the *Nashville Whig*, November 15, 1824, for Clay electors. Nonetheless, even the totals used here are really estimates.

8. These are the state totals found in Svend Petersen, *A Statistical History of the American Presidential Elections,* New York, NY: 1963, p. 18, and repeated in *Congressional Quarterly, Guide to U.S. Elections.* They are suspect in view of the returns I have located for the districts. *Tennessee Votes* has no returns for this election.

9. This combines the vote in districts where there was more than one electoral candidate pledged to the same candidate: Jackson 5th, 9th and 11th; and Clay 11th.

10. When Benton switched his allegiance from Crawford to Clay, Newland withdrew in mid–October. Jackson was unopposed in eight of the 11 districts.

1828

National Summary[1,2]
(electoral vote in parentheses)

State	Andrew Jackson (J)		John Quincy Adams (NR)		others	
Alabama	17,350 (89.78%)	(5)	1,976 (10.22%)			
Connecticut	4,488 (24.49%)		13,838 (75.51%)	(8)		
*Delaware				(3)		
Georgia	9,712 (53.05%)	(11)	605 (3.31%)		**7,991 (43.65%)	
Illinois	9,582 (67.18%)	(5)	4,681 (32.82%)			
Indiana	22,140 (56.60%)	(9)	16,978 (43.40%)			
Kentucky	39,085 (55.41%)	(14)	31,456 (44.59%)			
Louisiana	4,603 (53.04%)	(5)	4,076 (46.96%)			
Maine	13,808 (40.18%)	(1)	20,558 (59.82%)	(8)		
Maryland	24,465 (48.95%)	(5)	25,417 (51.05%)	(6)		
Massachusetts	6,016 (16.78%)		29,842 (83.22%)	(15)		
Mississippi	7,086 (81.56%)	(3)	1,602 (18.44%)			
Missouri	8,287 (69.30%)	(3)	3,672 (30.70%)			
New Hampshire	21,182 (46.76%)		24,120 (53.24%)	(8)		
New Jersey	21,951 (48.02%)		23,764 (51.98%)	(8)		
New York	140,763 (50.96%)	(20)	135,413 (49.04%)	(16)		
North Carolina	37,634 (72.97%)	(15)	13,938 (27.03%)			
Ohio	67,956 (51.60%)	(16)	63,394 (48.40%)			
Pennsylvania	102,151 (66.80%)	(28)	50,763 (33.20%)			
Rhode Island	820 (22.95%)		2,753 (77.03%)	(4)		
*South Carolina		(11)				
†Tennessee	44,092 (95.17%)	(11)	2,240 (4.83%)			
Vermont	8,335 (25.49%)		24,365 (74.51%)	(7)		
Virginia	26,842 (69.13%)	(24)	11,989 (30.87%)			
Total	**638,348 (55.33%) (178)**		**507,440 (43.98%) (83)**		**7,991**	**(0.69%)**

Electors chosen by the legislature.
**In Georgia two slates pledged to Jackson ran. See Georgia returns for a more complete explanation.*
†Combined vote of separate slate of Jackson electors. See Tennessee returns for an explanation.

Alabama

County	Jackson		Adams	
Autauga	595 (93.3%)		43 (6.7%)	
Baldwin	121 (80.7%)		29 (19.3%)	
Bibb	317 (83.4%)		63 (16.6%)	
Blount		no returns		
Butler	335 (87.5%)		48 (12.5%)	
Clarke	498 (93.1%)		37 (6.9%)	
Conecuh		no returns		
Covington	86 (95.6%)		4 (4.4%)	
Dale		no returns		
Dallas	744 (85.7%)		124 (14.3%)	
Fayette	276 (97.5%)		7 (2.5%)	
Franklin	644 (88.2%)		86 (11.8%)	
Greene	833 (70.8%)		344 (29.2%)	
Henry	266 (98.5%)		4 (1.5%)	
Jackson	1,088 (99.5%)		6 (0.5%)	
Jefferson	512 (95.7%)		23 (4.3%)	
Lauderdale	956 (89.8%)		108 (10.2%)	
Lawrence	1,078 (93.3%)		77 (6.7%)	
Limestone	946 (92.8%)		73 (7.2%)	
Madison	1,980 (90.7%)		204 (9.3%)	
Marengo		no returns		
Marion	367 (97.9%)		8 (2.1%)	
Mobile	396 (64.3%)		178 (35.7%)	
Monroe	676 (90.6%)		70 (9.4%)	
Montgomery	364 (90.8%)		37 (9.2%)	
Morgan	743 (98.9%)		8 (1.1%)	
Perry	636 (92.3%)		58 (7.7%)	
Pickens	408 (90.3%)		44 (9.7%)	
Pike		no returns		
St.Clair	459 (98.5%)		7 (1.5%)	

Shelby	591 (97.4%)	16 (2.6%)
Tuscaloosa	637 (80.5%)	154 (19.5%)
Walker	31 (100%)	0
Washington	185 (89.8%)	21 (10.2%)
Wilcox	582 (86.0%)	95 (14.0%)
Total	**17,350 (89.8%)**	**1,976 (10.2%)**
		*(1,993)

*Stated totals.

SOURCE—Loveman manuscript, state archives.

Connecticut

County	Jackson	Adams
Fairfield	384 (17.7%)	1,786 (82.3%)
Hartford	1,273 (33.0%)	2,583 (67.0%)
Litchfield	505 (18.5%)	2,222 (81.5%)
Middlesex	373 (29.6%)	889 (70.4%)
New Haven	234 (10.3%)	2,031 (89.7%)
New London	948 (31.7%)	2,042 (68.3%)
Tolland	515 (33.4%)	1,029 (66.6%)
Windham	256 (16.9%)	1,256 (83.1%)
Total	**4,488 (24.5%)**	**13,838 (75.5%)**
	*(4,448)	

*Stated totals.

SOURCE—Manuscript returns.

Delaware

Electors chosen by the legislature

Georgia

No complete listing of the county returns
has been located for this election

County	Jackson (Troup)	Jackson (Clarke)	Adams
Baldwin	547 (61.8%)	321 (36.3%)	21 (2.4%)
Bibb	138 (35.4%)	180 (46.3%)	72 (18.5%)
Hancock	347 (91.9%)	43 (7.2%)	5 (0.8%)
Jasper	355 (58.1%)	229 (37.5%)	27 (4.4%)
Jones	343 (56.6%)	248 (40.9%)	15 (2.5%)
Morgan	291 (78.0%)	81 (21.7%)	1 (0.3%)
Richmond	214 (30.7%)	244 (35.1%)	238 (34.2%)
Warren	565 (97.2%)	15 (2.6%)	1 (0.2%)
Wilkinson	76 (26.8%)	207 (72.9%)	1 (0.4%)
Total[3]	**9,712 (53.1%)**	**7,991 (43.6%)**	**605 (3.3%)**

SOURCE—(Milledgeville) Journal, November 24, 1828.

Illinois

County	Jackson	Adams
Adams	72 (52.9%)	64 (47.1%)
Alexander	37 (75.5%)	12 (24.5%)
Bond	151 (57.0%)	114 (43.0%)
Calhoun	42 (42.4%)	57 (57.6%)
Clark	100 (46.5%)	115 (53.5%)
Clay	102 (88.7%)	13 (11.3%)
Clinton	130 (63.7%)	74 (36.3%)
Crawford	224 (68.9%)	70 (31.1%)
Edgar	192 (61.5%)	120 (38.5%)
Edwards	184 (60.9%)	118 (39.1%)
Fayette	200 (74.1%)	70 (25.9%)
Franklin	320 (96.7%)	11 (3.3%)
Fulton	71 (45.5%)	85 (54.5%)
Gallatin	428 (79.4%)	111 (20.6%)
Greene	485 (70.3%)	205 (29.7%)
Hamilton	270 (96.1%)	11 (3.9%)
Jackson	142 (91.0%)	14 (9.0%)
Jefferson	224 (87.8%)	88 (12.2%)
Johnson	96 (94.1%)	6 (5.9%)
Lawrence	247 (65.3%)	131 (34.7%)
Madison	390 (52.9%)	347 (47.1%)
Marion	77 (85.6%)	13 (14.4%)
Monroe	167 (66.5%)	84 (33.5%)
Montgomery	208 (81.6%)	47 (18.4%)
Morgan	702 (71.3%)	282 (28.7%)
Peoria	46 (33.1%)	93 (66.9%)
Perry	31 (81.6%)	7 (18.4%)
Pike	54 (31.6%)	117 (68.4%)
Pope	255 (82.0%)	56 (18.0%)
Randolph	369 (69.6%)	161 (30.4%)
St. Clair	539 (61.5%)	337 (38.5%)
Sangamon	682 (61.3%)	431 (38.7%)
Schuyler	75 (57.3%)	56 (42.7%)
Shelby	238 (88.1%)	32 (11.9%)
Tazewell	149 (57.8%)	109 (42.2%)
Union	234 (89.0%)	30 (11.0%)
Vermilion	223 (67.0%)	110 (33.0%)
Wabash	109 (36.1%)	193 (63.9%)
Washington	71 (71.7%)	28 (28.3%)
Wayne	205 (87.2%)	30 (12.8%)
White	428 (66.8%)	213 (33.2%)
Total	**9,412 (67.7%)**	**4,681 (32.3%)**

SOURCE—Theodore Pease (ed.), Illinois Election Returns 1818–1848, Springfield, IL: Illinois State Historical Society Library, 1923, pp. 57–59.

Indiana

County	Jackson	Adams
Allen	64 (46.4%)	74 (53.6%)
Bartholomew	445 (65.4%)	235 (34.6%)
Clark	953 (60.8%)	615 (39.2%)
Clay	83 (76.9%)	25 (23.1%)
Crawford	230 (52.8%)	206 (47.2%)
Daviess	291 (58.1%)	210 (41.9%)
Dearborn	1,066 (51.9%)	986 (48.1%)
Decatur	346 (54.2%)	292 (45.8%)
Delaware	91 (59.1%)	63 (40.9%)
Dubois	180 (55.7%)	49 (44.3%)
Fayette	650 (55.7%)	516 (44.3%)
Floyd	590 (61.2%)	374 (38.8%)
Fountain	468 (67.6%)	224 (32.4%)
Franklin	693 (51.4%)	656 (48.6%)
Gibson	380 (61.4%)	239 (38.6%)
Greene	320 (66.5%)	161 (33.5%)
Hamilton	55 (26.1%)	156 (73.9%)
Hancock	65 (49.2%)	67 (50.8%)
Harrison	705 (60.7%)	457 (39.3%)
Hendricks	204 (55.4%)	164 (44.6%)
Henry	284 (46.4%)	328 (53.6%)
Jackson	405 (69.0%)	182 (31.0%)
Jefferson	627 (46.9%)	709 (53.1%)
Jennings	204 (40.5%)	290 (59.5%)
Johnson	298 (60.0%)	199 (40.0%)
Knox	420 (50.9%)	405 (49.1%)
Lawrence	823 (79.4%)	213 (20.6%)
Madison	58 (44.6%)	72 (55.4%)
Marion	379 (39.4%)	582 (60.6%)
Martin	191 (24.7%)	68 (75.3%)
Monroe	570 (89.3%)	223 (10.7%)
Montgomery	359 (59.6%)	243 (40.4%)

County	Jackson		Adams	
Morgan	235	(50.3%)	232	(49.7%)
Orange	631	(68.9%)	285	(31.1%)
Owen	187	(48.2%)	201	(51.8%)
Parke	480	(58.6%)	339	(41.4%)
Perry	134	(42.7%)	180	(57.3%)
Pike	149	(51.6%)	140	(48.4%)
Posey	646	(69.9%)	278	(30.1%)
Putnam	632	(67.2%)	309	(32.8%)
Randolph	123	(33.0%)	250	(67.0%)
Ripley	307	(49.8%)	325	(50.2%)
Rush	649	(65.2%)	345	(34.8%)
Scott	283	(65.8%)	147	(34.2%)
Shelby	458	(75.7%)	310	(24.3%)
Spencer	173	(68.4%)	80	(31.6%)
Sullivan	432	(72.0%)	168	(28.0%)
Switzerland	439	(56.7%)	335	(43.3%)
Tippecanoe	210	(53.3%)	184	(46.7%)
Union	547	(51.4%)	518	(48.6%)
Vanderburgh	108	(44.6%)	134	(55.4%)
Vermillion	282	(49.6%)	287	(50.4%)
Vigo	186	(25.5%)	544	(74.5%)
Warren	63	(45.0%)	77	(55.0%)
Warrick	318	(81.3%)	73	(18.7%)
Washington	1,083	(63.9%)	612	(36.1%)
Wayne	888	(39.8%)	1,342	(60.2%)
Total	**22,140**	**(56.6%)**	**16,978**	**(43.4%)**

SOURCE—Dorothy Riker and Gayle Thornbrough (eds.), *Indiana Election Returns 1816–1851*, Indianapolis, IN: Indiana Historical Bureau, 1960, pp. 10–13.

Kentucky

County	Jackson		Adams	
Adair	571	(63.2%)	333	(36.8%)
Allen	540	(70.8%)	223	(29.2%)
Anderson	444	(80.6%)	107	(19.4%)
Barren	839	(52.3%)	766	(47.7%)
Bath	548	(62.2%)	343	(37.8%)
Boone	485	(52.3%)	442	(47.7%)
Bourbon	849	(43.6%)	1,100	(56.4%)
Bracken	427	(48.6%)	452	(51.4%)
Breckinridge	369	(42.4%)	501	(57.6%)
Bullitt	453	(66.7%)	226	(33.3%)
Butler	218	(63.2%)	127	(36.8%)
Caldwell	637	(73.3%)	232	(26.7%)
Calloway	468	(90.5%)	49	(9.5%)
Campbell	813	(75.1%)	269	(24.9%)
Casey	278	(60.6%)	181	(39.4%)
Christian	530	(44.7%)	655	(55.3%)
Clark	537	(40.7%)	784	(59.3%)
Clay	53	(13.2%)	348	(86.8%)
Cumberland	435	(57.1%)	327	(42.9%)
Daviess	284	(63.8%)	161	(36.2%)
Edmonson	197	(61.6%)	123	(38.4%)
Estill	239	(52.6%)	215	(47.4%)
Fayette	1,021	(43.2%)	1,340	(56.8%)
Fleming	661	(49.4%)	676	(50.6%)
Floyd	380	(80.5%)	92	(19.5%)
Franklin	631	(62.2%)	384	(37.8%)
Gallatin	452	(57.0%)	341	(43.0%)
Garrard	262	(20.5%)	1,014	(79.5%)
Grant	186	(50.0%)	186	(50.0%)
Graves	141	(85.5%)	24	(14.5%)
Grayson	247	(51.6%)	232	(48.4%)
Green	993	(65.5%)	524	(34.5%)
Greenup	302	(50.7%)	294	(49.3%)
Hardin	908	(64.3%)	505	(35.7%)
Harlan	122	(36.3%)	214	(63.7%)
Harrison	966	(70.6%)	403	(29.4%)
Hart	366	(70.8%)	151	(29.2%)
Henderson	255	(44.3%)	321	(55.7%)
Henry	672	(65.9%)	338	(34.1%)
Hickman	260	(89.0%)	32	(11.0%)
Hopkins	362	(56.9%)	274	(43.1%)
Jefferson	1,460	(58.8%)	1,024	(41.2%)
Jessamine	520	(52.4%)	472	(47.6%)
Knox	134	(32.0%)	285	(68.0%)
Laurel	77	(35.3%)	141	(64.7%)
Lawrence	283	(72.6%)	107	(27.4%)
Lewis	404	(57.1%)	303	(42.9%)
Lincoln	576	(51.0%)	554	(49.0%)
Livingston	373	(63.7%)	213	(36.3%)
Logan	342	(27.9%)	883	(72.1%)
McCracken	94	(74.0%)	33	(26.0%)
Madison	653	(43.0%)	866	(57.0%)
Mason	660	(37.6%)	1,088	(62.4%)
Meade	150	(42.7%)	201	(57.3%)
Mercer	1,258	(70.6%)	525	(29.4%)
Monroe	463	(77.2%)	137	(22.8%)
Montgomery	600	(50.6%)	585	(49.4%)
Morgan	280	(81.9%)	62	(18.1%)
Muhlenberg	266	(42.6%)	359	(57.4%)
Nelson	784	(48.4%)	835	(51.6%)
Nicholas	536	(62.0%)	329	(38.0%)
Ohio	358	(62.7%)	213	(37.3%)
Oldham	657	(65.7%)	343	(34.3%)
Owen	502	(81.1%)	117	(18.9%)
Pendleton	267	(63.7%)	152	(36.3%)
Perry	59	(37.1%)	100	(62.9%)
Pike	194	(98.5%)	3	(1.5%)
Pulaski	519	(54.3%)	437	(45.7%)
Rockcastle	134	(35.0%)	249	(65.0%)
Russell	269	(57.6%)	198	(42.4%)
Scott	993	(64.1%)	555	(35.9%)
Shelby	946	(46.3%)	1,097	(53.7%)
Simpson	355	(51.5%)	334	(48.5%)
Spencer	437	(66.7%)	218	(33.3%)
Todd	296	(37.9%)	486	(62.1%)
Trigg	304	(60.3%)	200	(39.7%)
Union	249	(55.6%)	199	(44.4%)
Warren	478	(41.5%)	674	(58.5%)
Washington	1,486	(75.2%)	491	(24.8%)
Wayne	578	(68.1%)	271	(31.9%)
Whitley	177	(52.4%)	161	(47.6%)
Woodford	513	(44.2%)	647	(55.8%)
Total	**39,085**	**(55.4%)**	**31,456**	**(44.6%)**

SOURCE—(Frankfort) *Argus*, November 19 and 26, 1828.

Louisiana

Parish	Jackson		Adams	
Ascension	106	(50.0%)	106	(50.0%)
Assumption	140	(50.0%)	140	(50.0%)
Avoyelles	40	(24.5%)	123	(74.5%)
Catahoula	147	(79.5%)	38	(20.5%)
Claiborne & Natchitoches	242	(63.5%)	139	(36.5%)
Concordia	70	(62.5%)	42	(37.5%)
East Baton Rouge	247	(62.4%)	149	(37.6%)
East Feliciana	441	(84.6%)	80	(15.4%)
Iberville	190	(74.2%)	66	(25.8%)
Jefferson	24	(27.6%)	63	(73.4%)
Lafayette	208	(56.8%)	158	(43.2%)
Lafourche	39	(10.3%)	338	(89.7%)
Orleans	747	(52.9%)	665	(47.1%)
Ouachita	141	(60.8%)	91	(39.2%)
Plaquemines	29	(29.9%)	68	(70.1%)

	Jackson		Adams	
Point Coupee	93	(57.8%)	68	(42.2%)
Rapides	241	(74.6%)	82	(25.4%)
St. Bernard	56	(36.1%)	89	(63.9%)
St. Charles	37	(40.7%)	54	(59.3%)
St. Helena	294	(84.7%)	53	(15.3%)
St. James	76	(33.2%)	153	(66.8%)
St. John the Baptist	30	(28.0%)	77	(72.0%)
St. Landry	135	(19.9%)	543	(80.1%)
St. Martin	63	(19.7%)	257	(80.3%)
St. Mary	85	(39.5%)	130	(60.5%)
St. Tammany	164	(78.1%)	46	(21.9%)
Terrebone	42	(44.0%)	54	(56.0%)
Washington	181	(80.4%)	44	(19.6%)
West Baton Rouge	70	(53.0%)	62	(47.0%)
West Feliciana	225	(69.7%)	98	(30.3%)
Total	**4,603**	**(54.9%)**	**4,076**	**(45.1%)**

SOURCE—(New Orleans) *Louisiana Courier*, November 25, 1828.

Maine

Two electors chosen at large, the rest by districts.
Each county constituted a district except Hancock,
which was combined with Washington, and Penobscot,
which was combined with Somerset.
The figures are for the district electors.

County	Jackson		Adams	
Cumberland	4,227	(51.1%)	4,043	(48.9%)
Hancock	394	(31.6%)	853	(68.4%)
Kennebec	1,057	(25.6%)	3,075	(74.4%)
Lincoln	820	(29.8%)	1,933	(70.2%)
Oxford	2,812	(46.4%)	3,248	(53.6%)
Penobscot	1,040	(44.3%)	1,307	(55.7%)
Somerset	752	(31.5%)	1,637	(68.5%)
Washington	841	(37.3%)	1,415	(62.7%)
York	1,865	(38.0%)	3,047	(62.0%)
Total	**13,808**	**(40.2%)**	**20,558**	**(59.8%)**
	*(13,927)		*(20,558)	

*Stated totals.

SOURCE—(Portland) *Eastern Argus*, November, 1828, and June 15, 1844.

Maryland

Electors were chosen by district, and the returns are below
the county returns. The number in parentheses next to
each county indicates the electoral district the county was in.

County	Jackson		Adams	
(4) Allegany	856	(53.6%)	741	(46.4%)
(3) Anne Arundel	1,275	(47.2%)	1,428	(52.8%)
(5) Baltimore	2,942	(64.7%)	1,602	(35.3%)
(3) Baltimore (city)	4,783	(52.6%)	4,315	(47.4%)
(1) Calvert	181	(25.2%)	537	(74.8%)
(8) Caroline	537	(44.6%)	666	(55.4%)
(6) Cecil	1,118	(51.8%)	1,041	(48.2%)
(1) Charles	551	(42.7%)	739	(57.3%)
(8,9) Dorchester	804	(43.0%)	1,067	(57.0%)
(4) Frederick	3,234	(47.1%)	3,633	(52.9%)
(6) Harford	1,095	(47.7%)	1,201	(52.3%)
(7) Kent	461	(46.1%)	540	(53.9%)
(2) Montgomery	641	(38.2%)	1,036	(61.8%)
(2) Prince George's	687	(48.3%)	735	(51.7%)
(7) Queen Anne's	561	(49.7%)	568	(50.3%)
(1) St. Mary's	369	(32.9%)	751	(67.1%)
(9) Somerset	760	(37.5%)	1,265	(62.5%)

	Jackson		Adams	
(8) Talbot	421	(34.0%)	818	(66.0%)
(4) Washington	2,087	(54.4%)	1,743	(45.6%)
(9) Worcester	1,102	(52.7%)	991	(47.3%)
Total	**24,465**	**(49.0%)**	**25,417**	**(51.0%)**
1st District	1,101	(35.2%)	2,027	(64.8%)
2nd District	1,328	(42.9%)	1,771	(57.1%)
*3rd District (two elected)	6,058	(51.3%)	5,743	(48.7%)
*4th District (two elected)	6,177	(50.2%)	6,117	(49.8%)
5th District	2,942	(64.7%)	1,602	(35.3%)
6th District	2,213	(49.6%)	2,242	(50.4%)
7th District	1,022	(52.0%)	1,108	(48.0%)
8th District	1,050	(40.4%)	1,551	(59.6%)
9th District	2,574	(44.2%)	3,256	(55.8%)

*In the 3rd and 4th Districts, the vote represents the total for the high elector.

SOURCES—Hall of Records; John T. Willis, *Presidential Elections in Maryland*, Mt. Airy, MD: Lomond Publications, 1984, p. 169.

Massachusetts

County	Jackson		Adams	
Barnstable	25	(3.8%)	627	(96.2%)
Berkshire	1,355	(35.1%)	2,500	(64.9%)
Bristol	325	(15.7%)	1,740	(84.3%)
Dukes	14	(15.9%)	74	(84.1%)
Essex	800	(17.7%)	3,709	(82.3%)
Franklin	71	(3.4%)	2,015	(96.6%)
Hampden	676	(30.5%)	1,543	(69.5%)
Hampshire	88	(4.6%)	1,809	(95.4%)
Middlesex	525	(13.5%)	3,368	(86.5%)
Nantucket		no returns		
Norfolk	355	(12.4%)	2,516	(87.6%)
Plymouth	142	(8.0%)	1,642	(92.0%)
Suffolk	849	(21.2%)	3,153	(78.8%)
Worcester	791	(13.3%)	5,146	(86.7%)
Total	**6,016**	**(16.8%)**	**29,842**	**(83.2%)**
			*(29,836)	

*Stated totals.

SOURCE—State archives.

Mississippi

County	Jackson		Adams	
Adams	422	(57.2%)	335	(42.8%)
Amite	446	(85.0%)	79	(15.0%)
Claiborne	373	(61.7%)	232	(38.3%)
Copiah	495	(92.5%)	40	(7.5%)
Covington	209	(92.5%)	17	(7.5%)
Franklin	285	(87.2%)	42	(12.8%)
Greene	99	(75.6%)	20	(24.4%)
Hancock	61	(88.4%)	8	(11.6%)
Hinds	411	(87.8%)	57	(12.2%)
Jackson	73	(86.9%)	11	(13.1%)
Jefferson	491	(77.3%)	194	(22.7%)
Jones	124	(99.2%)	1	(0.8%)
Lawrence	490	(92.5%)	40	(7.5%)
Madison	149	(91.4%)	14	(8.6%)
Marion	250	(83.9%)	48	(16.1%)
Monroe	362	(95.8%)	16	(4.2%)
Perry	164	(94.3%)	10	(5.7%)
Pike	390	(94.0%)	25	(6.0%)
Rankin	51	(92.7%)	4	(7.3%)
Simpson	316	(93.8%)	21	(6.2%)
Warren	412	(70.8%)	170	(29.2%)
Washington	54	(75.0%)	18	(25.0%)

Wayne	156 (81.7%)	35 (18.3%)
Wilkinson	574 (78.1%)	161 (21.9%)
Yazoo	229 (98.3%)	4 (1.7%)
Total	**7,086 (81.6%)**	**1,602 (18.4%)**
	*(7,088)	

*Stated totals.

SOURCES—(Natchez) *Statesman & Gazette*, January 15, 1829; manuscript returns, state archives.

Missouri

County	Jackson	Adams
Boone	520 (63.7%)	296 (36.3%)
Callaway	267 (80.9%)	163 (19.1%)
Cape Girardeau	457 (75.5%)	148 (24.5%)
Chariton	361 (78.0%)	102 (22.0%)
Clinton	364 (74.4%)	125 (25.6%)
Cole	331 (87.8%)	46 (12.2%)
Cooper	458 (69.3%)	203 (30.7%)
Franklin	267 (89.6%)	31 (10.4%)
Gasconde	205 (97.2%)	6 (2.8%)
Howard	658 (65.0%)	355 (35.0%)
Jackson	210 (98.6%)	3 (1.4%)
Jefferson	152 (67.9%)	72 (32.1%)
Lafayette	322 (84.2%)	60 (15.8%)
Lincoln	231 (34.4%)	441 (65.6%)
Madison	271 (82.9%)	56 (17.1%)
Marion	159 (60.7%)	53 (39.3%)
Montgomery	234 (64.8%)	127 (35.2%)
New Madrid	58 (63.7%)	33 (36.3%)
Perry	196 (80.0%)	49 (20.0%)
Pike	260 (52.2%)	238 (47.8%)
Ralls	117 (70.1%)	50 (29.9%)
Ray	186 (89.9%)	21 (10.1%)
St. Charles	218 (65.2%)	116 (34.8%)
St. Francois	189 (68.0%)	89 (32.0%)
St. Louis	699 (61.2%)	443 (38.8%)
Ste. Genevieve	112 (70.0%)	48 (30.0%)
Saline	150 (83.3%)	30 (16.7%)
Scott	66 (74.2%)	23 (25.8%)
Washington	356 (65.2%)	190 (34.8%)
Wayne	213 (97.7%)	5 (2.3%)
Total	**8,287 (69.3%)**	**3,672 (30.7%)**

SOURCE—(St. Louis) *Missouri Republican*, November 25, 1828.

New Hampshire

County	Jackson	Adams
Cheshire	2,926 (35.6%)	5,287 (64.4%)
Coos	717 (62.8%)	426 (37.2%)
Grafton	2,896 (46.5%)	3,602 (53.5%)
Hillsborough	3,118 (46.9%)	3,531 (53.1%)
Merrimack	3,645 (57.7%)	2,672 (42.3%)
Rockingham	3,458 (46.3%)	4,005 (53.7%)
Strafford	4,422 (49.0%)	4,597 (51.0%)
Total	**21,182 (46.8%)**	**24,120 (53.2%)**

SOURCE—Manuscript returns.

New Jersey

County	Jackson	Adams
Bergen	1,413 (48.1%)	1,522 (51.9%)
Burlington	1,592 (36.2%)	2,806 (63.8%)
Cape May	204 (28.6%)	509 (71.4%)
Cumberland	1,138 (47.4%)	1,263 (52.6%)
Essex	2,292 (40.1%)	3,425 (59.9%)
Gloucester	1,551 (43.6%)	2,010 (56.4%)
Hunterdon	2,565 (54.1%)	2,180 (45.9%)
Mercer	1,853 (50.1%)	1,847 (49.9%)
Middlesex	1,302 (40.6%)	1,902 (59.4%)
Monmouth	1,933 (48.9%)	2,018 (51.1%)
Salem	979 (44.2%)	1,238 (55.8%)
Somerset	1,189 (48.1%)	1,283 (51.9%)
Sussex	2,249 (75.3%)	737 (24.7%)
Warren	1,691 (62.3%)	1,024 (37.7%)
Total	**21,951 (48.0%)**	**23,764 (52.0%)**

SOURCE—(Trenton) *True-American*, November 22, 1828.

New York

All but two electors were chosen from the congressional districts; the remaining two were chosen by those electors elected from the districts. The district returns are below the county returns. The number in parentheses next to each county indicates the electoral district the county was in.

County	Jackson	Adams
(10) Albany	3,924 (48.3%)	4,195 (51.7%)
(28) Allegany	1,614 (49.6%)	1,638 (50.4%)
(21) Broome	1,246 (58.4%)	889 (41.8%)
(28) Cattaraugus	855 (40.1%)	1,277 (59.9%)
(24) Cayuga	4,159 (63.3%)	2,416 (36.7%)
(30) Chautauqua	1,559 (35.0%)	2,893 (65.0%)
(21) Chenango	3,083 (58.1%)	2,227 (41.9%)
(19) Clinton	1,389 (50.4%)	1,367 (49.6%)
(8) Columbia	3,446 (48.6%)	3,642 (51.4%)
(22) Cortland	1,529 (47.0%)	1,721 (53.0%)
(11) Delaware	2,801 (64.0%)	1,573 (36.0%)
(5) Dutchess	4,680 (58.9%)	3,263 (41.1%)
(30) Erie	1,265 (21.2%)	3,331 (78.8%)
(19) Essex	1,282 (39.8%)	1,937 (60.2%)
(19) Franklin	679 (39.8%)	1,029 (60.2%)
(29) Genesee	2,320 (30.7%)	5,248 (69.3%)
(11) Greene	2,530 (58.4%)	1,799 (41.6%)
(15) Herkimer	3,177 (55.9%)	2,510 (44.1%)
(20) Jefferson	3,877 (53.2%)	3,417 (46.8%)
(2) Kings	1,349 (56.2%)	1,053 (43.8%)
(20) Lewis	1,035 (53.7%)	892 (46.3%)
(27) Livingston	1,486 (38.4%)	2,385 (61.6%)
(22) Madison	2,607 (44.5%)	3,253 (55.5%)
(27) Monroe	3,145 (40.1%)	4,694 (59.9%)
(16) Montgomery & Hamilton	3,778 (48.7%)	3,982 (51.3%)
(3) New York	15,435 (61.6%)	9,638 (38.4%)
(30) Niagara	836 (32.2%)	1,759 (67.8%)
(14) Oneida	5,136 (46.9%)	5,817 (53.1%)
(23) Onondaga	4,264 (52.9%)	3,796 (47.1%)
(26) Ontario	2,030 (33.0%)	4,120 (67.0%)
(6) Orange	3,798 (59.5%)	2,586 (40.5%)
(29) Orleans	936 (37.1%)	1,584 (62.9%)
(20) Oswego	2,077 (54.0%)	1,772 (46.0%)
(13) Otsego	4,241 (52.1%)	3,900 (47.9%)
(4) Putnam	1,119 (66.4%)	567 (33.6%)
(1) Queens	1,129 (45.0%)	1,379 (55.0%)
(9) Rensselaer	4,263 (47.8%)	4,650 (52.2%)
(2) Richmond	518 (52.2%)	475 (47.8%)
(2) Rockland	1,041 (71.1%)	424 (28.9%)
(20) St. Lawrence	2,576 (49.3%)	2,647 (50.7%)
(17) Saratoga	2,929 (45.2%)	3,545 (54.8%)
(12) Schenectady	1,143 (55.7%)	908 (44.3%)
(12) Schoharie	2,597 (60.8%)	1,676 (39.2%)

	Jackson	Adams
(26) Seneca	1,501 (48.3%)	1,606 (51.7%)
(28) Steuben	2,878 (66.0%)	1,480 (34.0%)
(1) Suffolk	1,946 (57.0%)	1,468 (43.0%)
(7) Sullivan	1,249 (65.2%)	688 (34.8%)
(25) Tioga	2,142 (57.2%)	1,601 (42.8%)
(25) Tompkins	3,236 (60.0%)	2,154 (40.0%)
(7) Ulster	3,375 (59.3%)	1,321 (40.7%)
(19) Warren	1,163 (65.0%)	626 (35.0%)
(18) Washington	2,658 (39.4%)	4,085 (60.6%)
(26) Wayne	1,907 (44.6%)	2,372 (55.4%)
(4) Westchester	2,669 (50.8%)	2,586 (49.2%)
(26) Yates	1,573 (58.8%)	1,101 (41.2%)
1st District	3,075 (51.9%)	2,847 (48.1%)
2nd District	2,936 (59.9%)	1,966 (40.1%)
3rd District (3 elected)	15,435 (61.6%)	9,638 (38.4%)
4th District	3,788 (54.6%)	3,153 (45.4%)
5th District	4,680 (58.9%)	3,263 (41.1%)
6th District	3,798 (59.5%)	2,586 (40.5%)
7th District	4,624 (69.7%)	2,009 (30.3%)
8th District	3,446 (48.6%)	3,642 (51.4%)
9th District	4,263 (47.8%)	4,650 (52.2%)
10th District	3,924 (48.3%)	4,195 (51.7%)
11th District	5,331 (61.3%)	3,370 (38.7%)
12th District	3,740 (39.4%)	2,584 (60.6%)
13th District	4,241 (67.1%)	3,900 (32.9%)
14th District	5,136 (46.9%)	5,817 (53.1%)
15th District	3,177 (55.9%)	2,510 (44.1%)
16th District	3,778 (55.9%)	3,982 (44.1%)
17th District	2,929 (53.5%)	3,545 (46.5%)
18th District	2,658 (39.6%)	4,085 (60.4%)
19th District	4,503 (52.1%)	5,042 (47.9%)
20th District (2 elected)	9,081 (49.8%)	9,164 (50.2%)
21st District	4,329 (58.5%)	3,116 (41.5%)
22nd District	4,136 (45.5%)	4,974 (54.5%)
23rd District	4,264 (52.9%)	3,796 (47.1%)
24th District	4,159 (63.3%)	2,416 (36.7%)
25th District	5,427 (59.1%)	3,755 (40.9%)
26th District (2 elected)	7,011 (43.5%)	9,119 (56.5%)
27th District	4,631 (39.6%)	7,079 (60.4%)
28th District	5,347 (61.2%)	4,395 (38.8%)
29th District	3,256 (32.3%)	6,832 (67.7%)
30th District	3,660 (31.4%)	7,983 (68.6%)
Total[4]	**140,763 (51.0%)**	**135,413 (49.0%)**

SOURCES—*Albany Argus*, November 15 and 27, 1828, and November 23, 1832; *Norwich Journal*, November 19, 1828; and *Plattsburgh Republican*, November 15, 1828.

North Carolina

County	Jackson	Adams
Anson	701 (58.7%)	494 (41.3%)
Ashe	319 (74.9%)	107 (25.1%)
Beaufort	372 (37.3%)	625 (62.7%)
Bertie	571 (73.1%)	210 (26.9%)
Bladen	384 (77.6%)	111 (22.4%)
Brunswick	149 (48.3%)	175 (51.7%)
Buncombe	762 (87.3%)	111 (12.7%)
Burke	1,314 (86.2%)	211 (13.8%)
Cabarrus	428 (57.1%)	321 (42.9%)
Camden	426 (86.8%)	65 (13.2%)
Carteret	325 (48.1%)	350 (51.9%)
Caswell	941 (97.3%)	26 (2.7%)
Chatham	698 (63.1%)	409 (36.9%)
Chowan	225 (76.5%)	69 (23.5%)
Columbus	300 (88.2%)	40 (11.8%)
Craven	550 (58.0%)	399 (42.0%)
Cumberland	821 (71.6%)	325 (28.4%)

County	Jackson	Adams
Currituck	396 (91.9%)	35 (8.1%)
Davidson	849 (78.4%)	234 (21.6%)
Duplin	546 (78.2%)	152 (21.8%)
Edgecombe	902 (89.0%)	111 (11.0%)
Franklin	630 (88.5%)	82 (11.5%)
Gates	424 (83.3%)	85 (16.7%)
Granville	842 (83.9%)	162 (16.1%)
Greene	203 (58.2%)	146 (41.8%)
Guilford	546 (36.0%)	970 (64.0%)
Halifax	765 (92.7%)	60 (7.3%)
Haywood	933 (99.3%)	3 (0.7%)
Hertford	379 (70.4%)	159 (29.6%)
Hyde	247 (73.7%)	88 (26.3%)
Iredell	563 (49.6%)	571 (50.4%)
Johnston	418 (69.6%)	183 (30.4%)
Jones	212 (49.6%)	215 (50.4%)
Lenoir	252 (69.4%)	111 (30.6%)
Lincoln	1,191 (73.5%)	429 (26.5%)
Martin	461 (70.0%)	198 (30.0%)
Mecklenburg	1,194 (76.1%)	376 (23.9%)
Montgomery	564 (63.0%)	331 (37.0%)
Moore	515 (81.9%)	90 (18.1%)
Nash	453 (88.8%)	57 (11.2%)
New Hanover	668 (82.0%)	147 (18.0%)
Northampton	362 (61.4%)	228 (38.6%)
Onslow	476 (81.9%)	105 (18.1%)
Orange	1,057 (70.6%)	440 (29.4%)
Pasquotank	373 (56.0%)	293 (44.0%)
Perquimans	301 (69.2%)	134 (30.8%)
Person	393 (94.2%)	24 (5.8%)
Pitt	329 (40.4%)	485 (59.6%)
Randolph	417 (40.3%)	619 (59.7%)
Richmond	315 (60.1%)	209 (39.9%)
Robeson	579 (68.9%)	264 (31.1%)
Rockingham	989 (90.0%)	110 (10.0%)
Rowan	1,197 (78.9%)	321 (21.1%)
Rutherford	1,214 (95.8%)	53 (4.2%)
Sampson	599 (83.3%)	120 (16.7%)
Stokes	1,190 (82.9%)	245 (17.1%)
Surry	1,190 (81.4%)	272 (18.6%)
Tyrrell	273 (93.2%)	20 (6.8%)
Wake	1,037 (79.6%)	266 (20.4%)
Warren	352 (91.4%)	33 (8.6%)
Washington	315 (83.6%)	62 (16.4%)
Wayne	538 (65.6%)	282 (34.4%)
Wilkes	699 (69.3%)	310 (30.7%)
Total	**37,634 (73.0%)**	**13,938 (27.0%)**
	(37,857)	**(13,918)**

SOURCE—Manuscript returns.

Ohio

County	Jackson	Adams
Adams	1,327 (78.1%)	373 (21.9%)
Ashtabula	179 (8.5%)	1,936 (71.5%)
Athens	482 (36.7%)	833 (63.3%)
Belmont	2,183 (50.2%)	2,162 (49.8%)
Brown	1,630 (69.9%)	703 (30.1%)
Butler	3,239 (77.3%)	953 (22.7%)
Champaign	595 (36.2%)	1,048 (63.8%)
Clark	637 (33.7%)	1,254 (66.3%)
Clermont	2,031 (67.0%)	1,002 (33.0%)
Clinton	715 (41.5%)	1,007 (58.5%)
Columbiana	2,431 (52.9%)	2,163 (47.1%)
Coshocton	1,031 (64.2%)	574 (35.8%)
Crawford	322 (60.5%)	210 (39.5%)
Cuyahoga	320 (20.1%)	1,269 (79.9%)

Darke	571 (75.0%)	190 (25.0%)
Delaware	472 (64.8%)	868 (35.2%)
Fairfield	2,606 (70.0%)	1,131 (30.0%)
Fayette	627 (54.1%)	533 (45.9%)
Franklin	868 (43.5%)	1,155 (56.5%)
Gallia	439 (37.0%)	746 (63.0%)
Geauga	347 (14.0%)	2,135 (86.0%)
Greene	964 (55.4%)	1,197 (44.6%)
Guernsey	1,259 (51.1%)	1,204 (48.9%)
Hamilton	4,917 (64.4%)	2,716 (35.6%)
Hancock	49 (60.5%)	32 (39.5%)
Harrison	1,594 (52.9%)	1,422 (47.1%)
Highland	991 (53.6%)	858 (46.4%)
Hocking	293 (57.9%)	213 (42.1%)
Holmes	863 (78.7%)	234 (21.3%)
Huron	583 (32.0%)	1,241 (68.0%)
Jackson	390 (50.5%)	383 (49.5%)
Jefferson	1,933 (55.4%)	1,556 (44.6%)
Knox	1,598 (68.5%)	736 (31.5%)
Lawrence	282 (48.0%)	306 (52.0%)
Licking	1,826 (63.7%)	1,040 (36.3%)
Logan & Hardin	275 (34.8%)	515 (65.2%)
Lorain	153 (20.5%)	595 (79.5%)
Madison	435 (50.6%)	424 (49.4%)
Marion	320 (55.0%)	254 (45.0%)
Medina	160 (16.6%)	803 (83.4%)
Meigs	306 (33.1%)	579 (66.9%)
Mercer, Allen & Van Wert	111 (60.7%)	72 (39.3%)
Miami	764 (41.2%)	1,089 (58.8%)
Monroe	741 (71.4%)	297 (28.6%)
Morgan	840 (54.7%)	697 (45.3%)
Montgomery	1,754 (50.6%)	1,709 (49.4%)
Muskingum	2,151 (49.6%)	2,184 (50.4%)
Perry	1,308 (67.1%)	640 (32.9%)
Pike	487 (66.8%)	242 (33.2%)
Pickaway	1,536 (57.4%)	1,139 (42.6%)
Portage	855 (28.9%)	2,107 (71.1%)
Preble	895 (44.6%)	1,113 (55.4%)
Richland	1,805 (58.5%)	1,283 (41.5%)
Ross	1,780 (47.7%)	1,951 (52.3%)
Sandusky	118 (36.4%)	206 (63.6%)
Scioto	465 (42.3%)	635 (57.7%)
Seneca	242 (40.7%)	353 (59.3%)
Shelby	273 (58.6%)	193 (41.4%)
Stark	1,770 (56.5%)	1,308 (43.5%)
Trumbull	1,590 (38.7%)	2,521 (61.3%)
Tuscarawas	1,041 (54.1%)	884 (45.9%)
Union	194 (51.7%)	181 (48.3%)
Warren	1,797 (49.2%)	1,835 (50.8%)
Washington	695 (61.0%)	1,086 (61.0%)
Wayne	2,045 (68.9%)	925 (31.1%)
Williams, Henry, Paulding & Putnam	50 (41.7%)	70 (58.3%)
Wood	46 (27.5%)	121 (72.5%)
Total	**67,596 (51.6%)**	**63,456 (48.4%)**
		*(63,394)

*Stated totals.

SOURCE—(Columbus) *Ohio State Journal*, November 20, 1828.

Pennsylvania

County	Jackson	Adams
Adams	1,242 (45.9%)	1,461 (54.1%)
Allegheny	3,866 (69.9%)	1,666 (30.1%)
Armstrong	1,133 (86.4%)	169 (13.6%)
Beaver	1,321 (49.4%)	1,352 (50.6%)
Bedford	2,260 (74.3%)	780 (25.7%)
Berks	4,583 (83.7%)	894 (16.3%)
Bradford	1,553 (63.1%)	910 (36.9%)
Bucks	3,223 (49.0%)	3,355 (51.0%)
Butler	1,068 (63.6%)	610 (36.4%)
Cambria	314 (77.0%)	94 (23.0%)
Centre	1,998 (81.5%)	453 (18.5%)
Chester	3,835 (52.0%)	3,535 (48.0%)
Clearfield	893 (80.9%)	211 (19.1%)
Columbia	1,869 (76.9%)	562 (23.1%)
Crawford	1,117 (53.9%)	958 (46.1%)
Cumberland	2,113 (70.2%)	898 (29.8%)
Dauphin	1,974 (63.4%)	1,140 (36.6%)
Delaware	953 (45.0%)	1,164 (55.0%)
Erie	773 (45.0%)	945 (55.0%)
Fayette	2,945 (70.5%)	1,230 (29.5%)
Franklin	2,586 (57.5%)	1,915 (42.5%)
Greene	1,498 (76.8%)	452 (23.2%)
Huntingdon	1,708 (59.9%)	1,144 (40.1%)
Indiana & Jefferson	926 (79.1%)	245 (20.9%)
Lancaster	5,186 (58.2%)	3,719 (41.8%)
Lebanon	1,439 (70.6%)	597 (29.4%)
Lehigh	2,000 (79.5%)	516 (20.5%)
Luzerne	1,645 (53.4%)	1,435 (46.6%)
Lycoming	1,534 (76.7%)	467 (23.3%)
McKean & Potter	175 (61.8%)	108 (38.2%)
Mercer	1,603 (68.5%)	738 (31.5%)
Mifflin	1,650 (76.5%)	506 (23.5%)
Montgomery	3,341 (59.1%)	2,311 (40.9%)
Northampton	3,628 (80.3%)	889 (19.7%)
Northumberland	1,669 (80.9%)	395 (19.1%)
Perry	1,060 (81.5%)	241 (18.5%)
Philadelphia	12,017 (66.0%)	6,200 (34.0%)
Pike	549 (88.1%)	74 (11.9%)
Schuylkill	863 (79.7%)	220 (20.3%)
Somerset	1,347 (85.0%)	238 (15.0%)
Susquehanna	1,062 (60.5%)	694 (39.5%)
Tioga	850 (85.5%)	193 (14.5%)
Union	1,697 (89.0%)	210 (11.0%)
Venango	769 (85.9%)	126 (14.1%)
Warren	340 (58.3%)	243 (41.7%)
Washington	3,883 (69.7%)	1,687 (30.3%)
Wayne	531 (62.4%)	320 (37.6%)
Westmoreland	3,917 (86.2%)	629 (13.8%)
York	3,645 (65.9%)	1,864 (34.1%)
Total	**102,151 (66.8%)**	**50,783 (33.2%)**
	(101,652)	**(50,848)**

SOURCES—(Harrisburg) *The Intelligencer*, November 18, 1828; and (Philadelphia) *Democratic Press*, November 19, 1828.

Rhode Island

County	Jackson	Adams
Bristol	90 (28.5%)	226 (71.5%)
Kent	93 (19.8%)	376 (80.2%)
Newport	87 (13.2%)	572 (86.8%)
Providence	332 (21.8%)	1,189 (78.2%)
Washington	218 (35.9%)	390 (64.1%)
Total	**820 (23.0%)**	**2,753 (77.0%)**
	*(821)	

*Stated totals.

SOURCE—(Newport) *Rhode Island Republican*, December 11, 1828.

South Carolina

Electors chosen by the legislature

Tennessee[5]

Electors chosen by district

1st Electoral District

County	Jackson				Adams	
Carter	273 (88.1%)	+ 37 (11.9%)	=	320 (100%)	0	
Greene	478 (70.6%)	+ 199 (29.4%)	=	677 (100%)	0	
Hawkins	821 (98.8%)	+ 10 (1.2%)	=	831 (100%)	0	
Sullivan	616 (89.7%)	+ 69 (10.3%)	=	685 (100%)	0	
Washington	608 (96.1%)	+ 25 (3.9%)	=	633 (100%)	0	
Total	2,796 (89.2%)	+ 340 (10.8%)	=	3,136 (100%)	0	

2nd Electoral District

County	Jackson				Adams	
Campbell	384 (87.1%)	+ 46 (10.7%)	=	430 (97.8%)	11	(2.6%)
Claiborne	407 (65.1%)	+ 210 (33.6%)	=	617 (98.7%)	13	(1.3%)
Cocke	270 (76.7%)	+ 82 (23.3%)	=	352 (100%)	0	
Grainger	888 (95.8%)	+ 13 (1.4%)	=	901 (97.2%)	26	(2.8%)
Jefferson	634 (65.9%)	+ 242 (25.2%)	=	876 (91.1%)	86	(8.9%)
Sevier	281 (84.4%)	+ 41 (12.3%)	=	322 (96.7%)	11	(3.3%)
Total	2,864 (78.6%)	+ 634 (17.4%)	=	3,498 (96.0%)	147	(4.0%)

3rd Electoral District

County	Jackson				Adams	
Anderson	491 (87.8%)	+ 68 (12.2%)	=	559 (100%)	0	
Blount	860 (85.7%)	+ 112 (11.2%)	=	972 (96.9%)	31	(3.0%)
Knox	1,076 (75.8%)	+ 115 (8.1%)	=	1,191 (83.9%)	218	(15.4%)
Morgan	127 (68.3%)	+ 55 (29.6%)	=	182 (97.9%)	4	(2.2%)
Roane	1,062 (93.7%)	+ 70 (6.2%)	=	1,132 (99.1%)	2	(0.2%)
Total	3,616 (84.3%)	+ 420 (9.8%)	=	4,036 (94.1%)	253	(5.9%)

7th Electoral District

County	Jackson	Adams
Davidson	1,939 (86.8%)	295 (13.2%)
Rutherford	1,545 (87.2%)	226 (12.8%)
Williamson	1,524 (88.9%)	190 (11.1%)
Total	5,008 (87.6%)	711 (12.4%)

10th Electoral District

County	Jackson				Adams	
Dickson	522 (98.5%)				8	(1.5%)
Humphreys	413 (98.3%)				7	(1.7%)
Montgomery	919 (87.9%)				127	(12.1%)
Perry	207 (98.6%)				3	(1.4%)
Robertson	825 (83.7%)	+ 149 (15.1%)	=	974 (98.8%)	12	(1.2%)
Stewart	446 (95.3%)				22	(4.7%)
Total	3,332 (91.0)	+ 149 (4.1%)	=	3,481 (95.1%)	179	(4.9%)

District	Jackson		Adams	
1st District	3,136	(100%)	0	
2nd District	3,418	(96.0%)	143	(4.0%)
3rd District	4,001	(94.0%)	254	(6.0%)
4th District	3,211	(99.8%)	7	(0.2%)
5th District	5,196	(98.6%)	74	(1.4%)
6th District	3,605	(100%)	0	
7th District	5,008	(87.4%)	715	(12.6%)
8th District	3,443	(99.8%)	6	(0.2%)
9th District	4,311	(95.1%)	220	(4.9%)
10th District	3,481	(95.1%)	179	(4.9%)
11th District	5,282	(89.2%)	642	(10.8%)
Total	**44,092**	**(95.2%)**	**2,240**	**(4.8%)**
	(44,195)			

SOURCES—*Knoxville Register,* November 19 and 26, and December 16, 1828; and *National Banner & Nashville Whig,* November 25, 1828.

Vermont

County	Jackson		Adams	
Addison	632	(19.7%)	2,581	(80.3%)
Bennington	386	(18.7%)	1,665	(81.3%)
Caledonia	497	(27.3%)	1,324	(72.7%)
Chittenden	1,096	(37.5%)	1,825	(62.5%)
Essex	198	(42.9%)	264	(57.1%)
Franklin	804	(30.6%)	1,820	(69.4%)
Grand Isle	138	(34.2%)	266	(65.8%)
Orange	1,200	(37.6%)	1,994	(62.4%)
Orleans	452	(34.0%)	879	(66.0%)
Rutland	671	(16.1%)	3,509	(83.9%)
Washington	1,192	(47.6%)	1,312	(52.4%)
Windham	585	(16.8%)	2,905	(83.2%)
Windsor	484	(10.7%)	4,021	(89.3%)

Total	8,335 (25.5%)	24,365 (74.5%)
	*(8,385)	

Stated totals.

Source—Manuscript returns, state archives.

Virginia

County	Jackson	Adams
Accomack	216 (47.4%)	240 (52.6%)
Albemarle	478 (79.4%)	124 (20.6%)
Alleghany	102 (87.2%)	15 (12.8%)
Amelia	223 (92.1%)	19 (7.9%)
Amherst	206 (64.2%)	15 (35.8%)
Augusta	359 (46.9%)	407 (53.1%)
Bath	133 (69.3%)	59 (30.7%)
Bedford	300 (50.5%)	294 (49.5%)
Berkeley	196 (37.0%)	334 (63.0%)
Botetourt	396 (78.7%)	73 (21.3%)
Brooke	315 (70.0%)	135 (30.0%)
Brunswick	218 (78.1%)	61 (21.9%)
Buckingham	437 (97.3%)	42 (2.7%)
Cabell	203 (74.4%)	70 (25.6%)
Campbell	311 (51.4%)	294 (48.6%)
Caroline	302 (75.3%)	99 (24.7%)
Charles City	66 (71.7%)	26 (28.3%)
Charlotte	319 (86.2%)	51 (13.8%)
Chesterfield	366 (78.2%)	102 (21.8%)
Culpeper	551 (81.3%)	119 (18.7%)
Cumberland	219 (71.8%)	86 (28.2%)
Dinwiddie	171 (83.4%)	34 (16.6%)
Elizabeth City	74 (50.0%)	74 (50.0%)
Essex	195 (80.9%)	46 (19.1%)
Fairfax	119 (49.2%)	123 (50.8%)
Fauquier	372 (59.9%)	249 (40.1%)
Fluvanna	269 (99.3%)	2 (0.7%)
Franklin	471 (83.1%)	96 (16.9%)
Frederick	637 (58.3%)	455 (41.7%)
Giles	292 (88.0%)	40 (12.0%)
Gloucester	168 (84.4%)	31 (15.6%)
Goochland	178 (85.6%)	30 (14.4%)
Grayson	289 (79.8%)	73 (20.1%)
Greenbrier	139 (36.2%)	255 (63.8%)
Greensville	101 (85.6%)	17 (14.4%)
Halifax	560 (88.1%)	76 (11.9%)
Hampshire	317 (52.1%)	292 (47.9%)
Hanover	280 (65.9%)	145 (34.1%)
Hardy	95 (39.7%)	144 (60.3%)
Harrison	437 (60.6%)	291 (39.4%)
Henrico	226 (65.3%)	120 (34.7%)
Henry	245 (90.1%)	27 (9.9%)
Isle of Wight	262 (79.4%)	68 (20.6%)
James City	83 (79.8%)	21 (20.2%)
Jefferson	207 (41.6%)	291 (58.4%)
Kanawha	167 (56.4%)	129 (43.6%)
King & Queen	182 (68.9%)	82 (31.1%)
King George	42 (33.6%)	83 (66.4%)
King William	178 (84.8%)	32 (15.2%)
Lancaster	59 (38.8%)	93 (61.2%)
Lee	275 (89.3%)	33 (10.7%)
Lewis	164 (47.5%)	181 (52.5%)
Logan	190 (95.0%)	10 (5.0%)
Loudoun	229 (30.4%)	525 (69.6%)
Louisa	435 (92.8%)	34 (7.2%)
Lunenburg	194 (93.7%)	13 (6.3%)
Madison	259 (93.8%)	17 (6.2%)
Mason	173 (57.3%)	129 (42.7%)
Mathews	113 (71.5%)	45 (28.5%)
Mecklenburg	461 (94.3%)	28 (5.7%)
Middlesex	102 (72.9%)	38 (27.1%)
Monongalia	490 (73.0%)	181 (27.0%)

Monroe	158 (37.1%)	268 (62.9%)
Montgomery	412 (91.2%)	40 (8.8%)
Morgan	75 (54.7%)	62 (45.3%)
Nansemond	234 (51.1%)	224 (48.9%)
Nelson	199 (73.7%)	71 (26.3%)
New Kent	96 (55.5%)	77 (44.5%)
Nicholas	116 (61.7%)	72 (38.3%)
Norfolk	156 (33.0%)	317 (67.0%)
Northampton	90 (75.6%)	29 (24.4%)
Northumberland	136 (52.9%)	121 (47.1%)
Nottoway	208 (99.0%)	2 (0.2%)
Ohio	330 (43.9%)	421 (56.1%)
Orange	424 (79.8%)	107 (20.2%)
Patrick	262 (83.2%)	53 (16.8%)
Pendleton	236 (62.1%)	144 (37.9%)
Pittsylvania	622 (84.3%)	116 (15.7%)
Pocahontas	94 (65.3%)	50 (34.7%)
Powhatan	158 (85.9%)	26 (14.1%)
Preston	228 (71.5%)	91 (28.5%)
Prince Edward	323 (97.6%)	8 (2.4%)
Prince George	186 (95.9%)	8 (4.1%)
Prince William	117 (62.9%)	69 (37.1%)
Princess Anne	105 (28.5%)	264 (71.5%)
Randolph	107 (42.0%)	148 (58.0%)
Richmond	73 (40.8%)	106 (59.2%)
Rockbridge	363 (56.8%)	276 (43.2%)
Rockingham	631 (83.9%)	121 (16.1%)
Russell	229 (93.9%)	15 (6.1%)
Scott	247 (98.4%)	4 (1.6%)
Shenandoah	990 (95.5%)	47 (4.5%)
Southampton	341 (74.8%)	115 (25.2%)
Spotsylvania	267 (77.6%)	77 (22.4%)
Stafford	106 (43.1%)	140 (56.9%)
Surry	160 (83.3%)	32 (16.7%)
Sussex	305 (97.4%)	8 (2.6%)
Tazewell	305 (99.0%)	3 (1.0%)
Tyler	124 (53.9%)	106 (46.1%)
Warwick	46 (86.8%)	7 (13.2%)
Washington	564 (98.9%)	16 (1.1%)
Westmoreland	101 (51.8%)	95 (48.2%)
Wood	125 (40.7%)	182 (59.3%)
Wythe	382 (95.0%)	20 (5.0%)
York	84 (92.3%)	7 (7.7%)
Norfolk (boro)	244 (52.8%)	218 (47.2%)
Petersburg (town)	124 (64.9%)	67 (35.1%)
Richmond (town)	107 (35.0%)	199 (65.0%)
Williamsburg (town)	36 (58.1%)	26 (41.9%)
Total	**26,842 (69.1%)**	**11,989 (30.9%)**
	*(26,808)	*(12,063)

Stated totals.

Source—Manuscript returns.

Notes

1. The electoral vote for vice president was John C. Calhoun (J) 171, Richard Rush (NR) 83 and William Smith (J) 7. The difference between the votes for the two offices was in Georgia where Smith received seven of the states's nine votes.

2. Both candidates were nominated by various state legislatures or conventions. The party names were hardly universal, partly because of an absence of any national nominating machinery. The Jacksonian name was only one of the names used by supporters; others were Democratic-Republicans or simply Republican or Democratic. National Republican seems more of a historical convience than a universal name. Other names used were Republican or Administration. Opposition newspapers frequently used the term Federalist. The titles chosen were the most common, although even this is debatable.

3. The only source for the county returns was the (Augusta) *Constitutionalist*, November 7, 1828. The two Jackson tickets repre-

sented factions of the party. Most sources combine the vote in reporting the Georgia data but this is legally incorrect. In determining the official returns, the state rejected returns from ten counties: Appling, Effingham, DeKalb, Glynn, Houston, Laurens, Merriwether, McIntosh, Wayne and Wilkinson plus a district in Gwinnett. In addition, no returns were received from eight counties: Baker, Bulloch, Early, Irwin, Marion, Telfair, Thomas and Ware. The statewide vote including the rejected vote was: Jackson-Troup 10,508, Jackson-Clark 8,854, and Adams 642.

4. The official returns were only reported by congressional district. The county returns were found in the *Albany Argus* of 1832. The sum of the county returns in the 2nd, 19th and 20th Districts for both candidates, and the 25th District for Jackson and the 26th District for Adams, differ from the stated district totals. Because I was unable to locate the certified returns at the county level, I could not reconcile these differences.

5. In at least four districts, more than one Jackson electoral candidate ran. Unfortunately the state totals combine the votes, which is legally incorrect. Since I could not obtain a breakdown of the vote in all districts, the district totals here represent votes for more than one Jackson candidate. This applies to an undetermined number of districts. No other county returns were located. The differences in district totals and the added county totals is due to the fact that the official returns, except for the 10th District, did not contain county returns.

1 8 3 2

National Summary[1,2]
(electoral vote in parentheses)

State	Andrew Jackson (D)			Henry Clay (NR)			William Wirt (AM)		Jackson (D)[3]		others	
Alabama	13,739	(86.34%)	(7)	5	(0.03%)				2,169	(13.63%)		
Connecticut	11,284	(34.89%)		17,736	(54.84%)	(8)	3,321	(10.27%)				
Delaware	4,105	(48.98%)		4,276	(51.02%)	(3)						
Georgia	13,881	(65.33%)	(11)						7,367	(34.67%)		
Illinois	14,617	(68.12%)	(5)	6,745	(31.43%)		97	(0.45%)				
Indiana	31,406	(55.42%)	(9)	25,238	(44.53%)		27	(0.05%)				
Kentucky	36,292	(45.51%)		43,449	(54.49%)	(15)						
Louisiana	4,059	(61.63%)	(5)	2,527	(38.37%)							
Maine	33,982	(54.66%)	(10)	27,341	(43.98%)		842	(1.35%)				
Maryland	18,448	(48.10%)	(3)	19,159	(49.95%)	(5)					*748 (1.95%)	(2)
Massachusetts	13,933	(23.05%)		31,829	(52.66%)	(14)	14,676	(24.28%)				
Mississippi	4,348	(73.71%)	(4)									
Missouri	8,904	(65.17%)	(4)	4,760	(34.83%)				1,551	(26.29%)		
New Hampshire	25,357	(56.25%)	(7)	19,629	(43.55%)		91	(0.20%)				
New Jersey	23,956	(50.07%)	(8)	23,393	(48.90%)		492	(1.03%)				
New York	168,585	(52.12%)	(42)	154,897	(47.88%)							
North Carolina	21,006	(70.51%)	(15)	4,532	(15.21%)				4,255	(14.28%)		
Ohio	81,246	(51.33%)	(21)	76,539	(48.35%)		509	(0.32%)				
Pennsylvania	90,973	(57.70%)	(30)				66,706	(42.30%)				
Rhode Island	2,126	(36.58%)		2,810	(48.35%)	(4)	876	(15.07%)				
South Carolina											(11)†	
Tennessee	29,031	(94.02%)	(15)	1,756	(5.69%)						**91 (0.29%)	
Vermont	7,868	(24.48%)		11,163	(34.73%)		13,107	(40.78%)	(7)			
Virginia	33,967	(74.41%)	(23)	11,433	(25.05%)		3	(0.01%)		244	(0.53%)	
Total	**693,113**	**(52.93%)**	**(219)**	**489,217**	**(37.36%)**	**(49)**	**110,760**	**(8.46%)**	**(7)**	**15,606**	**(1.19%)**	**838(0.06%)**	**(11)**

*See Maryland returns for a discussion of this vote.
**Independent electors.
†Electoral votes cast for John Floyd (D).

Alabama[4]

County	Jackson & Van Buren		Jackson & Barbour		Clay	
Autauga	no returns					
Baldwin	no returns					
Bibb	245	(98.4%)	4	(1.6%)		
Blount	443	(100%)	0			
Butler	202	(51.7%)	189	(48.3%)		
Clarke	323	(100%)	0			
Conecuh	133	(66.5%)	67	(33.5%)		
Covington	73	(73.0%)	27	(27.0%)		
Dale	no returns					
Dallas	278	(100%)	0			
Fayette	316	(99.8%)	4	(0.2%)		
Franklin	591	(97.5%)	10	(1.7%)	5	(0.1%)
Greene	825	(76.2%)	257	(23.8%)		

	Jackson					
Henry	no returns					
Jackson	1,035	(99.0%)	10	(1.0%)		
Jefferson	378	(98.7%)	5	(1.3%)		
Lauderdale	662	(90.8%)	67	(9.2%)		
Lawrence	942	(85.6%)	137	(14.4%)		
Limestone	838	(91.9%)	74	(8.1%)		
Lowndes	279	(61.3%)	142	(38.7%)		
Madison	1,426	(98.3%)	25	(1.7%)		
Marengo	393	(78.8%)	106	(21.2%)		
Marion	257	(100%)	0			
Mobile	331	(100%)	0			
Monroe	291	(86.6%)	45	(13.4%)		
Montgomery	681	(87.0%)	102	(13.0%)		
Morgan	494	(93.0%)	37	(7.0%)		
Perry	440	(87.3%)	64	(12.7%)		
Pickens	99	(22.8%)	345	(77.2%)		
Pike	no returns					
St. Clair	604	(99.8%)	1	(0.2%)		
Shelby	295	(77.6%)	85	(22.4%)		
Tuscaloosa	279	(65.2%)	149	(34.8%)		
Walker	no returns					
Washington	164	(100%)	0			
Wilcox	422	(65.7%)	220	(34.3%)		
Total	**13,739**	**(86.3%)**	**2,169**	**(13.6%)**	**5**	**(0.03%)**

SOURCES—*Loveman manuscript, state archives.*

Connecticut

County	Jackson		Clay		Wirt	
Fairfield	1,470	(32.5%)	2,612	(57.8%)	439	(9.7%)
Hartford	2,978	(42.2%)	3,549	(50.3%)	525	(7.4%)
Litchfield	1,653	(32.4%)	3,130	(61.4%)	313	(6.1%)
Middlesex	839	(36.9%)	1,348	(59.3%)	85	(3.7%)
New Haven	657	(16.2%)	3,310	(81.7%)	86	(2.1%)
New London	1,626	(41.2%)	1,860	(47.1%)	465	(11.8%)
Tolland	1,055	(43.0%)	850	(34.6%)	551	(22.4%)
Windham	1,006	(34.2%)	1,077	(36.6%)	857	(19.4%)
Total	**11,284**	**(34.9%)**	**17,736**	**(54.8%)**	**3,321**	**(10.3%)**

SOURCE—*Manuscript returns.*

Delaware

County	Jackson		Clay	
Kent	1,012	(46.4%)	1,167	(53.6%)
New Castle	1,715	(56.2%)	1,335	(43.8%)
Sussex	1,378	(43.7%)	1,774	(56.3%)
Total	**4,105**	**(49.0%)**	**4,276**	**(51.0%)**

SOURCE—*Governor's Register.*

Georgia[5]

County	Jackson & Van Buren	Jackson & Barbour
Total	**13,881** (65.3%)	**7,367** (34.7%)

SOURCE—*(Milledgeville) Journal,* December 10, 1832.

Illinois

County	Jackson		Clay		Wirt
Adams	259	(63.8%)	147	(36.2%)	
Alexander	26	(78.8%)	6	(21.2%)	

County	Jackson		Clay		Wirt	
Bond	202	(74.0%)	68	(24.9%)	3	(11.0%)
Calhoun	31	(79.5%)	8	(20.5%)		
Clark	228	(60.8%)	147	(39.2%)		
Clay	115	(97.5%)	3	(2.5%)		
Clinton	270	(78.9%)	72	(21.1%)		
Coles	293	(76.1%)	92	(23.9%)		
Cook	76	(48.7%)	80	(51.3%)		
Crawford	309	(76.1%)	97	(23.9%)		
Edgar	516	(72.9%)	192	(27.1%)		
Edwards	188	(59.9%)	126	(40.1%)		
Fayette	468	(99.6%)	85	(0.4%)		
Franklin	460	(99.6%)	2	(0.4%)		
Fulton	223	(64.3%)	124	(35.7%)		
Gallatin	572	(82.8%)	119	(17.2%)		
Greene	692	(66.9%)	286	(27.6%)	57	(5.5%)
Hamilton	376	(98.2%)	7	(1.8%)		
Hancock	39	(48.1%)	42	(51.9%)		
Jackson	125	(72.2%)	41	(27.8%)		
Jefferson	317	(97.2%)	6	(2.8%)		
Jo Daviess	156	(53.1%)	138	(46.9%)		
Johnson	113	(99.4%)	3	(0.6%)		
Knox	40	(54.8%)	33	(45.2%)		
La Salle	19	(43.2%)	25	(56.8%)		
Lawrence	294	(65.5%)	155	(34.5%)		
McDonough	128	(85.9%)	21	(14.1%)		
McLean	275	(68.4%)	127	(31.6%)		
Macon	173	(80.8%)	41	(19.2%)		
Macoupin	228	(87.7%)	32	(12.3%)		
Madison	553	(55.3%)	444	(44.4%)	3	(0.3%)
Marion	161	(79.3%)	13	(6.4%)	29	(14.3%)
Monroe	241	(67.3%)	114	(31.8%)	3	(0.8%)
Montgomery	281	(84.4%)	51	(15.3%)	1	(0.3%)
Morgan	1,226	(55.0%)	1,003	(45.0%)		
Peoria	77	(52.0%)	71	(48.0%)		
Perry	100	(80.0%)	25	(20.0%)		
Pike	131	(44.8%)	161	(55.2%)		
Pope	147	(69.7%)	64	(30.3%)		
Putnam	49	(33.3%)	98	(66.7%)		
Randolph	368	(74.3%)	126	(25.5%)	1	(0.2%)
St. Clair	507	(65.6%)	266	(34.4%)		
Sangamon	1,035	(56.1%)	810	(43.9%)		
Schuyler	238	(63.1%)	139	(36.9%)		
Shelby	324	(92.3%)	27	(7.7%)		
Tazewell	235	(49.4%)	241	(50.6%)		
Union	302	(96.5%)	11	(3.5%)		
Vermilion	500	(63.4%)	289	(36.6%)		
Wabash	142	(44.0%)	181	(56.0%)		
Warren	45	(44.6%)	56	(55.4%)		
Washington	151	(94.4%)	9	(5.6%)		
Wayne	188	(83.6%)	37	(16.4%)		
White	405	(68.8%)	184	(31.2%)		
Total	**14,617**	**(68.1%)**	**6,745**	**(31.4%)**	**97**	**(0.5%)**

SOURCE—Theodore Pease (ed.), *Illinois Election Returns 1818–1848,* Springfield, IL: Illinois State Historical Society Library, 1923, pp. 80–81.

Indiana

County	Jackson		Clay		Wirt	
Allen	126	(56.3%)	98	(43.7%)		
Bartholomew	489	(56.5%)	372	(43.0%)	5	(0.6%)
Boone	216	(63.3%)	125	(36.7%)		
Carroll	258	(59.9%)	173	(40.1%)		
Cass	162	(51.4%)	153	(48.6%)		
Clark	1,058	(67.8%)	502	(32.2%)		
Clay	230	(86.5%)	36	(13.5%)		
Clinton	252	(58.9%)	176	(41.1%)		
Crawford	222	(57.2%)	166	(42.8%)		

County	Jackson		Clay		Other	
Daviess	363	(75.9%)	315	(24.1%)		
Dearborn	1,198	(50.0%)	1,197	(49.9%)	3	(0.1%)
Decatur	405	(42.9%)	539	(57.0%)	1	(0.1%)
Delaware	197	(63.8%)	112	(36.2%)		
Dubois	191	(70.0%)	82	(30.0%)		
Elkhart	129	(68.3%)	60	(31.7%)		
Fayette	762	(50.0%)	762	(50.0%)		
Floyd	625	(58.9%)	436	(41.1%)		
Fountain	920	(62.2%)	559	(37.8%)		
Franklin	738	(48.1%)	790	(51.5%)	5	(0.3%)
Gibson	446	(51.9%)	414	(48.1%)		
Grant	34	(50.7%)	33	(49.3%)		
Greene	471	(72.4%)	180	(27.6%)		
Hamilton	166	(39.8%)	251	(60.2%)		
Hancock	310	(63.4%)	179	(36.6%)		
Harrison	603	(58.6%)	426	(41.4%)		
Hendricks	483	(56.3%)	374	(43.7%)		
Henry	583	(43.1%)	769	(56.9%)		
Jackson	533	(62.4%)	321	(37.6%)		
Jefferson	729	(51.0%)	700	(49.0%)		
Jennings	317	(46.8%)	355	(52.4%)	6	(0.9%)
Johnson	653	(70.2%)	270	(29.0%)	7	(0.8%)
Knox	481	(46.2%)	561	(53.8%)		
La Grange	44	(54.3%)	37	(45.7%)		
La Porte	46	(43.8%)	59	(56.2%)		
Lawrence	877	(70.4%)	368	(29.6%)		
Madison	287	(56.9%)	217	(43.1%)		
Marion	771	(48.6%)	817	(51.4%)		
Martin	202	(68.9%)	91	(31.1%)		
Monroe	811	(77.5%)	235	(22.5%)		
Montgomery	796	(55.5%)	639	(44.5%)		
Morgan	522	(55.6%)	417	(44.4%)		
Orange	615	(62.8%)	365	(37.7%)		
Owen	322	(53.6%)	279	(46.4%)		
Parke	882	(62.0%)	540	(38.0%)		
Perry	86	(31.5%)	187	(68.5%)		
Pike	186	(51.7%)	174	(48.3%)		
Posey	623	(67.3%)	303	(32.7%)		
Putnam	950	(65.8%)	493	(34.2%)		
Randolph	175	(40.8%)	254	(59.2%)		
Ripley	393	(47.0%)	444	(53.0%)		
Rush	927	(53.8%)	796	(46.2%)		
St. Joseph	121	(49.6%)	123	(50.4%)		
Scott	342	(66.7%)	171	(33.3%)		
Shelby	733	(60.2%)	485	(39.8%)		
Spencer	139	(62.3%)	84	(37.7%)		
Sullivan	648	(80.2%)	160	(19.8%)		
Switzerland	520	(49.3%)	535	(50.7%)		
Tippecanoe	618	(54.2%)	523	(45.8%)		
Union	568	(46.9%)	643	(53.1%)		
Vanderburgh	102	(37.5%)	170	(62.5%)		
Vermillion	545	(55.9%)	430	(44.1%)		
Vigo	425	(40.0%)	637	(60.0%)		
Warren	266	(46.9%)	301	(53.1%)		
Warrick	354	(74.5%)	121	(25.5%)		
Washington	1,088	(63.6%)	623	(36.4%)		
Wayne	1,072	(34.5%)	2,031	(65.5%)		
Total	**31,406**	**(55.4%)**	**25,238**	**(44.5%)**	**27**	**(0.1%)**

SOURCE—Dorothy F. Riker and Gayle Thornbrough (eds.), *Indiana Elections Returns 1816–1851*, Indianapolis, IN: Indiana Historical Bureau, 1960, pp. 14–16.

Kentucky

County	Jackson		Clay	
Adair	477	(61.1%)	304	(38.9%)
Allen	456	(61.1%)	290	(38.9%)
Anderson	425	(73.7%)	152	(26.3%)
Barren	835	(47.1%)	936	(52.9%)
Bath	496	(43.2%)	651	(56.8%)
Boone	477	(39.8%)	720	(60.2%)
Bourbon	594	(31.8%)	1,276	(68.2%)
Bracken	314	(36.9%)	537	(63.1%)
Breckinridge	290	(28.9%)	713	(71.1%)
Bullitt	451	(62.6%)	269	(37.4%)
Butler	231	(62.9%)	136	(37.1%)
Caldwell	621	(56.5%)	478	(43.5%)
Calloway	727	(85.8%)	120	(14.2%)
Campbell	794	(61.4%)	499	(38.6%)
Casey	226	(50.6%)	221	(49.4%)
Christian	570	(37.7%)	940	(62.3%)
Clarke	428	(29.8%)	1,009	(70.2%)
Clay	100	(25.1%)	299	(74.9%)
Cumberland	314	(50.9%)	303	(49.1%)
Daviess	291	(46.1%)	340	(53.9%)
Edmonson	173	(56.0%)	136	(44.0%)
Estill	227	(42.2%)	311	(57.8%)
Fayette	876	(34.7%)	1,645	(65.3%)
Fleming	604	(35.3%)	1,105	(64.7%)
Floyd	399	(72.9%)	148	(27.1%)
Franklin	541	(47.5%)	598	(52.5%)
Gallatin	418	(45.8%)	494	(54.2%)
Garrard	236	(17.6%)	1,108	(82.4%)
Grant	172	(42.9%)	229	(57.1%)
Graves	332	(79.8%)	84	(20.2%)
Grayson	194	(35.2%)	357	(64.8%)
Green	896	(72.1%)	347	(27.9%)
Greenup	320	(40.0%)	480	(60.0%)
Hancock	68	(45.0%)	83	(55.0%)
Hardin	813	(46.8%)	926	(53.2%)
Harlan	92	(29.5%)	220	(70.5%)
Harrison	966	(62.3%)	585	(37.7%)
Hart	313	(53.3%)	274	(46.7%)
Henry	727	(51.3%)	689	(48.7%)
Henderson	266	(42.6%)	359	(57.4%)
Hickman	621	(79.7%)	158	(20.3%)
Hopkins	430	(46.3%)	498	(53.7%)
Jefferson	1,552	(43.6%)	2,010	(56.4%)
Jessamine		no returns		
Knox	141	(27.3%)	376	(72.7%)
Laurel	102	(32.5%)	212	(67.5%)
Lawrence	203	(52.6%)	183	(47.4%)
Lewis	444	(53.8%)	381	(46.2%)
Lincoln	340	(37.6%)	768	(62.4%)
Livingston	384	(63.8%)	218	(36.2%)
Logan	352	(25.8%)	1,011	(74.2%)
McCracken	147	(61.2%)	93	(38.8%)
Madison	609	(32.8%)	1,250	(67.2%)
Mason	686	(33.3%)	1,377	(66.7%)
Meade	155	(31.9%)	331	(68.1%)
Mercer	1,046	(53.0%)	927	(47.0%)
Monroe	432	(69.2%)	192	(30.8%)
Montgomery	431	(37.2%)	727	(62.8%)
Morgan	259	(68.9%)	117	(31.1%)
Muhlenberg	273	(36.3%)	479	(63.7%)
Nelson	499	(31.1%)	1,108	(68.9%)
Nicholas	505	(47.7%)	553	(52.3%)
Ohio	316	(44.7%)	391	(55.3%)
Oldham	699	(60.9%)	449	(39.1%)
Owen	489	(67.0%)	241	(33.0%)
Pendleton	274	(57.4%)	203	(42.6%)
Perry	81	(35.7%)	146	(64.3%)
Pike	233	(85.7%)	39	(14.3%)
Pulaski	407	(43.0%)	540	(57.0%)
Rockcastle	63	(16.1%)	328	(83.9%)
Russell	191	(49.5%)	195	(50.5%)
Scott	928	(53.7%)	800	(46.3%)
Shelby	758	(35.2%)	1,396	(64.8%)

Simpson	380 (51.3%)	361	(48.7%)
Spencer	417 (50.6%)	407	(49.4%)
Todd	280 (30.6%)	634	(69.4%)
Trigg	439 (54.0%)	374	(46.0%)
Union	263 (51.1%)	252	(48.9%)
Warren	455 (36.4%)	795	(63.6%)
Washington	1,161 (50.9%)	1,119	(49.1%)
Wayne	485 (44.9%)	507	(55.1%)
Whitley	187 (46.1%)	219	(53.9%)
Woodford	425 (37.3%)	713	(62.7%)
Total	**36,292 (45.5%)**	**43,449**	**(54.5%)**

SOURCES—(Louisville) *Daily Louisville Public Advertiser*, November 24, 1832; (Lexington*) Observer & Reporter*, November 29, 1832.

Louisiana

Parish	Jackson	Clay
Ascension	117 (76.0%)	17 (24.0%)
Assumption	24 (15.5%)	131 (84.5%)
Avoyelles	91 (58.3%)	65 (41.7%)
Carroll	86 (83.5%)	17 (16.5%)
Catahoula	100 (75.2%)	33 (24.8%)
Claiborne & Natchitoches	382 (75.6%)	123 (24.4%)
Concordia	90 (67.2%)	44 (32.8%)
East Baton Rouge	200 (57.0%)	151 (43.0%)
East Feliciana	473 (92.4%)	39 (7.6%)
Iberville	101 (62.0%)	62 (38.0%)
Jefferson	12 (25.5%)	35 (74.5%)
Lafayette	167 (63.0%)	98 (37.0%)
Lafourche	35 (19.4%)	140 (80.6%)
Livingston	107 (79.9%)	27 (20.1%)
Plaquemines	34 (81.0%)	2 (19.0%)
Point Coupee	62 (84.9%)	11 (15.1%)
Orleans	542 (59.1%)	374 (40.9%)
Ouachita	180 (75.3%)	59 (24.7%)
Rapides	153 (65.9%)	79 (34.1%)
St. Bernard	33 (100%)	0
St. Charles	29 (93.5%)	2 (6.5%)
St. Helena	235 (92.5%)	19 (7.5%)
St. James	56 (62.2%)	34 (37.8%)
St. John the Baptist	8 (29.6%)	19 (70.4%)
St. Landry	141 (30.9%)	316 (69.1%)
St. Martin	50 (22.7%)	170 (77.3%)
St. Mary	56 (31.8%)	120 (68.2%)
St. Tammany	170 (74.9%)	57 (25.1%)
Terrebone	24 (18.9%)	103 (81.1%)
Washington	134 (83.2%)	27 (16.8%)
West Baton Rouge	18 (17.6%)	84 (82.4%)
West Feliciana	149 (68.3%)	69 (31.7%)
Total	**4,059 (61.6%)**	**2,527 (38.4%)**
	*(4,049)	*(2,528)

Stated totals.

SOURCE—(New Orleans) *Louisiana Courier*, November 28, 1832; and Benjamin Matthias, *Politician's Register*, Philadelphia, PA: 1835, p. 79.

Maine

County	Jackson	Clay	Wirt
Cumberland	5,846 (56.9%)	4,419 (43.0%)	10 (0.1%)
Hancock	1,738 (54.2%)	1,465 (45.7%)	1 (0.03%)
Kennebec	3,175 (38.4%)	4,863 (58.8%)	235 (2.8%)
Lincoln	4,079 (50.2%)	3,883 (47.8%)	161 (2.0%)
Oxford	3,496 (61.5%)	2,075 (36,5%)	118 (2.1%)
Penobscot	3,298 (60.1%)	2,113 (38.5%)	81 (1.5%)
Somerset	2,428 (47.5%)	2,629 (51.4%)	58 (1.1%)
Washington	1,554 (54.7%)	1,282 (45.1%)	7 (0.2%)
Waldo	3,283 (73.4%)	1,036 (23.2%)	151 (3.4%)
York	5,085 (58.6%)	3,576 (41.2%)	20 (0.2%)
Total	**33,982 (54.7%)**	**27,341 (44.0%)**	**842 (1.4%)**
	*(33,985)	*(841)	

Stated totals.

SOURCE—(Portland) *Eastern Argus*, November 28, 1832, and June 15, 1844.

Maryland

Electors were chosen by district, and the returns are below the county returns. The number in parentheses next to each county indicates the electoral district the county was in.

County	Jackson	Clay	other
(1) Allegany	815 (56.6%)	624 (43.4%)	
(1) Anne Arundel	753 (45.4%)	904 (54.6%)	
(3) Baltimore	2,198 (74.6%)	0	748 (25.4%)[6]
(2) Baltimore (city)	5,024 (54.2%)	4,247 (45.8%)	
(1) Calvert	265 (39.8%)	401 (60.2%)	
(4) Caroline	474 (46.0%)	556 (54.0%)	
(4) Cecil	1,099 (57.5%)	812 (42.5%)	
(1) Charles	404 (44.0%)	515 (56.0%)	
(4) Dorchester	664 (40.9%)	958 (59.1%)	
(1) Frederick	14 (0.5%)	2,670 (99.5%)	
(4) Harford	1,133 (55.9%)	893 (44.1%)	
(4) Kent	374 (45.5%)	448 (54.5%)	
(1) Montgomery	189 (20.8%)	718 (79.2%)	
(1) Prince George's	471 (42.4%)	641 (57.6%)	
(4) Queen Anne's	646 (53.6%)	560 (46.4%)	
(1) St. Mary's	255 (29.1%)	621 (70.9%)	
(4) Somerset	470 (39.5%)	719 (60.5%)	
(4) Talbot	413 (39.6%)	629 (60.4%)	
(1) Washington	1,931 (58.6%)	1,364 (41.4%)	
(4) Worcester	856 (48.5%)	879 (51.5%)	
Total	**18,448 (48.1%)**	**19,159 (50.0%)**	**748 (1.9%)**

1st District (4 elected)	5,097 (37.6%)	8,458 (62.4%)	
2nd District (2 elected)	5,024 (54.2%)	4,247 (45.8%)	
3rd District	2,198 (74.6%)	0 748	(25.4%)
4th District (3 elected)	6,129 (48.7%)	6,454 (51.3%)	

SOURCES—Manuscript returns; John T. Willis, *Presidential Elections in Maryland,* Mt. Airy, MD: Lomond Publications, 1984, p. 170.

Massachusetts

County	Jackson	Clay	Wirt
Barnstable	194 (14.6%)	1,013 (76.2%)	123 (9.2%)
Berkshire	1,612 (37.8%)	2,465 (57.8%)	185 (4.3%)
Bristol	499 (12.3%)	1,194 (29.5%)	2,360 (58.2%)
Dukes	67 (39.0%)	97 (56.4%)	8 (4.7%)
Essex	2,781 (34.3%)	4,603 (56.8%)	720 (8.9%)
Franklin	242 (8.1%)	1,533 (51.1%)	1,225 (40.8%)
Hampden	1,361 (36.9%)	1,899 (51.5%)	427 (11.6%)
Hampshire	164 (5.5%)	1,290 (43.3%)	1,522 (55.7%)
Middlesex	2,056 (26.0%)	4,198 (53.1%)	1,658 (21.0%)
Nantucket	35 (9.9%)	312 (88.6%)	5 (1.4%)
Norfolk	540 (12.1%)	1,846 (41.2%)	2,091 (46.7%)
Plymouth	797 (19.6%)	1,857 (45.7%)	1,406 (34.6%)
Suffolk	1,235 (23.6%)	3,093 (59.1%)	909 (17.4%)
Worcester	2,350 (21.5%)	6,529 (59.8%)	2,037 (18.7%)
Total	**13,933 (23.0%)**	**31,829 (52.7%)**	**14,676 (24.3%)**
		*(31,963)	*(14,692)

*Stated totals.

SOURCE—Manuscript returns.

Mississippi[7]

County	Jackson & Van Buren	Jackson & Barbour
Adams	165 (72.7%)	62 (27.3%)
Amite	270 (68.8%)	137 (31.2%)
Claiborne	215 (79.9%)	54 (20.1%)
Copiah	377 (87.9%)	52 (12.1%)
Covington	114 (86.4%)	18 (13.6%)
Franklin	155 (57.2%)	116 (42.8%)
Green	15 (41.7%)	21 (58.3%)
Hancock		no returns
Hinds	464 (80.8%)	110 (19.2%)
Jackson	17 (100%)	0
Jefferson	226 (75.6%)	73 (24.4%)
Jones	53 (98.1%)	1 (1.9%)
Lawrence	358 (98.1%)	7 (1.9%)
Lowndes	177 (100%)	0
Madison	144 (53.9%)	123 (46.1%)
Marion	66 (47.5%)	73 (52.5%)
Monroe	267 (100%)	0
Perry	70 (62.5%)	42 (37.5%)
Pike	192 (58.2%)	138 (41.8%)
Rankin	206 (98.1%)	4 (1.9%)
Simpson	135 (88.2%)	18 (11.8%)
Warren	124 (66.1%)	64 (33.9%)
Washington	57 (71.3%)	23 (28.7%)
Wayne	23 (62.2%)	14 (37.8%)
Wilkinson	121 (28.5%)	304 (71.5%)
Yazoo	337 (77.6%)	97 (22.4%)
Total	**4,348 (73.7%)**	**1,551 (26.9%)**

SOURCE—(Vicksburg) *Advocate & Register,* December 12, 1832.

Missouri[8]

Almost no county returns have been located for this election

County	Jackson	Clay
Boone		50 majority
Callaway	91 majority	
Coles	418 majority	
Crawford	130 majority	
Franklin	253 majority	
Howard	368 (37.5%)	613 (62.5%)
Jefferson	138 majority	
Montgomery		19 majority
Saint Charles	41 majority	
Saint Louis	554 (45.7%)	658 (54.3%)
Total	**8,904 (65.2%)**	**4,760 (34.8%)**

New Hampshire

County	Jackson	Clay	Wirt
Cheshire	1,720 (36.4%)	2,994 (63.3%)	17 (0.4%)
Coos	983 (75.4%)	308 (23.6%)	12 (0.9%)
Grafton	3,572 (56.5%)	2,700 (42.7%)	47 (0.7%)
Hillsborough	3,819 (56.7%)	2,917 (43.3%)	0
Merrimack	4,084 (65.9%)	2,103 (33.9%)	12 (0.2%)
Rockingham	3,774 (54.7%)	3,122 (45.3%)	0
Strafford	5,496 (58.8%)	3,841 (41.1%)	2 (0.02%)
Sullivan	1,909 (53.7%)	1,644 (46.3%)	1 (0.03%)
Total	**25,357 (56.3%)**	**19,629 (43.6%)**	**91 (0.2%)**

SOURCE—Manuscript returns.

New Jersey

County	Jackson	Clay	Wirt
Bergen	1,792 (53.2%)	1,537 (45.7%)	37 (1.1%)
Burlington	1,848 (38.6%)	2,931 (61.2%)	8 (1.7%)
Cape May	237 (32.8%)	486 (67.2%)	0
Cumberland	1,135 (48.7%)	1,182 (50.7%)	14 (0.6%)
Essex	2,457 (37.5%)	3,830 (58.5%)	265 (4.0%)
Gloucester	1,609 (46.4%)	1,841 (53.1%)	15 (0.4%)
Hunterdon	2,522 (57.4%)	1,858 (42.3%)	12 (0.3%)
Mercer	1,805 (48.1%)	1,937 (51.6%)	14 (0.4%)
Middlesex	1,793 (49.3%)	1,831 (50.3%)	14 (0.4%)
Monmouth	2,422 (53.1%)	2,117 (46.4%)	22 (0.5%)
Salem	943 (43.4%)	1,214 (55.9%)	14 (0.6%)
Somerset	1,296 (52.2%)	1,177 (47.4%)	10 (0.4%)
Sussex	2,422 (75.9%)	753 (23.6%)	18 (0.6%)
Warren	1,675 (69.1%)	699 (28.8%)	49 (2.0%)
Total	**23,956 (50.1%)**	**23,393 (48.9%)**	**492 (1.0%)**
	*(23,856)	*(480)	

*Stated totals.

SOURCE—(Trenton) *True-American,* November 24, 1832.

New York

County	Jackson	Clay
Albany	4,437 (50.6%)	4,333 (49.4%)
Allegany	2,112 (47.5%)	2,334 (52.5%)
Broome	1,421 (45.6%)	1,692 (54.4%)
Cattaraugus	1,355 (43.2%)	1,779 (56.8%)
Cayuga	4,463 (53.2%)	3,920 (46.8%)
Chautauqua	2,252 (36.2%)	3,970 (63.8%)

Chenango	3,704 (52.6%)	3,339 (47.4%)
Clinton	1,719 (61.2%)	1,092 (38.8%)
Columbia	3,967 (51.9%)	3,682 (48.1%)
Cortland	1,923 (48.4%)	2,014 (51.6%)
Delaware	2,919 (75.4%)	1,951 (24.6%)
Dutchess	4,895 (55.3%)	4,051 (44.7%)
Erie	1,812 (29.5%)	4,323 (70.5%)
Essex	1,347 (43.5%)	1,748 (56.5%)
Franklin	878 (45.2%)	1,064 (54.8%)
Genesee	3,212 (36.3%)	5,629 (63.7%)
Greene	3,086 (58.2%)	2,212 (41.8%)
Herkimer	3,649 (58.7%)	2,568 (41.3%)
Jefferson	4,381 (49.8%)	4,419 (50.2%)
Kings	1,741 (62.1%)	1,262 (37.9%)
Lewis	1,466 (63.9%)	828 (36.1%)
Livingston	1,760 (37.4%)	2,950 (62.6%)
Madison	3,496 (49.4%)	3,582 (50.6%)
Monroe	3,459 (41.4%)	4,906 (58.6%)
Montgomery & Hamilton	4,589 (56.7%)	3,510 (43.3%)
New York	18,028 (59.0%)	12,507 (41.0%)
Niagara	1,309 (37.6%)	2,168 (62.4%)
Oneida	6,413 (56.2%)	5,991 (43.8%)
Onondaga	5,362 (52.9%)	4,772 (47.1%)
Ontario	2,441 (36.9%)	4,174 (63.1%)
Orange	4,234 (59.5%)	2,884 (40.5%)
Orleans	1,424 (46.2%)	1,656 (53.8%)
Oswego	2,565 (51.9%)	2,379 (48.1%)
Otsego	4,956 (54.9%)	4,071 (45.1%)
Putnam	1,191 (64.0%)	669 (36.0%)
Queens	1,655 (54.1%)	1,402 (45.9%)
Rensselaer	4,818 (53.1%)	4,244 (46.9%)
Richmond	574 (51.7%)	537 (48.3%)
Rockland	975 (71.3%)	392 (28.7%)
St. Lawrence	3,321 (54.4%)	2,784 (45.6%)
Saratoga	3,550 (50.6%)	3,468 (49.4%)
Schenectady	1,342 (54.6%)	1,115 (45.4%)
Schoharie	2,747 (61.7%)	1,682 (38.3%)
Seneca	2,053 (54.0%)	1,752 (46.0%)
Steuben	3,966 (66.8%)	1,972 (33.2%)
Suffolk	2,580 (63.9%)	1,459 (36.1%)
Sullivan	1,267 (53.6%)	1,097 (46.4%)
Tioga	3,155 (62.5%)	1,890 (37.5%)
Tompkins	3,338 (52.3%)	3,045 (47.7%)
Ulster	3,974 (65.7%)	2,078 (34.3%)
Warren	1,256 (65.6%)	660 (34.4%)
Washington	2,175 (32.2%)	4,579 (67.8%)
Wayne	2,813 (51.1%)	2,695 (48.9%)
Westchester	3,134 (57.8%)	2,292 (42.2%)
Yates	1,926 (59.2%)	1,325 (40.8%)
Total	**168,585 (52.1%)**	**154,897 (47.9%)**

SOURCE—Manuscript returns.

North Carolina

County	Jackson & Van Buren	Jackson & Barbour	Clay
Anson	529 (77.9%)	39 (5.7%)	111 (16.3%)
Ashe	265 (76.1%)	34 (9.8%)	49 (4.1%)
Beaufort	55 (21.6%)	200 (61.2%)	53 (17.2%)
Bertie	261 (76.1%)	37 (10.8%)	45 (13.1%)
Bladen	210 (78.1%)	0	59 (21.9%)
Brunswick	103 (62.4%)	11 (6.7%)	51 (30.9%)
Buncombe	375 (54.0%)	259 (37.4%)	60 (8.6%)
Burke	490 (65.1%)	149 (26.3%)	114 (15.1%)
Cabarrus	79 (14.9%)	279 (52.5%)	173 (32.6%)
Camden	186 (93.0%)	3 (1.5%)	11 (5.5%)
Carteret	107 (62.6%)	5 (2.9%)	59 (34.5%)

County						
Caswell	620 (96.8%)	12	(2.0%)	8	(1.2%)	
Chatham	384 (77.0%)	34	(6.8%)	81	(16.2%)	
Chowan	109 (66.5%)	0		55	(33.5%)	
Columbus	169 (71.0%)	39	(16.4%)	30	(12.6%)	
Craven	288 (67.0%)	5	(1.1%)	137	(31.9%)	
Cumberland	593 (71.1%)	58	(7.0%)	183	(21.9%)	
Currituck	153 (100%)	0		0		
Davidson	55 (12.3%)	333	(81.6%)	58	(6.1%)	
Duplin	289 (96.3%)	0		11	(3.7%)	
Edgecombe	877 (93.3%)	48	(6.4%)	5	(0.3%)	
Franklin	459 (92.2%)	9	(1.7%)	30	(6.1%)	
Gates	321 (88.9%)	0		40	(11.1%)	
Granville	441 (91.7%)	0		40	(8.3%)	
Greene	174 (71.3%)	1	(0.4%)	69	(28.3%)	
Guilford	247 (38.1%)	27	(4.1%)	375	(57.8%)	
Halifax	243 (47.6%)	258	(49.2%)	10	(3.2%)	
Haywood	353 (98.6%)	5	(1.4%)	0		
Hertford	173 (81.2%)	25	(3.7%)	15	(15.1%)	
Hyde	99 (55.6%)	43	(24.2%)	36	(20.1%)	
Iredell	359 (45.2%)	104	(13.0%)	332	(41.8%)	
Johnston	360 (98.1%)	0		7	(1.9%)	
Jones	106 (63.5%)	5	(3.0%)	56	(33.5%)	
Lenoir	229 (90.9%)	4	(1.6%)	19	(7.5%)	
Lincoln	943 (63.9%)	306	(20.8%)	226	(15.3%)	
Macon	396 (89.4%)	44	(9.9%)	3	(0.7%)	
Martin	357 (79.5%)	75	(16.7%)	17	(3.8%)	
Mecklenburg	489 (50.2%)	273	(28.0%)	213	(21.8%)	
Montgomery	59 (12.4%)	331	(68.7%)	85	(17.9%)	
Moore	348 (96.7%)	7	(1.9%)	5	(1.4%)	
Nash	437 (98.2%)	8	(1.8%)	0		
New Hanover	541 (85.7%)	6	(2.4%)	74	(11.9%)	
Northampton	117 (74.5%)	2	(1.3%)	38	(24.2%)	
Onslow	373 (98.4%)	0		6	(1.6%)	
Orange	759 (81.2%)	6	(0.6%)	170	(18.2%)	
Pasquotank	233 (69.6%)	1	(0.1%)	101	(30.4%)	
Perquimans	135 (81.3%)	0		31	(18.7%)	
Person	251 (90.6%)	11	(4.0%)	15	(5.4%)	
Pitt	202 (50.0%)	121	(30.0%)	81	(20.0%)	
Randolph	289 (12.8%)	32	(46.4%)	221	(40.8%)	
Richmond	236 (52.1%)	48	(28.4%)	69	(19.5%)	
Robeson	407 (79.3%)	6	(1.2%)	100	(19.5%)	
Rockingham	383 (91.6%)	0		32	(8.4%)	
Rowan	158 (21.7%)	451	(62.1%)	118	(16.2%)	
Rutherford	775 (77.3%)	203	(20.3%)	24	(2.4%)	
Sampson	361 (95.0%)	9	(2.4%)	10	(2.6%)	
Stokes	667 (79.9%)	1	(17.5%)	167	(2.6%)	
Surry	482 (78.9%)	36	(6.3%)	90	(14.8%)	
Tyrrell	131 (89.7%)	7	(4.8%)	8	(5.5%)	
Wake	503 (80.4%)	22	(3.5%)	101	(16.1%)	
Warren	415 (45.8%)	10	(2.4%)	8	(1.8%)	
Washington	126 (72.0%)	25	(14.3%)	24	(16.7%)	
Wayne	422 (92.1%)	7	(1.6%)	34	(7.3%)	
Wilkes	250 (47.2%)	211	(21.4%)	69	(31.4%)	
Total	**21,006 (70.5%)**	**4,255**	**(14.3%)**	**4,532**	**(15.2%)**	

SOURCE—Manuscript returns.

Ohio

County	Jackson	Clay	Wirt
Adams	1,118 (66.4%)	563 (33.4%)	3 (0.2%)
Allen	114 (58.2%)	80 (40.8%)	2 (0.1%)
Ashtabula	489 (18.2%)	2,032 (75.4%)	173 (6.5%)
Athens	776 (47.5%)	856 (52.5%)	
Belmont	2,370 (52.0%)	2,191 (48.0%)	
Brown	1,597 (65.3%)	847 (34.6%)	3 (0.1%)
Butler	3,321 (72.6%)	1,250 (25.3%)	3 (0.1%)
Champaign	782 (34.1%)	1,468 (64.0%)	43 (1.9%)

County			
Clark	714 (29.6%)	1,693 (70.2%)	3 (0.1%)
Clermont	2,140 (63.7%)	1,217 (36.3%)	
Clinton	897 (43.6%)	1,158 (56.4%)	
Columbiana	3,109 (57.1%)	2,328 (42.7%)	12 (2.2%)
Coschocton	1,282 (68.4%)	592 (31.6%)	
Crawford	557 (68.3%)	259 (31.7%)	
Cuyahoga	691 (30.3%)	1,587 (69.7%)	
Darke	675 (73.1%)	242 (26.2%)	7 (0.8%)
Delaware	738 (41.7%)	1,015 (57.3%)	18 (1.0%)
Fairfield	2,648 (67.7%)	1,274 (32.5%)	2 (0.1%)
Fayette	694 (50.2%)	688 (49.8%)	
Franklin	1,157 (42.9%)	1,508 (56.0%)	29 (1.1%)
Gallia	527 (38.4%)	838 (61.0%)	9 (0.7%)
Geauga	782 (24.6%)	2,403 (75.4%)	
Greene	1,071 (42.0%)	1,397 (54.7%)	84 (3.3%)
Guernsey	1,356 (50.7%)	1,295 (48.4%)	22 (0.8%)
Hamilton	4,824 (58.3%)	3,454 (41.7%)	
Hancock	181 (68.0%)	85 (32.0%)	
Harrison	1,797 (52.6%)	1,610 (47.1%)	11 (0.3%)
Highland	1,350 (52.8%)	1,206 (47.2%)	
Hocking	356 (64.1%)	199 (35.9%)	
Holmes	1,164 (83.3%)	230 (16.5%)	3 (0.2%)
Huron	1,035 (38.4%)	1,646 (61.1%)	11 (0.4%)
Jackson	554 (60.2%)	367 (39.8%)	
Jefferson	2,118 (58.6%)	1,495 (41.4%)	1 (0.03%)
Knox	1,928 (61.9%)	1,184 (38.0%)	5 (0.2%)
Lawrence	414 (49.7%)	419 (50.3%)	
Licking	2,071 (55.2%)	1,684 (44.8%)	
Logan	446 (33.2%)	894 (66.6%)	3 (0.2%)
Lorain	511 (41.1%)	718 (57.8%)	14 (1.1%)
Madison	546 (48.1%)	581 (51.2%)	8 (0.6%)
Marion	721 (58.3%)	514 (41.6%)	1 (0.1%)
Medina	497 (30.4%)	1,137 (69.6%)	
Meigs	385 (34.9%)	717 (65.1%)	
Mercer	194 (64.7%)	106 (35.3%)	
Miami	957 (39.9%)	1,441 (60.1%)	1 (0.04%)
Monroe	916 (80.9%)	215 (19.0%)	1 (0.1%)
Montgomery	2,029 (48.8%)	2,131 (51.2%)	1 (0.02%)
Morgan	1,068 (53.2%)	919 (45.8%)	20 (1.0%)
Muskingum	2,394 (47.7%)	2,623 (52.3%)	2 (0.04%)
Perry	1,331 (67.2%)	651 (32.8%)	
Pickaway	1,458 (51.7%)	1,363 (48.3%)	
Pike	532 (61.4%)	335 (38.6%)	
Portage	1,406 (37.6%)	2,327 (62.3%)	2 (0.1%)
Preble	1,093 (42.6%)	1,357 (52.9%)	14 (5.5%)
Richland	2,552 (63.2%)	1,470 (36.4%)	15 (0.4%)
Ross	1,778 (42.9%)	2,367 (57.1%)	
Sandusky	279 (48.7%)	294 (51.3%)	
Scioto	595 (38.5%)	952 (61.5%)	
Seneca	555 (48.3%)	594 (51.7%)	
Shelby	433 (52.2%)	397 (47.8%)	
Stark	2,142 (56.7%)	1,635 (43.3%)	
Trumbull	2,359 (46.6%)	2,697 (53.3%)	1 (0.2%)
Tuscarawas	1,362 (58.8%)	944 (40.8%)	10 (0.4%)
Union	323 (52.1%)	296 (47.7%)	1 (0.2%)
Warren	1,735 (45.2%)	2,107 (54.8%)	
Washington	886 (43.9%)	1,134 (56.1%)	
Wayne	2,195 (69.3%)	973 (30.7%)	
Williams	93 (52.5%)	84 (47.5%)	
Wood	78 (27.8%)	203 (72.2%)	
**Total	81,246 (51.3%)	76,539 (48.4%)	509 (0.3%)

*Hardin   41 majority
*Putnam   154 (94.5%)   9 (5.5%)

*Not included in the official returns, Politician's Register, p. 87.
**No returns for Henry, Paulding and Van Wert. They also did not make any returns for the gubernatorial election held in October.

SOURCE—(Columbus) Ohio State Journal, November 17, 1832.

Pennsylvania[9]

County	Jackson	Wirt
Adams	1,071 (44.0%)	1,362 (56.0%)
Allegheny	3,321 (53.5%)	2,985 (46.5%)
Armstrong	1,437 (77.0%)	429 (23.0%)
Beaver	1,360 (49.5%)	1,388 (50.5%)
Bedford	1,970 (75.6%)	647 (24.4%)
Berks	4,472 (79.5%)	1,150 (20.5%)
Bradford	1,598 (56.7%)	1,221 (43.3%)
Bucks	2,681 (47.1%)	3,011 (52.9%)
Butler	1,076 (62.7%)	641 (37.3%)
Cambria	444 (82.5%)	94 (17.5%)
Centre	1,961 (73.0%)	725 (27.0%)
Chester	2,732 (38.9%)	4,286 (61.1%)
Clearfield	520 (71.5%)	207 (28.5%)
Columbia	1,658 (80.4%)	404 (19.6%)
Crawford	1,470 (56.5%)	1,130 (43.5%)
Cumberland	2,150 (61.7%)	1,337 (38.3%)
Dauphin	1,395 (50.9%)	1,348 (49.1%)
Delaware	955 (40.2%)	1,423 (59.8%)
Erie	1,049 (41.3%)	1,494 (58.7%)
Fayette	2,647 (69.2%)	1,176 (30.8%)
Franklin	1,979 (47.6%)	2,176 (52.4%)
Greene	1,443 (81.0%)	338 (19.0%)
Huntingdon	1,510 (51.2%)	1,441 (48.8%)
Indiana	654 (52.9%)	583 (47.1%)
Jefferson	175 (62.5%)	105 (37.5%)
Juniata	579 (68.4%)	268 (31.6%)
Lancaster	4,061 (44.1%)	5,140 (55.9%)
Lebanon	1,094 (55.4%)	882 (44.6%)
Lehigh	1,544 (62.3%)	933 (37.7%)
Luzerne	1,745 (56.9%)	1,325 (43.1%)
Lycoming	1,540 (69.7%)	669 (30.3%)
McKean & Potter	253 (65.9%)	131 (34.1%)
Mercer	1,366 (52.9%)	1,214 (47.1%)
Mifflin	784 (63.3%)	454 (36.7%)
Montgomery	3,315 (56.9%)	2,507 (43.1%)
Northampton	2,786 (71.8%)	1,092 (28.2%)
Northumberland	1,464 (78.1%)	411 (21.9%)
Perry	1,021 (74.8%)	346 (25.2%)
Philadelphia	10,029 (45.7%)	11,909 (54.3%)
Pike	506 (92.2%)	43 (7.8%)
Schuylkill	1,270 (72.5%)	482 (27.5%)
Somerset	778 (48.9%)	814 (51.1%)
Susquehanna	1,082 (55.5%)	868 (44.5%)
Tioga	1,035 (84.0%)	197 (16.0%)
Union	1,057 (55.0%)	864 (45.0%)
Venango	1,117 (79.2%)	294 (20.8%)
Warren	490 (71.6%)	194 (28.4%)
Washington	3,125 (62.3%)	1,888 (37.7%)
Wayne	633 (63.3%)	367 (36.7%)
Westmoreland	3,419 (79.9%)	861 (20.1%)
York	3,152 (68.5%)	1,452 (31.5%)
Total	**90,973 (57.7%)**	**66,706 (42.3%)**
	*(90,983)	*(66,716)

*Stated totals.

SOURCE—(Harrisburg) The Reporter & Democratic Herald, November 16, 1832.

Rhode Island

County	Jackson	Clay	Wirt
Bristol	109 (40.8%)	131 (49.1%)	27 (10.1%)
Kent	257 (32.0%)	365 (45.4%)	182 (22.6%)
Newport	275 (29.5%)	484 (52.0%)	172 (18.5%)
Providence	929 (32.5%)	1,522 (53.2%)	409 (14.3%)
Washington	556 (58.5%)	308 (32.4%)	86 (9.1%)
Total	**2,126 (36.6%)**	**2,810 (48.4%)**	**876 (15.1%)**

SOURCES—Manuscript returns.

South Carolina

Electors chosen by the legislature

Tennessee

County	Jackson	Clay	Independent
Anderson	261 (94.2%)	16 (5.8%)	
Bedford	1,394 (96.3%)	47 (3.2%)	6 (0.4%)
Bledsoe	174 (96.1%)	4 (2.2%)	3 (1.7%)
Blount	632 (93.9%)	36 (5.3%)	5 (0.7%)
Campbell	380 (100%)	0	
Carroll	577 (88.2%)	74(11.3%)	3 (0.5%)
Carter	225 (92.2%)	7 (2.9%)	12 (4.9%)
Claiborne	338 (99.1%)	3 (0.9%)	
Cocke	86 (81.9%)	5 (4.8%)	14(13.3%)
Davidson	827 (85.4%)	141(14.6%)	
Dickson	449 (97.4%)	12 (2.6%)	
Dyer	116 (95.1%)	6 (4.9%)	
Fayette	536 (94.7%)	26 (4.6%)	4 (0.7%)
Fentress	75 (44.6%)	93(55.4%)	
Franklin	943 (96.9%)	29 (2.9%)	1 (0.1%)
Gibson	183 (98.4%)	2 (1.1%)	1 (0.5%)
Giles	1,020 (99.8%)	2 (0.2%)	
Grainger	345 (98.6%)	5 (1.4%)	
Greene	722 (99.4%)	4 (0.6%)	
Hamilton	107 (100.%)	0	
Hardeman	451 (97.0%)	14 (3.0%)	
Hardin	201 (96.6%)	7 (3.4%)	
Hawkins	483 (99.2%)	4 (0.8%)	
Haywood	416 (93.9%)	25 (5.6%)	2 (0.5%)
Henderson	455 (99.3%)	3 (0.7%)	
Henry	662 (87.1%)	98(12.9%)	
Hickman	159 (99.4%)	1 (0.6%)	
Humphreys	353 (99.4%)	2 (0.6%)	
Jackson	172 (86.4%)	27(13.6%)	
Jefferson	337 (86.2%)	54(13.8%)	
Knox	948 (88.4%)	124(11.6%)	
Lawrence	63 (61.2%)	40(38.8%)	
Lincoln	813 (99.5%)	2 (0.2%)	2 (0.5%)
McMinn	515 (97.5%)	13 (2.5%)	
McNairy	260 (64.8%)	141(35.2%)	
Madison	539 (98.0%)	11 (2.0%)	
Marion	155 (98.7%)	2 (1.3%)	
Maury	1,396 (96.7%)	48 (3.3%)	
Monroe	515 (99.2%)	4 (0.8%)	
Montgomery	711 (91.2%)	69 (8.8%)	
Morgan	108 (100%)	0	
Obion	72 (96.0%)	3 (4.0%)	
Overton	399 (96.6%)	11 (2.6%)	3 (0.7%)
Perry	45 (100%)	0	
Rhea	160 (90.4%)	13 (7.3%)	4 (2.3%)
Roane	435 (91.4%)	39 (8.2%)	2 (0.4%)
Robertson	685 (99.9%)	1 (0.1%)	
Rutherford	898 (91.0%)	89 (9.0%)	
Sevier	222 (86.9%)	49(13.1%)	
Shelby	340 (96.6%)	12 (3.4%)	
Smith	583 (95.7%)	20 (3.3%)	6 (1.0%)
Stewart	589 (96.4%)	22 (3.6%)	
Sullivan	537 (99.3%)	4 (0.7%)	
Sumner	703 (98.6%)	10 (1.4%)	
Tipton	340 (81.7%)	76(18.3%)	
Warren	1,085 (99.0%)	11 (1.0%)	1 (0.1%)
Washington	718 (100%)	0	
Wayne	366 (98.1%)	7 (1.9%)	
Weakley	275 (85.3%)	44(14.7%)	
White	275 (91.7%)	25 (8.3%)	
Williamson	687 (83.6%)	114(13.9%)	21 (2.6%)
Wilson	515 (98.8%)	5 (1.0%)	1 (0.2%)
Total	**29,031 (94.0%)**	**1,756 (5.7%)**	**91 (0.3%)**
			*(90)

*Stated totals.

SOURCE—Manuscript returns.

Vermont

County	Jackson	Clay	Wirt
Addison	502 (15.1%)	936 (28.1%)	1,891 (56.8%)
Bennington	692 (37.8%)	805 (43.9%)	335 (18.3%)
Caledonia	367 (15.4%)	291 (12.2%)	1,726 (72.4%)
Chittenden	800 (38.0%)	875 (41.5%)	432 (20.5%)
Essex	181 (45.0%)	74 (18.4%)	147 (36.6%)
Franklin	489 (21.0%)	739 (31.7%)	1,101 (47.3%)
Grand Isle	134 (36.9%)	215 (59.2%)	14 (3.9%)
Orange	951 (29.2%)	1,108 (34.0%)	1,202 (36.9%)
Orleans	412 (29.2%)	418 (29.7%)	579 (41.1%)
Rutland	835 (19.7%)	1,772 (41.9%)	1,623 (38.4%)
Washington	1,134 (44.2%)	722 (28.1%)	711 (27.7%)
Windham	777 (26.8%)	1,352 (46.6%)	772 (26.6%)
Windsor	594 (11.8%)	1,856 (36.9%)	2,574 (51.2%)
Total	**7,868 (24.5%)**	**11,163 (34.7%)**	**13,107 (40.8%)**
	(*11,161)		

*Stated totals.

SOURCE—Manuscript returns.

Virginia

County	Jackson & Van Buren	Clay	Jackson & Barbour	Wirt
Accomack	378 (70.8%)	156 (29.2%)		
Albemarle	693 (84.0%)	109 (13.2%)	23 (2.8%)	
Alleghany	94 (85.5%)	16 (14.5%)		
Amelia	272 (97.1%)	8 (2.9%)		
Amherst	194 (56.7%)	148 (43.3%)		
Augusta	524 (59.4%)	358 (40.6%)		
Bath	187 (79.2%)	49 (20.8%)		
Bedford	420 (56.5%)	324 (43.5%)		
Berkeley	263 (43.2%)	346 (56.8%)		
Botetourt	749 (86.8%)	114 (13.2%)		
Brooke	437 (73.7%)	156 (26.3%)		
Brunswick	256 (89.8%)	29 (10.2%)		
Buckingham	667 (96.1%)	27 (3.9%)		
Cabell	92 (83.6%)	18 (16.4%)		
Campbell	440 (57.4%)	327 (42.6%)		
Caroline	330 (80.7%)	78 (19.1%)	1 (0.2%)	

County	Jackson & Van Buren	Clay	Jackson & Barbour	Wirt
Charles City	41 (71.9%)	16 (28.1%)		
Charlotte	468 (96.3%)	17 (3.5%)	1 (0.2%)	
Chesterfield	416 (88.1%)	56 (11.9%)		
Culpeper	681 (81.9%)	145 (17.4%)	2 (0.2%)	3 (0. 0.4%)
Cumberland	288 (84.2%)	54 (15.8%)		
Dinwiddie	238 (95.6%)	11 (4.4%)		
Elizabeth City	72 (100%)	0		
Essex	175 (92.1%)	14 (7.4%)	1 (0.5%)	
Fairfax	192 (58.5%)	136 (41.5%)		
Fauquier	599 (61.4%)	374 (38.4%)	2 (0.2%)	
Fayette	32 (66.7%)	16 (33.3%)		
Floyd	returns rejected			
Fluvanna	277 (98.6%)	4 (1.4%)		
Franklin	549 (84.5%)	77 (11.8%)	24 (3.7%)	
Frederick	1,084 (68.5%)	497 (31.4%)	1 (0.1%)	
Giles	no returns located			
Gloucester	260 (96.7%)	9 (3.3%)		
Goochland	222 (88.4%)	29 (11.6%)		
Grayson	223 (92.1%)	19 (7.9%)		
Greenbrier	300 (54.3%)	252 (45.7%)		
Greensville	114 (91.9%)	10 (8.1%)		
Halifax	663 (94.8%)	21 (3.0%)	15 (2.1%)	
Hampshire	525 (61.4%)	328 (38.4%)	2 (0.2%)	
Hanover	295 (80.6%)	67 (18.3%)	4 (1.1%)	
Hardy	57 majority			
Harrison	483 (72.7%)	171 (25.8%)	10 (1.5%)	
Henrico	274 (74.1%)	96 (25.9%)		
Henry	295 (91.9%)	26 (8.1%)		
Isle of Wight	272 (81.7%)	61 (18.3%)		
Jackson	165 (74.7%)	40 (18.1%)	16 (7.2%)	
James City	52 (88.1%)	7 (11.9%)		
Jefferson	279 (43.5%)	362 (56.5%)		
Kanawha	277 (80.7%)	201 (19.3%)		
King & Queen	222 (80.3%)	53 (19.7%)		
King George	89 (46.4%)	103 (53.6%)		
King William	154 (91.1%)	15 (8.9%)		
Lancaster	57 (46.7%)	65 (53.3%)		
Lee	349 (94.6%)	20 (5.4%)		
Lewis	215 (59.7%)	145 (40.3%)		
Logan	89 (96.7%)	3 (3.3%)		
Loudoun	319 (27.4%)	838 (72.0%)	7 (6.0%)	
Louisa	470 (93.8%)	31 (6.2%)		
Lunenburg	223 (98.2%)	4 (1.8%)		
Madison	297 (95.8%)	13 (4.2%)		
Mason	155 (60.3%)	102 (39.7%)		
Mathews	173 (87.4%)	25 (12.6%)		
Mecklenburg	515 (99.0%)	5 (1.0%)		
Middlesex	127 (88.2%)	17 (11.8%)		
Monongalia	861 (78.7%)	233 (21.3%)		
Monroe	346 (68.1%)	162 (31.9%)		
Montgomery	458 (90.0%)	51 (10.0%)		
Morgan	119 (72.6%)	45 (27.4%)		
Nansemond	252 (56.6%)	193 (43.4%)		
Nelson	217 (78.3%)	60 (21.7%)		
New Kent	71 (68.3%)	33 (31.7%)		
Nicholas	129 (71.7%)	51 (28.3%)		
Norfolk	241 (43.3%)	316 (56.7%)		
Northampton	203 (96.7%)	7 (3.3%)		
Northumberland	117 (90.7%)	12 (9.3%)		
Nottoway	200 (100%)	0		
Ohio	267 (34.9%)	497 (65.1%)		
Orange	470 (79.7%)	120 (20.3%)		
Page	267 (92.7%)	21 (7.3%)		
Patrick	287 (95.7%)	13 (4.3%)		
Pendleton	377 (80.9%)	89 (19.1%)		
Pittsylvania	1,007 (91.5%)	94 (8.5%)		
Pocahontas	140 (75.7%)	45 (24.3%)		
Powhatan	198 (93.0%)	15 (7.0%)		
Preston	328 (81.2%)	76 (18.8%)		

County	Jackson & Van Buren	Clay	Jackson & Barbour	Wirt
Prince Edward	323 (99.4%)	2 (0.6%)		
Prince George	167 (97.7%)	4 (2.3%)		
Prince William	295 (77.0%)	88 (23.0%)		
Princess Anne	158 (33.0%)	320 (66.8%)	1 (0.2%)	
Randolph	251 (61.7%)	156 (38.3%)		
Richmond	102 (63.0%)	60 (37.0%)		
Rockbridge	444 (57.5%)	328 (42.5%)		
Rockingham	804 (91.4%)	76 (8.6%)		
Russell	412 (100%)	0		
Scott	316 (99.4%)	1 (0.3%)	1 (0.3%)	
Shenandoah	973 (94.0%)	62 (6.0%)		
Smyth	200 (98.5%)	3 (1.5%)		
Southampton	260 (91.2%)	25 (8.8%)	1 (0.2%)	
Spotsylvania	426 (75.9%)	134 (23.9%)		
Stafford	228 (64.0%)	128 (36.0%)		
Surry	139 (87.4%)	14 (8.8%)	6 (3.8%)	
Sussex	251 (100%)	0		
Tazewell	249 (100%)	0		
Tyler	172 (51.7%)	137 (41.1%)	24 (7.2%)	
Warwick	15 (40.0%)	25 (60.0%)		
Washington	563 (95.6%)	18 (3.1%)	8 (1.4%)	
Westmoreland	123 (71.5%)	49 (28.5%)		
Wood	288 (54.6%)	239 (45.4%)		
Wythe	318 (91.6%)	29 (8.4%)		
York	65 (83.3%)	9 (11.5%)	4 (5.1%)	
Norfolk (boro)	217 (42.1%)	288 (55.9%)	10 (1.9%)	
Petersburg (town)	223 (75.6%)	72 (24.4%)		
Richmond (town)	154 (40.2%)	229 (59.8%)		
Williamsburg (town)	15 (41.7%)	11 (30.6%)	10 (27.8%)	3 (0.01%)
Total	**33,967 (74.4%)**	**11,433 (25.0%)**	**244 (0.5%)**	**3 (0.01%)**

SOURCE—Manuscript returns; *Politician's Register*, p. 66.

NOTES

1. The vice presidential electoral vote was Martin Van Buren (D) 189, John Sergeant (NR) 49, William Wilkins (J) 30, Henry Lee 11, and Amos Ellmaker (AM) 7. Pennsylvania electors voted for Wilkins rather than Van Buren.

2. All the candidates were nominated at national conventions, the first ever held.

3. Electoral slate pledged to Jackson and Philip P. Barbour of Virginia.

4. Two slates of Jackson electors ran in the state, pledged as indicated to different vice presidential candidates. Although other sources combine the total, this is incorrect.

5. Two slates of electors both pledged to Jackson but with different vice presidential candidates ran in the state. They also represented the two factions of the Democratic Party. One slate supported Jackson and Van Buren and was known as the Troup faction. The other backed Jackson and Barbour, this was the Clark or Union faction. Although other sources combine the two slates, this is incorrect.

6. Elias Brown received 707 votes, but his party affiliation is unclear. He was a Jackson elector in 1824 and 1828 but was chosen as a Whig elector in 1836. Several sources include his total with the Jacksonian vote. He is considered an Anti–Van Buren Jacksonian. Cornelius Howard received 41 votes, and his affiliation is also unknown.

7. Two separate sets of electors ran. While each was pledged to Jackson, they were, as indicated, pledged to different vice presidential candidates, as was the case in Georgia. Although other sources list the Jackson vote as the total of both slates, this is incorrect.

8. Other sources have indicated a majority of 5,159 or 5,192 for Jackson without indicating the vote for any candidate. See *Politician's Textbook* and (St. Louis) *The Mill Boy*, January, 1845. *Politician's Register*, published in 1835, is the earliest reference to this statistic I have uncovered. Over the years, some sources have inaccurately interpreted this to mean Jackson was unopposed and the figures cited above represent his total vote. See Svend Petersen, *A Statistical History of the American Presidential Elections*, New York, NY: 1963. See also *Congressional Quarterly*.

While meager newspaper coverage was given to the returns in Missouri newspapers, this much is clear: Clay did run a slate of electors throughout the state and carried, based on the above, at least four counties, probably more. The statewide vote appears in only a single source, the (Jefferson City) *Jeffersonian*, September 21, 1833. Unfortunately, I could not locate the same paper for the relevant 1832 issues.

The listing of the county majorities and the St. Louis vote were taken from the (St. Louis) *Missouri Republican*, November 13 and 20, 1832; the Howard vote from the (Columbia) *Missouri Intelligencer*, November 17, 1832.

9. The National Republicans withdrew their slate of electors and supported the Anti-Masons.

1 8 3 6

National Summary[1]
(electoral vote is in parentheses)

State	Martin Van Buren			Whigs[2]			
*Alabama	21,231 (55.45%)	(7)		17,055 (44.55%)			
*Arkansas	2,557 (65.23%)	(3)		1,363 (34.17%)			
Connecticut	19,291 (50.72%)	(8)		18,745 (49.28%)			
Delaware	4,154 (46.73%)			4,736 (53.27%)	(3)		
*Georgia	22,020 (47.10%)			24,732 (52.90%)	(11)		
†Illinois	18,448 (54.76%)	(5)		15,240 (45.24%)			
Indiana	32,978 (44.41%)			41,281 (55.59%)	(9)		
Kentucky	33,435 (47.50%)			36,955 (52.50%)	(15)		
*Louisiana	3,653 (51.90%)	(5)		3,386 (48.10%)			
Maine	22,890 (60.09%)	(10)		15,200 (39.91%)	(10)		
Maryland	22,270 (46.28%)			25,854 (53.72%)			
**Massachusetts	32,991 (45.11%)			40,149 (54.89%)	(14)		
Michigan[3]	7,381 (64.53%)	(3)		4,057 (35.47%)			
*Mississippi	10,317 (51.26%)	(4)		9,808 (48.74%)			
Missouri	10,953 (59.55%)	(4)		7,440 (40.45%)			
New Hampshire	18,701 (75.08%)	(7)		6,228 (24.92%)			
New Jersey	25,592 (49.47%)			26,137 (50.53%)	(8)		
New York	166,884 (54.60%)	(42)		138,765 (45.40%)			
*North Carolina	25,993 (53.41%)	(15)		22,676 (46.59%)			
Ohio	96,238 (47.83%)			104,960 (52.17%)	(21)		
Pennsylvania	91,414 (51.21%)	(30)		87,088 (48.79%)			
Rhode Island	2,964 (52.24%)	(4)		2,710 (47.76%)			
South Carolina	electors chosen by the legislature					‡(11)	
*Tennessee	26,122 (42.14%)			35,862 (57.86%)	(15)		
Vermont	14,037 (40.07%)			20,994 (59.93%)	(7)		
*Virginia	30,251 (56.41%)	(23)		23,368 (43.59%)			
Total	**762,765 (50.93%) (170)**			**734,829 (49.07%)**	**(113)[4]**	**(11)**	

*Whig electors pledged to Hugh L. White.
**Whig electors pledged to Daniel Webster.
†See Illinois returns for explanation.
‡Electoral vote cast for William P. Magnum (D).

Alabama

County	Van Buren(D)		White (W)	
Autauga	565	(48.1%)	609	(51.9%)
Baldwin	74	(63.2%)	43	(36.8%)
Barbour	291	(47.6%)	320	(52.4%)
Benton	637	(68.9%)	287	(31.1%)
Bibb	297	(75.4%)	97	(24.6%)
Blount	480	(89.7%)	55	(10.3%)
Butler	144	(29.7%)	341	(70.3%)
Chambers	no returns			
Cherokee	180	(42.7%)	242	(57.3%)
Choctaw	no returns			
Clarke	386	(73.0%)	143	(27.0%)
Coffee	no returns			
Conecuh	88	(23.6%)	285	(76.4%)
Coosa	130	(70.3%)	55	(29.7%)
Covington	27	(30.3%)	62	(69.7%)
Dale	133	(71.5%)	53	(28.5%)
Dallas	456	(33.2%)	916	(66.8%)
DeKalb	378	(90.0%)	42	(10.0%)
Fayette	580	(86.6%)	90	(13.4%)
Franklin	593	(59.9%)	397	(40.1%)
Greene	672	(32.6%)	1,113	(67.4%)
Henry	131	(52.6%)	118	(47.4%)
Jackson	1,626	(94.8%)	89	(5.2%)
Jefferson	536	(70.0%)	230	(30.0%)
Lauderdale	917	(68.8%)	415	(31.2%)
Lawrence	600	(51.5%)	564	(48.5%)
Limestone	715	(69.1%)	319	(30.9%)
Lowndes	316	(26.7%)	869	(73.3%)
Macon	34	(18.5%)	150	(81.5%)
Madison	1,678	(80.5%)	420	(19.5%)
Marengo	422	(44.7%)	523	(55.3%)
Marion	299	(67.8%)	142	(32.2%)
Marshall	539	(84.2%)	101	(15.8%)
Mobile	866	(54.0%)	739	(46.0%)
Monroe	307	(40.7%)	447	(59.3%)
Montgomery	723	(43.4%)	944	(56.6%)
Morgan	568	(54.5%)	475	(45.5%)
Perry	290	(26.0%)	827	(74.0%)
Pickens	432	(47.9%)	469	(52.1%)
Pike	304	(49.3%)	313	(50.7%)
Randolph	56	(46.3%)	65	(53.7%)
Russell	40	(20.6%)	154	(79.4%)
St. Clair	464	(94.7%)	26	(5.3%)
Shelby	198	(36.6%)	343	(63.4%)

	Van Buren (D)	White (W)
Sumter	631 (44.5%)	789 (55.5%)
Talladega	413 (52.3%)	376 (47.7%)
Tallapoosa	63 (39.1%)	98 (60.9%)
Tuscaloosa	841 (53.5%)	730 (46.5%)
Walker	110 (59.6%)	76 (40.4%)
Washington	166 (64.8%)	90 (35.2%)
Wilcox	242 (28.5%)	607 (71.5%)
Total	**21,231 (55.5%)**	**17,055 (44.5%)**

SOURCE—Loveman manuscript, state archives.

Arkansas

County	Van Buren (D)	White (W)
Arkansas	38 (31.7%)	82 (68.3%)
Carroll	73 (92.4%)	6 (7.6%)
Chicot	43 (45.7%)	51 (54.3%)
Clark	41 (85.4%)	7 (14.6%)
Conway	23 (32.4%)	48 (67.6%)
Crawford	109 (47.8%)	119 (52.2%)
Crittenden	38 (58.5%)	27 (41.5%)
Greene		no returns
Hempstead	110 (57.0%)	83 (43.0%)
Hot Spring	11 (68.8%)	5 (31.2%)
Independence	134 (54.3%)	113 (45.7%)
Izard	87 (85.3%)	15 (14.7%)
Jackson	56 (53.8%)	48 (46.2%)
Jefferson	50 (51.0%)	48 (49.0%)
Johnson	107 (72.8%)	40 (27.2%)
Lafayette	30 (73.2%)	11 (26.8%)
Lawrence	82 (72.6%)	31 (27.4%)
Miller		no returns
Mississippi		no returns
Monroe	17 (32.7%)	35 (67.3%)
Phillips	96 (59.6%)	65 (40.4%)
Pike	33 (100%)	0
Pope	93 (66.9%)	46 (33.1%)
Pulaski	234 (55.1%)	191 (44.9%)
Randolph	138 (89.0%)	17 (11.0%)
St. Francis	108 (85.7%)	18 (14.3%)
Saline	81 (60.9%)	52 (39.1%)
Scott		no returns
Searcy		no returns
Sevier	67 (66.3%)	34 (33.7%)
Union		no returns
Van Buren	19 (67.9%)	9 (32.1%)
Washington	622 (82.4%)	133 (17.6%)
White	17 (37.0%)	29 (63.0%)
Total	**2,557 (65.2%)**	**1,363 (34.8%)**

SOURCE—(Little Rock) *Gazette*, December 20, 1836.

Connecticut

County	Van Buren (D)	Harrison (W)
Fairfield	2,711 (53.8%)	2,326 (46.2%)
Hartford	3,768 (48.6%)	3,979 (51.4%)
Litchfield	2,957 (49.3%)	3,036 (50.7%)
Middlesex	1,618 (57.7%)	1,187 (42.3%)
New Haven	3,420 (49.6%)	3,476 (50.4%)
New London	2,059 (52.3%)	1,880 (47.7%)
Tolland	1,190 (50.0%)	1,191 (50.0%)
Windham	1,568 (48.8%)	1,670 (51.2%)
Total	**19,291 (50.7%)**	**18,745 (49.3%)**
		*(18,765)

*Stated totals.

SOURCE—Manuscript returns.

Delaware

County	Van Buren (D)	Harrison (W)
Kent	1,039 (46.3%)	1,205 (53.7%)
New Castle	1,814 (52.0%)	1,673 (48.0%)
Sussex	1,301 (41.2%)	1,858 (58.8%)
Total	**4,154 (46.7%)**	**4,736 (53.3%)**

SOURCE—*Governor's Register.*

Georgia

County	Van Buren (D)	White (W)
Appling	34 (60.7%)	22 (39.3%)
Baker	91 (64.1%)	51 (35.9%)
Baldwin	502 (49.9%)	499 (50.1%)
Bibb	625 (48.9%)	654 (51.1%)
Bryan	29 (39.2%)	45 (60.8%)
Bulloch	217 (100%)	0
Burke	136 (30.1%)	316 (69.9%)
Butts	259 (55.2%)	210 (44.8%)
Camden	113 (52.8%)	101 (47.2%)
Campbell	296 (67.0%)	146 (33.0%)
Carroll	402 (76.9%)	121 (23.1%)
Cass	328 (67.6%)	205 (32.4%)
Chatham	527 (60.0%)	351 (40.0%)
Cherokee	174 (55.4%)	140 (44.6%)
Clarke	313 (40.4%)	461 (59.6%)
Cobb	197 (55.1%)	119 (44.9%)
Columbia	106 (27.4%)	281 (72.6%)
Coweta	408 (47.7%)	447 (52.3%)
Crawford	373 (60.3%)	246 (39.7%)
Decatur	149 (36.9%)	255 (63.1%)
De Kalb	467 (54.7%)	387 (45.3%)
Dooly	162 (43.5%)	117 (56.5%)
Early	150 (75.8%)	48 (24.2%)
Effingham	81 (62.0%)	132 (38.0%)
Elbert	77 (18.3%)	549 (81.7%)
Emanuel	55 (91.7%)	5 (8.3%)
Fayette	307 (61.8%)	190 (38.2%)
Floyd	136 (61.0%)	87 (39.0%)
Forsyth	258 (57.5%)	152 (42.5%)
Franklin	484 (69.8%)	209 (30.2%)
Gilmer	78 (61.9%)	48 (38.1%)
Glynn	31 (37.3%)	52 (62.7%)
Greene	31 (5.3%)	551 (94.7%)
Gwinnett	632 (53.8%)	543 (46.2%)
Habersham	576 (70.5%)	241 (29.5%)
Hall	473 (61.9%)	291 (38.1%)
Hancock	243 (41.5%)	343 (58.5%)
Harris	330 (35.3%)	606 (64.7%)
Heard	241 (54.2%)	204 (45.8%)
Henry	392 (40.2%)	584 (59.8%)
Houston	450 (44.6%)	560 (55.4%)
Irwin	77 (95.1%)	4 (4.9%)
Jackson	484 (61.9%)	298 (38.1%)
Jasper	406 (40.3%)	596 (59.7%)
Jefferson	119 (18.4%)	526 (81.6%)
Jones	350 (48.3%)	375 (51.7%)
Laurens	1 (0.3%)	288 (99.7%)
Lee	57 (33.5%)	113 (66.5%)
Liberty	89 (41.4%)	126 (58.6%)
Lincoln	155 (39.8%)	284 (60.2%)
Lowndes	73 (30.9%)	163 (69.1%)
Lumpkin	599 (69.0%)	269 (31.0%)
McIntosh	38 (41.3%)	54 (58.7%)
Madison	159 (41.8%)	221 (58.2%)
Marion	212 (60.9%)	346 (39.1%)
Merriwether	509 (52.6%)	459 (47.4%)

Monroe	568 (44.4%)	710 (55.6%)
Montgomery	11 (14.1%)	67 (85.9%)
Morgan	171 (33.4%)	341 (66.6%)
Murray	128 (84.8%)	23 (15.2%)
Muscogee	325 (31.4%)	711 (68.6%)
Newton	337 (34.6%)	636 (65.4%)
Oglethorpe	76 (21.0%)	286 (79.0%)
Paulding	40 (61.5%)	25 (38.5%)
Pike	427 (59.8%)	287 (40.2%)
Pulaski	149 (59.8%)	119 (40.2%)
Putnam	218 (41.6%)	446 (58.4%)
Rabun	185 (97.4%)	5 (2.6%)
Randolph	239 (55.3%)	193 (44.7%)
Richmond	324 (39.3%)	501 (60.7%)
Scriven	135 (40.7%)	197 (59.3%)
Stewart	374 (51.3%)	355 (48.7%)
Sumter	159 (39.9%)	239 (60.1%)
Talbot	621 (48.7%)	653 (51.3%)
Taliaferro	25 (6.5%)	361 (93.5%)
Tattnall	13 (92.0%)	149 (8.0%)
Telfair	44 (32.6%)	90 (67.4%)
Thomas	22 (9.9%)	201 (90.1%)
Troup	219 (18.8%)	945 (81.2%)
Twiggs	303 (50.7%)	295 (49.3%)
Union	178 (97.3%)	5 (2.7%)
Upson	297 (41.6%)	489 (58.4%)
Walker	159 (56.8%)	122 (43.2%)
Walton	538 (63.7%)	306 (36.3%)
Ware		no returns
Warren	317 (48.5%)	337 (51.5%)
Washington	375 (51.0%)	360 (49.0%)
Wayne	56 (100%)	0
Wilkes	474 (57.2%)	355 (42.8%)
Wilkinson	252 (52.2%)	231 (47.8%)
Total	**22,020 (47.1%)**	**24,732 (52.8%)**
	*(22,043)	*(24,702)

*Stated totals.

SOURCE—(Savannah) *Daily Republican*, December 2, 1836.

Illinois

County	Van Buren (D)	(W)[5]
Adams	651 (63.1%)	380 (36.9%)
Alexander	149 (41.8%)	28 (58.2%)
Bond	108 (38.4%)	173 (61.6%)
Calhoun	48 (47.5%)	53 (52.5%)
Champaign	86 (58.5%)	61 (41.5%)
Clark	218 (53.4%)	190 (46.6%)
Clay	85 (61.2%)	54 (38.8%)
Clinton	149 (54.6%)	124 (45.4%)
Coles	151 (45.6%)	180 (54.4%)
Cook	519 (49.8%)	524 (50.2%)
Crawford	203 (56.9%)	154 (43.1%)
Edgar	409 (61.1%)	260 (38.9%)
Edwards	95 (39.9%)	143 (60.1%)
Effingham	45 (97.8%)	1 (2.2%)
Fayette	268 (77.0%)	80 (23.0%)
Franklin	374 (97.4%)	10 (2.6%)
Fulton	376 (51.9%)	348 (48.1%)
Gallatin	452 (75.1%)	150 (24.9%)
Greene	1,037 (59.3%)	711 (40.7%)
Hamilton	265 (90.1%)	29 (9.9%)
Hancock	260 (43.3%)	340 (56.7%)
Iroquois	96 (81.4%)	22 (18.6%)
Jackson	164 (66.1%)	84 (33.9%)
Jasper	12 (63.2%)	7 (36.8%)
Jefferson	227 (93.0%)	17 (7.0%)
Jo Daviess	367 (37.4%)	615 (62.6%)
Johnson	37 (88.1%)	5 (11.9%)
Kane	235 (71.6%)	93 (28.4%)
Knox	265 (60.1%)	176 (39.9%)
La Salle	248 (62.5%)	149 (37.5%)
Lawrence	224 (48.3%)	240 (51.7%)
McDonough	158 (56.0%)	124 (44.0%)
McLean	427 (50.1%)	425 (49.9%)
Macon	313 (77.1%)	93 (22.9%)
Macoupin	486 (64.4%)	269 (35.6%)
Madison	682 (41.6%)	959 (58.4%)
Marion	142 (78.9%)	38 (21.1%)
Mercer	24 (25.3%)	71 (74.7%)
Monroe	118 (52.0%)	109 (48.0%)
Montgomery	266 (68.9%)	120 (31.1%)
Morgan	1,720 (52.1%)	1,582 (47.9%)
Peoria	300 (56.5%)	231 (43.5%)
Perry	127 (58.8%)	89 (41.2%)
Pike	366 (52.5%)	331 (47.5%)
Pope	84 (44.0%)	107 (56.0%)
Putnam	263 (38.8%)	415 (61.2%)
Randolph	411 (50.2%)	408 (49.8%)
Rock Island	35 (25.2%)	104 (74.8%)
St. Clair	551 (60.9%)	354 (39.1%)
Sangamon	903 (38.1%)	1,464 (61.9%)
Schuyler	490 (56.1%)	384 (43.9%)
Shelby	333 (84.7%)	60 (15.3%)
Tazewell	356 (41.1%)	510 (58.9%)
Union	221 (96.1%)	9 (3.9%)
Vermilion	465 (45.4%)	560 (54.6%)
Wabash	102 (26.7%)	280 (73.3%)
Warren	181 (52.0%)	167 (48.0%)
Washington	123 (88.6%)	15 (11.4%)
Wayne	227 (88.0%)	31 (12.0%)
White	357 (56.6%)	274 (43.4%)
Will	306 (62.2%)	186 (37.8%)
Winnebago	88 (55.7%)	70 (44.3%)
Total	**18,448 (54.8%)**	**15,240 (45.2%)**

SOURCE—Theodore Pease (ed.), *Illinois Election Returns 1818–1848*, Springfield, IL: Illinois State Historical Society Library, 1923, pp. 104–106.

Indiana

County	Van Buren (D)	Harrison (W)
Adams	28 (29.2%)	68 (70.8%)
Allen	266 (43.0%)	353 (57.0%)
Bartholomew	412 (40.4%)	608 (59.6%)
Boone	421 (47.6%)	464 (52.4%)
Carroll	565 (60.1%)	375 (39.9%)
Cass	286 (35.8%)	513 (64.2%)
Clark	978 (52.3%)	893 (47.7%)
Clay	251 (62.1%)	153 (37.9%)
Clinton	427 (56.3%)	331 (43.7%)
Crawford	166 (45.9%)	196 (54.1%)
Daviess	253 (36.6%)	438 (63.4%)
Dearborn	1,282 (51.6%)	1,203 (48.4%)
Decatur	513 (35.1%)	950 (64.9%)
Delaware	307 (45,4%)	369 (54.6%)
Dubois	127 (43.5%)	165 (56.5%)
Elkhart	305 (46.3%)	354 (53.7%)
Fayette	545 (40.1%)	965 (59.9%)
Floyd	999 (65.2%)	574 (34.8%)
Fountain	948 (57.6%)	697 (42.4%)
Franklin	875 (47.6%)	963 (52.4%)
Fulton	39 (41.5%)	55 (58.5%)
Gibson	425 (49.1%)	496 (50.9%)
Grant	130 (35.3%)	238 (64.7%)
Greene	330 (47.4%)	366 (52.6%)
Hamilton	262 (31.5%)	569 (68.5%)

County	Van Buren (D)	Harrison (W)
Hancock	293 (44.5%)	366 (55.5%)
Harrison	456 (37.9%)	747 (62.1%)
Hendricks	390 (28.4%)	731 (71.6%)
Henry	712 (35.1%)	1,304 (64.9%)
Huntington	67 (56.3%)	52 (43.7%)
Jackson	307 (41.2%)	439 (58.8%)
Jefferson	679 (36.7%)	1,172 (63.3%)
Jennings	292 (31.8%)	626 (68.2%)
Johnson	559 (56.1%)	438 (43.9%)
Knox	437 (37.3%)	736 (62.7%)
Kosciusko	149 (48.2%)	160 (51.8%)
La Grange	150 (52.1%)	138 (47.9%)
La Porte	452 (48.0%)	490 (52.0%)
Lawrence	815 (54.9%)	670 (45.1%)
Madison	367 (57.0%)	487 (43.0%)
Marion	1,043 (42.5%)	1,409 (57.5%)
Marshall	42 (30.9%)	94 (69.1%)
Martin	197 (58.1%)	142 (41.9%)
Miami	80 (37.6%)	133 (62.4%)
Monroe	604 (58.8%)	424 (41.2%)
Montgomery	752 (41.4%)	1,066 (58.6%)
Morgan	543 (44.9%)	666 (55.1%)
Noble	80 (63.5%)	46 (36.5%)
Orange	564 (53.9%)	483 (46.1%)
Owen	286 (59.9%)	427 (40.1%)
Parke	534 (39.2%)	828 (60.8%)
Perry	114 (22.5%)	392 (77.5%)
Pike	218 (49.1%)	226 (50.9%)
Porter	69 (44.2%)	87 (55.8%)
Posey	751 (69.5%)	330 (30.5%)
Putnam	694 (39.4%)	1,067 (60.6%)
Randolph	234 (27.0%)	633 (73.0%)
Ripley	453 (40.6%)	663 (59.4%)
Rush	749 (39.1%)	1,167 (60.9%)
St. Joseph	255 (34.9%)	480 (65.1%)
Scott	267 (47.6%)	294 (52.4%)
Shelby	675 (49.5%)	688 (50.5%)
Spencer	179 (51.1%)	171 (48.9%)
Sullivan	558 (73.3%)	203 (26.7%)
Switzerland	519 (45.2%)	630 (54.8%)
Tippecanoe	1,041 (45.6%)	1,244 (54.4%)
Union	568 (44.8%)	700 (55.2%)
Vanderburgh	130 (32.6%)	269 (67.4%)
Vermillion	433 (43.0%)	574 (57.0%)
Vigo	287 (23.6%)	963 (76.4%)
Wabash	47 (27.8%)	122 (72.2%)
Warren	329 (37.8%)	541 (62.2%)
Warrick	380 (70.8%)	157 (29.2%)
Washington	947 (59.1%)	656 (40.9%)
Wayne	985 (30.1%)	2,285 (69.9%)
White	106 (49.3%)	109 (50.7%)
Total	**32,978 (44.4%)**	**41,281 (55.6%)**

SOURCE—Dorothy F. Riker and Gayle Thornbrough (eds.), *Indiana Election Returns 1816–1851*, Indianapolis, IN: Indiana Historical Bureau, 1960, pp. 4–9.

Kentucky

County	Van Buren (D)	Harrison (W)
Adair	401 (64.3%)	223 (35.7%)
Allen	373 (65.0%)	201 (35.0%)
Anderson	375 (67.4%)	181 (32.6%)
Barren	825 (51.2%)	787 (48.8%)
Bath	470 (49.2%)	485 (50.8%)
Boone	488 (45.7%)	580 (54.3%)
Bourbon	416 (29.5%)	992 (70.5%)
Bracken	275 (36.1%)	486 (63.9%)
Breckinridge	176 (18.9%)	755 (81.1%)
Bullitt	319 (60.4%)	209 (39.6%)
Butler	187 (59.0%)	130 (41.0%)
Caldwell	497 (62.2%)	302 (37.8%)
Calloway	716 (88.2%)	99 (11.8%)
Campbell	1,026 (67.9%)	484 (32.1%)
Casey	224 (56.0%)	176 (44.0%)
Christian	470 (41.2%)	670 (58.8%)
Clark	226 (21.2%)	838 (78.8%)
Clay	153 (42.5%)	207 (57.5%)
Clinton	206 (68.7%)	94 (31.3%)
Cumberland	144 (32.1%)	304 (67.9%)
Daviess	344 (43.6%)	445 (56.4%)
Edmonson	149 (45.0%)	122 (55.0%)
Estill	318 (54.2%)	269 (45.8%)
Fayette	689 (35.2%)	1,266 (64.8%)
Fleming	464 (33.3%)	898 (66.7%)
Floyd	549 (87.3%)	80 (12.7%)
Franklin	560 (52.4%)	509 (47.6%)
Gallatin	525 (52.1%)	483 (47.9%)
Garrard	218 (21.1%)	814 (78.9%)
Grant	225 (47.7%)	247 (52.3%)
Graves	363 (69.7%)	158 (30.3%)
Grayson	153 (36.3%)	268 (63.7%)
Green	890 (76.5%)	274 (23.5%)
Greenup	265 (42.6%)	357 (57.4%)
Hancock	72 (32.1%)	152 (67.9%)
Hardin	526 (43.0%)	698 (57.0%)
Harlan	53 (23.3%)	174 (76.7%)
Harrison	714 (61.6%)	445 (38.4%)
Hart	387 (64.2%)	216 (35.8%)
Henderson	360 (49.7%)	364 (50.3%)
Henry	794 (56.0%)	625 (44.0%)
Hickman	521 (72.5%)	198 (27.5%)
Hopkins	381 (48.6%)	403 (51.4%)
Jefferson	1,544 (42.6%)	2,083 (57.4%)
Jessamine	339 (39.8%)	513 (60.2%)
Knox	95 (23.5%)	309 (76.5%)
Laurel	100 (36.9%)	171 (63.1%)
Lawrence	207 (75.3%)	68 (24.7%)
Lewis	302 (46.7%)	345 (53.3%)
Lincoln	317 (34.1%)	613 (65.9%)
Livingston	361 (61.6%)	225 (38.4%)
Logan	289 (24.3%)	902 (75.7%)
McCracken	106 (41.6%)	149 (58.4%)
Madison	420 (30.2%)	972 (69.8%)
Marion	616 (66.2%)	314 (33.8%)
Mason	508 (29.2%)	1,231 (70.8%)
Meade	128 (27.4%)	339 (72.6%)
Mercer	938 (55.9%)	739 (44.1%)
Monroe	220 (55.1%)	179 (44.9%)
Montgomery	341 (39.5%)	522 (60.5%)
Morgan	335 (85.5%)	57 (14.5%)
Muhlenberg	227 (39.8%)	344 (60.2%)
Nelson	425 (35.7%)	765 (64.3%)
Nicholas	439 (50.6%)	428 (49.4%)
Ohio	247 (44.1%)	313 (55.9%)
Oldham	590 (62.5%)	354 (37.5%)
Owen	649 (78.9%)	174 (21.1%)
Pendleton	342 (72.0%)	133 (28.0%)
Perry	172 (67.5%)	83 (32.5%)
Pike	213 (89.9%)	24 (10.1%)
Pulaski	443 (46.3%)	514 (53.7%)
Rockcastle	58 (12.7%)	400 (87.3%)
Russell	127 (36.0%)	226 (64.0%)
Scott	993 (64.6%)	544 (35.4%)
Shelby	586 (30.6%)	1,327 (69.4%)
Simpson	257 (44.0%)	327 (56.0%)
Spencer	347 (54.3%)	292 (45.7%)
Todd	212 (27.8%)	550 (72.2%)
Trigg	359 (57.0%)	271 (43.0%)
Union	266 (56.5%)	205 (43.5%)

	Van Buren	Harrison
Warren	440 (36.6%)	763 (63.4%)
Washington	636 (71.6%)	252 (28.4%)
Wayne	349 (47.7%)	383 (52.3%)
Whitley	80 (22.9%)	269 (77.1%)
Woodford	325 (34.6%)	615 (65.4%)
Total	**33,435 (47.5%)**	**36,955 (52.5%)**

SOURCE—(Frankfort) *Commonwealth*, November 23, 1836.

Louisiana

Parish	Van Buren (D)	White (W)
Ascension	159 (76.1%)	50 (23.9%)
Assumption	84 (45.2%)	102 (54.8%)
Avoyelles	41 (18.2%)	184 (81.8%)
Carroll	63 (53.8%)	54 (46.2%)
Catahoula	85 (56.3%)	66 (43.8%)
Claiborne	no returns	
Concordia	49 (35.0%)	91 (65.0%)
East Baton Rouge	214 (55.7%)	170 (44.3%)
East Feliciana	296 (66.4%)	150 (33.6%)
Iberville	91 (60.3%)	60 (39.7%)
Jefferson	26 (39.4%)	40 (60.6%)
Lafayette	158 (81.4%)	36 (18.6%)
Lafourche	58 (26.6%)	160 (73.4%)
Livingston	100 (50.0%)	100 (50.0%)
Natchitoches	no returns	
Ouachita	129 (56.6%)	99 (43.4%)
Orleans	665 (49.5%)	678 (50.5%)
Plaquemines	44 (83.0%)	9 (17.0%)
Point Coupee	51 (56.0%)	40 (44.0%)
Rapides	120 (61.5%)	175 (38.5%)
St. Bernard	25 (71.4%)	10 (28.6%)
St. Charles	33 (97.1%)	1 (2.9%)
St. Helena	264 (84.1%)	50 (15.9%)
St. James	22 (32.8%)	45 (67.2%)
St. John the Baptist	4 (100%)	0
St. Landry	165 (30.0%)	385 (70.0%)
St. Martin	36 (24.8%)	109 (75.2%)
St. Mary	63 (29.3%)	152 (70.7%)
St. Tammany	194 (76.4%)	60 (23.6%)
Terrebone	50 (34.5%)	95 (65.5%)
Washington	183 (83.2%)	37 (16.8%)
West Baton Rouge	28 (25.9%)	80 (74.1%)
West Feliciana	153 (61.0%)	98 (39.0%)
Total	**3,653 (51.9%)**	**3,386 (48.1%)**

SOURCE—*New Orleans Bee*, November 29, 1836.

Maine

County	Van Buren (D)	Harrison (W)
Cumberland	4,812 (57.1%)	3,608 (42.9%)
Hancock	1,001 (61.8%)	619 (38.2%)
Kennebec	1,791 (49.0%)	1,867 (51.0%)
Lincoln	2,526 (52.8%)	2,262 (47.2%)
Oxford	2,149 (72.1%)	832 (27.9%)
Penobscot	2,423 (62.1%)	1,481 (37.9%)
Somerset	1,654 (52.1%)	1,521 (47.9%)
Waldo	1,611 (84.5%)	305 (15.5%)
Washington	1,530 (65.9%)	792 (34.1%)
York	3,393 (63.9%)	1,913 (36.1%)
Total	**22,890 (60.1%)**	**15,200 (39.9%)**

SOURCE—Manuscript returns.

Maryland

County	Van Buren (D)	Harrison (W)
Allegany	705 (43.2%)	926 (56.8%)
Anne Arundel	1,009 (44.7%)	1,248 (55.3%)
Baltimore	2,482 (54.5%)	2,074 (45.5%)
Baltimore (city)	5,740 (50.5%)	5,630 (49.5%)
Calvert	284 (44.0%)	362 (56.0%)
Caroline	492 (46.1%)	576 (53.9%)
Cecil	1,092 (51.7%)	1,020 (48.3%)
Charles	256 (33.2%)	514 (66.8%)
Dorchester	697 (41.9%)	966 (58.1%)
Frederick	3,015 (49.1%)	3,130 (50.9%)
Harford	920 (46.0%)	1,080 (54.0%)
Kent	367 (38.4%)	589 (61.6%)
Montgomery	515 (35.5%)	936 (64.5%)
Prince George's	450 (38.2%)	727 (61.8%)
Queen Anne's	517 (44.8%)	636 (55.2%)
St. Mary's	190 (22.8%)	643 (77.2%)
Somerset	523 (33.7%)	1,030 (66.3%)
Talbot	480 (42.3%)	656 (57.7%)
Washington	1,995 (49.0%)	2,079 (51.0%)
Worcester	541 (34.4%)	1,032 (65.6%)
Total	**22,270 (46.3%)**	**25,854 (53.7%)**

SOURCE—Manuscript returns.

Massachusetts

County	Van Buren (D)	Webster (W)
Barnstable	883 (42.7%)	1,187 (57.3%)
Berkshire	2,090 (49.4%)	2,138 (50.6%)
Bristol	2,568 (57.2%)	1,923 (42.8%)
Dukes	138 (44.7%)	171 (55.3%)
Essex	5,266 (45.5%)	6,299 (54.5%)
Franklin	1,163 (34.3%)	2,232 (65.7%)
Hampden	2,440 (51.0%)	2,344 (49.0%)
Hampshire	675 (29.8%)	1,592 (70.2%)
Middlesex	5,797 (55.9%)	4,877 (44.1%)
Nantucket	92 (24.5%)	283 (75.5%)
Norfolk	2,231 (49.6%)	2,269 (50.4%)
Plymouth	2,821 (60.5%)	2,844 (39.5%)
Suffolk	2,980 (38.1%)	4,842 (61.9%)
Worcester	3,847 (35.0%)	7,148 (65.0%)
Total	**32,911 (45.1%)** *(33,297)	**40,149 (54.9%)** *(41,099)

*Stated totals.

SOURCE—Manuscript returns.

Michigan

County	Van Buren (D)	Harrison (W)
Allegan	92 (100%)	0
Berrien	409 (99.8%)	1 (0.2%)
Branch	65 (100%)	0
Calhoun	401 (100%)	0
Cass	164 (100%)	0
Chippewa	37 (100%)	0
Clinton	no returns	
Genesee	90 (42.1%)	124 (57.9%)
Hillsdale	180 (96.3%)	7 (3.7%)
Iona	no returns	
Jackson & Ingham	355 (50.1%)	353 (49.9%)
Kalamazoo	213 (100%)	0
Kent	55 (100%)	0
Lapeer	129 (69.4%)	57 (30.6%)
Lenawaee	567 (68.7%)	260 (31.3%)
Livingston	142 (66.0%)	73 (34.0%)

Macomb	397 (90.0%)	44	(10.0%)
Michilmackinac		no returns	
Monroe	2 (0.2%)	1,143	(99.8%)
Oakland	820 (43.7%)	1,057	(56.3%)
Ottawa		no returns	
St. Joseph	42 (100%)	0	
Saginaw	65 (100%)	0	
Washtenaw	1,633 (61.3%)	1,032	(38.7%)
Wayne	1,576 (87.4%)	27	(12.6%)
Total[6]	**7,434 (64.0%)**	**4,177**	**(36.0%)**
	*(7,534)	*(4,085)	
St. Clair	93 (98.9%)	1	(1.1%)
Van Buren	64 (100%)	0	

Totals as stated in (New York) Albany Argus.

Mississippi

County	Van Buren (D)	White (W)
Adams	342 (38.1%)	556 (61.9%)
Amite	274 (47.2%)	307 (52.8%)
Atalla	87 (43.9%)	111 (56.1%)
Bolivar	16 (43.2%)	21 (56.8%)
Carroll	218 (42.7%)	292 (57.3%)
Chickasaw	58 (70.7%)	24 (29.3%)
Choctaw	74 (44.8%)	91 (55.2%)
Claiborne	258 (42.4%)	350 (57.6%)
Clarke	102 (90.3%)	11 (9.7%)
Coahoma	no returns	
Copiah	464 (63.9%)	268 (36.1%)
Covington	237 (82.0%)	52 (18.0%)
De Soto	76 (53.1%)	67 (46.9%)
Franklin	189 (71.6%)	75 (28.4%)
Greene	38 (30.4%)	87 (69.6%)
Hancock	105 (79.5%)	27 (20.5%)
Hinds	559 (39.0%)	876 (61.0%)
Holmes	254 (45.1%)	309 (54.9%)
Itawamba	131 (89.1%)	16 (10.9%)
Jackson	88 (98.9%)	1 (1.1%)
Jasper	261 (77.7%)	75 (22.3%)
Jefferson	202 (40.5%)	297 (59.5%)
Jones	25 (80.6%)	6 (19.4%)
Kemper	196 (49.9%)	197 (50.1%)
Lafayette	93 (38.4%)	151 (61.6%)
Lauderdale	101 (90.2%)	11 (9.8%)
Lawrence	429 (94.1%)	47 (5.9%)
Leake	68 (60.2%)	45 (39.8%)
Lowndes	572 (56.8%)	435 (43.2%)
Madison	282 (28.3%)	714 (71.7%)
Marion	178 (73.0%)	66 (27.0%)
Marshall	352 (44.7%)	436 (55.3%)
Monroe	447 (70.0%)	162 (30.0%)
Neshoba	59 (80.8%)	14 (19.2%)
Newton	103 (83.1%)	21 (16.9%)
Noxubee	312 (53.7%)	269 (46.3%)
Oktibbeha	108 (60.0%)	72 (40.0%)
Perry	no returns	
Pike	348 (79.1%)	92 (20.9%)
Ponola	192 (71.9%)	75 (28.1%)
Pontotoc	217 (45.9%)	256 (54.1%)
Rankin	133 (34.9%)	248 (65.1%)
Scott	71 (74.7%)	24 (25.3%)
Simpson	148 (64.6%)	81 (35.4%)
Smith	81 (85.3%)	14 (14.7%)
Tallahatchie	80 (31.9%)	171 (68.1%)
Tippah	245 (59.3%)	168 (40.7%)
Tishomingo	149 (70.3%)	63 (29.7%)
Tunica	no returns	
Warren	265 (33.5%)	525 (66.5%)

Washington	29 (38.7%)	46	(61.3%)
Wayne	75 (75.8%)	24	(24.2%)
Wilkinson	143 (21.5%)	422	(78.5%)
Winston	185 (71.2%)	75	(28.8%)
Yalobusha	411 (48.5%)	436	(51.5%)
Yazoo	187 (26.1%)	529	(73.9%)
Total	**10,317 (51.3%)**	**9,808**	**(48.7%)**

SOURCES—(Jackson) *The Mississippian*, December 9, 1836; Manuscript returns, state archives.

Missouri

County	Van Buren (D)	Harrison (W)
Barry	55 (100%)	0
Benton	75 (94.1%)	4 (5.9%)
Boone	567 (44.3%)	714 (55.7%)
Callaway	616 (58.0%)	446 (42.0%)
Cape Girardeau	435 (74.5%)	149 (25.5%)
Carroll	142 (81.1%)	33 (18.9%)
Chariton	188 (69.1%)	84 (30.9%)
Clay	347 (55.2%)	282 (44.8%)
Clinton	129 (73.3%)	47 (26.7%)
Cole	576 (88.8%)	73 (11.2%)
Cooper	no returns	
Crawford	86 (59.3%)	59 (40.7%)
Franklin	238 (64.2%)	133 (35.8%)
Gasconde	115 (58.7%)	81 (41.3%)
Greene	140 (92.7%)	11 (7.3%)
Howard	619 (63.6%)	354 (36.4%)
Jackson	489 (72.8%)	183 (27.2%)
Jefferson	138 (60.8%)	89 (39.2%)
Johnson	240 (75.5%)	78 (24.5%)
Lafayette	294 (64.1%)	165 (35.9%)
Lewis	298 (60.2%)	197 (39.8%)
Lincoln	236 (46.2%)	275 (53.8%)
Madison	109 (64.5%)	55 (35.5%)
Marion	338 (49.6%)	343 (50.4%)
Monroe	317 (53.1%)	280 (46.9%)
Montgomery	92 (35.2%)	169 (64.8%)
Morgan	216 (80.9%)	51 (19.1%)
New Madrid	no returns	
Perry	173 (91.0%)	17 (9.0%)
Pettis	161 (71.6%)	64 (28.4%)
Pike	415 (50.6%)	405 (49.4%)
Polk	80 (55.2%)	65 (44.8%)
Pulaski	230 (82.4%)	49 (17.6%)
Randolph	399 (67.2%)	195 (32.8%)
Ralls	151 (55.3%)	122 (44.7%)
Ray	221 (48.8%)	232 (51.2%)
Ripley	70 (7.2%)	2 (92.8%)
Rives	108 (73.0%)	40 (27.0%)
St. Charles	237 (45.7%)	282 (54.3%)
St. Francois	137 (48.8%)	144 (51.2%)
St. Genevieve	97 (67.4%)	47 (32.6%)
St. Louis	681 (47.8%)	843 (52.2%)
Saline	178 (56.9%)	135 (43.1%)
Scott	no returns	
Shelby	63 (67.0%)	31 (33.0%)
Stoddard	70 (80.5%)	17 (19.5%)
Van Buren	no returns	
Warren	76 (33.6%)	150 (66.4%)
Washington	311 (55.9%)	245 (44.1%)
Wayne	no returns	
Total	**10,953 (59.5%)**	**7,440 (40.5%)**
	*(10,995)	*(7,337)

Stated totals.

SOURCE—(St. Louis) *The Republican*, December 2, 1836.

New Hampshire

County	Van Buren (D)	Harrison (W)
Cheshire	1,507 (51.0%)	1,446 (49.0%)
Coos	670 (89.3%)	80 (10.7%)
Grafton	2,708 (82.3%)	584 (17.7%)
Hillsborough	2,877 (79.3%)	750 (20.7%)
Merrimack	3,190 (84.3%)	594 (15.7%)
Rockingham	2,564 (75.6%)	828 (24.4%)
Strafford	3,696 (77.6%)	1,068 (22.4%)
Sullivan	1,489 (62.9%)	878 (37.1%)
Total	**18,701 (75.0%)**	**6,228 (25.0%)**

SOURCE—Manuscript returns.

New Jersey

County	Van Buren (D)	Harrison (W)
Bergen	1,942 (53.1%)	1,716 (46.9%)
Burlington	2,123 (41.1%)	3,032 (58.9%)
Cape May	234 (32.4%)	489 (67.6%)
Cumberland	993 (45.4%)	1,193 (54.6%)
Essex	3,334 (43.4%)	4,343 (56.6%)
Gloucester	2,203 (48.1%)	2,377 (51.9%)
Hunterdon	2,349 (52.6%)	2,114 (47.4%)
Middlesex	1,719 (46.2%)	2,002 (53.8%)
Monmouth	2,549 (52.0%)	2,349 (48.0%)
Morris	1,774 (49.6%)	1,801 (50.4%)
Salem	1,036 (43.7%)	1,334 (56.3%)
Somerset	1,343 (48.3%)	1,436 (51.7%)
Sussex	2,389 (27.6%)	910 (72.4%)
Warren	1,604 (60.6%)	1,041 (39.4%)
Total	**25,592 (49.5%)**	**26,137 (50.5%)**

SOURCE—(Trenton) *True-American*, December 3, 1836.

New York

County	Van Buren (D)	Harrison (W)
Albany	4,947 (53.7%)	4,261 (46.3%)
Allegany	2,615 (40.5%)	2,696 (59.5%)
Broome	1,642 (52.8%)	1,465 (47.2%)
Cattaraugus	1,888 (55.9%)	1,489 (44.1%)
Cayuga	4,284 (53.5%)	3,724 (46.5%)
Chatauqua	3,120 (44.5%)	3,895 (55.5%)
Chemung	1,724 (63.3%)	1,000 (36.7%)
Chenango	3,611 (56.9%)	2,734 (43.1%)
Clinton	1,331 (60.9%)	854 (39.1%)
Columbia	3,767 (55.3%)	3,051 (44.7%)
Cortland	1,724 (46.1%)	2,017 (53.9%)
Delaware	2,823 (77.9%)	800 (22.1%)
Dutchess	3,981 (62.7%)	2,366 (37.3%)
Erie	2,661 (35.3%)	4,882 (64.7%)
Essex	1,603 (46.4%)	1,855 (53.6%)
Franklin	862 (48.6%)	910 (51.4%)
Genesee	3,271 (38.2%)	5,282 (61.8%)
Greene	2,976 (61.2%)	1,883 (38.8%)
Herkimer	3,036 (71.9%)	1,184 (28.1%)
Jefferson	4,595 (55.0%)	3,761 (45.0%)
Kings	2,321 (55.4%)	1,868 (44.6%)
Lewis	1,096 (72.7%)	411 (27.3%)
Livingston	1,902 (41.8%)	2,643 (58.2%)
Madison	2,909 (63.1%)	1,703 (36.9%)
Monroe	3,931 (44.6%)	4,887 (55.4%)
Montgomery	4,303 (57.6%)	3,170 (42.4%)
New York	17,469 (51.7%)	16,348 (48.3%)
Niagara	2,143 (48.6%)	2,267 (51.4%)
Oneida	5,476 (60.2%)	3,621 (39.8%)
Onondaga	4,776 (61.6%)	2,981 (38.4%)
Ontario	2,732 (44.2%)	3,435 (55.8%)
Orange	3,541 (61.2%)	2,242 (38.8%)
Orleans	1,825 (49.5%)	1,859 (50.5%)
Oswego	3,105 (61.5%)	1,946 (38.5%)
Otsego	4,627 (65.2%)	2,469 (34.8%)
Putnam	818 (77.6%)	236 (22.4%)
Queens	1,654 (54.2%)	1,399 (45.8%)
Rensselaer	4,983 (51.8%)	4,634 (48.2%)
Richmond	649 (50.0%)	649 (50.0%)
Rockland	1,045 (73.8%)	371 (26.2%)
St. Lawrence	3,089 (58.0%)	2,235 (42.0%)
Saratoga	3,338 (52.6%)	3,013 (47.4%)
Schenectady	1,480 (56.3%)	1,149 (43.7%)
Schoharie	2,437 (63.2%)	1,422 (36.8%)
Seneca	2,036 (57.6%)	1,501 (42.4%)
Steuben	3,650 (60.5%)	2,384 (39.5%)
Suffolk	2,071 (66.6%)	1,037 (33.4%)
Sullivan	1,227 (59.6%)	833 (40.4%)
Tioga	1,626 (56.5%)	1,253 (43.5%)
Tompkins	2,935 (51.3%)	2,786 (48.7%)
Ulster	3,658 (62.8%)	2,167 (37.2%)
Warren	1,316 (69.8%)	570 (30.2%)
Washington	2,592 (41.9%)	3,593 (58.1%)
Wayne	2,968 (52.8%)	2,653 (47.2%)
Westchester	3,009 (63.2%)	1,749 (36.8%)
Yates	1,686 (59.0%)	1,172 (41.0%)
Total	**166,884 (54.6%)**	**138,765 (45.4%)**

SOURCE—Manuscript returns.

North Carolina

The manuscript returns are incomplete for this election

	Van Buren (D)	White (W)
*Anson	329 (32.3%)	690 (67.7%)
*Ashe	14 (100%)	0
Beaufort	180 (22.6%)	616 (77.4%)
Bertie	442 (58.6%)	312 (41.4%)
Bladen	263 (57.4%)	195 (42.6%)
Brunswick	99 (38.8%)	156 (61.2%)
Buncombe	350 (32.6%)	724 (67.4%)
Burke	333 (30.9%)	744 (69.1%)
Cabarrus	231 (34.4%)	440 (65.6%)
Camden	88 (35.9%)	157 (64.1%)
Carteret	152 (55.3%)	123 (44.7%)
Caswell	1,055 (90.8%)	107 (9.2%)
Chatham	599 (43.0%)	718 (57.0%)
*Chowan	0	63 (100%)
*Columbus	110 (100%)	0
Craven	323 (63.3%)	187 (36.7%)
Cumberland	667 (61.8%)	418 (38.2%)
*Currituck	424 (92.8%)	33 (7.2%)
Davidson	109 (15.5%)	593 (84.5%)
*Duplin	662 (77.1%)	197 (22.9%)
Edgecombe	1,175 (92.9%)	90 (7.1%)
*Franklin	584 (71.5%)	233 (28.5%)
Gates	281 (67.9%)	133 (32.1%)
*Granville	494 (42.7%)	664 (57.3%)
Greene	178 (55.5%)	143 (44.5%)
*Guilford	378 (32.4%)	788 (67.6%)
Halifax	282 (42.2%)	387 (57.8%)
Haywood	205 (60.1%)	136 (39.9%)
Hertford	214 (45.8%)	253 (54.2%)
Hyde	74 (30.5%)	169 (69.5%)
Iredell	337 (30.4%)	772 (69.6%)
*Johnston	173 (100%)	0

Jones	90 (36.7%)	155 (63.3%)
Lenoir	281 (62.0%)	172 (38.0%)
Lincoln	1,386 (70.1%)	591 (29.9%)
Macon	288 (61.3%)	182 (38.7%)
Martin	559 (75.7%)	179 (24.3%)
Mecklenburg	985 (58.0%)	712 (42.0%)
Montgomery	106 (14.1%)	644 (85.9%)
Moore	493 (73.1%)	181 (26.9%)
Nash	481 (83.5%)	95 (16.5%)
New Hanover	735 (83.1%)	150 (16.9%)
Northampton	183 (33.8%)	359 (66.2%)
Onslow	446 (76.1%)	140 (23.9%)
Orange	1,103 (54.9%)	905 (45.1%)
Pasquotank	155 (43.7%)	200 (56.3%)
Perquimans	50 (23.1%)	166 (76.9%)
Person	507 (76.0%)	160 (24.0%)
Pitt	368 (49.4%)	377 (50.6%)
*Randolph	180 (34.0%)	349 (66.0%)
Richmond	57 (11.5%)	438 (88.5%)
Robeson	472 (61.7%)	293 (38.3%)
Rockingham	860 (79.4%)	223 (20.6%)
Rowan	108 (7.9%)	1,131 (92.1%)
Rutherford	449 (32.5%)	929 (67.5%)
Sampson	559 (65.3%)	297 (34.7%)
Stokes	978 (58.8%)	684 (41.2%)
Surry	723 (57.0%)	546 (43.0%)
Tyrrell	35 (15.6%)	189 (84.4%)
Wake	813 (55.0%)	665 (45.0%)
Warren	661 (88.5%)	86 (11.5%)
Washington	48 (9.9%)	193 (90.1%)
Wayne	551 (77.3%)	162 (22.7%)
Wilkes	209 (21.9%)	744 (78.1%)
Yancey	267 (65.9%)	138 (34.1%)
Total	**25,993 (53.4%)**	**22,676 (46.6%)**
	*(30,648)	

*Stated totals.

*The returns for these counties are taken from Thad Eure (Secretary of State), North Carolina Government 1585–1979, Raleigh, NC: 1979, pp. 1328–9.

Ohio

County	Van Buren (D)	Harrison (W)
Adams	1,060 (57.4%)	786 (42.6%)
Allen	416 (46.1%)	487 (53.9%)
Ashtabula	805 (22.4%)	2,792 (77.6%)
Athens	957 (46.6%)	1,098 (53.4%)
Belmont	2,358 (46.9%)	2,666 (53.1%)
Brown	1,675 (57.8%)	1,223 (42.2%)
Butler	3,004 (66.9%)	1,487 (33.1%)
Carroll	1,187 (49.0%)	1,233 (51.0%)
Champaign	907 (35.6%)	1,641 (64.4%)
Clark	731 (27.1%)	1,964 (72.9%)
Clermont	2,029 (58.0%)	1,467 (42.0%)
Clinton	807 (35.8%)	1,448 (64.2%)
Columbiana	2,992 (53.0%)	2,656 (47.0%)
Coshocton	1,410 (58.5%)	1,000 (41.5%)
Crawford	702 (50.9%)	677 (49.1%)
Cuyahoga	1,694 (40.1%)	2,529 (59.9%)
Darke	668 (50.5%)	656 (49.5%)
Delaware	1,254 (44.7%)	1,550 (55.3%)
Fairfield	2,906 (61.1%)	1,846 (38.9%)
Fayette	703 (47.9%)	764 (52.1%)
Franklin	1,375 (38.8%)	2,166 (61.2%)
Gallia	490 (36.0%)	873 (64.0%)
Geauga	1,465 (31.3%)	3,219 (68.7%)
Greene	903 (32.1%)	1,908 (67.9%)
Guernsey	1,652 (44.3%)	2,074 (55.7%)
Hamilton	4,871 (54.7%)	4,032 (45.3%)
Hancock	701 (60.2%)	464 (39.8%)
Hardin	196 (41.7%)	274 (58.3%)
Harrison	1,683 (51.5%)	1,584 (48.5%)
Henry	87 (48.1%)	94 (51.9%)
Highland	1,476 (49.7%)	1,492 (50.3%)
Hocking	536 (64.7%)	292 (35.3%)
Holmes	1,101 (66.6%)	551 (33.4%)
Huron	2,143 (43.4%)	2,798 (56.6%)
Jackson	437 (49.5%)	445 (50.5%)
Jefferson	1,992 (56.2%)	1,552 (43.8%)
Knox	2,095 (54.7%)	1,732 (45.3%)
Lawrence	370 (47.2%)	414 (52.8%)
Licking	2,605 (55.6%)	2,083 (44.4%)
Logan	622 (30.9%)	1,388 (69.1%)
Lorain	1,410 (49.1%)	1,460 (50.9%)
Lucas	396 (36.0%)	630 (64.0%)
Madison	574 (37.1%)	973 (62.9%)
Marion	844 (45.4%)	1,016 (54.6%)
Medina	1,094 (37.1%)	1,858 (62.9%)
Meigs	446 (38.1%)	724 (61.9%)
Mercer	315 (55.4%)	245 (44.6%)
Miami	1,050 (37.0%)	1,787 (63.0%)
Monroe	1,182 (70.6%)	492 (29.4%)
Montgomery	2,310 (47.5%)	2,554 (52.5%)
Morgan	1,262 (53.3%)	1,107 (46.7%)
Muskingum	2,069 (38.4%)	3,321 (61.6%)
Paulding	no returns	
Perry	1,503 (58.2%)	1,080 (41.8%)
Pickaway	1,591 (51.4%)	1,508 (48.6%)
Pike	491 (53.8%)	422 (46.2%)
Portage	2,683 (44.8%)	3,302 (55.2%)
Preble	978 (35.5%)	1,777 (64.5%)
Putnam	238 (58.5%)	179 (41.5%)
Richland	3,283 (59.4%)	2,247 (40.6%)
Ross	1,905 (43.1%)	2,515 (56.9%)
Sandusky	799 (55.4%)	642 (44.6%)
Scioto	568 (34.9%)	1,049 (65.1%)
Shelby	1,129 (54.4%)	948 (45.6%)
Stark	2,418 (55.4%)	1,946 (44.6%)
Trumbull	2,892 (46.1%)	3,386 (53.9%)
Tuscarawas	1,370 (48.4%)	1,459 (51.6%)
Union	439 (40.4%)	648 (59.6%)
Van Wert	no returns	
Warren	1,326 (37.1%)	2,260 (62.9%)
Washington	906 (45.9%)	1,070 (54.1%)
Wayne	2,696 (62.3%)	1,630 (37.7%)
Williams	198 (52.9%)	176 (47.1%)
Wood	275 (64.1%)	490 (35.9%)
Total	**96,238 (47.8%)**	**104,960 (52.2%)**

Source—(Columbus) Ohio State Journal, November 4, 1836.

Pennsylvania

County	Van Buren (D)	Harrison (W)
Adams	1,186 (43.8%)	1,520 (56.2%)
Allegheny	3,074 (45.9%)	3,623 (54.1%)
Armstrong	1,528 (60.1%)	1,014 (39.9%)
Beaver	1,075 (34.1%)	2,077 (65.9%)
Bedford	1,587 (45.3%)	1,920 (54.7%)
Berks	4,967 (75.8%)	1,584 (24.2%)
Bradford	1,463 (49.0%)	1,521 (51.0%)
Bucks	3,081 (48.4%)	3,289 (51.6%)
Butler	1,008 (46.4%)	1,166 (54.0%)
Cambria	450 (44.8%)	554 (55.2%)
Centre	1,809 (66.2%)	924 (33.8%)
Chester	3,277 (45.5%)	3,921 (54.5%)
Clearfield	499 (63.7%)	284 (36.3%)
Columbia	1,560 (74.1%)	544 (25.9%)
Crawford	1,614 (56.7%)	1,232 (43.3%)

County	Van Buren (D)	Harrison (W)
Cumberland	1,904 (52.9%)	1,696 (47.1%)
Dauphin	1,372 (40.8%)	1,993 (59.2%)
Delaware	1,030 (45.7%)	1,224 (54.3%)
Erie	1,312 (38.1%)	2,134 (61.9%)
Fayette	2,016 (54.7%)	1,669 (45.3%)
Franklin	2,155 (45.6%)	2,575 (54.4%)
Greene	1,138 (55.4%)	915 (44.6%)
Huntingdon	1,340 (33.8%)	2,628 (66.2%)
Indiana	692 (37.2%)	1,169 (62.8%)
Jefferson	244 (51.6%)	229 (48.4%)
Juniata	627 (51.3%)	596 (48.7%)
Lancaster	4,144 (39.9%)	6,250 (60.1%)
Lebanon	1,168 (44.0%)	1,487 (56.0%)
Lehigh	1,987 (52.7%)	1,784 (47.3%)
Luzerne	2,008 (58.7%)	1,415 (41.3%)
Lycoming	1,705 (64.5%)	938 (35.5%)
Mercer	1,253 (38.6%)	1,991 (61.4%)
Mifflin	917 (55.1%)	748 (44.9%)
Monroe	796 (82.7%)	166 (17.3%)
Montgomery	3,446 (55.1%)	2,409 (44.9%)
Northampton	2,378 (62.5%)	1,426 (37.5%)
Northumberland	1,421 (66.6%)	712 (33.4%)
Perry	1,107 (70.1%)	473 (29.9%)
Philadelphia	10,932 (47.3%)	12,196 (52.7%)
Pike	358 (87.3%)	52 (12.7%)
Potter & McKean	312 (69.8%)	135 (30.2%)
Schuylkill	1,380 (66.8%)	687 (33.2%)
Somerset	511 (21.2%)	1,905 (78.8%)
Susquehanna	1,145 (57.2%)	856 (42.8%)
Tioga	1,027 (72.0%)	400 (28.0%)
Union	1,143 (46.3%)	1,328 (53.7%)
Venango	967 (61.7%)	600 (38.3%)
Warren	498 (66.2%)	254 (33.8%)
Wayne	2,445 (46.6%)	2,805 (53.4%)
Washington	724 (68.0%)	340 (32.0%)
Westmoreland	2,878 (62.5%)	1,725 (37.5%)
York	2,756 (57.9%)	2,005 (42.1%)
Total	**91,414 (51.2%)**	**87,088 (48.8%)**
	*(91,475)	*(87,111)

*Stated totals.

SOURCE—(Harrisburg) *Pennsylvania Reporter & State Journal*, November 24, 1836.

Rhode Island

County	Van Buren (D)	Harrison (W)
Bristol	184 (45.8%)	218 (54.2%)
Kent	426 (57.0%)	321 (43.0%)
Newport	511 (47.4%)	568 (52.6%)
Providence	1,247 (51.0%)	1,196 (49.0%)
Washington	596 (59.4%)	407 (40.6%)
Total	**2,964 (52.2%)**	**2,710 (47.8%)**

SOURCE—*Newport Mercury*, November 26, 1836.

South Carolina

Electors chosen by the legislature

Tennessee

County	Van Buren (D)	White (W)
Anderson	81 (26.8%)	221 (73.2%)
Bedford	1,614 (51.8%)	1,500 (48.2%)
Benton	153 (61.7%)	95 (38.3%)
Bledsoe	15 (6.3%)	223 (93.7%)
Blount	153 (21.3%)	564 (78.7%)
Campbell	147 (48.4%)	157 (51.6%)
Carroll	202 (22.3%)	802 (77.7%)
Carter	46 (8.5%)	495 (91.5%)
Claiborne	90 (21.5%)	329 (78.5%)
Cocke	7 (2.2%)	309 (97.8%)
Davidson	985 (42.5%)	1,334 (57.5%)
Dickson	426 (67.7%)	203 (32.3%)
Dyer	55 (27.4%)	146 (72.6%)
Fayette	879 (49.8%)	886 (50.2%)
Fentress	7 (4.0%)	166 (96.0%)
Franklin	1,199 (72.8%)	448 (27.2%)
Gibson	152 (17.8%)	702 (82.2%)
Giles	796 (46.7%)	908 (53.3%)
Grainger	16 (2.6%)	601 (97.4%)
Greene	724 (51.0%)	695 (49.0%)
Hamilton	158 (41.9%)	215 (58.1%)
Hardeman	531 (53.6%)	459 (46.4%)
Hardin	141 (35.9%)	252 (64.1%)
Hawkins	481 (38.4%)	770 (61.6%)
Haywood	268 (32.8%)	551 (67.2%)
Henderson	87 (9.5%)	831 (90.5%)
Henry	498 (38.2%)	645 (61.8%)
Hickman	621 (80.6%)	149 (19.4%)
Humphreys	175 (58.5%)	124 (41.5%)
Jackson	263 (27.0%)	710 (73.0%)
Jefferson	23 (96.2%)	577 (96.2%)
Johnson	24 (12.4%)	169 (87.6%)
Knox	86 (8.2%)	965 (91.8%)
Lawrence	272 (54.4%)	228 (45.6%)
Lincoln	1,479 (66.3%)	752 (33.7%)
McMinn	428 (34.2%)	824 (65.8%)
McNairy	152 (28.9%)	374 (71.1%)
Madison	169 (13.2%)	1,111 (86.8%)
Marion	170 (37.2%)	287 (56.8%)
Maury	1,997 (62.3%)	1,210 (37.7%)
Meigs	106 (39.4%)	163 (60.6%)
Monroe	288 (33.8%)	563 (66.2%)
Montgomery	467 (38.5%)	745 (61.5%)
Morgan	3 (3.4%)	85 (96.6%)
Obion	105 (39.0%)	164 (61.0%)
Overton	557 (69.0%)	250 (31.0%)
Perry	120 (21.9%)	427 (78.1%)
Rhea	63 (18.9%)	271 (81.1%)
Roane	110 (19.3%)	460 (80.7%)
Robertson	609 (41.4%)	862 (58.6%)
Rutherford	1,000 (45.9%)	1,179 (54.1%)
Sevier	2 (0.8%)	153 (99.2%)
Shelby	310 (38.8%)	488 (61.2%)
Smith	332 (20.4%)	1,296 (79.6%)
Stewart	402 (70.4%)	169 (29.6%)
Sullivan	934 (75.6%)	302 (24.4%)
Sumner	1,160 (60.8%)	748 (39.2%)
Tipton	331 (48.9%)	346 (51.1%)
Warren	1,172 (56.7%)	394 (43.3%)
Washington	760 (63.4%)	439 (36.6%)
Wayne	155 (36.3%)	272 (63.7%)
Weakley	311 (55.6%)	248 (44.4%)
White	100 (11.8%)	750 (88.2%)
Williamson	402 (21.2%)	1,491 (78.8%)
Wilson	553 (25.6%)	1,610 (74.4%)
Total	**26,122 (42.1%)**	**35,862 (57.9%)**
	*(26,120)	*(35,962)

*Stated totals.

*Bradley   49 (45.4%)   59 (54.6%)

*The vote of Bradley County was not included in the above. The returns were located in the manuscript returns at the Tennessee state archives. The document indicated that they did not arrive at the capitol until December 2, 1836.

SOURCE—(Nashville) *Republican*, November 24, 1836.

Vermont

County	Van Buren (D)	Harrison (W)
Addison	939 (35.8%)	1,684 (64.2%)
Bennington	1,090 (46.4%)	1,260 (53.6%)
Caledonia	1,028 (42.2%)	1,410 (57.8%)
Chittenden	1,062 (43.8%)	1,360 (56.2%)
Essex	192 (53.9%)	164 (46.1%)
Franklin	970 (50.5%)	949 (49.5%)
Grand Isle	148 (38.2%)	239 (61.8%)
Orange	1,641 (45.0%)	2,003 (55.0%)
Orleans	873 (44.7%)	1,081 (55.3%)
Rutland	1,271 (31.5%)	2,769 (68.5%)
Washington	1,927 (50.2%)	1,913 (49.8%)
Windham	1,458 (39.1%)	2,271 (60.9%)
Windsor	1,438 (27.0%)	3,891 (73.0%)
Total	**14,037 (40.1%)**	**20,994 (59.9%)**

SOURCE—Manuscript returns.

Virginia

County	Van Buren (D)	White (W)
Accomack	30 (4.6%)	617 (95.4%)
Albemarle	676 (56.3%)	524 (43.7%)
Alleghany	153 (83.6%)	30 (16.4%)
Amelia	180 (68.4%)	83 (31.6%)
Amherst	255 (50.9%)	246 (49.1%)
Augusta	302 (26.9%)	821 (73.1%)
Bath	206 (64.4%)	114 (35.6%)
Bedford	482 (48.5%)	511 (51.5%)
Berkeley	260 (40.6%)	380 (59.4%)
Botetourt	799 (81.5%)	181 (18.5%)
Brooke	413 (69.5%)	181 (30.5%)
Brunswick	258 (59.3%)	177 (40.7%)
Buckingham	468 (61.3%)	296 (38.7%)
Braxton	42 (73.7%)	15 (16.3%)
Cabell	206 (51.8%)	192 (48.2%)
Campbell	477 (49.9%)	478 (50.1%)
Caroline	317 (59.1%)	219 (40.9%)
Charles City	31 (23.1%)	103 (76.9%)
Charlotte	332 (57.5%)	245 (42.5%)
Chesterfield	353 (59.2%)	243 (40.8%)
Clarke	138 (57.5%)	102 (42.5%)
Culpeper	242 (40.8%)	251 (59.2%)
Cumberland	216 (47.3%)	241 (52.7%)
Dinwiddie	161 (48.9%)	168 (51.1%)
Elizabeth City	28 (26.2%)	79 (73.8%)
Essex	87 (40.1%)	130 (59.9%)
Fairfax	176 (43.3%)	230 (56.7%)
Fauquier	363 (45.8%)	429 (54.2%)
Fayette	136 (51.3%)	129 (48.7%)
Fluvanna	300 (84.3%)	56 (15.7%)
Franklin	530 (60.4%)	348 (39.6%)
Frederick	518 (64.8%)	281 (35.2%)
Giles	254 (61.5%)	159 (38.5%)
Gloucester	126 (41.6%)	177 (58.4%)
Goochland	282 (80.8%)	67 (19.2%)
Grayson	377 (88.3%)	50 (11.7%)
Greenbrier	212 (36.4%)	371 (63.6%)
Greensville	171 (62.6%)	102 (37.4%)
Halifax	732 (80.0%)	183 (20.0%)
Hampshire	407 (50.7%)	396 (49.3%)
Hanover	386 (59.0%)	268 (41.0%)
Hardy	137 (32.5%)	285 (67.5%)
Harrison	601 (71.0%)	246 (29.0%)
Henrico	246 (46.2%)	287 (53.8%)
Henry	213 (47.2%)	238 (52.8%)
Isle of Wight	253 (83.8%)	49 (16.2%)
Jackson	152 (57.4%)	113 (42.6%)
James City	4 (3.5%)	109 (96.5%)
Jefferson	269 (38.7%)	400 (61.3%)
Kanawha	228 (31.4%)	497 (68.6%)
King & Queen	275 (58.0%)	199 (42.0%)
King George	52 (26.0%)	148 (74.0%)
King William	185 (75.2%)	61 (24.8%)
Lancaster	76 (45.0%)	93 (55.0%)
Lee	330 (84.2%)	62 (15.8%)
Lewis	243 (62.8%)	144 (37.2%)
Logan	157 (73.4%)	57 (26.6%)
Loudoun	254 (21.4%)	935 (78.6%)
Louisa	458 (79.8%)	116 (20.2%)
Lunenburg	202 (60.5%)	132 (39.5%)
Madison	307 (90.6%)	32 (9.4%)
Marshall	297 (56.5%)	229 (43.5%)
Mason	170 (45.5%)	204 (54.5%)
Mathews	131 (67.2%)	64 (32.8%)
Mecklenburg	420 (67.1%)	206 (32.9%)
Middlesex	96 (60.8%)	62 (39.2%)
Monongalia	681 (68.8%)	309 (31.2%)
Monroe	358 (60.6%)	223 (39.4%)
Montgomery	389 (70.4%)	163 (29.6%)
Morgan	100 (68.5%)	46 (31.5%)
Nansemond	76 (29.1%)	185 (70.9%)
Nelson	249 (67.8%)	118 (32.2%)
New Kent	57 (34.5%)	108 (65.5%)
Nicholas	53 (30.8%)	119 (69.2%)
Norfolk	163 (33.7%)	320 (66.3%)
Northampton	6 (2.1%)	284 (97.9%)
Northumberland	185 (70.6%)	77 (29.4%)
Nottoway	174 (71.3%)	70 (28.7%)
Ohio	239 (30.8%)	536 (69.2%)
Orange	386 (64.0%)	217 (36.0%)
Page	247 (93.2%)	18 (6.8%)
Patrick	294 (62.4%)	177 (37.6%)
Pendleton	382 (63.8%)	217 (36.2%)
Pittsylvania	529 (45.2%)	641 (54.8%)
Pocahontas	85 (75.2%)	28 (24.8%)
Powhatan	176 (52.2%)	161 (47.8%)
Preston	300 (65.8%)	156 (34.2%)
Prince Edward	273 (55.8%)	216 (44.2%)
Princess Anne	56 (22.3%)	195 (77.8%)
Prince George	154 (68.4%)	71 (31.6%)
Prince William	232 (70.7%)	96 (29.3%)
Randolph	160 (35.3%)	293 (64.7%)
Rappahannock	196 (54.9%)	171 (45.1%)
Richmond	108 (48.4%)	115 (51.6%)
Rockbridge	379 (48.2%)	408 (51.8%)
Rockingham	792 (86.0%)	129 (14.0%)
Russell	385 (97.7%)	9 (2.3%)
Scott	316 (96.9%)	10 (3.1%)
Shenandoah	735 (93.4%)	52 (6.6%)
Smyth	229 (75.1%)	76 (24.9%)
Southampton	192 (50.9%)	185 (49.1%)
Spotsylvania	282 (57.7%)	207 (42.3%)
Stafford	178 (54.6%)	148 (45.4%)
Surry	108 (72.5%)	41 (27.5%)
Sussex	213 (82.2%)	46 (17.8%)
Tazewell	259 (99.2%)	2 (0.8%)
Tyler	223 (60.9%)	143 (39.1%)
Warwick	5 (10.9%)	41 (89.1%)
Warren	163 (74.4%)	56 (25.6%)
Washington	608 (89.7%)	70 (10.3%)
Westmoreland	52 (25.7%)	150 (74.3%)
Wood	249 (44.1%)	315 (55.9%)
Wythe	369 (76.7%)	112 (23.3%)
York	3 (5.0%)	57 (95.0%)
Norfolk (boro)	98 (29.5%)	234 (70.5%)
Petersburg (boro)	125 (40.6%)	183 (59.4%)

Richmond (city)	138 (23.3%)	455 (76.7%)
Williamsburg (town)	4 (5.6%)	68 (94.4%)
Total[7]	**30,251 (56.4%)**	23,368 (43.6%)
	*(30,261)	

Stated totals.

SOURCE—(Richmond) *Enquirer*, December 6, 1836.

NOTES

1. The electoral vote for vice president was Richard Johnson (D) 147, Francis Granger (W) 77, John Tyler (W) 47, and William Smith (D) 23. No candidate having received a majority of the electoral vote, the Senate elected Johnson vice president on the first ballot: 33 for Johnson, 17 for Granger.

2. The Whigs held no national convention but through a series of state nominations ran essentially a northern and a southern ticket in addition to Daniel Webster's candidacy in Massachusetts. This was their first presidential campaign. But the term Whig is really a fiction as a single national name (see Illinois returns). In addition, in Georgia, White was the candidate of the States Rights Party; in Tennessee he really was the anti–Van Buren candidate and the term Whig was not used there. In several other states, the term Whig was often part of a hyphenated term used with States Rights. See: Richard P. McCormick, *The Second American Party System*, Chapel Hill, NC: University of North Carolina Press, 1966; Paul Murray, *The Whig Party in Georgia, 1825–1853,* Chapel Hill, NC: University of North Carolina Press, 1948; Michael F. Holt, *The Rise and Fall of the American Whig Party*, New York: Oxford University Press, 1999; Jonathan M. Atkins, *Parties, Politics, and the Sectional Conflict in Tennessee 1832–1861,* Knoxville, TN: University of Tennessee Press, 1997.

3. The vote of Michigan, similar to Missouri's in 1820, was challenged on the grounds that Michigan was not yet a state. As in the Missouri case, the returns were read both with and without Michigan's vote, thus the matter was never resolved.

4. The Whig vote broken down by candidate was Harrison (541,190, 36.14%) (73), White (138,250, 9.23%) (26), Webster (40,149, 2.68%) (14) Illinois (15,240, 1.02%).

5. According to Pease, three of the five Whig electors agreed to support either Harrison or White depending upon who stood a better chance of being elected. There is no indication who the other two electors supported. Pease lists the Whig slate as "Union anti–Van Buren." Peterson places the Whig vote under White's totals. See: Theodore Pease (ed.), *Illinois Election Returns 1818–1848*, Springfield, IL: Illinois State Historical Society Library, 1923; and Svend Petersen, *A Statistical History of the American Presidential Elections*, New York, NY: 1963.

6. There is no one set of definitive returns. The (New York) *Albany Argus*, December 13, 1836, reports, as official, returns from 21 counties. Most of these returns were also found in the files of the state archives and are largely the same. The *Argus* vote is the same as the returns in the archives if you combine the vote in the archives files under different spellings, they add to the returns listed in the *Argus*. However returns for Cass and Wayne counties were reported in the *Argus* but not found in the archives, they are included here. Returns for St. Clair and Van Buren counties were found only in the archives file and are listed separately from the other county returns because of the nature of the data. The St. Clair vote is but 93 while the vote for other officials elected at the same time exceeded 900. In addition the vote for electors was found on a page as part of the returns for state senator from the 5th District. The Van Buren vote was only from Lafayette township. The document also indicated that the vote from the entire county was suspect and was sent to the governor after the date for counting the vote. The full county vote was not found.

The archives' files are only by county and lack a state total as well as a county summary page. Interestingly many editions of the *Michigan Manual* state that there are no records of this election and cite the *Whig Almanac, 1841* as the basis for returns. *Presidential Ballots* in turn used the *Manual*.

The state totals used here are the added returns of the counties and the totals as listed in the *Argus* are in parentheses below the figures.

7. The following votes were rejected by the state:

County	Van Buren (D)	White (W)
Floyd	293 (92.7%)	23 (7.3%)
Monongalia (part)	231	21
Pocahontas (part)	60	0

1 8 4 0

National Summary[1]

(electoral vote in parentheses)

State	William H. Harrison (W)		Martin Van Buren (D)		James G. Birney (Lty)
Alabama	28,515 (45.62%)		33,996 (54.38%)	(7)	
Arkansas	4,664 (43.66%)		6,018 (56.34%)	(3)	
Connecticut	31,597 (55.50%)	(8)	25,282 (44.40%)		57 (0.10%)
Delaware	5,967 (55.05%)	(3)	4,872 (44.95%)		
Georgia	40,246 (55.77%)	(11)	31,922 (44.23%)		
Illinois	45,576 (48.91%)		47,443 (50.92%)	(5)	160 (0.17%)
Indiana	65,305 (55.82%)	(9)	51,691 (44.15%)		30 (0.03%)
Kentucky	58,489 (64.20%)	(15)	32,616 (35.80%)		
Louisiana	11,297 (59.73%)	(5)	7,617 (40.27%)		
Maine	46,613 (50.12%)	(10)	46,200 (49.67%)		194 (0.21%)
Maryland	33,533 (53.83%)	(10)	28,759 (46.17%)		
Massachusetts	72,532 (57.48%)	(14)	52,047 (41.24%)		*1,618 (1.28%)
Michigan	22,933 (51.71%)	(3)	21,096 (47.57%)		321 (0.72%)

State	William H. Harrison (W)		Martin Van Buren (D)		James G. Birney (Lty)
Mississippi	19,515 (53.43%)	(4)	17,010 (46.57%)		
Missouri	22,971 (43.64%)		29,668 (56.36%)	(4)	
New Hampshire	26,294 (44.45%)		32,744 (55.36%)	(7)	114 (0.19%)
New Jersey	33,351 (51.74%)	(8)	31,034 (48.15%)		69 (0.11%)
New York	225,817 (51.19%)	(42)	212,528 (48.18%)		2,799 (0.63%)
North Carolina	46,376 (57.86%)	(15)	33,779 (42.14%)		
Ohio	148,141 (54.10%)	(21)	124,770 (45.57%)		903 (0.33%)
Pennsylvania	144,023 (49.98%)	(30)	143,784 (49.90%)		343 (0.12%)
Rhode Island	5,213 (61.37%)	(4)	3,263 (38.41%)		19 (0.22%)
South Carolina	electors chosen by the legislature (11)				
Tennessee	60,391 (55.57%)	(15)	48,289 (44.43%)		
Vermont	32,440 (63.90%)	(7)	18,007 (35.47%)		319 (0.63%)
Virginia	42,501 (49.19%)		43,893 (50.81%)	(23)	
Total	**1,274,304 (52.88%) (234)**		**1,128,348 (46.83%) (60)**		**6,946 (0.29%)**

See Massachusetts returns for an explanation of the vote.

Alabama

County	Harrison (W)	Van Buren (D)
Autauga	591 (50.8%)	574 (49.2%)
Baldwin	137 (53.7%)	118 (46.3%)
Barbour	1,028 (61.6%)	642 (38.6%)
Benton	482 (27.9%)	1,248 (72.1%)
Bibb	583 (54.9%)	478 (45.1%)
Blount	105 (12.7%)	720 (87.3%)
Butler	710 (72.2%)	274 (27.8%)
Chambers	1,039 (60.5%)	678 (39.5%)
Cherokee	377 (33.2%)	759 (66.8%)
Clarke	230 (27.8%)	596 (72.2%)
Conecuh	541 (72.2%)	208 (27.8%)
Coosa	361 (40.1%)	539 (59.9%)
Covington	188 (74.3%)	65 (25.7%)
Dale	367 (35.3%)	672 (64.7%)
Dallas	1,024 (59.8%)	689 (40.2%)
De Kalb	157 (16.9%)	771 (83.1%)
Fayette	203 (19.9%)	819 (80.1%)
Franklin	637 (41.4%)	903 (58.6%)
Greene	1,366 (63.4%)	790 (36.6%)
Henry	325 (45.4%)	391 (54.6%)
Jackson	57 (2.6%)	2,147 (97.4%)
Jefferson	315 (35.1%)	582 (64.9%)
Lauderdale	645 (39.5%)	987 (60.5%)
Lawrence	649 (45.4%)	782 (54.6%)
Limestone	356 (28.4%)	897 (71.6%)
Lowndes	896 (63.2%)	522 (36.8%)
Macon	731 (68.3%)	340 (31.7%)
Madison	393 (16.5%)	1,985 (83.5%)
Marengo	842 (58.6%)	595 (41.4%)
Marion	196 (26.8%)	535 (73.2%)
Marshall	142 (13.3%)	924 (86.7%)
Mobile	1,481 (56.9%)	1,121 (43.1%)
Monroe	646 (64.2%)	361 (35.8%)
Montgomery	1,134 (58.3%)	812 (41.7%)
Morgan	358 (30.8%)	804 (69.2%)
Perry	973 (54.1%)	825 (45.9%)
Pickens	1,062 (57.7%)	779 (42.3%)
Pike	653 (51.0%)	627 (49.0%)
Randolph	279 (34.7%)	524 (65.3%)
Russell	691 (63.0%)	406 (37.0%)
St. Clair	42 (5.8%)	679 (94.2%)
Shelby	573 (58.5%)	407 (41.5%)
Sumter	1,308 (52.6%)	1,180 (47.4%)
Talladega	669 (63.0%)	788 (37.0%)
Tallapoosa	412 (48.6%)	436 (51.4%)
Tuscaloosa	1,276 (57.6%)	938 (42.4%)
Walker	244 (39.9%)	367 (60.1%)
Washington	263 (48.8%)	276 (51.2%)
Wilcox	778 (64.1%)	436 (35.9%)
Total	**28,515 (45.6%)**	**33,996 (54.4%)**

SOURCE—Manuscript returns.

Arkansas

No returns for Franklin and Searcy counties

County	Harrison (W)	Van Buren (D)
Arkansas	120 (50.5%)	78 (49.5%)
Benton	72 (22.7%)	245 (77.3%)
Carroll	68 (23.4%)	223 (76.6%)
Chicot	191 (81.6%)	43 (18.4%)
Clarke	119 (56.8%)	87 (43.2%)
Conway	177 (46.8%)	201 (53.2%)
Crittenden	95 (57.2%)	71 (42.8%)
Desha	173 (68.9%)	78 (31.1%)
Hempstead	210 (45.6%)	251 (54.4%)
Hot Spring	55 (34.8%)	103 (65.2%)
Independence	370 (65.1%)	198 (34.9%)
Izard	79 (31.2%)	174 (68.8%)
Jackson	107 (42.8%)	143 (57.2%)
Jefferson	173 (61.3%)	109 (38.7%)
Johnson	160 (33.3%)	321 (66.7%)
Lafayette	43 (63.2%)	25 (36.8%)
Lawrence	138 (39.2%)	214 (60.8%)
Madison	135 (54.9%)	253 (45.1%)
Mississippi	90 (55.2%)	73 (44.8%)
Phillips	238 (50.9%)	247 (49.1%)
Pike	23 (20.9%)	87 (79.1%)
Poinsett	4 (3.0%)	130 (97.0%)
Pope	183 (41.3%)	263 (58.7%)
Pulaski	607 (54.8%)	500 (45.2%)
Randolph	45 (15.2%)	252 (84.8%)
St. Francis	82 (22.1%)	216 (77.9%)
Saline	142 (51.3%)	135 (48.7%)
Scott	32 (22.1%)	112 (77.9%)
Sevier	76 (27.8%)	197 (72.2%)
Union	124 (41.2%)	173 (58.8%)
Van Buren	29 (16.2%)	150 (83.8%)
Washington	422 (40.5%)	620 (59.5%)
White	82 (64.0%)	46 (36.0%)
Total	**4,664 (43.7%)**	**6,018 (56.3%)**
	(4,363)	***(6,019)***

County	Harrison		Van Buren	
**Crawford	335	(49.1%)	347	(50.9%)
**Greene	18	(14.6%)	105	(85.4%)
**Marion	21	(15.8%)	121	(84.2%)
**Monroe	124	(73.8%)	44	(26.2%)
Total	5,201		6,635	

*Stated totals listed in parentheses.

**Not listed in the official returns. They are listed in the December 2, 1840, table but not in the official statement signed by Governor Archibald Yell, dated November 21, 1840, and published in the Gazette on December 9, 1840.

SOURCES—(Little Rock) *Arkansas Gazette*, December 2 and 9, 1840; W. Dean Burnham, *Presidential Ballots, 1836–1892*, New York, NY: Arno Press, 1976, pp. 276–292; and *Political Textbook for 1860*, New York, NY: Tribune Association, 1860, pp. 234–5.

Connecticut

County	Harrison		Van Buren		Birney (Lty)	
Fairfield	4,870	(55.8%)	3,862	(44.2%)	0	
Hartford	6,215	(58.0%)	4,495	(42.0%)	2	(0.2%)
Litchfield	4,542	(54.4%)	3,784	(45.3%)	19	(2.3%)
Middlesex	2,276	(49.81%)	2,274	(49.77%)	19	(4.2%)
New Haven	5,100	(56.0%)	4,013	(44.0%)	1	(0.1%)
New London	3,814	(54.8%)	3,147	(45.2%)	3	(0.4%)
Tolland	1,990	(56.7%)	1,509	(43.0%)	12	(0.3%)
Windham	2,790	(55.9)	2,198	(44.1%)	1	(0.2%)
Total	**31,597**	**(55.5%)**	**25,282**	**(44.4%)**	**57**	**(1.0%)**
	*(31,598)					

*Stated totals.

SOURCE— Manuscript returns.

Delaware

County	Harrison		Van Buren	
Kent	1,593	(59.3%)	1,095	(40.7%)
New Castle	2,321	(51.4%)	2,195	(48.6%)
Sussex	2,053	(56.5%)	1,582	(43.5%)
Total	**5,967**	**(55.1%)**	**4,872**	**(44.9%)**

SOURCE— *Governor's Register, 1840.*

Georgia

County	Harrison		Van Buren	
Baker	182	(47.2%)	204	(52.8%)
Baldwin	731	(58.0%)	530	(42.0%)
Bibb	758	(50.3%)	748	(49.7%)
Bryan	80	(78.4%)	22	(21.6%)
Bulloch	25	(6.1%)	384	(93.9%)
Burke	593	(74.5%)	203	(25.5%)
Butts	185	(35.3%)	339	(64.7%)
Camden	166	(46.5%)	191	(53.5%)
Campbell	163	(27.6%)	427	(72.4%)
Carroll	276	(39.3%)	437	(60.7%)
Cass	561	(44.3%)	705	(55.7%)
Chatham	590	(47.7%)	647	(52.3%)
Chattooga	186	(48.1%)	201	(51.9%)
Cherokee	369	(47.0%)	416	(53.0%)
Clark	617	(66.0%)	318	(34.0%)
Cobb	428	(39.4%)	658	(60.6%)
Columbia	470	(67.8%)	223	(32.2%)
Coweta	792	(50.8%)	768	(49.2%)
Crawford	435	(48.7%)	458	(51.3%)
Dade	38	(18.9%)	163	(81.1%)
Decatur	432	(68.0%)	203	(32.0%)
De Kalb	665	(46.7%)	759	(53.3%)
Dooly	226	(43.3%)	296	(56.7%)
Early	258	(46.8%)	293	(53.2%)
Effingham	158	(76.2%)	55	(23.8%)
Elbert	957	(90.1%)	105	(9.9%)
Emanuel	80	(41.5%)	113	(58.5%)
Fayette	337	(38.3%)	542	(61.7%)
Floyd	275	(50.7%)	267	(49.3%)
Forsyth	348	(43.2%)	457	(56.8%)
Franklin	353	(37.8%)	581	(62.2%)
Gilmer	127	(43.6%)	164	(56.4%)
Glynn	88	(86.3%)	14	(13.7%)
Greene	889	(87.6%)	126	(12.4%)
Gwinnett	745	(54.4%)	624	(45.6%)
Habersham	290	(27.6%)	761	(72.4%)
Hall	445	(46.9%)	504	(53.1%)
Hancock	481	(66.7%)	240	(33.3%)
Harris	853	(74.5%)	292	(25.5%)
Heard	315	(47.2%)	352	(52.8%)
Henry	931	(54.0%)	793	(46.0%)
Houston	667	(53.8%)	572	(46.2%)
Irwin	59	(32.8%)	121	(67.2%)
Jackson	572	(51.3%)	542	(48.7%)
Jasper	495	(50.0%)	495	(50.0%)
Jefferson	458	(83.7%)	89	(16.3%)
Jones	461	(56.7%)	352	(43.3%)
Laurens	556	(99.3%)	4	(0.7%)
Lee	304	(79.8%)	77	(20.2%)
Liberty	144	(64.9%)	78	(35.1%)
Lincoln	317	(72.0%)	123	(28.0%)
Lowndes	422	(82.4%)	90	(17.6%)
Lumpkin	355	(31.1%)	786	(68.9%)
Macon	369	(54.9%)	303	(45.1%)
Madison	357	(55.5%)	286	(44.5%)
Marion	404	(67.7%)	193	(32.3%)
McIntosh	119	(46.9%)	135	(53.1%)
Meriwether	755	(51.8%)	702	(48.2%)
Monroe	796	(54.1%)	675	(45.9%)
Montgomery	167	(95.4%)	8	(4.6%)
Morgan	478	(63.1%)	280	(36.9%)
Murray	273	(37.7%)	452	(62.3%)
Muscogee	1,044	(56.3%)	811	(43.7%)
Newton	988	(73.8%)	351	(26.2%)
Oglethorpe	654	(65.9%)	127	(34.1%)
Paulding	227	(52.3%)	207	(47.7%)
Pike	560	(47.3%)	624	(52.7%)
Pulaski	241	(46.7%)	275	(53.3%)
Putnam	468	(60.2%)	310	(39.8%)
Rabun	30	(12.4%)	212	(87.6%)
Randolph	509	(49.5%)	519	(50.5%)
Richmond	939	(69.8%)	407	(30.2%)
Scriven	180	(47.5%)	199	(52.5%)
Stewart	882	(58.0%)	639	(42.0%)
Sumter	449	(71.8%)	176	(28.2%)
Talbot	912	(53.1%)	807	(46.9%)
Taliaferro	431	(90.2%)	47	(9.8%)
Tatnall	253	(90.0%)	28	(10.0%)
Telfair	203	(79.3%)	53	(20.7%)
Thomas	426	(87.7%)	60	(12.3%)
Troup	1,071	(76.4%)	330	(23.6%)
Twiggs	411	(52.4%)	373	(47.6%)
Union	107	(22.9%)	360	(77.1%)
Upson	632	(68.3%)	293	(31.7%)
Walker	387	(41.7%)	541	(58.3%)
Walton	516	(45.5%)	619	(54.5%)
Ware	215	(86.0%)	35	(14.0%)
Warren	552	(69.4%)	243	(30.6%)
Washington	593	(56.7%)	453	(43.3%)
Wayne	74	(59.2%)	51	(40.8%)

Wilkes	438 (55.4%)	352 (44.6%)	
Wilkinson	428 (47.5%)	474 (52.5%)	
Total[2]	**40,246 (55.8%)**	**31,922 (44.2%)**	
	*(40,261)	*(31,921)	

Stated totals.

*Appling	93 (60.4)	61 (39.6)	

Not included in the official returns.

Sources—(Milledgeville) *Southern Journal,* November 24, 1860; *Whig Almanac 1844,* pp. 62–3; W. Dean Burnham, *Presidential Ballots 1836–1892,* reprint edition, New York, NY: Arno Press, 1976, pp. 332–62; and (New York) *Log Cabin,* January 23, 1841.

Illinois

County	Van Buren (D)	Harrison (W)	Birney (Lty)
Adams	1,352 (44.9%)	1,617 (53.7%)	42 (1.4%)
Alexander	424 (58.6%)	299 (41.4%)	
Bond	551 (51.8%)	513 (48.2%)	
Boone	222 (50.2%)	220 (49.8%)	
Brown	434 (59.0%)	301 (41.0%)	
Bureau	279 (38.4%)	434 (59.8%)	13 (1.8%)
Calhoun	133 (38.4%)	213 (61.6%)	
Carroll	69 (22.0%)	244 (78.0%)	
Cass	315 (44.3%)	397 (55.7%)	
Champaign	141 (47.8%)	154 (52.2%)	
Christian	147 (62.3%)	89 (37.7%)	
Clark	611 (47.8%)	667 (52.2%)	
Clay	338 (60.8%)	218 (39.2%)	
Clinton	417 (56.1%)	326 (43.9%)	
Coles	695 (38.5%)	1,109 (61.5%)	
Cook	1,989 (65.8%)	1,034 (34.2%)	1 (0.03%)
Crawford	392 (48.2%)	421 (51.8%)	
De Kalb	197 (53.2%)	172 (46.5%)	
De Witt	316 (51.9%)	293 (48.1%)	
Du Page	373 (46.4%)	428 (53.2%)	3 (0.04%)
Edgar	720 (47.9%)	783 (52.1%)	
Edwards	212 (40.5%)	311 (59.5%)	
Effingham	207 (79.9%)	52 (20.1%)	
Fayette	645 (59.3%)	442 (40.7%)	
Franklin	542 (88.4%)	71 (11.6%)	
Fulton	1,347 (51.8%)	1,253 (48.2%)	1 (0.04%)
Gallatin	1,286 (72.0%)	500 (28.0%)	
Greene	1,175 (57.4%)	870 (42.5%)	3 (0.01%)
Hamilton	557 (81.6%)	126 (28.4%)	
Hancock	624 (31.6%)	1,352 (68.4%)	
Hardin	132 (46.2%)	154 (53.8%)	
Henry	86 (34.3%)	162 (64.5%)	3 (1.2%)
Iroquois	175 (53.2%)	154 (46.8%)	
Jackson	337 (61.6%)	210 (38.4%)	
Jasper	178 (69.5%)	78 (30.5%)	
Jefferson	727 (77.6%)	210 (22.4%)	
Jersey	360 (40.5%)	517 (58.2%)	11 (1.2%)
Jo Daviess	680 (38.7%)	1,079 (61.3%)	
Johnson	440 (80.1%)	109 (19.9%)	
Kane	774 (48.8%)	810 (51.1%)	1 (0.01%)
Knox	541 (41.8%)	740 (57.2%)	13 (1.0%)
Lake	267 (48.7%)	281 (51.3%)	
La Salle	1,638 (60.1%)	1,080 (39.6%)	6 (0.2%)
Lawrence	597 (46.9%)	676 (53.1%)	
Lee	230 (48.3%)	241 (50.6%)	5 (1.1%)
Livingston	78 (47.9%)	85 (52.1%)	
Logan	167 (39.1%)	260 (60.9%)	
McDonough	428 (47.6%)	472 (52.4%)	
McHenry	271 (43.9%)	346 (56.1%)	
McLean	531 (43.7%)	683 (56.2%)	2 (0.02%)
Macon	377 (60.1%)	250 (39.9%)	
Macoupin	812 (56.2%)	632 (43.8%)	

County	Van Buren (D)	Harrison (W)	Birney (Lty)
Madison	1,184 (41.0%)	1,704 (58.9%)	3 (0.01%)
Marion	573 (76.7%)	174 (23.3%)	
Marshall	183 (46.7%)	209 (53.3%)	
Menard	374 (46.3%)	434 (53.7%)	
Mercer	193 (38.0%)	315 (62.0%)	
Monroe	563 (60.3%)	370 (39.7%)	
Montgomery	523 (62.7%)	311 (37.3%)	
Morgan	1,293 (45.7%)	1,533 (54.2%)	5 (0.2%)
Ogle	266 (35.0%)	491 (64.5%)	4 (0.5%)
Peoria	767 (50.5%)	744 (48.9%)	9 (0.6%)
Perry	331 (65.5%)	174 (34.5%)	
Pike	1,037 (47.4%)	1,149 (52.6%)	
Pope	268 (40.7%)	391 (59.3%)	
Putnam	151 (35.7%)	259 (61.2%)	13 (3.1%)
Randolph	817 (53.3%)	715 (46.7%)	
Rock Island	224 (34.5%)	426 (65.5%)	
Saint Clair	1,783 (64.3%)	989 (35.7%)	
Sangamon	1,249 (38.4%)	2,000 (61.6%)	
Schuyler	611 (45.5%)	732 (54.5%)	1 (0.01%)
Scott	575 (45.6%)	685 (54.4%)	
Shelby	751 (64.8%)	408 (35.2%)	
Stark	154 (45.2%)	187 (54.8%)	
Stephenson	241 (39. 4%)	371 (60.6%)	
Tazewell	661 (35.9%)	1,181 (64.1%)	
Union	636 (89.1%)	78 (10.9%)	
Vermilion	587 (36.0%)	1,044 (64.0%)	
Wabash	254 (33.3%)	509 (66.7%)	
Warren	524 (42.4%)	711 (57.6%)	
Washington	493 (76.8%)	149 (23.2%)	
Wayne	500 (70.9%)	205 (29.1%)	
White	639 (45.4%)	770 (54.6%)	
Whiteside	236 (38.6%)	375 (61.4%)	
Will	1,367 (64.0%)	753 (35.3%)	16 (0.7%)
Williamson	578 (84.9%)	103 (15.1%)	
Winnebago	321 (28.8%)	789 (70.8%)	4 (0.4%)
Total	**47,443 (50.9%)**	**45,576 (48.9%)**	**160 (0.2%)**

Source—Theodore Pease (ed.), *Illinois Election Returns 1818–1848,* Springfield, IL: Illinois State Historical Society Library, 1923, pp. 117–8.

Indiana

County	Harrison (W)	Van Buren (D)	Birney (Lty)
Adam	193 (55.8%)	153 (44.2%)	
Allen	640 (61.9%)	394 (38.1%)	
Bartholomew	982 (58.3%)	703 (41.7%)	
Benton	26 (38.2%)	42 (61.8%)	
Blackford	77 (34.3%)	147 (65.7%)	
Boone	700 (50.5%)	686 (49.5%)	
Brown	54 (16.7%)	270 (83.3%)	
Carroll	699 (47.7%)	765 (52.3%)	
Cass	649 (63.6%)	372 (36.4%)	
Clark	1,132 (47.0%)	1,278 (53.0%)	
Clay	398 (45.0%)	487 (55.0%)	
Clinton	582 (45.7%)	698 (54.3%)	
Crawford	435 (60.8%)	281 (39.2%)	
Daviess	738 (59.2%)	509 (40.8%)	
Dearborn	1,771 (52.8%)	1,583 (47.2%)	3 (0.1%)
Decatur	1,298 (63.1%)	759 (36.9%)	
De Kalb	177 (51.2%)	169 (48.8%)	
Delaware	920 (63.4%)	531 (36.6%)	
Dubois	264 (52.5%)	239 (47.5%)	
Elkhart	640 (51.8%)	596 (48.2%)	
Fayette	1,090 (60.0%)	728 (40.0%)	
Floyd	869 (60.0%)	796 (40.0%)	
Fountain	938 (44.6%)	1,166 (55.4%)	

Franklin	1,188 (51.6%)	1,115 (48.4%)			
Fulton	241 (69.3%)	107 (30.7%)			
Gibson	788 (58.3%)	594 (41.7%)			
Grant	470 (56.4%)	364 (43.6%)			
Greene	704 (52.6%)	634 (47.4%)			
Hamilton	972 (58.6%)	688 (41.4%)			
Hancock	721 (57.3%)	537 (42.7%)			
Harrison	1,285 (59.9%)	861 (40.1%)			
Hendricks	1,190 (64.6%)	651 (35.4%)			
Henry	1,652 (66.3%)	839 (33.7%)			
Huntington	143 (44.7%)	177 (55.3%)			
Jackson	680 (48.0%)	737 (52.0%)			
Jasper	73 (43.5%)	95 (56.5%)			
Jay	283 (51.5%)	267 (48.5%)			
Jefferson	1,674 (61.9%)	1,026 (38.0%)	3	(0.1%)	
Jennings	908 (64.0%)	503 (35.4%)	8	(0.6%)	
Johnson	631 (40.0%)	948 (60.0%)			
Knox	1,077 (62.1%)	658 (37.9%)			
Kosciusko	496 (60.1%)	329 (39.9%)			
LaGrange	391 (63.5%)	225 (36.5%)			
Lake	115 (47.9%)	125 (52.1%)			
LaPorte	1,068 (62.5%)	640 (37.5%)			
Lawrence	989 (52.4%)	898 (47.6%)			
Madison	911 (59.3%)	625 (40.7%)			
Marion	1,636 (56.1%)	1,279 (43.9%)			
Marshall	154 (44.3%)	194 (55.7%)			
Martin	311 (46.0%)	366 (54.0%)			
Miami	312 (56.1%)	244 (43.9%)			
Monroe	719 (43.3%)	943 (56.7%)			
Montgomery	1,413 (53.6%)	1,222 (46.4%)			
Morgan	1,012 (54.9%)	815 (44.2%)	16	(0.9%)	
Noble	241 (51.4%)	228 (48.6%)			
Orange	708 (44.6%)	879 (55.4%)			
Owen	709 (54.0%)	604 (46.0%)			
Parke	1,360 (58.9%)	948 (41.1%)			
Perry	560 (71.7%)	221 (28.3%)			
Pike	474 (59.8%)	318 (40.2%)			
Porter	220 (53.1%)	194 (46.9%)			
Posey	706 (42.3%)	965 (57.7%)			
Pulaski	51 (45.9%)	60 (54.1%)			
Putnam	1,571 (60.0%)	1,049 (40.0%)			
Randolph	1,068 (65.9%)	553 (34.1%)			
Ripley	1,000 (61.6%)	623 (38.4%)			
Rush	1,526 (56.6%)	1,170 (43.4%)			
Saint Joseph	809 (64.8%)	440 (35.2%)			
Scott	399 (52.5%)	361 (47.5%)			
Shelby	1,016 (48.7%)	1,070 (51.3%)			
Spencer	589 (64.5%)	324 (35.5%)			
Steuben	238 (57.5%)	176 (42.5%)			
Sullivan	417 (29.1%)	1,074 (70.9%)			
Switzerland	1,023 (58.2%)	735 (41.3%)			
Tippecanoe	1,508 (55.7%)	1,200 (44.3%)			
Union	760 (55.3%)	614 (44.7%)			
Vanderburgh	628 (62.9%)	370 (37.1%)			
Vermillion	847 (56.1%)	663 (43.9%)			
Vigo	1,511 (72.2%)	583 (27.8%)			
Wabash	307 (60.8%)	198 (39.2%)			
Warren	737 (67.8%)	347 (32.2%)			
Warrick	355 (34.9%)	662 (65.1%)			
Washington	1,138 (45.2%)	1,381 (54.8%)			
Wayne	2,869 (69.5%)	1,258 (30.5%)			
Wells	131 (48.3%)	140 (51.7%)			
White	206 (58.9%)	144 (41.1%)			
Whitley	144 (50.5%)	141 (49.5%)			
Total	**65,305 (55.8%)**	**51,691 (44.2%)**	**30**	**(0.03%)**	

SOURCE—Dorothy F. Riker and Gayle Thornbrough (eds.), *Indiana Election Returns 1816–1851*, Indianapolis, IN: Indiana Historical Bureau, 1960, pp. 29–37.

Kentucky

County	Harrison (W)	Van Buren (D)
Adair	518 (57.9%)	376 (42.1%)
Allen	410 (52.1%)	377 (47.9%)
Anderson	292 (47.0%)	329 (53.0%)
Barren	1,216 (62.4%)	732 (37.6%)
Bath	605 (56.0%)	475 (44.0%)
Boone	843 (64.1%)	473 (35.9%)
Bourbon	1,126 (74.0%)	396 (26.0%)
Bracken	712 (71.8%)	279 (28.2%)
Breathitt	159 (77.9%)	45 (22.1%)
Breckinridge	989 (82.2%)	214 (17.8%)
Bullitt	465 (64.8%)	253 (35.2%)
Butler	258 (57.9%)	189 (42.1%)
Caldwell	687 (50.6%)	670 (49.4%)
Calloway	201 (16.0%)	1,055 (84.0%)
Campbell	355 (43.2%)	466 (56.8%)
Carroll	359 (62.0%)	220 (38.0%)
Carter	163 (41.7%)	228 (58.3%)
Casey	392 (84.5%)	72 (15.5%)
Christian	1,080 (64.6%)	591 (35.4%)
Clark	1,001 (83.4%)	199 (16.6%)
Clay	438 (82.8%)	91 (17.2%)
Clinton	314 (68.9%)	122 (31.1%)
Cumberland	567 (87.8%)	79 (12.2%)
Daviess	690 (61.7%)	428 (38.3%)
Edmonson	209 (60.9%)	134 (39.1%)
Estill	459 (74.8%)	155 (25.2%)
Fayette	1,435 (70.7%)	596 (29.3%)
Fleming	1,142 (70.8%)	472 (29.2%)
Floyd	233 (36.6%)	404 (73.4%)
Franklin	656 (60.2%)	434 (39.8%)
Gallatin	326 (55.4%)	262 (44.6%)
Garrard	1,026 (88.1%)	138 (11.9%)
Grant	354 (52.5%)	320 (47.5%)
Graves	304 (33.4%)	607 (66.6%)
Grayson	445 (68.4%)	206 (31.6%)
Green	766 (53.5%)	666 (46.5%)
Greenup	599 (69.1%)	268 (30.9%)
Hancock	214 (75.6%)	69 (24.4%)
Hardin	1,342 (71.5%)	524 (28.5%)
Harlan	438 (97.8%)	10 (2.2%)
Harrison	741 (51.6%)	694 (48.4%)
Hart	499 (62.2%)	303 (37.8%)
Henderson	616 (57.8%)	451 (42.2%)
Henry	807 (48.8%)	845 (51.2%)
Hickman	393 (36.5%)	684 (63.5%)
Hopkins	654 (57.6%)	481 (42.4%)
Jefferson	3,110 (64.6%)	1,707 (35.4%)
Jessamine	652 (70.5%)	273 (29.5%)
Kenton	518 (45.6%)	618 (54.4%)
Knox	690 (87.5%)	99 (12.5%)
Laurel	406 (80.9%)	96 (19.1%)
Lawrence	335 (73.1%)	123 (26.9%)
Lewis	523 (62.0%)	321 (38.0%)
Lincoln	922 (83.5%)	182 (16.5%)
Livingston	632 (56.9%)	478 (43.1%)
Logan	1,223 (85.2%)	213 (14.8%)
Madison	1,318 (77.1%)	391 (22.9%)
Marion	698 (71.6%)	277 (28.4%)
Mason	1,556 (73.4%)	564 (26.6%)
McCracken	388 (59.5%)	264 (40.5%)
Meade	646 (81.1%)	151 (18.9%)
Mercer	1,145 (54.5%)	954 (45.5%)
Monroe	478 (71.9%)	187 (28.1%)
Montgomery	625 (61.6%)	390 (38.4%)
Morgan	260 (45.1%)	318 (54.9%)
Muhlenberg	652 (74.9%)	219 (25.1%)
Nelson	1,208 (78.9%)	324 (21.1%)

Nicholas	627 (56.1%)	491 (43.9%)
Ohio	552 (68.7%)	252 (31.3%)
Oldham	465 (49.2%)	480 (50.8%)
Owen	454 (45.6%)	541 (54.4%)
Pendleton	257 (39.7%)	390 (60.3%)
Perry	185 (80.4%)	45 (19.6%)
Pike	170 (58.2%)	122 (41.8%)
Pulaski	738 (67.6%)	354 (32.4%)
Rockcastle	467 (95.5%)	22 (4.5%)
Russell	504 (89.8%)	77 (10.2%)
Scott	729 (47.8%)	797 (52.2%)
Shelby	1,570 (73.4%)	568 (26.6%)
Simpson	453 (71.8%)	178 (28.2%)
Spencer	472 (61.1%)	300 (38.9%)
Todd	705 (78.1%)	198 (21.9%)
Trigg	455 (49.9%)	457 (50.1%)
Trimble	284 (41.3%)	404 (58.7%)
Union	484 (53.6%)	419 (46.4%)
Warren	997 (69.5%)	437 (30.5%)
Washington	697 (67.3%)	338 (32.7%)
Wayne	579 (77.4%)	169 (22.6%)
Whitley	439 (89.4%)	52 (10.6%)
Woodford	723 (71.1%)	294 (28.9%)
Total	**58,489 (64.2%)**	**32,616 (35.8%)**

SOURCE—(Frankfort) *Commonwealth*, November 24, 1840.

Louisiana

No returns from Caldwell, Claiborne, and Lafayette parishes.

Parish	Harrison (W)	Van Buren (D)
Ascension	218 (50.0%)	218 (50.0%)
Assumption	289 (45.9%)	340 (54.1%)
Avoyelles	250 (54.9%)	205 (45.1%)
Carroll	96 (45.7%)	114 (54.3%)
Catahoula	259 (52.9%)	231 (47.1%)
Concordia	269 (70.4%)	113 (29.6%)
East Baton Rouge	324 (51.3%)	308 (48.7%)
East Feliciana	360 (45.6%)	430 (54.4%)
Iberville	204 (52.8%)	182 (47.2%)
Jefferson	252 (74.6%)	86 (25.4%)
Lafourche	538 (92.4%)	44 (7.6%)
Livingston	127 (38.0%)	207 (62.0%)
Madison	147 (57.0%)	111 (43.0%)
Natchitoches & Caddo	668 (51.4%)	631 (48.6%)
Orleans	2,681 (60.5%)	1,748 (39.5%)
Ouachita	243 (65.1%)	130 (34.9%)
Plaquemines	40 (13.7%)	250 (86.3%)
Point Coupee	147 (51.4%)	139 (48.6%)
Rapides	475 (55.4%)	382 (44.6%)
St. Bernard	173 (65.5%)	91 (34.5%)
St. Charles	69 (67.6%)	33 (32.4%)
St. Helena	172 (42.0%)	238 (58.0%)
St. James	379 (91.1%)	37 (8.9%)
St. John the Baptist	133 (74.7%)	45 (25.3%)
St. Landry & Calcasieu	836 (66.3%)	434 (33.7%)
St. Martin	463 (81.8%)	103 (18.2%)
St. Mary	308 (78.0%)	87 (22.0%)
St. Tammany	204 (71.8%)	80 (28.2%)
Terrebone	313 (94.0%)	20 (6.0%)
Union	74 (48.7%)	76 (51.3%)
Washington	150 (52.8%)	134 (47.2%)
West Baton Rouge	183 (68.5%)	84 (31.5%)
West Feliciana	253 (46.9%)	286 (53.1%)
Total	**11,297 (59.7%)**	**7,617 (40.3%)**

SOURCE—*New Orleans Bee*, November 24, 1840.

Maine

County	Harrison (W)	Van Buren (D)	Birney (Lty)
Aroostook	289 (37.6%)	480 (62.4%)	0
Cumberland	6,791 (51.2%)	6,438 (48.6%)	28 (0.2%)
Franklin	1,848 (47.0%)	2,058 (52.4%)	22 (0.6%)
Hancock	2,434 (49.2%)	2,509 (50.8%)	0
Kennebec	6,905 (66.0%)	3,520 (33.6%)	43 (0.4%)
Lincoln	6,286 (54.7%)	5,188 (45.2%)	14 (0.1%)
Oxford	2,932 (37.8%)	4,800 (61.9%)	19 (0.2%)
Penobscot	4,333 (49.3%)	4,445 (50.6%)	4 (0.05%)
Piscataquis	1,275 (52.3%)	1,136 (46.6%)	27 (1.1%)
Somerset	3,684 (60.4%)	2,597 (41.2%)	21 (0.3%)
Waldo	2,694 (34.7%)	5,069 (65.3%)	3 (0.04%)
Washington	2,357 (51.2%)	2,235 (48.6%)	9 (0.2%)
York	4,785 (45.5%)	5,725 (54.5%)	4 (0.04%)
Total	**46,613 (50.1%)**	**46,200 (49.7%)**	**194 (0.2%)**

SOURCES—(Portland) *Eastern Argus*, November 21 and 23, 1840; and *Kennebec Journal*, November 27, 1840.

Maryland

County	Harrison (W)	Van Buren (D)
Allegany	1,271 (53.8%)	1,093 (46.2%)
Anne Arundel	1,605 (53.7%)	1,384 (46.3%)
Baltimore	1,941 (42.6%)	2,620 (57.4%)
Calvert	494 (60.3%)	325 (39.7%)
Caroline	690 (56.2%)	537 (43.8%)
Carroll	1,554 (49.1%)	1,610 (50.9%)
Cecil	1,448 (52.4%)	1,314 (47.6%)
Charles	841 (62.6%)	502 (37.4%)
Dorchester	1,381 (62.2%)	839 (37.8%)
Frederick	2,958 (53.0%)	2,624 (47.0%)
Harford	1,342 (51.8%)	1,248 (48.2%)
Kent	678 (58.8%)	475 (41.2%)
Montgomery	1,099 (62.3%)	665 (37.7%)
Prince George's	1,017 (62.5%)	609 (37.5%)
Queen Anne's	778 (54.1%)	661 (45.9%)
Saint Mary's	896 (68.3%)	415 (31.7%)
Somerset	1,516 (64.1%)	848 (35.9%)
Talbot	749 (52.3%)	683 (47.7%)
Washington	2,485 (52.0%)	2,290 (48.0%)
Worcester	1,494 (68.4%)	691 (31.6%)
Baltimore (city)	7,296 (49.9%)	7,326 (50.1%)
Total	**33,533 (53.8%)**	**28,759 (46.7%)**

SOURCE—Manuscript returns.

Massachusetts

County	Harrison (W)	Van Buren (D)	Birney (Lty)[3]
Barnstable	2,751 (62.9%)	1,554 (35.5%)	68 (1.6%)
Berkshire	3,931 (50.6%)	3,779 (48.6%)	66 (0.8%)
Bristol	4,892 (50.5%)	4,679 (48.3%)	117 (1.2%)
Dukes	346 (53.1%)	294 (45.2%)	11 (1.7%)
Essex	10,053 (60.0%)	6,473 (38.7%)	216 (1.3%)
Franklin	3,660 (60.8%)	2,304 (38.3%)	57 (0.9%)
Hampden	3,438 (50.1%)	3,312 (48.2%)	117 (1.7%)
Hampshire	4,082 (69.6%)	1,628 (27.8%)	153 (2.6%)
Middlesex	9,673 (52.4%)	8,500 (46.1%)	302 (1.6%)
Nantucket	671 (67.6%)	320 (32.3%)	1 (0.1%)
Norfolk	5,408 (55.4%)	4,254 (43.6%)	98 (1.0%)
Plymouth	4,811 (53.8%)	4,015 (44.9%)	114 (1.3%)
Suffolk	7,499 (62.7%)	4,338 (36.3%)	115 (1.0%)
Worcester	11,317 (62.5%)	6,597 (36.5%)	183 (1.0%)

| Total | 72,532 (57.5%) | 52,047 (41.3%) | 1,618 (1.3%) |
| | *(72,626) | *(52,132) | |

Stated totals.

SOURCE— Manuscript returns.

Michigan

County	Harrison (W)	Van Buren (D)	Birney (Lty)
Allegan	257 (59.5%)	174 (40.3%)	1 (0.2%)
Barry	128 (54.7%)	105 (44.8%)	1 (0.5%)
Berrien	548 (49.6%)	553 (50.1%)	3 (0.3%)
Branch	543 (46.4%)	616 (52.6%)	11 (0.9%)
Calhoun	1,153 (49.0%)	1,169 (49.6%)	33 (1.4%)
Cass	670 (55.6%)	527 (43.8%)	7 (0.6%)
Clinton	221 (60.4%)	145 (39.6%)	0
Eaton	337 (59.5%)	229 (40.5%)	0
Genesee	513 (56.6%)	380 (41.9%)	13 (1.4%)
Hillsdale	843 (53.7%)	721 (45.9%)	6 (0.4%)
Ingham	265 (49.3%)	261 (48.6%)	11 (2.0%)
Ionia	266 (54.7%)	219 (45.0%)	2 (0.4%)
Jackson	1,504 (55.9%)	1,121 (41.6%)	67 (2.5%)
Kalamazoo	954 (55.3%)	744 (43.1%)	27 (1.6%)
Kent	319 (49.7%)	320 (49.8%)	3 (0.5%)
Lapeer	492 (54.4%)	413 (45.6%)	0
Lenawee	2,117 (53.0%)	1,865 (46.7%)	10 (0.3%)
Livingston	700 (45.3%)	844 (54.7%)	0
Michelmackinac	85 (51.8%)	79 (48.2%)	0
Macomb	982 (46.9%)	1,124 (53.1%)	0
Monroe	939 (47.8%)	1,023 (52.1%)	1 (0.1%)
Oakland	2,372 (49.7%)	2,365 (49.5%)	40 (0.8%)
Ottawa	81 (47.9%)	88 (52.1%)	0
Saginaw	89 (47.3%)	100 (52.7%)	0
St. Clair	517 (53.7%)	446 (46.3%)	0
St. Joseph	800 (51.2%)	761 (48.8%)	0
Shiawassee	283 (64.0%)	159 (36.0%)	0
Van Buren	182 (42.0%)	251 (58.0%)	0
Washtenaw	2,527 (54.4%)	2,057 (44.3%)	60 (1.3%)
Wayne	2,246 (49.8%)	2,237 (49.6%)	25 (0.6%)
Total	**22,933 (51.7%)**	**21,096 (47.6%)**	**321 (0.7%)**

SOURCES—*Michigan Manual*, 1913; manuscript returns.

Mississippi

County	Harrison (W)	Van Buren (D)
Adams	862 (66.3%)	438 (33.7%)
Amite	500 (63.0%)	294 (37.0%)
Attala	272 (47.1%)	306 (52.9%)
Bolivar	62 (58.5%)	44 (41.5%)
Carroll	711 (57.4%)	527 (42.6%)
Chickasaw	142 (41.0%)	204 (59.0%)
Choctaw	388 (47.4%)	430 (52.6%)
Claiborne	538 (58.0%)	390 (42.0%)
Clark	124 (34.3%)	238 (65.7%)
Coahoma	181 (62.4%)	109 (37.6%)
Copiah	571 (51.7%)	545 (48.3%)
Covington	116 (33.2%)	233 (66.8%)
De Soto	371 (51.5%)	349 (48.5%)
Franklin	186 (44.4%)	233 (55.6%)
Green	91 (42.1%)	125 (57.9%)
Hancock	281 (72.4%)	107 (27.6%)
Hinds	1,207 (64.7%)	658 (35.3%)
Holmes	556 (63.6%)	318 (36.4%)
Itawamba	170 (30.1%)	394 (69.9%)
Jackson	25 (12.7%)	172 (87.3%)
Jasper	239 (47.1%)	268 (52.9%)
Jefferson	412 (64.3%)	229 (35.7%)
Jones	56 (35.2%)	103 (64.8%)
Kemper	326 (43.8%)	(4) 418 (56.2%)
Lafayette	382 (51.1%)	366 (48.9%)
Lauderdale	239 (35.0%)	444 (65.0%)
Lawrence	123 (21.4%)	453 (78.6%)
Leake	145 (52.3%)	132 (47.7%)
Lowndes	620 (50.0%)	620 (50.0%)
Madison	691 (31.1%)	312 (68.9%)
Marion	136 (43.8%)	175 (56.2%)
Marshall	1,006 (55.3%)	814 (44.7%)
Monroe	452 (48.1%)	487 (51.9%)
Neshoba	113 (40.8%)	164 (59.2%)
Newton	109 (36.0%)	194 (64.0%)
Noxubee	514 (58.0%)	372 (42.0%)
Oktibbeha	195 (45.8%)	219 (54.2%)
Panola	332 (61.7%)	206 (38.3%)
Perry	110 (53.9%)	94 (46.1%)
Pike	314 (45.5%)	376 (54.5%)
Pontotoc	237 (41.9%)	329 (58.1%)
Rankin	331 (55.8%)	262 (44.2%)
Scott	41 (27.5%)	108 (72.5%)
Simpson	201 (47.9%)	219 (52.1%)
Smith	89 (33.2%)	179 (66.8%)
Tallahatchie	186 (60.0%)	124 (40.0%)
Tippah	681 (53.8%)	584 (46.2%)
Tishomingo	321 (35.5%)	583 (64.5%)
Tunica	76 (58.9%)	53 (41.1%)
Warren	1,006 (70.4%)	422 (29.6%)
Washington	159 (72.3%)	61 (27.7%)
Wayne	94 (51.9%)	87 (48.1%)
Wilkinson	663 (82.2%)	148 (17.8%)
Winston	262 (47.6%)	288 (52.4%)
Yalobusha	739 (53.5%)	643 (46.5%)
Yazoo	561 (60.9%)	360 (39.1%)
Total⁴	**19,515 (53.4%)**	**17,010 (46.6%)**

Missouri

County	Harrison (W)	Van Buren (D)
Audrain	132 (52.0%)	122 (48.0%)
Barry	98 (18.4%)	436 (81.6%)
Benton	150 (23.0%)	501 (77.0%)
Boone	1,112 (69.0%)	500 (31.0%)
Buchanan	340 (23.2%)	1,128 (76.8%)
Caldwell	133 (46.3%)	154 (53.7%)
Callaway	881 (58.5%)	626 (41.5%)
Cape Girardeau	455 (37.3%)	764 (62.7%)
Carroll	112 (38.1%)	182 (61.9%)
Chariton	246 (38.6%)	391 (61.4%)
Clark	240 (47.6%)	264 (52.4%)
Clay	649 (58.7%)	457 (41.3%)
Clinton	137 (33.8%)	268 (66.2%)
Cole	348 (26.6%)	962 (73.4%)
Cooper	778 (52.9%)	694 (47.1%)
Crawford	240 (53.8%)	264 (46.2%)
Daviess	170 (39.2%)	264 (39.2%)
Franklin	355 (39.1%)	552 (60.9%)
Gasconade	136 (17.6%)	636 (82.4%)
Greene	171 (28.4%)	432 (71.6%)
Howard	753 (45.5%)	901 (54.5%)
Jackson	427 (37.5%)	711 (62.5%)
Jefferson	298 (48.1%)	321 (51.9%)
Johnson	225 (37.6%)	374 (62.4%)
Lafayette	500 (51.3%)	475 (48.7%)
Lewis	542 (47.3%)	602 (52.7%)
Lincoln	462 (46.0%)	543 (54.0%)
Linn	93 (28.4%)	235 (71.6%)
Livingston	249 (33.8%)	487 (66.2%)
Macon	374 (42.8%)	500 (57.2%)
Madison	152 (35.6%)	275 (64.4%)

Marion	827	(60.8%)	534	(39.2%)
Miller	21	(6.2%)	317	(93.8%)
Monroe	815	(56.9%)	618	(43.1%)
Montgomery	344	(56.8%)	262	(43.2%)
Morgan	169	(29.5%)	404	(70.5%)
New Madrid	363	(65.2%)	194	(34.8%)
Newton	178	(22.0%)	630	(78.0%)
Perry	319	(48.5%)	339	(51.5%)
Pettis	157	(37.5%)	262	(62.5%)
Pike	732	(49.5%)	746	(50.5%)
Platte	451	(32.0%)	960	(68.0%)
Polk	241	(21.9%)	860	(78.1%)
Pulaski	196	(21.2%)	729	(78.8%)
Ralls	400	(54.4%)	335	(45.6%)
Randolph	515	(56.0%)	405	(44.0%)
Ray	432	(43.4%)	563	(56.6%)
Ripley	15	(4.4%)	325	(95.6%)
Rives	299	(41.5%)	421	(58.5%)
St. Charles	586	(56.1%)	459	(43.9%)
Ste. Genevieve	170	(43.4%)	222	(56.6%)
St. Francois	221	(52.5%)	199	(47.5%)
St. Louis	2,515	(57.3%)	1,874	(42.7%)
Saline	375	(53.8%)	322	(46.2%)
Scott	284	(36.2%)	500	(63.8%)
Shelby	233	(50.8%)	226	(49.2%)
Stoddard	69	(18.3%)	308	(81.7%)
†Taney	0		258	(100%)
Van Buren	208	(36.6%)	360	(63.4%)
Warren	342	(49.6%)	348	(50.4%)
Washington	479	(84.3%)	514	(15.7%)
Wayne	57	(21.3%)	211	(78.7%)
Total	**22,971**	**(43.6%)**	**29,668**	**(56.4%)**
	*(23,470)		*(29,758)	

*Stated totals.

†41 votes cast for Whig presidential candidate, but because of an error by the county clerk, no list of Whig electors was provided and therefore these vote were not counted.

SOURCES—(Jefferson City) *Jefferson Enquirer*, November 26, 1840; manuscript returns; W. Dean Burnham, *Presidential Ballots 1836–1892*, reprint edition, New York, NY: Arno Press, 1976.

New Hampshire

County	Harrison (W)	Van Buren (D)	Birney (Lty)
Cheshire	3,634 (60.9%)	2,310 (38.7%)	23 (0.4%)
Coos	532 (28.9%)	1,306 (71.1%)	0
Grafton	3,697 (42.6%)	4,969 (57.3%)	9 (0.1%)
Hillsborough	5,091 (55.3%)	4,086 (44.4%)	28 (0.3%)
Merrimack	2,755 (35.3%)	5,030 (64.5%)	14 (0.2%)
Rockingham	4,115 (45.2%)	4,983 (54.7%)	13 (0.1%)
Strafford	5,377 (44.3%)	6,756 (55.6%)	13 (0.1%)
Sullivan	2,098 (47.6%)	2,299 (52.1%)	14 (0.3%)
Total	**26,294 (44.5%)**	**32,744 (55.4%)**	**114 (0.2%)**
	*(26,434)	*(32,670)	*(126)

*Stated totals.

SOURCE—Manuscript returns.

New Jersey

County	Harrison (W)	Van Buren (D)	Birney (Lty)
Atlantic	425 (33.4%)	846 (66.6%)	
Bergen	977 (42.1%)	1,346 (57.9%)	
Burlington	3,417 (58.7%)	2,405 (41.3%)	
Cape May	696 (78.3%)	194 (21.7%)	
Cumberland	1,497 (55.7%)	1,190 (44.3%)	
Essex	4,636 (61.9%)	2,832 (37.8%)	25 (0.3%)
Gloucester	2,388 (57.4%)	1,773 (42.6%)	2 (0.05%)
Hudson	732 (59.1%)	501 (40.4%)	6 (0.5%)
Hunterdon	1,830 (40.1%)	2,733 (59.9%)	
Mercer	2,022 (57.5%)	1,494 (42.5%)	
Middlesex	2,014 (54.5%)	1,683 (45.5%)	
Monmouth	2,953 (50.6%)	2,880 (49.4%)	2 (0.03%)
Morris	2,509 (53.7%)	2,150 (46.0%)	13 (0.3%)
Passaic	1,362 (58.2%)	962 (41.1%)	18 (0.8%)
Salem	1,582 (54.8%)	1,302 (45.1%)	1 (0.03%)
Somerset	1,721 (56.1%)	1,345 (43.9%)	
Sussex	1,171 (28.5%)	2,932 (71.4%)	2 (0.05%)
Warren	1,419 (36.5%)	2,466 (63.5%)	
Total	**33,351 (51.7%)**	**31,034 (48.2%)**	**69 (0.1%)**

SOURCES—(Trenton) *New Jersey State Gazette*, November 27, 1840; and (Newark) *Sentinel of Freedom*, December 1, 1840.

New York

County	Harrison (W)	Van Buren (D)	Birney (Lty)
Albany	6,371 (51.5%)	5,944 (48.1%)	45 (0.4%)
Allegany	4,132 (54.4%)	3,381 (44.5%)	79 (1.0%)
Broome	2,395 (52.7%)	2,131 (46.9%)	21 (0.5%)
Cattaraugus	2,966 (53.9%)	2,475 (45.0%)	64 (1.1%)
Cayuga	5,172 (51.2%)	4,863 (48.1%)	73 (0.7%)
Chautauqua	5,985 (64.0%)	3,345 (35.8%)	23 (0.2%)
Chemung	1,698 (42.5%)	2,296 (57.5%)	0
Chenango	4,386 (52.1%)	3,995 (47.5%)	25 (0.3%)
Clinton	2,023 (52.1%)	1,828 (47.1%)	31 (0.8%)
Columbia	4,290 (48.9%)	4,479 (51.0%)	5 (0.1%)
Cortland	2,664 (54.0%)	2,229 (45.1%)	44 (0.9%)
Delaware	2,988 (43.4%)	3,847 (55.9%)	42 (0.6%)
Dutchess	5,355 (49.9%)	5,362 (50.0%)	16 (0.1%)
Erie	6,787 (64.6%)	3,687 (35.1%)	36 (0.3%)
Essex	2,617 (59.4%)	1,789 (40.6%)	1 (0.02%)
Franklin	1,440 (56.3%)	1,110 (43.4%)	6 (0.2%)
Fulton	1,964 (54.0%)	1,645 (45.2%)	29 (0.8%)
Genesee	7,057 (64.0%)	3,808 (34.6%)	156 (1.4%)
Greene	2,990 (47.8%)	3,258 (52.1%)	7 (0.1%)
Hamilton	123 (35.6%)	222 (64.4%)	0
Herkimer	3,118 (41.4%)	4,350 (57.7%)	70 (0.9%)
Jefferson	6,257 (52.4%)	5,630 (47.1%)	59 (0.5%)
Kings	3,293 (50.9%)	3,157 (48.8%)	23 (0.4%)
Lewis	1,718 (48.9%)	1,755 (50.0%)	37 (1.1%)
Livingston	3,916 (59.3%)	2,634 (39.9%)	52 (0.8%)
Madison	4,266 (49.5%)	4,115 (47.7%)	240 (2.8%)
Monroe	6,468 (56.8%)	4,835 (42.5%)	77 (0.7%)
Montgomery	2,828 (46.1%)	3,298 (53.8%)	9 (0.1%)
New York	20,961 (48.7%)	21,936 (51.0%)	153 (0.4%)
Niagara	2,964 (56.4%)	2,219 (42.2%)	72 (1.4%)
Oneida	7,156 (46.7%)	7,769 (50.7%)	393 (2.6%)
Onondaga	6,557 (49.6%)	6,562 (49.6%)	105 (0.8%)
Ontario	4,828 (57.3%)	3,451 (40.9%)	152 (1.8%)
Orange	4,371 (47.4%)	4,845 (52.6%)	3 (0.03%)
Orleans	2,606 (55.3%)	2,031 (43.1%)	77 (1.6%)
Oswego	4,192 (50.7%)	3,907 (47.3%)	166 (2.0%)
Otsego	4,856 (46.3%)	5,580 (53.2%)	60 (0.6%)
Putnam	920 (36.8%)	1,583 (53.2%)	0
Queens	2,522 (49.7%)	2,550 (50.3%)	2 (0.04%)
Rensselaer	5,751 (51.3%)	5,424 (48.3%)	33 (0.3%)
Richmond	903 (51.2%)	861 (48.8%)	0
Rockland	637 (27.8%)	1,657 (72.2%)	0
St. Lawrence	4,803 (50.1%)	4,751 (49.5%)	41 (0.4%)
Saratoga	4,416 (53.2%)	3,873 (46.6%)	16 (0.2%)
Schenectady	1,752 (52.5%)	1,579 (47.3%)	5 (0.1%)
Schoharie	2,692 (46.0%)	3,137 (53.6%)	26 (0.4%)
Seneca	2,466 (49.8%)	2,472 (49.9%)	13 (0.3%)
Steuben	4,081 (45.6%)	4,820 (53.9%)	42 (0.5%)
Suffolk	2,415 (41.0%)	3,482 (59.0%)	0
Sullivan	1,475 (46.6%)	1,679 (53.1%)	9 (0.3%)

Tioga	1,925 (46.8%)	2,180 (53.0%)	5 (0.1%)	
Tompkins	3,969 (52.5%)	3,558 (47.1%)	32 (0.4%)	
Ulster	4,492 (51.2%)	4,280 (48.8%)	2 (0.02%)	
Warren	1,306 (48.0%)	1,411 (51.8%)	5 (0.2%)	
Washington	5,070 (62.4%)	3,024 (37.2%)	28 (0.3%)	
Wayne	4,309 (51.6%)	3,998 (47.9%)	36 (0.4%)	
Westchester	4,083 (48.3%)	4,354 (51.6%)	9 (0.1%)	
Yates	2,072 (49.3%)	2,087 (49.7%)	44 (1.0%)	
Total	**225,817 (51.2%)**	**212,528 (48.2%)**	**2,799 (0.6%)**	

SOURCE—Manuscript returns.

North Carolina

County	Harrison (W)	Van Buren (D)
Anson	1,194 (75.1%)	395 (24.9%)
Ashe	578 (55.7%)	460 (44.3%)
Beaufort	961 (75.7%)	309 (24.3%)
Bertie	496 (56.3%)	385 (43.7%)
Bladen	346 (45.5%)	414 (54.5%)
Brunswick	350 (60.3%)	230 (39.7%)
Buncombe & Henderson	1,436 (76.1%)	452 (23.9%)
Burke	1,623 (84.0%)	309 (16.0%)
Cabarrus	891 (71.6%)	354 (28.4%)
Camden	612 (86.0%)	100 (14.0%)
Carteret	454 (70.9%)	186 (29.1%)
Caswell	276 (19.1%)	1,169 (80.9%)
Chatham	1,124 (66.4%)	568 (33.6%)
Cherokee	414 (78.6%)	113 (21.4%)
Chowan	330 (67.6%)	158 (32.4%)
Columbus	204 (39.3%)	315 (60.7%)
Craven	666 (55.2%)	540 (44.8%)
Cumberland	612 (39.2%)	950 (60.8%)
Currituck	142 (23.3%)	468 (76.7%)
Davidson	1,441 (78.7%)	390 (21.3%)
Duplin	253 (23.9%)	807 (76.1%)
Edgecombe	135 (8.9%)	1,374 (91.1%)
Franklin	374 (35.2%)	689 (64.8%)
Gates	378 (53.5%)	328 (46.5%)
Granville	933 (54.5%)	778 (45.5%)
Greene	297 (58.0%)	215 (42.0%)
Guilford	2,300 (84.7%)	414 (15.3%)
Halifax	604 (62.9%)	356 (37.1%)
Haywood	431 (66.1%)	221 (33.9%)
Hertford	396 (66.6%)	199 (33.4%)
Hyde	431 (82.9%)	89 (17.1%)
Iredell	1,780 (84.4%)	328 (15.6%)
Johnson	597 (68.4%)	549 (31.6%)
Jones	243 (64.5%)	132 (35.5%)
Lincoln	1,000 (33.8%)	1,958 (66.2%)
Macon	433 (72.0%)	168 (28.0%)
Martin	291 (32.8%)	596 (67.2%)
Mecklenburg	1,000 (44.5%)	1,246 (55.5%)
Montgomery	1,136 (91.5%)	105 (8.5%)
Moore	529 (51.5%)	495 (48.5%)
Nash	78 (8.9%)	797 (91.1%)
New Hanover	293 (28.1%)	1,042 (71.9%)
Northampton	550 (62.2%)	383 (37.8%)
Onslow	143 (17.2%)	690 (82.8%)
Orange	1,639 (53.1%)	1,448 (46.9%)
Pasquotank	693 (82.3%)	149 (17.7%)
Pender	214 (25.0%)	597 (75.0%)
Perquimans	596 (81.6%)	134 (18.4%)
Pitt	627 (61.6%)	391 (38.4%)
Randolph	1,344 (83.3%)	269 (16.7%)
Richmond	820 (88.9%)	102 (11.1%)
Robeson	579 (53.4%)	506 (46.6%)
Rockingham	547 (37.7%)	905 (62.3%)
Rowan & Davie	1,630 (69.2%)	725 (30.8%)

County	Harrison (W)	Van Buren (D)
Rutherford	1,802 (76.9%)	540 (23.1%)
Sampson	553 (42.7%)	741 (57.3%)
Stokes	1,212 (53.3%)	1,061 (46.7%)
Surry	1,191 (59.5%)	812 (40.5%)
Tyrrell	380 (82.1%)	83 (17.9%)
Wake	1,026 (47.2%)	1,149 (52.8%)
Warren	105 (12.2%)	754 (87.8%)
Washington	432 (88.9%)	54 (11.1%)
Wayne	306 (29.5%)	731 (70.5%)
Wilkes	1,450 (92.7%)	114 (7.3%)
Yancey	415 (58.9%)	290 (41.1%)
Total	**46,376 (57.9%)**	**33,779 (42.1%)**
		*(33,782)

*Stated totals.

*Lenoir	252 (39.5%)	386 (60.5%)

*Not included in the official returns.

SOURCE— Manuscript returns.

Ohio

County	Harrison (W)	Van Buren (D)	Birney (Lty)
Adams	1,205 (45.5%)	1,431 (54.0%)	15 (0.6%)
Allen	763 (46.4%)	883 (53.6%)	0
Ashtabula	3,738 (79.0%)	896 (18.9%)	95 (2.0%)
Athens	2,094 (61.2%)	1,322 (38.6%)	7 (0.2%)
Belmont	3,166 (54.6%)	2,602 (44.8%)	34 (0.6%)
Brown	1,798 (47.9%)	1,931 (51.4%)	28 (0.7%)
Butler	2,101 (39.6%)	3,192 (60.2%)	12 (0.2%)
Carroll	1,677 (52.1%)	1,545 (48.0%)	8 (0.2%)
Champaign	2,062 (63.1%)	1,207 (36.9%)	0
Clark	2,381 (72.7%)	895 (27.3%)	1 (0.03%)
Clermont	2,044 (46.5%)	2,315 (52.6%)	39 (0.9%)
Clinton	1,847 (64.5%)	1,006 (35.2%)	9 (0.3%)
Columbiana	3,602 (49.5%)	3,660 (50.3%)	9 (1.2%)
Coshocton	1,830 (64.5%)	2,009 (35.5%)	0
Crawford	1,009 (45.5%)	1,206 (54.4%)	2 (0.1%)
Cuyahoga	3,102 (62.6%)	1,814 (36.6%)	38 (0.8%)
Darke	1,303 (54.4%)	1,092 (45.6%)	0
Delaware	2,360 (58.7%)	1,644 (40.9%)	19 (0.5%)
Erie	1,324 (55.9%)	1,042 (44.0%)	2 (0.1%)
Fairfield	2,463 (42.6%)	3,318 (57.4%)	2 (0.3%)
Fayette	1,132 (59.0%)	771 (40.2%)	16 (0.8%)
Franklin	2,866 (61.6%)	1,774 (38.1%)	13 (0.3%)
Gallia	1,479 (67.1%)	725 (32.9%)	1 (0.05%)
Geauga	2,310 (71.8%)	893 (27.8%)	14 (0.4%)
Greene	2,321 (66.4%)	1,172 (33.5%)	3 (0.1%)
Guernsey	2,606 (54.2%)	2,186 (45.5%)	13 (0.3%)
Hamilton	5,873 (50.0%)	5,835 (49.7%)	44 (0.4%)
Hancock	693 (36.4%)	1,064 (63.6%)	0
Hardin	431 (53.4%)	376 (46.6%)	0
Harrison	2,008 (53.3%)	1,739 (46.2%)	18 (0.5%)
Henry	191 (51.3%)	181 (48.7%)	0
Highland	2,145 (52.9%)	1,899 (46.8%)	12 (0.3%)
Hocking	649 (41.8%)	903 (58.2%)	0
Holmes	1,109 (36.8%)	1,906 (63.2%)	0
Huron	2,291 (59.6%)	1,531 (39.8%)	24 (0.6%)
Jackson	794 (50.2%)	785 (49.7%)	2 (0.1%)
Jefferson	2,300 (50.8%)	2,218 (49.0%)	6 (0.1%)
Knox	2,441 (46.4%)	2,789 (53.1%)	29 (0.6%)
Lake	1,887 (74.0%)	653 (25.6%)	11 (0.4%)
Lawrence	1,118 (71.1%)	454 (28.9%)	0
Licking	3,357 (48.8%)	3,516 (51.1%)	12 (0.2%)
Logan	1,574 (64.8%)	845 (34.8%)	9 (0.4%)
Lorain	1,868 (57.2%)	1,313 (40.2%)	82 (2.5%)
Lucas	931 (64.3%)	516 (35.6%)	1 (0.1%)
Madison	1,201 (67.8%)	571 (32.2%)	1 (0.1%)
Marion	1,358 (54.5%)	1,128 (45.2%)	7 (0.3%)
Medina	1,793 (55.3%)	1,436 (44.3%)	13 (0.4%)

Meigs	1,284	(66.4%)	649	(33.5%)	2	(0.1%)
Mercer	551	(28.9%)	1,349	(70.8%)	5	(0.3%)
Miami	2,469	(64.8%)	1,339	(35.1%)	5	(0.1%)
Monroe	1,086	(34.3%)	2,075	(65.6%)	2	(0.1%)
Montgomery	3,427	(53.7%)	2,951	(46.2%)	7	(0.1%)
Morgan	1,851	(49.1%)	1,910	(50.6%)	12	(0.3%)
Muskingum	4,367	(61.0%)	2,771	(38.7%)	21	(0.3%)
Ottawa	232	(58.0%)	168	(42.0%)	0	
Paulding	65	(29.5%)	155	(70.5%)	0	
Perry	1,471	(41.2%)	2,097	(58.8%)	0	
Pickaway	2,201	(54.9%)	1,807	(45.1%)	0	
Pike	650	(48.9%)	674	(50.7%)	5	(0.4%)
Portage	2,524	(56.1%)	1,963	(43.6%)	16	(0.4%)
Preble	2,299	(63.3%)	1,331	(36.6%)	3	(0.1%)
Putnam	401	(40.6%)	582	(59.0%)	4	(0.4%)
Richland	3,331	(42.3%)	4,539	(57.6%)	12	(0.2%)
Ross	3,081	(59.6%)	2,071	(40.1%)	16	(0.3%)
Sandusky	919	(50.1%)	917	(49.9%)	0	
Scioto	1,472	(66.2%)	749	(33.7%)	1	(0.1%)
Seneca	1,483	(47.8%)	1,616	(38.8%)	6	(0.2%)
Shelby	955	(48.2%)	1,027	(51.8%)	0	
Stark	2,701	(46.5%)	3,107	(53.5%)	1	(0.02%)
Summit	2,562	(60.4%)	1,646	(38.8%)	35	(0.8%)
Trumbull	4,106	(54.7%)	3,325	(44.3%)	82	(1.1%)
Tuscarawas	2,329	(56.6%)	1,787	(43.4%)	0	
Union	946	(62.0%)	577	(38.0%)	3	(0.2%)
Van Wert	119	(38.4%)	191	(61.6%)	0	
Warren	2,813	(65.1%)	1,504	(34.8%)	6	(0.1%)
Washington	2,109	(59.1%)	1,458	(40.9%)	2	(0.1%)
Wayne	2,798	(45.7%)	3,321	(54.2%)	6	(0.1%)
Williams	396	(49.3%)	407	(50.7%)	0	
Wood	548	(51.4%)	518	(48.6%)	0	
Total	**148,141**	**(54.1%)**	**124,710**	**(45.6%)**	**903**	**(0.3%)**
			*(124,780)			

*Stated totals.

SOURCE—(Columbus) *Ohio State Journal*, November 18, 1840.

Pennsylvania

County	Harrison (W)		Van Buren (D)		Birney (Lty)[5]
Adams	2,453	(60.1%)	1,628	(39.9%)	3
Allegheny	7,619	(62.5%)	4,573	(37.5%)	?
Armstrong	1,260	(41.9%)	1,744	(58.1%)	?
Beaver	3,143	(64.8%)	1,710	(35.2%)	20
Bedford	2,910	(54.3%)	2,446	(45.7%)	0
Berks	3,582	(32.5%)	7,425	(67.5%)	?
Bradford	2,631	(47.1%)	2,958	(52.9%)	26
Bucks	4,705	(51.2%)	4,488	(48.8%)	0
Butler	2,100	(53.8%)	1,804	(46.2%)	0
Cambria	811	(46.9%)	920	(53.1%)	?
Centre	1,448	(39.2%)	2,242	(60.8%)	?
Chester	5,643	(53.6%)	4,882	(46.4%)	22
Clarion	648	(32.2%)	1,366	(67.8%)	0
Clearfield	638	(49.6%)	649	(50.4%)	0
Clinton	499	(38.1%)	812	(61.9%)	?
Columbia	1,325	(31.9%)	2,829	(68.1%)	0
Crawford	2,469	(45.9%)	2,908	(54.1%)	3
Cumberland	2,791	(50.9%)	2,695	(49.1%)	3
Dauphin	3,124	(58.8%)	2,187	(41.2%)	3
Delaware	2,031	(60.3%)	1,335	(39.7%)	5
Erie	3,636	(63.8%)	2,061	(36.2%)	0
Fayette	2,755	(47.6%)	3,035	(52.4%)	?
Franklin	3,586	(55.4%)	2,892	(44.6%)	?
Greene	1,350	(40.2%)	2,010	(59.8%)	?
Huntingdon	3,826	(62.8%)	2,266	(37.2%)	0
Indiana	1,953	(61.8%)	1,209	(38.2%)	?
Jefferson	476	(44.6%)	592	(55.4%)	?
Juniata	966	(48.1%)	1,043	(51.9%)	?

Lancaster	9,678	(63.9%)	5,470	(36.1%)	1
Lebanon	2,370	(62.8%)	1,402	(37.2%)	0
Lehigh	2,405	(62.8%)	2,450	(37.2%)	0
Luzerne	2,776	(40.3%)	4,119	(59.7%)	0
Lycoming	1,504	(40.8%)	2,181	(59.2%)	?
McKean	263	(48.8%)	276	(51.2%)	?
Mercer	3,247	(58.2%)	2,334	(41.8%)	?
Mifflin	1,226	(49.1%)	1,269	(50.9%)	0
Monroe	345	(19.3%)	1,447	(80.7%)	?
Montgomery	4,068	(45.5%)	4,869	(54.5%)	?
Northampton	2,846	(42.6%)	3,838	(57.4%)	0
Northumberland	1,351	(38.2%)	2,187	(61.8%)	0
Perry	1,072	(35.2%)	1,970	(64.8%)	0
Philadelphia	17,843	(49.7%)	18,076	(50.3%)	107
Pike	135	(20.5%)	524	(79.5%)	0
Potter	180	(33.1%)	363	(66.9%)	0
Schuylkill	1,881	(46.3%)	2,184	(53.9%)	2
Somerset	2,501	(76.6%)	765	(23.4%)	?
Susquehanna	1,560	(43.6%)	2,022	(56.4%)	0
Tioga	895	(34.2%)	1,721	(65.8%)	0
Union	2,423	(61.5%)	1,518	(38.5%)	?
Venango	855	(40.1%)	1,276	(59.9%)	?
Warren	827	(47.1%)	929	(52.9%)	?
Washington	4,149	(53.5%)	3,611	(46.5%)	?
Wayne	675	(36.2%)	1,188	(63.8%)	0
Westmoreland	2,778	(37.1%)	4,704	(62.9%)	0
York	3,792	(46.4%)	4,382	(53.6%)	0
Total	**144,023**	**(50.04%)**	**143,784**	**(49.96%)**	
	*(144,021)				

*Stated totals.

SOURCE—*Harrisburg Telegraph*, December 2, 1840.

Rhode Island

County	Harrison (W)		Van Buren (D)		Birney (Lty)	
Bristol	476	(77.8%)	136	(22.2%)		
Kent	669	(64.3%)	372	(35.7%)		
Newport	849	(68.1%)	379	(30.4%)	19[6]	(1.5%)
Providence	2,483	(59.2%)	1,711	(40.8%)		
Washington	737	(52.6%)	665	(47.4%)		
Total	**5,213**	**(61.4%)**	**3,263**	**(38.4%)**	**19**	**(0.2%)**

SOURCE— Manuscript returns, *Providence Journal*, November 11, 1840.

South Carolina

Electors chosen by the state legislature

Tennessee

County	Harrison (W)		Van Buren (D)	
Anderson	626	(73.4%)	227	(26.6%)
Bedford	1,878	(46.6%)	2,156	(53.4%)
Benton	259	(46.3%)	301	(53.7%)
Bledsoe	645	(76.2%)	202	(23.8%)
Blount	1,198	(65.2%)	640	(34.8%)
Bradley	467	(37.1%)	791	(62.9%)
Campbell	481	(59.5%)	328	(40.5%)
Carroll	1,361	(79.5%)	352	(20.5%)
Carter	837	(89.4%)	99	(10.6%)
Claiborne	631	(46.3%)	733	(53.7%)
Cocke	917	(92.0%)	80	(8.0%)
Davidson	1,960	(60.6%)	1,274	(39.4%)
Dickson	396	(37.8%)	653	(62.2%)
Dyer	446	(68.4%)	206	(31.6%)
Fayette	1,140	(55.8%)	902	(44.2%)

Fentress	140 (30.2%)	323 (69.8%)
Franklin	645 (30.6%)	1,461 (69.4%)
Gibson	1,272 (75.3%)	418 (24.7%)
Giles	1,190 (48.9%)	1,242 (51.1%)
Grainger	1,095 (70.9%)	449 (29.1%)
Greene	1,032 (39.8%)	1,559 (60.2%)
Hamilton	606 (56.2%)	473 (43.8%)
Hardeman	676 (44.0%)	860 (56.0%)
Hardin	562 (49.2%)	581 (50.8%)
Hawkins	1,053 (45.7%)	1,251 (54.3%)
Haywood	807 (58.4%)	576 (41.6%)
Henderson	1,318 (82.6%)	277 (17.4%)
Henry	862 (44.4%)	1,079 (55.6%)
Hickman	293 (23.5%)	952 (76.5%)
Humphreys	191 (36.5%)	333 (63.5%)
Jackson	1,302 (68.8%)	591 (31.2%)
Jefferson	1,811 (93.3%)	131 (6.7%)
Johnson	390 (88.8%)	49 (11.2%)
Knox	2,096 (87.0%)	314 (13.0%)
Lawrence	537 (59.1%)	372 (40.9%)
Lincoln	831 (24.7%)	2,531 (75.3%)
Madison	1,312 (71.0%)	537 (29.0%)
Marion	503 (57.7%)	368 (42.3%)
Maury	1,497 (42.5%)	2,025 (57.5%)
McMinn	1,022 (53.3%)	897 (46.7%)
McNairy	906 (65.5%)	477 (34.5%)
Meigs	119 (18.2%)	535 (81.8%)
Monroe	923 (49.9%)	928 (50.1%)
Montgomery	1,101 (58.2%)	790 (41.8%)
Morgan	211 (56.7%)	161 (43.3%)
Obion	267 (42.8%)	357 (57.2%)
Overton	329 (25.0%)	988 (75.0%)
Perry	781 (69.2%)	348 (30.8%)
Polk	195 (36.6%)	338 (63.4%)
Rhea	209 (35.3%)	383 (64.7%)
Roane	1,047 (65.8%)	545 (34.2%)
Robertson	1,167 (64.2%)	650 (35.8%)
Rutherford	1,706 (53.6%)	1,475 (46.4%)
Sevier	926 (95.4%)	45 (4.6%)
Shelby	950 (58.2%)	681 (41.8%)
Smith	2,657 (79.4%)	688 (20.6%)
Stewart	457 (41.6%)	642 (58.4%)
Sullivan	327 (19.1%)	1,386 (80.9%)
Sumner	794 (31.4%)	1,738 (68.6%)
Tipton	573 (49.4%)	588 (50.6%)
Warren	513 (20.9%)	1,944 (79.1%)
Washington	892 (45.2%)	1,083 (54.8%)
Wayne	760 (74.1%)	266 (25.9%)
Weakley	528 (42.2%)	723 (57.8%)
White	1,201 (75.7%)	386 (24.3%)
Williamson	2,017 (74.8%)	681 (25.2%)
Wilson	2,550 (74.6%)	870 (25.4%)
Total	**60,391 (55.6%)**	**48,289 (44.4%)**

SOURCE—*Nashville Whig*, November 30, 1840.

Vermont

County	Harrison (W)	Van Buren (D)	Birney (Lty)
Addison	2,806 (74.9%)	916 (24.4%)	26 (0.7%)
Bennington	1,796 (55.3%)	1,423 (43.4%)	30 (0.9%)
Caledonia	2,025 (54.2%)	1,713 (45.8%)	0
Chittenden	2,281 (62.0%)	1,381 (37.5%)	18 (0.5%)
Essex	448 (59.7%)	303 (40.3%)	0
Franklin	2,186 (64.0%)	1,190 (34.8%)	39 (1.1%)
Grand Isle	363 (69.1%)	162 (30.9%)	0
Lamoille	907 (50.2%)	888 (49.1%)	12 (0.7%)
Orange	2,874 (55.7%)	2,216 (42.9%)	72 (1.4%)
Orleans	1,294 (62.9%)	745 (36.2%)	17 (0.8%)
Rutland	4,114 (72.5%)	1,551 (27.3%)	10 (0.2%)
Washington	2,057 (50.1%)	1,984 (48.3%)	65 (1.6%)
Windham	3,472 (66.7%)	1,714 (32.9%)	18 (0.3%)
Windsor	5,817 (76.0%)	1,821 (23.8%)	12 (0.2%)
Total	**32,440 (63.9%)**	**18,007 (35.5%)**	**319 (0.6%)**

SOURCE— Manuscript returns.

Virginia

County	Harrison (W)	Van Buren (D)
Accomac	739 (75.6%)	239 (24.4%)
Albemarle	714 (58.0%)	517 (42.0%)
Alleghany	84 (32.9%)	171 (67.1%)
Amelia	166 (41.1%)	240 (58.9%)
Amherst	372 (53.1%)	329 (46.9%)
Augusta	1,204 (72.6%)	454 (27.4%)
Bath	203 (48.2%)	218 (51.8%)
Bedford	919 (62.2%)	558 (37.8%)
Berkeley	599 (61.7%)	372 (38.3%)
Botetourt	407 (41.4%)	575 (58.6%)
Brooke	350 (40.4%)	516 (59.6%)
Brunswick	261 (40.7%)	380 (59.3%)
Buckingham	475 (43.4%)	520 (56.6%)
Braxton	202 (65.0%)	109 (35.0%)
Cabell	481 (52.5%)	436 (47.5%)
Campbell	718 (59.6%)	487 (40.4%)
Caroline	399 (46.1%)	467 (53.9%)
Charles City	173 (85.2%)	30 (14.8%)
Charlotte	318 (49.3%)	327 (50.7%)
Chesterfield	298 (35.1%)	580 (64.9%)
Clarke	174 (47.7%)	191 (52.3%)
Culpeper	351 (54.3%)	295 (45.7%)
Cumberland	262 (53.5%)	228 (46.5%)
Dinwiddie	302 (56.2%)	235 (43.8%)
Elizabeth City	141 (62.4%)	85 (37.6%)
Essex	241 (65.8%)	125 (34.2%)
Fairfax	366 (53.3%)	321 (46.7%)
Fauquier	683 (56.2%)	533 (43.8%)
Fayette	199 (52.1%)	183 (47.9%)
Fluvanna	334 (68.6%)	153 (31.4%)
Floyd	143 (33.9%)	279 (66.1%)
Franklin	569 (52.5%)	515 (47.5%)
Frederick	755 (50.4%)	743 (49.6%)
Giles	226 (43.6%)	293 (56.4%)
Gloucester	247 (51.9%)	179 (48.1%)
Goochland	120 (73.5%)	333 (26.5%)
Grayson	455 (43.7%)	587 (56.3%)
Greenbrier	568 (64.8%)	308 (35.2%)
Greensville	110 (41.4%)	156 (58.6%)
Greene	62 (21.2%)	230 (78.8%)
Halifax	422 (30.4%)	964 (69.6%)
Hampshire	729 (54.6%)	605 (45.4%)
Hanover	450 (49.3%)	462 (50.7%)
Hardy	497 (68.4%)	230 (31.6%)
Harrison	828 (38.2%)	1,341 (61.8%)
Henrico	445 (52.9%)	398 (47.1%)
Henry	311 (62.0%)	191 (38.0%)
Isle of Wight	89 (14.3%)	533 (85.7%)
Jackson	258 (55.0%)	211 (45.0%)
James City	141 (94.0%)	9 (6.0%)
Jefferson	667 (53.0%)	592 (47.0%)
Kanawha	827 (71.9%)	324 (28.1%)
King & Queen	282 (48.0%)	305 (52.0%)
King George	168 (56.6%)	129 (43.4%)
King William	115 (27.3%)	306 (72.7%)
Lancaster	170 (66.1%)	87 (33.9%)
Lee	275 (36.0%)	489 (64.0%)

Lewis	386	(38.5%)	616	(61.5%)
Logan	136	(41.8%)	189	(58.2%)
Loudoun	1,269	(76.9%)	381	(23.1%)
Louisa	375	(44.1%)	475	(55.9%)
Lunenburg	228	(43.0%)	302	(57.0%)
Madison	53	(9.1%)	532	(90.9%)
Marshall	458	(49.7%)	462	(50.3%)
Mason	405	(57.1%)	304	(42.9%)
Mathews	180	(55.0%)	220	(45.0%)
Mecklenburg	319	(36.3%)	561	(63.7%)
Mercer	146	(54.1%)	124	(45.9%)
Middlesex	101	(45.1%)	123	(54.9%)
Monongalia	681	(35.5%)	1,236	(64.5%)
Monroe	408	(49.3%)	420	(50.7%)
Montgomery	338	(56.4%)	261	(43.6%)
Morgan	179	(55.2%)	145	(44.8%)
Nansemond	383	(59.7%)	259	(40.3%)
Nelson	404	(63.0%)	237	(37.0%)
New Kent	198	(55.9%)	156	(44.1%)
Nicholas	173	(59.0%)	120	(41.0%)
Norfolk	561	(54.0%)	478	(46.0%)
Northampton	334	(93.3%)	24	(6.7%)
Northumberland	183	(37.9%)	300	(62.1%)
Nottoway	132	(41.0%)	190	(59.0%)
Ohio	922	(76.3%)	287	(23.7%)
Orange	231	(49.6%)	235	(50.4%)
Page	45	(7.9%)	528	(92.1%)
Patrick	342	(55.5%)	274	(44.5%)
Pendleton	389	(45.4%)	468	(54.6%)
Pittsylvania	876	(58.7%)	616	(41.3%)
Pocahontas	107	(33.8%)	210	(66.2%)
Powhatan	176	(45.6%)	210	(54.4%)
Preston	396	(46.0%)	464	(54.0%)
Prince Edward	268	(42.6%)	361	(57.4%)
Prince George	124	(34.3%)	237	(65.7%)
Princess Anne	402	(59.5%)	274	(40.5%)
Prince William	167	(29.8%)	393	(70.2%)
Pulaski	142	(46.9%)	161	(53.1%)
Randolph	450	(58.4%)	321	(41.6%)
Rappahannock	318	(51.5%)	300	(48.5%)
Richmond	177	(54.0%)	151	(46.0%)
Roanoke	159	(77.2%)	255	(22.8%)
Rockbridge	635	(45.4%)	528	(54.6%)
Rockingham	256	(15.1%)	1,444	(84.9%)
Russell	264	(47.4%)	293	(52.6%)
Scott	284	(39.2%)	441	(60.8%)
Shenandoah	102	(7.7%)	1,218	(92.3%)
Smyth	259	(45.9%)	305	(54.1%)
Southampton	378	(50.4%)	372	(49.6%)
Spotsylvania	358	(49.3%)	368	(50.7%)
Stafford	265	(47.3%)	295	(52.7%)
Surry	95	(32.8%)	195	(67.2%)
Sussex	109	(23.9%)	347	(76.1%)
Tazewell	113	(18.9%)	486	(81.1%)
Tyler	325	(42.6%)	438	(57.4%)
Warren	110	(26.8%)	300	(73.2%)
Warwick	92	(96.8%)	3	(3.2%)
Washington	364	(36.8%)	625	(63.2%)
Westmoreland	286	(77.9%)	81	(22.1%)
Wood	513	(56.7%)	392	(43.3%)
Wythe	279	(37.1%)	474	(62.9%)
York	192	(94.1%)	12	(5.9%)

Cities, towns, boroughs

Norfolk	529	(64.0%)	298	(36.0%)
Petersburg	245	(48.3%)	262	(51.7%)
Richmond	580	(76.7%)	176	(23.3%)
Williamsburg	83	(92.2%)	7	(7.8%)
Total	**42,501**	**(49.2%)**	**43,893**	**(50.8%)**

SOURCE—*Richmond Enquirer*, December 22, 1840.

NOTES

1. The vice presidential electoral vote was John Tyler (W) 234, Richard M. Johnson (D) 48, Littleton W. Tazewell (D) 11, and James K. Polk (D) 1.

2. The official county returns appear in the (New York) *Log Cabin*, January 23, 1841, and also in the *Whig Almanac, 1844*, pp. 62–3. Georgia newspapers and the *Executive Minutes* only give the statewide vote for each elector.

3. Some sources credit Birney with all these votes. This is in fact the total of the scattering votes as listed in the manuscript returns. In fact both the *Providence Journal,* December 12, 1840, and the *Whig Almanac, 1844,* p. 55, list the votes as "ballot for all others" or scattering. Only later sources list the votes as being solely for Birney. In the election for governor, held at the same time, the Liberty candidate received 1,081 votes with 181 additional scattering votes. At the Congressional level there were 1,419 votes cast for other candidates. Of these, 1,057 were listed as scattering. In four districts, more than one candidate received votes in this category. Thus it is unlikely that Birney received all 1,618 votes. But I could not determine his actual total. Most likely a substantial majority of the scattering votes were for Birney electors but certainly not all. Although I list this vote under Birney's column, in reality a more accurate listing would be Birney and scattering.

4. These returns are taken from the (Jackson) *Mississippian*, November 20, 1840. W. Dean Burnham's *Presidential Ballots* cites a manuscript from the files of the secretary of state that differs in the vote for Van Buren in Kemper County which is used here. In addition, the votes of Jackson, Marshall and Washington counties are listed as "reported" in the *Mississippian*. The manuscript returns I located give the same vote for the first two counties but no returns for Washington. *Presidential Ballots'* total for Washington is used here, but its statewide totals are three less for each candidate compared to the newspaper returns. The *Mississippian* totals were Harrison—19,518 and Van Buren—16,992 and these are also found in Svend Petersen's *A Statistical History of the American Presidential Elections* and the *Whig Almanac 1843.* However *Congressional Quarterly, Guide to U.S. Elections* gives the same total as *Presidential Ballots* and agrees with my figures.

5. The official statewide vote for Birney is widely reported as 343, I have uncovered no source that gives his vote by county. What is listed here is the result of a search of many Pennsylvania papers. As a consequence I list an incomplete set of county returns for Birney, hence no county percentage breakdown for his vote. Where a ? appears, this means that I could not locate any information about that county's vote for Birney. The county vote listed here accounts for 195 votes for Birney. Birney's statewide total is, however, included in the national summary.

6. The manuscript returns list a total of 42 votes as scattering with 19 in Newport identified as "abolitionist." W. Dean Burnham's *Presidential Ballots*, p. 340, citing returns furnished by the secretary of state, credits Birney with 34. Svend Petersen's *A Statistical History of the American Presidential Elections* lists his vote as 42. CQ lists Birney's vote as 19.

1 8 4 4

National Summary[1]
(electoral vote in parentheses)

State	James K. Polk (D)		Henry Clay (W)		James G. Birney (Lty)	
Alabama	37,401 (58.99%)	(9)	26,002 (41.01%)			
Arkansas	9,546 (63.13%)	(3)	5,604 (36.87%)			
Connecticut	29,841 (46.18%)		32,832 (50.81%)	(6)	1,944 (3.01%)	
Delaware	5,970 (48.77%)		6,271 (51.23%)	(3)		
Georgia	43,397 (50.84%)	(10)	41,975 (49.16%)			
Illinois	58,982 (54.44%)	(9)	45,931 (42.39%)		3,433 (3.17%)	
Indiana	70,183 (50.07%)	(12)	67,866 (48.42%)		2,107 (1.50%)	
Kentucky	52,053 (45.98%)		61,167 (54.02%)	(12)		
Louisiana	13,782 (51.31%)	(6)	13,080 (48.69%)			
Maine	45,719 (53.84%)	(9)	34,378 (40.49%)		4,816 (5.67%)	
Maryland	32,676 (47.59%)		35,984 (52.41%)	(8)		
Massachusetts	53,403 (40.67%)		67,062 (51.08%)	(12)	10,830 (8.25%)	
Michigan	27,737 (49.92%)	(5)	24,185 (43.53%)		3,637 (6.54%)	
Mississippi	25,926 (56.61%)	(6)	19,874 (43.39%)			
Missouri	41,324 (56.94%)	(7)	31,250 (43.06%)			
New Hampshire	27,232 (55.39%)	(6)	17,769 (36.14%)		4,160 (8.46%)	
New Jersey	37,495 (49.57%)		38,018 (50.26%)	(7)	131 (0.17%)	
New York	237,588 (48.90%)	(36)	232,482 (47.85%)		15,814 (3.25%)	
North Carolina	39,287 (47.61%)		43,232 (52.39%)	(11)		
Ohio	149,011 (47.73%)		155,112 (49.69%)	(23)	8,050 (2.58%)	
Pennsylvania	167,535 (50.48%)	(26)	161,203 (48.57%)		3,133 (0.94%)	
Rhode Island	4,876 (39.93%)		7,322 (60.07%)	(4)		
South Carolina	(9)	electors chosen by the legislature				
Tennessee	59,917 (49.95%)		60,030 (50.05%)	(13)		
Vermont	18,049 (36.99%)		26,777 (54.88%)	(6)	3,970 (8.14%)	
Virginia	51,383 (53.43%)	(17)	44,791 (46.57%)			
Total	**1,340,313 (49.59%) (170)**		**1,300,197 (48.11%) (105)**		**62,025 (2.30%)**	

Alabama

County	Polk (D)	Clay (W)
Autauga	633 (57.1%)	475 (42.9%)
Baldwin	120 (44.6%)	149 (55.4%)
Barbour	860 (43.6%)	1,113 (56.4%)
Benton	1,382 (78.7%)	373 (21.3%)
Bibb	596 (57.0%)	450 (43.0%)
Blount	774 (90.2%)	84 (9.8%)
Butler	405 (37.8%)	666 (62.2%)
Chambers	936 (44.7%)	1,158 (55.3%)
Cherokee	955 (72.8%)	356 (27.2%)
Clarke	631 (73.1%)	232 (26.9%)
Coffee	315 (68.9%)	142 (31.1%)
Conecuh	277 (38.6%)	441 (61.4%)
Coosa	796 (66.6%)	400 (33.4%)
Covington	139 (48.4%)	148 (51.6%)
Dale	616 (74.7%)	209 (25.3%)
Dallas	722 (45.5%)	864 (54.5%)
De Kalb	700 (77.2%)	207 (22.8%)
Fayette	796 (83.9%)	153 (16.1%)
Franklin	983 (67.9%)	465 (32.1%)
Greene	819 (42.9%)	1,090 (57.1%)
Henry	546 (59.8%)	367 (40.2%)
Jackson	1,751 (95.3%)	87 (4.7%)
Jefferson	585 (68.9%)	264 (31.1%)
Lauderdale	919 (66.0%)	474 (34.0%)
Lawrence	783 (62.5%)	469 (37.5%)
Limestone	965 (74.8%)	325 (25.2%)
Lowndes	678 (48.8%)	710 (51.2%)
Macon	626 (36.5%)	1,087 (63.5%)
Madison	1,720 (82.8%)	357 (17.2%)
Marengo	634 (46.6%)	726 (53.4%)
Marion	638 (84.2%)	120 (15.8%)
Marshall	875 (84.4%)	162 (15.6%)
Mobile	1,347 (49.0%)	1,403 (51.0%)
Monroe	359 (38.8%)	567 (61.2%)
Montgomery	836 (45.1%)	1,016 (54.9%)
Morgan	682 (71.6%)	271 (28.4%)
Perry	849 (49.4%)	869 (50.6%)
Pickens	967 (52.0%)	892 (48.0%)
Pike	768 (47.1%)	862 (52.9%)
Randolph	747 (72.2%)	288 (27.8%)
Russell	624 (45.9%)	736 (54.1%)
Saint Clair	644 (93.3%)	46 (6.7%)
Shelby	472 (48.0%)	511 (52.0%)
Sumter	1,061 (53.4%)	927 (46.6%)
Talladega	851 (57.3%)	633 (42.7%)
Tallapoosa	705 (49.2%)	728 (50.8%)
Tuscaloosa	964 (51.7%)	902 (48.3%)
Walker	442 (72.2%)	170 (27.8%)
Washington	279 (50.5%)	273 (49.5%)
Wilcox	629 (51.8%)	585 (48.2%)
Total	**37,401 (59.0%)**	**26,002 (41.0%)**

SOURCE—Manuscript returns.

Arkansas

County	Polk (D)	Clay (W)
Arkansas	93 (53.8%)	80 (46.2%)
Benton	351 (78.5%)	96 (21.5%)
Bradley	154 (51.7%)	144 (48.3%)
Carroll	no returns	
Chicot	158 (42.9%)	210 (57.1%)
Clark	217 (55.5%)	174 (44.5%)
Conway	288 (63.3%)	167 (36.7%)
Crawford	565 (59.5%)	385 (40.5%)
Crittenden	129 (54.2%)	109 (45.8%)
Desha	55 (30.2%)	127 (69.8%)
Franklin	261 (64.1%)	146 (35.9%)
Fulton	no returns	
Greene	206 (84.8%)	37 (15.2%)
Hempstead	359 (53.3%)	314 (46.7%)
Hot Springs & Montgomery	237 (66.4%)	120 (33.6%)
Independence	335 (55.6%)	278 (44.4%)
Izard	no returns	
Jackson	184 (59.7%)	124 (40.3%)
Jefferson	147 (51.4%)	139 (48.6%)
Johnson	431 (75.3%)	141 (24.7%)
Lafayette	70 (64.2%)	39 (35.8%)
Lawrence	267 (70.4%)	112 (29.6%)
Madison	366 (85.3%)	63 (14.7%)
Marion	no returns	
Mississippi	no returns	
Monroe	73 (44.2%)	92 (55.8%)
Newton	140 (89.7%)	16 (10.3%)
Ouachita	184 (45.5%)	220 (54.5%)
Perry	65 (66.3%)	33 (33.7%)
Phillips	276 (50.4%)	280 (50.4%)
Pike	no returns	
Poinsett	171 (85.5%)	29 (14.5%)
Pope	308 (56.1%)	241 (43.9%)
Pulaski	528 (54.7%)	438 (45.3%)
Randolph	341 (85.3%)	59 (14.7%)
St. Francis	269 (73.3%)	99 (26.7%)
Saline	219 (62.8%)	130 (37.2%)
Scott	167 (81.5%)	35 (18.5%)
Searcy	no returns	
Sevier	301 (72.5%)	114 (27.5%)
Union	409 (65.7%)	214 (34.3%)
Van Buren	121 (72.5%)	46 (27.5%)
Washington	729 (65.9%)	378 (34.1%)
White	123 (56.4%)	95 (43.6%)
Yell	249 (75.7%)	80 (24.3%)
Total[2]	**9,546 (63.0%)**	**5,604 (37.0%)**

SOURCES—W. Dean Burnham, *Presidential Ballots 1836–1892* (reprint edition), New York, NY: Arno Press, 1976, pp. 274–292, citing the *Arkansas Gazette*, December 4, 1844; and *Political Textbook for 1860*, Tribune Association, New York, NY: 1860, pp. 234–5.

Connecticut

County	Polk (D)	Clay (W)	Birney (Lty)
Fairfield	4,599 (45.5%)	5,368 (53.1%)	142 (1.4%)
Hartford	5,624 (46.2%)	6,259 (51.4%)	287 (2.4%)
Litchfield	4,335 (46.3%)	4,668 (49.8%)	369 (3.9%)
Middlesex	2,354 (49.0%)	2,324 (48.3%)	130 (2.7%)
New Haven	4,726 (45.0%)	5,546 (52.8%)	229 (2.2%)
New London	3,709 (45.8%)	4,081 (50.4%)	304 (3.8%)
Tolland	1,950 (48.3%)	1,964 (48.7%)	120 (3.0%)
Windham	2,544 (46.0%)	2,622 (47.4%)	363 (6.6%)
Total	**29,841 (46.2%)**	**32,832 (50.8%)**	**1,944 (3.0%)**

SOURCE—Manuscript returns.

Delaware

County	Polk (D)	Clay (W)
Kent	1,415 (47.2%)	1,583 (52.8%)
New Castle	2,678 (48.7%)	2,819 (51.3%)
Sussex	1,877 (50.1%)	1,869 (49.9%)
Total	**5,970 (48.8%)**	**6,271 (51.2%)**

SOURCE—*Governor's Register*, 1844.

Georgia

County	Polk (D)	Clay (W)
Appling	142 (48.3%)	152 (51.7%)
Baker	506 (69.4%)	223 (30.6%)
Baldwin	307 (48.7%)	324 (51.3%)
Bibb	862 (55.0%)	706 (45.0%)
Bryan	72 (41.1%)	103 (58.9%)
Burke	410 (42.4%)	556 (57.6%)
Butts	434 (64.1%)	243 (35.9%)
Camden	218 (67.7%)	104 (32.3%)
Campbell	543 (72.6%)	205 (27.4%)
Carroll	766 (68.3%)	355 (31.7%)
Cass	1,139 (63.6%)	652 (36.4%)
Chatham	839 (50.7%)	817 (49.3%)
Chattooga	323 (53.3%)	285 (46.7%)
Cherokee	813 (61.1%)	517 (38.9%)
Clarke	420 (41.3%)	596 (58.7%)
Cobb	943 (58.9%)	658 (41.1%)
Columbia	307 (38.4%)	492 (61.6%)
Coweta	744 (48.9%)	777 (51.1%)
Crawford	454 (54.6%)	377 (45.4%)
Dade	246 (84.2%)	46 (15.8%)
Decatur	346 (47.5%)	383 (52.5%)
De Kalb	967 (62.5%)	580 (37.5%)
Dooly	507 (65.3%)	269 (34.7%)
Early	419 (66.5%)	211 (33.5%)
Effingham	87 (31.1%)	193 (68.9%)
Elbert	186 (15.7%)	999 (84.3%)
Fayette	705 (63.1%)	412 (36.9%)
Floyd	425 (54.8%)	350 (45.2%)
Forsyth	731 (61.7%)	454 (38.3%)
Franklin	1,057 (73.6%)	380 (26.4%)
Gilmer	511 (70.0%)	219 (30.0%)
Glynn	23 (20.0%)	92 (80.0%)
Greene	132 (14.5%)	780 (85.5%)
Gwinnett	763 (49.4%)	780 (50.6%)
Habersham	966 (74.9%)	323 (25.1%)
Hall	697 (58.8%)	489 (41.2%)
Hancock	330 (39.1%)	515 (60.9%)
Harris	464 (35.4%)	845 (64.6%)
Heard	436 (59.8%)	293 (40.2%)
Henry	819 (48.8%)	858 (51.2%)
Houston	723 (52.3%)	659 (47.7%)
Irwin	223 (91.4%)	21 (8.6%)
Jackson	663 (57.4%)	491 (42.6%)
Jasper	536 (55.0%)	438 (45.0%)
Jefferson	108 (15.7%)	579 (84.3%)
Jones	455 (53.4%)	397 (46.6%)
Lawrence	15 (23.3%)	628 (76.7%)
Lee	121 (26.5%)	335 (73.5%)
Liberty	191 (51.6%)	179 (48.4%)
Lincoln	179 (38.5%)	286 (61.5%)
Lowndes	362 (45.9%)	427 (54.1%)
Lumpkin	1,254 (65.3%)	665 (34.7%)
Macon	245 (42.5%)	331 (57.5%)
Madison	327 (48.5%)	347 (51.5%)
Marion	256 (38.1%)	416 (61.9%)
McIntosh	114 (47.3%)	127 (52.7%)

Meriwether	926 (57.4%)	688 (42.6%)	
Monroe	706 (46.9%)	798 (53.1%)	
Montgomery	34 (12.5%)	238 (87.5%)	
Morgan	348 (44.1%)	442 (55.9%)	
Murray	699 (69.8%)	303 (30.2%)	
Muscogee	980 (45.2%)	1,190 (54.8%)	
Newton	553 (35.0%)	1,025 (65.0%)	
Oglethorpe	241 (27.8%)	626 (72.2%)	
Paulding	394 (64.4%)	218 (35.6%)	
Pike	871 (56.9%)	659 (43.1%)	
Pulaski	457 (64.9%)	247 (35.1%)	
Putnam	350 (44.9%)	430 (55.1%)	
Rabun	224 (87.2%)	33 (12.8%)	
Randolph	735 (54.9%)	605 (35.1%)	
Richmond	647 (41.7%)	903 (58.3%)	
Scriven	278 (52.0%)	257 (48.0%)	
Stewart	813 (47.7%)	891 (52.3%)	
Sumter	444 (40.6%)	650 (59.4%)	
Talbot	912 (51.6%)	855 (48.4%)	
Taliaferro	67 (14.8%)	386 (85.2%)	
Tattnall	64 (15.9%)	338 (84.1%)	
Telfair	198 (73.8%)	177 (26.2%)	
Thomas	267 (43.4%)	348 (56.6%)	
Troup	487 (37.6%)	1,053 (62.4%)	
Twiggs	467 (54.6%)	389 (45.4%)	
Union	554 (70.0%)	237 (30.0%)	
Upson	384 (37.4%)	643 (62.6%)	
Walker	686 (60.5%)	447 (39.5%)	
Walton	762 (57.9%)	554 (42.1%)	
Ware	125 (40.1%)	187 (59.9%)	
Warren	368 (36.5%)	641 (63.5%)	
Washington	595 (50.3%)	629 (49.7%)	
Wayne	96 (47.0%)	138 (53.0%)	
Wilkes	389 (47.5%)	430 (52.5%)	
Wilkinson	445 (53.9%)	381 (46.1%)	
Total	**43,397 (50.8%)**	**41,975 (49.2%)**	
*Bulloch	410 (96.0%)	47 (4.0%)	
*Emanuel	251 (68.3%)	107 (31.7%)	
*Wilkinson (part)	115	5	

*The votes of these counties were rejected due to "irregularities."

SOURCES—*Executive Council Minutes of Georgia*, December, 1844, p. 93; and W. Dean Burnham, *Presidential Ballots 1836–1892* (reprint edition), New York, NY: Arno Press, 1976, pp. 332–362.

Illinois

County	Polk (D)	Clay (W)	Birney (Lty)
Adams	1,495 (51.1%)	1,280 (43.8%)	149 (5.1%)
Alexander	138 (63.0%)	81 (37.0%)	0
Bond	635 (51.8%)	564 (46.0%)	26 (2.1%)
Boone	398 (47.9%)	375 (45.1%)	58 (7.0%)
Brown	551 (62.6%)	329 (37.4%)	0
Bureau	379 (41.7%)	369 (40.6%)	160 (17.6%)
Calhoun	269 (51.8%)	247 (47.6%)	3 (0.6%)
Carroll	178 (41.3%)	247 (57.3%)	6 (1.4%)
Cass	408 (49.1%)	423 (50.9%)	0
Champaign	191 (51.8%)	178 (48.2%)	0
Christian	216 (54.3%)	182 (45.7%)	0
Clark	756 (54.7%)	625 (45.3%)	0
Clay	408 (68.7%)	186 (31.3%)	0
Clinton	552 (60.1%)	366 (39.8%)	1 (0.1%)
Coles	582 (42.9%)	776 (39.8%)	0
Cook	2,027 (58.5%)	1,119 (32.3%)	317 (9.2%)
Crawford	496 (53.9%)	425 (46.1%)	0
Cumberland	189 (49.7%)	191 (50.3%)	0
De Kalb	242 (47.0%)	142 (27.6%)	131 (25.4%)
De Witt	361 (53.0%)	317 (46.5%)	3 (0.4%)
Du Page	551 (50.3%)	372 (33.9%)	173 (15.8%)
Edgar	884 (54.9%)	701 (43.6%)	24 (1.5%)
Edwards	185 (32.5%)	385 (67.5%)	0
Effingham	364 (81.6%)	82 (18.4%)	0
Fayette	653 (61.2%)	414 (38.8%)	0
Franklin	634 (86.1%)	102 (13.9%)	0
Fulton	1,537 (49.9%)	1,434 (46.6%)	108 (3.5%)
Gallatin	1,202 (74.6%)	410 (25.4%)	0
Greene	1,250 (61.0%)	800 (39.0%)	0
Grundy	91 (61.9%)	49 (33.3%)	7 (4.8%)
Hamilton	629 (83.2%)	127 (16.8%)	0
Hancock	1,399 (65.2%)	747 (34.8%)	1 (0.5%)
Hardin	167 (55.1%)	136 (44.9%)	0
Henderson	294 (40.7%)	428 (59.3%)	0
Henry	166 (48.7%)	147 (43.1%)	28 (8.2%)
Iroquois	281 (57.9%)	204 (42.1%)	0
Jackson	347 (65.6%)	182 (34.4%)	0
Jasper	276 (65.9%)	143 (34.1%)	0
Jefferson	863 (79.1%)	227 (20.8%)	1 (0.1%)
Jersey	459 (43.2%)	555 (52.3%)	48 (4.5%)
Jo Daviess	1,585 (50.9%)	1,514 (48.6%)	14 (0.4%)
Johnson	382 (92.2%)	32 (7.8%)	0
Kane	1,046 (50.0%)	748 (35.7%)	299 (14.3%)
Kendall	479 (49.0%)	357 (36.5%)	142 (14.5%)
Knox	689 (43.1%)	746 (46.7%)	162 (10.1%)
Lake	620 (54.5%)	386 (33.9%)	131 (11.5%)
La Salle	1,006 (61.2%)	511 (31.1%)	126 (7.7%)
Lawrence	611 (58.9%)	427 (41.1%)	0
Lee	315 (51.9%)	244 (40.1%)	48 (7.9%)
Livingston	109 (62.2%)	66 (37.7%)	0
Logan	251 (44.7%)	310 (55.3%)	0
Macon	328 (59.7%)	221 (40.3%)	0
Macoupin	974 (60.1%)	641 (39.5%)	6 (0.4%)
Madison	1,496 (47.3%)	1,657 (52.4%)	12 (0.4%)
Marion	722 (79.3%)	182 (21.0%)	6 (0.7%)
Marquette	149 (37.6%)	247 (62.4%)	0
Marshall	263 (50.9%)	237 (45.8%)	17 (3.3%)
Mason	254 (49.9%)	255 (50.1%)	0
Massac	398 (70.7%)	165 (29.3%)	0
McDonough	493 (51.4%)	458 (46.7%)	9 (0.9%)
McHenry	668 (54.1%)	493 (39.9%)	74 (6.0%)
McLean	477 (44.0%)	586 (54.0%)	22 (2.0%)
Menard	378 (48.8%)	397 (51.1%)	0
Mercer	321 (43.9%)	410 (56.1%)	0
Monroe	740 (70.9%)	304 (29.1%)	0
Montgomery	661 (65.1%)	355 (34.9%)	0
Morgan	1,421 (48.6%)	1,444 (49.4%)	59 (2.0%)
Moultrie	204 (51.0%)	196 (49.0%)	0
Ogle	383 (35.7%)	595 (55.4%)	95 (8.9%)
Peoria	1,169 (51.5%)	846 (40.9%)	55 (2.7%)
Perry	477 (66.4%)	219 (30.5%)	22 (3.1%)
Piatt	120 (59.7%)	81 (40.3%)	0
Pike	1,456 (50.6%)	1,411 (49.0%)	11 (0.4%)
Pope	348 (63.4%)	201 (36.6%)	0
Pulaski	208 (69.8%)	90 (30.2%)	0
Putnam	228 (37.7%)	237 (39.2%)	140 (23.1%)
Randolph	771 (47.4%)	713 (43.9%)	141 (8.7%)
Richland	322 (52.7%)	289 (47.3%)	0
Rock Island	397 (46.3%)	461 (53.7%)	0
St. Clair	1,945 (65.1%)	1,042 (34.9%)	2 (0.1%)
Sangamon	1,371 (42.7%)	1,837 (57.3%)	0
Schuyler	743 (54.8%)	610 (45.0%)	4 (0.3%)
Scott	610 (47.4%)	670 (52.1%)	7 (0.5%)
Shelby	683 (68.4%)	315 (31.6%)	0
Stark	206 (48.4%)	187 (43.9%)	33 (0.8%)
Stephenson	465 (49.8%)	483 (49.7%)	24 (2.5%)
Tazewell	628 (37.6%)	1,011 (60.5%)	33 (2.0%)
Union	617 (86.8%)	94 (13.2%)	0
Vermilion	768 (46.1%)	869 (52.2%)	28 (1.7%)
Wabash	315 (39.6%)	479 (60.2%)	2 (0.3%)

Warren	503 (48.5%)	500 (48.2%)	35 (3.4%)
Washington	565 (68.4%)	254 (30.8%)	7 (0.8%)
Wayne	637 (70.5%)	266 (29.5%)	0
White	748 (50.4%)	736 (49.6%)	0
Whiteside	290 (40.2%)	384 (53.3%)	47 (6.5%)
Will	810 (53.0%)	510 (33.4%)	209 (13.7%)
Williamson	766 (81.1%)	179 (18.9%)	0
Winnebago	368 (34.3%)	547 (50.9%)	159 (14.8%)
Woodford	322 (65.8%)	159 (32.5%)	8 (1.6%)
Total	**58,982 (54.4%)**	**45,931 (42.4%)**	**3,433 (3.2%)**

SOURCE—Theodore Pease (ed.), *Illinois Election Returns, 1818–1848,* Springfield, IL: Illinois State Historical Society Library, 1923, pp. 149–152.

Indiana

County	Polk (D)	Clay (W)	Birney (Lty)
Adams	296 (61.2%)	198 (38.8%)	0
Allen	849 (49.6%)	861 (50.4%)	0
Bartholomew	1,068 (50.5%)	1,035 (48.9%)	13 (0.6%)
Benton	60 (59.4%)	40 (39.6%)	1 (0.1%)
Blackford	205 (70.9%)	81 (28.0%)	3 (1.0%)
Boone	871 (51.4%)	816 (48.1%)	8 (0.5%)
Brown	432 (88.0%)	59 (12.0%)	0
Carroll	965 (57.3%)	712 (42.3%)	8 (0.5%)
Cass	671 (46.1%)	768 (52.7%)	18 (1.2%)
Clark	1,417 (55.6%)	1,132 (44.4%)	0
Clay	662 (60.7%)	429 (39.3%)	0
Clinton	944 (59.0%)	645 (40.3%)	12 (0.7%)
Crawford	397 (46.2%)	462 (53.8%)	0
Daviess	764 (48.6%)	807 (51.4%)	0
Dearborn	1,971 (54.2%)	1,616 (44.4%)	50 (1.4%)
Decatur	1,091 (44.8%)	1,275 (52.3%)	68 (2.8%)
De Kalb	327 (54.3%)	269 (44.7%)	6 (1.0%)
Delaware	732 (43.7%)	940 (56.1%)	3 (0.2%)
Dubois	501 (68.6%)	229 (31.4%)	0
Elkhart	964 (55.9%)	758 (44.0)	1 (0.1%)
Fayette	908 (46.0%)	1,051 (53.2%)	17 (0.9%)
Floyd	981 (50.6%)	956 (49.4%)	0
Fountain	1,387 (59.4%)	947 (40.6%)	0
Franklin	1,584 (54.3%)	1,325 (45.4%)	8 (0.3%)
Fulton	308 (46.8%)	344 (52.3%)	6 (0.9%)
Gibson	810 (50.1%)	796 (49.3%)	8 (0.5%)
Grant	423 (43.5%)	353 (36.3%)	196 (20.2%)
Greene	909 (54.4%)	762 (45.6%)	0
Hamilton	766 (43.4%)	859 (48.7%)	139 (7.9%)
Hancock	736 (50.5%)	719 (49.3%)	2 (0.1%)
Harrison	1,144 (47.7%)	1,252 (52.3%)	0
Hendricks	844 (39.6%)	1,262 (59.2%)	26 (1.2%)
Henry	1,005 (38.0%)	1,458 (55.1%)	188 (7.1%)
Huntington	316 (52.6%)	277 (46.1%)	8 (1.3%)
Jackson	1,048 (61.3%)	662 (38.7%)	1 (0.1%)
Jasper	175 (56.3%)	128 (41.2%)	8 (2.6%)
Jay	352 (48.6%)	331 (45.7%)	42 (5.8%)
Jefferson	1,427 (43.1%)	1,835 (55.4%)	50 (1.5%)
Jennings	669 (43.0%)	872 (56.1%)	14 (0.9%)
Johnson	1,150 (63.0%)	659 (36.1%)	15 (0.8%)
Knox	821 (43.2%)	1,079 (56.8%)	1 (0.1%)
Kosciusko	553 (46.8%)	623 (52.8%)	5 (0.4%)
LaGrange	457 (42.1%)	590 (54.4%)	38 (3.5%)
Lake	206 (63.4%)	114 (35.1%)	5 (1.5%)
LaPorte	831 (43.9%)	1,009 (53.3%)	53 (2.8%)
Lawrence	1,085 (51.5%)	1,019 (48.4%)	3 (0.1%)
Madison	854 (50.6%)	813 (48.2%)	20 (1.2%)
Marion	1,634 (48.4%)	1,715 (50.8%)	25 (0.7%)
Marshall	256 (50.3%)	199 (39.1%)	54 (10.6%)
Martin	516 (65.2%)	276 (34.8%)	0
Miami	517 (47.6%)	569 (52.4%)	0

County	Polk (D)	Clay (W)	Birney (Lty)
Monroe	1,118 (60.4%)	721 (39.0%)	12 (0.6%)
Montgomery	1,521 (51.1%)	1,450 (48.7%)	8 (0.3%)
Morgan	1,078 (50.7%)	1,023 (48.1%)	24 (1.1%)
Noble	438 (52.9%)	390 (47.1%)	0
Ohio	168 (46.5%)	193 (53.5%)	0
Orange	1,036 (59.2%)	707 (40.6%)	3 (0.2%)
Owen	888 (54.0%)	754 (45.9%)	1 (0.1%)
Parke	1,329 (48.9%)	1,377 (50.7%)	12 (0.4%)
Perry	334 (37.3%)	564 (62.7%)	0
Pike	491 (51.7%)	459 (48.3%)	0
Porter	305 (48.4%)	311 (49.4%)	14 (2.2%)
Posey	1,154 (63.2%)	673 (36.8%)	0
Pulaski	124 (50.0%)	123 (49.6%)	1 (0.4%)
Putnam	1,367 (46.9%)	1,540 (52.8%)	9 (0.3%)
Randolph	809 (44.1%)	818 (44.6%)	206 (11.2%)
Richardville	133 (48.2%)	129 (46.7%)	14 (5.1%)
Ripley	908 (44.1%)	1,060 (51.5%)	89 (4.3%)
Rush	1,362 (45.6%)	1,580 (52.9%)	42 (1.4%)
Saint Joseph	683 (43.3%)	863 (54.7%)	33 (2.1%)
Scott	441 (47.8%)	481 (52.1%)	1 (0.1%)
Shelby	1,342 (54.6%)	1,107 (45.1%)	7 (0.3%)
Spencer	496 (45.8%)	586 (54.2%)	0
Steuben	303 (45.0%)	328 (48.7%)	42 (6.2%)
Sullivan	1,221 (70.7%)	464 (26.9%)	1 (0.1%)
Switzerland	1,006 (50.9%)	961 (48.7%)	8 (0.4%)
Tippecanoe	1,551 (49.4%)	1,550 (49.4%)	38 (1.2%)
Tipton	119 (54.3%)	100 (45.7%)	0
Union	672 (47.5%)	682 (48.2%)	60 (4.2%)
Vanderburgh	556 (45.1%)	675 (54.8%)	1 (0.1%)
Vermillion	762 (27.4%)	787 (72.6%)	0
Vigo	856 (36.1%)	1,515 (63.9%)	0
Wabash	575 (48.1%)	601 (50.2%)	19 (1.6%)
Warren	470 (37.4%)	778 (61.8%)	10 (0.8%)
Warrick	850 (68.3%)	394 (31.7%)	0
Washington	1,660 (59.0%)	1,149 (40.8%)	5 (0.2%)
Wayne	1,437 (35.2%)	2,321 (56.9%)	319 (7.8%)
Wells	306 (61.9%)	185 (37.4%)	3 (0.6%)
White	218 (45.7%)	259 (54.3%)	0
Whitley	237 (51.4%)	222 (48.2%)	2 (0.4%)
Total	**70,183 (50.1%)**	**67,866 (48.4%)**	**2,107 (1.5%)**

SOURCE—Dorothy F. Riker and Gayle Thornbrough (eds.), *Indiana Election Returns 1816–1851*, Indianapolis, IN: Indiana Historical Bureau, 1960, pp. 38–52.

Kentucky

County	Polk (D)	Clay (W)
Adair	639 (53.8%)	548 (46.2%)
Allen	635 (61.3%)	401 (38.7%)
Anderson	552 (66.3%)	281 (33.7%)
Ballard	400 (58.7%)	282 (41.3%)
Barren	1,108 (45.9%)	1,306 (54.1%)
Bath	783 (56.2%)	611 (43.8%)
Boone	712 (47.1%)	800 (52.9%)
Bourbon	521 (30.1%)	1,208 (69.9%)
Boyle	352 (36.3%)	617 (63.7%)
Bracken	443 (37.0%)	753 (63.0%)
Breathitt	231 (64.2%)	129 (35.8%)
Breckinridge	464 (33.4%)	924 (66.6%)
Bullitt	436 (45.2%)	528 (54.8%)
Butler	290 (45.2%)	351 (54.8%)
Caldwell	966 (55.3%)	780 (44.7%)
Calloway	772 (79.1%)	204 (20.9%)
Campbell	618 (63.3%)	358 (36.7%)
Carroll	370 (49.2%)	382 (50.8%)
Carter	508 (77.4%)	148 (22.6%)
Casey	214 (31.4%)	468 (68.6%)
Christian	825 (42.4%)	1,122 (57.6%)

	Polk (D)	Clay (W)
Clark	314 (24.0%)	996 (76.0%)
Clay	92 (21.5%)	335 (78.5%)
Clinton	315 (54.6%)	262 (45.4%)
Crittenden	399 (58.4%)	284 (41.6%)
Cumberland	167 (22.1%)	590 (77.9%)
Daviess	622 (43.5%)	808 (56.5%)
Edmonson	251 (59.1%)	174 (40.9%)
Estill	216 (35.5%)	392 (64.5%)
Fayette	824 (32.7%)	1,695 (67.3%)
Fleming	771 (40.3%)	1,143 (59.7%)
Floyd	340 (64.2%)	190 (35.8%)
Franklin	634 (43.7%)	816 (56.3%)
Gallatin	351 (50.2%)	348 (49.8%)
Garrard	229 (16.9%)	1,128 (83.1%)
Grant	493 (55.5%)	396 (44.5%)
Graves	884 (69.6%)	386 (30.4%)
Grayson	386 (47.2%)	432 (52.8%)
Green	1,042 (55.8%)	827 (44.2%)
Greenup	385 (39.4%)	593 (60.6%)
Hancock	213 (43.5%)	277 (56.5%)
Hardin	702 (39.1%)	1,095 (60.9%)
Harlan	75 (22.1%)	334 (77.9%)
Harrison	975 (53.2%)	859 (46.8%)
Hart	558 (49.1%)	579 (50.9%)
Henderson	638 (47.0%)	719 (53.0%)
Henry	1,044 (59.6%)	708 (40.4%)
Hickman	740 (70.9%)	304 (29.1%)
Hopkins	814 (53.7%)	701 (46.3%)
Jefferson	2,706 (43.4%)	3,527 (56.6%)
Jessamine	469 (43.2%)	616 (56.8%)
Johnson	252 (74.8%)	85 (25.2%)
Kenton	920 (57.2%)	687 (42.8%)
Knox	164 (21.8%)	589 (78.2%)
Larue	333 (46.6%)	382 (53.4%)
Laurel	124 (24.4%)	384 (75.6%)
Lawrence	345 (49.9%)	347 (50.1%)
Letcher	161 (84.7%)	29 (15.3%)
Lewis	543 (51.8%)	506 (48.2%)
Lincoln	335 (69.7%)	769 (30.3%)
Livingston	327 (43.5%)	424 (56.5%)
Logan	374 (21.0%)	1,407 (79.0%)
Madison	633 (34.5%)	1,202 (65.5%)
Marion	737 (50.8%)	715 (49.2%)
Marshall	600 (86.5%)	94 (13.5%)
Mason	799 (33.2%)	1,608 (66.8%)
McCracken	195 (43.2%)	256 (56.8%)
Meade	223 (25.5%)	650 (74.5%)
Mercer	985 (63.9%)	557 (36.1%)
Monroe	473 (51.2%)	451 (48.8%)
Montgomery	597 (47.0%)	673 (53.0%)
Morgan	512 (67.5%)	247 (32.5%)
Muhlenberg	489 (42.7%)	657 (57.3%)
Nelson	608 (31.4%)	1,326 (68.6%)
Nicholas	703 (50.9%)	678 (49.1%)
Ohio	513 (46.1%)	601 (53.9%)
Oldham	625 (59.5%)	426 (40.5%)
Owen	937 (65.9%)	485 (34.1%)
Owsley	129 (43.9%)	165 (56.1%)
Pendleton	530 (64.9%)	287 (35.1%)
Perry	84 (42.6%)	113 (57.4%)
Pike	238 (48.7%)	251 (51.3%)
Pulaski	708 (49.3%)	727 (50.7%)
Rockcastle	73 (13.9%)	451 (86.1%)
Russell	178 (29.2%)	431 (70.8%)
Scott	938 (53.9%)	803 (46.1%)
Shelby	796 (35.6%)	1,441 (64.4%)
Simpson	418 (47.9%)	455 (52.1%)
Spencer	508 (52.0%)	469 (48.0%)
Todd	406 (34.1%)	784 (65.9%)
Trigg	651 (53.9%)	557 (46.1%)
Trimble	507 (65.4%)	268 (34.6%)
Union	584 (53.5%)	507 (46.5%)
Warren	687 (37.7%)	1,132 (62.3%)
Washington	709 (51.8%)	660 (48.2%)
Wayne	342 (39.0%)	535 (61.0%)
Whitley	99 (18.7%)	431 (81.3%)
Woddford	473 (38.7%)	750 (61.3%)
Total	**52,053 (46.0%)**	**61,167 (54.0%)**
	*(51,988)	*(61,255)

*Stated totals.

SOURCE—(Frankfort) *Commonwealth*, December 3, 1844.

Louisiana

Parish	Polk (D)	Clay (W)
Ascension	264 (53.5%)	239 (46.5%)
Assumption	279 (49.5%)	285 (50.5%)
Avoyelles	364 (65.8%)	189 (34.2%)
Bossier	103 (63.6%)	59 (36.4%)
*Calcasieu	128 (75.3%)	42 (24.7%)
Caldwell	194 (73.8%)	69 (26.2%)
Carroll	221 (53.8%)	190 (46.2%)
Catahoula	304 (55.6%)	243 (44.4%)
Claiborne	375 (66.0%)	193 (34.0%)
Concordia	95 (33.6%)	188 (66.4%)
De Soto	150 (74.3%)	52 (25.7%)
East Baton Rouge	399 (55.1%)	325 (44.9%)
East Feliciana	419 (56.0%)	329 (44.0%)
Franklin	158 (54.1%)	134 (45.9%)
Iberville	235 (48.2%)	253 (51.8%)
Jefferson	403 (47.9%)	434 (52.1%)
Lafayette	399 (61.4%)	193 (38.6%)
Lafourche Interior	137 (22.5%)	471 (77.5%)
Livingston	229 (69.6%)	100 (30.4%)
Madison	198 (49.0%)	206 (51.0%)
Morehouse	31 (22.5%)	107 (77.5%)
Natchitoches	650 (59.0%)	452 (41.0%)
Orleans	2,612 (46.3%)	3,026 (53.7%)
Ouachita	206 (66.0%)	106 (34.0%)
Plaquemines	1,007 (96.5%)	37 (3.5%)
Point Coupee	175 (50.1%)	174 (49.9%)
Rapides	586 (58.2%)	419 (41.8%)
Sabine	383 (60.0%)	255 (40.0%)
St. Bernard	84 (31.2%)	185 (68.8%)
St. Charles	42 (30.4%)	96 (69.6%)
St. Helena	222 (59.0%)	154 (41.0%)
St. James	181 (34.0%)	351 (66.0%)
St. John the Baptist	113 (44.3%)	142 (55.7%)
†St. Landry	406 (34.0%)	789 (66.0%)
St. Martin	303 (38.7%)	479 (61.3%)
St. Mary	142 (36.0%)	352 (64.0%)
St. Tammany	199 (54.1%)	169 (45.9%)
Tensas	108 (40.8%)	157 (59.2%)
Terrebone	164 (38.2%)	265 (61.8%)
Union	213 (50.8%)	206 (49.2%)
Vermillion	104 (37.1%)	176 (62.9%)
Washington	230 (64.4%)	127 (35.6%)
West Baton Rouge	104 (33.2%)	209 (66.8%)
West Feliciana	308 (55.9%)	243 (44.1%)
Total[3]	**13,782 (51.3%)**	**13,080 (48.7%)**
	*(13,477)	(12,818)

*Stated totals.

†*Calcasieu and St. Landry parishes reported as one in the* Bee *and the* Whig Almanac *but separately in W. Dean Burnham's* Presidential Ballots. *The separate totals add up to the combined total.*

SOURCES—*New Orleans Bee*, November 26, 1844; *Whig Almanac 1845*, p. 59; and W. Dean Burnham, *Presidential Ballots 1836–1892* (reprint edition), New York, NY: Arno Press, 1976, pp. 486–500.

Maine

County	Polk (D)	Clay (W)	Birney (Lty)
Aroostook	907 (68.4%)	398 (30.0%)	21 (1.6%)
Cumberland	6,367 (55.2%)	4,483 (38.8%)	694 (6.0%)
Franklin	1,609 (51.4%)	1,132 (36.1%)	392 (1.3%)
Hancock	2,608 (57.2%)	1,849 (40.5%)	105 (2.3%)
Kennebec	3,535 (37.3%)	5,393 (56.8%)	561 (5.9%)
Lincoln	5,354 (51.6%)	4,566 (44.0%)	461 (4.4%)
Oxford	4,395 (65.8%)	1,887 (28.3%)	397 (5.9%)
Penobscot	4,895 (54.6%)	3,376 (37.6%)	701 (7.8%)
Piscataquis	1,136 (46.6%)	1,074 (44.1%)	228 (9.4%)
Somerset	2,530 (43.5%)	2,849 (49.0%)	435 (7.5%)
Waldo	4,661 (68.5%)	1,826 (26.8%)	316 (4.6%)
Washington	2,605 (52.0%)	2,329 (46.5%)	74 (1.5%)
York	5,117 (58.4%)	3,216 (36.7%)	431 (4.9%)
Total	**45,719 (53.8%)**	**34,378 (40.5%)**	**4,816 (5.7%)**

SOURCES—(Augusta) *Kennebec Journal*, December 6, 1844; (Portland) *Eastern Argus*, December 9, 1844.

Maryland

County	Polk (D)	Clay (W)
Allegany	1,491 (51.1%)	1,424 (48.9%)
Anne Arundel	1,503 (45.8%)	1,777 (54.2%)
Baltimore	2,716 (54.1%)	2,301 (45.9%)
Calvert	344 (43.3%)	451 (56.7%)
Caroline	552 (44.8%)	680 (55.2%)
Carroll	1,694 (48.7%)	1,784 (51.3%)
Cecil	1,504 (49.6%)	1,527 (50.4%)
Charles	519 (39.8%)	785 (60.2%)
Dorchester	903 (39.6%)	1,377 (60.4%)
Frederick	2,994 (48.4%)	3,190 (51.6%)
Harford	1,247 (45.1%)	1,517 (54.9%)
Kent	527 (42.3%)	718 (57.7%)
Montgomery	852 (43.1%)	1,124 (56.9%)
Prince George's	666 (38.7%)	1,054 (61.3%)
Queen Anne's	722 (49.1%)	749 (50.9%)
St Mary's	468 (37.4%)	783 (62.6%)
Somerset	902 (38.4%)	1,449 (61.6%)
Talbot	712 (47.2%)	795 (52.8%)
Washington	2,565 (49.3%)	2,633 (50.7%)
Worcester	909 (38.5%)	1,453 (61.5%)
Baltimore (city)	8,886 (51.4%)	8,413 (48.6%)
Total	**32,676 (47.6%)**	**35,984 (52.4%)**

SOURCE—Manuscript records.

Massachusetts

County	Polk (D)	Clay (W)	Birney (Lty)
Barnstable	1,472 (36.6%)	2,285 (56.8%)	264 (6.6%)
Berkshire	3,729 (47.3%)	3,760 (47.7%)	387 (4.9%)
Bristol	5,003 (47.3%)	4,922 (46.6%)	647 (6.1%)
Dukes	255 (43.8%)	303 (52.1%)	24 (4.1%)
Essex	6,237 (37.8%)	8,415 (51.0%)	1,838 (11.1%)
Franklin	2,066 (39.5%)	2,677 (51.2%)	486 (9.3%)
Hampden	3,506 (47.9%)	3,386 (46.3%)	427 (5.8%)
Hampshire	1,596 (26.9%)	3,725 (62.8%)	609 (10.3%)
Middlesex	9,470 (45.8%)	9,523 (46.0%)	1,687 (8.2%)
Nantucket	236 (26.4%)	633 (70.8%)	25 (2.8%)
Norfolk	4,297 (41.4%)	5,204 (50.1%)	889 (8.6%)
Plymouth	3,183 (39.9%)	4,073 (51.0%)	723 (9.1%)
Suffolk	4,812 (33.9%)	8,709 (61.4%)	663 (4.7%)
Worcester	7,541 (39.4%)	9,447 (49.3%)	2,161 (11.3%)
Total	**53,403 (40.7%)** *(53,039)	**67,062 (51.1%)**	**10,830 (8.3%)**

*Stated totals.

SOURCE—Manuscript returns.

Michigan

County	Polk (D)	Clay (W)	Birney (Lty)
Allegan	299 (47.2%)	323 (51.0%)	11 (1.7%)
Barry	249 (50.5%)	228 (46.2%)	16 (3.2%)
Berrien	828 (52.5%)	713 (45.2%)	35 (2.2%)
Branch	888 (54.8%)	644 (39.7%)	89 (5.5%)
Calhoun	1,528 (49.1%)	1,357 (43.6%)	226 (7.3%)
Cass	715 (46.6%)	760 (49.5%)	59 (3.8%)
Chippewa	34 (41.5%)	48 (58.5%)	0
Clinton	283 (50.8%)	255 (45.8%)	19 (3.4%)
Eaton	376 (44.4%)	410 (48.4%)	61 (7.2%)
Genesee	676 (42.5%)	733 (46.1%)	182 (11.4%)
Hillsdale	1,088 (48.0%)	968 (42.7%)	212 (9.3%)
Ingham	441 (48.0%)	432 (47.7%)	45 (4.9%)
Ionia	398 (45.5%)	418 (47.8%)	59 (6.7%)
Jackson	1,389 (43.9%)	1,302 (41.1%)	475 (15.0%)
Kalamazoo	828 (40.7%)	932 (45.8%)	276 (13.6%)
Kent	564 (52.6%)	476 (44.4%)	33 (3.1%)
Lapeer	502 (50.8%)	399 (40.3%)	88 (8.9%)
Lenawee	2,272 (48.6%)	2,178 (46.6%)	228 (4.9%)
Livingston	1,087 (61.0%)	587 (32.9%)	108 (6.1%)
Mackinac	100 (69.9%)	43 (30.1%)	0
Macomb	1,359 (55.2%)	963 (39.1%)	140 (5.7%)
Monroe	1,282 (58.3%)	870 (39.5%)	48 (2.2%)
Oakland	2,833 (52.1%)	2,225 (40.9%)	377 (6.9%)
Ottawa	116 (66.3%)	42 (24.0%)	17 (9.7%)
Saginaw	104 (48.8%)	107 (50.2%)	2 (0.9%)
St. Clair	617 (50.9%)	569 (46.9%)	27 (2.2%)
St. Joseph	976 (48.9%)	935 (46.9%)	84 (4.2%)
Shiawassee	269 (40.5%)	300 (45.1%)	96 (14.4%)
Van Buren	350 (52.3%)	273 (40.8%)	46 (6.9%)
Washtenaw	2,550 (48.2%)	2,349 (44.4%)	386 (7.3%)
Wayne	2,736 (51.9%)	2,346 (44.5%)	192 (3.6%)
Total	**27,737 (49.9%)**	**24,185 (43.5%)**	**3,637 (6.5%)**

SOURCES—Manuscript returns; *Michigan Manual 1913*, pp. 690–1; and W. Dean Burnham, *Presidential Ballots 1836–1892* (reprint edition), New York, NY: Arno Press, 1976, pp. 514–532.

Mississippi

County	Polk (D)	Clay (W)
Adams	452 (37.4%)	755 (62.6%)
Amite	351 (44.4%)	429 (55.6%)
Attala	505 (64.7%)	276 (35.3%)
Bolivar	61 (52.6%)	55 (47.4%)
Carroll	742 (52.6%)	678 (47.4%)
Chickasaw	632 (63.3%)	366 (36.7%)
Choctaw	644 (60.2%)	426 (39.8%)
Claiborne	429 (49.8%)	433 (50.2%)
Clarke	353 (75.4%)	115 (24.6%)
Coahoma	162 (53.1%)	143 (46.9%)
Copiah	649 (59.2%)	447 (40.8%)
Covington	308 (75.9%)	98 (24.1%)
De Soto	709 (51.4%)	671 (48.6%)
Franklin	220 (56.1%)	172 (43.9%)
Greene	175 (73.8%)	62 (26.2%)
Hancock	127 (69.0%)	57 (31.0%)
Harrison	169 (62.1%)	103 (37.9%)

County	Polk (D)	Clay (W)
Hinds	915 (43.3%)	1,198 (56.7%)
Holmes	498 (46.3%)	578 (53.7%)
Itawamba	825 (69.2%)	368 (30.8%)
*Jackson	216 (92.7%)	17 (7.3%)
Jasper	403 (65.7%)	210 (34.3%)
Jefferson	333 (47.8%)	364 (52.2%)
Jones	117 (61.9%)	72 (38.1%)
Kemper	515 (63.9%)	291 (36.1%)
Lafayette	632 (53.8%)	542 (46.2%)
Lauderdale	631 (71.1%)	256 (28.9%)
Lawrence	545 (85.3%)	94 (14.7%)
Leake	235 (55.2%)	190 (44.8%)
Lowndes	850 (56.9%)	644 (43.1%)
Madison	486 (44.3%)	612 (55.7%)
Marion	254 (78.9%)	68 (21.1%)
*Marshall	1,184 (53.4%)	1,035 (46.6%)
Monroe	911 (62.4%)	549 (37.6%)
Neshoba	577 (52.6%)	519 (47.4%)
Newton	269 (65.3%)	143 (34.7%)
Noxubee	260 (62.5%)	156 (37.5%)
Oktibbeha	336 (58.2%)	241 (41.8%)
Panola	408 (48.2%)	439 (51.8%)
Perry	71 (36.2%)	125 (63.8%)
Pike	444 (65.7%)	232 (34.3%)
Pontotoc	709 (64.9%)	384 (35.1%)
Rankin	406 (56.6%)	311 (43.4%)
Scott	259 (69.8%)	112 (30.2%)
Simpson	300 (52.8%)	178 (37.2%)
Smith	249 (72.6%)	94 (27.4%)
Sunflower	14 (66.7%)	7 (33.3%)
Tallahatchie	218 (54.9%)	179 (45.1%)
Tippah	1,170 (62.8%)	692 (37.2%)
Tishomingo	1,003 (67.6%)	480 (32.4%)
Tunica	24 (40.0%)	36 (60.0%)
Warren	507 (35.5%)	922 (64.5%)
*Washington & Issaquena	108 (34.1%)	209 (65.9%)
Wayne	95 (48.2%)	102 (51.8%)
Wilkinson	355 (44.6%)	441 (55.4%)
Winston	475 (70.3%)	201 (29.7%)
Yalobusha	895 (55.5%)	719 (44.5%)
Yazoo	530 (47.8%)	578 (52.2%)
Total	**25,926 (56.6%)**	**19,874 (43.4%)**

*Listed in manuscript returns as unofficial but the Whig Almanac 1845, p. 63, gives the same returns.

SOURCES—Manuscript returns; Whig Almanac 1845, p. 63.

Missouri

County	Polk (D)	Clay (W)
Adair	450 (60.5%)	294 (39.5%)
Andrew	941 (71.0%)	384 (29.0%)
Audrain	163 (48.2%)	175 (51.8%)
Barry	478 (77.1%)	142 (22.9%)
Bates	307 (59.8%)	206 (40.2%)
Benton	664 (72.5%)	252 (27.5%)
Boone	602 (33.6%)	1,190 (66.4%)
Buchanan	1,162 (66.0%)	599 (34.0%)
Caldwell	212 (62.2%)	129 (37.8%)
Callaway	793 (45.8%)	940 (54.2%)
Camden	247 (77.9%)	70 (22.1%)
Cape Girardeau	914 (63.8%)	518 (36.2%)
Carroll	311 (56.2%)	242 (43.8%)
Chariton	602 (61.9%)	371 (38.1%)
Clark	220 (49.4%)	225 (50.6%)
Clay	552 (39.0%)	765 (61.0%)
Clinton	567 (64.7%)	310 (35.3%)
Cole	1,122 (72.9%)	418 (27.1%)
Cooper	783 (46.5%)	901 (53.5%)
Crawford	367 (90.8%)	237 (9.2%)
Dade	690 (73.0%)	255 (27.0%)
Daviess	446 (58.4%)	318 (41.6%)
Decatur	208 (78.5%)	57 (21.5%)
Franklin	796 (67.3%)	386 (32.7%)
Gasconade	326 (82.5%)	71 (17.5%)
Greene	817 (69.9%)	351 (30.1%)
Grundy	365 (51.3%)	346 (48.7%)
Henry	283 (50.3%)	280 (49.7%)
Holt	378 (67.1%)	185 (32.9%)
Howard	969 (48.9%)	1,013 (51.1%)
Jackson	852 (58.1%)	614 (41.9%)
Jasper	242 (67.8%)	115 (32.2%)
Jefferson	349 (51.6%)	327 (48.4%)
Johnson	511 (58.2%)	367 (41.8%)
Lafayette	576 (41.3%)	820 (58.7%)
Lewis	403 (51.5%)	380 (48.5%)
Lincoln	683 (54.2%)	578 (45.8%)
Linn	494 (64.7%)	269 (35.3%)
Livingston	351 (63.9%)	198 (36.1%)
Macon	457 (58.3%)	327 (41.7%)
Madison	399 (68.6%)	183 (31.4%)
Marion	723 (41.6%)	1,017 (58.4%)
Miller	369 (83.3%)	74 (16.7%)
Monroe	578 (42.2%)	792 (57.8%)
Montgomery	232 (39.3%)	359 (60.7%)
Morgan	544 (67.5%)	262 (32.5%)
New Madrid	208 (41.1%)	298 (58.9%)
Newton	663 (77.8%)	189 (22.2%)
Niangua	345 (81.9%)	76 (18.1%)
Osage	434 (78.3%)	120 (21.7%)
Perry	463 (54.6%)	385 (45.4%)
Pettis	319 (58.3%)	228 (41.7%)
Pike	809 (48.4%)	861 (51.6%)
Platte	1,386 (60.6%)	900 (39.4%)
Polk	636 (70.0%)	273 (30.0%)
Pulaski	325 (79.1%)	86 (20.9%)
Ralls	322 (43.3%)	422 (56.7%)
Randolph	571 (48.9%)	596 (51.1%)
Ray	734 (55.1%)	599 (44.9%)
Ripley	266 (89.6%)	31 (10.4%)
St. Charles	503 (51.2%)	480 (48.8%)
St. Clair	342 (65.9%)	177 (34.1%)
St. Francois	234 (43.7%)	301 (56.3%)
Ste. Genevieve	245 (55.9%)	193 (44.1%)
St. Louis	3,329 (47.4%)	3,688 (52.6%)
Saline	446 (43.0%)	591 (57.0%)
Scotland	442 (58.2%)	317 (41.8%)
Scott	480 (65.0%)	258 (35.0%)
Shannon	271 (82.6%)	57 (17.4%)
Shelby	209 (46.1%)	244 (53.9%)
Stoddard	323 (95.6%)	115 (4.4%)
Taney	297 (89.2%)	36 (10.8%)
Van Buren	443 (63.3%)	257 (36.7%)
Warren	341 (48.4%)	364 (51.6%)
Washington	588 (49.0%)	613 (51.0%)
Wayne	366 (81.0%)	86 (19.0%)
Wright	486 (83.4%)	97 (16.6%)
Total	**41,324 (56.9%)** *(41,369)	**31,250 (43.1%)** *(31,251)

*Stated totals.

SOURCE—(Jefferson City) Jefferson Inquirer, November 28, 1844.

New Hampshire

County	Polk (D)	Clay (W)	Birney (Lty)
Belknap	1,701 (60.5%)	864 (30.7%)	248 (8.8%)
Carroll	1,848 (65.7%)	732 (26.0%)	233 (8.3%)

Cheshire	2,067	(41.3%)	2,558	(51.2%)	374	(7.5%)			
Coos	1,366	(74.8%)	351	(19.2%)	108	(5.9%)			
Grafton	4,048	(55.9%)	2,566	(35.4%)	631	(8.7%)			
Hillsborough	4,617	(54.9%)	3,124	(37.1%)	675	(8.0%)			
Merrimack	3,825	(63.3%)	1,589	(26.3%)	628	(10.4%)			
Rockingham	4,007	(54.7%)	2,730	(37.3%)	583	(8.0%)			
Strafford	1,808	(47.1%)	1,702	(44.3%)	330	(8.6%)			
Sullivan	1,945	(50.5%)	1,553	(40.4%)	350	(9.1%)			
Total	**27,232**	**(55.4%)**	**17,769**	**(36.1%)**	**4,160**	**(8.5%)**			
	*(27,016)		*(17,776)		*(4,152)				

*Stated totals.

SOURCE—Manuscript returns.

New Jersey

County	Clay (W)		Polk (D)		Birney (Lty)	
Atlantic	493	(37.0%)	848	(63.0%)	0	
Bergen	679	(32.0%)	1,440	(68.0%)	0	
Burlington	3,730	(55.2%)	3,017	(44.7%)	7	(0.1%)
Camden	1,448	(54.4%)	1,208	(45.4%)	4	(0.2%)
Cape May	780	(71.3%)	314	(28.7%)	0	
Cumberland	1,549	(53.0%)	1,371	(47.0%)	0	
Essex	5,471	(59.8%)	3,655	(39.9%)	29	(0.3%)
Gloucester	1,411	(60.3%)	902	(38.5%)	27	(1.2%)
Hudson	1,129	(61.4%)	703	(38.2%)	8	(0.4%)
Hunterdon	2,544	(42.9%)	3,386	(57.1%)	0	
Mercer	1,883	(54.4%)	1,577	(45.6%)	0	
Middlesex	2,321	(53.4%)	2,023	(46.6%)	0	
Monmouth	3,221	(48.4%)	3,434	(51.6%)	3	(0.05%)
Morris	2,903	(53.7%)	2,466	(45.6%)	34	(0.6%)
Passaic	1,602	(55.2%)	1,291	(44.5%)	9	(0.3%)
Salem	1,775	(54.3%)	1,493	(45.6%)	3	(0.1%)
Somerset	2,139	(52.0%)	1,978	(48.0%)	0	
Sussex	1,295	(27.0%)	3,490	(72.8%)	7	(0.1%)
Warren	1,645	(36.2%)	2,899	(63.8%)	0	
Total	**38,018**	**(50.3%)**	**37,495**	**(49.6%)**	**131**	**(0.2%)**
	(38,318)					

SOURCE—(Trenton) *New Jersey State Gazette*, November 18, 1844.

New York

County	Polk (D)		Clay (W)		Birney (Lty)	
Albany	6,916	(48.9%)	7,109	(50.2%)	124	(0.9%)
Allegany	3,640	(45.6%)	3,913	(49.0%)	436	(5.5%)
Broome	2,508	(47.5%)	2,661	(50.4%)	106	(2.0%)
Cattaraugus	2,634	(44.9%)	2,743	(46.8%)	487	(8.3%)
Cayuga	5,202	(49.6%)	4,908	(46.8%)	376	(3.6%)
Chautauqua	3,407	(36.5%)	5,612	(60.1%)	314	(3.4%)
Chemung	2,592	(57.7%)	1,791	(39.9%)	106	(2.4%)
Chenango	4,495	(50.2%)	4,215	(47.1%)	243	(2.7%)
Clinton	2,218	(48.8%)	1,919	(42.2%)	410	(9.0%)
Columbia	4,691	(52.0%)	4,322	(47.9%)	11	(0.1%)
Cortland	2,358	(44.7%)	2,378	(45.1%)	542	(10.3%)
Delaware	4,230	(56.4%)	3,071	(40.9%)	205	(2.7%)
Dutchess	5,627	(49.2%)	5,767	(50.5%)	37	(0.3%)
Erie	5,050	(40.8%)	6,905	(55.8%)	415	(3.4%)
Essex	1,998	(42.0%)	2,612	(55.0%)	143	(3.0%)
Franklin	1,501	(48.1%)	1,524	(48.9%)	93	(3.0%)
Fulton & Hamilton	2,192	(49.8%)	2,107	(47.9%)	100	(2.3%)
Genesee	2,105	(35.0%)	3,604	(60.0%)	298	(5.0%)
Greene	3,488	(53.8%)	2,968	(45.8%)	30	(0.5%)
Herkimer	4,346	(55.6%)	2,868	(36.7%)	608	(7.8%)
Jefferson	6,291	(50.0%)	5,576	(44.3%)	712	(5.7%)
Kings	4,648	(47.3%)	5,107	(51.9%)	77	(0.8%)
Lewis	2,073	(53.6%)	1,640	(42.4%)	154	(4.0%)
Livingston	2,709	(40.5%)	3,773	(56.4%)	210	(3.1%)
Madison	3,848	(43.5%)	3,683	(41.7%)	1,311	(14.8%)
Monroe	5,611	(43.4%)	6,873	(53.2%)	430	(3.3%)
Montgomery	3,278	(52.8%)	2,849	(45.9%)	85	(1.4%)
New York	28,296	(51.6%)	26,385	(48.1%)	117	(0.2%)
Niagara	2,589	(43.2%)	3,100	(51.7%)	309	(5.2%)
Oneida	7,717	(48.7%)	6,983	(44.1%)	1,144	(7.2%)
Onondaga	6,878	(48.8%)	6,495	(46.0%)	733	(5.2%)
Ontario	3,659	(42.2%)	4,568	(52.7%)	435	(5.0%)
Orange	5,303	(53.2%)	4,626	(46.4%)	37	(0.4%)
Orleans	2,311	(44.6%)	2,600	(50.1%)	276	(5.3%)
Oswego	4,382	(48.7%)	3,771	(41.9%)	851	(9.5%)
Otsego	6,050	(54.0%)	4,743	(42.3%)	413	(3.7%)
Putnam	1,731	(63.9%)	979	(36.1%)	0	
Queens	2,751	(51.9%)	2,547	(48.1%)	0	
Rensselaer	5,618	(46.2%)	6,361	(52.3%)	181	(1.5%)
Richmond	1,063	(50.3%)	1,049	(49.6%)	1	(0.05%)
Rockland	1,679	(67.9%)	794	(32.1%)	1	(0.04%)
St. Lawrence	6,008	(53.9%)	4,672	(41.9%)	468	(4.2%)
Saratoga	4,200	(47.4%)	4,550	(51.3%)	119	(1.3%)
Schenectady	1,679	(47.6%)	1,814	(51.5%)	31	(0.9%)

County	Polk (D)	Clay (W)	Birney (Lty)
Schoharie	3,523 (53.2%)	2,986 (45.1%)	111 (1.7%)
Seneca	2,569 (51.1%)	2,327 (46.4%)	124 (2.5%)
Steuben	5,512 (54.4%)	4,385 (43.2%)	243 (2.4%)
Suffolk	3,375 (57.4%)	2,487 (42.3%)	14 (0.2%)
Sullivan	1,964 (52.6%)	1,739 (46.6%)	30 (0.8%)
Tioga	2,548 (54.9%)	1,999 (43.1%)	90 (1.9%)
Tompkins	4,013 (49.0%)	3,845 (47.0%)	324 (4.0%)
Ulster	4,783 (49.8%)	4,804 (50.0%)	12 (0.1%)
Warren	1,791 (55.3%)	1,330 (41.1%)	118 (3.6%)
Washington	3,270 (37.9%)	5,024 (58.2%)	338 (3.9%)
Wayne	4,046 (47.3%)	3,953 (46.2%)	563 (6.6%)
Westchester	4,412 (50.8%)	4,258 (49.0%)	19 (0.2%)
Wyoming	2,102 (39.7%)	2,754 (52.0%)	442 (8.3%)
Yates	2,110 (48.3%)	2,056 (47.0%)	207 (4.7%)
Total	**237,588 (48.9%)**	**232,482 (47.8%)**	**15,814 (3.3%)**

SOURCE—Manuscript returns.

North Carolina

County	Polk (D)	Clay (W)
Anson	481 (32.2%)	1,012 (67.8%)
Ashe	477 (47.7%)	522 (52.3%)
Beaufort	527 (36.1%)	932 (63.9%)
Bertie	439 (47.9%)	475 (52.4%)
Bladen	486 (63.4%)	280 (36.6%)
Brunswick	283 (44.6%)	351 (55.4%)
Buncombe	412 (26.2%)	961 (73.8%)
Burke	228 (15.6%)	1,234 (84.4%)
Cabarrus	374 (34.2%)	718 (65.8%)
Caldwell	219 (26.8%)	598 (73.2%)
Camden	101 (15.4%)	556 (84.6%)
Carteret	315 (42.1%)	434 (57.9%)
Caswell	1,182 (80.7%)	283 (19.3%)
Chatham	729 (39.1%)	1,136 (60.9%)
Cherokee	225 (36.6%)	390 (63.4%)
Chowan	166 (64.8%)	305 (35.2%)
Cleveland	624 (63.0%)	366 (37.0%)
Columbus	363 (72.9%)	135 (27.1%)
Craven	628 (49.0%)	654 (51.0%)
Cumberland	1,101 (64.6%)	703 (35.4%)
Currituck	551 (77.8%)	157 (22.2%)
Davidson	610 (35.9%)	1,091 (64.1%)
Davie	272 (34.0%)	529 (66.0%)
Duplin	936 (80.8%)	223 (19.2%)
Edgecombe	1,503 (92.3%)	126 (7.7%)
Franklin	760 (69.3%)	336 (30.7%)
Gates	355 (50.0%)	355 (50.0%)
Granville	942 (50.2%)	936 (49.8%)
Greene	276 (47.8%)	302 (52.2%)
Guilford	515 (19.5%)	2,130 (80.5%)
Halifax	456 (43.5%)	592 (56.5%)
Haywood	267 (43.8%)	342 (56.2%)
Henderson	141 (20.3%)	555 (79.7%)
Hertford	253 (38.2%)	309 (61.8%)
Hyde	164 (34.0%)	318 (66.0%)
Jackson	330 (17.3%)	1,582 (82.7%)
Johnston	650 (52.2%)	595 (47.8%)
Jones	142 (41.2%)	203 (58.8%)
Lenoir	356 (61.3%)	225 (38.7%)
Lincoln	1,736 (68.7%)	790 (31.3%)
Macon	224 (37.5%)	374 (62.5%)
Madison	580 (65.2%)	310 (34.8%)
Mecklenburg	1,201 (56.9%)	909 (43.1%)
Montgomery	139 (17.4%)	658 (82.6%)
Moore	500 (48.1%)	540 (51.9%)
Nash	894 (92.7%)	74 (7.3%)
New Hanover	1,122 (74.6%)	382 (25.4%)
Northampton	364 (41.2%)	519 (58.8%)
Onslow	717 (78.7%)	194 (21.3%)
Orange	1,589 (48.5%)	1,686 (51.5%)
Pasquotank	232 (25.9%)	663 (74.1%)
Perquimans	223 (33.6%)	441 (66.4%)
Person	649 (70.2%)	275 (29.8%)
Pitt	476 (42.9%)	634 (57.1%)
Randolph	312 (21.0%)	1,171 (79.0%)
Richmond	117 (12.7%)	802 (87.3%)
Robeson	591 (51.4%)	559 (48.6%)
Rockingham	1,022 (70.4%)	430 (29.6%)
Rowan	586 (41.3%)	833 (58.7%)
Rutherford	296 (18.4%)	1,310 (81.6%)
Sampson	878 (61.8%)	533 (38.2%)
Stanly	48 (8.3%)	530 (91.7%)
Stokes	1,153 (51.5%)	1,084 (48.5%)
Surry	880 (46.9%)	996 (53.1%)
Tyrrell	92 (24.5%)	283 (75.5%)
Wake	1,374 (36.7%)	1,044 (63.3%)
Warren	810 (86.3%)	128 (13.7%)
Washington	124 (35.1%)	329 (64.9%)
Wayne	911 (78.3%)	254 (21.7%)
Wilkes	181 (13.0%)	1,208 (87.0%)
Yancey	427 (55.8%)	338 (44.2%)
Total	**39,287 (47.6%)**	**43,232 (52.4%)**

SOURCE—Manuscript returns.

Ohio

County	Polk (D)	Clay (W)	Birney (Lty)
Adams	1,611 (54.6%)	1,252 (42.4%)	87 (2.9%)
Allen	1,062 (57.4%)	779 (42.1%)	9 (0.5%)
Ashtabula	1,123 (22.3%)	3,383 (67.1%)	537 (10.6%)
Athens	1,425 (38.6%)	2,050 (55.5%)	220 (6.0%)
Belmont	2,821 (45.9%)	3,140 (51.1%)	184 (3.0%)

County	Polk (D)	Clay (W)	Birney (Lty)
Brown	2,342 (54.8%)	1,798 (42.1%)	130 (3.0%)
Butler	3,546 (61.5%)	2,158 (37.4%)	61 (1.1%)
Carroll	1,584 (46.2%)	1,701 (49.7%)	140 (4.1%)
Champaign	1,409 (40.1%)	2,069 (58.9%)	32 (0.9%)
Clark	1,155 (31.4%)	2,477 (67.4%)	43 (1.1%)
Clermont	2,627 (53.4%)	2,189 (44.5%)	105 (2.1%)
Clinton	1,137 (37.3%)	1,736 (57.0%)	172 (5.6%)
Columbiana	3,743 (50.7%)	3,416 (46.3%)	217 (2.9%)
Coshocton	2,281 (54.0%)	1,885 (44.6%)	60 (1.4%)
Crawford	1,734 (59.0%)	1,197 (40.7%)	8 (0.3%)
Cuyahoga	2,338 (39.1%)	3,331 (55.7%)	312 (5.2%)
Darke	1,409 (49.6%)	1,408 (49.5%)	25 (0.9%)
Delaware	2,017 (43.1%)	2,548 (54.4%)	118 (2.5%)
Erie	1,261 (45.3%)	1,458 (52.4%)	65 (2.3%)
Fairfield	3,637 (58.7%)	2,542 (41.0%)	15 (0.2%)
Fayette	878 (40.4%)	1,229 (56.5%)	67 (3.1%)
Franklin	2,498 (45.1%)	2,965 (53.6%)	72 (1.3%)
Gallia	957 (38.7%)	1,484 (60.0%)	31 (1.3%)
Geauga	1,101 (30.5%)	2,274 (63.0%)	233 (6.5%)
Greene	1,380 (35.1%)	2,422 (61.7%)	126 (3.2%)
Guernsey	2,628 (47.0%)	2,746 (49.1%)	218 (3.9%)
Hamilton	8,983 (54.5%)	7,201 (43.7%)	298 (1.8%)
Hancock	1,247 (53.0%)	907 (38.5%)	2 (0.1%)
Hardin	495 (49.0%)	510 (50.4%)	6 (0.6%)
Harrison	1,750 (44.2%)	2,039 (51.2%)	195 (4.9%)
Henry	245 (51.7%)	229 (48.3%)	0
Highland	2,164 (43.9%)	2,148 (43.6%)	114 (2.3%)
Hocking	1,289 (64.1%)	719 (35.8%)	2 (0.1%)
Holmes	2,317 (66.9%)	1,142 (33.0%)	5 (0.1%)
Huron	2,136 (44.2%)	2,564 (53.0%)	138 (2.9%)
Jackson	1,046 (53.2%)	908 (46.2%)	13 (0.7%)
Jefferson	2,354 (48.7%)	2,385 (49.3%)	95 (2.0%)
Knox	3,324 (53.6%)	2,746 (44.3%)	134 (2.2%)
Lake	901 (31.9%)	1,818 (64.3%)	109 (3.9%)
Lawrence	658 (36.5%)	1,140 (63.3%)	3 (0.2%)
Licking	3,840 (50.7%)	3,500 (46.2%)	238 (3.1%)
Logan	1,015 (37.1%)	1,625 (59.5%)	93 (3.4%)
Lorain	1,793 (42.5%)	1,956 (46.3%)	473 (11.2%)
Lucas	881 (42.8%)	1,167 (56.7%)	12 (0.6%)
Madison	643 (33.5%)	1,269 (66.1%)	8 (0.4%)
Marion	1,480 (49.4%)	1,425 (47.6%)	88 (2.9%)
Medina	1,920 (45.9%)	2,045 (48.9%)	221 (5.3%)
Meigs	880 (38.9%)	1,341 (59.3%)	41 (1.8%)
Mercer	812 (65.5%)	423 (34.1%)	4 (0.3%)
Miami	1,657 (38.1%)	2,572 (59.1%)	113 (2.6%)
Monroe	2,548 (65.8%)	1,210 (31.3%)	114 (2.9%)
Montgomery	3,101 (47.2%)	3,388 (51.6%)	83 (1.3%)
Morgan	2,021 (42.2%)	2,107 (44.0%)	64 (1.3%)
Muskingum	3,196 (41.1%)	4,489 (57.8%)	86 (1.1%)
Ottawa	233 (48.2%)	241 (49.9%)	9 (1.9%)
Paulding	192 (75.6%)	62 (24.4%)	0
Perry	2,273 (59.8%)	1,527 (40.2%)	3 (0.1%)
Pickaway	2,012 (47.4%)	2,219 (52.3%)	10 (0.2%)
Pike	836 (50.6%)	800 (48.4%)	16 (1.0%)
Portage	2,247 (44.9%)	2,510 (50.2%)	244 (4.9%)
Preble	1,526 (39.6%)	2,262 (58.6%)	70 (1.8%)
Putnam	697 (60.6%)	451 (39.2%)	2 (0.2%)
Richland	5,574 (61.1%)	3,443 (37.7%)	111 (1.2%)
Ross	2,380 (41.1%)	3,321 (57.3%)	90 (1.6%)
Sandusky	1,214 (54.6%)	997 (44.8%)	12 (0.5%)
Scioto	1,095 (41.9%)	1,519 (58.1%)	0
Seneca	2,316 (56.7%)	1,727 (42.3%)	41 (1.0%)
Shelby	1,014 (49.1%)	1,026 (49.7%)	26 (1.3%)
Stark	3,575 (54.1%)	2,952 (44.7%)	76 (1.2%)
Summit	2,056 (40.5%)	2,841 (55.9%)	184 (3.6%)
Trumbull	3,544 (43.7%)	3,837 (47.3%)	738 (9.1%)
Tuscarawas	2,358 (46.3%)	2,696 (53.0%)	35 (0.7%)
Union	710 (40.5%)	1,009 (57.6%)	32 (1.8%)
Van Wert	270 (63.1%)	158 (36.9%)	0

County	Polk (D)	Clay (W)	Birney (Lty)
Warren	1,795 (38.2%)	2,822 (60.0%)	85 (1.8%)
Washington	1,686 (41.8%)	2,194 (54.4%)	151 (3.7%)
Wayne	3,765 (57.0%)	2,759 (41.8%)	75 (1.1%)
Williams	673 (54.9%)	553 (45.1%)	0
Wood	570 (49.7%)	576 (50.2%)	1 (0.1%)
Total	**149,011 (47.7%)**	**155,112 (49.7%)**	**8,050 (2.6%)**
	*(149,061)	*(155,113)	

*Stated totals.

SOURCE—(Columbus) *Ohio State Journal*, November 16, 1844.

Pennsylvania

County	Polk (D)	Clay (W)	Birney (Lty)
Adams	1,891 (41.9%)	2,609 (57.9%)	6 (1.3%)
Allegheny	5,743 (40.3%)	8,083 (56.7%)	435 (3.1%)
Armstrong	1,983 (57.1%)	1,453 (41.8%)	38 (1.1%)
Beaver	2,172 (41.5%)	2,792 (53.3%)	270 (5.2%)
Bedford	2,989 (48.7%)	3,147 (51.2%)	5 (0.1%)
Berks	8,674 (68.4%)	4,000 (31.6%)	3 (0.2%)
Bradford	3,568 (51.8%)	3,235 (47.1%)	63 (0.9%)
Bucks	5,251 (51.8%)	4,862 (47.9%)	27 (2.7%)
Butler	2,112 (47.0%)	2,247 (50.0%)	135 (3.0%)
Cambria	1,123 (52.9%)	996 (47.0%)	2 (0.1%)
Carbon	905 (63.0%)	531 (37.0%)	0
Centre	2,425 (56.5%)	1,860 (43.3%)	7 (0.2%)
Chester	5,550 (47.3%)	6,070 (51.8%)	106 (0.9%)
Clarion	1,883 (69.6%)	814 (30.1%)	7 (0.3%)
Clearfield	874 (61.6%)	544 (38.4%)	0
Clinton	875 (52.6%)	788 (47.4%)	0
Columbia	3,370 (66.0%)	1,738 (34.0%)	1 (0.2%)
Crawford	3,334 (54.6%)	2,636 (43.1%)	139 (2.3%)
Cumberland	3,155 (50.5%)	3,092 (49.5%)	5 (0.1%)
Dauphin	2,401 (42.1%)	3,285 (57.6%)	16 (0.3%)
Delaware	1,466 (41.1%)	2,090 (58.5%)	15 (0.4%)
Elk	128 (53.8%)	101 (42.4%)	9 (3.8%)
Erie	2,226 (37.6%)	3,621 (61.1%)	74 (1.2%)
Fayette	3,429 (54.7%)	2,804 (44.7%)	35 (0.6%)
Franklin	3,298 (45.8%)	3,901 (54.2%)	0
Greene	2,354 (62.1%)	1,418 (37.4%)	18 (0.5%)
Huntingdon	2,575 (38.7%)	4,086 (61.3%)	0
Indiana	1,448 (38.9%)	2,200 (59.1%)	80 (2.1%)
Jefferson	731 (55.1%)	591 (44.5%)	5 (0.4%)
Juniata	1,260 (53.6%)	1,089 (46.4%)	0
Lancaster	5,943 (36.6%)	10,295 (63.3%)	21 (0.1%)
Lebanon	1,791 (40.5%)	2,636 (59.5%)	0
Lehigh	2,811 (52.4%)	2,553 (47.6%)	0
Luzerne	3,950 (59.1%)	2,699 (40.4%)	29 (0.4%)
Lycoming	2,629 (56.4%)	2,012 (43.2%)	19 (0.4%)
McKean	419 (55.2%)	340 (44.8%)	0
Mercer	2,869 (45.4%)	2,840 (45.0%)	604 (9.6%)
Mifflin	1,519 (49.9%)	1,518 (49.8%)	9 (0.3%)
Monroe	1,806 (81.3%)	414 (18.6%)	1 (0.05%)
Montgomery	5,596 (55.2%)	4,491 (44.3%)	49 (0.5%)
Northampton	3,870 (58.2%)	2,776 (41.8%)	0
Northumberland	2,446 (61.2%)	1,547 (38.7%)	7 (0.2%)
Perry	2,321 (62.9%)	1,370 (37.1%)	0
Philadelphia	18,851 (44.5%)	23,289 (55.0%)	222 (0.5%)
Pike	769 (83.6%)	151 (16.4%)	0
Potter	554 (65.6%)	240 (28.4%)	50 (15.9%)
Schuylkill	3,404 (56.9%)	2,571 (43.0%)	3 (0.5%)
Somerset	1,035 (28.0%)	2,660 (71.9%)	6 (0.2%)
Susquehanna	2,697 (58.7%)	1,802 (39.2%)	93 (2.0%)
Tioga	2,193 (64.8%)	1,169 (34.5%)	23 (0.7%)
Union	1,765 (38.6%)	2,788 (61.0%)	18 (0.4%)
Venango	1,377 (57.2%)	966 (40.1%)	65 (2.7%)
Warren	1,149 (55.6%)	899 (43.5%)	17 (0.8%)
Washington	3,973 (48.8%)	3,872 (47.6%)	296 (3.6%)

County	Polk (D)	Clay (W)	Birney (Lty)
Wayne	1,657 (64.4%)	899 (35.0%)	15 (0.6%)
Westmoreland	4,978 (64.5%)	2,672 (34.6%)	71 (0.9%)
Wyoming	899 (52.5%)	814 (47.2%)	13 (0.8%)
York	5,071 (54.5%)	4,237 (45.5%)	1 (0.1%)
Total	**167,535 (50.5%)**	**161,203 (48.6%)**	**3,133 (0.9%)**

SOURCES—(Harrisburg) *Democratic Union; Whig Almanac 1845*, pp. 55–56.

Rhode Island

County	Polk (D)	Clay (W)
Bristol	109 (15.6%)	589 (84.4%)
Kent	381 (32.6%)	786 (67.4%)
Newport	473 (27.8%)	1,229 (72.2%)
Providence	3,192 (46.0%)	3,751 (54.0%)
Washington	712 (42.4%)	967 (57.6%)
Total	**4,867[4] (39.9%)**	**7,322 (60.1%)**

SOURCES—*Providence Journal*, November 13, 1844; *Whig Almanac, 1845*, p. 53; and W. Dean Burnham, *Presidential Ballots 1836–1892* (reprint edition), New York, NY: Arno Press, 1976.

South Carolina

Electors chosen by the legislature

Tennessee

County	Polk (D)	Clay (W)
Anderson	325 (34.3%)	629 (65.7%)
Bedford	1,526 (51.2%)	1,455 (48.8%)
Benton	481 (62.2%)	292 (37.8%)
Bledsoe	259 (32.9%)	529 (67.1%)
Blount	735 (41.3%)	1,046 (58.7%)
Bradley	958 (62.6%)	572 (37.4%)
Campbell	318 (48.5%)	337 (51.5%)
Cannon	761 (70.6%)	318 (29.4%)
Carroll	524 (27.9%)	1,356 (72.1%)
Carter	177 (19.3%)	739 (80.7%)
Claiborne	857 (59.7%)	578 (40.3%)
Cocke	187 (18.1%)	844 (81.9%)
Coffee	1,000 (78.1%)	280 (21.9%)
Davidson	1,683 (42.6%)	2,266 (57.4%)
De Kalb	491 (50.2%)	488 (49.8%)
Dickson	706 (67.6%)	339 (32.4%)
Dyer	272 (43.3%)	356 (56.7%)
Fayette	1,151 (48.9%)	1,205 (51.1%)
Fentress	456 (88.4%)	60 (11.6%)
Franklin	1,123 (75.3%)	358 (24.7%)
Gibson	611 (31.6%)	1,320 (68.4%)
Giles	1,387 (51.6%)	1,301 (48.4%)
Grainger	548 (35.4%)	998 (64.6%)
Greene	1,701 (62.3%)	1,031 (37.7%)
Hamilton	624 (49.2%)	614 (50.8%)
Hardeman	1,077 (61.0%)	689 (39.0%)
Hardin	732 (59.2%)	505 (40.8%)
Hawkins	1,388 (54.2%)	1,173 (45.8%)
Haywood	668 (46.9%)	756 (53.1%)
Henderson	492 (28.9%)	1,209 (71.1%)
Henry	1,312 (65.1%)	835 (34.9%)
Hickman	1,034 (80.2%)	255 (19.8%)
Humphreys	523 (63.2%)	305 (36.8%)
Jackson	807 (40.0%)	1,211 (60.0%)
Jefferson	247 (13.6%)	1,563 (86.4%)
Johnson	79 (17.6%)	370 (82.4%)
Knox	507 (20.1%)	2,015 (79.9%)
Lauderdale	211 (42.5%)	286 (57.5%)
Lawrence	547 (52.8%)	489 (47.2%)
Lincoln	2,494 (79.1%)	658 (20.9%)
Madison	768 (36.1%)	1,357 (63.9%)
Marion	381 (43.1%)	503 (56.9%)
Marshall	1,398 (68.8%)	635 (31.2%)
Maury	1,988 (60.6%)	1,292 (39.4%)
McMinn	1,061 (54.7%)	873 (45.3%)
McNairy	741 (48.9%)	773 (51.1%)
Meigs	620 (83.8%)	120 (16.2%)
Monroe	1,086 (55.8%)	859 (44.2%)
Montgomery	1,029 (44.7%)	1,271 (55.3%)
Morgan	232 (52.3%)	211 (47.7%)
Obion	536 (65.5%)	282 (34.5%)
Overton	1,145 (77.3%)	336 (22.7%)
Perry	513 (40.8%)	744 (59.2%)
Polk	488 (65.2%)	260 (34.8%)
Rhea	368 (61.3%)	232 (38.7%)
Roane	735 (45.0%)	900 (55.0%)
Robertson	871 (42.2%)	1,193 (57.8%)
Rutherford	1,500 (46.4%)	1,730 (53.6%)
Sevier	78 (9.6%)	738 (90.4%)
Shelby	1,352 (45.4%)	1,625 (54.6%)
Smith	788 (25.3%)	2,328 (74.7%)
Stewart	704 (58.0%)	510 (42.0%)
Sullivan	1,533 (81.4%)	350 (18.6%)
Sumner	2,017 (69.6%)	881 (30.4%)
Tipton	502 (58.2%)	360 (41.8%)
Van Buren	190 (62.1%)	116 (37.9%)
Warren	1,190 (78.0%)	335 (22.0%)
Washington	1,225 (58.2%)	881 (41.8%)
Wayne	446 (40.1%)	665 (59.9%)
Weakley	1,084 (65.9%)	560 (34.1%)
White	468 (35.3%)	857 (64.7%)
Williamson	859 (30.2%)	1,986 (69.8%)
Wilson	1,042 (28.6%)	2,607 (71.4%)
Total	**59,917 (49.95%)**	**60,030 (50.05%)**

SOURCES—(Nashville) *American*, November 9, 1848; *Whig Almanac 1845*, p. 60.

Vermont

County	Polk (D)	Clay (W)	Birney (Lty)
Addison	772 (21.4%)	2,527 (70.0%)	312 (8.6%)
Bennington	1,451 (44.3%)	1,656 (50.6%)	168 (5.1%)
Caledonia	1,730 (47.1%)	1,762 (47.9%)	184 (5.0%)
Chittenden	1,445 (38.4%)	1,932 (51.3%)	386 (10.3%)
Essex	331 (44.7%)	392 (52.9%)	18 (2.4%)
Franklin	1,439 (40.3%)	1,872 (52.4%)	261 (7.3%)
Grand Isle	165 (32.7%)	339 (67.3%)	0
Lamoille	759 (45.9%)	485 (29.3%)	411 (24.8%)
Orange	1,911 (43.3%)	2,077 (47.0%)	427 (9.7%)
Orleans	833 (36.7%)	1,192 (52.5%)	246 (10.8%)
Rutland	1,582 (28.8%)	3,585 (65.2%)	332 (6.0%)
Washington	2,085 (51.5%)	1,650 (40.7%)	300 (7.4%)

Windham	1,703 (36.0%)	2,641 (55.9%)	384 (8.1%)
Windsor	1,843 (26.1%)	4,667 (66.2%)	541 (7.7%)
Total	**18,049 (37.0%)**	**26,777 (54.9%)**	**3,970 (8.1%)**

SOURCE—Manuscript returns.

Virginia

County	Polk (D)	Clay (W)
Accomac	472 (45.5%)	566 (54.5%)
Albemarle	702 (43.5%)	912 (56.5%)
Alleghany	180 (61.2%)	114 (38.8%)
Amelia	274 (63.3%)	159 (36.7%)
Amherst	461 (50.5%)	451 (49.5%)
Augusta	665 (32.2%)	1,398 (67.8%)
Barbour	468 (67.9%)	221 (32.1%)
Bath	250 (56.1%)	196 (43.9%)
Bedford	639 (40.4%)	941 (59.6%)
Berkeley	539 (45.2%)	663 (54.8%)
Botetourt	695 (63.8%)	394 (36.2%)
Braxton	156 (45.6%)	186 (54.4%)
Brooke	543 (56.0%)	427 (44.0%)
Brunswick	408 (67.8%)	194 (32.2%)
Buckingham	596 (52.1%)	548 (47.9%)
Cabell	346 (54.7%)	287 (45.3%)
Campbell	656 (44.1%)	833 (55.9%)
Caroline	463 (49.3%)	476 (50.7%)
Carroll	968 (88.9%)	121 (11.1%)
Charles City	43 (4.6%)	202 (95.4%)
Charlotte	346 (50.7%)	337 (49.3%)
Chesterfield	604 (64.1%)	338 (35.9%)
Clarke	220 (52.5%)	199 (47.5%)
Culpeper	298 (44.9%)	396 (55.1%)
Cumberland	207 (43.0%)	274 (57.0%)
Dinwiddie	318 (54.1%)	270 (45.9%)
Elizabeth City	123 (48.0%)	133 (52.0%)
Essex	186 (44.8%)	229 (55.2%)
Fairfax	391 (48.8%)	410 (51.2%)
Fauquier	607 (44.4%)	761 (55.6%)
Fayette	163 (39.6%)	249 (60.4%)
Fluvanna	244 (44.4%)	305 (55.6%)
Floyd	297 (70.5%)	124 (29.5%)
Franklin	674 (52.1%)	619 (47.9%)
Frederick	887 (52.4%)	805 (47.6%)
Giles	350 (56.7%)	267 (43.3%)
Gloucester	220 (39.8%)	233 (60.2%)
Goochland	303 (66.9%)	150 (33.1%)
Grayson	331 (68.8%)	150 (31.2%)
Greenbrier	351 (33.1%)	709 (66.9%)
Greene	300 (82.0%)	66 (18.0%)
Greensville	146 (63.8%)	83 (36.2%)
Halifax	1,041 (75.2%)	344 (24.8%)
Hampshire	694 (50.7%)	675 (49.3%)
Hanover	482 (46.3%)	558 (53.7%)
Hardy	272 (46.2%)	533 (53.8%)
Harrison	760 (61.3%)	479 (38.7%)
Henrico	405 (41.2%)	578 (58.8%)
Henry	258 (45.7%)	306 (54.3%)
Isle of Wight	470 (83.5%)	93 (16.5%)
Jackson	265 (56.6%)	203 (43.4%)
James City	39 (27.5%)	103 (72.5%)
Jefferson	624 (46.3%)	725 (53.7%)
Kanawha	442 (31.0%)	983 (69.0%)
King & Queen	328 (56.7%)	250 (43.3%)
King George	117 (41.4%)	165 (58.6%)
King William	337 (75.6%)	109 (24.4%)
Lancaster	99 (41.6%)	139 (58.4%)
Lee	578 (70.9%)	237 (29.1%)
Lewis	684 (67.5%)	329 (32.5%)
Logan	177 (59.0%)	123 (41.0%)
Loudoun	474 (24.0%)	1,505 (76.0%)
Louisa	525 (59.1%)	364 (40.9%)
Lunenburg	333 (62.9%)	196 (37.1%)
Madison	512 (88.7%)	65 (11.3%)
Matthews	222 (56.3%)	172 (43.7%)
Marion	677 (70.3%)	286 (29.7%)
Mason	363 (46.7%)	415 (53.3%)
Mecklenburg	618 (69.1%)	276 (69.1%)
Mercer	177 (50.6%)	173 (49.4%)
Middlesex	118 (47.4%)	131 (52.6%)
Monongalia	780 (66.5%)	393 (33.5%)
Marshall	473 (51.4%)	447 (48.6%)
Monroe	460 (52.0%)	425 (48.0%)
Montgomery	345 (48.7%)	364 (48.7%)
Morgan	216 (54.1%)	183 (45.9%)
Nansemond	244 (40.3%)	361 (59.7%)
Nelson	291 (39.6%)	443 (60.4%)
New Kent	178 (47.3%)	198 (52.7%)
Nicholas	135 (46.1%)	158 (53.9%)
Northampton	116 (32.6%)	240 (67.4%)
Northumberland	276 (59.9%)	185 (40.1%)
Norfolk	590 (48.5%)	627 (51.5%)
Nottoway	182 (49.3%)	187 (50.7%)
Ohio	402 (30.9%)	897 (69.1%)
Orange	288 (54.6%)	239 (45.4%)
Page	628 (92.6%)	50 (7.4%)
Patrick	386 (51.1%)	369 (48.9%)
Pendleton	552 (57.4%)	409 (42.6%)
Pittsylvania	635 (43.1%)	838 (56.9%)
Pocahontas	227 (73.7%)	81 (26.3%)
Powhatan	210 (49.4%)	215 (50.6%)
Preston	504 (56.9%)	382 (43.1%)
Prince Edward	377 (58.8%)	264 (41.2%)
Prince George	226 (61.9%)	139 (38.1%)
Princess Anne	251 (43.3%)	329 (56.7%)
Prince William	457 (74.2%)	159 (25.8%)
Pulaski	174 (51.1%)	166 (48.9%)
Randolph	199 (49.0%)	207 (51.0%)
Rappahannock	314 (46.7%)	359 (53.3%)
Richmond	154 (43.3%)	202 (56.7%)
Ritchie	254 (70.9%)	104 (29.1%)
Roanoke	279 (61.1%)	177 (38.9%)
Rockbridge	543 (43.8%)	697 (56.2%)
Rockingham	1,716 (85.5%)	290 (14.5%)
Russell	416 (50.1%)	415 (49.9%)
Scott	531 (65.8%)	276 (34.2%)
Shenandoah	1,372 (89.0%)	170 (11.0%)
Smyth	371 (57.4%)	275 (42.6%)
Southampton	390 (54.5%)	325 (45.5%)
Spotsylvania	442 (50.2%)	438 (49.8%)
Stafford	346 (59.8%)	233 (40.2%)
Surry	168 (58.7%)	118 (41.3%)
Sussex	325 (72.4%)	124 (27.6%)
Taylor	259 (51.5%)	244 (48.5%)
Tazewell	627 (86.2%)	100 (13.8%)
Tyler	511 (53.7%)	441 (46.3%)
Warren	321 (71.8%)	126 (28.2%)
Warwick	24 (26.4%)	67 (73.6%)
Washington	723 (66.1%)	371 (33.9%)
Wayne	184 (49.2%)	190 (50.8%)
Westmoreland	67 (18.0%)	305 (82.0%)
Wood	330 (38.2%)	533 (61.8%)
Wythe	553 (64.1%)	309 (35.9%)
York	109 (49.1%)	113 (50.9%)

Cities & Towns

	Polk (D)	Clay (W)
Norfolk	403 (30.9%)	634 (69.1%)
Petersburg	336 (47.2%)	376 (52.8%)
Richmond	282 (25.0%)	847 (75.0%)

Williamsburg	50 (43.1%)	66 (56.9%)	
Total	**51,383 (53.4%)**	**44,790 (46.6%)**	
	*(50,683)		

*Stated totals.

SOURCE—*Richmond Enquirer*, November 14, 1848.

NOTES

1. The electoral vote for vice president was George M. Dallas (D) 170, and Thomas Frelinghuysen (W) 105.

2. The returns are reported in W. Dean Burnham's *Presidential Ballots*, pp. 274–292 citing the (Little Rock) *Arkansas Gazette*, December 4, 1844; they are also found in *Political Textbook*, pp. 234–5. The *Whig Almanac* for the years following this election gives no presidential returns for Arkansas.

3. The official returns as published in the *New Orleans Bee*, November 26, 1844, did not include any votes for Caddo and De Soto parishes. These returns were found in the *Whig Almanac, 1845*. I have included these two parishes in the official returns, however. The *Almanac's* returns are the same for all parishes except that the vote for Clay in Claiborne is three more than here. The totals in parentheses are the *Bee's* totals without any votes from Caddo and De Soto.

4. The *Manual* states that Polk's total was 4,876, which appears to be a transposing error of the last two digits. Contemporary sources list Polk's total as stated here with the county returns adding to the same total. However, the *Providence Journal* of November 13, 1844, in reporting the official figures, gives Polk 362 votes in Kent County. *The Whig Almanac, 1845*, and W. Dean Burnham's *Presidential Ballots*, citing the *Journal*, both give Polk 381 votes in Kent. There are no surviving manuscript returns.

1 8 4 8

National Summary[1]

(electoral vote in parentheses)

State	Zachary Taylor (W)		Lewis Cass (D)		Martin Van Buren (FS)	Gerrit Smith (Lty)
Alabama	30,482 (49.44%)		31,173 (50.56%)	(9)		
Arkansas	7,587 (44.93%)		9,301 (55.07%)	(3)		
Connecticut	30,318 (48.59%)	(6)	27,051 (43.36%)		5,005 (8.02%)	18 (0.03%)
Delaware	6,440 (51.81%)	(3)	5,910 (47.55%)		80 (0.64%)	
Florida	4,546 (58.36%)	(3)	3,243 (41.64%)			
Georgia	47,538 (51.49%)	(10)	44,794 (48.51%)			
Illinois	52,853 (42.45%)		55,952 (44.94%)	(9)	15,702 (12.61%)	
Indiana	70,175 (45.88%)		74,684 (48.83%)	(12)	8,100 (5.30%)	
Iowa	10,617 (44.62%)		12,051 (50.65%)	(4)	1,126 (4.73%)	
Kentucky	67,141 (57.45%)	(12)	49,720 (42.55%)			
Louisiana	18,248 (54.81%)	(6)	15,248 (45.19%)			
Maine	35,125 (40.33%)		39,880 (45.79%)	(9)	12,096 (13.89%)	
Maryland	37,704 (52.10%)	(8)	34,533 (47.72%)		128 (0.18%)	
Massachusetts[2]	61,072 (45.34%)	(12)	35,284 (26.20%)		38,333 (28.46%)	
Michigan	23,940 (36.86%)		30,617 (47.14%)	(5)	10,393 (16.00%)	
Mississippi	25,918 (49.39%)		26,556 (50.61%)	(6)		
Missouri	32,670 (44.91%)		40,093 (55.09%)	(7)		
New Hampshire	14,789 (29.51%)		27,761 (55.40%)	(6)	7,559 (15.09%)	
New Jersey	40,015 (51.43%)	(7)	36,881 (47.40%)		829 (1.07%)	77 (0.10%)
New York	218,590 (47.94%)	(36)	114,320 (25.07%)		120,515 (26.43%)	2,545 (0.56%)
North Carolina	43,981 (55.04%)	(11)	35,923 (44.96%)			
Ohio	138,357 (42.09%)		154,773 (47.09%)	(23)	35,452 (10.79%)	111 (0.03%)
Pennsylvania	185,535 (50.31%)	(26)	171,979 (46.63%)		11,263 (3.05%)	
Rhode Island	6,779 (60.77%)	(4)	3,646 (32.68%)		730 (6.54%)	
South Carolina	electors chosen by the legislature			(9)		
Tennessee	64,705 (52.53%)	(13)	58,479 (47.47%)			
Texas	3,777 (30.03%)		8,801 (69.97%)	(4)		
Vermont	22,932 (48.06%)	(6)	10,948 (22.94%)		13,837 (29.00%)	
Virginia	45,219 (49.16%)		46,764 (50.84%)	(17)		
Wisconsin	13,639 (35.13%)		14,924 (38.44%)	(4)	10,261 (26.43%)	
Total	**1,360,692 (47.31%) (163)**		**1,221,289 (42.46%) (127)**		**291,409 (10.13%)**	**2,751 (0.10%)**

Alabama

County	Taylor (W)	Cass (D)
Autauga	553 (54.0%)	471 (46.0%)
Baldwin	100 (42.9%)	133 (57.1%)
Barbour	1,205 (66.2%)	614 (33.8%)
Benton	566 (30.8%)	1,272 (69.2%)
Bibb	474 (53.3%)	416 (46.7%)
Blount	134 (20.3%)	526 (79.7%)
Butler	772 (73.6%)	277 (26.4%)
Chambers	1,323 (65.8%)	689 (34.2%)
Cherokee	630 (40.6%)	921 (59.4%)
Choctaw	373 (57.3%)	278 (42.7%)
Clarke	120 (26.8%)	327 (73.2%)
Coffee	192 (52.5%)	174 (47.5%)
Conecuh	426 (64.8%)	231 (35.2%)
Coosa	626 (41.4%)	883 (58.6%)
Covington	248 (72.9%)	92 (27.1%)
Dale	368 (39.9%)	555 (60.1%)
Dallas	860 (58.2%)	618 (41.8%)
De Kalb	257 (28.3%)	650 (71.7%)
Fayette	272 (24.4%)	841 (75.6%)
Franklin	510 (39.1%)	795 (60.9%)
Greene	1,088 (60.4%)	712 (39.6%)
Henry	504 (50.4%)	496 (49.6%)
Jackson	136 (21.2%)	1,589 (78.8%)
Jefferson	288 (42.8%)	385 (57.2%)
Lauderdale	695 (47.4%)	772 (52.6%)
Lawrence	663 (50.3%)	656 (49.7%)
Limestone	374 (31.0%)	833 (69.0%)
Lowndes	761 (63.7%)	434 (36.3%)
Macon	464 (73.3%)	532 (26.7%)
Madison	465 (25.1%)	1,385 (74.9%)
Marengo	739 (57.2%)	553 (42.8%)
Marion	193 (27.3%)	514 (72.7%)
Marshall	246 (25.8%)	708 (74.2%)
Mobile	1,319 (55.1%)	1,073 (44.9%)
Monroe	479 (68.9%)	216 (31.1%)
Montgomery	1,176 (63.7%)	669 (36.3%)
Morgan	361 (51.9%)	335 (48.1%)
Perry	826 (56.7%)	631 (43.3%)
Pickens	1,044 (52.9%)	931 (47.1%)
Pike	935 (58.5%)	663 (41.5%)
Randolph	461 (37.7%)	770 (62.3%)
Russell	970 (62.7%)	577 (37.3%)
St. Clair	150 (24.8%)	456 (75.2%)
Shelby	557 (60.2%)	368 (39.8%)
Sumter	820 (51.5%)	771 (48.5%)
Talladega	869 (51.5%)	820 (48.5%)
Tallapoosa	972 (51.4%)	920 (48.6%)
Tuscaloosa	976 (58.4%)	694 (41.6%)
Walker	231 (37.6%)	383 (62.4%)
Washington	72 (45.9%)	85 (54.1%)
Wilcox	639 (57.2%)	479 (42.8%)
Total	**30,482 (49.4%)**	**31,173 (50.6%)**

SOURCE—Loveman manuscript.

Arkansas

The returns of Franklin and Montgomery Counties were rejected.

County	Taylor (W)	Cass (D)
Arkansas	80 (51.9%)	74 (48.1%)
Benton	90 (23.7%)	290 (76.3%)
Bradley	227 (64.7%)	124 (35.3%)
Carroll	139 (34.8%)	261 (65.2%)
Chocot	146 (57.0%)	110 (43.0%)
Clark	193 (46.4%)	223 (53.6%)
Conway	149 (46.6%)	171 (53.4%)
Crawford	345 (43.0%)	457 (57.0%)
Crittenden	104 (60.5%)	68 (39.5%)
Dallas	203 (43.5%)	265 (56.5%)
Desha	208 (58.3%)	149 (41.7%)
Drew	198 (44.3%)	249 (55.7%)
Fulton	52 (35.9%)	93 (64.1%)
Greene	13 (22.0%)	46 (78.0%)
Hempstead	375 (53.2%)	330 (46.8%)
Hot Spring	141 (44.2%)	178 (55.8%)
Independence	422 (50.8%)	408 (49.2%)
Izard	no returns	
Jackson	194 (45.3%)	235 (54.7%)
Jefferson	195 (52.4%)	177 (47.6%)
Johnson	194 (35.7%)	350 (64.3%)
Lafayette	85 (46.4%)	98 (53.6%)
Lawrence	239 (47.8%)	291 (52.2%)
Madison	87 (28.9%)	214 (71.1%)
Marion	49 (50.0%)	49 (50.0%)
Mississippi	118 (51.8%)	110 (48.2%)
Monroe	113 (53.6%)	98 (46.4%)
Newton	2 (3.6%)	54 (96.4%)
Ouachita	571 (57.2%)	428 (42.8%)
Perry	29 (49.2%)	30 (50.8%)
Phillips	no returns	
Pike	67 (33.5%)	133 (66.5%)
Poinsett	44 (27.5%)	116 (72.5%)
Polk	17 (22.4%)	59 (77.6%)
Pope	240 (45.2%)	292 (54.8%)
Prairie	41 (27.0%)	111 (73.0%)
Pulaski	438 (49.0%)	455 (51.0%)
Randolph	50 (27.9%)	129 (72.1%)
St. Francis	208 (44.4%)	260 (55.6%)
Saline	147 (37.6%)	244 (62.4%)
Scott	61 (25.3%)	180 (74.7%)
Searcy	no returns	
Sevier	103 (34.6%)	195 (65.4%)
Union	553 (46.5%)	635 (53.5%)
Van Buren	95 (41.1%)	136 (58.9%)
Washington	377 (44.0%)	480 (56.0%)
White	48 (44.4%)	60 (55.6%)
Yell	137 (42.4%)	186 (57.6%)
Total	**7,587 (44.9%)** *(7,588)	**9,300 (55.1%)**

*Stated totals.

SOURCE— *Whig Almanac 1850*, p. 60. This is the only known source for these returns. There is no indication of whether or not they were official.

Connecticut

County	Taylor (W)	Cass (D)	Van Buren (FS)	Smith (Lty)
Fairfield	5,036 (52.6%)	4,064 (42.5%)	462 (4.8%)	7 (0.1%)
Hartford	6,001 (49.4%)	5,347 (44.0%)	810 (6.7%)	
Litchfield	3,918 (46.6%)	3,674 (43.7%)	800 (9.5%)	11 (0.1%)
Middlesex	2,136 (45.9%)	2,152 (46.3%)	361 (7.8%)	

New Haven	5,273 (49.8%)	4,517 (42.6%)	806 (7.6%)	
New London	4,021 (48.9%)	3,423 (41.6%)	776 (9.4%)	
Tolland	1,666 (48.0%)	1,612 (46.5%)	191 (5.5%)	
Windham	2,267 (42.55%)	2,262 (42.45%)	799 (15.0%)	
Total	**30,318 (48.6%)**	**27,051 (43.4%)**	**5,005 (8.0%)**	**18 (0.03%)**

SOURCE—Manuscript returns.

Delaware

County	Taylor (W)	Cass (D)	Van Buren (FS)
Kent	1,497 (52.8%)	1,337 (47.2%)	1 (0.04%)
New Castle	3,091 (52.5%)	2,717 (46.2%)	79 (1.3%)
Sussex	1,852 (49.9%)	1,856 (50.1%)	0
Total	**6,440 (51.8%)**	**5,910 (47.6%)**	**80 (0.6%)**

SOURCE—Governor's Register.

Florida

County	Taylor (W)	Cass (D)
Alachua	176 (53.0%)	156 (47.0%)
Benton	39 (38.6%)	62 (61.4%)
Calhoun	50 (45.0%)	61 (55.0%)
Columbia	285 (50.2%)	283 (49.8%)
Duval	312 (59.0%)	217 (41.0%)
Escambia	226 (59.3%)	155 (40.7%)
Franklin	131 (48.3%)	140 (51.7%)
Gadsden	452 (63.3%)	262 (36.7%)
Hamilton	129 (50.0%)	120 (50.0%)
Hillsborough	71 (40.3%)	105 (59.7%)
Holmes	111 (80.4%)	27 (19.6%)
Jackson	422 (71.8%)	166 (28.2%)
Jefferson	213 (45.7%)	253 (54.3%)
Levy	444 (61.4%)	279 (38.6%)
Liberty	39 (62.9%)	23 (37.1%)
Madison	272 (65.0%)	148 (35.0%)
Marion	209 (58.4%)	149 (41.6%)
Monroe	63 (42.3%)	86 (57.7%)
Nassau	73 (73.0%)	27 (27.0%)
Orange	17 (27.4%)	45 (72.6%)
St. Johns	137 (46.6%)	157 (53.4%)
St. Lucie	0	5 (100%)
Santa Rosa	204 (76.4%)	63 (23.6%)
Wakulla	165 (65.7%)	86 (34.3%)
Walton	216 (72.2%)	83 (27.8%)
Washington	88 (47.8%)	96 (52.2%)
Total[3]	**4,546 (58.4%)** [3] (4,535)	**3,243 (41.6%)** [3] (3,254)
Dade[4]	0	5 (100%)

Georgia

County	Taylor (W)	Cass (D)
Appling	14 (57.1%)	108 (42.9%)
Baker	341 (35.0%)	634 (65.0%)
Baldwin	382 (54.2%)	323 (45.8%)
Bibb	704 (46.7%)	805 (53.3%)
Bryan	123 (67.2%)	60 (32.8%)
Bulloch	43 (10.2%)	377 (89.8%)
Burke	598 (73.6%)	215 (26.4%)
Butts	269 (39.0%)	420 (61.0%)
Camden	106 (32.5%)	220 (67.5%)
Campbell	281 (32.6%)	582 (67.4%)
Carroll	475 (36.3%)	834 (63.7%)
Cass	987 (39.3%)	1,527 (60.7%)
Chatham	843 (53.3%)	739 (46.7%)
Chattooga	402 (48.1%)	434 (51.9%)
Cherokee	660 (40.4%)	984 (59.6%)
Clarke	624 (55.8%)	495 (44.2%)
Cobb	861 (40.6%)	1,262 (59.4%)
Columbia	519 (67.5%)	250 (32.5%)
Coweta	821 (55.4%)	662 (44.6%)
Crawford	402 (48.1%)	434 (51.9%)
Dade	102 (28.3%)	259 (71.7%)
Decatur	493 (58.5%)	350 (41.5%)
De Kalb	799 (42.1%)	1,097 (57.9%)
Dooly	349 (37.9%)	571 (62.1%)
Early	200 (28.4%)	505 (71.6%)
Effingham	183 (64.9%)	99 (35.1%)
Elbert	991 (86.3%)	157 (13.7%)
Emanuel	155 (42.8%)	207 (57.2%)
Fayette	521 (42.1%)	717 (57.9%)
Floyd	680 (50.4%)	670 (49.6%)
Forsyth	629 (45.7%)	747 (54.3%)
Franklin	364 (27.4%)	965 (72.6%)
Gilmer	402 (32.0%)	855 (68.0%)
Glynn	132 (85.7%)	22 (14.3%)
Greene	827 (85.6%)	139 (14.4%)
Gwinnett	744 (53.9%)	636 (46.1%)
Habersham	425 (35.3%)	778 (64.7%)
Hall	522 (44.0%)	665 (56.0%)
Hancock	472 (62.5%)	283 (37.5%)
Harris	870 (68.3%)	403 (31.7%)
Heard	415 (46.7%)	473 (53.3%)
Henry	939 (53.3%)	824 (46.7%)
Houston	697 (50.8%)	674 (49.2%)
Irwin	86 (19.5%)	355 (80.5%)
Jackson	561 (44.9%)	688 (55.1%)
Jasper	409 (44.4%)	512 (55.6%)
Jefferson	607 (84.5%)	111 (15.5%)
Jones	404 (49.3%)	415 (50.7%)
Laurens	567 (95.8%)	25 (4.2%)
Lee	323 (64.1%)	181 (35.9%)
Liberty	171 (56.4%)	132 (43.6%)
Lincoln	238 (66.5%)	120 (33.5%)
Lowndes	507 (56.1%)	397 (43.9%)
Lumpkin	652 (37.3%)	1,095 (62.7%)
Macon	388 (58.9%)	271 (41.1%)
Madison	336 (50.8%)	326 (49.2%)
Marion	510 (51.6%)	478 (48.4%)
McIntosh	117 (54.4%)	98 (45.6%)
Meriwether	717 (48.3%)	768 (51.7%)
Monroe	791 (54.4%)	664 (45.6%)
Montgomery	231 (90.6%)	24 (9.4%)
Morgan	467 (61.0%)	299 (39.0%)
Murray	799 (42.7%)	1,072 (57.3%)
Muscogee	1,330 (60.8%)	856 (39.2%)
Newton	1,045 (67.6%)	502 (32.4%)
Oglethorpe	636 (76.7%)	193 (23.3%)
Paulding	352 (45.4%)	423 (54.6%)
Pike	828 (48.1%)	892 (51.9%)
Pulaski	320 (43.1%)	423 (56.9%)
Putnam	399 (57.6%)	294 (42.4%)
Rabun	55 (21.0%)	207 (79.0%)
Randolph	780 (51.9%)	724 (48.1%)

Richmond	908 (60.4%)	595 (39.6%)	Walker	784 (44.8%)	965 (55.2%)
Scriven	265 (54.3%)	223 (45.7%)	Walton	544 (42.3%)	741 (57.7%)
Stewart	926 (57.4%)	686 (42.6%)	Ware	193 (54.5%)	161 (45.5%)
Sumter	733 (55.5%)	587 (44.5%)	Warren	614 (63.0%)	360 (37.0%)
Talbot	817 (52.5%)	738 (47.5%)	Washington	692 (52.5%)	626 (47.5%)
Taliaferro	388 (87.6%)	55 (12.4%)	Wayne	58 (45.7%)	69 (54.3%)
Tattnall	361 (89.1%)	44 (10.9%)	Wilkes	452 (60.7%)	293 (39.3%)
Telfair	160 (51.6%)	150 (48.4%)	Wilkinson	473 (48.7%)	498 (51.3%)
Thomas	526 (67.8%)	250 (32.2%)			
Troup	1,122 (74.5%)	384 (25.5%)	**Total**	**47,538 (51.5%)**	**44,794 (48.5%)**
Twiggs	331 (44.4%)	414 (55.6%)			*(44,809)
Union	412 (39.1%)	641 (60.9%)			
Upson	657 (65.6%)	344 (34.4%)			

*Stated totals.

SOURCE—*Executive Council Minutes.*

Illinois

County	Taylor (W)	Cass (D)	Van Buren (FS)
Adams	1,992 (44.8%)	2,205 (49.6%)	251 (5.6%)
Alexander	101 (32.1%)	212 (67.3%)	2 (0.6%)
Bond	391 (48.6%)	371 (46.1%)	43 (5.3%)
Boone	414 (32.9%)	395 (31.4%)	450 (35.7%)
Brown	408 (37.3%)	666 (60.9%)	20 (1.8%)
Bureau	376 (30.1%)	306 (24.5%)	566 (45.4%)
Calhoun	215 (45.3%)	257 (54.1%)	3 (0.6%)
Carroll	426 (55.8%)	222 (29.1%)	116 (15.2%)
Cass	761 (50.9%)	724 (48.4%)	11 (0.7%)
Champaign	213 (53.2%)	187 (46.7%)	0
Christian	183 (41.9%)	254 (58.1%)	0
Clark	743 (48.6%)	759 (49.6%)	27 (1.8%)
Clay	207 (33.8%)	405 (66.2%)	0
Clinton	351 (44.7%)	431 (54.9%)	3 (0.4%)
Coles	877 (57.8%)	633 (41.8%)	6 (0.4%)
Cook	1,708 (31.3%)	1,622 (29.8%)	2,120 (38.9%)
Crawford	493 (49.3%)	507 (50.7%)	0
Cumberland	108 (51.4%)	102 (48.6%)	0
De Kalb	223 (21.8%)	374 (36.5%)	427 (41.7%)
De Witt	373 (49.3%)	363 (48.0%)	20 (2.6%)
Du Page	313 (21.4%)	623 (42.6%)	528 (36.1%)
Edgar	829 (49.1%)	816 (48.4%)	42 (2.5%)
Edwards	288 (68.6%)	113 (26.9%)	19 (4.5%)
Effingham	99 (23.1%)	330 (76.9%)	0
Fayette	407 (47.4%)	452 (52.6%)	0
Franklin	139 (23.2%)	459 (76.8%)	0
Fulton	1,635 (44.3%)	1,684 (45.6%)	371 (10.1%)
Gallatin	235 (30.2%)	537 (69.0%)	6 (0.8%)
Greene	853 (42.3%)	1,128 (55.9%)	36 (1.8%)
Grundy	123 (31.3%)	207 (52.7%)	63 (16.0%)
Hamilton	125 (20.7%)	478 (79.3%)	0
Hancock	1,087 (48.8%)	1,074 (48.2%)	67 (3.0%)
Hardin	234 (49.7%)	237 (50.3%)	0
Henderson	408 (53.4%)	291 (38.1%)	65 (8.5%)
Iroquois	268 (43.4%)	322 (52.1%)	28 (4.5%)
Jackson	177 (41.6%)	243 (57.2%)	5 (1.2%)
Jasper	154 (40.3%)	228 (59.7%)	0
Jefferson	280 (31.6%)	605 (68.2%)	2 (0.2%)
Jersey	530 (49.2%)	454 (42.2%)	93 (8.6%)
Jo Daviess	1,772 (53.7%)	1,392 (42.2%)	134 (4.1%)
Johnson	67 (18.8%)	290 (81.2%)	0
Kane	855 (30.2%)	753 (26.6%)	1,220 (43.1%)
Kendall	392 (29.8%)	378 (28.7%)	547 (41.5%)
Knox	830 (42.6%)	727 (37.3%)	392 (20.1%)
La Salle	862 (29.0%)	1,238 (41.6%)	873 (29.4%)
Lake	321 (17.3%)	446 (24.0%)	1,088 (58.7%)
Lawrence	464 (46.6%)	532 (53.4%)	0
Lee	300 (36.9%)	367 (45.2%)	135 (16.6%)
Livingston	82 (38.0%)	130 (60.2%)	4 (1.9%)
Logan	465 (55.5%)	369 (44.0%)	4 (0.5%)
Macon	253 (43.5%)	323 (55.6%)	5 (0.9%)
Macoupin	710 (47.2%)	698 (46.4%)	96 (6.4%)

County	Taylor (W)	Cass (D)	Van Buren (FS)
Madison	1,820 (52.2%)	1,503 (43.1%)	162 (4.6%)
Marion	227 (25.8%)	639 (72.5%)	15 (1.7%)
Marshall	465 (55.5%)	369 (44.0%)	4 (0.5%)
Mason	391 (48.8%)	403 (50.3%)	7 (0.9%)
Massac	204 (40.2%)	303 (59.8%)	0
McDonough	440 (49.9%)	416 (47.2%)	25 (2.8%)
McHenry	618 (27.1%)	565 (24.8%)	1,096 (48.1%)
McLean	758 (51.3%)	626 (42.4%)	94 (6.4%)
Menard	605 (55.3%)	488 (44.6%)	1 (0.1%)
Mercer	430 (51.4%)	315 (37.7%)	90 (10.8%)
Monroe	355 (39.4%)	546 (60.6%)	0
Montgomery	332 (37.8%)	533 (60.7%)	13 (1.5%)
Morgan	1,372 (48.7%)	1,309 (46.4%)	139 (4.9%)
Moultrie	248 (56.5%)	191 (43.5%)	0
Ogle	682 (43.3%)	480 (30.5%)	413 (26.2%)
Peoria	1,237 (44.7%)	1,161 (42.0%)	368 (13.3%)
Perry	239 (38.1%)	344 (54.9%)	44 (7.0%)
Piatt	132 (48.9%)	138 (51.1%)	0
Pike	1,609 (47.3%)	1,636 (48.1%)	159 (4.7%)
Pope	224 (48.9%)	234 (51.1%)	0
Pulaski	84 (37.3%)	141 (62.7%)	0
Putnam	266 (35.5%)	185 (24.7%)	299 (39.9%)
Randolph	580 (37.0%)	689 (43.9%)	300 (19.1%)
Richland	235 (53.0%)	208 (47.0%)	0
Rock Island	583 (52.5%)	431 (38.8%)	96 (8.6%)
St. Clair	1,109 (34.7%)	2,023 (63.3%)	63 (2.0%)
Saline	122 (28.1%)	312 (71.9%)	0
Sangamon	1,943 (58.4%)	1,336 (40.2%)	47 (1.4%)
Schuyler	807 (49.1%)	804 (48.9%)	34 (2.1%)
Scott	798 (54.6%)	649 (44.4%)	15 (1.0%)
Shelby	332 (33.5%)	658 (66.4%)	1 (0.1%)
Stark	214 (45.3%)	174 (36.9%)	84 (17.8%)
Stephenson	730 (44.2%)	763 (46.2%)	157 (9.5%)
Tazewell	1,097 (61.4%)	593 (33.2%)	96 (5.4%)
Union	108 (17.5%)	503 (81.7%)	5 (0.8%)
Vermilion	942 (53.3%)	758 (42.9%)	68 (3.8%)
Wabash	456 (59.0%)	303 (39.2%)	14 (1.8%)
Warren	537 (44.2%)	529 (43.5%)	149 (12.3%)
Washington	204 (25.2%)	577 (71.4%)	27 (3.3%)
Wayne	318 (39.8%)	479 (60.0%)	1 (0.1%)
White	674 (56.2%)	513 (42.7%)	13 (1.1%)
Whiteside	391 (43.2%)	235 (26.0%)	279 (30.8%)
Will	713 (33.2%)	897 (41.7%)	540 (25.1%)
Williamson	211 (26.8%)	575 (73.2%)	0
Winnebago	866 (45.3%)	240 (12.5%)	807 (42.2%)
Woodford	186 (34.2%)	306 (56.3%)	52 (9.6%)
Total[5]	**52,853 (42.5%)**	**55,952 (44.9%)**	**15,702 (12.6%)**

SOURCE—Adler, Howard and Vincent A. Lacey (ed.), *Illinois Election Returns 1818–1990*, Carbondale, IL: Southern Illinois Univ. Press, 1993, pp. 128–130.

Indiana

County	Taylor (W)	Cass (D)	Van Buren (FS)
Adams	261 (39.5%)	398 (60.3%)	1 (0.2%)
Allen	991 (48.0%)	1,059 (51.3%)	13 (0.6%)
Bartholomew	1,011 (45.8%)	1,167 (52.9%)	28 (1.3%)
Benton	60 (42.6%)	78 (55.3%)	3 (2.1%)
Blackford	61 (19.7%)	231 (65.6%)	28 (8.8%)
Boone	773 (44.0%)	916 (52.2%)	66 (3.8%)
Brown	70 (12.2%)	503 (87.8%)	0
Carroll	822 (43.4%)	1,008 (53.2%)	76 (4.0%)
Cass	881 (49.9%)	829 (47.0%)	55 (3.1%)
Clark	1,200 (43.8%)	1,510 (55.1%)	28 (1.0%)
Clay	500 (40.4%)	734 (59.2%)	5 (0.4%)
Clinton	726 (40.9%)	964 (54.2%)	87 (4.9%)
Crawford	520 (56.7%)	397 (43.3%)	0

County	Taylor (W)	Cass (D)	Van Buren (FS)
Daviess	735 (51.1%)	701 (48.7%)	2 (0.1%)
Dearborn	1,378 (41.1%)	1,801 (53.7%)	176 (5.2%)
Decatur	1,245 (50.1%)	1,096 (44.1%)	143 (5.8%)
De Kalb	347 (35.8%)	577 (59.5%)	45 (4.6%)
Delaware	822 (52.2%)	694 (44.1%)	58 (3.7%)
Dubois	258 (30.4%)	579 (68.3%)	1 (0.1%)
Elkhart	756 (38.8%)	1,050 (53.9%)	142 (7.3%)
Fayette	1,040 (55.0%)	765 (40.5%)	86 (4.5%)
Floyd	1,018 (46.5%)	1,154 (52.7%)	17 (0.8%)
Fountain	840 (36.8%)	1,304 (57.1%)	138 (6.0%)
Franklin	1,411 (44.7%)	1,694 (53.7%)	51 (0.2%)
Fulton	423 (48.8%)	404 (46.7%)	39 (4.5%)
Gibson	860 (51.3%)	802 (47.8%)	15 (0.9%)
Grant	325 (24.9%)	623 (47.7%)	359 (27.5%)
Greene	918 (49.8%)	921 (49.9%)	6 (0.3%)
Hamilton	809 (41.9%)	805 (41.7%)	317 (16.4%)
Hancock	665 (44.0%)	806 (53.3%)	40 (2.6%)
Harrison	1,277 (55.0%)	1,046 (45.0%)	1 (0.04%)
Hendricks	1,158 (55.0%)	775 (36.8%)	173 (8.2%)
Henry	1,215 (45.4%)	1,005 (37.6%)	455 (17.0%)
Howard	275 (35.2%)	355 (45.4%)	152 (19.4%)
Huntington	457 (47.3%)	463 (47.9%)	46 (4.8%)
Jackson	632 (37.0%)	1,071 (62.6%)	7 (0.4%)
Jasper	86 (21.3%)	190 (47.0%)	128 (31.6%)
Jay	276 (34.1%)	392 (48.4%)	142 (17.5%)
Jefferson	2,075 (53.9%)	1,609 (41.8%)	167 (4.3%)
Jennings	926 (51.3%)	784 (43.4%)	96 (5.3%)
Johnson	676 (36.8%)	1,114 (60.7%)	46 (2.5%)
Knox	1,044 (58.5%)	741 (41.5%)	0
Kosciusko	797 (51.9%)	676 (44.0%)	64 (4.2%)
LaGrange	629 (45.6%)	636 (46.1%)	114 (8.3%)
Lake	138 (27.4%)	208 (42.9%)	139 (28.7%)
LaPorte	1,027 (48.2%)	876 (41.1%)	226 (10.6%)
Lawrence	1,070 (50.5%)	1,030 (48.6%)	18 (0.8%)
Madison	824 (44.0%)	993 (53.0%)	55 (2.9%)
Marion	1,877 (49.7%)	1,789 (47.4%)	109 (2.9%)
Marshall	305 (37.0%)	428 (51.9%)	91 (11.0%)
Martin	342 (40.4%)	497 (58.7%)	7 (0.8%)
Miami	731 (46.5%)	770 (49.0%)	70 (4.5%)
Monroe	780 (40.6%)	1,084 (56.4%)	59 (3.1%)
Montgomery	1,509 (47.7%)	1,547 (48.9%)	109 (3.4%)
Morgan	986 (46.2%)	1,029 (48.2%)	121 (5.7%)
Noble	497 (42.7%)	613 (52.7%)	53 (4.6%)
Ohio	439 (48.6%)	459 (50.8%)	6 (0.7%)
Orange	760 (44.1%)	959 (55.6%)	6 (0.3%)
Owen	882 (47.7%)	953 (51.6%)	13 (0.7%)
Parke	1,398 (50.4%)	1,318 (47.5%)	57 (2.1%)
Perry	599 (63.6%)	335 (35.6%)	8 (0.8%)
Pike	519 (50.4%)	510 (49.6%)	1 (0.1%)
Porter	343 (41.8%)	401 (48.8%)	77 (9.4%)
Posey	763 (38.0%)	1,226 (61.1%)	19 (0.9%)
Pulaski	135 (37.5%)	224 (62.2%)	1 (0.3%)
Putnam	1,647 (55.3%)	1,300 (43.7%)	29 (1.0%)
Randolph	631 (32.5%)	789 (40.6%)	523 (26.9%)
Ripley	1,114 (49.0%)	988 (43.4%)	173 (7.6%)
Rush	1,442 (49.4%)	1,392 (47.7%)	87 (3.0%)
St. Joseph	817 (45.0%)	667 (36.7%)	332 (18.3%)
Scott	487 (49.7%)	477 (48.7%)	16 (1.6%)
Shelby	1,122 (43.9%)	1,414 (55.4%)	18 (0.7%)
Spencer	681 (59.1%)	471 (55.4%)	0
Steuben	315 (32.2%)	352 (48.0%)	194 (19.8%)
Sullivan	465 (28.9%)	1,142 (70.9%)	3 (0.2%)
Switzerland	1,093 (48.7%)	1,106 (49.3%)	44 (2.0%)
Tippecanoe	1,269 (39.7%)	1,523 (47.6%)	405 (12.7%)
Tipton	183 (43.5%)	235 (55.8%)	3 (0.3%)
Union	526 (38.4%)	637 (46.4%)	208 (15.2%)
Vanderburgh	734 (51.6%)	667 (46.9%)	22 (1.5%)
Vermillion	830 (51.8%)	763 (47.6%)	9 (0.6%)
Vigo	1,585 (64.8%)	852 (34.8%)	10 (0.4%)

County	Taylor (W)	Cass (D)	Van Buren (FS)
Wabash	847 (49.1%)	739 (42.8%)	140 (8.1%)
Warren	708 (57.3%)	460 (37.2%)	68 (5.5%)
Warrick	457 (34.1%)	862 (64.3%)	21 (1.6%)
Washington	1,126 (40.3%)	1,643 (58.9%)	22 (0.8%)
Wayne	2,085 (47.9%)	1,432 (32.9%)	839 (19.3%)
Wells	252 (36.7%)	416 (60.6%)	18 (2.6%)
White	268 (36.7%)	305 (50.2%)	34 (5.6%)
Whitey	318 (44.7%)	373 (52.4%)	21 (2.9%)
Total	**70,175 (45.9%)**	**74,684 (48.8%)** *(74,692)	**8,100 (5.3%)**

*Stated totals.

Source—Dorothy F. Riker and Gayle Thornbrough (eds.), *Indiana Election Returns 1816–1851*, Indianapolis, IN: Indiana Historical Bureau, pp. 53–67.

Iowa

County	Taylor (W)	Cass (D)	Van Buren (FS)
Appanoose	44 (27.2%)	118 (72.8%)	0
Benton	22 (33.8%)	43 (66.2%)	0
Buchanan	21 (33.3%)	37 (58.7%)	5 (7.9%)
Cedar	205 (39.5%)	276 (53.2%)	38 (7.3%)
Clayton	148 (40.9%)	188 (51.9%)	26 (7.2%)
Clinton	168 (44.8%)	207 (55.2%)	0
Dallas	30 (53.6%)	26 (46.4%)	0
Davis	364 (49.2%)	375 (50.7%)	1 (0.1%)
Delaware	124 (53.0%)	104 (44.4%)	6 (3.0%)
Des Moines	954 (45.0%)	1,070 (50.5%)	95 (4.5%)
Dubuque	585 (43.2%)	764 (56.5%)	4 (0.3%)
Henry	655 (50.2%)	459 (35.2%)	190 (14.6%)
Iowa	25 (29.1%)	59 (68.6%)	1 (1.1%)
Jackson	397 (41.2%)	559 (58.0%)	8 (0.8%)
Jasper	66 (48.9%)	69 (51.1%)	0
Jefferson	637 (45.5%)	739 (52.8%)	23 (1.6%)
Johnson	286 (42.3%)	359 (53.2%)	30 (4.4%)
Jones	154 (38.3%)	207 (51.5%)	41 (10.2%)
Keokuk	220 (36.9%)	355 (59.6%)	21 (3.5%)
Lee	1,222 (40.2%)	1,614 (53.1%)	204 (6.7%)
Linn	293 (40.9%)	383 (53.4%)	41 (5.7%)
Louisa	428 (55.6%)	286 (37.1%)	56 (7.2%)
Mahaska	402 (48.8%)	400 (48.6%)	21 (2.6%)
Marion	277 (46.8%)	306 (51.7%)	9 (1.5%)
Monroe	111 (35.1%)	195 (61.7%)	10 (3.2%)
Muscatine	395 (50.3%)	377 (48.0%)	13 (1.7%)
Polk	193 (45.2%)	234 (54.8%)	0
Poweshiek	20 (50.0%)	20 (50.0%)	0
Scott	335 (42.7%)	366 (46.7%)	30 (3.8%)
Van Buren	926 (46.1%)	978 (48.7%)	104 (5.2%)
Wapello	570 (49.3%)	584 (50.4%)	2 (0.2%)
Washington	340 (43.5%)	295 (37.7%)	147 (18.8%)
Total	**10,617 (44.6%)**	**12,052 (50.7%)** *(12,051)	**1,126 (4.7%)**

*Stated totals.

*Pottawatamie	527 (92.6%)	42 (7.4%)	0

*Unorganized and not counted.

Source—(Iowa City) *Iowa Capitol Reporter*, November 29, 1848.

Kentucky

No returns have been located for this election
for Letcher and Perry Counties.

County	Taylor (W)	Cass (D)
Adair	568 (50.9%)	549 (49.1%)
Allen	423 (43.3%)	553 (56.7%)
Anderson	334 (37.9%)	547 (62.1%)
Ballard	277 (49.6%)	281 (50.4%)
Barren	1,462 (58.2%)	1,048 (41.8%)
Bath	724 (48.1%)	782 (51.9%)
Boone	935 (54.9%)	769 (45.1%)
Bourbon	1,172 (70.7%)	486 (29.3%)
Boyle	773 (69.0%)	347 (31.0%)
Bracken	795 (62.7%)	472 (37.3%)
Breathitt	143 (48.6%)	151 (51.4%)
Breckinridge	1,006 (70.4%)	422 (29.6%)
Bullitt	499 (55.6%)	399 (44.4%)

Butler	349 (63.1%)	204 (36.9%)	
Caldwell	826 (49.6%)	841 (50.4%)	
Calloway	227 (25.5%)	664 (74.5%)	
Campbell	511 (38.6%)	814 (61.4%)	
Carroll	433 (50.3%)	428 (49.7%)	
Carter	243 (32.2%)	510 (67.8%)	
Casey	529 (73.0%)	196 (27.0%)	
Christian	1,132 (59.0%)	786 (41.0%)	
Clark	1,046 (76.6%)	319 (23.4%)	
Clay	377 (75.1%)	125 (24.9%)	
Clinton	286 (49.3%)	294 (50.7%)	
Crittenden	342 (46.2%)	399 (53.8%)	
Cumberland	642 (80.8%)	153 (19.2%)	
Daviess	986 (62.0%)	605 (38.0%)	
Edmonson	249 (54.4%)	209 (45.6%)	
Estill	485 (67.1%)	238 (32.9%)	
Fayette	1,541 (66.4%)	781 (33.6%)	
Fleming	1,159 (62.3%)	700 (37.7%)	
Floyd	260 (53.6%)	225 (46.4%)	
Franklin	926 (58.2%)	664 (41.8%)	
Fulton	191 (41.2%)	273 (58.8%)	
Gallatin	360 (49.5%)	368 (50.5%)	
Garrard	1,187 (86.1%)	191 (13.9%)	
Grant	485 (47.8%)	529 (52.2%)	
Graves	468 (37.7%)	772 (62.3%)	
Grayson	507 (59.5%)	345 (40.5%)	
Green	517 (50.2%)	512 (49.8%)	
Greenup	640 (55.4%)	516 (44.6%)	
Hancock	304 (64.7%)	166 (35.3%)	
Hardin	1,239 (66.3%)	631 (33.7%)	
Harlan	350 (86.2%)	56 (13.8%)	
Harrison	891 (49.9%)	896 (50.1%)	
Hart	586 (52.6%)	528 (47.4%)	
Henderson	731 (56.7%)	559 (43.3%)	
Henry	827 (44.7%)	1,022 (55.3%)	
Hickman	169 (32.4%)	353 (67.6%)	
Hopkins	796 (51.0%)	766 (49.0%)	
Jefferson	3,997 (57.2%)	2,990 (42.8%)	
Jessamine	682 (60.8%)	439 (39.2%)	
Johnson	106 (33.1%)	214 (66.9%)	
Kenton	985 (44.5%)	1,228 (55.5%)	
Knox	648 (80.3%)	159 (19.7%)	
Larue	478 (57.8%)	349 (42.2%)	
Laurel	488 (77.1%)	145 (22.9%)	
Lawrence	414 (56.6%)	318 (43.4%)	
Lewis	521 (47.9%)	566 (52.1%)	
Lincoln	832 (71.9%)	325 (28.1%)	
Livingston	403 (60.3%)	265 (9.7%)	
Logan	1,402 (79.7%)	358 (20.3%)	
Madison	1,313 (70.0%)	564 (30.0%)	
Marion	765 (54.9%)	629 (45.1%)	
Marshall	120 (19.5%)	496 (80.5%)	
Mason	1,631 (63.1%)	953 (36.9%)	
McCracken	407 (56.9%)	308 (43.1%)	
Meade	713 (76.0%)	225 (24.0%)	
Mercer	734 (40.5%)	1,088 (59.5%)	
Monroe	586 (60.7%)	379 (39.3%)	
Montgomery	688 (55.7%)	548 (44.3%)	
Morgan	413 (45.7%)	490 (54.3%)	
Muhlenberg	746 (63.1%)	437 (36.9%)	
Nelson	1,149 (71.2%)	464 (28.8%)	
Nicholas	673 (48.9%)	704 (51.1%)	
Ohio	718 (57.0%)	542 (43.0%)	
Oldham	476 (49.4%)	488 (50.6%)	
Owen	533 (39.7%)	810 (60.3%)	
Owesley	330 (57.2%)	248 (42.8%)	
Pendleton	375 (38.5%)	599 (61.5%)	
Pike	225 (61.6%)	140 (38.4%)	
Pulaski	947 (56.3%)	734 (43.7%)	
Rockcastle	497 (84.0%)	95 (16.0%)	

Russell	519 (74.2%)	180 (25.8%)	
Scott	797 (52.1%)	734 (47.9%)	
Shelby	1,434 (66.7%)	716 (33.3%)	
Simpson	448 (51.1%)	428 (48.9%)	
Spencer	460 (56.7%)	351 (43.3%)	
Taylor	324 (40.9%)	469 (59.1%)	
Todd	808 (66.4%)	409 (33.6%)	
Trigg	588 (48.2%)	632 (51.8%)	
Trimble	361 (42.6%)	486 (57.4%)	
Union	501 (52.2%)	458 (47.8%)	
Warren	1,226 (67.0%)	603 (33.0%)	
Washington	721 (51.5%)	678 (48.5%)	
Wayne	689 (63.0%)	405 (37.0%)	
Whitley	584 (86.3%)	93 (13.7%)	
Woodford	778 (69.8%)	337 (30.2%)	
Total	**67,141 (57.5%)**	**49,720 (42.5%)**	

SOURCE—*Louisville Daily Journal*, December 2, 1848.

Louisiana

Parish	Taylor (W)	Cass (D)
Ascension	288 (55.0%)	236 (45.0%)
Assumption	469 (55.0%)	286 (45.0%)
Avoyelles	299 (45.4%)	359 (54.6%)
Bienville	114 (37.6%)	189 (62.4%)
Bossier	183 (53.2%)	161 (46.8%)
Caddo	281 (48.4%)	300 (51.6%)
Calcasieu	44 (19.6%)	181 (80.4%)
Caldwell	90 (37.7%)	149 (62.3%)
Carroll	268 (53.3%)	235 (46.7%)
Catahoula	320 (45.3%)	386 (54.7%)
Claiborne	221 (40.6%)	323 (59.4%)
Concordia	188 (66.2%)	96 (33.8%)
De Soto	149 (40.7%)	217 (59.3%)
East Baton Rouge	400 (49.6%)	406 (50.4%)
East Feliciana	349 (47.0%)	394 (53.0%)
Franklin	124 (43.4%)	162 (56.6%)
Iberville	429 (59.3%)	295 (40.7%)
Jefferson	717 (52.1%)	660 (47.9%)
Lafayette	108 (32.9%)	220 (67.1%)
Lafourche Interior	739 (82.0%)	162 (18.0%)
Livingston	144 (37.2%)	243 (62.8%)
Madison	283 (59.6%)	192 (40.4%)
Morehouse	178 (63.8%)	101 (36.2%)
Natchitoches	386 (43.8%)	495 (56.2%)
Orleans	5,551 (54.8%)	4,579 (45.2%)
Ouachita	168 (18.8%)	176 (81.2%)
Plaquemines	187 (34.8%)	350 (65.2%)
Pointe Coupee	288 (43.8%)	370 (56.2%)
Rapides	383 (41.4%)	543 (58.6%)
Sabine	246 (47.6%)	271 (52.4%)
St. Bernard	124 (58.2%)	89 (41.8%)
St. Charles	135 (79.4%)	35 (20.6%)
St. Helena	169 (47.3%)	188 (52.7%)
St. James	431 (78.6%)	117 (21.4%)
St. John the Baptist	228 (64.0%)	128 (36.0%)
St. Landry	754 (73.9%)	276 (26.1%)
St. Martin	456 (65.5%)	240 (34.5%)
St. Mary	470 (73.9%)	166 (26.1%)
St. Tammany	275 (60.0%)	183 (40.0%)
Tensas	177 (61.5%)	111 (38.5%)
Terrebone	353 (73.2%)	129 (26.8%)
Union	307 (56.4%)	237 (43.6%)
Vermillion	130 (71.4%)	52 (28.6%)
Washington	158 (45.4%)	190 (54.6%)
West Baton Rouge	255 (74.1%)	109 (25.9%)
West Feliciana	232 (47.1%)	261 (52.9%)
Total	**18,248 (54.8%)**	**15,248 (45.2%)**

*Jackson   127 (39.7%)   193 (60.3%)

Not included in the official returns. See the Whig Almanac 1849, *p. 58.*

SOURCES—(New Orleans) *Courier*, November 30, 1848; *Daily Picayune*, November 28, 1848; and the *Whig Almanac 1849.*

Maine

County	Taylor (W)	Cass (D)	Van Buren (FS)
Aroostook	431 (30.7%)	868 (61.8%)	106 (7.5%)
Cumberland	4,797 (38.3%)	5,989 (47.8%)	1,744 (13.9%)
Franklin	886 (28.3%)	1,431 (45.8%)	810 (25.9%)
Hancock	2,075 (44.7%)	2,318 (50.0%)	247 (5.3%)
Kennebec	5,056 (54.1%)	2,634 (28.2%)	1,656 (17.7%)
Lincoln	5,316 (48.5%)	4,670 (42.6%)	967 (8.8%)
Oxford	1,531 (24.2%)	3,601 (56.9%)	1,201 (19.0%)
Penobscot	3,916 (39.0%)	4,591 (45.7%)	1,528 (15.2%)
Piscataquis	937 (36.9%)	1,168 (46.0%)	432 (17.0%)
Somerset	2,445 (44.1%)	2,085 (37.6%)	1,008 (18.2%)
Waldo	1,768 (28.3%)	3,382 (54.1%)	1,107 (17.7%)
Washington	2,501 (46.3%)	2,446 (45.3%)	449 (8.3%)
York	3,466 (38.5%)	4,697 (52.2%)	841 (9.3%)
Total	**35,125 (40.3%)**	**39,880 (45.8%)**	**12,096 (13.9%)**

SOURCES—(Augusta) *Kennebec Journal*, November 30, 1848; and (Portland) *Eastern Argus*, November 30, 1848.

Maryland

County	Taylor (W)	Cass (D)	Van Buren (FS)
Allegany	1,579 (49.3%)	1,620 (50.6%)	3 (0.1%)
Anne Arundel	1,693 (53.2%)	1,486 (46.7%)	5 (0.2%)
Baltimore	2,527 (48.6%)	2,669 (51.3%)	7 (0.1%)
Calvert	432 (56.3%)	335 (43.7%)	0
Caroline	492 (45.9%)	580 (54.1%)	0
Carroll	1,763 (51.3%)	1,670 (48.5%)	7 (0.2%)
Cecil	1,503 (50.9%)	1,444 (48.9%)	4 (0.1%)
Charles	769 (72.1%)	398 (27.9%)	0
Dorchester	1,367 (62.5%)	821 (37.5%)	0
Frederick	3,159 (51.2%)	2,989 (48.5%)	20 (0.3%)
Harford	1,521 (54.8%)	1,253 (45.1%)	3 (0.1%)
Kent	645 (59.1%)	447 (40.9%)	0
Montgomery	1,056 (57.8%)	771 (42.2%)	1 (0.1%)
Prince George's	1,051 (58.9%)	733 (41.1%)	1 (0.1%)
Queen Anne's	725 (64.2%)	612 (35.8%)	0
St. Mary's	788 (65.1%)	422 (34.9%)	0
Somerset	1,414 (58.5%)	1,005 (41.5%)	0
Talbot	706 (49.5%)	719 (50.5%)	0
Washington	2,688 (52.5%)	2,434 (47.5%)	1 (0.1%)
Worcester	1,352 (54.5%)	1,130 (45.5%)	0
Baltimore (city)	10,474 (48.6%)	10,995 (51.0%)	76 (0.4%)
Total	**37,704 (52.1%)**	**34,533 (47.7%)**	**128 (0.2%)**

SOURCES—Manuscript returns; John T. Willis, *Presidential Elections in Maryland*, Mt. Airy, MD: Lomond Publications, 1984, p. 174.

Massachusetts

County	Taylor (W)	Cass (D)	Van Buren (FS)
Barnstable	2,015 (60.5%)	802 (24.1%)	516 (15.5%)
Berkshire	3,549 (47.4%)	2,387 (31.9%)	1,549 (20.7%)
Bristol	4,841 (49.2%)	2,170 (22.0%)	2,832 (28.8%)
Dukes	290 (57.5%)	133 (26.4%)	81 (16.1%)
Essex	8,554 (46.9%)	4,679 (25.6%)	5,021 (27.5%)
Franklin	2,133 (40.1%)	1,542 (29.0%)	1,645 (30.9%)
Hampden	3,306 (43.2%)	3,061 (40.0%)	1,285 (16.8%)
Hampshire	3,055 (51.5%)	1,070 (18.0%)	1,806 (30.5%)
Middlesex	9,855 (43.5%)	6,821 (30.1%)	5,965 (26.3%)
Nantucket	444 (64.2%)	89 (12.9%)	159 (23.0%)
Norfolk	4,740 (43.9%)	2,451 (22.7%)	3,608 (33.4%)

County	Taylor (W)	Cass (D)	Van Buren (FS)
Plymouth	3,569 (41.5%)	1,848 (21.5%)	3,188 (37.1%)
Suffolk	8,896 (62.6%)	3,173 (22.3%)	2,136 (15.0%)
Worcester	5,825 (30.0%)	5,058 (26.0%)	8,542 (44.0%)
Total	**61,072 (45.3%)**	**35,284 (26.2%)**	**38,333 (28.5%)**

SOURCE—Manuscript returns.

Michigan

County	Taylor (W)	Cass (D)	Van Buren (FS)
Allegan	274 (36.5%)	303 (40.3%)	174 (23.2%)
Barry	243 (33.8%)	382 (53.2%)	93 (13.0%)
Berrien	953 (43.2%)	1,146 (51.9%)	108 (4.9%)
Branch	665 (31.0%)	1,083 (50.4%)	400 (18.6%)
Calhoun	1,254 (31.0%)	1,487 (42.7%)	745 (21.4%)
Cass	783 (41.8%)	901 (48.1%)	191 (10.2%)
Chippewa	51 (54.3%)	43 (45.7%)	0
Clinton	213 (31.6%)	340 (50.4%)	131 (19.4%)
Eaton	356 (31.8%)	546 (48.8%)	218 (19.5%)
Genesee	877 (43.5%)	823 (40.8%)	315 (15.6%)
Hillsdale	1,027 (36.7%)	1,290 (46.1%)	482 (17.2%)
Ingham	473 (31.6%)	692 (46.2%)	332 (32.4%)
Ionia	379 (25.9%)	608 (41.5%)	477 (32.6%)
Jackson	969 (27.0%)	1,547 (43.1%)	1,070 (29.8%)
Kalamazoo	1,010 (42.3%)	880 (36.9%)	495 (20.8%)
Kent	653 (37.1%)	768 (43.7%)	337 (19.2%)
Lapeer`	369 (33.1%)	542 (48.6%)	205 (18.4%)
Lenawaee	1,886 (38.9%)	2,171 (44.7%)	795 (16.4%)
Livingston	764 (35.2%)	1,127 (51.9%)	280 (12.9%)
Mackinac	51 (28.7%)	127 (71.3%)	0
Macomb	855 (35.7%)	1,339 (55.8%)	204 (8.5%)
Monroe	791 (34.3%)	1,155 (50.1%)	398 (17.2%)
Oakland	1,942 (35.9%)	2,781 (51.3%)	694 (12.8%)
Ottawa	143 (30.8%)	269 (57.8%)	53 (11.4%)
Saginaw	118 (33.9%)	183 (52.6%)	47 (13.5%)
St. Clair	665 (42.6%)	814 (52.1%)	83 (5.3%)
St. Joseph	963 (40.3%)	1,011 (42.3%)	418 (17.5%)
Shiawassee	281 (31.3%)	426 (47.4%)	192 (21.4%)
Van Buren	353 (36.1%)	508 (51.9%)	117 (12.0%)
Washtenaw	2,029 (40.4%)	2,080 (41.4%)	918 (18.3%)
Wayne	2,540 (40.5%)	3,305 (52.7%)	421 (6.7%)
Total	**23,947 (36.8%)**	**30,742 (47.2%)**	**10,393 (16.0%)**
*Houghton	17 (12.2%)	65 (87.8%)	0

*Not included in the official returns.

SOURCES—Manuscript returns; *Michigan Manual 1913*, pp. 690–1.

Mississippi

County	Taylor (W)	Cass (D)
Adams	643 (63.8%)	365 (36.2%)
Amite	426 (58.0%)	309 (42.0%)
Attala	480 (42.4%)	653 (57.6%)
Bolivar	89 (64.5%)	49 (35.5%)
Carroll	885 (49.0%)	921 (51.0%)
Chickasaw	846 (47.2%)	948 (52.8%)
Choctaw	642 (46.4%)	743 (53.6%)
Claiborne	464 (56.4%)	358 (43.6%)
Clarke	211 (42.8%)	282 (57.2%)
Coahoma	189 (59.1%)	130 (40.9%)
Copiah	491 (45.5%)	587 (54.5%)
Covington	135 (28.1%)	346 (71.9%)
De Soto	836 (53.6%)	723 (46.4%)
Franklin	226 (47.6%)	249 (52.4%)
Greene	184 (70.0%)	79 (30.0%)
Hancock	157 (57.5%)	116 (42.5%)
Harrison	165 (77.1%)	172 (22.9%)
Hinds	1,206 (59.5%)	822 (40.5%)
Holmes	643 (55.3%)	520 (44.7%)
Issaquena	85 (59.4%)	58 (40.6%)
Itawamba	567 (36.7%)	880 (63.3%)
Jackson	32 (16.2%)	166 (83.8%)
Jasper	343 (52.7%)	308 (47.3%)
Jefferson	382 (56.8%)	290 (43.2%)
Jones	95 (41.3%)	135 (58.7%)
Kemper	416 (48.0%)	450 (52.0%)
Lafayette	730 (49.0%)	760 (51.0%)
Lauderdale	474 (41.5%)	667 (58.5%)
Lawrence	145 (24.9%)	438 (75.1%)
Leake	328 (53.2%)	289 (46.8%)
Lowndes	801 (50.7%)	780 (49.3%)
Madison	614 (55.3%)	497 (44.7%)
Marion	99 (37.9%)	162 (62.1%)
Marshall	1,306 (49.3%)	1,344 (50.7%)

County	Taylor (W)	Cass (D)
Monroe	921 (46.4%)	1,062 (53.6%)
Neshoba	241 (48.9%)	254 (51.1%)
Newton	184 (48.3%)	197 (51.7%)
Noxubee	617 (48.1%)	667 (51.9%)
Oktibbeha	388 (47.8%)	424 (52.2%)
Panola	578 (62.7%)	344 (37.3%)
Perry	143 (67.5%)	69 (32.5%)
Pike	277 (41.0%)	398 (59.0%)
Pontotoc	757 (43.1%)	999 (56.9%)
Rankin	356 (49.0%)	370 (51.0%)
Scott	152 (35.8%)	273 (64.2%)
Simpson	236 (47.2%)	264 (52.8%)
Smith	210 (42.3%)	287 (57.7%)
Sunflower	33 (60.0%)	22 (40.0%)
Tallahatchie	206 (48.5%)	219 (51.5%)
Tippah	981 (44.2%)	1,236 (55.8%)
Tishomingo	840 (41.4%)	1,190 (58.6%)
Tunica	51 (67.1%)	25 (32.9%)
Warren	890 (65.1%)	478 (34.9%)
Washington	179 (71.6%)	71 (28.4%)
Wayne	97 (65.1%)	52 (34.9%)
Wilkinson	455 (61.0%)	291 (39.0%)
Winston	307 (41.9%)	425 (58.1%)
Yalobusha	843 (49.9%)	846 (50.1%)
Yazoo	641 (56.8%)	497 (43.2%)
Total[6]	**25,918 (49.4%)**	**26,556 (50.6%)**

SOURCES—(Jackson) *Mississippian and State Gazette*, November 24, 1848; the *Whig Almanac 1849*, pp. 58–9; and W. Dean Burnham, *Presidential Ballots 1836–1892* (reprint edition), New York, NY: Arno Press, 1976, pp. 552–570.

Missouri

County	Taylor (W)	Cass (D)
Adair	110 (35.5%)	200 (64.5%)
Andrew	384 (35.8%)	689 (64.2%)
Atchison	77 (36.2%)	136 (63.8%)
Audrain	185 (52.7%)	166 (47.3%)
Barry	55 (20.2%)	217 (79.8%)
Bates	146 (43.7%)	186 (56.3%)
Benton	208 (35.3%)	382 (64.7%)
Boone	1,102 (65.2%)	588 (34.8%)
Buchanan	704 (39.9%)	1,061 (60.1%)
Caldwell	128 (43.2%)	168 (56.8%)
Callaway	849 (57.4%)	631 (42.6%)
Camden	155 (35.5%)	282 (64.5%)
Cape Girardeau	485 (40.6%)	709 (59.4%)
Carroll	266 (44.8%)	298 (55.2%)
Cedar	116 (30.0%)	271 (70.0%)
Chariton	414 (37.9%)	577 (62.1%)
Clark	284 (54.0%)	242 (46.0%)
Clay	626 (60.0%)	418 (40.0%)
Clinton	290 (50.3%)	285 (49.7%)
Cole	277 (34.3%)	531 (65.7%)
Cooper	813 (43.8%)	633 (56.2%)
Crawford	264 (49.0%)	275 (51.0%)
Dade	166 (35.2%)	306 (64.8%)
Dallas	105 (27.1%)	283 (72.9%)
Daviess	269 (42.9%)	358 (57.1%)
De Kalb	37 (20.2%)	146 (79.8%)
Dunklin	42 (50.0%)	42 (50.0%)
Franklin	339 (33.3%)	680 (66.7%)
Gasconade	87 (20.0%)	349 (80.0%)
Gentry	152 (27.7%)	396 (72.3%)
Greene	401 (32.8%)	825 (67.2%)
Grundy	225 (54.6%)	187 (45.4%)
Harrison	63 (30.4%)	144 (69.6%)
Henry	274 (53.4%)	239 (46.6%)
Hickory	98 (30.4%)	224 (69.6%)
Holt	148 (37.4%)	248 (62.6%)
Howard	801 (47.4%)	888 (52.6%)
Jackson	695 (42.1%)	954 (57.9%)
Jasper	161 (35.4%)	294 (64.6%)
Jefferson	246 (44.2%)	311 (55.8%)
Johnson	334 (42.5%)	451 (57.5%)
Knox	196 (49.5%)	197 (50.5%)
Lafayette	915 (61.0%)	585 (39.0%)
Lawrence	170 (31.3%)	374 (68.7%)
Lewis	479 (50.0%)	479 (50.0%)
Lincoln	556 (44.4%)	696 (55.6%)
Linn	230 (43.6%)	297 (56.4%)
Livingston	195 (34.3%)	373 (65.7%)
Macon	360 (43.4%)	470 (56.6%)
Madison	231 (38.0%)	377 (62.0%)
Marion	1,046 (56.8%)	797 (43.2%)
Mercer	144 (44.0%)	183 (56.0%)
Miller	76 (16.9%)	373 (83.1%)
Mississippi	138 (43.3%)	181 (56.7%)
Montgomery	379 (67.1%)	186 (32.9%)
Moniteau	161 (25.7%)	466 (74.3%)
Monroe	807 (59.0%)	561 (41.0%)
Morgan	167 (32.8%)	342 (67.2%)
New Madrid	323 (65.8%)	168 (34.2%)
Newton	161 (25.9%)	461 (74.1%)
Nodaway	43 (14.8%)	148 (85.2%)
Oregon	7 (5.9%)	111 (94.1%)
Osage	92 (22.8%)	312 (77.2%)
Ozark	39 (25.7%)	113 (74.3%)
Perry	322 (45.3%)	389 (54.7%)
Pettis	230 (46.5%)	265 (53.5%)
Pike	793 (50.3%)	784 (49.7%)
Platte	1,102 (42.4%)	1,494 (57.6%)
Polk	231 (30.9%)	516 (69.1%)
Pulaski	124 (34.0%)	241 (66.0%)
Putnam	74 (38.1%)	120 (61.9%)
Ralls	397 (57.0%)	299 (43.0%)
Randolph	607 (54.4%)	508 (45.6%)
Ray	509 (44.8%)	626 (55.2%)
Reynolds	21 (12.4%)	148 (87.6%)
Ripley	14 (8.3%)	154 (91.7%)
St. Charles	477 (45.6%)	569 (54.4%)
St. Clair	148 (47.6%)	263 (52.4%)
St. Francois	285 (51.0%)	274 (49.0%)
St. Genevieve	142 (45.8%)	168 (54.2%)
St. Louis	4,827 (50.3%)	4,778 (49.7%)
Saline	536 (55.0%)	438 (45.0%)
Schuyler	204 (51.5%)	192 (48.5%)
Scotland	131 (35.3%)	240 (64.7%)
Scott	147 (40.4%)	217 (59.6%)
Shannon	35 (39.3%)	54 (60.7%)
Shelby	175 (40.0%)	263 (60.0%)
Stoddard	97 (33.1%)	196 (66.9%)
Sullivan	154 (38.1%)	250 (61.9%)
Taney	54 (14.2%)	325 (85.8%)
Texas	81 (30.5%)	185 (69.5%)
Van Buren	270 (39.1%)	420 (60.9%)
Warren	351 (51.1%)	336 (48.9%)
Washington	473 (52.8%)	423 (47.2%)
Wayne	91 (27.1%)	245 (72.9%)
Wright	72 (28.5%)	181 (71.5%)
Total	**32,670 (44.9%)**	**40,082 (55.1%)**
	*(32,680)	*(40,093)

*Stated totals.

SOURCE—(Jefferson City) *Jefferson Inquirer*, November 25 and December 2, 1848.

New Hampshire

County	Taylor (W)	Cass (D)	Van Buren (FS)
Belknap	609 (22.5%)	1,769 (65.2%)	334 (12.3%)
Carroll	539 (18.0%)	1,835 (61.2%)	624 (20.8%)
Cheshire	1,881 (38.4%)	2,076 (42.4%)	945 (19.3%)
Coos	230 (13.3%)	1,282 (74.1%)	219 (12.7%)
Grafton	1,925 (27.2%)	4,060 (57.3%)	1,104 (15.6%)
Hillsborough	2,798 (31.7%)	4,772 (54.1%)	1,258 (14.3%)
Merrimack	1,245 (19.0%)	4,218 (64.5%)	1,075 (16.4%)
Rockingham	2,710 (35.4%)	3,971 (51.8%)	980 (12.8%)
Strafford	1,676 (41.0%)	1,912 (46.8%)	497 (12.2%)
Sullivan	1,176 (33.0%)	1,866 (52.3%)	523 (14.7%)
Total	**14,789 (29.5%)**	**27,761 (55.4%)** *(27,762)	**7,559 (15.1%)**

*Stated total.

SOURCE—Manuscript returns.

New Jersey

County	Taylor (W)	Cass (D)	Van Buren (FS)	Smith (Lty)
Atlantic	472 (37.7%)	780 (62.3%)	0	
Bergen	1,004 (44.0%)	1,262 (55.3%)	15 (0.7%)	
Burlington	3,898 (56.2%)	3,014 (43.4%)	30 (0.4%)	
Camden	1,967 (88.4%)	236 (10.6%)	23 (1.0%)	
Cape May	657 (74.4%)	226 (25.6%)	0	
Cumberland	1,666 (55.8%)	1,319 (44.2%)	0	
Essex	5,997 (60.0%)	3,824 (38.3%)	127 (1.3%)	41 (0.4%)
Gloucester	1,297 (57.7%)	862 (38.4%)	88 (3.9%)	
Hudson	1,434 (63.1%)	760 (33.4%)	80 (3.5%)	
Hunterdon	2,191 (40.4%)	3,220 (59.4%)	9 (0.2%)	
Mercer	2,631 (51.8%)	2,424 (47.7%)	26 (0.5%)	1 (0.02%)
Middlesex	2,469 (56.0%)	1,807 (41.0%)	129 (2.9%)	
Monmouth	3,119 (47.2%)	3,450 (52.2%)	4 (0.1%)	35 (0.5%)
Morris	2,889 (53.5%)	2,424 (44.9%)	91 (1.7%)	
Passaic	1,749 (55.1%)	1,304 (41.1%)	120 (3.8%)	
Salem	1,702 (51.3%)	1,586 (47.8%)	28 (0.8%)	
Somerset	2,028 (55.6%)	1,617 (44.4%)	0	
Sussex	1,211 (25.8%)	3,443 (73.3%)	46 (1.0%)	
Warren	1,634 (37.7%)	2,689 (62.0%)	13 (0.3%)	
Total	**40,015 (51.4%)**	**36,881 (47.4%)** *(36,901)	**829 (1.1%)** *(819)	**77 (0.1%)**

*Stated totals.

SOURCE—(Newark) *Sentinel of Freedom*, November 28, 1848.

New York

County	Taylor (W)	Van Buren (FS)	Cass (D)	Smith (Lty)
Albany	7,068 (52.3%)	2,407 (17.8%)	4,002 (29.6%)	34 (0.3%)
Allegany	2,789 (45.3%)	2,040 (33.2%)	1,283 (20.9%)	41 (0.7%)
Broome	2,490 (47.6%)	777 (14.9%)	1,959 (37.4%)	6 (0.1%)
Cattaraugus	2,604 (46.8%)	1,236 (22.2%)	1,677 (30.2%)	45 (0.8%)
Cayuga	4,318 (46.0%)	3,979 (42.4%)	1,034 (11.0%)	58 (0.6%)
Chautauqua	4,207 (54.2%)	1,628 (21.0%)	1,911 (24.6%)	11 (0.1%)
Chemung	1,943 (40.2%)	2,166 (44.8%)	728 (15.1%)	0
Chenango	3,587 (46.6%)	1,481 (19.2%)	2,616 (34.0%)	19 (0.2%)
Clinton	1,941 (41.8%)	1,221 (26.3%)	1,472 (31.7%)	9 (0.2%)
Columbia	3,943 (48.3%)	2,100 (25.7%)	2,121 (26.0%)	5 (0.1%)
Cortland	1,879 (39.9%)	1,803 (38.3%)	946 (20.1%)	77 (1.6%)
Delaware	2,832 (43.2%)	2,908 (44.3%)	790 (12.0%)	31 (0.5%)
Dutchess	5,376 (54.3%)	1,295 (13.1%)	3,227 (32.6%)	7 (0.1%)
Erie	7,647 (57.1%)	2,357 (17.6%)	3,360 (25.1%)	24 (0.2%)
Essex	2,629 (55.3%)	1,119 (23.5%)	1,002 (21.1%)	7 (0.1%)
Franklin	1,353 (41.8%)	911 (28.1%)	974 (30.1%)	0

County	Taylor (W)	Van Buren (FS)	Cass (D)	Smith (Lty)
Fulton & Hamilton	1,976 (49.8%)	1,602 (40.4%)	380 (9.6%)	9 (0.2%)
Genesee	2,890 (55.2%)	1,111 (21.2%)	1,180 (22.5%)	55 (1.1%)
Greene	2,707 (42.8%)	1,425 (22.5%)	1,551 (24.5%)	648 (10.2%)
Herkimer	2,430 (34.5%)	3,893 (55.2%)	699 (9.9%)	29 (0.4%)
Jefferson	4,841 (41.5%)	4,342 (37.2%)	2,445 (20.9%)	43 (0.4%)
Kings	7,511 (56.6%)	817 (6.2%)	4,881 (36.8%)	50 (0.4%)
Lewis	1,223 (37.3%)	1,258 (38.3%)	789 (24.0%)	13 (0.4%)
Livingston	3,730 (55.1%)	2,100 (31.0%)	889 (13.1%)	46 (0.7%)
Madison	2,898 (39.1%)	2,739 (36.9%)	1,565 (21.1%)	219 (3.0%)
Monroe	6,539 (51.5%)	4,671 (36.8%)	1,443 (11.4%)	47 (0.4%)
Montgomery	2,924 (50.2%)	1,602 (27.5%)	1,285 (22.0%)	19 (0.3%)
New York	29,057 (54.5%)	5,106 (9.6%)	18,975 (35.6%)	159 (0.3%)
Niagara	2,828 (45.3%)	2,080 (33.3%)	1,313 (21.0%)	24 (0.4%)
Oneida	6,032 (41.5%)	4,816 (33.1%)	3,585 (24.7%)	103 (0.7%)
Onondaga	5,442 (43.0%)	4,942 (39.1%)	2,229 (17.6%)	39 (0.3%)
Ontario	3,848 (49.2%)	2,627 (33.6%)	1,272 (16.2%)	82 (1.0%)
Orange	4,172 (47.5%)	1,434 (16.3%)	3,170 (36.1%)	0
Orleans	2,402 (47.2%)	1,722 (33.8%)	918 (18.0%)	51 (1.0%)
Oswego	3,655 (39.9%)	4,254 (46.4%)	1,134 (12.3%)	122 (1.3%)
Otsego	3,929 (41.0%)	1,941 (20.3%)	3,674 (38.3%)	38 (0.4%)
Putnam	816 (36.7%)	415 (18.6%)	995 (44.7%)	0
Queens	2,444 (53.7%)	800 (17.6%)	1,310 (28.8%)	0
Rensselaer	6,241 (52.5%)	2,930 (24.7%)	2,685 (22.6%)	25 (0.2%)
Richmond	1,099 (52.8%)	123 (5.9%)	860 (41.3%)	0
Rockland	918 (40.9%)	255 (11.3%)	1,064 (47.4%)	6 (0.3%)
St. Lawrence	3,667 (35.6%)	6,028 (58.5%)	614 (6.0%)	1 (0.01%)
Saratoga	4,438 (52.7%)	1,405 (16.7%)	2,515 (29.9%)	61 (0.7%)
Schenectady	1,716 (53.0%)	444 (13.7%)	1,070 (33.1%)	6 (0.2%)
Schoharie	2,724 (44.8%)	654 (10.8%)	2,671 (44.0%)	25 (0.4%)
Seneca	1,767 (37.9%)	1,523 (32.6%)	1,360 (29.2%)	15 (0.3%)
Steuben	4,357 (43.7%)	3,623 (36.4%)	1,975 (19.8%)	4 (0.04%)
Suffolk	2,180 (46.9%)	1,400 (30.1%)	1,051 (22.6%)	15 (0.3%)
Sullivan	1,672 (46.8%)	534 (15.0%)	1,363 (38.2%)	1 (0.03%)
Tioga	1,782 (41.8%)	789 (18.5%)	1,683 (39.4%)	14 (0.3%)
Tompkins	3,003 (43.3%)	2,648 (38.2%)	1,270 (18.3%)	11 (0.2%)
Ulster	4,659 (52.3%)	2,277 (25.7%)	1,969 (22.1%)	0
Warren	1,270 (42.9%)	618 (20.9%)	1,019 (34.5%)	50 (0.2%)
Washington	4,486 (57.7%)	2,024 (26.1%)	1,225 (15.8%)	33 (0.4%)
Wayne	3,567 (44.0%)	3,690 (45.5%)	797 (9.8%)	48 (0.6%)
Westchester	4,112 (54.2%)	1,312 (17.3%)	2,146 (28.3%)	15 (0.2%)
Wyoming	2,381 (44.3%)	1,630 (30.3%)	1,337 (24.9%)	27 (0.5%)
Yates	1,651 (38.6%)	1,483 (36.9%)	862 (21.5%)	18 (0.4%)
Total	**218,590 (47.9%)**	**120,515 (26.4%)**	**114,320 (25.1%)**	**2,545 (0.6%)**
	*(218,603)	*(120,510)		

Stated totals.

SOURCE—Manuscript returns.

North Carolina

County	Taylor (W)	Cass (D)
Alexander	367 (70.8%)	151 (29.2%)
Anson	1,084 (75.1%)	359 (24.9%)
Ashe	660 (64.8%)	358 (35.2%)
Beaufort	923 (66.6%)	463 (33.4%)
Bertie	524 (63.4%)	302 (36.6%)
Bladen	280 (45.1%)	341 (54.9%)
Brunswick	319 (57.3%)	237 (42.7%)
Buncombe	996 (69.7%)	434 (30.3%)
Burke	1,210 (80.9%)	286 (19.1%)
Cabarrus	756 (66.7%)	377 (33.3%)
Caldwell	503 (84.0%)	96 (16.0%)
Camden	493 (87.6%)	70 (12.4%)
Carteret	474 (59.9%)	317 (40.1%)
Caswell	293 (21.2%)	1,087 (78.8%)
Chatham	1,033 (66.1%)	519 (33.9%)
Cherokee	549 (75.8%)	175 (24.2%)
Chowan	295 (62.5%)	177 (37.5%)
Cleveland	314 (42.5%)	425 (57.5%)
Columbus	169 (38.1%)	274 (61.9%)
Craven	696 (53.0%)	616 (47.0%)
Cumberland	812 (40.5%)	1,191 (59.5%)
Currituck	193 (29.3%)	466 (70.7%)
Davidson	1,087 (67.6%)	520 (32.4%)
Davie	448 (62.3%)	251 (37.7%)
Duplin	318 (25.4%)	939 (74.6%)
Edgecombe	143 (3.3%)	1,335 (96.7%)
Franklin	341 (34.1%)	658 (65.9%)
Gates	379 (56.7%)	289 (43.3%)
Granville	959 (53.6%)	831 (46.4%)
Greene	318 (57.3%)	237 (42.7%)
Guilford	1,714 (82.1%)	373 (17.9%)
Halifax	582 (56.6%)	446 (43.4%)
Haywood	418 (66.2%)	213 (33.8%)
Henderson	541 (82.3%)	116 (17.7%)
Hertford	316 (68.7%)	144 (31.3%)
Hyde	495 (67.5%)	238 (32.5%)
Iredell	1,146 (84.5%)	211 (15.5%)
Johnston	646 (46.4%)	746 (53.6%)

Jones	242 (64.0%)	136	(36.0%)
Lenoir	282 (45.8%)	334	(54.2%)
Lincoln	828 (34.2%)	1,593	(65.8%)
Macon	427 (67.4%)	207	(32.6%)
Martin	361 (39.8%)	545	(60.2%)
McDowell	59 (26.8%)	161	(73.2%)
Mecklenburg	775 (45.1%)	945	(54.9%)
Montgomery	583 (87.7%)	82	(12.3%)
Moore	538 (57.0%)	406	(43.0%)
Nash	113 (12.4%)	798	(87.6%)
New Hanover	464 (27.0%)	1,255	(73.0%)
Northampton	493 (50.3%)	488	(49.7%)
Onslow	211 (23.5%)	686	(76.5%)
Orange	1,667 (51.3%)	1,585	(48.7%)
Pasquotank	570 (70.0%)	244	(30.0%)
Perquimans	434 (63.2%)	253	(36.8%)
Person	346 (40.0%)	518	(60.0%)
Pitt	636 (57.0%)	479	(43.0%)
Randolph	1,196 (84.2%)	225	(15.8%)
Richmond	699 (90.8%)	71	(9.2%)

Robeson	633 (53.8%)	545	(46.2%)
Rockingham	380 (33.2%)	766	(66.8%)
Rowan	859 (60.5%)	560	(39.5%)
Rutherford	958 (88.4%)	126	(11.6%)
Sampson	612 (45.2%)	741	(54.8%)
Stanly	725 (98.1%)	14	(1.9%)
Stokes	1,014 (52.6%)	912	(47.4%)
Surry	1,132 (57.1%)	852	(42.9%)
Tyrrell	300 (75.8%)	96	(24.2%)
Union	775 (45.1%)	945	(54.9%)
Wake	1,028 (45.2%)	1,247	(54.8%)
Warren	156 (19.0%)	667	(81.0%)
Washington	373 (71.4%)	149	(28.6%)
Wayne	258 (22.2%)	903	(77.8%)
Wilkes	1,060 (89.8%)	121	(10.2%)
Total	**43,981 (55.0%)**	**35,923**	**(45.0%)**
	*(44,207)	*(35,975)	

Stated totals.

SOURCES—Manuscript returns; Thad Eure (Secretary of State), *North Carolina Government, 1585–1979*, Raleigh, NC: 1979, pp. 1330–1.

Ohio

County	Taylor (W)	Cass (D)	Van Buren (FS)	Smith (Lty)[7]
Adams	1,259 (40.0%)	1,690 (53.7%)	196 (6.2%)	
Allen	728 (40.4%)	1,070 (59.4%)	2 (0.1%)	
Ashland	1,341 (32.4%)	2,519 (60.9%)	275 (6.7%)	
Ashtabula	1,124 (25.2%)	878 (19.6%)	2,467 (55.2%)	
Athens	1,846 (50.2%)	1,509 (41.0%)	320 (8.7%)	
Auglaize	457 (30.3%)	1,039 (68.8%)	14 (0.9%)	
Belmont	2,723 (44.2%)	2,892 (47.0%)	543 (8.8%)	
Brown	1,771 (37.4%)	2,557 (54.0%)	403 (8.5%)	
Butler	1,959 (33.3%)	3,536 (60.2%)	381 (6.5%)	
Carroll	1,453 (45.5%)	1,395 (43.7%)	345 (10.8%)	
Champaign	1,878 (50.5%)	1,508 (40.6%)	330 (8.9%)	
Clark	2,506 (61.3%)	1,375 (33.6%)	208 (5.1%)	
Clermont	2,204 (40.5%)	2,833 (52.0%)	408 (7.5%)	
Clinton	1,233 (39.9%)	1,122 (36.3%)	735 (23.8%)	
Columbiana	1,850 (34.0%)	2,732 (50.2%)	865 (15.9%)	
Coshocton	1,814 (41.5%)	2,422 (55.4%)	137 (3.1%)	
Crawford	952 (35.0%)	1,678 (61.7%)	90 (3.3%)	
Cuyahoga	1,776 (26.4%)	2,368 (35.1%)	2,594 (38.5%)	
Darke	1,508 (48.0%)	1,554 (49.4%)	81 (2.6%)	
Defiance	384 (39.3%)	567 (58.0%)	23 (2.4%)	
Delaware	1,866 (50.3%)	1,574 (42.5%)	268 (7.2%)	
Erie	1,409 (45.6%)	999 (32.3%)	681 (22.0%)	
Fairfield	2,438 (40.7%)	3,515 (58.6%)	42 (0.7%)	
Fayette	1,157 (51.9%)	946 (52.4%)	128 (5.7%)	
Franklin	3,199 (49.1%)	3,029 (46.5%)	284 (4.4%)	
Gallia	1,630 (58.1%)	1,081 (38.5%)	95 (3.4%)	
Geauga	872 (27.5%)	922 (29.1%)	1,373 (43.4%)	
Greene	2,035 (51.7%)	1,256 (31.9%)	644 (16.4%)	
Guernsey	2,375 (44.2%)	2,504 (46.6%)	489 (9.1%)	
Hamilton	9,018 (41.3%)	10,834 (49.6%)	1,986 (9.1%)	
Hancock	1,016 (40.0%)	1,501 (59.1%)	22 (0.9%)	
Hardin	596 (49.6%)	605 (48.3%)	51 (4.1%)	
Harrison	1,564 (41.5%)	1,658 (44.0%)	543 (14.4%)	
Henry	217 (40.9%)	297 (55.9%)	17 (3.2%)	
Highland	2,114 (45.2%)	2,224 (49.5%)	344 (7.3%)	
Hocking	856 (39.0%)	1,319 (60.1%)	23 (1.0%)	
Holmes	1,118 (33.0%)	2,224 (65.7%)	45 (1.3%)	
Huron	1,950 (42.4%)	1,769 (38.5%)	876 (19.1%)	
Jackson	987 (46.0%)	1,108 (51.7%)	50 (2.3%)	
Jefferson	2,147 (44.4%)	2,231 (46.2%)	455 (9.4%)	
Knox	1,910 (35.8%)	2,890 (54.1%)	539 (10.1%)	
Lake	777 (32.4%)	716 (29.9%)	904 (37.8%)	
Lawrence	1,164 (59.3%)	745 (38.0%)	53 (2.7%)	
Licking	3,030 (43.1%)	3,468 (49.3%)	534 (7.6%)	
Logan	1,652 (53.9%)	1,137 (37.1%)	275 (9.0%)	

County	Taylor (W)	Cass (D)	Van Buren (FS)	Smith (Lty)[7]
Lorain	647 (17.3%)	1,473 (39.4%)	1,616 (43.3%)	
Lucas	1,298 (46.0%)	1,197 (42.4%)	327 (11.6%)	
Madison	1,329 (62.7%)	712 (33.6%)	80 (3.8%)	
Mahoning	720 (19.1%)	1,953 (51.9%)	1,042 (27.7%)	
Marion	1,001 (44.5%)	1,193 (53.0%)	55 (2.4%)	
Medina	1,140 (28.0%)	1,836 (45.1%)	1,098 (27.0%)	
Meigs	1,327 (50.2%)	1,014 (38.3%)	305 (11.5%)	
Mercer	360 (35.4%)	641 (63.0%)	16 (1.6%)	
Miami	2,542 (54.8%)	1,822 (39.3%)	272 (5.9%)	
Monroe	999 (25.6%)	2,574 (65.9%)	330 (8.5%)	
Montgomery	3,561 (49.5%)	3,331 (46.3%)	304 (4.2%)	
Morgan	2,320 (45.7%)	2,448 (48.2%)	314 (6.2%)	
Morrow	1,166 (33.7%)	1,884 (54.5%)	407 (11.8%)	
Muskingum	4,427 (55.1%)	3,380 (42.1%)	228 (2.8%)	
Ottawa	190 (40.8%)	231 (49.6%)	45 (9.7%)	
Paulding	70 (26.1%)	198 (73.9%)	0	
Perry	1,488 (40.2%)	2,192 (59.3%)	19 (0.5%)	
Pickaway	2,115 (51.6%)	1,960 (47.8%)	24 (0.6%)	
Pike	843 (47.2%)	909 (50.9%)	33 (1.8%)	
Portage	1,270 (27.9%)	2,149 (47.3%)	1,127 (24.8%)	
Preble	2,106 (53.5%)	1,519 (38.6%)	314 (8.0%)	
Putnam	402 (38.7%)	634 (61.0%)	3 (0.3%)	
Richland	2,087 (38.3%)	3,177 (58.3%)	188 (3.4%)	
Ross	3,395 (57.8%)	2,306 (39.3%)	174 (3.0%)	
Sandusky	928 (42.2%)	1,148 (51.1%)	125 (5.7%)	
Scioto	1,838 (58.9%)	1,268 (40.7%)	13 (0.4%)	
Seneca	1,536 (35.4%)	2,326 (53.5%)	483 (11.1%)	
Shelby	1,021 (46.4%)	1,129 (51.3%)	49 (2.2%)	
Stark	2,382 (36.9%)	3,495 (54.2%)	570 (8.8%)	
Summit	1,892 (39.7%)	1,815 (38.1%)	1,058 (22.2%)	
Trumbull	1,364 (25.3%)	1,951 (36.2%)	2,075 (38.5%)	
Tuscarawas	2,662 (47.5%)	2,553 (47.5%)	164 (3.0%)	
Union	1,030 (51.5%)	797 (39.9%)	173 (8.7%)	
Van Wert	223 (37.6%)	381 (62.4%)	0	
Warren	2,526 (52.7%)	1,861 (38.9%)	402 (8.4%)	
Washington	2,079 (46.5%)	1,930 (43.2%)	462 (10.3%)	
Wayne	2,284 (39.0%)	3,380 (57.7%)	190 (3.2%)	
Williams	328 (32.9%)	515 (51.7%)	154 (15.4%)	
Wood	647 (49.3%)	636 (48.4%)	29 (2.2%)	
Wyandot	951 (46.3%)	1,059 (51.5%)	46 (2.2%)	
Total	**138,357 (42.1%)** *(138,359)	**154,773 (47.1%)**	**35,452 (10.8%)** *(35,346)	

*Stated totals.

SOURCE—(Columbus) *Ohio State Journal*, November 25, 1848.

Pennsylvania

County	Taylor (W)	Cass (D)	Van Buren (FS)
Adams	2,576 (59.0%)	1,762 (40.4%)	25 (0.6%)
Allegheny	10,112 (57.8%)	6,591 (37.7%)	779 (4.5%)
Armstrong	2,030 (47.2%)	2,126 (49.5%)	141 (3.3%)
Beaver	2,655 (48.4%)	2,303 (42.0%)	530 (9.7%)
Bedford	2,836 (50.2%)	2,816 (49.8%)	1 (0.02%)
Berks	5,082 (34.8%)	9,484 (64.9%)	51 (0.3%)
Blair	2,476 (63.2%)	1,438 (36.7%)	4 (0.1%)
Bradford	3,274 (47.2%)	1,889 (27.2%)	1,780 (25.6%)
Bucks	5,140 (48.2%)	5,364 (50.3%)	163 (1.5%)
Butler	2,505 (50.9%)	2,247 (45.6%)	173 (3.5%)
Cambria	1,233 (46.9%)	1,386 (52.7%)	12 (0.5%)
Carbon	889 (42.9%)	1,181 (57.0%)	1 (0.05%)
Centre	1,856 (41.5%)	2,611 (58.4%)	4 (0.1%)
Chester	5,949 (50.3%)	5,370 (45.4%)	507 (4.3%)
Clarion	1,372 (36.9%)	2,306 (62.1%)	37 (1.0%)
Clearfield	761 (39.0%)	1,168 (59.8%)	23 (1.2%)
Clinton	911 (48.5%)	967 (51.5%)	1 (0.1%)
Columbia	2,263 (39.8%)	3,396 (59.7%)	29 (0.5%)
Crawford	2,205 (39.6%)	2,748 (49.3%)	621 (11.1%)

County	Taylor (W)	Cass (D)	Van Buren (FS)
Cumberland	3,242 (50.3%)	3,178 (49.3%)	25 (0.4%)
Dauphin	3,705 (61.9%)	2,251 (37.6%)	34 (0.6%)
Delaware	2,194 (57.4%)	1,547 (40.4%)	84 (2.2%)
Elk	134 (34.2%)	242 (61.7%)	16 (4.1%)
Erie	3,418 (59.0%)	2,022 (34.9%)	357 (6.2%)
Fayette	3,045 (46.4%)	3,441 (52.5%)	73 (1.1%)
Franklin	4,006 (55.6%)	3,199 (44.4%)	4 (0.1%)
Greene	1,476 (37.8%)	2,379 (60.9%)	52 (1.3%)
Huntingdon	2,590 (57.1%)	1,922 (42.4%)	25 (0.6%)
Indiana	2,410 (58.0%)	1,544 (37.1%)	204 (4.9%)
Jefferson	850 (46.2%)	972 (52.8%)	19 (1.0%)
Juniata	888 (50.9%)	856 (49.1%)	1 (0.1%)
Lancaster	11,390 (64.6%)	6,080 (34.5%)	163 (0.9%)
Lebanon	2,996 (61.6%)	1,862 (38.3%)	2 (0.04%)
Lehigh	2,978 (48.2%)	3,199 (51.8%)	3 (0.05%)
Luzerne	3,516 (45.8%)	3,991 (51.9%)	176 (2.3%)
Lycoming	1,992 (46.9%)	2,244 (52.9%)	9 (0.2%)
McKean	367 (45.5%)	418 (51.8%)	22 (2.7%)
Mercer	2,977 (41.6%)	3,094 (43.3%)	1,080 (15.1%)
Mifflin	1,543 (48.9%)	1,586 (50.3%)	26 (0.8%)
Monroe	518 (22.0%)	1,830 (77.8%)	3 (0.1%)
Montgomery	5,040 (46.2%)	5,627 (51.5%)	251 (2.3%)
Northampton	3,191 (42.9%)	4,203 (56.6%)	38 (0.5%)
Northumberland	1,765 (43.8%)	2,258 (56.0%)	8 (0.2%)
Perry	1,562 (40.4%)	2,295 (59.4%)	5 (0.1%)
Philadelphia	31,229 (58.2%)	21,508 (40.1%)	877 (1.6%)
Pike	216 (21.2%)	799 (78.5%)	3 (0.3%)
Potter	226 (24.0%)	468 (49.7%)	248 (26.3%)
Schuylkill	4,808 (57.7%)	3,490 (41.9%)	35 (0.4%)
Somerset	3,018 (72.4%)	1,127 (27.0%)	21 (0.5%)
Sullivan	147 (31.3%)	303 (64.6%)	19 (4.1%)
Susquehanna	1,853 (39.3%)	2,563 (54.3%)	301 (6.4%)
Tioga	1,264 (34.7%)	1,344 (36.9%)	1,039 (28.5%)
Union	3,129 (65.1%)	1,656 (34.4%)	25 (0.5%)
Venango	1,061 (38.4%)	1,538 (55.7%)	164 (5.9%)
Warren	948 (43.6%)	1,088 (50.1%)	136 (6.3%)
Washington	3,898 (47.6%)	3,820 (46.7%)	468 (5.7%)
Wayne	997 (35.1%)	1,642 (57.8%)	202 (7.1%)
Westmoreland	3,124 (37.0%)	5,197 (61.6%)	122 (1.4%)
Wyoming	861 (48.1%)	892 (49.8%)	37 (2.1%)
York	4,838 (48.4%)	5,151 (51.5%)	4 (0.04%)
Total	**185,535 (50.3%)**	**171,979 (46.6%)**	**11,263 (3.1%)**

*Stated totals. *(185,537)

SOURCE—*Journal of the Pennsylvania Senate, 1849*, pp. 468–475.

Rhode Island

County	Taylor (W)	Cass (D)	Van Buren (FS)
Bristol	590 (79.8%)	131 (17.7%)	18 (2.4%)
Kent	690 (65.1%)	318 (30.0%)	52 (4.9%)
Newport	1,207 (77.8%)	232 (14.9%)	113 (7.3%)
Providence	3,542 (54.9%)	2,515 (39.0%)	398 (6.2%)
Washington	750 (55.6%)	450 (33.4%)	149 (11.0%)
Total	**6,779 (60.8%)**	**3,646 (32.7%)**	**730 (6.5%)**

SOURCE—*Providence Journal*, November 30, 1848.

South Carolina

Electors chosen by the legislature

Tennessee

County	Taylor (W)	Cass (D)
Anderson	602 (70.7%)	250 (29.3%)
Bedford	1,497 (52.0%)	1,381 (48.0%)
Benton	392 (46.1%)	459 (53.9%)
Bledsoe	508 (68.9%)	229 (31.1%)
Blount	965 (59.3%)	663 (40.7%)
Bradley	760 (45.1%)	927 (54.9%)
Campbell	473 (62.9%)	279 (37.1%)
Cannon	469 (36.2%)	827 (63.8%)
Carroll	1,493 (72.7%)	560 (27.3%)
Carter	745 (85.2%)	129 (14.8%)
Claiborne	700 (48.5%)	744 (51.5%)
Cocke	815 (81.2%)	189 (18.8%)
Coffee	332 (26.0%)	943 (74.0%)
Davidson	2,698 (57.7%)	1,976 (42.3%)
Decatur	384 (58.1%)	277 (41.9%)
De Kalb	571 (49.9%)	573 (50.1%)
Dickson	386 (36.4%)	674 (63.6%)
Dyer	383 (58.6%)	271 (41.4%)
Fayette	1,217 (53.4%)	1,060 (46.6%)
Fentress	113 (20.7%)	432 (79.3%)
Franklin	390 (24.4%)	1,207 (75.6%)
Gibson	1,423 (67.4%)	688 (32.6%)
Giles	1,389 (47.9%)	1,511 (52.1%)
Grainger	1,094 (69.1%)	489 (30.9%)
Greene	963 (39.4%)	1,483 (60.6%)
Hamilton	685 (51.9%)	634 (48.1%)

County	Taylor/Whig	Cass/Dem
Hardeman	723 (41.6%)	1,016 (58.4%)
Hardin	621 (44.6%)	770 (55.4%)
Hawkins	1,252 (50.2%)	1,243 (49.8%)
Haywood	800 (54.3%)	672 (45.7%)
Henderson	1,286 (73.7%)	460 (26.3%)
Henry	860 (38.9%)	1,349 (61.1%)
Hickman	301 (23.4%)	988 (76.6%)
Humphreys	309 (39.1%)	482 (60.9%)
Jackson	1,269 (61.3%)	801 (38.7%)
Jefferson	1,468 (84.7%)	265 (15.3%)
Johnson	382 (83.4%)	76 (16.6%)
Knox	2,140 (83.0%)	439 (17.0%)
Lauderdale	279 (50.5%)	274 (49.5%)
Lawrence	596 (52.3%)	544 (47.7%)
Lincoln	680 (20.8%)	2,584 (79.2%)
Marshall	730 (34.1%)	1,408 (65.9%)
McMinn	960 (48.4%)	1,024 (51.6%)
McNairy	939 (54.4%)	786 (45.6%)
Madison	1,562 (67.9%)	737 (32.1%)
Marion	562 (62.6%)	336 (37.4%)
Maury	1,516 (43.5%)	1,970 (56.5%)
Meigs	150 (21.9%)	534 (78.1%)
Monroe	962 (50.1%)	960 (49.9%)
Montgomery	1,288 (57.1%)	969 (42.9%)
Morgan	229 (55.0%)	187 (45.0%)
Obion	357 (42.3%)	487 (57.7%)
Overton	467 (29.6%)	1,112 (70.4%)
Perry	433 (60.1%)	287 (39.9%)
Polk	367 (41.5%)	517 (58.5%)
Rhea	298 (47.9%)	324 (52.1%)
Roane	998 (59.8%)	671 (40.2%)
Robertson	1,236 (59.6%)	839 (40.4%)
Rutherford	1,754 (54.9%)	1,439 (45.1%)
Sevier	787 (93.2%)	57 (6.8%)
Shelby	1,828 (53.2%)	1,607 (46.8%)
Smith	2,380 (76.8%)	719 (23.2%)
Stewart	574 (44.9%)	705 (55.1%)
Sullivan	436 (24.1%)	1,375 (75.9%)
Sumner	922 (48.1%)	1,994 (51.9%)
Tipton	352 (42.2%)	482 (57.8%)
Van Buren	130 (39.6%)	198 (60.4%)
Warren	407 (29.6%)	1,161 (70.4%)
Washington	862 (45.9%)	1,016 (54.1%)
Wayne	673 (63.6%)	386 (36.4%)
Weakley	669 (38.3%)	1,080 (61.7%)
White	1,064 (67.9%)	503 (32.1%)
Williamson	1,883 (70.4%)	793 (29.6%)
Wilson	2,517 (71.6%)	998 (28.4%)
Total	**64,705 (52.5%)**	**58,479 (47.5%)**
	*Stated totals.	*(58,419)

SOURCES—(Nashville) *Daily Union*, August 2, 1849; and *Whig Almanac 1849*, p. 59.

Texas

No returns have been located for this election for Refugio County plus three counties created in 1848: Cooke, Gillespie and Webb.

County	Taylor (W)	Cass (D)
Anderson	83 (26.6%)	229 (73.4%)
Austin	45 (39.7%)	175 (60.3%)
Bastrop	42 (18.0%)	191 (82.0%)
Bexar	189 (36.3%)	332 (63.7%)
Brazoria	83 (32.5%)	172 (67.5%)
Brazos	0	33 (100%)
Burleson	9 (12.3%)	64 (87.7%)
Caldwell	27 (21.4%)	99 (78.6%)
Calhoun	71 (47.8%)	76 (52.2%)
Cherokee	110 (26.7%)	302 (73.3%)
Collin	43 (30.3%)	99 (69.7%)
Colorado	20 (22.7%)	68 (77.3%)
Comal	14 (11.8%)	105 (88.2%)
Dallas	57 (21.4%)	209 (78.6%)
Denton	7 (13.2%)	45 (86.8%)
De Witt	16 (16.5%)	81 (83.5%)
Fannin	88 (26.4%)	245 (73.6%)
Fayette	92 (33.5%)	175 (66.5%)
Fort Bend	39 (22.4%)	135 (77.6%)
Galveston	217 (47.9%)	235 (52.1%)
Goliad	27 (44.3%)	34 (55.7%)
Gonzales	58 (38.7%)	92 (61.3%)
Grimes	53 (22.2%)	186 (77.8%)
Guadeloupe	31 (25.8%)	72 (74.2%)
Harris	289 (39.5%)	443 (60.5%)
Harrison	364 (48.9%)	381 (51.1%)
Hays	12 (21.8%)	43 (78.2%)
Houston	24 (13.0%)	161 (87.0%)
Hunt	11 (14.3%)	66 (85.7%)
Jackson	13 (17.6%)	61 (82.4%)
Jasper	53 (31.4%)	113 (68.6%)
Lamar	186 (34.2%)	358 (65.8%)
Lavaca	13 (27.7%)	34 (72.3%)
Leon	26 (15.5%)	142 (84.5%)
Liberty	68 (32.1%)	144 (67.9%)
Matagorda	69 (46.6%)	79 (53.4%)
Medina	0	45 (100%)
Milam	38 (24.2%)	119 (75.8%)
Montgomery	59 (26.6%)	163 (73.4%)
Nacogdoches	97 (23.7%)	313 (76.3%)
Nueces	66 (54.1%)	56 (45.9%)
Panola	43 (18.1%)	194 (81.9%)
Polk	56 (34.4%)	107 (65.6%)
Robertson	5 (8.1%)	57 (91.9%)
Rusk	202 (30.7%)	455 (69.3%)
Sabine	38 (17.4%)	181 (82.6%)
San Augustine	70 (23.0%)	234 (77.0%)
San Patricio	5 (16.1%)	26 (83.9%)
Titus	123 (29.4%)	296 (70.6%)
Travis	29 (10.4%)	249 (89.6%)
Van Zandt	26 (27.7%)	68 (72.3%)
Victoria	87 (50.3%)	86 (49.7%)
Walker	119 (36.5%)	207 (63.5%)
Washington	123 (24.8%)	373 (75.2%)
Williamson	16 (28.1%)	41 (71.9%)
Wharton	26 (33.8%)	51 (66.2%)
Total[8]	**3,777 (30.0%)**	**8,801 (70.0%)**

SOURCES—*Governor's Register*, November 27, 1848; W. Dean Burnham, *Presidential Ballots 1836–1892* (reprint edition), New York, NY: Arno Press, 1976, pp. 764–812, 943; and the *Whig Almanac 1852*, p. 58.

Vermont

County	Taylor (W)	Cass (D)	Van Buren (FS)
Addison	2,558 (65.4%)	319 (8.2%)	1,035 (26.5%)
Bennington	1,559 (46.9%)	1,150 (34.6%)	616 (18.5%)
Caledonia	1,367 (40.1%)	1,158 (33.9%)	888 (26.0%)
Chittenden	1,763 (45.8%)	571 (14.8%)	1,516 (39.4%)
Essex	370 (49.8%)	331 (44.5%)	42 (5.7%)
Franklin	1,266 (40.1%)	691 (21.9%)	1,204 (38.1%)
Grand Isle	311 (57.1%)	130 (23.9%)	104 (19.1%)
Lamoille	289 (19.1%)	474 (31.2%)	754 (49.7%)
Orange	1,780 (39.5%)	1,414 (31.4%)	1,308 (29.1%)
Orleans	1,056 (49.0%)	562 (26.1%)	536 (24.9%)
Rutland	2,911 (57.8%)	744 (14.8%)	1,377 (27.4%)
Washington	1,398 (33.3%)	1,693 (40.3%)	1,106 (26.4%)

Windham	2,648 (46.5%)	608 (10.7%)	1,443 (25.3%)	
Windsor	3,656 (54.8%)	1,103 (16.5%)	1,908 (28.6%)	
Total	**22,932 (48.1%)**	**10,948 (22.9%)**	**13,837 (29.0%)**	
	*(23,122)			

*Stated totals.

Source—Manuscript returns.

Virginia

County	Taylor (W)	Cass (D)
Accomac	544 (64.8%)	295 (35.2%)
Albemarle	833 (57.4%)	619 (42.6%)
Alleghany	104 (41.1%)	149 (58.9%)
Amelia	163 (45.2%)	198 (54.8%)
Amherst	416 (50.2%)	413 (49.8%)
Appomattox	190 (36.7%)	328 (63.3%)
Augusta	1,354 (65.2%)	723 (34.8%)
Barbour	287 (37.2%)	484 (62.8%)
Bath	152 (55.1%)	124 (44.9%)
Bedford	886 (62.4%)	534 (37.6%)
Berkeley	608 (52.8%)	544 (47.2%)
Boone	68 (34.7%)	128 (65.3%)
Botetourt	452 (40.3%)	683 (59.7%)
Brooke	227 (45.1%)	276 (54.9%)
Brunswick	213 (38.7%)	337 (61.3%)
Braxton	191 (62.6%)	114 (37.4%)
Buckingham	344 (47.4%)	381 (52.6%)
Cabell	287 (55.2%)	233 (44.8%)
Campbell	794 (58.9%)	554 (41.1%)
Caroline	367 (49.3%)	425 (50.7%)
Carroll	179 (40.1%)	267 (59.9%)
Charles City	142 (71.0%)	58 (29.0%)
Charlotte	290 (48.9%)	303 (51.1%)
Chesterfield	296 (37.0%)	505 (63.0%)
Clarke	209 (51.0%)	201 (49.0%)
Culpeper	354 (52.7%)	318 (47.3%)
Cumberland	235 (59.2%)	162 (40.8%)
Dinwiddie	285 (55.6%)	228 (44.4%)
Doddridge	28 (17.0%)	137 (83.0%)
Elizabeth City	133 (52.6%)	120 (47.4%)
Essex	188 (57.9%)	135 (42.1%)
Fairfax	489 (60.4%)	320 (39.6%)
Fauquier	685 (57.7%)	503 (42.3%)
Fayette	257 (65.7%)	134 (34.3%)
Fluvanna	271 (58.8%)	190 (41.2%)
Floyd	271 (54.6%)	225 (45.4%)
Franklin	608 (50.1%)	606 (49.9%)
Frederick	795 (42.3%)	884 (57.7%)
Giles	274 (44.5%)	342 (55.5%)
Gilmer	77 (30.2%)	178 (69.8%)
Gloucester	185 (48.4%)	197 (51.6%)
Goochland	168 (39.8%)	254 (60.2%)
Grayson	193 (49.2%)	200 (50.8%)
Greenbrier	658 (68.4%)	303 (31.6%)
Greene	63 (18.9%)	270 (81.1%)
Greensville	77 (37.2%)	130 (62.8%)
Halifax	395 (31.9%)	843 (68.1%)
Hampshire	581 (46.9%)	657 (53.1%)
Hancock	161 (42.7%)	216 (57.3%)
Hanover	410 (49.0%)	427 (51.0%)
Hardy	525 (66.0%)	271 (34.0%)
Harrison	443 (42.0%)	611 (58.0%)
Henrico	592 (60.1%)	393 (39.9%)
Henry	315 (55.7%)	251 (44.3%)
Highland	101 (26.0%)	288 (74.0%)
Isle of Wight	105 (21.1%)	393 (78.9%)
James City	99 (72.8%)	37 (27.2%)
Jackson	229 (49.6%)	233 (50.4%)
Jefferson	738 (55.4%)	594 (44.6%)
Kanawha	742 (73.2%)	272 (26.8%)
King & Queen	224 (46.5%)	258 (53.5%)
King George	149 (57.1%)	112 (42.9%)
King William	93 (28.4%)	234 (71.6%)
Lancaster	137 (56.1%)	107 (43.9%)
Lee	324 (38.3%)	521 (61.7%)
Lewis	331 (38.8%)	522 (61.2%)
Logan	99 (45.8%)	117 (54.2%)
Loudoun	1,453 (77.6%)	420 (22.4%)
Louisa	307 (41.0%)	441 (59.0%)
Lunenburg	169 (38.3%)	272 (61.7%)
Madison	69 (12.4%)	486 (87.6%)
Marshall	558 (51.4%)	527 (48.6%)
Marion	324 (32.6%)	669 (67.4%)
Mason	349 (56.0%)	274 (44.0%)
Matthews	136 (41.8%)	189 (58.2%)
Mecklenburg	342 (40.8%)	497 (59.2%)
Mercer	191 (50.9%)	184 (49.1%)
Middlesex	116 (48.1%)	125 (51.9%)
Monongalia	434 (34.9%)	809 (65.1%)
Monroe	488 (51.0%)	469 (49.0%)
Montgomery	342 (52.8%)	306 (47.2%)
Morgan	188 (48.3%)	201 (51.7%)
Nansemond	311 (52.6%)	280 (47.4%)
Nelson	304 (57.0%)	229 (43.0%)
New Kent	176 (63.5%)	101 (36.5%)
Nicholas	213 (70.3%)	90 (29.7%)
Norfolk	629 (49.2%)	650 (50.8%)
Northampton	170 (64.2%)	95 (35.8%)
Northumberland	161 (40.8%)	234 (59.2%)
Nottoway	117 (45.0%)	143 (55.0%)
Ohio	977 (67.1%)	478 (32.9%)
Orange	296 (51.3%)	281 (48.7%)
Page	69 (10.4%)	595 (89.6%)
Patrick	387 (58.7%)	272 (41.3%)
Pendleton	285 (48.0%)	309 (48.0%)
Pittsylvania	834 (58.6%)	589 (41.4%)
Pocahontas	106 (33.3%)	212 (66.7%)
Powhatan	154 (43.3%)	202 (56.7%)
Preston	460 (46.6%)	527 (53.4%)
Prince Edward	211 (45.5%)	253 (54.5%)
Prince George	127 (37.1%)	215 (62.9%)
Prince William	207 (33.4%)	412 (66.6%)
Princess Anne	373 (55.5%)	299 (44.5%)
Pulaski	131 (48.2%)	141 (51.8%)
Putnam	192 (51.2%)	183 (48.8%)
Randolph	201 (48.6%)	213 (51.4%)
Rappahannock	304 (56.0%)	239 (44.0%)
Richmond	182 (55.1%)	148 (44.9%)
Ritchie	124 (26.8%)	339 (73.2%)
Roanoke	183 (42.4%)	249 (57.6%)
Rockbridge	665 (57.0%)	501 (43.0%)
Rockingham	395 (19.3%)	1,655 (80.7%)
Russell	482 (60.4%)	316 (39.6%)
Scott	296 (39.6%)	452 (60.4%)
Shenandoah	176 (11.1%)	1,404 (88.9%)
Smyth	396 (51.3%)	309 (48.7%)
Southampton	338 (52.4%)	307 (47.6%)
Spotsylvania	413 (50.5%)	405 (49.5%)
Stafford	230 (47.4%)	255 (52.6%)
Surry	94 (37.3%)	158 (62.7%)
Sussex	82 (23.1%)	273 (76.9%)
Taylor	266 (51.9%)	247 (48.1%)
Tazewell	215 (28.2%)	548 (71.8%)
Tyler	324 (52.8%)	290 (47.2%)
Warren	122 (30.0%)	285 (70.0%)
Warwick	62 (80.5%)	15 (19.5%)
Washington	485 (41.7%)	679 (58.3%)
Wayne	105 (48.8%)	110 (51.2%)

Westmoreland	249 (80.6%)	60 (19.4%)	Norfolk	652 (59.3%)	448 (40.7%)
Wetzel	80 (20.2%)	317 (79.8%)	Petersburg	392 (54.1%)	333 (45.9%)
Wirt	122 (48.4%)	130 (51.6%)	Richmond	1,064 (75.5%)	345 (24.5%)
Wood	430 (57.0%)	325 (43.0%)	Williamsburg	47 (58.0%)	34 (42.0%)
Wythe	347 (50.8%)	336 (49.2%)	**Total**	**45,219 (49.2%)**	**46,764 (50.8%)**
York	118 (57.8%)	86 (42.2%)	*Stated totals.*	*(45,265)	*(46,738)
Cities & Towns					
Alexandria	539 (70.5%)	225 (29.5%)			

SOURCE—*Richmond Enquirer,* January 26, 1849.

Wisconsin

No returns were located for this election for La Pointe County.
They might have been included with Crawford and Chippewa, just as they were in the gubernatorial election of May, 1848.

County	Taylor (W)	Cass (D)	Van Buren (FS)
Brown	238 (42.7%)	309 (55.4%)	10 (1.8%)
Calumet	65 (45.1%)	79 (54.7%)	0
Columbia	300 (49.3%)	145 (23.6%)	166 (27.0%)
Crawford & Chippewa	109 (32.4%)	215 (64.0%)	12 (3.6%)
Dane	724 (37.6%)	757 (39.3%)	443 (23.0%)
Dodge	527 (26.9%)	797 (40.6%)	637 (32.5%)
Fond du Lac	445 (31.2%)	483 (33.9%)	497 (34.9%)
Grant	1,649 (56.1%)	1,148 (39.0%)	144 (4.9%)
Green	479 (41.4%)	391 (33.8%)	287 (24.8%)
Iowa & Richland	884 (47.8%)	848 (45.8%)	118 (6.4%)
Jefferson	713 (33.7%)	840 (39.7%)	562 (26.6%)
Lafayette	921 (44.8%)	1,105 (53.7%)	31 (1.5%)
Manitowoc	77 (25.2%)	159 (52.0%)	70 (22.9%)
Marquette	214 (38.1%)	174 (31.0%)	174 (31.0%)
Milwaukee	1,189 (30.0%)	2,150 (54.2%)	626 (15.8%)
Portage	216 (49.0%)	225 (51.0%)	0
Racine	908 (26.1%)	644 (18.5%)	1,930 (55.4%)
Rock	1,300 (41.5%)	491 (15.7%)	1,338 (42.8%)
St. Croix	45 (39.8%)	67 (59.3%)	1 (0.1%)
Sheboygan	371 (37.6%)	442 (44.7%)	175 (17.7%)
Walworth	804 (28.2%)	550 (19.3%)	1,494 (52.5%)
Washington	355 (14.8%)	1,720 (71.7%)	324 (13.5%)
Waukesha	806 (29.1%)	963 (34.8%)	1,002 (36.2%)
Winnebago	300 (46.4%)	222 (29.9%)	220 (29.6%)
Total	**13,639 (35.1%)**	**14,924 (38.4%)**	**10,261 (26.4%)**
Stated totals.	*(13,642)		
*Sauk	159 (34.1%)	158 (33.9%)	149 (32.0%)

These returns were not included in the official returns and were located in the Whig Almanac 1849, *p. 63, and in W. Dean Burnham's* Presidential Ballots, *pp. 876, 952, citing the* Milwaukee Sentinel, *November 29, 1852.*

SOURCES—Manuscript returns; the *Whig Almanac 1849*; and W. Dean Burnham, *Presidential Ballots 1836–1892* (reprint edition), New York, NY: Arno Press, 1976.

NOTES

1. The electoral vote for vice president was Millard Fillmore (W) 163, and William O. Butler (D) 127.

2. The Massachusetts legislature cast the electoral vote because none of the electors had received a majority of the vote, as must happen under the law of the commonwealth.

3. The official statewide totals were published in the (Tallahassee) *Floridian*, December 9, 1848, without any county returns. The high electoral candidates for each party, whose totals are used here and in the national summary, were: Samuel Spencer (Whig) and Charles H. Dupont (Democrat). No contemporary source has been located that contains the county returns. The *Floridian* on November 25, 1848, published returns for 12 counties and the majority in nine others. The *Whig Almanac* did not contain county returns until its 1851 edition, and only reported returns for 13 counties and the majority in the remaining counties.

The county returns used are largely those supplied by the state archives. They are precinct returns without benefit of any county or state totals. The only other source for county returns is W. Dean Burnham's *Presidential Ballots*, pp. 320–332, citing "Manuscript records furnished by the Secretary of State." While these returns largely agree with the material I used, there are some differences. The statewide total is significantly less than the statewide total reported here primarily due to absence of any returns from Jackson County. The totals found in Burnham's *Presidential Ballots* are Taylor 4,081 (stated), 4,120 (added), and Cass 3,014 (stated), 3,083 (added). Adding the Jackson County vote to the added totals produced the following: Taylor 4,542 and Cass 3,249. The returns for Jackson County were found in the returns furnished to me by the archives and are obviously part of the official tally. The majority vote for Jackson County appears in the *Floridian* and the 1851 *Whig Almanac*. In addition, Burnham's *Presidential Ballots* reports the vote for Holmes County as 119 for Taylor and 19 for Cass, but the precinct returns add up to the returns used here and are the same totals as found in the sources cited above. The returns for Columbia, Marion and Madison are taken from Burnham's *Presidential Ballots* because the precinct returns I received are apparently incomplete.

Clearly there is no definitive set of county returns. The totals in parentheses are the added returns used here.

4. Dade County was apparently not included in the official returns, but it was located in the returns I used. See Burnham's *Presidential Ballots*, p. 902.

5. A slate of electors pledged to Henry Clay received 89 votes in ten counties: Adams 9, Du Page 11, Fulton 2, Kendall 7, Knox 7, Lee 13, Mc Henry 1, Mercer 2, Peoria 34, Putnam 2 and Winnebago 1.

The vote of Henry County was not included in the official returns but was reported in the Whig Almanac 1849, p. 62, as follows:

	Taylor (W)	Cass (D)	Van Buren (FS)
Henry	133 (30.2%)	80 (18.1%)	228 (51.7%)

6. The official returns as published in the (Jackson) *Mississippian and State Gazette*, November 24, 1848, do not include returns for Coahoma and Tunica Counties, but they are listed both in the *Whig Almanac 1849* and in *Presidential Ballots* by W. Dean Burnham, both of which cite the Secretary of State as the source. As a result, they are included here. I also found the Tunica returns in the manuscript returns. The totals listed here are the added totals.

7. Although the statewide vote for each Smith elector was found in the *Ohio State Journal*, I was unable to locate the vote by county. See the national summary for his statewide vote.

8. These official returns dated November 27, 1848, which include the statement "the returns so far as received," only have the vote of 56 counties. W. Dean Burnham's *Presidential Ballots* gives returns for 18 additional counties citing "Official manuscript returns fur-

nished by the State Librarian," p. 943. Because these additional returns were received after the above date, they were not included in the official returns; they are listed below. The returns as reported in Burnham's *Presidential Ballots* are the same as those given here, except for Jackson County where Cass is credited with 64 votes instead of 61.

County	Taylor (W)		Cass (D)	
Angelina	29	(35.8%)	52	(64.2%)
Bowie	111	(46.6%)	127	(53.4%)
Cameron	476	(57.6%)	350	(42.4%)
Cass	107	(31.9%)	228	(68.1%)
Grayson	47	(26.0%)	134	(74.0%)
Henderson	42	(38.1%)	68	(61.9%)
Hopkins	70	(23.6%)	227	(76.4%)
Jefferson	21	(36.2%)	37	(63.8%)
Kaufman	25	(41.7%)	35	(58.3%)
Limestone	40	(20.6%)	154	(79.4%)
Navarro	44	(26.2%)	124	(73.8%)
Newton	20	(26.3%)	56	(73.7%)
Red River	177	(34.0%)	344	(66.0%)
Shelby	99	(22.8%)	336	(77.2%)
Smith	57	(28.4%)	144	(71.6%)
Starr	37	(18.0%)	168	(82.0%)
Tyler	38	(35.8%)	68	(64.2%)
Upshur	64	(25.4%)	188	(74.6%)
Total	5,281		11,641	

1 8 5 2

National Summary[1]

(electoral vote in parentheses)

State	Franklin Pierce (D)		Winfield Scott (W)		John P. Hale (FS)		all others	
Alabama	26,681 (60.89%)	(9)	15,061 (34.16%)				2,205[2]	(4.99%)
Arkansas	12,179 (62.11%)	(4)	7,430 (37.89%)					
California	40,585 (53.17%)	(4)	35,752 (46.83%)					
Connecticut	33,249 (49.80%)	(6)	30,359 (45.47%)		3,161 (4.73%)			
Delaware	6,330 (49.87%)	(3)	6,299 (49.63%)		63 (0.50%)			
Florida	4,318 (60.03%)	(3)	2,875 (39.97%)					
Georgia	34,708 (55.56%)	(10)	16,639 (26.63%)				11,125[3]	(17.81%)
Illinois	80,368 (51.86%)	(11)	64,733 (41.77%)		9,863 (6.36%)			
Indiana	94,890 (51.93%)	(13)	80,901 (44.28%)		6,928 (3.79%)			
Iowa	17,824 (50.02%)	(4)	16,195 (45.45%)		1,612 (4.52%)			
Kentucky	53,807 (48.40%)		57,108 (51.37%)	(12)	256 (0.23%)			
Louisiana	18,653 (51.95%)	(6)	17,255 (48.05%)					
Maine	41,609 (50.63%)	(8)	32,543 (39.60%)		8,030 (9.77%)			
Maryland	40,428 (53.50%)	(8)	35,080 (46.42%)		56 (0.07%)			
Massachusetts	45,875 (35.72%)		52,863 (41.16%)	(13)	28,023 (21.82%)		1,670[4]	(1.30%)
Michigan	41,842 (50.45%)	(6)	33,860 (40.83%)		7,237 (8.73%)			
Mississippi	26,110 (60.89%)	(7)	16,773 (39.11%)					
Missouri	38,610 (56.32%)	(9)	29,947 (43.68%)					
New Hampshire	28,503 (56.40%)	(5)	15,486 (30.64%)		6,546 (12.95%)			
New Jersey	44,301 (52.79%)	(7)	38,551 (45.93%)		336 (0.40%)		738[5]	(0.88%)
New York	262,083 (50.12%)	(35)	234,896 (44.92%)		25,435 (4.86%)		459[6]	(0.08%)
North Carolina	39,784 (50.39%)	(10)	39,108 (49.53%)		59 (0.07%)			
Ohio	169,190 (47.94%)	(23)	152,577 (43.24%)		31,133 (8.82%)			
Pennsylvania	198,591 (51.17%)	(27)	179,216 (46.18%)		8,596 (2.22%)		1,677[7]	(0.43%)
Rhode Island	8,735 (51.37%)	(4)	7,626 (44.85%)		644 (3.79%)			

State	Franklin Pierce (D)		Winfield Scott (W)		John P. Hale (FS)	all others
South Carolina		**(8)**	electors chosen by the legislature			
Tennessee	57,056 (49.24%)		58,807 (50.76%) **(12)**			
Texas	11,519 (73.34%)	**(4)**	4,187 (26.66%)			
Vermont	13,044 (29.77%)		22,156 (50.56%)	**(5)**	8,621 (19.67%)	
Virginia	73,833 (55.70%)	**(15)**	58,732 (44.30%)			
Wisconsin	33,658 (51.99%)	**(5)**	22,240 (34.35%)		8,842 (13.66%)	
Total	**1,598,363 (50.63%) (254)**		**1,385,255 (43.88%) (42)**		**155,441 (4.93%)**	**17,741[8] (0.57%)**

Alabama

County	Pierce (D)	Scott (W)	Troup (SoR)
Autauga	322 (44.5%)	196 (7.1%)	205 (28.4%)
Baldwin	72 (53.7%)	62 (46.3%)	0
Barbour	309 (26.6%)	297 (25.2%)	571 (48.5%)
Benton	918 (92.5%)	74 (7.5%)	0
Bibb	346 (58.9%)	238 (40.5%)	3 (0.5%)
Blount	422 (88.5%)	55 (11.5%)	0
Butler	251 (42.3%)	345 (57.7%)	0
Chambers	616 (47.2%)	668 (51.1%)	21 (1.6%)
Cherokee	735 (75.2%)	242 (24.8%)	0
Choctaw	334 (59.3%)	227 (40.3%)	2 (3.6%)
Clarke	479 (80.2%)	98 (16.4%)	19 (3.2%)
Coffee	239 (64.6%)	113 (30.5%)	18 (4.9%)
Conecuh	287 (55.4%)	216 (41.7%)	15 (2.9%)
Coosa	709 (67.8%)	294 (28.1%)	42 (4.0%)
Covington	117 (66.1%)	52 (29.4%)	8 (4.5%)
Dale	406 (66.9%)	170 (28.0%)	31 (5.7%)
Dallas	440 (41.1%)	386 (36.1%)	244 (22.8%)
De Kalb	501 (78.3%)	139 (21.7%)	0
Fayette	516 (86.4%)	81 (13.6%)	0
Franklin	993 (68.1%)	462 (31.6%)	5 (3.4%)
Greene	555 (38.0%)	694 (47.5%)	10 (6.9%)
Hancock	65 (87.8%)	9 (12.2%)	0
Henry	184 (44.0%)	94 (22.5%)	140 (33.4%)
Jackson	1,154 (93.3%)	83 (6.7%)	0
Jefferson	339 (74.8%)	114 (25.6%)	0
Lauderdale	803 (64.5%)	441 (35.5%)	0
Lawrence	588 (53.2%)	512 (46.3%)	5 (0.5%)
Limestone	662 (85.9%)	227 (14.1%)	0
Lowndes	186 (35.9%)	126 (24.3%)	206 (39.8%)
Macon	658 (43.0%)	772 (50.5%)	99 (6.5%)
Madison	1,300 (78.6%)	354 (21.4%)	0
Marengo	526 (52.8%)	450 (45.2%)	20 (2.0%)
Marion	467 (79.8%)	118 (20.2%)	0
Marshall	568 (83.6%)	111 (16.4%)	0
Mobile	1,380 (53.1%)	1,123 (43.2%)	94 (3.6%)
Monroe	260 (45.7%)	264 (46.4%)	45 (7.9%)
Montgomery	557 (40.6%)	717 (52.3%)	98 (7.1%)
Morgan	482 (69.7%)	208 (30.0%)	2 (0.3%)
Perry	512 (65.1%)	261 (33.2%)	13 (1.7%)
Pickens	752 (56.6%)	568 (42.7%)	9 (0.7%)
Pike	703 (61.0%)	379 (32.9%)	71 (6.2%)
Randolph	707 (87.1%)	102 (12.6%)	3 (0.4%)
Russell	522 (53.3%)	434 (44.3%)	24 (2.4%)
St. Clair	455 (91.2%)	44 (8.8%)	0
Shelby	315 (49.6%)	317 (49.9%)	3 (0.5%)
Sumter	497 (50.6%)	482 (49.0%)	4 (0.4%)
Talladega	672 (64.1%)	372 (35.5%)	4 (0.4%)
Tallapoosa	845 (69.5%)	351 (28.9%)	19 (1.6%)
Tuscaloosa	475 (47.3%)	527 (52.4%)	3 (0.3%)
Walker	217 (80.1%)	54 (19.9%)	0
Washington	65 (54.6%)	52 (43.7%)	2 (1.7%)
Wilcox	398 (47.9%)	286 (34.4%)	147 (17.7%)
Total	**26,881 (60.9%)**	**15,061 (34.2%)**	**2,205 (5.0%)**

SOURCE—Loveman manuscript.

Arkansas

County	Pierce (D)	Scott (W)
Arkansas	140 (53.8%)	120 (46.2%)
Ashley	146 (62.4%)	88 (37.6%)
Benton	334 (76.8%)	91 (23.2%)
Bradley	180 (48.9%)	188 (51.1%)
Calhoun	151 (74.4%)	52 (25.6%)
Carroll	333 (72.9%)	124 (27.1%)
Chicot	118 (58.1%)	85 (41.9%)
Clark	205 (60.1%)	136 (39.9%)
Conway	259 (70.2%)	110 (29.8%)
Crawford	236 (60.7%)	153 (39.3%)
Crittenden	97 (50.5%)	95 (49.5%)
Dallas	194 (56.4%)	150 (43.6%)
Desha	199 (51.8%)	185 (48.2%)
Drew	135 (53.4%)	118 (46.6%)
Franklin	224 (67.9%)	106 (32.1%)
Fulton	77 (67.0%)	38 (33.0%)
Green	211 (69.2%)	94 (30.8%)
Hempstead	362 (54.8%)	298 (45.2%)
Hot Spring	269 (68.3%)	125 (31.7%)
Independence	612 (57.5%)	452 (42.5%)
Izard	226 (76.6%)	69 (23.4%)
Jackson	335 (53.4%)	292 (46.6%)
Jefferson	306 (57.7%)	224 (42.3%)
Johnson	384 (66.6%)	193 (33.4%)
Lafayette	175 (54.0%)	149 (46.0%)
Lawrence	417 (58.2%)	299 (41.8%)
Madison	274 (78.3%)	76 (21.7%)
Marion	137 (77.4%)	40 (22.6%)
Mississippi	88 (66.7%)	44 (33.3%)
Monroe	92 (61.7%)	57 (38.3%)
Montgomery	111 (79.9%)	28 (20.1%)
Newton	79 (90.8%)	8 (9.2%)
Ouachita	496 (52.3%)	452 (47.7%)
Perry	33 (68.8%)	15 (31.2%)
Phillips	378 (49.7%)	383 (50.3%)
Pike	168 (80.8%)	40 (19.2%)
Poinsett	132 (73.3%)	48 (26.7%)
Polk	94 (84.7%)	17 (15.3%)
Pope	325 (64.0%)	183 (36.0%)
Prairie	171 (68.7%)	78 (31.3%)
Pulaski	419 (59.5%)	285 (40.5%)
Randolph	95 (74.8%)	32 (25.2%)
St. Francis	307 (64.1%)	172 (35.9%)
Saline	277 (67.0%)	137 (33.0%)
Scott	83 (78.3%)	23 (21.7%)
Searcy	197 (67.5%)	75 (32.5%)
Sebastian	283 (61.6%)	180 (38.4%)
Sevier	125 (71.4%)	50 (28.6%)
Union	531 (58.0%)	384 (42.0%)
Van Buren	no returns	
Washington	495 (60.3%)	326 (39.7%)
White	139 (58.9%)	97 (41.1%)
Yell	325 (66.2%)	166 (33.8%)
Total	**12,179 (62.1%)**	**7,430 (37.9%)**

SOURCE—(Little Rock) *Arkansas Gazette*, December 3, 1852.

California

County	Pierce (D)	Scott (W)
Butte	1,741 (54.1%)	1,478 (45.9%)
Calaveras	2,838 (55.4%)	2,288 (44.6%)
Colusa	232 (50.7%)	226 (49.3%)
Contra Costa	590 (58.9%)	413 (41.1%)
El Dorado	6,106 (54.3%)	5,144 (45.7%)
Klamath	210 (49.2%)	217 (50.8%)
Los Angeles	574 (53.6%)	496 (46.4%)
Marin	137 (48.6%)	145 (51.4%)
Mariposa	1,292 (60.2%)	854 (39.8%)
Monterey	273 (83.5%)	54 (16.5%)
Napa	267 (56.9%)	202 (43.1%)
Nevada	2,855 (52.2%)	2,618 (47.8%)
Placer	2,830 (55.5%)	2,273 (44.5%)
Sacramento	3,279 (47.4%)	3,635 (52.6%)
San Diego	105 (49.5%)	107 (50.5%)
San Francisco	4,241 (50.5%)	4,162 (49.5%)
San Joaquin	1,198 (50.8%)	1,159 (49.2%)
San Luis Obispo	11 (8.9%)	112 (91.1%)
Santa Barbara	104 (60.5%)	68 (39.5%)
Santa Clara	780 (48.4%)	831 (51.6%)
Santa Cruz	306 (62.2%)	186 (37.8%)
Shasta	971 (56.2%)	757 (43.8%)
Sierra	1,619 (54.6%)	1,348 (45.4%)
Siskiyou	492 (51.7%)	459 (48.3%)
Solano	355 (53.5%)	308 (46.5%)
Sonoma	474 (64.0%)	267 (36.0%)
Sutter	205 (48.9%)	214 (51.1%)
Trinity	784 (53.4%)	683 (46.6%)
Tulare	40 (55.6%)	32 (44.4%)
Tuolumne	3,131 (55.2%)	2,541 (44.8%)
Yolo	350 (46.8%)	398 (53.2%)
Yuba	2,195 (51.4%)	2,077 (48.6%)
Total	**40,585 (53.2%)**	**35,752 (46.8%)**
	*(40,885)	*(36,052)

*Stated totals.

SOURCE—Manuscript returns.

Connecticut

County	Pierce (D)	Scott (W)	Hale (FS)
Fairfield	5,155 (50.9%)	4,814 (47.5%)	167 (1.6%)
Hartford	6,639 (49.4%)	6,329 (47.1%)	461 (3.4%)
Litchfield	4,082 (48.4%)	3,946 (46.7%)	414 (4.9%)
Middlesex	2,734 (54.3%)	2,065 (41.0%)	238 (4.7%)
New Haven	6,097 (48.5%)	6,046 (48.1%)	424 (3.4%)
New London	4,079 (50.5%)	3,361 (41.6%)	637 (7.9%)
Tolland	2,015 (51.4%)	1,703 (43.4%)	202 (5.2%)
Windham	2,448 (47.5%)	2,095 (40.7%)	618 (12.0%)
Total	**33,249 (49.8%)**	**30,359 (45.5%)**	**3,161 (4.7%)**

Source — Manuscript returns.

Delaware

County	Pierce (D)	Scott (W)	Hale (FS)
Kent	1,432 (47.4%)	1,592 (52.6%)	0
New Castle	3,039 (51.8%)	2,767 (47.1%)	63 (1.1%)
Sussex	1,859 (48.9%)	1,940 (51.1%)	0
Total	**6,330 (49.9%)**	**6,299 (49.6%)**	**63 (0.5%)**

SOURCES—Manuscript returns; Hall of Records.

Florida

County	Pierce (D)	Scott (W)
Alachua	209 (65.3%)	111 (34.7%)
Calhoun	61 (82.4%)	13 (17.6%)
Columbia	337 (63.1%)	197 (36.9%)
Duval	314 (53.4%)	274 (46.6%)
Escambia	213 (51.3%)	202 (48.7%)
Franklin	173 (66.5%)	87 (33.5%)
Gadsden	306 (64.3%)	170 (35.7%)
Hamilton	117 (81.3%)	27 (18.7%)
Holmes	59 (44.7%)	73 (55.3%)
Hernando	93 (66.4%)	47 (33.6%)
Hillsborough	165 (70.2%)	70 (29.8%)
Jackson	261 (50.1%)	260 (49.9%)
Jefferson	320 (79.0%)	85 (21.0%)
Leon	384 (62.8%)	227 (37.2%)
Levy	43 (61.4%)	27 (38.6%)
Madison	183 (64.4%)	101 (35.6%)
Marion	206 (60.1%)	137 (39.9%)
Monroe	116 (55.0%)	95 (45.0%)
Nassau	29 (37.7%)	48 (62.3%)
Orange	35 (50.0%)	35 (50.0%)
Putnam	47 (56.0%)	37 (44.0%)
St. Johns	140 (59.1%)	97 (40.9%)
St. Lucie	7 (100%)	0
Santa Rosa	159 (42.2%)	218 (57.8%)
Walton	78 (40.8%)	113 (59.2%)
Wakalla	154 (63.1%)	90 (36.9%)
Washington	109 (76.2%)	34 (23.8%)
Total	**4,318 (60.0%)**	**2,875 (40.0%)**

SOURCE—(Tallahassee) *Floridian and Journal*, December 4, 1852.

Georgia

No returns have been found for this election for Hancock County.

County	Pierce (D)	Scott (W)	*Pierce (ID)[9]	Webster (UW)
Appling	77 (85.6%)	13 (14.4%)	0	0
Baker	630 (83.6%)	101 (13.4%)	4 (0.5%)	19 (2.5%)
Baldwin	269 (51.1%)	176 (33.5%)	30 (5.7%)	51 (9.7%)
Bibb	780 (68.8%)	318 (28.1%)	7 (0.6%)	28 (2.5%)

County	Pierce (D)	Scott (W)	*Pierce (ID)[9]	Webster (UW)
Bryan	66 (52.4%)	60 (47.6%)	0	0
Bulloch	287 (100%)	0	0	0
Burke	177 (67.8%)	15 (5.7%)	1 (0.4%)	68 (26.1%)
Butts	434 (84.8%)	11 (2.1%)	0	67 (13.1%)
Camden	211 (87.2%)	31 (12.8%)	0	0
Campbell	538 (73.7%)	158 (21.6%)	5 (0.7%)	29 (4.0%)
Carroll	850 (76.6%)	185 (16.7%)	43 (3.9%)	32 (2.9%)
Cass	654 (44.8%)	263 (18.0%)	530 (36.3%)	12 (0.8%)
Chatham	1,175 (78.3%)	305 (20.3%)	15 (1.0%)	6 (0.4%)
Chattooga	316 (55.3%)	114 (20.0%)	62 (10.9%)	79 (13.8%)
Cherokee	660 (50.9%)	81 (6.3%)	545 (42.1%)	10 (50.9%)
Clark	226 (29.6%)	139 (18.2%)	257 (33.7%)	142 (18.6%)
Clinch	48 (38.4%)	4 (3.2%)	2 (1.6%)	71 (57.7%)
Cobb	975 (68.7%)	307 (21.6%)	117 (8.2%)	20 (1.4%)
Columbia	259 (53.3%)	110 (22.6%)	2 (0.4%)	115 (23.7%)
Coweta	650 (63.1%)	215 (20.9%)	5 (0.5%)	160 (15.5%)
Crawford	367 (67.0%)	161 (29.4%)	0	20 (3.6%)
Dade	126 (45.5%)	65 (23.5%)	86 (31.0%)	0
Decatur	295 (51.7%)	220 (38.5%)	0	56 (9.8%)
De Kalb	1,016 (61.2%)	565 (34.1%)	26 (1.6%)	52 (3.1%)
Dooly	474 (72.2%)	175 (26.7%)	0	7 (1.1%)
Early	374 (71.5%)	129 (24.7%)	14 (2.7%)	6 (1.1%)
Effingham	64 (36.0%)	18 (10.1%)	0	96 (53.9%)
Elbert	107 (13.0%)	159 (9.3%)	73 (8.9%)	485 (58.9%)
Emanuel	174 (87.0%)	5 (2.5%)	0	21 (10.5%)
Fayette	582 (64.4%)	267 (29.5%)	16 (1.8%)	39 (4.3%)
Floyd	494 (52.0%)	368 (38.7%)	58 (6.1%)	40 (4.2%)
Forsyth	589 (76.1%)	106 (13.7%)	40 (5.2%)	39 (5.0%)
Franklin	435 (66.1%)	66 (10.0%)	157 (23.9%)	0
Gilmer	309 (36.3%)	116 (13.6%)	426 (50.1%)	0
Glynn	40 (50.6%)	29 (36.7%)	0	10 (12.7%)
Gordon	584 (61.1%)	264 (27.6%)	105 (11.0%)	3 (0.3%)
Greene	172 (27.4%)	311 (49.5%)	0	145 (23.1%)
Gwinnett	427 (47.1%)	61 (6.7%)	74 (8.2%)	345 (38.0%)
Habersham	59 (8.9%)	98 (14.7%)	499 (74.9%)	10 (1.5%)
Hall	186 (29.8%)	43 (6.9%)	382 (61.1%)	14 (29.8%)
Harris	339 (40.5%)	468 (55.9%)	1 (1.2%)	29 (3.5%)
Heard	410 (61.3%)	258 (38.6%)	0	1 (0.1%)
Henry	525 (54.3%)	428 (44.3%)	3 (0.3%)	10 (1.0%)
Houston	503 (63.2%)	273 (34.3%)	0	20 (2.5%)
Irwin	192 (90.6%)	12 (5.7%)	0	8 (3.8%)
Jackson	103 (15.0%)	45 (6.6%)	488 (71.1%)	50 (7.3%)
Jasper	372 (67.0%)	132 (23.8%)	17 (3.1%)	34 (6.1%)
Jefferson	93 (24.4%)	91 (23.9%)	1 (0.3%)	196 (51.4%)
Jones	340 (65.1%)	166 (31.8%)	0	16 (3.1%)
Laurens	63 (21.1%)	67 (22.5%)	0	168 (56.4%)
Lee	223 (48.1%)	189 (40.7%)	10 (2.2%)	42 (9.1%)
Liberty	133 (67.1%)	58 (29.3%)	0	7 (3.5%)
Lincoln	155 (63.5%)	17 (7.0%)	5 (2.0)	67 (27.5%)
Lowndes	273 (61.3%)	22 (4.9%)	0	150 (33.7%)
Lumpkin	295 (41.5%)	178 (25.0%)	232 (32.6%)	6 (0.8%)
Macon	386 (55.1%)	296 (42.3%)	0	18 (2.6%)
Madison	69 (17.0%)	23 (5.7%)	198 (48.9%)	115 (28.4%)
Marion	425 (54.2%)	351 (44.8%)	0	8 (1.0%)
McIntosh	90 (77.6%)	16 (13.8%)	0	10 (8.6%)
Meriwether	634 (64.8%)	323 (33.0%)	0	22 (2.2%)
Monroe	631 (59.1%)	379 (35.5%)	1 (0.1%)	56 (5.2%)
Montgomery	36 (25.5%)	14 (10.0%)	0	91 (64.5%)
Morgan	285 (47.2%)	189 (31.3%)	11 (1.8%)	119 (19.7%)
Murray	323 (55.9%)	237 (41.0%)	16 (2.8%)	2 (0.3%)
Muscogee	875 (56.3%)	651 (41.9%)	9 (0.6%)	19 (56.3%)
Newton	386 (41.1%)	336 (35.7%)	23 (2.4%	195 (20.7%)
Oglethorpe	179 (39.0%)	60 (13.1%)	16 (3.5%)	204 (44.4%)
Paulding	327 (72.2%)	45 (9.9%)	79 (17.4%)	2 (0.4%)
Pike	508 (68.6%)	184 (24.8%)	1 (0.1%)	48 (6.5%)
Polk	147 (35.7%)	119 (28.9%)	92 (22.3%)	54 (13.1%)
Pulaski	231 (71.7%)	33 (10.2%)	1 (0.3%)	57 (17.7%)
Putnam	284 (53.8%)	229 (43.4%)	2 (0.4%)	13 (2.5%)
Rabun	144 (52.0%)	4 (1.4%)	127 (45.8%)	2 (0.7%)

County	Pierce (D)	Scott (W)	*Pierce (ID)[9]	Webster (UW)
Randolph	677 (64.4%)	362 (34.4%)	2 (0.2%)	11 (64.4%)
Richmond	626 (51.3%)	411 (33.7%)	38 (3.1%)	145 (11.9%)
Scriven	171 (79.5%)	8 (3.7%)	0	36 (16.7%)
Spalding	376 (49.0%)	356 (46.4%)	0	36 (4.7%)
Stewart	491 (55.1%)	325 (36.5%)	0	75 (8.4%)
Sumter	452 (57.6%)	325 (41.4%)	0	8 (1.0%)
Talbot	411 (46.9%)	431 (49.2%)	0	34 (3.9%)
Taliaferro	76 (22.2%)	19 (5.5%)	0	248 (72.3%)
Tattnall	55 (30.7%)	121 (67.6%)	0	3 (1.7%)
Taylor	264 (71.5%)	105 (28.5%)	0	0
Telfair	88 (59.1%)	47 (31.5%)	0	14 (9.4%)
Thomas	259 (70.2%)	89 (24.1%)	4 (1.1%)	17 (4.6%)
Troup	422 (39.4%)	596 (55.6%)	3 (0.3%)	50 (4.7%)
Twiggs	268 (69.6%)	113 (29.4%)	0	4 (1.0%)
Union	223 (34.3%)	97 (14.9%)	331 (50.8%)	0
Upson	338 (43.9%)	355 (46.1%)	0	77 (10.0%)
Walker	784 (63.5%)	372 (30.1%)	29 (2.3%)	50 (4.0%)
Walton	395 (48.4%)	111 (13.6%)	200 (24.5%)	110 (13.5%)
Ware	37 (67.3%)	1 (1.8%)	0	17 (30.9%)
Warren	306 (61.0%)	25 (5.0%)	26 (5.2%)	145 (28.9%)
Washington	451 (61.4%)	236 (32.2%)	2 (0.3%)	45 (6.1%)
Wayne	65 (82.3%)	10 (12.7%)	0	4 (5.1%)
Whitfield	644 (67.9%)	293 (30.9%)	8 (0.8%)	3 (0.3%)
Wilkes	193 (39.0%)	12 (2.4%)	247 (49.9%)	43 (8.7%)
Wilkinson	501 (82.8%)	94 (15.5%)	0	10 (1.7%)
Total	**34,708 (55.6%)**	**16,639 (26.6%)**	**5,804 (9.3%)**	**5,321 (8.5%)**

SOURCES—(Augusta) *Chronicle & Sentinel*, November 24, 1852; (Milledgeville) *Southern Recorder* November 16, 1856; the *Whig Almanac 1853*, p. 54; and W. Dean Burnhams *Presidential Ballots 1836–1892* (reprint edition), New York, NY: Arno Press, 1976, pp. 332–362, 904–5.

Illinois

County	Pierce (D)	Scott (W)	Hale (FS)
Adams	2,635 (52.9%)	2,236 (44.9%)	107 (2.1%)
Alexander	296 (73.8%)	105 (26.2%)	0
Bond	485 (48.2%)	494 (49.1%)	27 (2.7%)
Boone	525 (36.9%)	551 (38.7%)	338 (23.7%)
Brown	661 (59.8%)	445 (40.2%)	0
Bureau	670 (37.0%)	712 (39.3%)	431 (23.8%)
Calhoun	335 (61.4%)	211 (38.6%)	0
Carroll	351 (38.1%)	499 (54.1%)	72 (7.8%)
Cass	830 (51.4%)	784 (48.6%)	0
Champaign	251 (42.0%)	347 (58.0%)	0
Christian	426 (54.3%)	356 (45.4%)	2 (0.3%)
Clark	966 (53.3%)	842 (46.4%)	6 (0.3%)
Clay	530 (65.1%)	284 (34.9%)	0
Clinton	670 (64.1%)	375 (35.9%)	0
Coles	733 (42.3%)	997 (57.6%)	2 (0.1%)
Cook	3,767 (57.6%)	2,089 (31.9%)	689 (10.5%)
Crawford	827 (58.7%)	571 (40.5%)	11 (0.8%)
Cumberland	444 (60.2%)	293 (39.8%)	0
De Kalb	583 (41.8%)	456 (32.7%)	355 (25.5%)
De Witt	540 (50.2%)	516 (48.0%)	20 (1.9%)
Du Page	586 (43.3%)	381 (28.2%)	386 (28.5%)
Edgar	924 (50.0%)	892 (48.2%)	33 (1.8%)
Edwards	162 (35.8%)	291 (64.2%)	0
Effingham	527 (75.1%)	175 (24.9%)	0
Fayette	678 (60.8%)	437 (39.2%)	0
Franklin	709 (78.3%)	196 (21.7%)	0
Fulton	2,192 (50.6%)	1,843 (42.5%)	298 (6.9%)
Gallatin	592 (64.6%)	324 (35.4%)	0
Greene	1,297 (59.7%)	864 (39.8%)	12 (0.6%)
Grundy	338 (52.0%)	248 (38.2%)	64 (9.8%)
Hamilton	754 (77.2%)	223 (22.8%)	0
Hancock	1,466 (52.6%)	1,286 (46.2%)	34 (1.2%)
Hardin	212 (46.5%)	244 (53.5%)	0
Henderson	414 (41.6%)	547 (55.0%)	34 (3.4%)

County	Pierce (D)	Scott (W)	Hale (FS)
Henry	475 (51.5%)	357 (38.7%)	91 (9.9%)
Iroquois	482 (54.6%)	378 (42.9%)	22 (2.5%)
Jackson	531 (60.5%)	347 (39.5%)	0
Jasper	461 (64.1%)	258 (35.9%)	0
Jefferson	865 (68.7%)	395 (31.3%)	0
Jersey	564 (43.3%)	651 (49.9%)	89 (6.8%)
Jo Daviess	1,425 (47.1%)	1,481 (48.9%)	122 (4.0%)
Johnson	751 (84.8%)	135 (15.2%)	0
Kane	1,308 (42.1%)	1,160 (37.3%)	642 (20.6%)
Kendall	532 (41.0%)	515 (39.6%)	252 (19.4%)
Knox	1,119 (43.2%)	1,080 (41.7%)	391 (15.1%)
La Salle	1,894 (51.9%)	1,204 (33.0%)	552 (15.1%)
Lake	812 (40.0%)	697 (34.4%)	519 (25.6%)
Lawrence	589 (53.6%)	510 (46.4%)	0
Lee	573 (50.8%)	478 (42.4%)	77 (6.8%)
Livingston	214 (54.9%)	164 (42.1%)	12 (3.1%)
Logan	489 (46.3%)	568 (53.7%)	0
Macon	486 (57.3%)	355 (41.9%)	7 (0.8%)
Macoupin	1,176 (56.2%)	841 (40.2%)	74 (3.5%)
Madison	1,715 (52.1%)	1,548 (47.0%)	31 (0.9%)
Marion	762 (70.9%)	285 (26.5%)	28 (2.6%)
Marshall	579 (48.8%)	546 (46.0%)	61 (5.1%)
Mason	621 (52.3%)	561 (47.3%)	5 (0.4%)
Massac	449 (62.6%)	268 (37.4%)	0
McDonough	838 (49.7%)	840 (49.8%)	9 (0.5%)
McHenry	1,199 (44.2%)	866 (32.0%)	645 (23.8%)
McLean	1,058 (44.9%)	1,256 (53.4%)	40 (1.7%)
Menard	698 (52.0%)	644 (48.0%)	1 (0.1%)
Mercer	498 (42.7%)	575 (49.4%)	92 (7.9%)
Monroe	1,125 (79.3%)	294 (20.7%)	0
Montgomery	655 (61.2%)	415 (38.8%)	0
Morgan	1,411 (47.6%)	1,397 (47.1%)	158 (5.3%)
Moultree	263 (47.4%)	292 (52.6%)	0
Ogle	755 (38.8%)	899 (46.1%)	294 (15.1%)
Peoria	1,805 (50.0%)	1,556 (43.1%)	252 (7.0%)
Perry	564 (62.7%)	277 (30.8%)	59 (6.6%)
Piatt	161 (45.6%)	192 (54.4%)	0
Pike	1,762 (49.8%)	1,745 (49.3%)	34 (1.0%)
Pope	439 (57.8%)	320 (42.2%)	0
Pulaski	245 (68.6%)	112 (31.4%)	0
Putnam	248 (31.9%)	300 (38.6%)	230 (29.6%)
Randolph	814 (50.6%)	575 (35.7%)	220 (13.7%)
Richland	109 (38.5%)	174 (61.5%)	0
Rock Island	686 (44.4%)	764 (49.4%)	96 (6.2%)
St. Clair	2,571 (72.0%)	998 (28.0%)	0
Saline	633 (75.2%)	209 (24.8%)	0
Sangamon	1,606 (42.8%)	2,125 (56.6%)	22 (0.6%)
Schuyler	980 (53.3%)	844 (45.9%)	16 (0.9%)
Scott	708 (49.1%)	730 (50.7%)	3 (0.2%)
Shelby	958 (68.2%)	446 (31.8%)	0
Stark	350 (45.6%)	336 (43.8%)	82 (10.7%)
Stephenson	1,061 (48.1%)	976 (44.2%)	170 (7.7%)
Tazewell	869 (37.5%)	1,369 (59.1%)	80 (3.5%)
Union	630 (78.7%)	169 (21.1%)	1 (0.1%)
Vermilion	761 (42.4%)	997 (55.6%)	36 (2.0%)
Wabash	355 (43.1%)	469 (56.9%)	0
Warren	781 (44.9%)	806 (46.3%)	153 (8.8%)
Washington	763 (73.2%)	251 (24.1%)	28 (2.7%)
Wayne	757 (67.8%)	359 (32.1%)	1 (0.1%)
White	782 (51.1%)	749 (48.9%)	0
Whiteside	518 (42.4%)	554 (45.3%)	151 (12.3%)
Will	1,450 (48.0%)	1,251 (41.4%)	320 (10.6%)
Williamson	799 (69.9%)	344 (30.1%)	0
Winnebago	820 (31.9%)	1,023 (39.8%)	725 (28.2%)
Woodford	339 (33.1%)	635 (62.1%)	49 (4.8%)
Total	**80,368 (51.9%)**	**64,733 (41.8%)**	**9,863 (6.4%)**

SOURCE—Adler, Howard and Vincent A. Lacey (ed.), *Illinois Election Returns 1818–1990*, Carbondale, IL: Southern Illinois Univ. Press, 1993, pp. 128–130.

Indiana

County	Pierce (D)	Scott (W)	Hale (FS)
Adams	672 (64.1%)	362 (34.5%)	14 (1.3%)
Allen	1,964 (61.1%)	1,225 (38.1%)	24 (0.7%)
Bartholomew	1,512 (54.3%)	1,245 (44.7%)	26 (0.9%)
Benton	138 (51.7%)	110 (41.2%)	19 (7.1%)
Blackford	263 (68.1%)	108 (28.0%)	15 (3.9%)
Boone	1,161 (52.6%)	936 (42.4%)	109 (4.9%)
Brown	532 (83.9%)	102 (16.1%)	0
Carroll	1,256 (53.2%)	1,075 (45.6%)	29 (1.2%)
Cass	1,190 (49.3%)	1,176 (48.7%)	50 (2.1%)
Clark	1,812 (60.0%)	1,186 (39.2%)	24 (0.8%)
Clay	743 (60.7%)	474 (38.7%)	8 (0.7%)
Clinton	1,250 (55.5%)	929 (41.2%)	75 (3.3%)
Crawford	499 (49.9%)	502 (50.1%)	0
Daviess	720 (49.6%)	726 (50.0%)	6 (0.4%)
Dearborn	2,486 (61.4%)	1,474 (36.4%)	89 (2.2%)
Decatur	1,394 (48.1%)	1,364 (47.1%)	138 (4.8%)
De Kalb	780 (58.4%)	391 (29.2%)	164 (12.3%)
Delaware	937 (46.1%)	1,083 (53.3%)	11 (0.5%)
Dubois	717 (75.7%)	229 (24.3%)	0
Elkhart	1,343 (55.1%)	1,068 (43.8%)	28 (1.1%)
Fayette	872 (44.2%)	1,019 (51.7%)	80 (4.1%)
Floyd	1,815 (57.7%)	1,328 (42.2%)	1 (0.3%)
Fountain	1,496 (57.9%)	1,023 (39.6%)	64 (2.5%)
Franklin	1,956 (56.5%)	1,473 (42.6%)	30 (0.9%)
Fulton	581 (50.6%)	559 (48.8%)	6 (0.5%)
Gibson	1,127 (53.9%)	942 (45.1%)	20 (1.0%)
Grant	336 (26.3%)	599 (46.8%)	345 (22.0%)
Greene	944 (51.5%)	884 (48.3%)	4 (0.2%)
Hamilton	961 (41.2%)	971 (41.6%)	401 (17.2%)
Hancock	1,002 (53.8%)	823 (44.2%)	40 (2.1%)
Harrison	1,278 (49.9%)	1,284 (50.1%)	0
Hendricks	980 (41.0%)	1,252 (52.4%)	156 (6.5%)
Henry	1,226 (37.8%)	1,559 (48.1%)	456 (14.1%)
Howard	526 (42.8%)	539 (43.8%)	165 (13.4%)
Huntington	888 (54.4%)	706 (43.3%)	37 (2.3%)
Jackson	1,188 (65.9%)	614 (34.1%)	0
Jasper	347 (47.1%)	357 (48.4%)	33 (4.5%)
Jay	500 (49.5%)	375 (37.1%)	135 (13.4%)
Jefferson	2,263 (49.6%)	2,016 (44.2%)	286 (6.3%)
Jennings	1,104 (51.1%)	998 (45.2%)	59 (2.7%)
Johnson	1,333 (59.3%)	896 (39.8%)	20 (0.9%)
Knox	1,003 (46.2%)	1,167 (53.8%)	0
Kosciusko	938 (46.7%)	1,045 (52.0%)	26 (1.3%)
La Grange	677 (46.3%)	667 (55.7%)	117 (8.0%)
Lake	334 (53.7%)	230 (37.0%)	58 (9.3%)
Laporte	1,468 (49.6%)	1,357 (45.8%)	136 (4.6%)
Lawrence	1,113 (51.0%)	1,054 (48.3%)	14 (0.6%)
Madison	1,282 (54.1%)	1,004 (42.4%)	83 (0.4%)
Marion	2,599 (53.4%)	2,158 (44.3%)	110 (2.3%)
Marshall	511 (56.2%)	343 (37.7%)	56 (6.2%)
Martin	519 (57.7%)	377 (41.9%)	5 (0.6%)
Miami	1,196 (52.8%)	994 (43.9%)	76 (3.4%)
Monroe	1,085 (60.5%)	622 (34.7%)	87 (4.8%)
Montgomery	1,852 (52.7%)	1,559 (44.4%)	100 (2.8%)
Morgan	1,181 (48.8%)	1,109 (45.8%)	132 (5.5%)
Noble	807 (54.1%)	606 (40.6%)	79 (5.3%)
Ohio	455 (51.1%)	432 (48.6%)	2 (0.2%)
Orange	1,022 (57.7%)	747 (42.2%)	3 (0.2%)
Owen	1,060 (53.5%)	901 (45.5%)	20 (1.0%)
Parke	1,084 (43.3%)	1,312 (52.5%)	105 (4.2%)
Perry	659 (49.0%)	684 (50.8%)	3 (0.2%)
Pike	688 (56.1%)	538 (43.8%)	1 (0.1%)
Porter	527 (49.8%)	444 (41.9%)	88 (8.3%)
Posey	1,433 (63.9%)	784 (35.0%)	26 (1.2%)
Pulaski	333 (61.2%)	210 (38.6%)	1 (0.2%)
Putnam	1,466 (44.4%)	1,712 (51.9%)	22 (0.7%)
Randolph	993 (41.0%)	900 (37.1%)	530 (21.9%)

County	Pierce (D)	Scott (W)	Hale (FS)
Ripley	1,386 (52.9%)	1,119 (42.7%)	113 (4.3%)
Rush	1,480 (47.6%)	1,507 (48.6%)	119 (3.8%)
St. Joseph	1,052 (47.3%)	998 (44.9%)	174 (7.8%)
Scott	559 (47.1%)	518 (43.6%)	11 (0.9%)
Shelby	1,627 (55.3%)	1,286 (43.7%)	27 (0.9%)
Spencer	710 (50.9%)	685 (49.1%)	1 (0.1%)
Starke	122 (64.9%)	66 (35.1%)	0
Steuben	543 (48.5%)	487 (43.5%)	90 (8.0%)
Sullivan	1,203 (69.5%)	529 (30.5%)	0
Switzerland	1,147 (47.6%)	1,134 (49.6%)	7 (0.3%)
Tippecanoe	2,446 (54.3%)	1,918 (42.6%)	143 (3.2%)
Tipton	461 (57.1%)	340 (42.1%)	7 (0.9%)
Union	626 (46.1%)	584 (43.0%)	149 (11.0%)
Vanderburgh	1,317 (58.7%)	945 (41.7%)	6 (0.3%)
Vermillion	783 (47.8%)	852 (52.0%)	4 (0.2%)
Vigo	1,155 (40.4%)	1,694 (59.3%)	8 (0.3%)
Wabash	959 (43.7%)	1,145 (52.2%)	91 (4.2%)
Warren	552 (37.9%)	850 (58.3%)	56 (3.8%)
Warrick	1,034 (66.6%)	487 (31.4%)	31 (2.0%)
Washington	1,613 (59.4%)	1,093 (40.2%)	11 (0.4%)
Wayne	1,874 (37.8%)	2,304 (46.4%)	786 (15.8%)
Wells	710 (61.8%)	415 (36.1%)	23 (2.0%)
White	536 (50.6%)	510 (48.2%)	13 (1.2%)
Whitley	568 (52.8%)	497 (46.2%)	11 (4.6%)
*Totals	**94,890 (51.9%)**	**80,901 (44.3%)**	**6,928 (3.8%)**
	*(95,311)	*(80,914)	*(6,906)

*Stated totals.

SOURCE—(Indianapolis) *Indiana Daily Sentinel,* November 24, 1852.

Iowa

County	Pierce (D)	Scott (W)	Hale (FS)
Alamakee	123 (46.4%)	142 (53.6%)	0
Appanoose	335 (55.2%)	247 (40.7%)	25 (4.1%)
Benton	89 (52.7%)	80 (47.3%)	0
Boone	84 (67.7%)	40 (32.3%)	0
Buchanan	148 (54.6%)	123 (45.4%)	0
Cedar	354 (44.6%)	338 (42.6%)	102 (12.8%)
Clark	32 (36.0%)	20 (22.5%)	37 (41.6%)
Clayton	461 (49.4%)	471 (50.6%)	0
Clinton	398 (58.9%)	278 (41.1%)	0
Dallas	89 (53.0%)	79 (47.0%)	0
Davis	614 (50.4%)	592 (48.6%)	12 (1.1%)
Decatur	133 (70.0%)	55 (28.9%)	2 (1.1%)
Delaware	206 (45.1%)	233 (51.0%)	18 (3.9%)
Des Moines	1,154 (52.1%)	983 (44.3%)	80 (3.6%)
Dubuque	1,150 (55.4%)	917 (44.2%)	6 (0.3%)
Fayette	117 (38.4%)	167 (54.8%)	21 (6.9%)
Fremont	67 (41.4%)	95 (58.6%)	0
Guthrie	39 (84.8%)	7 (15.2%)	0
Henry	513 (32.7%)	832 (53.1%)	223 (14.2%)
Iowa	101 (47.2%)	112 (52.3%)	1 (0.5%)
Jackson	739 (56.6%)	554 (42.5%)	12 (0.9%)
Jasper	113 (40.9%)	160 (45.9%)	3 (1.1%)
Jefferson	795 (48.3%)	756 (42.2%)	97 (5.9%)
Johnson	531 (54.0%)	415 (42.2%)	38 (3.9%)
Jones	338 (54.0%)	266 (42.5%)	22 (3.5%)
Keokuk	403 (52.2%)	325 (42.2%)	42 (5.4%)
Lee	1,708 (51.9%)	1,379 (41.9%)	201 (6.1%)
Linn	593 (49.6%)	522 (43.7%)	80 (6.7%)
Louisa	368 (39.1%)	468 (49.7%)	105 (11.1%)
Lucas	85 (50.6%)	80 (47.6%)	3 (1.8%)
Madison	150 (59.3%)	103 (40.7%)	0
Mahaska	541 (45.7%)	599 (50.5%)	45 (3.8%)
Marion	488 (53.5%)	411 (45.1%)	13 (1.5%)
Marshall	52 (62.7%)	31 (37.3%)	0
Mills	91 (59.1%)	63 (40.9%)	0

County	Pierce (D)	Scott (W)	Hale (FS)
Monroe	295 (55.2%)	203 (38.0%)	36 (6.7%)
Muscatine	604 (50.5%)	564 (47.1%)	30 (2.5%)
Page	40 (58.0%)	29 (42.0%)	0
Polk	439 (51.4%)	401 (47.0) %	13 (1.5%)
Pottawattamie	182 (62.1%)	111 (37.9%)	0
Poweshiek	45 (41.7%)	61 (56.5%)	2 (1.9%)
Scott	641 (51.7%)	517 (41.7%)	81 (6.5%)
Taylor	9 (69.2%)	4 (30.8%)	0
Van Buren	1,027 (50.0%)	981 (47.7%)	48 (2.3%)
Wapello	762 (52.0%)	683 (46.6%)	20 (1.4%)
Warren	82 (43.2%)	95 (50.0%)	13 (6.8%)
Washington	369 (36.1%)	472 (46.3%)	181 (17.7%)
Wayne	59 (48.4%)	63 (51.6%)	0
Winneshick	68 (50.0%)	68 (50.0%)	0
Total	**17,824 (50.0%)**	**16,195 (45.5%)**	**1,612 (4.5%)**

Stated totals.   *(17,823)*   *(15,895)*

SOURCE—(Iowa City) *Iowa Republican*, November 27, 1852.

Kentucky

County	Pierce (D)	Scott (W)	Hale (FS)
Adair	597 (56.6%)	457 (43.4%)	
Allen	454 (61.9%)	280 (38.1%)	
Anderson	606 (67.4%)	292 (32.5%)	1 (0.1%)
Ballard	328 (55.8%)	260 (44.2%)	
Barren	967 (46.1%)	1,119 (53.3%)	13 (0.6%)
Bath	785 (57.2%)	587 (42.8%)	
Boone	769 (49.0%)	800 (51.0%)	
Bourbon	528 (35.1%)	978 (64.9%)	
Boyle	323 (34.9%)	603 (65.1%)	
Bracken	517 (44.3%)	638 (54.7%)	11 (0.9%)
Breathitt	234 (71.0%)	96 (29.0%)	
Breckinridge	440 (34.4%)	842 (65.6%)	
Bullitt	446 (52.5%)	403 (47.5%)	
Butler	269 (46.3%)	312 (53.7%)	
Caldwell	874 (54.5%)	731 (45.5%)	
Calloway	815 (81.2%)	189 (18.8%)	
Campbell	1,098 (65.4%)	577 (34.4%)	4 (0.2%)
Carroll	473 (51.5%)	446 (48.5%)	
Carter	497 (73.4%)	180 (26.6%)	
Casey	230 (32.7%)	474 (67.3%)	
Christian	806 (45.3%)	973 (54.7%)	
Clark	322 (27.7%)	842 (72.3%)	
Clay	185 (40.0%)	278 (60.0%)	
Clinton	318 (53.5%)	276 (46.5%)	
Crittenden	486 (55.1%)	396 (44.9%)	
Cumberland	157 (23.9%)	501 (76.1%)	
Daviess	711 (40.9%)	1,027 (59.1%)	
Edmonson	218 (51.1%)	208 (48.9%)	
Estill	322 (46.8%)	358 (52.0%)	8 (1.6%)
Fayette	810 (37.2%)	1,376 (63.1%)	3 (0.1%)
Fleming	698 (44.0%)	888 (56.0%)	1 (0.1%)
Floyd	222 (57.4%)	165 (42.6%)	
Franklin	759 (47.7%)	833 (52.3%)	
Fulton	233 (60.5%)	152 (39.5%)	
Gallatin	411 (52.5%)	372 (47.5%)	
Garrard	236 (21.5%)	862 (78.4%)	2 (0.2%)
Grant	572 (56.7%)	437 (43.3%)	
Graves	971 (68.5%)	446 (31.5%)	
Grayson	394 (47.6%)	433 (52.4%)	
Green	487 (53.6%)	422 (46.4%)	
Greenup	660 (50.9%)	637 (49.1%)	
Hancock	205 (45.2%)	249 (54.8%)	
Hardin	619 (38.1%)	1,007 (61.9%)	
Harlan	65 (16.6%)	327 (83.4%)	
Harrison	947 (54.1%)	802 (45.8%)	1 (0.1%)
Hart	578 (56.0%)	455 (44.0%)	
Henderson	635 (50.8%)	616 (49.2%)	
Henry	983 (56.9%)	744 (43.1%)	
Hickman	379 (71.0%)	155 (29.0%)	
Hopkins	809 (52.3%)	737 (47.7%)	
Jefferson	3,791 (50.8%)	3,665 (49.1%)	1 (0.01%)
Jessamine	476 (46.1%)	556 (53.9%)	
Johnson	299 (82.4%)	64 (17.6%)	
Kenton	1,384 (58.6%)	975 (41.3%)	1 (0.04%)
Knox	164 (25.2%)	487 (74.8%)	
Larue	348 (45.5%)	417 (54.5%)	
Laurel	187 (33.5%)	372 (66.5%)	
Lawrence	362 (48.5%)	385 (51.5%)	
Letcher	78 (55.3%)	63 (44.7%)	
Lewis	503 (55.4%)	400 (44.1%)	5 (0.6%)
Lincoln	338 (33.4%)	674 (66.6%)	
Livingston	267 (46.1%)	312 (53.9%)	
Logan	384 (22.8%)	1,294 (77.0%)	3 (0.2%)
Madison	541 (32.4%)	976 (58.4%)	155 (9.3%)
Marion	763 (49.4%)	782 (50.6%)	
Marshall	425 (76.2%)	132 (23.7%)	1 (0.2%)
Mason	896 (40.1%)	1,337 (59.8%)	3 (0.1%)
McCracken	416 (51.9%)	385 (48.1%)	
Meade	230 (26.2%)	647 (73.8%)	
Mercer	914 (60.6%)	594 (39.4%)	1 (0.1%)
Monroe	389 (42.9%)	518 (57.1%)	
Montgomery	350 (47.8%)	377 (51.5%)	5 (0.7%)
Morgan	509 (61.7%)	316 (38.3%)	
Muhlenberg	553 (40.5%)	814 (59.5%)	
Nelson	487 (33.7%)	958 (66.3%)	
Nicholas	721 (54.9%)	592 (45.1%)	1 (0.1%)
Ohio	624 (47.1%)	701 (52.9%)	
Oldham	486 (55.6%)	388 (44.4%)	
Owen	1,186 (70.1%)	505 (29.9%)	
Owsley	326 (52.6%)	294 (47.4%)	
Pendleton	570 (68.5%)	262 (31.5%)	
Perry	77 (37.2%)	130 (62.8%)	
Pike	194 (46.7%)	221 (53.3%)	
Powell	133 (54.5%)	111 (45.5%)	
Pulaski	622 (46.8%)	707 (53.2%)	
Rockcastle	97 (21.2%)	326 (71.2%)	35 (7.6%)
Russell	195 (30.9%)	437 (69.1%)	
Scott	888 (54.9%)	729 (45.1%)	
Shelby	753 (38.9%)	1,184 (61.1%)	
Simpson	380 (49.4%)	389 (50.6%)	
Spencer	340 (50.7%)	331 (49.3%)	
Taylor	527 (66.6%)	264 (33.4%)	
Todd	422 (39.3%)	652 (60.7%)	1 (0.1%)
Trigg	629 (52.9%)	560 (47.1%)	

Trimble	491 (62.1%)	300 (37.9%)
Union	612 (55.1%)	499 (44.9%)
Warren	600 (37.9%)	982 (62.1%)
Washington	680 (51.6%)	637 (48.4%)
Wayne	342 (42.5%)	463 (57.5%)
Woodford	410 (36.7%)	706 (63.3%)
Total	**53,807 (48.4%)**	**57,108 (51.4%)** **256 (0.2%)**
*Whitley	503 (58.3%)	360 (41.7%)

Not included in the official returns.

SOURCES—(Frankfort) *Commonwealth*, December 7, 1852; *Presidential Politics in Kentucky*.

Louisiana

Parish	Pierce (D)	Scott (W)
Ascension	360 (54.9%)	296 (45.1%)
Assumption	553 (52.0%)	511 (48.0%)
Avoyelles	387 (56.3%)	300 (43.7%)
Bienville	313 (64.5%)	172 (35.5%)
Bossier	248 (57.9%)	180 (42.1%)
Caddo	342 (49.9%)	344 (50.1%)
Calcasieu	221 (86.7%)	34 (13.3%)
Caldwell	158 (74.5%)	54 (25.5%)
Carroll	261 (54.4%)	219 (45.6%)
Catahoula	310 (52.5%)	280 (47.5%)
Clayton	506 (60.5%)	330 (39.5%)
Concordia	86 (41.5%)	121 (58.5%)
De Soto	288 (54.4%)	241 (45.6%)
East Baton Rouge	485 (50.1%)	484 (49.9%)
East Feliciana	443 (56.4%)	342 (43.6%)
Franklin	192 (63.6%)	110 (36.4%)
Iberville	426 (57.3%)	318 (42.7%)
Jackson	341 (66.2%)	174 (33.8%)
Jefferson	943 (50.4%)	928 (49.6%)
Lafayette	277 (70.3%)	117 (29.7%)
Lafource Interior	135 (16.6%)	676 (83.4%)
Livingston	337 (67.9%)	159 (32.1%)
Madison	147 (46.2%)	171 (53.8%)
Morehouse	137 (41.1%)	196 (58.9%)
Natchitoches	407 (58.5%)	289 (41.5%)
Orleans	4,843 (50.9%)	4,724 (49.1%)
Ouachita	240 (55.8%)	190 (44.2%)
Plaquemines	372 (71.1%)	151 (28.9%)
Point Coupee	364 (60.1%)	242 (39.9%)
Rapides	623 (60.8%)	401 (39.2%)
Sabine	251 (51.4%)	237 (48.6%)
St. Bernard	120 (48.0%)	130 (52.0%)
St. Charles	39 (27.9%)	101 (72.1%)
St. Helena	246 (54.1%)	209 (45.9%)
St. James	158 (33.0%)	321 (67.0%)
St. John the Baptist	160 (44.3%)	202 (55.7%)
St. Landry	568 (45.1%)	692 (54.9%)
St. Martin	298 (38.4%)	479 (61.6%)
St. Mary	243 (38.4%)	390 (61.6%)
St. Tammany	208 (45.0%)	254 (55.0%)
Tensas	107 (47.1%)	120 (52.9%)
Terrebone	97 (33.0%)	197 (67.0%)
Union	465 (51.7%)	435 (48.3%)

Vermillion	126 (48.1%)	136 (51.9%)
Washington	258 (67.4%)	125 (32.6%)
West Baton Rouge	118 (34.9%)	220 (65.1%)
West Feliciana	308 (61.8%)	190 (38.2%)
Wynn	138 (70.8%)	57 (29.2%)
Total	**18,653 (52.09%)** *(18,647)	**17,255 (48.0%)**

Stated totals.

SOURCE—(New Orleans) *Daily Picayune*, November 25, 1852.

Maine

County	Pierce (D)	Scott (W)	Hale (FS)
Aroostook	787 (49.5%)	724 (45.5%)	80 (5.0%)
Cumberland	6,504 (52.6%)	4,471 (36.2%)	1,379 (11.2%)
Franklin	1,310 (45.1%)	997 (34.3%)	596 (20.5%)
Hancock	2,619 (56.4%)	1,809 (39.0%)	214 (4.6%)
Kennebec	2,703 (33.2%)	4,489 (55.1%)	954 (11.7%)
Lincoln	5,168 (47.2%)	5,224 (47.7%)	563 (5.1%)
Oxford	4,049 (64.2%)	1,560 (24.7%)	697 (11.1%)
Penobscot	4,513 (46.3%)	3,132 (36.2%)	1,015 (11.7%)
Piscataquis	851 (44.2%)	693 (36.0%)	381 (19.8%)
Somerset	2,019 (41.5%)	2,394 (49.2%)	457 (9.4%)
Waldo	3,126 (59.4%)	1,379 (26.2%)	757 (14.4%)
Washington	2,690 (51.9%)	2,278 (44.0%)	211 (4.1%)
York	5,270 (56.1%)	3,393 (36.1%)	726 (7.7%)
Total	**41,609 (50.6%)**	**32,543 (39.6%)**	**8,030 (9.8%)**

SOURCES—(Augusta) *Kennebec Journal*, December 2, 1852; and *Maine Legislative Documents, 1857*.

Maryland

County	Pierce (D)	Scott (W)	Hale (FS)
Allegany	1,976 (57.8%)	1,454 (42.2%)	
Anne Arundel	889 (51.6%)	833 (48.4%)	
Baltimore	3,001 (60.7%)	1,946 (39.3%)	
Calvert	353 (50.0%)	353 (50.0%)	
Caroline	500 (47.4%)	554 (52.6%)	
Carroll	1,919 (52.9%)	1,702 (46.9%)	16 (0.4%)
Cecil	1,550 (50.9%)	1,494 (49.1%)	
Charles	411 (38.5%)	657 (61.5%)	
Dorchester	933 (43.0%)	1,239 (57.0%)	
Frederick	3,344 (51.0%)	3,204 (48.8%)	13 (0.2%)
Harford	1,378 (50.4%)	1,353 (49.5%)	1 (0.04%)
Howard	625 (52.3%)	570 (47.7%)	
Kent	552 (45.4%)	664 (54.6%)	
Montgomery	843 (44.3%)	1,060 (55.7%)	
Prince George's	724 (44.1%)	918 (55.9%)	
Queen Anne's	735 (50.4%)	723 (49.6%)	
St. Mary's	440 (39.3%)	681 (60.7%)	
Somerset	1,114 (43.6%)	1,443 (56.4%)	
Talbot	796 (51.8%)	741 (48.2%)	
Washington	2,723 (50.5%)	2,669 (49.5%)	
Worcester	1,185 (48.6%)	1,253 (51.4%)	
Baltimore City	14,437 (60.1%)	9,569 (39.8%)	26 (0.1%)
Total	**40,428 (53.5%)**	**35,080 (46.4%)**	**56 (0.1%)**

SOURCE—Manuscript returns.

Massachusetts

County	Pierce (D)	Scott (W)	Hale (FS)	Webster (W)
Barnstable	892 (32.4%)	1,379 (50.1%)	473 (17.2%)	9 (0.3%)
Berkshire	2,973 (41.4%)	3,579 (49.8%)	631 (8.8%)	2 (0.3%)
Bristol	3,269 (35.5%)	3,827 (41.6%)	2,091 (22.7%)	11 (0.1%)

County	Pierce (D)	Scott (W)	Hale (FS)	Webster (W)
Dukes	225 (42.9%)	250 (47.7%)	48 (9.2%)	1 (0.2%)
Essex	5,750 (36.2%)	6,539 (41.2%)	3,485 (22.0%)	107 (0.7%)
Franklin	1,726 (31.4%)	2,552 (46.4%)	1,218 (22.2%)	0
Hampden	3,458 (45.1%)	3,445 (44.9%)	757 (9.9%)	10 (0.1%)
Hampshire	1,425 (23.9%)	3,300 (55.3%)	1,243 (20.8%)	2 (0.3%)
Middlesex	8,976 (40.4%)	8,750 (39.3%)	4,231 (19.0%)	280 (1.3%)
Nantucket	189 (26.7%)	329 (46.5%)	189 (26.7%)	1 (0.1%)
Norfolk	3,456 (35.7%)	3,589 (37.1%)	2,479 (25.6%)	161 (1.7%)
Plymouth	2,082 (27.6%)	2,993 (39.6%)	2,440 (32.3%)	40 (0.5%)
Suffolk	5,412 (41.9%)	4,868 (37.7%)	1,600 (12.4%)	1,029 (8.0%)
Worcerster	6,042 (29.5%)	7,283 (35.6%)	7,138 (34.9%)	17 (0.1%)
Total	**45,875 (35.7%)**	**52,863 (41.2%)**	**28,023 (21.8%)**	**1,670 (1.3%)**

SOURCE—Manuscript returns.

Michigan

No returns were located for this election for Houghton County.

County	Pierce (D)	Scott (W)	Hale (FS)
Allegan	582 (48.7%)	547 (45.8%)	66 (5.5%)
Barry	652 (52.7%)	478 (38.6%)	107 (8.6%)
Berrien	1,234 (53.9%)	1,015 (44.3%)	41 (1.8%)
Branch	1,380 (51.9%)	1,077 (40.5%)	202 (7.6%)
Calhoun	1,824 (45.1%)	1,784 (44.1%)	440 (10.9%)
Cass	984 (47.6%)	988 (47.8%)	95 (4.6%)
Clinton	437 (41.5%)	469 (44.6%)	146 (13.9%)
Eaton	786 (47.7%)	637 (38.7%)	225 (13.7%)
Genesee	1,145 (42.9%)	1,221 (45.8%)	301 (11.2%)
Hillsdale	1,596 (46.9%)	1,417 (41.6%)	391 (11.5%)
Ingham	929 (50.4%)	786 (42.6%)	128 (6.9%)
Ionia	864 (47.3%)	659 (36.1%)	302 (16.5%)
Jackson	1,840 (45.4%)	1,726 (42.6%)	484 (12.0%)
Kalamazoo	1,257 (41.3%)	1,374 (45.2%)	411 (13.5%)
Keweenaw	1,519 (52.2%)	1,226 (42.1%)	166 (5.7%)
Lapeer	819 (51.9%)	618 (39.1%)	142 (9.0%)
Lenawee	2,857 (48.3%)	2,418 (40.9%)	640 (10.8%)
Livingston	1,419 (57.1%)	931 (37.5%)	133 (5.4%)
Mackinac	292 (88.5%)	38 (11.5%)	0
Macomb	1,634 (51.0%)	1,060 (33.1%)	509 (15.9%)
Monroe	1,582 (55.3%)	1,112 (38.8%)	169 (5.9%)
Montcalm	156 (55.3%)	120 (42.6%)	6 (2.1%)
Newaygo	104 (72.2%)	40 (27.8%)	0
Oakland	3,178 (52.0%)	2,376 (38.9%)	552 (9.0%)
Ottawa	756 (64.2%)	363 (30.8%)	59 (5.0%)
Saginaw	694 (61.2%)	367 (32.4%)	73 (6.4%)
St. Clair	1,110 (55.1%)	852 (42.3%)	53 (2.6%)
St. Joseph	1,259 (47.1%)	1,164 (43.5%)	252 (9.4%)
Sanilac	252 (69.8%)	109 (30.2%)	0
Shiawassee	584 (50.6%)	519 (44.9%)	52 (4.5%)
Tuscola	62 (35.2%)	80 (45.5%)	34 (19.3%)
Van Buren	771 (52.4%)	613 (41.7%)	87 (5.9%)
Washtenaw	2,604 (47.5%)	2,274 (41.5%)	603 (11.0%)
Wayne	4,680 (55.4%)	3,402 (40.3%)	368 (4.4%)
Total	**41,842 (50.5%)**	**33,860 (40.8%)**	**7,237 (8.7%)**
*Stated totals.		*(33,800)	

SOURCE—*Michigan Manual, 1913*, pp. 688-9.

Mississippi

County	Pierce (D)	Scott (W)
Adams	442 (46.2%)	514 (53.8%)
Attala	673 (67.9%)	318 (32.1%)
Amite	354 (52.1%)	325 (47.9%)
Bolivar	38 (36.2%)	67 (63.8%)
Calhoun	467 (68.5%)	215 (31.5%)
Carroll	783 (59.7%)	528 (40.3%)
Chickasaw	719 (60.1%)	478 (39.9%)
Choctaw	610 (64.8%)	332 (35.2%)
Claiborne	358 (57.0%)	270 (43.0%)
Clarke	343 (71.5%)	137 (28.5%)
Coahoma	115 (42.0%)	159 (58.0%)
Copiah	607 (69.1%)	272 (30.9%)
Covington	303 (75.8%)	97 (24.2%)
Franklin	254 (61.7%)	158 (38.3%)
Green	114 (65.1%)	61 (34.9%)
Hancock	112 (71.8%)	44 (28.2%)
Harrison	276 (63.9%)	156 (36.1%)
Hinds	839 (46.3%)	975 (53.7%)
Holmes	484 (53.6%)	419 (46.4%)
Issaquena	54 (52.9%)	48 (47.1%)
Itawamba	1,015 (71.6%)	402 (28.4%)
Jackson	213 (94.2%)	13 (5.8%)
Jasper	421 (63.4%)	243 (36.6%)
Jefferson	317 (61.0%)	203 (39.0%)
Jones	114 (75.0%)	38 (25.0%)
Kemper	511 (61.9%)	317 (38.1%)
Lafayette	690 (63.2%)	401 (36.8%)
Lauderdale	688 (69.1%)	308 (30.9%)
Lawrence	395 (80.3%)	97 (19.7%)
Leake	335 (62.9%)	198 (37.1%)
Lowndes	745 (59.9%)	499 (40.1%)
Madison	497 (53.0%)	440 (47.0%)
Marion	207 (81.2%)	48 (18.8%)
Marshall	1,304 (54.5%)	1,087 (45.5%)
Monroe	972 (67.6%)	466 (32.4%)
Neshoba	248 (82.9%)	51 (17.1%)
Newton	217 (67.0%)	107 (33.0%)
Noxubee	413 (52.3%)	377 (47.7%)
Oktibbeha	344 (62.0%)	211 (38.0%)
Panola	383 (47.3%)	427 (52.7%)
Perry	112 (54.4%)	94 (45.6%)
Pike	412 (74.5%)	141 (25.5%)
Pontotoc	1,030 (68.4%)	475 (31.6%)
Rankin	351 (56.2%)	274 (43.8%)
Scott	247 (71.6%)	98 (28.4%)
Simpson	244 (60.5%)	159 (39.5%)
Smith	270 (76.1%)	85 (23.9%)
Sunflower	43 (55.1%)	35 (44.9%)
Tallahatchie	186 (56.5%)	143 (43.5%)
Tippah	1,233 (68.4%)	569 (31.6%)
Tishemingo	1,312 (63.3%)	760 (36.7%)
Tunica	34 (63.0%)	20 (37.0%)
Warren	494 (40.6%)	723 (59.4%)
Washington	90 (41.1%)	129 (58.9%)
Wayne	61 (46.2%)	71 (53.8%)
Wilkinson	365 (57.4%)	271 (42.6%)

	Pierce (D)	Scott (W)
Winston	448 (67.3%)	218 (32.7%)
Yalobusha	644 (54.0%)	549 (46.0%)
Yazoo	560 (55.3%)	453 (44.7%)
Total	**26,110 (60.9%)**	**16,773 (39.1%)**
*De Soto	888 (53.2%)	781 (46.8%)

*The vote of the county was not included in the manuscript returns and is listed as "not official" in the (Jackson) Mississippian, November 26, 1852.

SOURCES—(Jackson) *Mississippian*, November 26, 1852; and manuscript returns.

Missouri

No returns were located for this election for Shannon county.

County	Pierce (D)	Scott (W)
Adair	201 (64.0%)	113 (36.0%)
Andrew	784 (62.7%)	466 (37.3%)
Atchinson	150 (58.6%)	106 (41.4%)
Audrain	160 (43.2%)	210 (56.8%)
Barry	253 (43.2%)	72 (56.8%)
Bates	116 (52.7%)	104 (47.3%)
Benton	328 (66.3%)	167 (33.7%)
Bollinger	112 (80.0%)	28 (20.0%)
Boone	613 (35.5%)	1,112 (64.5%)
Buchanan	857 (54.6%)	712 (45.4%)
Butler	26 (61.9%)	16 (38.1%)
Caldwell	209 (57.1%)	157 (42.9%)
Callaway	595 (49.7%)	601 (50.3%)
Camden	109 (61.9%)	67 (38.1%)
Cape Girardeau	487 (59.8%)	328 (40.2%)
Carroll	286 (54.5%)	239 (45.5%)
Cass	237 (51.0%)	228 (49.0%)
Cedar	162 (71.4%)	65 (28.6%)
Charlton	498 (58.9%)	348 (41.1%)
Clark	289 (47.1%)	325 (52.9%)
Clay	406 (39.3%)	626 (60.7%)
Clinton	290 (50.6%)	283 (49.4%)
Cole	463 (68.2%)	216 (31.8%)
Cooper	535 (45.3%)	645 (54.7%)
Crawford	278 (53.7%)	240 (46.3%)
Dade	276 (61.2%)	175 (38.8%)
Dallas	344 (77.1%)	102 (22.9%)
Daviess	351 (78.5%)	296 (21.5%)
De Kalb	167 (71.7%)	66 (28.3%)
Dent	69 (54.3%)	58 (45.7%)
Dodge	55 (64.0%)	31 (36.0%)
Dunklin		no legal election held
Franklin	619 (69.1%)	277 (30.9%)
Gasconade	304 (77.4%)	89 (22.6%)
Gentry	233 (63.7%)	133 (36.3%)
Greene	921 (65.5%)	485 (34.5%)
Grundy	184 (46.1%)	215 (53.9%)
Harrison	164 (59.6%)	111 (40.4%)
Henry	245 (48.1%)	266 (51.9%)
Hickory	194 (72.1%)	75 (27.9%)
Holt	291 (60.6%)	189 (39.4%)
Howard	762 (53.0%)	675 (47.0%)
Jackson	858 (54.1%)	728 (45.9%)
Jasper	355 (67.7%)	169 (32.3%)
Jefferson	210 (55.0%)	172 (45.0%)
Johnson	456 (55.9%)	360 (44.1%)
Knox	255 (54.8%)	210 (45.2%)
Laclede	184 (71.9%)	72 (28.1%)
Lafayette	532 (39.9%)	803 (60.1%)
Lawrence	390 (70.7%)	162 (29.3%)
Lewis	408 (50.6%)	398 (49.4%)
Lincoln	587 (57.2%)	440 (42.8%)
Linn	282 (53.1%)	249 (46.9%)

County	Pierce (D)	Scott (W)
Livingston	321 (56.1%)	251 (43.9%)
Macon	473 (57.1%)	355 (42.9%)
Madison	259 (68.9%)	117 (31.1%)
Marion	751 (45.7%)	894 (54.3%)
McDonald	194 (75.5%)	63 (24.5%)
Mercer	186 (50.0%)	186 (50.0%)
Miller	279 (81.8%)	62 (18.2%)
Mississippi	168 (58.9%)	117 (41.1%)
Moniteau	453 (70.6%)	189 (29.4%)
Monroe	611 (44.6%)	760 (55.4%)
Montgomery	266 (40.8%)	386 (59.2%)
Morgan	290 (68.7%)	132 (31.3%)
New Madrid	32 (25.6%)	93 (74.4%)
Newton	323 (75.1%)	107 (24.9%)
Nodaway	111 (64.5%)	61 (35.5%)
Oregon	95 (89.6%)	11 (10.4%)
Osage	372 (72.2%)	143 (27.8%)
Ozark	58 (64.4%)	32 (35.6%)
Pemiscot	34 (37.4%)	57 (62.6%)
Perry	213 (55.5%)	171 (44.5%)
Pettis	301 (55.1%)	245 (44.9%)
Pike	758 (48.6%)	803 (51.4%)
Platte	1,060 (53.7%)	915 (46.3%)
Polk	504 (66.0%)	260 (34.0%)
Pulaski	169 (81.3%)	39 (18.7%)
Putnam	121 (53.8%)	104 (46.2%)
Ralls	278 (44.9%)	341 (55.1%)
Randolph	502 (51.4%)	476 (48.6%)
Ray	618 (56.1%)	483 (43.9%)
Reynolds	98 (95.1%)	5 (4.9%)
Ripley	83 (83.8%)	16 (16.2%)
St. Charles	595 (61.1%)	378 (38.9%)
St. Clair	225 (60.2%)	149 (39.8%)
St. Francois	328 (56.7%)	250 (43.3%)
Ste. Genevieve	165 (57.5%)	122 (42.5%)
St. Louis	5,826 (52.4%)	4,298 (47.6%)
Saline	443 (46.3%)	514 (53.7%)
Schuyler	222 (55.6%)	177 (44.4%)
Scotland	283 (56.7%)	216 (43.3%)
Scott	97 (62.2%)	59 (37.8%)
Shelby	328 (61.5%)	205 (38.5%)
Stoddard	177 (60.4%)	116 (39.6%)
Stone	94 (84.7%)	17 (15.3%)
Sullivan	274 (68.3%)	127 (31.7%)
Taney	168 (93.9%)	11 (6.1%)
Texas	167 (63.7%)	95 (36.3%)
Vernon	153 (70.8%)	63 (29.2%)
Wayne	144 (78.3%)	40 (21.7%)
Warren	301 (50.0%)	301 (50.0%)
Washington	334 (48.1%)	360 (51.9%)
Wright	165 (63.5%)	95 (36.5%)
Total	**38,610 (56.3%)**	**29,947 (43.7%)**

SOURCES—Manuscript returns; state archives.

New Hampshire

County	Pierce (D)	Scott (W)	Hale (FS)
Belknap	1,837 (64.8%)	737 (26.0%)	262 (9.2%)
Carroll	1,931 (69.5%)	499 (17.9%)	350 (12.6%)
Cheshire	2,001 (44.2%)	1,877 (41.4%)	653 (14.4%)
Coos	1,088 (68.3%)	347 (21.8%)	159 (10.0%)
Grafton	4,140 (59.9%)	2,015 (29.2%)	754 (10.9%)
Hillsborough	4,622 (51.8%)	2,889 (32.4%)	1,405 (15.8%)
Merrimack	4,213 (64.1%)	1,385 (21.1%)	976 (14.8%)
Rockingham	4,502 (55.7%)	2,507 (31.0%)	1,071 (13.3%)
Strafford	2,250 (47.4%)	2,003 (42.2%)	498 (10.5%)
Sullivan	1,919 (53.8%)	1,227 (34.4%)	418 (11.7%)
Total	**28,503 (56.4%)**	**15,486 (30.6%)**	**6,546 (13.0%)**

SOURCE—*New Hampshire Manual 1889.*

New Jersey

County	Pierce (D)		Scott (W)		Hale (FS)		Broome (A)	
Atlantic	751	(68.3%)	349	(31.7%)	0			
Bergen	1,414	(60.4%)	926	(39.6%)	0			
Burlington	3,796	(48.9%)	3,820	(49.2%)	114	(1.5%)	31	(0.4%)
Camden	1,696	(45.6%)	1,568	(42.2%)	27	(0.7%)	442	(11.4%)
Cape May	352	(36.9%)	603	(63.1%)	0			
Cumberland	1,613	(54.1%)	1,371	(45.9%)	0			
Essex	5,630	(47.3%)	6,241	(52.4%)	35	(0.3%)		
Gloucester	1,083	(41.3%)	1,221	(46.5%)	55	(2.1%)	265	(10.1%)
Hudson	1,645	(50.4%)	1,596	(48.9%)	21	(0.6%)		
Hunterdon	3,578	(61.0%)	2,290	(39.0%)	0			
Mercer	2,567	(49.0%)	2,657	(50.7%)	13	(0.2%)		
Middlesex	2,400	(49.0%)	2,495	(51.0%)	0			
Monmouth	3,178	(63.7%)	1,806	(36.2%)	5	(0.1%)		
Morris	2,800	(52.1%)	2,548	(47.4%)	25	(0.5%)		
Ocean	567	(34.0%)	1,102	(66.0%)	0			
Passaic	1,825	(52.2%)	1,670	(47.8%)	0			
Salem	1,783	(50.3%)	1,723	(48.6%)	31	(0.9%)		
Somerset	1,680	(48.1%)	1,814	(51.9%)	0			
Sussex	3,184	(73.0%)	1,177	(27.0%)	0			
Warren	2,759	(63.5%)	1,574	(36.2%)	10	(0.2%)		
Total	**44,301**	**(52.8%)**	**38,551**	**(45.9%)**	**336**	**(0.4%)**	**738**	**(0.9%)**
					*(344)		*(714)	

*Stated totals.

Source—(Newark) *Sentinel of Freedom*, November 16, 1852.

New York

County	Pierce (D)		Scott (W)		Hale (FS)		Webster (W)		Smith (Ab)	
Albany	8,363	(53.1%)	7,244	(46.0%)	133	(0.8%)	8	(0.1%)		
Allegany	4,009	(48.0%)	3,670	(43.9%)	678	(8.1%)				
Broome	3,064	(50.4%)	2,674	(43.9%)	347	(5.7%)				
Cattaraugus	3,493	(44.9%)	3,688	(47.3%)	607	(7.8%)				
Cayuga	4,550	(44.1%)	4,838	(46.9%)	916	(8.9%)	1	(0.01%)	6	(0.1%)
Chauatauqua	3,703	(35.2%)	5,612	(53.3%)	1,209	(11.5%)				
Chemung	3,189	(54.5%)	2,326	(39.7%)	339	(5.8%)				
Chenango	4,481	(51.7%)	3,880	(44.8%)	303	(3.5%)			2	(0.02%)
Clinton	2,812	(52.6%)	2,286	(42.8%)	245	(4.6%)				
Columbia	4,455	(51.8%)	4,142	(48.1%)	7	(0.1%)				
Cortland	2,064	(40.9%)	2,328	(46.1%)	655	(13.0%)				
Delaware	4,052	(52.8%)	3,289	(42.8%)	339	(4.4%)				
Dutchess	5,600	(50.3%)	5,495	(49.4%)	33	(0.3%)				
Erie	7,033	(45.2%)	8,023	(51.5%)	510	(3.3%)				
Essex	1,973	(40.2%)	2,756	(56.2%)	174	(3.5%)				
Franklin	2,074	(52.5%)	1,747	(44.2%)	130	(3.2%)				
Fulton	2,070	(47.5%)	2,171	(49.8%)	115	(2.6%)				
Genesee	2,166	(37.1%)	3,358	(57.5%)	313	(5.4%)				
Greene	3,242	(53.5%)	2,803	(46.2%)	16	(0.3%)				
Hamilton	342	(73.1%)	126	(26.9%)	0					
Herkimer	4,220	(56.6%)	2,679	(35.9%)	555	(7.4%)			2	(0.02%)
Jefferson	6,279	(49.4%)	5,656	(44.5%)	757	(6.0%)			13	(0.1%)
Kings	10,621	(55.1%)	8,491	(44.0%)	66	(0.3%)	106	(0.5%)		
Lewis	2,535	(55.5%)	1,727	(32.8%)	303	(6.6%)				
Livingston	3,055	(41.0%)	4,096	(54.9%)	308	(4.1%)			1	(0.01%)
Madison	3,435	(40.8%)	3,379	(40.1%)	1,584	(18.8%)			20	(0.2%)
Monroe	6,314	(43.4%)	7,467	(51.3%)	775	(5.3%)	1	(0.1%)		
Montgomery	3,373	(52.6%)	3,000	(46.8%)	40	(0.6%)	1	(0.02%)		
New York	34,226	(59.2%)	23,115	(40.0%)	200	(0.3%)	236	(0.4%)		
Niagara	2,862	(39.0%)	3,413	(46.6%)	1,056	(1.4%)				
Oneida	8,636	(49.3%)	7,831	(44.7%)	1,046	(6.0%)				
Onondaga	6,415	(45.1%)	6,097	(42.9%)	1,701	(2.0%)	7	(0.05%)	1	(0.01%)
Ontario	3,437	(41.0%)	4,402	(52.5%)	547	(6.5%)	1	(0.01%)	3	(0.04%)
Orange	5,171	(55.0%)	4,221	(44.9%)	16	(0.2%)	1	(0.01%)		
Orleans	2,267	(41.5%)	2,586	(47.4%)	605	(11.1%)				
Oswego	4,973	(43.2%)	4,375	(38.0%)	2,148	(18.7%)			9	(0.1%)
Otsego	5,486	(51.9%)	4,454	(42.1%)	634	(6.0%)				
Putnam	1,521	(64.8%)	826	(35.2%)	0					

County	Pierce (D)	Scott (W)	Hale (FS)	Webster (W)	Smith (Ab)
Queens	2,899 (56.6%)	2,209 (43.1%)	12 (0.2%)	5 (0.1%)	
Rensselaer	6,563 (50.6%)	6,184 (47.7%)	218 (1.7%)	7 (0.1%)	
Richmond	1,324 (52.9%)	1,147 (45.8%)	30 (1.2%)	2 (0.1%)	
Rockland	1,785 (70.9%)	733 (29.1%)	0		
St. Lawrence	5,583 (48.4%)	4,570 (39.6%)	1,385 (12.0%)		
Saratoga	4,291 (48.4%)	4,498 (50.8%)	71 (0.8%)	1 (0.01%)	
Schenectady	1,900 (53.5%)	1,654 (46.5%)	0	1 (0.03%)	
Schoharie	3,846 (56.4%)	2,958 (43.4%)	18 (0.3%)		
Seneca	2,511 (50.9%)	2,213 (44.9%)	200 (4.1%)	1 (0.02%)	5 (0.1%)
Steuben	6,880 (55.2%)	5,236 (42.0%)	345 (2.8%)		
Suffolk	3,306 (63.3%)	1,917 (36.7%)	0	2 (0.04%)	
Sullivan	2,681 (56.0%)	2,059 (43.0%)	44 (0.9%)		
Tioga	2,815 (53.7%)	2,234 (42.6%)	197 (3.8%)		
Tompkins	3,472 (44.8%)	3,410 (44.0%)	862 (11.1%)		
Ulster	5,916 (53.3%)	5,156 (46.5%)	26 (0.2%)		
Warren	1,713 (57.0%)	1,174 (39.1%)	119 (4.0%)		
Washington	3,174 (40.4%)	4,231 (53.9%)	451 (5.7%)		
Wayne	4,050 (44.8%)	4,033 (44.6%)	941 (10.4%)		10 (0.1%)
Westchester	5,279 (56.3%)	4,033 (43.0%)	55 (0.6%)	6 (0.1%)	
Wyoming	2,471 (39.8%)	3,005 (48.4%)	727 (11.7%)		
Yates	2,153 (48.4%)	1,974 (44.3%)	324 (7.3%)		
Total	**262,083 (50.1%)**	**234,896 (44.9%)**	**25,435 (4.9%)**	**387 (0.1%)**	**72 (0.01%)**
	*(262,456)	*(234,906)	*(25,433)		

*Stated totals.

SOURCE—*Albany Argus*, December 13, 1852.

North Carolina

County	Pierce (D)	Scott (W)	Hale (FS)
Alexander	98 (30.9%)	219 (69.1%)	
Anson	369 (27.1%)	992 (72.9%)	
Ashe	302 (44.4%)	378 (55.6%)	
Beaufort	574 (61.3%)	910 (38.7%)	
Bertie	444 (47.1%)	498 (52.9%)	
Bladen	582 (61.1%)	371 (38.9%)	
Brunswick	301 (46.1%)	352 (53.9%)	
Buncombe	376 (59.7%)	557 (40.3%)	
Burke	389 (33.8%)	761 (66.2%)	
Cabarrus	371 (36.6%)	642 (63.4%)	
Caldwell	146 (22.8%)	493 (77.2%)	
Camden	107 (17.5%)	503 (82.5%)	
Carteret	388 (48.4%)	414 (51.6%)	
Caswell	931 (19.5%)	226 (80.5%)	
Chatham	725 (41.5%)	1,008 (57.7%)	15 (0.9%)
Cherokee	290 (35.2%)	534 (64.8%)	
Chowan	219 (49.3%)	225 (50.7%)	
Cleveland	494 (70.1%)	211 (29.9%)	
Columbus	357 (67.3%)	178 (32.7%)	
Craven	694 (54.3%)	583 (45.7%)	
Cumberland	1,488 (64.7%)	811 (35.3%)	
Currituck	490 (78.5%)	134 (21.5%)	
Davidson	497 (32.8%)	1,019 (67.2%)	
Davie	259 (38.5%)	414 (61.5%)	
Duplin	930 (83.3%)	187 (16.7%)	
Edgecombe	1,454 (94.2%)	89 (5.8%)	
Franklin	704 (65.7%)	367 (34.3%)	
Gates	368 (50.0%)	368 (50.0%)	
Granville	945 (48.8%)	991 (51.2%)	
Greene	326 (50.1%)	325 (49.9%)	
Guilford	389 (19.2%)	1,596 (78.7%)	44 (2.2%)
Halifax	424 (46.0%)	497 (54.0%)	
Haywood	302 (49.0%)	314 (51.0%)	
Henderson	210 (29.9%)	493 (70.1%)	
Hertford	236 (44.9%)	290 (55.1%)	
Hyde	227 (40.4%)	335 (59.6%)	
Iredell	280 (23.5%)	909 (76.5%)	
Johnston	870 (55.1%)	708 (44.9%)	
Jones	201 (48.9%)	192 (51.1%)	
Lenoir	397 (58.5%)	282 (41.5%)	
Lincoln	1,418 (69.5%)	621 (30.5%)	
Macon	240 (43.7%)	309 (56.3%)	
Martin	567 (66.2%)	289 (33.8%)	
Mecklenburg	1,115 (62.1%)	680 (37.9%)	
Montgomery	132 (17.6%)	620 (82.4%)	
Moore	484 (47.0%)	546 (53.0%)	
Nash	1,030 (92.1%)	88 (7.9%)	
New Hanover	1,400 (78.5%)	383 (21.5%)	
Northampton	530 (53.8%)	455 (46.2%)	
Onslow	597 (77.3%)	175 (22.7%)	
Orange	1,307 (47.6%)	1,441 (52.4%)	
Pasquotank	316 (37.0%)	539 (63.0%)	
Perquimans	270 (45.5%)	324 (54.5%)	
Person	471 (64.2%)	263 (35.8%)	
Pitt	602 (47.0%)	679 (53.0%)	
Randolph	277 (21.1%)	1,036 (78.9%)	
Richmond	146 (17.7%)	678 (82.3%)	
Robeson	732 (52.6%)	660 (47.4%)	
Rockingham	823 (70.6%)	342 (29.4%)	
Rowan	672 (44.6%)	836 (55.4%)	
Rutherford	301 (28.3%)	761 (71.7%)	
Sampson	867 (58.9%)	604 (41.1%)	
Stanly	58 (7.5%)	714 (92.5%)	
Stokes	1,237 (53.4%)	1,081 (46.6%)	
Surry	937 (47.3%)	1,046 (52.7%)	
Tyrrell	87 (23.3%)	286 (76.7%)	
Wake	1,357 (56.8%)	1,032 (43.2%)	
Warren	691 (80.5%)	167 (19.5%)	
Washington	210 (41.0%)	302 (59.0%)	
Watauga	94 (34.3%)	180 (65.7%)	
Wayne	1,067 (78.9%)	286 (21.1%)	
Wilkes	242 (18.4%)	1,073 (81.6%)	
Yancey	357 (60.2%)	236 (39.8%)	
Total	**39,784 (50.4%)**	**39,108 (49.5%)**	**59 (0.1%)**
	*(39,744)		

SOURCE—Manuscript returns.

Ohio

County	Pierce (D)	Scott (W)	Hale (FS)
Adams	1,736 (54.6%)	1,213 (38.1%)	233 (7.3%)
Allen	1,536 (61.0%)	958 (38.1%)	23 (0.9%)
Ashland	2,434 (59.4%)	1,368 (33.4%)	297 (7.2%)
Ashtabula	1,075 (18.7%)	2,174 (37.8%)	2,502 (43.5%)
Athens	1,383 (39.5%)	1,750 (50.0%)	366 (10.5%)
Auglaize	1,480 (70.7%)	588 (28.1%)	24 (1.1%)
Belmont	2,694 (45.4%)	2,786 (46.9%)	454 (7.7%)
Brown	2,460 (54.0%)	1,703 (37.4%)	393 (8.6%)
Butler	3,579 (60.5%)	2,210 (37.4%)	122 (2.1%)
Carroll	1,355 (43.1%)	1,543 (49.1%)	242 (7.7%)
Champaign	1,687 (43.4%)	1,994 (51.3%)	206 (5.3%)
Clarke	1,374 (32.6%)	2,662 (63.1%)	183 (4.3%)
Clermont	2,765 (51.3%)	2,213 (41.1%)	409 (7.6%)
Clinton	1,063 (33.3%)	1,424 (44.7%)	702 (22.0%)
Columbiana	2,911 (47.4%)	2,237 (36.4%)	993 (16.2%)
Coshocton	2,618 (57.0%)	1,898 (41.4%)	73 (1.6%)
Crawford	2,106 (65.0%)	1,074 (33.2%)	58 (1.8%)
Cuyahoga	3,571 (41.4%)	2,945 (34.2%)	2,107 (24.4%)
Darke	1,797 (49.8%)	1,719 (47.6%)	92 (2.5%)
Defiance	895 (60.1%)	551 (37.0%)	43 (2.9%)
Delaware	1,591 (39.1%)	2,083 (51.2%)	391 (9.6%)
Erie	1,401 (42.9%)	1,589 (48.7%)	275 (8.4%)
Fairfield	3,211 (60.2%)	2,117 (39.7%)	10 (1.9%)
Fayette	893 (39.2%)	1,221 (53.6%)	166 (7.3%)
Franklin	3,652 (49.4%)	3,498 (47.3%)	242 (3.3%)
Fulton	727 (52.5%)	587 (42.4%)	71 (5.1%)
Gallia	1,103 (39.3%)	1,567 (55.9%)	135 (4.8%)
Geauga	664 (20.4%)	1,147 (35.3%)	1,439 (44.3%)
Greene	1,490 (33.7%)	2,430 (55.0%)	500 (11.3%)
Guernsey	1,809 (42.5%)	1,941 (45.6%)	503 (11.8%)
Hamilton	13,207 (57.1%)	9,253 (40.0%)	684 (3.0%)
Hancock	1,617 (59.3%)	1,076 (39.4%)	35 (1.3%)
Hardin	847 (47.0%)	882 (48.9%)	74 (4.1%)
Harrison	1,462 (40.5%)	1,723 (47.8%)	422 (11.7%)
Henry	536 (61.3%)	325 (37.1%)	14 (1.6%)
Highland	2,299 (50.4%)	1,982 (43.4%)	281 (6.2%)
Hocking	1,852 (67.6%)	865 (31.6%)	21 (7.7%)
Holmes	2,100 (65.5%)	1,066 (33.2%)	42 (13.1%)
Huron	1,819 (36.7%)	2,242 (42.3%)	893 (18.0%)
Jackson	1,093 (50.1%)	1,069 (49.0%)	19 (0.9%)
Jefferson	2,169 (48.1%)	1,995 (44.3%)	343 (5.4%)
Knox	2,692 (56.2%)	1,874 (39.1%)	226 (4.7%)
Lake	670 (23.7%)	1,046 (37.0%)	1,111 (39.3%)
Lawrence	981 (42.7%)	1,299 (56.6%)	15 (0.7%)
Licking	3,569 (51.5%)	2,779 (40.1%)	582 (8.4%)
Logan	1,361 (37.1%)	2,118 (57.7%)	191 (5.2%)
Lorain	1,553 (33.3%)	1,332 (28.6%)	1,777 (38.1%)
Lucas	1,271 (48.2%)	1,238 (46.9%)	129 (4.9%)
Madison	655 (31.0%)	1,400 (66.2%)	61 (2.9%)
Mahoning	1,873 (48.5%)	955 (24.7%)	1,033 (26.8%)
Marion	1,270 (56.1%)	914 (40.4%)	79 (3.5%)
Medina	1,754 (40.4%)	1,579 (36.4%)	1,008 (23.2%)
Meigs	1,399 (42.8%)	1,573 (48.1%)	297 (9.1%)
Mercer	829 (61.9%)	500 (37.3%)	11 (0.8%)
Miami	2,004 (40.1%)	2,754 (55.2%)	235 (4.7%)
Monroe	2,422 (67.3%)	997 (27.7%)	180 (5.0%)
Montgomery	3,744 (48.0%)	3,886 (49.8%)	177 (2.3%)
Morgan	1,708 (42.6%)	2,084 (51.9%)	220 (5.5%)
Morrow	1,710 (49.0%)	1,029 (29.5%)	748 (21.5%)
Muskingum	3,500 (44.1%)	4,228 (53.2%)	213 (2.7%)
Noble	1,487 (53.0%)	885 (31.5%)	435 (15.5%)
Ottawa	400 (59.2%)	274 (40.5%)	2 (0.3%)
Paulding	347 (73.4%)	121 (25.6%)	5 (1.1%)
Perry	2,246 (60.1%)	1,471 (39.4%)	17 (0.5%)
Pickaway	2,041 (48.0%)	2,175 (51.2%)	35 (0.8%)
Pike	1,029 (52.2%)	927 (47.0%)	16 (0.8%)
Portage	2,007 (41.3%)	1,551 (32.0%)	1,296 (26.7%)

County	Pierce (D)	Scott (W)	Hale (FS)
Preble	1,633 (40.0%)	2,253 (55.2%)	197 (4.8%)
Putnam	890 (63.0%)	461 (32.6%)	61 (4.3%)
Richland	3,234 (58.0%)	2,133 (38.3%)	209 (3.7%)
Ross	2,465 (43.0%)	3,091 (53.9%)	179 (3.1%)
Sandusky	1,619 (58.4%)	1,064 (38.4%)	88 (3.2%)
Scioto	1,424 (43.7%)	1,804 (55.4%)	29 (0.9%)
Seneca	2,809 (57.3%)	1,972 (40.3%)	118 (2.4%)
Shelby	1,309 (52.2%)	1,147 (45.7%)	54 (2.2%)
Stark	3,634 (54.0%)	2,740 (40.7%)	356 (5.3%)
Summit	1,965 (39.6%)	2,336 (47.1%)	660 (13.3%)
Trumbull	2,039 (35.5%)	1,968 (34.2%)	1,739 (30.3%)
Tuscarawas	2,685 (49.2%)	2,659 (48.7%)	112 (2.1%)
Union	943 (38.5%)	1,249 (51.0%)	255 (10.4%)
Van Wert	737 (63.3%)	422 (36.2%)	6 (0.5%)
Vinton	912 (51.2%)	774 (43.5%)	95 (5.3%)
Warren	1,919 (38.6%)	2,823 (56.8%)	224 (4.5%)
Washington	2,139 (44.2%)	2,369 (48.9%)	332 (6.9%)
Wayne	3,143 (57.4%)	2,288 (41.8%)	49 (0.9%)
Williams	832 (54.1%)	546 (35.5%)	160 (10.4%)
Wood	986 (53.7%)	831 (45.2%)	20 (1.1%)
Wyandot	1,290 (56.4%)	990 (43.3%)	9 (0.4%)
Total	**169,190 (48.0%)**	**152,577 (43.2%)**	**31,133 (8.9%)**
	*(168,933)	*(152,523)	*(31,732)

*Stated totals.

SOURCE—*Executive Documents, 1865.*

Pennsylvania

County	Pierce (D)	Scott (W)	Hale (FS)	Broome (A)
Adams	2,018 (42.3%)	2,725 (57.1%)	31 (0.6%)	
Allegheny	7,226 (40.0%)	9,615 (53.3%)	965 (5.3%)	239 (1.3%)
Armstrong	2,430 (52.0%)	2,093 (44.8%)	142 (3.0%)	9 (0.2%)
Beaver	1,943 (46.0%)	1,805 (42.8%)	361 (8.6%)	111 (2.6%)
Bedford	2,319 (50.5%)	2,273 (49.5%)	0	
Berks	9,503 (65.9%)	4,913 (34.1%)	5 (0.03%)	2 (0.01%)
Blair	1,931 (42.7%)	2,590 (57.2%)	5 (0.1%)	
Bradford	3,930 (50.8%)	3,526 (45.6%)	281 (3.6%)	
Bucks	5,766 (53.5%)	4,928 (45.7%)	58 (0.5%)	22 (0.2%)
Butler	2,533 (45.8%)	2,833 (51.2%)	165 (3.0%)	1 (0.02%)
Cambria	2,035 (58.0%)	1,461 (41.6%)	15 (0.4%)	
Carbon	1,311 (63.6%)	749 (36.4%)	0	
Centre	2,993 (61.0%)	1,916 (39.0%)	0	
Chester	5,520 (47.8%)	5,700 (49.3%)	338 (2.9%)	
Clarion	2,642 (68.0%)	1,218 (31.3%)	28 (0.7%)	
Clearfield	1,733 (62.9%)	997 (36.2%)	24 (0.9%)	
Clinton	1,318 (56.9%)	996 (43.0%)	2 (0.1%)	
Columbia	2,102 (64.3%)	1,165 (35.7%)	0	
Crawford	3,427 (47.6%)	2,775 (38.6%)	996 (13.8%)	
Cumberland	3,188 (52.6%)	2,878 (47.4%)	0	
Dauphin	2,675 (41.9%)	3,673 (57.6%)	29 (0.5%)	
Delaware	1,737 (44.2%)	2,083 (53.0%)	107 (2.7%)	
Elk	423 (70.4%)	163 (27.1%)	14 (2.3%)	
Erie	2,748 (37.3%)	4,016 (54.5%)	611 (8.3%)	
Fayette	3,867 (55.5%)	3,030 (43.5%)	72 (1.0%)	
Franklin	3,358 (46.2%)	3,904 (53.7%)	3 (0.04%)	
Fulton	831 (53.2%)	729 (46.7%)	1 (0.1%)	
Greene	2,602 (62.1%)	1,559 (37.2%)	30 (0.7%)	
Huntingdon	2,041 (44.8%)	2,511 (55.1%)	2 (0.04%)	
Indiana	1,827 (40.7%)	2,387 (53.1%)	278 (6.2%)	
Jefferson	1,484 (56.6%)	1,115 (42.5%)	22 (0.8%)	
Juniata	823 (59.6%)	559 (40.4%)	0	
Lancaster	6,578 (36.0%)	11,637 (63.7%)	53 (0.3%)	3 (0.02%)
Lawrence	1,064 (29.9%)	1,984 (55.7%)	514 (14.4%)	
Lebanon	2,118 (40.5%)	3,105 (59.4%)	1 (0.02%)	
Lehigh	3,493 (53.8%)	2,993 (46.1%)	2 (0.03%)	
Luzerne	5,340 (61.0%)	3,339 (38.1%)	79 (0.9%)	
Lycoming	2,790 (57.2%)	2,085 (42.7%)	5 (0.1%)	1 (0.02%)

County	Pierce (D)	Scott (W)	Hale (FS)	Broome (A)
McKean	597 (55.3%)	405 (37.5%)	78 (7.2%)	
Mercer	2,693 (47.5%)	2,211 (39.0%)	769 (13.6%)	
Mifflin	1,620 (53.8%)	1,392 (46.2%)	0	
Monroe	2,098 (83.4%)	418 (16.6%)	0	
Montgomery	5,767 (53.8%)	4,791 (44.7%)	160 (1.5%)	4 (0.04%)
Montour	1,455 (62.7%)	866 (37.3%)	0	
Northampton	4,403 (59.5%)	2,979 (40.3%)	16 (0.2%)	
Northumberland	2,451 (60.2%)	1,619 (39.7%)	4 (0.1%)	
Perry	2,159 (60.4%)	1,413 (39.6%)	0	
Philadelphia	26,026 (49.7%)	24,572 (46.9%)	626 (1.2%)	1,148 (2.2%)
Pike	834 (80.5%)	202 (19.5%)	0	
Potter	661 (52.9%)	263 (21.1%)	325 (26.0%)	
Schuylkill	4,758 (52.6%)	4,170 (46.1%)	10 (0.1%)	104 (1.2%)
Somerset	1,203 (28.5%)	2,986 (70.8%)	28 (0.7%)	
Susquehanna	3,046 (57.5%)	2,034 (38.4%)	215 (4.1%)	
Sullivan	426 (64.4%)	177 (26.7%)	59 (8.9%)	
Tioga	2,614 (61.4%)	1,564 (36.7%)	81 (1.9%)	
Union	2,003 (39.5%)	3,072 (60.5%)	0	
Venango	1,899 (58.1%)	1,164 (35.6%)	204 (6.2%)	2 (0.1%)
Warren	1,433 (50.9%)	1,138 (40.4%)	243 (8.6%)	
Washington	4,064 (49.2%)	3,810 (46.1%)	370 (4.5%)	20 (0.2%)
Wayne	2,362 (65.4%)	1,232 (34.1%)	20 (0.6%)	
Westmoreland	5,509 (62.4%)	3,203 (36.3%)	119 (1.3%)	
Wyoming	1,258 (60.3%)	807 (38.7%)	19 (0.9%)	
York	5,585 (54.2%)	4,700 (45.6%)	11 (1.1%)	11 (1.1%)
Total	**198,591 (51.2%)**	**179,216 (46.2%)**	**8,596 (2.2%)**	**1,677 (0.4%)**
	*(198,590)	*(179,128)	*(8,496)	

SOURCE—*Legislative Documents of the Commonwealth of Pennsylvania*, Harrisburg, PA: 1857, pp. 680–690.

Rhode Island

County	Pierce (D)	Scott (W)	Hale (FS)
Bristol	367 (36.8%)	628 (63.0%)	2 (0.2%)
Kent	748 (44.8%)	839 (50.2%)	83 (5.0%)
Newport	1,005 (43.7%)	1,249 (54.3%)	48 (2.1%)
Providence	5,529 (56.1%)	3,888 (39.5%)	431 (4.4%)
Washington	1,086 (49.6%)	1,022 (46.7%)	80 (3.7%)
Total	**8,735 (51.4%)**	**7,626 (44.9%)**	**644 (3.8%)**

SOURCE—*Providence Daily Patriot*, November 15, 1852.

Tennessee

County	Pierce (D)	Scott (W)
Anderson	267 (30.7%)	602 (69.3%)
Bedford	1,356 (49.4%)	1,390 (50.6%)
Benton	485 (58.8%)	340 (41.2%)
Bledsoe	209 (31.1%)	464 (68.9%)
Blount	566 (40.6%)	827 (59.4%)
Bradley	778 (58.3%)	547 (41.7%)
Campbell	251 (44.5%)	313 (55.5%)
Cannon	727 (61.6%)	453 (38.4%)
Carroll	649 (30.2%)	1,498 (69.8%)
Carter	139 (19.2%)	585 (80.8%)
Claiborne	519 (50.8%)	508 (49.2%)
Cocke	196 (20.9%)	743 (79.1%)
Coffee	722 (77.9%)	205 (22.1%)
Davidson	2,058 (44.0%)	2,617 (56.0%)
Decatur	315 (44.1%)	400 (55.9%)
De Kalb	588 (51.3%)	559 (48.7%)
Dickson	607 (65.3%)	323 (34.7%)
Dyer	411 (44.7%)	508 (55.3%)
Fayette	1,034 (50.7%)	1,006 (49.3%)
Fentress	411 (72.9%)	153 (27.1%)
Franklin	1,133 (77.4%)	330 (22.6%)
Gibson	901 (36.5%)	1,570 (63.5%)
Giles	1,447 (52.6%)	1,303 (47.4%)
Grainger	477 (35.9%)	852 (64.1%)
Greene	1,301 (62.5%)	780 (37.5%)
Grundy	327 (88.1%)	44 (11.9%)
Hamilton	648 (45.6%)	774 (54.4%)
Hancock	336 (58.2%)	241 (41.8%)
Hardeman	1,024 (58.8%)	717 (41.2%)
Hardin	808 (55.7%)	643 (44.3%)
Hawkins	831 (51.6%)	778 (48.4%)
Haywood	732 (48.1%)	790 (51.9%)
Henderson	511 (30.0%)	1,193 (70.0%)
Henry	1,516 (62.8%)	899 (37.2%)
Hickman	839 (77.7%)	241 (22.3%)
Humphreys	471 (63.7%)	263 (36.3%)
Jackson	803 (40.7%)	1,170 (59.3%)
Jefferson	307 (20.8%)	1,168 (79.2%)
Johnson	93 (20.3%)	365 (79.7%)
Knox	565 (23.3%)	1,863 (76.7%)
Lauderdale	277 (45.6%)	330 (54.4%)
Lawrence	583 (51.6%)	547 (48.4%)
Lewis	186 (81.2%)	43 (18.8%)
Lincoln	2,297 (79.1%)	606 (20.9%)
Macon	374 (37.7%)	617 (62.3%)
Madison	819 (36.5%)	1,426 (63.5%)
Marion	292 (39.2%)	453 (60.8%)
Marshall	1,340 (66.8%)	666 (33.2%)
Maury	1,799 (57.6%)	1,324 (42.4%)
McMinn	866 (52.1%)	796 (47.9%)
McNairy	872 (48.6%)	921 (51.4%)
Meigs	442 (75.8%)	141 (24.2%)
Monroe	847 (51.3%)	805 (48.7%)
Montgomery	903 (41.7%)	1,260 (58.3%)
Morgan	222 (48.1%)	240 (51.9%)
Obion	644 (59.9%)	431 (40.1%)
Overton	1,089 (75.9%)	345 (24.1%)
Perry	314 (49.1%)	325 (50.9%)
Polk	470 (63.3%)	272 (36.7%)

Rhea	307 (50.5%)	300 (49.5%)
Roane	678 (45.3%)	820 (54.7%)
Robertson	769 (43.2%)	1,013 (56.8%)
Rutherford	1,313 (46.8%)	1,495 (53.2%)
Scott	127 (39.0%)	199 (61.0%)
Sevier	80 (11.4%)	621 (88.6%)
Shelby	1,628 (47.2%)	1,824 (52.8%)
Smith	520 (23.0%)	1,742 (77.0%)
Stewart	725 (57.6%)	533 (42.4%)
Sullivan	1,114 (81.1%)	260 (18.9%)
Sumner	1,563 (65.5%)	825 (34.5%)
Tipton	565 (61.3%)	357 (38.7%)
Van Buren	165 (60.7%)	107 (39.3%)
Warren	922 (72.8%)	344 (27.2%)
Washington	853 (60.2%)	565 (39.8%)
Wayne	380 (36.3%)	666 (63.7%)
Weakley	1,149 (59.5%)	783 (40.5%)
White	518 (35.3%)	949 (64.7%)
Williamson	763 (32.5%)	1,583 (67.5%)
Wilson	923 (29.1%)	2,248 (70.9%)
Total	**57,056 (49.2%)**	**58,807 (50.8%)**
*Stated totals.	*(57,123)	*(58,807)

SOURCE—*Nashville True Whig*, August 10, 1853.

Texas

No returns were located for this election for Smith County.

County	Pierce (D)	Scott (W)
Anderson	412 (73.3%)	150 (26.7%)
Angelina	56 (66.7%)	28 (33.3%)
Bastrop	243 (72.1%)	94 (27.9%)
Bell	157 (85.8%)	26 (14.2%)
Bexar	804 (72.9%)	299 (27.1%)
Brazos	34 (79.1%)	9 (20.9%)
Bueleson	103 (84.4%)	19 (15.6%)
Burnet	21 (100%)	0
Caldwell	235 (73.7%)	84 (26.3%)
Cass	75 (71.4%)	30 (28.6%)
Cherokee	696 (73.7%)	248 (26.3%)
Collin	133 (69.6%)	58 (30.4%)
Colorado	92 (75.4%)	30 (24.6%)
Comal	112 (94.9%)	6 (5.1%)
Cooke	14 (73.7%)	5 (26.3%)
Dallas	383 (75.8%)	108 (24.2%)
Denton	37 (100%)	0
Ellis	90 (67.7%)	43 (32.3%)
Fannin	208 (76.8%)	63 (23.2%)
Fayette	341 (67.4%)	165 (32.6%)
Fort Bend	86 (73.5%)	31 (26.5%)
Galveston	324 (69.7%)	141 (30.3%)
Gillespie	74 (97.4%)	2 (2.6%)
Gonzales	208 (65.0%)	112 (35.0%)
Grayson	198 (80.5%)	48 (19.5%)
Grimes	142 (72.4%)	54 (27.6%)
Guadalupe	145 (68.1%)	68 (31.9%)
Harris	468 (70.9%)	195 (29.1%)
Harrison	400 (58.6%)	283 (41.4%)
Hays	55 (74.3%)	21 (25.7%)
Henderson	74 (76.3%)	23 (23.7%)
Houston	125 (73.1%)	46 (26.9%)
Hunt	121 (86.4%)	19 (13.6%)
Jackson	90 (73.2%)	33 (26.8%)
Jasper	121 (80.1%)	30 (19.9%)
Lamar	189 (76.8%)	57 (23.2%)
Lavaca	85 (72.0%)	33 (28.0%)
Leon	124 (72.1%)	48 (27.9%)
Liberty	87 (68.5%)	40 (31.5%)
Limestone	176 (82.2%)	38 (17.8%)

Matagorda	74 (71.2%)	30 (28.8%)
McLennan	45 (90.0%)	5 (10.0%)
Medina	42 (95.5%)	2 (4.5%)
Milam	119 (68.4%)	55 (31.6%)
Montgomery	120 (61.9%)	74 (38.1%)
Nacogdoches	312 (79.8%)	79 (20.2%)
Newton	111 (88.9%)	16 (11.1%)
Nueces	52 (71.2%)	21 (28.8%)
Orange	39 (62.9%)	23 (37.1%)
Red River	233 (73.0%)	86 (27.0%)
Robertson	95 (67.6%)	53 (32.4%)
Rusk	588 (70.8%)	242 (29.2%)
Sabine	81 (86.2%)	13 (13.8%)
San Augustine	158 (84.5%)	29 (15.5%)
San Patricio	30 (100%)	0
Shelby	106 (85.5%)	19 (14.5%)
Tarrant	60 (98.4%)	1 (1.6%)
Titus	240 (70.6%)	100 (29.4%)
Travis	370 (75.8%)	118 (24.2%)
Trinity	17 (100%)	0
Van Zandt	43 (100%)	0
Victoria	96 (53.3%)	84 (46.7%)
Walker	228 (76.0%)	72 (24.0%)
Washington	519 (72.3%)	199 (27.7%)
Wharton	59 (77.6%)	17 (22.4%)
Williamson	143 (69.8%)	62 (30.2%)
Total[10]	**11,519 (73.3%)**	**4,187 (26.7%)**

SOURCES—Manuscript returns; and W. Dean Burnham, *Presidential Ballots 1836–1892* (reprint edition), New York, NY: Arno Press, 1976.

Vermont

County	Pierce (D)	Scott (W)	Hale (FS)
Addison	378 (12.3%)	2,041 (66.7%)	642 (21.0%)
Bennington	1,150 (42.3%)	1,388 (51.0%)	181 (6.7%)
Caledonia	1,480 (40.7%)	1,673 (46.0%)	487 (13.4%)
Chittenden	803 (23.7%)	1,672 (49.4%)	908 (26.8%)
Essex	382 (44.2%)	567 (54.0%)	16 (1.8%)
Franklin	1,211 (35.5%)	1,675 (49.1%)	526 (15.4%)
Grand Isle	186 (36.3%)	295 (57.6%)	31 (6.1%)
Lamoille	462 (29.9%)	394 (25.5%)	689 (44.6%)
Orange	1,555 (37.9%)	1,799 (43.8%)	752 (18.3%)
Orleans	859 (36.3%)	1,199 (50.7%)	308 (13.0%)
Rutland	938 (21.0%)	2,758 (61.7%)	773 (17.3%)
Washington	1,231 (32.0%)	1,402 (36.4%)	1,217 (31.6%)
Windham	881 (22.6%)	2,035 (52.2%)	986 (25.3%)
Windsor	1,528 (25.5%)	3,358 (56.1%)	1,105 (18.5%)
Total	**13,044 (29.8%)**	**22,156 (50.6%)**	**8,621 (19.7%)**

SOURCE—Manuscript returns.

Virginia

County	Pierce (D)	Scott (W)
Accomac	564 (49.5%)	576 (50.5%)
Albemarle	1,106 (48.7%)	1,163 (51.3%)
Alexandria	577 (42.4%)	784 (57.6%)
Alleghany	206 (68.9%)	93 (31.1%)
Amelia	237 (62.0%)	145 (38.0%)
Amherst	559 (55.4%)	450 (44.6%)
Appomattox	352 (79.3%)	192 (20.7%)
Augusta	1,388 (45.3%)	1,674 (54.7%)
Barbour	592 (64.6%)	324 (35.4%)
Bath	179 (53.2%)	157 (46.8%)
Bedford	965 (44.8%)	1,189 (55.2%)
Berkeley	924 (55.2%)	751 (44.8%)

Boone	212 (64.4%)	117	(35.6%)
Botetourt	738 (63.7%)	421	(36.3%)
Braxton	290 (42.8%)	387	(57.2%)
Brooke	460 (62.1%)	281	(37.9%)
Brunswick	462 (71.2%)	187	(28.8%)
Buckingham	530 (54.7%)	438	(45.3%)
Cabell	424 (48.5%)	457	(51.5%)
Campbell	879 (44.4%)	1,101	(55.6%)
Caroline	621 (58.4%)	443	(41.6%)
Carroll	488 (69.6%)	213	(30.4%)
Charles City	89 (33.6%)	176	(66.4%)
Charlotte	369 (52.3%)	337	(47.7%)
Chesterfield	854 (67.6%)	409	(32.4%)
Clarke	386 (51.5%)	363	(48.5%)
Craig	238 (72.1%)	92	(27.9%)
Culpeper	461 (50.8%)	447	(49.2%)
Cumberland	252 (49.6%)	256	(50.4%)
Dinwiddie	304 (48.8%)	319	(51.2%)
Doddridge	285 (76.8%)	86	(23.2%)
Elizabeth City	211 (57.5%)	156	(42.5%)
Essex	233 (46.0%)	273	(54.0%)
Fairfax	606 (49.9%)	608	(50.1%)
Fauquier	1,045 (53.0%)	928	(47.0%)
Fayette	243 (47.8%)	265	(52.2%)
Floyd	301 (43.9%)	384	(56.1%)
Fluvanna	378 (46.2%)	440	(53.8%)
Franklin	802 (59.6%)	620	(40.4%)
Frederick	1,421 (58.1%)	1,024	(41.9%)
Giles	350 (54.9%)	287	(45.1%)
Gilmer	324 (74.0%)	114	(26.0%)
Gloucester	372 (58.2%)	267	(41.8%)
Goochland	396 (67.0%)	195	(33.0%)
Grayson	267 (54.6%)	222	(45.4%)
Greenbrier	498 (43.6%)	644	(56.4%)
Greene	416 (82.7%)	87	(17.3%)
Greensville	168 (71.4%)	67	(28.6%)
Halifax	1,096 (73.0%)	405	(27.0%)
Hampshire	1,115 (60.0%)	743	(40.0%)
Hancock	349 (59.2%)	241	(40.8%)
Hanover	554 (55.2%)	450	(44.8%)
Hardy	532 (38.3%)	858	(61.7%)
Harrison	992 (62.3%)	601	(37.7%)
Henrico	548 (45.9%)	646	(54.1%)
Henry	332 (50.2%)	330	(49.8%)
Highland	431 (71.7%)	170	(28.3%)
Isle of Wight	645 (79.0%)	171	(21.0%)
Jackson	459 (51.1%)	439	(48.9%)
James City	45 (31.7%)	97	(68.3%)
Jefferson	898 (48.4%)	958	(51.6%)
Kanawha	776 (38.8%)	1,226	(61.2%)
King & Queen	349 (67.3%)	169	(32.7%)
King George	166 (55.7%)	132	(44.3%)
King William	246 (71.3%)	99	(28.7%)
Lancaster	122 (47.3%)	136	(52.7%)
Lee	773 (62.5%)	463	(37.5%)
Lewis	566 (71.6%)	224	(28.4%)
Logan	308 (64.0%)	173	(36.0%)
Loudoun	788 (30.3%)	1,813	(69.7%)
Louisa	503 (58.6%)	356	(41.4%)
Lunenburg	374 (70.2%)	159	(29.8%)
Madison	646 (85.8%)	107	(14.2%)
Marion	1,197 (68.1%)	560	(31.9%)
Marshall	721 (49.2%)	743	(50.8%)
Mason	476 (47.0%)	536	(53.0%)
Matthews	255 (59.0%)	177	(41.0%)
Mecklenburg	680 (69.1%)	304	(30.9%)
Mercer	279 (51.1%)	268	(48.9%)
Middlesex	157 (62.3%)	95	(37.7%)
Monongalia	1,308 (65.5%)	688	(34.5%)
Monroe	499 (50.1%)	497	(49.9%)
Montgomery	490 (49.4%)	501	(50.6%)

Morgan	259 (47.3%)	270	(52.7%)
Nansemond	462 (48.0%)	500	(52.0%)
Nelson	444 (42.9%)	591	(57.1%)
New Kent	148 (46.0%)	174	(54.0%)
Nicholas	167 (39.9%)	252	(60.1%)
Norfolk	1,224 (57.1%)	921	(42.9%)
Northampton	144 (32.6%)	298	(67.4%)
Northumberland	279 (57.3%)	208	(42.7%)
Nottoway	185 (60.2%)	122	(39.8%)
Ohio	1,186 (45.0%)	1,452	(55.0%)
Orange	343 (54.2%)	290	(45.8%)
Page	870 (88.8%)	110	(11.2%)
Patrick	399 (44.9%)	489	(55.1%)
Pendleton	381 (50.4%)	375	(49.6%)
Pleasants	237 (60.9%)	152	(39.1%)
Pittsylvania	877 (50.4%)	864	(49.6%)
Pocahontas	240 (67.4%)	116	(32.6%)
Powhatan	243 (66.6%)	122	(33.4%)
Preston	923 (58.8%)	647	(41.2%)
Prince Edward	302 (57.1%)	227	(42.9%)
Prince George	282 (75.6%)	91	(24.4%)
Princess Anne	342 (45.5%)	409	(54.5%)
Prince William	534 (73.8%)	190	(26.2%)
Pulaski	223 (56.2%)	174	(43.8%)
Putnam	370 (51.5%)	348	(48.5%)
Raleigh	68 (34.7%)	128	(65.3%)
Randolph	337 (52.8%)	301	(47.2%)
Rappahannock	436 (56.8%)	331	(43.2%)
Richmond	181 (43.6%)	234	(56.4%)
Ritchie	381 (67.0%)	188	(33.0%)
Roanoke	384 (64.9%)	208	(35.1%)
Rockbridge	1,084 (51.3%)	1,031	(48.7%)
Rockingham	2,473 (81.1%)	575	(18.9%)
Russell	275 (47.7%)	301	(52.3%)
Scott	577 (62.0%)	354	(38.0%)
Shenandoah	2,094 (87.8%)	291	(12.2%)
Smyth	479 (52.5%)	434	(47.5%)
Southampton	456 (47.8%)	498	(52.2%)
Spotsylvania	565 (56.2%)	440	(43.8%)
Stafford	447 (62.4%)	269	(37.6%)
Surry	201 (57.8%)	147	(42.2%)
Sussex	322 (75.1%)	107	(24.9%)
Taylor	383 (52.2%)	351	(47.8%)
Tazewell	612 (71.6%)	243	(28.4%)
Tyler	383 (53.0%)	340	(47.0%)
Upshur	439 (57.5%)	324	(42.5%)
Warren	520 (75.5%)	169	(24.5%)
Warwick	14 (17.5%)	66	(82.5%)
Washington	924 (56.3%)	715	(43.7%)
Wayne	206 (47.8%)	225	(52.2%)
Westmoreland	83 (22.9%)	280	(77.1%)
Wetzel	488 (82.7%)	102	(17.3%)
Wirt	288 (56.5%)	222	(43.5%)
Wood	607 (48.5%)	645	(51.5%)
Wyoming	29 (40.8%)	42	(59.2%)
Wythe	615 (64.9%)	333	(35.1%)
York	90 (41.1%)	129	(58.9%)

Cities & Towns

Norfolk	792 (50.8%)	767	(49.2%)
Petersburg	759 (59.6%)	515	(40.4%)
Richmond	1,012 (35.3%)	1,854	(64.7%)
Williamsburg	68 (64.8%)	37	(35.2%)
Total	**73,833 (55.7%)**	**58,732**	**(44.3%)**
	*(73,872)		

*Stated total.

SOURCES—*Richmond Enquirer*, December 14, 1852; W. Dean Burnham, *Presidential Ballots 1836–1892* (reprint edition), New York, NY: Arno Press, 1976, pp.816–843, 852–864, 948; and *Politicians Text Book*.

Wisconsin

County	Pierce (D)	Scott (W)	Hale (FS)
Bad Ax	87 (55.8%)	69 (44.2%)	0
Brown	515 (60.8%)	326 (38.5%)	6 (7.1%)
Calumet	294 (60.5%)	171 (35.2%)	21 (4.3%)
Columbia	1,233 (51.9%)	1,111 (46.8%)	31 (1.3%)
Crawford	173 (56.9%)	131 (43.1%)	0
Dane	2,138 (60.6%)	1,104 (31.3%)	287 (8.1%)
Dodge	2,264 (58.1%)	1,204 (30.9%)	430 (11.0%)
Fond du Lac	1,635 (52.6%)	1,065 (34.3%)	408 (13.1%)
Grant	1,379 (48.4%)	1,341 (47.1%)	129 (4.5%)
Green	865 (50.6%)	659 (38.5%)	186 (10.9%)
Iowa	948 (50.7%)	895 (47.9%)	27 (1.4%)
Jefferson	1,693 (52.0%)	1,203 (37.0%)	359 (11.0%)
Kenosha	590 (34.5%)	483 (28.3%)	636 (37.2%)
Kewaunee	23 (82.1%)	5 (17.9%)	0
La Crosse	281 (59.4%)	182 (38.5%)	10 (2.1%)
Lafayette	1,389 (61.6%)	850 (37.7%)	16 (0.7%)
Manitowoc	874 (80.0%)	209 (19.1%)	9 (0.8%)
Marathon	202 (59.1%)	140 (40.9%)	0
Marquette	982 (50.1%)	748 (38.1%)	232 (11.8%)
Milwaukee	3,639 (58.9%)	2,017 (32.6%)	527 (8.5%)
Outagamie	412 (68.3%)	140 (23.2%)	51 (8.5%)
Portage	377 (58.5%)	267 (41.5%)	0
Racine	1,308 (44.6%)	840 (28.6%)	787 (26.8%)
Richland	166 (47.6%)	167 (47.9%)	16 (4.6%)
Rock	1,690 (41.0%)	1,509 (36.6%)	920 (22.3%)
St. Croix	166 (60.4%)	107 (38.9%)	2 (0.7%)
Sauk	681 (46.7%)	622 (42.6%)	156 (10.7%)
Sheboygan	1,340 (60.6%)	656 (29.7%)	214 (9.7%)
Walworth	1,141 (40.5%)	965 (27.3%)	1,433 (40.5%)
Washington	2,350 (63.7%)	1,156 (31.3%)	182 (4.9%)
Waukesha	1,614 (44.4%)	949 (26.1%)	1,075 (29.5%)
Waupeca	86 (47.3%)	95 (52.2%)	1 (0.5%)
Waushara	174 (39.8%)	147 (33.6%)	116 (26.5%)
Winnebago	949 (42.5%)	707 (31.7%)	575 (25.8%)
Total	**33,658 (52.0%)**	**22,240 (34.4%)**	**8,842 (13.7%)**
*Adams	86 (43.1%)	111 (56.9%)	0
*Oconto	101 (58.7%)	71 (41.3%)	0

Not included in the official returns.

SOURCES—James R. Donoghue, *How Wisconsin Voted, 1848–1872,* 3rd Edition, Madison, WI: Institute of Governmental Affairs, University of Wisconsin, p. 73; and the *Whig Almanac* 1853, p. 61.

NOTES

1. The electoral vote for vice president was William R. D. King (D) 254, and William A. Graham (W) 42.

2. George T. Troup (SoR) 2,205.

3. Independent Democrat 5,811 (5,804) and Webster (UW) 5,321.

4. Daniel Webster (UW) 1,670.

5. Jacob Broome (A) 738.

6. Daniel Webster (UW) 387 and Gerrit Smith (Ab) 72.

7. Jacob Broome (A) 1,677.

8. The national totals for those listed under "all others" were: Troup (SoR) 2,205 (0.07%); Independent Democrats, 5,811 (0.18%), (5,804 [0.18%]); Daniel Webster (UW and W) 7,378 (0.23%); Jacob Broome (A) 2,415 (0.08%); and Gerrit Smith (Ab) 72 (0.002%).

9. This was a separate slate of independent Democrats pledged to Pierce.

10. The official returns dated November 29, 1852, include the vote of 65 counties. However W. Dean Burnham's *Presidential Ballots* includes the vote of 17 additional counties listed below, citing "Official manuscript returns furnished by the State Librarian" as the source. They were received after the deadline and thus not included in the official returns.

County	Pierce (D)	Scott (W)
Austin	163 (75.8%)	52 (24.2%)
Brazoria	145 (75.5%)	47 (24.5%)
Caldwell	235 (73.7%)	84 (26.3%)
Calhoun	125 (57.1%)	94 (42.9%)
Cameron	329 (57.6%)	242 (42.4%)
De Witt	138 (67.6%)	66 (32.4%)
Goliad	37 (86.0%)	6 (14.0%)
Hidalgo	119 (71.3%)	48 (28.7%)
Hopkins	116 (80.0%)	29 (20.0%)
Navarro	220 (71.2%)	89 (18.8%)
Panola	192 (80.3%)	47 (19.7%)
Polk	175 (70.0%)	75 (30.0%)
Starr	72 (51.8%)	67 (48.2%)
Tyler	52 (91.2%)	5 (8.8%)
Upshur	361 (72.5%)	137 (27.5%)
Webb	116 (87.9%)	16 (12.1%)
Wood	42 (73.7%)	15 (26.3%)
Total	*2,637*	*1,119*

1 8 5 6

National Summary[1]

(electoral vote in parentheses)

State	James Buchanan (D)		John C. Frémont (R)		Millard Fillmore (A&W)[2]		others	
Alabama	46,739 (62.08%)	**(9)**	0		28,552 (37.92%)			
Arkansas	21,910 (67.12%)	**(4)**	0		10,732 (32.88%)			
California	53,359 (48.39%)	**(4)**	20,710 (18.78%)		36,195 (32.83%)			
Connecticut	34,997 (43.57%)		42,717 (53.18%)	**(6)**	2,615 (3.26%)			
Delaware	8,003 (55.25%)	**(3)**	306 (2.11%)		6,175 (42.63%)			
Florida	6,358 (56.81%)	**(3)**	0		4,833 (43.19%)			
Georgia	56,579 (57.05%)	**(10)**	0		42,603 (42.95%)			
Illinois	105,528 (44.09%)	**(11)**	96,278 (40.23%)		37,531 (15.68%)			
Indiana	118,670 (50.41%)	**(13)**	94,376 (40.09%)		22,386 (9.51%)			
Iowa	37,568 (40.66%)		45,163 (48.88%)	**(4)**	9,663 (10.46%)			
Kentucky	69,509 (52.18%)	**(12)**	314 (0.02%)		63,391 (47.59%)			
Louisiana	22,164 (51.70%)	**(6)**	0		20,709 (48.30%)			
Maine	39,080 (35.60%)		67,379 (61.37%)	**(8)**	3,325 (3.02%)			
Maryland	39,115 (45.03%)		285 (0.33%)		47,462 (54.64%)	**(8)**		
Massachusetts	39,240 (23.49%)		108,190 (64.76%)	**(13)**	19,626 (11.75%)			
Michigan	52,139 (41.52%)		71,762 (57.15%)	**(6)**	1,660 (1.32%)			
Mississippi	35,386 (59.40%)	**(7)**	0		24,191 (40.60%)			
Missouri	58,360 (54.62%)	**(9)**	0		48,495 (45.38%)			
New Hampshire	31,891 (45.71%)		37,473 (53.71%)	**(5)**	410 (0.59%)			
New Jersey	46,943 (47.23%)	**(7)**	28,338 (28.51%)		24,115 (24.26%)			
New York	195,878 (32.90%)		274,705 (46.14%)	**(35)**	124,667 (20.94%)		165 (0.03%)[3]	
North Carolina	46,771 (56.41%)	**(10)**	0		36,143 (43.59%)			
Ohio	170,874 (44.19%)		187,517 (48.50%)	**(23)**	28,121 (7.27%)		155 (0.04%)[4]	
Pennsylvania	230,686 (50.13%)	**(27)**	147,286 (32.01%)		55,852 (12.14%)		26,337 (5.72%)[5]	
Rhode Island	6,680 (33.70%)		11,467 (57.85%)	**(4)**	1,675 (8.45%)			
South Carolina	**(8)** electors chosen by the legislature							
Tennessee	73,406 (52.50%)	**(12)**	0		66,425 (47.50%)			
Texas	29,139 (65.65%)	**(4)**	0		15,244 (34.35%)			
Vermont	10,579 (20.87%)		39,563 (78.05%)	**(5)**	545 (1.08%)			
Virginia	90,352 (59.93%)	**(15)**	286 (0.19%)		60,112 (39.88%)			
Wisconsin	52,843 (44.22%)		66,090 (55.30%)	**(5)**	579 (0.48%)			
Total	**1,830,746 (45.30%) (174)**		**1,340,205 (33.16%) (114)**		**844,032 (20.88%) (8)**		**26,657 (0.66%)[6]**	

Alabama

County	Buchanan (D)	Fillmore (A)
Autauga	621 (56.7%)	475 (43.3%)
Baldwin	144 (39.7%)	219 (60.3%)
Barbour	1,445 (62.8%)	857 (37.2%)
Benton	1,687 (79.2%)	443 (20.8%)
Bibb	539 (52.9%)	479 (47.1%)
Blount	770 (95.4%)	37 (4.6%)
Butler	777 (49.5%)	792 (50.5%)
Chambers	1,141 (54.1%)	967 (45.9%)
Cherokee	1,537 (77.2%)	455 (22.8%)
Choctaw	643 (61.4%)	404 (38.6%)
Clarke	754 (77.3%)	222 (22.7%)
Coffee	703 (70.0%)	301 (30.0%)
Conecuh	425 (51.0%)	408 (49.0%)
Coosa	1,167 (59.3%)	802 (40.7%)
Covington	304 (51.4%)	288 (48.6%)
Dale	945 (69.3%)	419 (30.7%)
Dallas	831 (55.1%)	676 (44.9%)
De Kalb	900 (87.4%)	130 (12.6%)
Fayette	799 (64.5%)	440 (35.5%)
Franklin	1,056 (59.8%)	711 (40.2%)
Greene	694 (47.0%)	784 (53.0%)
Hancock	221 (94.0%)	14 (6.0%)
Henry	966 (67.2%)	471 (32.8%)
Jackson	1,790 (94.9%)	97 (5.1%)
Jefferson	697 (78.1%)	196 (21.9%)
Lauderdale	1,141 (67.3%)	555 (32.7%)
Lawrence	699 (52.6%)	631 (47.4%)
Limestone	790 (73.8%)	281 (26.2%)
Lowndes	699 (49.9%)	703 (50.1%)
Macon	1,039 (45.6%)	1,239 (54.4%)
Madison	1,476 (78.6%)	401 (21.4%)
Marengo	789 (58.2%)	567 (41.8%)
Marion	700 (78.0%)	198 (22.0%)
Marshall	883 (90.8%)	89 (9.2%)
Mobile	1,838 (50.9%)	1,771 (49.1%)
Monroe	604 (56.3%)	469 (43.7%)
Montgomery	1,100 (48.7%)	1,158 (51.3%)
Morgan	808 (78.4%)	222 (21.6%)
Perry	808 (49.5%)	824 (50.5%)
Pickens	1,037 (60.8%)	669 (39.2%)
Pike	1,262 (51.7%)	1,178 (48.3%)
Randolph	1,460 (68.1%)	683 (31.9%)
Russell	994 (53.8%)	855 (46.2%)
St. Clair	818 (90.8%)	83 (9.2%)
Shelby	787 (62.7%)	468 (37.3%)

Sumter	703 (56.9%)	532 (43.1%)	
Talladega	1,134 (55.9%)	896 (44.1%)	
Tallapoosa	1,478 (53.7%)	1,276 (46.3%)	
Tuscaloosa	680 (41.1%)	973 (58.9%)	
Walker	449 (75.5%)	146 (24.5%)	
Washington	194 (56.1%)	152 (43.9%)	
Wilcox	813 (64.6%)	446 (35.4%)	
Total	**46,739 (62.1%)**	**28,552 (37.9%)**	

SOURCE—Loveman manuscript.

Arkansas

County	Buchanan (D)	Fillmore (A)
Arkansas	226 (50.2%)	224 (49.8%)
Ashley		no returns
Benton	753 (90.9%)	75 (9.1%)
Bradley	398 (53.7%)	343 (46.3%)
Calhoun	291 (81.5%)	56 (18.5%)
Carroll	655 (78.1%)	184 (21.9%)
Chicot	165 (51.2%)	157 (48.8%)
Clark	528 (73.3%)	192 (26.7%)
Columbia	676 (57.3%)	504 (42.7%)
Conway	408 (73.5%)	147 (26.5%)
Crawford	371 (69.7%)	161 (30.3%)
Crittenden		no returns
Dallas	335 (60.6%)	218 (39.4%)
Desha	334 (59.7%)	225 (40.3%)
Drew	377 (66.3%)	192 (33.7%)
Franklin	449 (79.5%)	116 (20.5%)
Fulton	210 (80.5%)	51 (19.5%)
Greene		no returns
Hempstead	610 (59.5%)	415 (40.5%)
Hot Spring	478 (78.5%)	131 (21.5%)
Independence	860 (58.4%)	612 (41.6%)

County	Buchanan (D)	Fillmore (A)
Izard	495 (84.0%)	94 (16.0%)
Jackson	591 (57.5%)	436 (42.5%)
Jefferson	515 (57.5%)	381 (42.5%)
Johnson	453 (80.0%)	113 (20.0%)
Lafayette	176 (59.5%)	120 (40.5%)
Lawrence	717 (71.8%)	282 (28.2%)
Madison	649 (89.1%)	79 (10.9%)
Marion	393 (75.7%)	126 (24.3%)
Mississippi	188 (60.8%)	121 (39.2%)
Monroe	233 (64.3%)	129 (35.7%)
Montgomery	356 (88.8%)	45 (11.2%)
Newton	132 (80.5%)	32 (19.5%)
Ouachita	701 (58.3%)	501 (41.7%)
Perry	125 (74.0%)	44 (26.0%)
Phillips	526 (53.1%)	464 (46.9%)
Pike	296 (86.3%)	47 (13.7%)
Poinsett	248 (77.3%)	73 (22.7%)
Polk		no returns
Pope	568 (77.7%)	163 (22.3%)
Prairie	393 (63.2%)	229 (36.8%)
Pulaski	739 (56.6%)	566 (43.4%)
Randolph	416 (86.1%)	67 (13.9%)
St. Francis	498 (61.8%)	308 (38.2%)
Saline	404 (65.5%)	213 (34.5%)
Scott	215 (68.7%)	98 (31.3%)
Searcy	303 (83.2%)	61 (16.8%)
Sebastian	302 (43.5%)	392 (56.5%)
Sevier	523 (68.9%)	236 (31.1%)
Union	626 (54.8%)	516 (45.2%)
Van Buren	305 (79.6%)	78 (20.4%)
Washington	917 (71.4%)	367 (28.6%)
White	403 (66.7%)	201 (33.3%)
Yell	383 (72.3%)	147 (27.7%)
Total	**21,910 (67.0%)**	**10,787 (33.0%)**

SOURCE—*Politicians' Text Book*, pp. 234–5.

California

No returns have been located for this election for Buena Vista County.

County	Buchanan (D)	Frémont (R)	Fillmore (A)
Alameda	729 (43.7%)	723 (43.4%)	213 (12.8%)
Amador	1,784 (44.6%)	657 (16.4%)	1,557 (38.4%)
Butte	2,501 (50.6%)	744 (15.0%)	1,702 (34.4%)
Calaveras	2,615 (55.7%)	561 (12.0%)	1,515 (32.3%)
Colusa	289 (47.2%)	18 (3.0%)	305 (49.8%)
Contra Costa	451 (48.3%)	190 (20.3%)	293 (31.4%)
El Dorado	4,048 (48.2%)	1,392 (16.6%)	2,959 (35.2%)
Fresno	218 (63.6%)	1 (0.3%)	124 (36.2%)
Humboldt	204 (41.0%)	103 (20.7%)	191 (38.4%)
*Klamath	832 (61.4%)	82 (6.1%)	440 (32.5%)
Los Angeles	722 (52.4%)	522 (37.9%)	135 (9.8%)
Marin	350 (59.4%)	157 (26.7%)	82 (13.9%)
Mariposa	1,255 (57.3%)	165 (7.5%)	771 (35.2%)
Merced	249 (64.3%)	14 (3.6%)	124 (32.1%)
Monterey	266 (40.7%)	219 (33.5%)	169 (25.8%)
Napa	444 (47.1%)	158 (16.8%)	341 (36.2%)
Nevada	3,498 (48.6%)	1,462 (20.3%)	2,241 (31.1%)
Placer	2,807 (47.6%)	992 (16.8%)	2,096 (35.6%)
Plumas	1,124 (51.0%)	217 (9.8%)	865 (39.2%)
Sacramento	3,437 (44.3%)	939 (12.1%)	3,387 (43.6%)
San Bernardino	314 (75.8%)	93 (22.5%)	7 (1.7%)
San Diego	172 (75.4%)	18 (7.9%)	38 (16.7%)
San Francisco	5,334 (44.3%)	5,097 (42.4%)	1,601 (13.3%)
San Joaquin	1,288 (44.8%)	547 (19.0%)	1,040 (36.2%)
San Luis Obispo	83 (40.5%)	107 (52.2%)	15 (7.3%)
San Mateo	282 (44.5%)	238 (37.6%)	113 (17.9%)
Santa Barbara	175 (47.6%)	183 (49.7%)	10 (2.7%)

County	Buchanan (D)	Frémont (R)	Fillmore (A)
Santa Cruz	576 (28.0%)	809 (39.3%)	674 (32.7%)
Santa Clara	320 (39.8%)	196 (24.4%)	288 (35.8%)
Shasta	1,537 (55.1%)	169 (6.0%)	1,083 (38.9%)
Sierra	2,504 (46.4%)	693 (12.8%)	2,203 (40.8%)
Siskiyou	2,072 (47.9%)	464 (10.7%)	1,790 (41.4%)
Solano	799 (49.2%)	190 (11.7%)	634 (39.1%)
Sonoma & Mendocino	1,519 (63.3%)	382 (15.9%)	498 (20.8%)
Stanislaus	436 (63.6%)	21 (3.1%)	228 (33.3%)
Sutter	491 (52.8%)	92 (9.9%)	347 (37.3%)
Tehama	436 (55.1%)	44 (5.6%)	312 (39.4%)
Trinity	1,011 (48.6%)	188 (9.0%)	882 (42.4%)
Tulare	248 (60.5%)	23 (5.6%)	139 (33.9%)
Tuolumne	2,935 (48.1%)	1,059 (17.3%)	2,113 (34.6%)
Yolo	553 (43.7%)	130 (10.3%)	583 (46.0%)
Yuba	2,451 (47.2%)	652 (12.6%)	2,087 (40.2%)
Total	**52,534 (48.3%)**	**20,622 (18.9%)**	**35,733 (32.8%)**

The manuscript returns do not include any vote for Klamath County. The vote included here was in the (San Francisco) Daily Alta of December 6, 1856, whose returns are listed as official.

SOURCES—Manuscript returns; and (San Francisco) *Daily Alta*, December 6, 1856.

Connecticut

County	Buchanan (D)	Frémont (R)	Fillmore (A&W)
Fairfield	5,539 (43.6%)	6,234 (49.1%)	928 (7.3%)
Hartford	7,038 (44.6%)	8,416 (53.4%)	309 (2.0%)
Litchfield	3,986 (41.4%)	5,482 (57.0%)	150 (1.6%)
Middlesex	2,965 (49.1%)	2,887 (47.8%)	183 (3.0%)
New Haven	7,315 (46.0%)	7,975 (50.2%)	604 (3.8%)
New London	3,953 (40.7%)	5,403 (55.7%)	350 (3.6%)
Tolland	1,953 (44.4%)	2,407 (54.8%)	35 (0.8%)
Windham	2,248 (36.2%)	3,913 (62.9%)	56 (0.9%)
Total	**34,997 (43.6%)**	**42,717 (53.2%)**	**2,615 (3.3%)**

SOURCE—(Connecticut) *State Register & Manual, 1889.*

Delaware

County	Buchanan (D)	Frémont (R)	Fillmore (A)
Kent	2,083 (57.7%)	0	1,530 (42.3%)
New Castle	3,576 (55.0%)	306 (4.7%)	2,625 (40.3%)
Sussex	2,344 (53.7%)	0	2,020 (46.3%)
Total	**8,003 (55.3%)**	**306 (2.1%)**	**6,175 (42.6%)**

SOURCE—(Wilmington) *Delaware Gazette*, November 18, 1856.

Florida

County	Buchanan (D)	Fillmore (A)
Alachua	361 (71.8%)	142 (38.2%)
Calhoun	71 (58.7%)	50 (41.3%)
Columbia	462 (50.1%)	460 (49.9%)
Duval	341 (44.0%)	434 (56.0%)
Escambia	249 (51.6%)	234 (48.4%)
Franklin	177 (64.8%)	96 (35.2%)
Gadsden	328 (52.2%)	300 (47.8%)
Hamilton	180 (53.4%)	157 (46.6%)
Hernando	101 (71.6%)	40 (28.4%)
Hillsborough	365 (67.8%)	173 (32.2%)
Holmes	76 (46.6%)	87 (53.4%)
Jackson	431 (48.5%)	457 (51.5%)
Jefferson	390 (72.9%)	145 (27.1%)
Leon	414 (58.5%)	294 (41.5%)
Levy	45 (45.0%)	55 (55.0%)
Liberty	88 (58.3%)	63 (41.7%)
Madison	454 (55.8%)	360 (44.2%)
Manatee	24 (43.6%)	31 (56.4%)
Marion	324 (60.7%)	210 (39.3%)
Monroe	222 (80.4%)	54 (19.6%)
Nassau	133 (65.5%)	70 (34.5%)
Orange	51 (60.7%)	33 (39.3%)
Putnam	70 (73.7%)	25 (26.3%)
St. Johns	198 (72.5%)	75 (27.5%)
Santa Rosa	200 (37.5%)	334 (62.5%)
Sumpter	100 (67.1%)	49 (32.9%)
Volusia	52 (55.9%)	41 (44.1%)
Wakulla	169 (53.1%)	149 (46.9%)
Walton	129 (47.4%)	143 (52.6%)
Washington	153 (68.0%)	72 (32.0%)
Total	**6,358 (56.8%)**	**4,833 (43.2%)**

SOURCE—(Tallahassee) *Floridian & Journal*, December 6, 1856.

Georgia

County	Buchanan (D)	Fillmore (A)
Appling	268 (73.6%)	96 (26.4%)
Baker	453 (72.1%)	175 (27.9%)
Baldwin	300 (53.0%)	266 (47.0%)
Berrien	220 (69.4%)	97 (30.6%)
Bibb	959 (55.3%)	774 (44.7%)
Bryan	134 (58.8%)	94 (41.2%)
Bulloch	460 (92.9%)	35 (7.1%)

County		
Burke	490 (72.8%)	183 (27.2%)
Butts	387 (57.8%)	283 (42.2%)
Calhoun	251 (81.8%)	56 (18.2%)
Camden	186 (86.9%)	28 (13.1%)
Campbell	754 (62.7%)	448 (37.3%)
Carroll	1,176 (72.1%)	456 (27.9%)
Cass	1,205 (61.6%)	751 (38.4%)
Catoosa	365 (51.3%)	346 (48.7%)
Chariton	129 (77.2%)	38 (22.8%)
Chatham	1,445 (59.8%)	971 (40.2%)
Chattahoochee	320 (58.1%)	231 (41.9%)
Chattooga	506 (56.7%)	386 (43.3%)
Cherokee	1,147 (71.1%)	566 (28.9%)
Clarke	487 (44.7%)	603 (55.3%)
Clay	279 (59.7%)	188 (40.3%)
Clinch	133 (43.8%)	171 (56.2%)
Cobb	1,251 (62.1%)	764 (37.9%)
Coffee	16 (50.0%)	16 (50.0%)
Colquitt	106 (58.6%)	75 (41.4%)
Columbia	456 (57.2%)	341 (42.8%)
Coweta	882 (60.2%)	584 (39.8%)
Crawford	378 (62.4%)	228 (37.6%)
Dade	240 (60.8%)	155 (39.2%)
Decatur	396 (46.6%)	454 (53.4%)
De Kalb	665 (59.5%)	453 (40.5%)
Dooly	419 (67.1%)	205 (32.9%)
Dougherty	266 (57.5%)	197 (42.5%)
Early	299 (66.7%)	149 (33.3%)
Effingham	192 (39.3%)	296 (60.7%)
Elbert	524 (59.7%)	354 (40.3%)
Emanuel	273 (51.3%)	259 (48.7%)
Fannin	571 (79.0%)	152 (21.0%)
Fayette	734 (61.7%)	455 (38.3%)
Floyd	847 (51.1%)	812 (48.9%)
Forsyth	798 (63.5%)	458 (36.5%)
Franklin	972 (82.7%)	183 (17.3%)
Fulton	832 (47.7%)	911 (52.3%)
Gilmer	820 (83.3%)	164 (16.7%)
Glynn	109 (54.5%)	91 (45.5%)
Gordon	890 (59.9%)	595 (40.1%)
Greene	283 (32.9%)	576 (67.1%)
Gwinnett	1,092 (59.3%)	749 (40.7%)
Habersham	858 (77.0%)	256 (23.0%)
Hall	696 (60.7%)	451 (39.3%)
Hancock	306 (41.7%)	427 (58.3%)
Haralson	272 (80.5%)	66 (19.5%)
Harris	528 (41.2%)	753 (58.8%)
Hart	610 (80.1%)	152 (19.9%)
Heard	516 (55.3%)	417 (44.7%)
Henry	590 (43.7%)	759 (56.3%)
Houston	602 (51.2%)	574 (48.8%)
Irwin	155 (83.8%)	30 (16.2%)
Jackson	773 (63.1%)	453 (36.9%)
Jasper	418 (52.3%)	382 (47.7%)
Jefferson	353 (48.4%)	376 (51.6%)
Jones	308 (69.5%)	135 (30.5%)
Laurens	70 (14.7%)	406 (85.3%)
Lee	250 (52.2%)	229 (47.1%)
Liberty	191 (59.0%)	133 (41.0%)
Lincoln	219 (50.8%)	212 (49.2%)
Lowndes	443 (60.4%)	291 (39.6%)
Lumpkin	736 (61.1%)	468 (38.9%)
Macon	274 (41.6%)	385 (58.4%)
Madison	415 (65.9%)	215 (34.1%)
Marion	494 (49.9%)	495 (50.1%)
McIntosh	155 (76.0%)	49 (24.0%)
Meriwether	703 (52.0%)	648 (48.0%)
Miller	153 (88.4%)	20 (11.6%)
Monroe	505 (43.5%)	656 (56.5%)
Montgomery	26 (11.5%)	201 (88.5%)
Morgan	234 (39.2%)	363 (60.8%)
Murray	567 (70.3%)	240 (29.7%)
Muscogee	740 (44.2%)	933 (55.8%)
Newton	844 (48.1%)	910 (51.9%)
Oglethorpe	451 (60.5%)	394 (39.5%)
Paulding	776 (80.2%)	191 (19.8%)
Pickens	425 (68.2%)	198 (31.8%)
Pike	630 (56.2%)	494 (43.8%)
Polk	259 (41.1%)	371 (58.9%)
Pulaski	417 (63.4%)	240 (36.6%)
Putnam	353 (54.6%)	294 (45.4%)
Rabun	407 (85.0%)	72 (15.0%)
Randolph	656 (58.8%)	459 (41.2%)
Richmond	891 (43.8%)	1,143 (56.2%)
Scriven	268 (61.6%)	167 (38.4%)
Spalding	545 (50.2%)	540 (49.8%)
Stewart	558 (48.3%)	598 (51.7%)
Sumter	701 (45.1%)	855 (54.9%)
Talbot	442 (44.7%)	547 (55.3%)
Taliaferro	238 (68.6%)	109 (31.4%)
Tattnall	186 (48.6%)	197 (51.4%)
Taylor	429 (57.9%)	312 (42.1%)
Telfair	110 (47.6%)	121 (52.4%)
Terrell	233 (42.7%)	313 (57.3%)
Thomas	463 (57.6%)	341 (42.4%)
Towns	265 (81.5%)	60 (18.5%)
Troup	412 (29.1%)	1,005 (70.9%)
Twiggs	287 (61.7%)	178 (38.3%)
Union	454 (63.5%)	261 (36.5%)
Upson	305 (33.1%)	617 (66.9%)
Walker	824 (59.3%)	565 (40.7%)
Walton	684 (60.3%)	450 (39.7%)
Ware	125 (95.4%)	6 (4.6%)
Warren	589 (69.5%)	259 (30.5%)
Washington	564 (44.7%)	699 (55.3%)
Wayne	131 (77.1%)	39 (22.9%)
Webster	213 (44.7%)	263 (55.3%)
Whitfield	733 (55.1%)	598 (44.9%)
Wilkinson	531 (65.3%)	282 (34.7%)
Wilkes	428 (60.5%)	279 (39.5%)
Worth	227 (73.2%)	83 (26.8%)
Total	**56,579 (57.0%)**	**42,603 (43.0%)**
	*(56,417)	*(42,352)

*Stated totals.

SOURCE—(Milledgeville) *Southern Recorder*, November 18, 1856.

Illinois

County	Buchanan (D)	Frémont (R)	Fillmore (A)
Adams	3,311 (53.2%)	2,256 (36.2%)	662 (10.6%)
Alexander	401 (62.1%)	15 (2.3%)	230 (35.6%)
Bond	607 (42.8%)	153 (10.8%)	659 (46.4%)
Boone	243 (12.0%)	1,748 (86.6%)	27 (1.3%)
Brown	903 (60.0%)	169 (11.2%)	433 (28.8%)
Bureau	1,234 (31.8%)	2,603 (67.0%)	48 (1.2%)
Calhoun	391 (62.7%)	70 (11.2%)	163 (26.1%)

County	Buchanan (D)	Frémont (R)	Fillmore (A)
Carroll	237 (15.3%)	1,161 (74.9%)	153 (9.9%)
Cass	914 (55.2%)	303 (18.3%)	438 (26.5%)
Champaign	550 (36.2%)	732 (48.2%)	236 (15.5%)
Christian	884 (62.2%)	239 (16.8%)	299 (21.0%)
Clark	1,318 (55.9%)	709 (30.1%)	330 (14.0%)
Clay	731 (56.2%)	29 (2.2%)	540 (41.5%)
Clinton	840 (61.6%)	161 (11.8%)	362 (26.6%)
Coles	1,178 (42.7%)	783 (28.4%)	796 (28.9%)
Cook	5,680 (37.8%)	9,020 (60.0%)	342 (2.3%)
Crawford	961 (57.1%)	477 (28.4%)	244 (14.5%)
Cumberland	641 (57.1%)	246 (21.9%)	235 (20.9%)
De Kalb	381 (14.1%)	2,254 (83.2%)	75 (2.8%)
De Witt	679 (40.4%)	623 (37.1%)	378 (22.5%)
Du Page	542 (28.1%)	1,387 (71.8%)	2 (0.1%)
Edgar	1,342 (51.6%)	952 (36.6%)	308 (11.8%)
Edwards	283 (36.8%)	176 (22.9%)	310 (40.3%)
Effingham	784 (75.6%)	90 (8.7%)	163 (15.7%)
Fayette	949 (52.3%)	68 (3.7%)	799 (44.0%)
Franklin	1,051 (80.4%)	5 (0.4%)	251 (19.2%)
Fulton	2,724 (48.3%)	2,021 (35.8%)	898 (15.9%)
Gallatin	764 (63.1%)	24 (2.0%)	423 (34.9%)
Greene	1,565 (61.9%)	245 (9.7%)	719 (28.4%)
Grundy	618 (31.0%)	923 (59.6%)	7 (0.5%)
Hamilton	1,185 (87.4%)	9 (0.7%)	162 (11.9%)
Hancock	2,111 (49.9%)	1,120 (26.5%)	999 (23.6%)
Hardin	333 (58.8%)	4 (0.7%)	229 (40.5%)
Henderson	610 (40.1%)	757 (49.8%)	153 (10.1%)
Henry	883 (31.0%)	1,914 (67.3%)	47 (1.7%)
Iroquois	460 (34.9%)	750 (56.9%)	108 (8.2%)
Jackson	1,056 (75.9%)	14 (1.0%)	322 (23.1%)
Jasper	679 (63.5%)	233 (21.8%)	158 (14.8%)
Jefferson	1,278 (72.4%)	60 (3.4%)	426 (24.1%)
Jersey	702 (43.4%)	387 (23.9%)	530 (32.7%)
Jo Daviess	1,509 (41.2%)	2,110 (57.7%)	41 (1.1%)
Johnson	1,144 (93.8%)	2 (0.2%)	74 (6.1%)
Kane	912 (19.4%)	3,750 (79.9%)	29 (0.6%)
Kankakee	260 (15.2%)	1,383 (81.1%)	63 (3.7%)
Kendall	334 (17.0%)	1,622 (82.4%)	13 (0.7%)
Knox	1,490 (32.3%)	2,851 (61.7%)	277 (6.0%)
La Salle	2,665 (41.0%)	3,721 (57.2%)	121 (1.9%)
Lake	558 (19.1%)	2,347 (80.5%)	10 (0.3%)
Lawrence	729 (54.0%)	89 (6.6%)	533 (39.5%)
Lee	601 (23.8%)	1,894 (75.0%)	32 (1.3%)
Livingston	480 (42.2%)	585 (51.5%)	72 (6.3%)
Logan	823 (41.9%)	655 (33.4%)	484 (24.7%)
Macon	821 (47.9%)	500 (29.2%)	393 (22.9%)
Macoupin	1,778 (49.2%)	823 (22.8%)	1,010 (28.0%)
Madison	1,451 (34.4%)	1,111 (26.3%)	1,658 (39.3%)
Marion	1,150 (67.1%)	150 (8.8%)	413 (24.1%)
Marshall	834 (42.6%)	1,008 (51.5%)	115 (5.9%)
Mason	737 (47.4%)	267 (17.2%)	553 (35.6%)
Massac	628 (71.5%)	4 (0.5%)	246 (28.0%)
McDonough	1,370 (48.5%)	590 (20.9%)	864 (30.6%)
McHenry	945 (24.5%)	2,867 (74.4%)	43 (1.1%)
McLean	1,517 (37.7%)	1,937 (48.2%)	566 (14.1%)
Menard	854 (52.4%)	109 (6.7%)	668 (41.0%)
Mercer	769 (37.5%)	1,141 (55.7%)	140 (6.8%)
Monroe	900 (51.0%)	346 (19.6%)	518 (29.4%)
Montgomery	992 (53.8%)	167 (9.1%)	686 (37.2%)
Morgan	1,656 (47.3%)	963 (27.5%)	885 (25.3%)
Moultrie	432 (48.5%)	154 (17.3%)	305 (34.2%)
Ogle	730 (20.9%)	2,469 (70.8%)	289 (8.3%)
Peoria	2,534 (49.2%)	2,156 (41.8%)	465 (9.0%)
Perry	671 (51.4%)	200 (15.3%)	434 (33.3%)
Piatt	310 (41.6%)	85 (11.4%)	350 (47.0%)
Pike	2,163 (51.2%)	1,053 (24.9%)	1,010 (23.9%)
Pope	855 (79.2%)	11 (1.0%)	214 (19.8%)
Pulaski	473 (71.7%)	21 (3.2%)	166 (25.2%)
Putnam	307 (32.2%)	532 (55.8%)	115 (12.1%)

County	Buchanan (D)	Frémont (R)	Fillmore (A)
Randolph	1,222 (49.3%)	709 (28.6%)	546 (22.0%)
Richland	785 (62.1%)	39 (3.1%)	440 (34.8%)
Rock Island	1,114 (39.4%)	1,439 (50.9%)	276 (9.8%)
Saline	1,004 (81.2%)	4 (0.3%)	229 (18.5%)
Sangamon	2,475 (47.0%)	1,174 (22.3%)	1,612 (30.6%)
Schuyler	1,369 (58.8%)	388 (16.7%)	570 (24.5%)
Scott	843 (54.0%)	183 (11.7%)	536 (34.3%)
Shelby	1,414 (70.1%)	152 (7.5%)	451 (22.4%)
St. Clair	1,728 (36.8%)	1,996 (42.5%)	973 (20.7%)
Stark	353 (28.9%)	718 (58.7%)	152 (12.4%)
Stephenson	1,308 (39.0%)	1,997 (59.5%)	50 (1.5%)
Tazewell	1,313 (42.5%)	1,023 (33.1%)	757 (24.5%)
Union	1,283 (81.5%)	46 (2.9%)	246 (15.6%)
Vermilion	1,111 (39.5%)	1,506 (53.6%)	194 (6.9%)
Wabash	481 (44.2%)	122 (11.2%)	485 (44.6%)
Warren	1,117 (41.3%)	1,282 (47.4%)	307 (11.3%)
Washington	1,132 (68.2%)	244 (14.7%)	283 (17.1%)
Wayne	1,218 (69.6%)	129 (7.4%)	402 (23.0%)
White	1,062 (54.9%)	27 (1.4%)	845 (43.7%)
Whiteside	613 (22.5%)	1,902 (69.8%)	210 (7.7%)
Will	1,575 (39.6%)	2,393 (60.2%)	10 (0.3%)
Williamson	1,419 (87.8%)	10 (0.6%)	188 (11.6%)
Woodford	747 (48.8%)	596 (38.9%)	189 (12.3%)
Winnebago	457 (11.0%)	3,636 (87.5%)	61 (1.5%)
Total	**105,528 (44.1%)**	**96,278 (40.2%)**	**37,531 (15.7%)**

SOURCE—Adler, Howard and Vincent A. Lacey (ed.), *Illinois Election Returns 1818–1990*, Carbondale, IL: Southern Illinois Univ. Press, 1993, pp. 135–7.

Indiana

County	Buchanan (D)	Frémont (R)	Fillmore (A)
Adams	847 (63.7%)	413 (31.1%)	69 (5.2%)
Allen	3,211 (64.9%)	1,593 (32.2%)	145 (2.9%)
Bartholomew	1,844 (56.3%)	1,292 (39.4%)	142 (4.3%)
Benton	217 (33.9%)	315 (49.2%)	8 (1.3%)
Blackford	404 (58.7%)	238 (34.6%)	81 (2.8%)
Boone	1,493 (52.0%)	1,299 (45.2%)	81 (2.8%)
Brown	681 (74.1%)	148 (16.1%)	90 (9.8%)
Carroll	1,344 (51.2%)	1,261 (48.0%)	22 (0.8%)
Cass	1,539 (49.9%)	1,504 (48.8%)	40 (1.3%)
Clark	1,950 (55.5%)	492 (14.0%)	1,074 (30.5%)
Clay	1,108 (62.6%)	365 (20.6%)	296 (16.7%)
Clinton	1,364 (51.3%)	1,261 (47.4%)	34 (1.3%)
Crawford	735 (58.0%)	24 (1.9%)	509 (40.1%)
Daviess	1,115 (53.3%)	26 (1.2%)	939 (44.9%)
Dearborn	2,619 (58.3%)	1,573 (35.0%)	297 (6.6%)
Decatur	1,639 (48.0%)	1,718 (50.3%)	61 (1.8%)
De Kalb	1,247 (51.6%)	1,097 (45.3%)	75 (3.1%)
Delaware	992 (35.9%)	1,736 (62.9%)	32 (1.2%)
Dubois	1,191 (82.3%)	21 (1.5%)	236 (16.3%)
Elkhart	1,651 (45.4%)	1,971 (54.1%)	18 (0.5%)
Fayette	1,002 (44.9%)	1,189 (53.3%)	40 (1.8%)
Floyd	1,767 (54.5%)	228 (7.0%)	1,262 (38.7%)
Fountain	1,588 (49.2%)	1,606 (49.7%)	36 (1.1%)
Franklin	2,259 (60.4%)	1,437 (38.5%)	41 (1.1%)
Fulton	835 (50.1%)	822 (49.3%)	9 (0.5%)
Gibson	1,286 (53.2%)	365 (15.1%)	766 (31.7%)
Grant	1,035 (40.9%)	1,395 (55.2%)	99 (3.9%)
Greene	1,129 (55.3%)	379 (18.6%)	533 (26.1%)
Hamilton	1,185 (39.9%)	1,748 (58.8%)	38 (1.3%)
Hancock	1,343 (57.7%)	962 (41.3%)	24 (1.0%)
Harrison	1,681 (54.6%)	773 (25.1%)	623 (20.2%)
Hendricks	1,378 (44.0%)	1,680 (53.6%)	74 (2.4%)
Henry	1,229 (30.6%)	2,741 (68.3%)	49 (1.2%)
Howard	686 (38.6%)	1,057 (59.5%)	33 (1.9%)
Huntington	1,181 (47.8%)	1,232 (49.9%)	58 (2.3%)
Jackson	1,700 (70.4%)	299 (12.4%)	516 (21.4%)

County	Buchanan (D)	Frémont (R)	Fillmore (A)
Jasper	548 (44.1%)	633 (50.9%)	63 (5.1%)
Jay	880 (48.4%)	883 (48.1%)	54 (3.0%)
Jefferson	1,936 (41.4%)	2,314 (49.5%)	425 (9.1%)
Jennings	1,159 (44.2%)	1,293 (49.3%)	172 (6.6%)
Johnson	1,608 (56.3%)	1,095 (38.3%)	153 (5.4%)
Knox	1,512 (58.1%)	557 (21.4%)	535 (20.5%)
Kosciusko	1,075 (39.1%)	1,662 (60.4%)	13 (0.5%)
Lagrange	640 (31.2%)	1,406 (68.5%)	6 (0.2%)
Lake	346 (27.2%)	923 (72.6%)	3 (0.2%)
Laporte	2,239 (46.5%)	2,533 (52.6%)	45 (0.9%)
Lawrence	1,126 (49.7%)	480 (21.1%)	660 (29.1%)
Madison	1,603 (53.5%)	1,309 (43.7%)	84 (2.8%)
Marion	3,738 (48.6%)	3,696 (43.7%)	205 (2.7%)
Marshall	1,039 (52.8%)	927 (47.2%)	0
Martin	769 (64.4%)	76 (6.4%)	350 (29.3%)
Miami	1,513 (51.4%)	1,390 (47.3%)	38 (1.3%)
Monroe	1,191 (57.2%)	498 (23.9%)	392 (18.8%)
Montgomery	2,088 (50.4%)	1,910 (46.1%)	142 (3.4%)
Morgan	1,528 (48.2%)	1,573 (49.6%)	68 (2.1%)
Noble	1,198 (47.9%)	1,257 (50.2%)	48 (1.9%)
Ohio	505 (51.1%)	104 (10.5%)	379 (38.4%)
Orange	1,207 (64.8%)	49 (2.6%)	606 (32.5%)
Owen	1,289 (54.6%)	487 (20.6%)	586 (24.8%)
Parke	1,283 (43.2%)	1,494 (50.3%)	192 (6.5%)
Perry	1,066 (59.4%)	96 (5.4%)	632 (35.2%)
Pike	772 (54.1%)	80 (5.6%)	574 (40.3%)
Porter	614 (41.7%)	847 (57.6%)	10 (0.7%)
Posey	1,819 (66.1%)	306 (11.1%)	625 (22.7%)
Pulaski	557 (60.2%)	341 (36.9%)	27 (2.9%)
Putnam	1,882 (51.6%)	1,345 (36.8%)	423 (11.6%)
Randolph	1,253 (37.4%)	2,042 (60.9%)	59 (1.8%)
Ripley	1,661 (50.8%)	1,425 (43.6%)	184 (5.6%)
Rush	1,685 (49.4%)	1,644 (48.2%)	83 (2.4%)
St. Joseph	1,509 (45.4%)	1,812 (54.5%)	6 (0.2%)
Scott	693 (56.1%)	278 (22.5%)	264 (21.4%)
Shelby	2,075 (55.7%)	1,510 (40.5%)	142 (3.8%)
Spencer	1,260 (54.7%)	235 (9.2%)	808 (35.1%)
Starke	155 (56.6%)	112 (40.9%)	7 (2.6%)
Steuben	553 (30.9%)	1,215 (68.0%)	19 (1.1%)
Sullivan	1,650 (71.6%)	257 (11.2%)	397 (17.2%)
Switzerland	1,121 (46.9%)	228 (9.5%)	1,040 (43.5%)
Tippecanoe	2,307 (45.0%)	2,778 (54.2%)	45 (0.9%)
Tipton	738 (56.9%)	546 (42.1%)	14 (1.1%)
Union	710 (47.6%)	763 (51.1%)	19 (1.3%)
Vanderburgh	1,880 (60.8%)	372 (12.0%)	840 (27.2%)
Vermillion	824 (46.6%)	866 (48.9%)	80 (4.5%)
Vigo	1,808 (46.9%)	1,165 (30.2%)	883 (22.9%)
Wabash	1,096 (36.7%)	1,785 (59.7%)	108 (3.6%)
Warren	767 (38.2%)	1,167 (58.1%)	76 (3.8%)
Warrick	1,506 (72.0%)	107 (5.1%)	480 (22.9%)
Washington	1,778 (63.5%)	331 (11.8%)	691 (24.7%)
Wayne	1,958 (34.1%)	3,688 (64.1%)	100 (1.7%)
Wells	931 (55.6%)	726 (43.4%)	16 (1.0%)
White	746 (50.0%)	703 (47.1%)	42 (2.8%)
Whitley	851 (49.9%)	797 (46.7%)	57 (3.3%)
Total	**118,670 (50.4%)** *(118,672)	**94,376 (40.1%)**	**22,386 (9.5%)**

*Stated totals.

SOURCE—(Indianapolis) *Daily Journal*, November 26, 1856.

Iowa

County	Buchanan (D)	Frémont (R)	Fillmore (A)
Adair	27 (26.2%)	72 (69.9%)	4 (3.9%)
Adams	73 (38.6%)	113 (59.8%)	3 (1.6%)
Allamakee	560 (46.0%)	630 (51.7%)	28 (2.3%)
Appanoose	853 (55.7%)	191 (12.5%)	487 (31.8%)
Audubon	31 (49.2%)	28 (44.4%)	4 (6.3%)

County	Buchanan (D)	Frémont (R)	Fillmore (A)
Benton	426 (38.5%)	558 (50.4%)	123 (11.1%)
Black Hawk	292 (32.8%)	566 (63.5%)	33 (3.7%)
Boone	359 (57.2%)	203 (32.3%)	66 (10.5%)
Bremer	172 (31.4%)	327 (59.8%)	48 (8.8%)
Butler	141 (35.9%)	223 (56.7%)	29 (7.4%)
Buchanan	343 (32.0%)	709 (66.1%)	21 (2.0%)
Calhoun	14 (60.9%)	9 (39.1%)	0
Cass	84 (38.9%)	132 (61.1%)	0
Cedar	701 (35.2%)	1,116 (56.0%)	176 (8.8%)
Cerro Gordo	40 (28.2%)	101 (71.1%)	1 (0.7%)
Chickasaw	102 (21.0%)	351 (72.4%)	32 (6.6%)
Clarke	338 (44.4%)	346 (45.5%)	77 (10.1%)
Clayton	754 (33.6%)	1,420 (63.4%)	67 (3.0%)
Clinton	839 (37.7%)	1,245 (55.9%)	142 (6.4%)
Crawford	8 (18.2%)	36 (81.8%)	0
Dallas	319 (38.6%)	487 (59.0%)	20 (2.4%)
Davis	1,019 (51.7%)	201 (10.2%)	752 (38.1%)
Decatur	583 (57.8%)	243 (24.1%)	183 (18.1%)
Delaware	500 (34.5%)	801 (55.2%)	149 (10.3%)
Des Moines	1,413 (43.2%)	1,338 (40.9%)	522 (15.9%)
Dubuque	2,427 (60.6%)	1,322 (33.0%)	256 (6.4%)
Fayette	452 (28.0%)	1,043 (64.7%)	117 (7.3%)
Floyd	124 (26.8%)	324 (70.1%)	14 (3.0%)
Franklin	32 (22.5%)	110 (77.5%)	0
Frémont	203 (43.5%)	156 (33.4%)	108 (23.1%)
Greene	117 (61.6%)	73 (38.4%)	0
Grundy	2 (3.0%)	65 (97.0%)	0
Guthrie	205 (49.6%)	196 (47.5%)	12 (2.9%)
Harrison	124 (40.9%)	170 (56.1%)	9 (3.0%)
Hardin	195 (24.6%)	580 (73.1%)	12 (2.3%)
Henry	767 (27.0%)	1,767 (62.2%)	308 (10.8%)
Howard	63 (23.3%)	207 (76.7%)	0
Iowa	326 (36.3%)	492 (54.8%)	79 (8.8%)
Jackson	1,332 (48.1%)	1,163 (42.0%)	276 (10.0%)
Jasper	455 (33.2%)	878 (64.0%)	38 (2.8%)
Jefferson	1,023 (42.3%)	1,188 (49.2%)	206 (8.5%)
Johnson	961 (39.1%)	1,215 (49.4%)	282 (11.5%)
Jones	663 (40.5%)	964 (58.9%)	10 (0.6%)
Keokuk	830 (45.3%)	895 (48.9%)	107 (5.8%)
Kossuth	12 (12.4%)	85 (87.6%)	0
Lee	2,158 (47.0%)	1,780 (38.8%)	650 (14.2%)
Linn	971 (33.8%)	1,632 (56.7%)	273 (9.5%)
Louisa	642 (35.0%)	993 (54.1%)	200 (10.9%)
Lucas	355 (43.3%)	288 (35.2%)	176 (21.5%)
Madison	519 (44.7%)	580 (50.0%)	61 (5.3%)
Mahaska	940 (38.7%)	1,224 (50.3%)	268 (11.0%)
Marion	1,322 (50.5%)	1,069 (40.9%)	225 (8.6%)
Marshall	199 (32.0%)	531 (63.7%)	104 (5.3%)
Mills	153 (28.2%)	287 (53.0%)	102 (18.8%)
Mitchell	135 (28.7%)	334 (71.1%)	1 (0.2%)
Monroe	603 (45.6%)	622 (47.0%)	98 (7.4%)
Monona	56 (50.9%)	41 (37.3%)	13 (12.3%)
Montgomery	58 (42.0%)	63 (45.7%)	17 (12.3%)
Muscatine	895 (27.8%)	1,094 (34.0%)	328 (10.2%)
Page	171 (38.9%)	100 (22.7%)	169 (38.4%)
Polk	888 (43.4%)	1,065 (52.1%)	91 (4.5%)
Pottawattamie	353 (50.6%)	259 (37.2%)	84 (12.1%)
Poweshiek	255 (31.8%)	459 (57.3%)	87 (10.9%)
Ringggold	52 (25.0%)	92 (44.2%)	64 (30.8%)
Sac	35 (58.3%)	25 (41.7%)	0
Scott	1,119 (35.8%)	1,675 (53.6%)	329 (10.5%)
Shelby	19 (23.5%)	62 (76.5%)	0
Story	272 (46.8%)	232 (39.8%)	79 (13.6%)
Tama	206 (26.9%)	470 (61.4%)	90 (11.7%)
Taylor	183 (55.0%)	119 (35.7%)	31 (9.3%)
Union	121 (50.4%)	102 (42.5%)	17 (7.1%)
Van Buren	1,396 (49.6%)	1,092 (38.8%)	324 (11.5%)
Wapello	1,175 (46.5%)	1,098 (43.5%)	252 (10.0%)
Warren	519 (34.9%)	855 (57.5%)	112 (7.5%)

County	Buchanan (D)	Frémont (R)	Fillmore (A)
Washington	629 (28.3%)	1,188 (53.5%)	403 (18.1%)
Wayne	363 (50.7%)	183 (25.6%)	170 (23.7%)
Webster	269 (39.0%)	389 (56.5%)	31 (4.5%)
Winneshiek	209 (21.1%)	770 (77.6%)	13 (1.3%)
Wright	24 (32.0%)	51 (68.0%)	0
Total	**37,568 (40.7%)**	**45,163 (48.9%)**	**9,663 (10.5%)**
	*(37,663)	*(45,196)	*(9,669)

Stated totals.

SOURCE—(Frankford) *Tri-Weekly Commonwealth*, December 10, 1956.

Kentucky

County	Buchanan (D)	Frémont (R)	Fillmore (A)
Adair	1,033 (69.4%)	2 (0.1%)	455 (30.5%)
Allen	713 (57.0%)		537 (43.0%)
Anderson	737 (71.1%)		299 (28.9%)
Ballard	655 (67.0%)		323 (33.0%)
Barren	1,232 (44.0%)	6 (0.3%)	1,561 (55.8%)
Bath	1,028 (61.6%)		642 (38.4%)
Boone	818 (46.6%)		937 (53.4%)
Bourbon	601 (38.6%)		957 (61.4%)
Boyle	362 (34.9%)		676 (65.1%)
Breathitt	502 (81.6%)	1 (0.2%)	112 (18.2%)
Breckinridge	628 (38.4%)	1 (0.1%)	1,008 (61.6%)
Bullitt	561 (50.7%)		545 (49.3%)
Butler	451 (44.1%)		571 (55.9%)
Caldwell	607 (56.7%)	1 (0.1%)	463 (43.2%)
Calloway	1,209 (85.4%)		206 (14.6%)
Campbell	1,219 (54.3%)	119 (5.3%)	906 (40.4%)
Carroll	511 (53.8%)		439 (46.2%)
Carter	787 (72.5%)		298 (27.5%)
Casey	415 (40.8%)		601 (59.2%)
Christian	1,098 (50.4%)	2 (0.1%)	1,080 (49.6%)
Clarke	418 (30.6%)	1 (0.1%)	946 (69.3%)
Clay	369 (46.7%)		421 (53.3%)
Clinton	522 (66.7%)		261 (33.3%)
Cumberland	335 (34.5%)	1 (0.1%)	635 (65.4%)
Daviess	965 (50.3%)		954 (49.7%)
Edmonson	421 (72.1%)	2 (0.3%)	161 (27.6%)
Estill	543 (52.9%)	9 (0.9%)	474 (46.2%)
Fayette	1,006 (41.7%)	1 (0.04%)	1,404 (58.2%)
Fleming	848 (47.2%)	1 (0.1%)	949 (52.8%)
Floyd	939 (91.7%)		85 (8.3%)
Franklin	794 (47.3%)		883 (52.7%)
Fulton	460 (57.5%)		340 (42.5%)
Gallatin	269 (46.5%)		310 (53.5%)
Garrard	423 (32.8%)		866 (67.2%)
Graves	1,380 (74.4%)		475 (25.6%)
Grayson	651 (57.7%)	1 (0.1%)	477 (42.2%)
Green	639 (61.0%)		408 (39.0%)
Greenup	865 (49.9%)	1 (0.1%)	866 (50.0%)
Hancock	407 (48.9%)		425 (51.1%)
Hardin	932 (43.2%)		1,226 (56.8%)
Harrison	1,095 (53.1%)	1 (0.05%)	965 (46.8%)
Hart	816 (61.6%)		509 (38.4%)
Henderson	767 (47.0%)		865 (53.0%)
Henry	1,050 (59.1%)		727 (40.9%)
Hickman	631 (72.1%)		244 (27.9%)
Hopkins	1,133 (56.9%)		857 (43.1%)
Jefferson	2,972 (37.3%)	14 (0.2%)	4,982 (62.5%)
Jessamine	553 (47.3%)	1 (0.1%)	614 (52.6%)
Johnson	708 (98.1%)		14 (1.9%)
Kenton	1,643 (56.4%)	26 (0.9%)	1,246 (42.7%)
Knox	271 (31.5%)	1 (0.1%)	588 (68.4%)
Larue	489 (47.2%)	1 (0.1%)	546 (52.7%)
Laurel	365 (47.2%)	1 (0.1%)	408 (47.2%)
Lawrence	478 (50.6%)		466 (49.4%)

County	Buchanan (D)	Frémont (R)	Fillmore (A)
Lewis	631 (47.6%)	13 (1.1%)	586 (47.6%)
Lincoln	459 (36.6%)		796 (63.4%)
Livingston	372 (44.9%)		457 (55.1%)
Logan	506 (23.8%)	7 (0.3%)	1,613 (75.9%)
Lyon	390 (60.7%)		253 (39.3%)
Madison	832 (41.7%)	77 (3.9%)	1,087 (54.5%)
Marshall	943 (90.1%)		104 (9.9%)
Mason	994 (43.1%)	6 (0.3%)	1,308 (56.7%)
McCracken	505 (43.3%)		660 (56.7%)
McLean	476 (54.1%)	2 (0.2%)	404 (45.8%)
Meade	402 (36.0%)		714 (64.0%)
Mercer	1,121 (64.6%)		615 (35.4%)
Monroe	451 (45.1%)	4 (0.4%)	546 (54.5%)
Montgomery	661 (54.1%)		561 (45.9%)
Morgan	1,068 (78.7%)		289 (21.3%)
Muhlenberg	747 (50.4%)	1 (0.1%)	733 (49.5%)
Nelson	1,041 (56.8%)		793 (43.2%)
Nicholas	709 (51.6%)		666 (48.4%)
Ohio	901 (52.6%)	3 (0.2%)	813 (47.4%)
Oldham	528 (57.7%)		387 (42.3%)
Owen	1,579 (74.0%)		554 (26.0%)
Owsley	401 (54.5%)		335 (45.5%)
Pendleton	732 (49.5%)	2 (0.1%)	746 (50.4%)
Perry	295 (63.0%)		173 (37.0%)
Pike	706 (81.4%)		161 (18.6%)
Powell	177 (51.5%)		167 (48.5%)
Pulaski	1,336 (58.3%)		956 (41.7%)
Russell	429 (48.9%)		448 (51.1%)
Scott	1,049 (60.9%)		674 (39.1%)
Shelby	773 (38.0%)		1,262 (62.0%)
Simpson	537 (55.1%)		437 (44.9%)
Spencer	434 (52.6%)		391 (47.4%)
Taylor	672 (67.9%)		317 (32.1%)
Todd	573 (42.9%)	1 (0.1%)	762 (57.0%)
Trigg	859 (59.7%)		581 (40.3%)
Trimble	599 (68.5%)		275 (31.5%)
Warren	695 (33.9%)	1 (0.05%)	1,354 (66.0%)
Washington	1,145 (72.1%)	1 (0.1%)	441 (27.8%)
Wayne	699 (57.5%)	2 (0.1%)	515 (42.4%)
Whitley	338 (37.1%)		572 (62.9%)
Woodford	420 (38.5%)		672 (61.5%)
Total[7]	**69,509 (52.2%)**	**314 (0.02%)**	**63,391 (47.6%)**

SOURCES—(Frankfort) *Tri-Weekly Commonwealth*, December 10, 1856.

Louisiana

Parish	Buchanan (D)	Fillmore (A)
Ascension	479 (63.4%)	276 (36.6%)
Assumption	837 (81.1%)	195 (18.9%)
Avoyelles	584 (64.4%)	323 (35.6%)
Bienville	706 (70.5%)	296 (29.5%)
Bossier	475 (70.2%)	202 (29.8%)
Caddo	458 (48.2%)	493 (51.8%)
Calcasieu	296 (92.2%)	25 (7.8%)
Caldwell	308 (75.1%)	102 (24.9%)
Carroll	441 (60.5%)	288 (39.5%)
Catahoula	448 (52.2%)	411 (47.8%)
Claiborne	852 (55.7%)	678 (44.3%)
Concordia	135 (46.6%)	155 (53.4%)
De Soto	510 (63.3%)	296 (36.7%)
East Baton Rouge	593 (52.3%)	540 (47.7%)
East Feliciana	464 (57.3%)	346 (42.7%)
Franklin	264 (59.1%)	183 (40.9%)
Iberville	517 (66.1%)	265 (33.9%)
Jackson	538 (58.2%)	387 (41.8%)
Jefferson	122 (11.5%)	937 (88.5%)
Lafayette	453 (78.0%)	128 (22.0%)
Lafourche	753 (71.5%)	300 (28.5%)
Livingston	391 (62.9%)	231 (37.1%)
Madison	210 (46.8%)	239 (53.2%)
Morehouse	332 (48.6%)	351 (51.4%)
Natchitoches	588 (58.3%)	420 (41.7%)
Orleans	2,626 (30.3%)	6,052 (69.7%)
Ouachita	390 (60.0%)	260 (40.0%)
Plaquemines	248 (54.7%)	205 (45.3%)
Point Coupee	521 (66.2%)	266 (33.8%)
Rapides	763 (56.6%)	584 (43.4%)
Sabine	349 (64.9%)	189 (35.1%)
St. Bernard	122 (49.8%)	123 (50.2%)
St. Charles	104 (60.8%)	67 (39.2%)
St. James	172 (31.2%)	380 (68.8%)
St. John the Baptist	217 (52.5%)	196 (47.5%)
St. Helena	272 (46.8%)	309 (53.2%)
St. Landry	1,103 (57.7%)	807 (42.3%)
St. Martin	423 (43.9%)	541 (56.1%)

St. Mary	374 (45.4%)	449 (54.6%)	
St. Tammany	227 (42.7%)	304 (57.3%)	
Tensas	205 (56.6%)	157 (43.4%)	
Terrebone	382 (49.0%)	397 (51.0%)	
Union	623 (53.3%)	545 (46.7%)	
Vermillion	234 (66.9%)	116 (33.1%)	
Washington	304 (68.2%)	142 (31.8%)	

West Baton Rouge	593 (52.3%)	540 (47.7%)
West Feliciana	464 (57.3%)	346 (42.7%)
Winn	314 (66.7%)	157 (33.3%)
Total	**22,164 (51.7%)**	**20,709 (48.3%)**

SOURCE—(New Orleans) *Louisiana Courier*, November 25, 1856.

Maine

County	Buchanan (D)	Frémont (R)	Fillmore (A&W)
Androscoggin	1,699 (31.0%)	3,588 (65.6%)	186 (3.4%)
Aroostook	795 (48.5%)	837 (51.0%)	8 (0.5%)
Cumberland	5,258 (37.4%)	8,211 (58.3%)	605 (4.3%)
Franklin	1,358 (34.7%)	2,529 (64.7%)	21 (0.5%)
Hancock	2,142 (35.9%)	3,667 (61.4%)	161 (2.7%)
Kennebec	2,487 (24.5%)	7,320 (72.1%)	340 (3.4%)
Lincoln	3,598 (40.3%)	4,935 (55.3%)	392 (4.4%)
Oxford	3,116 (41.5%)	4,364 (58.1%)	28 (0.4%)
Penobscot	3,793 (31.6%)	7,861 (65.5%)	341 (2.8%)
Piscataquis	915 (33.3%)	1,734 (63.1%)	97 (3.5%)
Sagadahoc	934 (21.8%)	2,956 (69.0%)	397 (9.3%)
Somerset	1,926 (29.1%)	4,283 (64.6%)	417 (6.3%)
Waldo	3,138 (37.3%)	5,159 (61.3%)	114 (1.4%)
Washington	2,867 (46.0%)	3,299 (53.0%)	64 (1.0%)
York	5,054 (42.7%)	6,636 (56.0%)	154 (1.3%)
*Total	**39,080 (35.6%)**	**67,379 (61.4%)**	**3,325 (3.0%)**
	*(38,036)	*(65,514)	*(3,235)

*Returns from 15 towns arrived after the legal deadline. However, several sources, including Maine Legislative Documents, 1857, include these towns in the returns and they are included in the above. The state totals without these towns are listed in parentheses below the totals in bold.

SOURCES—(Augusta) *Kennebec Journal*, December 26, 1856; (Portland) *Eastern Argus*, December 13, 1856; *Oxford Democrat*, January 2, 1857; and *Maine Legislative Documents, 1857*.

Maryland

County	Buchanan (D)	Frémont (R)	Fillmore (A)
Allegany	2,248 (53.7%)	1,938 (46.3%)	
Anne Arundel	927 (47.1%)		1,043 (52.9%)
Baltimore	3,155 (47.3%)	8 (0.1%)	3,504 (52.6%)
Calvert	356 (47.0%)		401 (53.0%)
Caroline	743 (53.8%)	1 (0.1%)	638 (46.2%)
Carroll	2,099 (47.1%)	6 (0.1%)	2,347 (52.7%)
Cecil	1,845 (49.2%)	20 (0.5%)	1,884 (50.3%)
Charles	758 (62.1%)		461 (37.9%)
Dorchester	979 (43.0%)	4 (0.2%)	1,292 (56.7%)
Frederick	3,304 (46.9%)	21 (0.3%)	3,724 (52.8%)
Harford	1,405 (37.1%)	4 (0.1%)	2,074 (54.8%)
Howard	633 (41.3%)		899 (58.7%)
Kent	550 (39.7%)	3 (0.2%)	834 (60.1%)
Montgomery	1,126 (48.2%)		1,208 (51.8%)
Prince George's	983 (52.7%)		881 (47.3%)
Queen Anne's	741 (45.0%)		904 (55.0%)
St. Mary's	1,052 (81.0%)		247 (19.0%)
Somerset	1,321 (45.3%)	1 (0.03%)	1,593 (54.6%)
Talbot	910 (54.9%)		749 (45.1%)
Washington	2,670 (49.5%)	3 (0.1%)	2,717 (50.4%)
Worcester	1,428 (53.8%)		1,224 (46.2%)
Baltimore (City)	9,882 (36.6%)	214 (0.8%)	16,900 (62.6%)
Total	**39,115 (45.0%)**	**285 (0.3%)**	**47,462 (54.6%)**

SOURCES—Manuscript returns; John T. Willis, *Presidential Elections*, Mt. Airy, MD: Lomond Publications, p. 176.

Massachusetts

County	Buchanan (D)	Frémont (R)	Fillmore (A&W)
Barnstable	703 (19.2%)	2,667 (72.7%)	300 (8.2%)
Berkshire	2,749 (32.4%)	5,344 (63.1%)	377 (4.5%)

County	Buchanan (D)	Frémont (R)	Fillmore (A&W)
Bristol	2,465 (20.1%)	8,845 (72.2%)	936 (7.6%)
Dukes	161 (26.8%)	317 (52.8%)	122 (20.3%)
Essex	4,577 (19.8%)	15,885 (68.8%)	2,612 (11.3%)
Franklin	1,266 (21.2%)	4,445 (74.4%)	260 (4.4%)
Hampden	2,730 (30.7%)	5,533 (62.2%)	631 (7.1%)
Hampshire	832 (13.3%)	5,166 (82.3%)	277 (4.4%)
Middlesex	7,705 (26.5%)	17,222 (59.3%)	4,095 (14.1%)
Nantucket	126 (16.1%)	583 (74.6%)	73 (9.3%)
Norfolk	3,697 (25.0%)	8,402 (56.9%)	2,670 (18.1%)
Plymouth	1,772 (16.9%)	7,228 (68.9%)	1,496 (14.3%)
Suffolk	5,853 (30.7%)	8,582 (45.0%)	4,648 (24.4%)
Worcester	4,604 (19.4%)	17,971 (75.8%)	1,129 (4.8%)
Total	**39,240 (23.5%)**	**108,190 (64.8%)**	**19,626 (11.8%)**

SOURCE—Manuscript returns.

Michigan

County	Buchanan (D)	Frémont (R)	Fillmore (A)
Allegan	1,027 (39.8%)	1,526 (59.1%)	29 (1.1%)
Barry	873 (36.1%)	1,495 (61.9%)	49 (2.0%)
Berrien	1,540 (42.8%)	1,926 (53.5%)	132 (3.7%)
Branch	1,322 (33.5%)	2,608 (66.1%)	14 (0.3%)
Calhoun	2,151 (37.3%)	3,495 (60.6%)	122 (2.1%)
Cass	1,165 (40.0%)	1,703 (58.5%)	41 (1.4%)
Clinton	1,034 (43.0%)	1,358 (56.4%)	14 (0.6%)
Eaton	1,228 (39.2%)	1,888 (60.3%)	15 (0.5%)
Genesee	1,538 (35.9%)	2,635 (61.5%)	110 (2.6%)
Grand Traverse	243 (60.4%)	157 (39.1%)	2 (0.5%)
Gratiot	136 (26.0%)	388 (74.0%)	0
Hillsdale	1,408 (28.8%)	3,446 (70.5%)	37 (0.8%)
Houghton	398 (66.3%)	201 (33.5%)	1 (0.2%)
Ingham	1,534 (45.0%)	1,849 (54.3%)	25 (0.7%)
Ionia	1,154 (36.3%)	2,002 (63.0%)	22 (0.7%)
Jackson	2,119 (41.1%)	2,996 (58.1%)	46 (41.1%)
Kalamazoo	1,620 (36.2%)	2,803 (62.7%)	50 (1.1%)
Kent	2,516 (45.4%)	2,931 (52.9%)	93 (1.7%)
Lapeer	995 (38.2%)	1,579 (60.6%)	31 (1.2%)
Lenawee	2,779 (37.3%)	4,499 (60.4%)	167 (2.2%)
Livingston	1,711 (49.0%)	1,765 (50.5%)	18 (0.5%)
Macomb	1,846 (45.2%)	2,210 (54.1%)	30 (0.7%)
Marquette	77 (43.8%)	79 (44.9%)	20 (11.4%)
Mason	12 (27.3%)	32 (72.7%)	0
Midland	43 (20.1%)	169 (79.0%)	2 (0.9%)
Monroe	1,703 (48.5%)	1,777 (50.6%)	34 (1.0%)
Montcalm	265 (38.6%)	414 (60.3%)	7 (1.5%)
Oakland	3,276 (44.0%)	4,105 (55.1%)	71 (1.0%)
Oceana	21 (20.4%)	82 (79.6%)	0
Ottawa	998 (41.1%)	1,392 (57.3%)	39 (16.1%)
Saginaw	1,222 (53.6%)	1,042 (45.7%)	17 (0.7%)
St. Clair	1,521 (45.4%)	1,807 (54.0%)	21 (0.6%)
St. Joseph	1,475 (38.7%)	2,324 (61.0%)	12 (0.3%)
Sanilac	201 (20.0%)	803 (79.9%)	1 (1.0%)
Shiawasee	1,105 (45.2%)	1,304 (53.3%)	36 (1.5%)
Tuscola	242 (35.2%)	442 (64.2%)	4 (0.6%)
Van Buren	1,031 (37.2%)	1,710 (61.6%)	34 (1.2%)
Washtenaw	2,833 (43.5%)	3,570 (54.8%)	109 (1.7%)
Wayne	5,777 (51.4%)	5,250 (46.7%)	205 (1.8%)
***Total[8]**	**52,139 (41.5%)**	**71,762 (57.2%)**	**1,660 (1.3%)**

SOURCES—Manuscript returns; *Michigan Manual 1877, 1913*; W. Dean Burnham, *Presidential Ballots 1836–1892* (reprint edition), New York, NY: Arno Press, 1976, pp. 514–532, 920–922.

Mississippi

County	Buchanan (D)	Fillmore (A)
Adams	380 (42.9%)	505 (57.1%)
Amite	364 (45.3%)	440 (54.7%)
Attala	928 (64.9%)	501 (35.1%)
Bolivar	106 (38.7%)	168 (61.3%)
Calhoun	840 (76.2%)	263 (23.8%)
Carroll	938 (52.6%)	846 (47.4%)
Chickasaw	861 (57.8%)	629 (41.2%)
Choctaw	1,127 (67.4%)	539 (32.6%)
Claiborne	387 (53.5%)	337 (46.5%)
Clark	522 (57.2%)	390 (42.8%)
Coahoma	111 (32.9%)	226 (67.1%)
Copiah	731 (63.8%)	415 (36.2%)
Covington	387 (81.5%)	88 (18.5%)
De Soto	1,159 (62.0%)	709 (38.0%)
Franklin	342 (61.3%)	216 (38.7%)
Hancock	186 (61.0%)	109 (39.0%)
Harrison	414 (69.5%)	182 (30.5%)
Hinds	751 (40.1%)	1,122 (59.9%)
Holmes	585 (53.9%)	500 (46.5%)
Issaquena	76 (40.0%)	114 (60.0%)
Itawamba	1,239 (36.6%)	715 (63.4%)
Jackson	326 (84.5%)	60 (15.5%)
Jasper	599 (61.7%)	372 (38.3%)
Jefferson	356 (53.6%)	308 (46.4%)
Jones	236 (77.1%)	70 (22.9%)
Kemper	655 (57.3%)	489 (42.7%)
Lafayette	975 (64.8%)	529 (35.2%)
Lauderdale	863 (71.8%)	339 (28.2%)
Lawrence	604 (82.4%)	129 (17.6%)
Leake	615 (64.0%)	346 (36.0%)
Lowndes	801 (59.2%)	553 (40.8%)
Madison	541 (48.5%)	575 (51.5%)
Marion	285 (80.5%)	69 (19.5%)
Marshall	1,465 (54.0%)	1,250 (46.0%)
Monroe	1,065 (63.5%)	612 (36.5%)
Neshoba	464 (73.5%)	167 (6.5%)
Newton	427 (67.4%)	207 (32.6%)
Noxubee	601 (55.8%)	476 (44.2%)
Oktibbeha	595 (68.9%)	268 (31.1%)
Panola	561 (48.0%)	607 (52.0%)
Perry	185 (62.1%)	113 (37.9%)
Pike	533 (65.6%)	279 (34.4%)
Pontotoc	1,392 (55.4%)	1,121 (44.6%)
Rankin	546 (57.2%)	409 (42.8%)
Scott	442 (72.7%)	166 (27.3%)
Simpson	341 (71.3%)	137 (28.7%)
Smith	433 (65.8%)	225 (34.2%)
Sunflower	89 (42.6%)	120 (57.4%)
Tallahatchie	276 (61.1%)	176 (38.9%)
Tippah	1,601 (66.2%)	816 (33.8%)
Tishomingo	1,862 (65.4%)	983 (34.6%)
Tunica	4 (8.3%)	44 (91.7%)
Warren	447 (33.4%)	890 (66.6%)
Washington	135 (47.7%)	148 (52.3%)
Wilkinson	400 (51.8%)	372 (48.2%)
Winston	776 (72.1%)	301 (27.9%)
Yalobusha	848 (54.2%)	716 (45.8%)
Yazoo	608 (45.3%)	735 (54.7%)
Total[9]	35,386 (59.4%)	24,191 (40.6%)

Missouri

County	Buchanan (D)	Fillmore (A)
Adair	410 (59.2%)	283 (40.8%)
Andrew	889 (67.5%)	428 (32.5%)
Atchison	345 (72.3%)	132 (27.7%)
Audrain	521 (48.0%)	565 (52.0%)
Barry	488 (76.7%)	148 (23.3%)
Barton	64 (54.7%)	53 (45.3%)
Bates	409 (61.6%)	255 (38.4%)
Benton	467 (74.6%)	159 (25.4%)
Bollinger	413 (67.5%)	199 (32.5%)
Boone	958 (41.9%)	1,329 (58.1%)
Buchanan	1,036 (57.4%)	768 (42.6%)
Butler	143 (80.8%)	34 (19.2%)
Caldwell	295 (55.5%)	237 (44.5%)
Callaway	805 (42.4%)	1,095 (57.6%)
Camden	269 (56.2%)	210 (43.8%)
Cape Girardeau	898 (57.5%)	664 (42.5%)
Carroll	659 (62.3%)	399 (37.7%)
Cass	561 (48.5%)	596 (51.5%)
Cedar	391 (70.6%)	163 (29.4%)
Chariton	559 (56.0%)	440 (44.0%)
Clark	587 (44.9%)	721 (55.1%)
Clay	675 (47.2%)	756 (52.8%)
Clinton	397 (49.4%)	406 (50.6%)
Cole	552 (68.1%)	259 (31.9%)
Cooper	778 (49.7%)	787 (50.3%)
Crawford	434 (48.5%)	460 (51.5%)
Dade	418 (55.7%)	333 (44.3%)
Dallas	454 (77.5%)	132 (22.5%)
Daviess	572 (60.1%)	380 (39.9%)
Dent	396 (74.8%)	77 (25.2%)
De Kalb	336 (66.1%)	172 (33.9%)
Dunklin	147 (59.3%)	101 (40.7%)
Franklin	846 (61.4%)	531 (38.6%)
Gasconade	403 (64.7%)	220 (35.3%)
Gentry	757 (65.7%)	396 (34.3%)
Green	1,029 (50.7%)	1,003 (49.3%)
Grundy	335 (48.9%)	350 (51.1%)
Harrison	495 (60.9%)	318 (39.1%)
Henry	369 (47.9%)	402 (52.1%)
Hickory	333 (76.4%)	103 (23.6%)
Holt	409 (63.0%)	240 (37.0%)
Howard	867 (52.1%)	798 (47.9%)
Jackson	1,168 (56.6%)	894 (43.4%)
Jasper	398 (57.5%)	294 (42.5%)
Jefferson	387 (42.5%)	523 (57.5%)
Johnson	540 (39.0%)	844 (61.0%)
Knox	471 (54.6%)	391 (45.4%)
Laclede	821 (58.8%)	225 (41.2%)
Lafayette	654 (33.6%)	1,293 (66.4%)
Lawrence	574 (61.6%)	358 (38.4%)
Lewis	761 (58.4%)	642 (41.6%)
Lincoln	846 (59.7%)	572 (40.3%)
Linn	400 (51.1%)	383 (48.9%)
Livingston	501 (53.8%)	430 (46.2%)
Macon	934 (68.2%)	435 (31.8%)
Madison	418 (54.1%)	355 (45.9%)
Maries	246 (78.6%)	67 (21.4%)
Marion	727 (35.5%)	1,321 (64.5%)
McDonald	299 (83.1%)	61 (16.9%)
Mercer	450 (51.9%)	417 (48.1%)
Miller	224 (67.5%)	108 (32.5%)
Mississippi	327 (50.8%)	317 (49.2%)
Moniteau	427 (52.5%)	387 (47.5%)
Monroe	762 (43.0%)	1,012 (57.0%)
Montgomery	365 (37.8%)	603 (62.2%)
Morgan	403 (64.0%)	227 (36.0%)
New Madrid	234 (44.2%)	295 (55.8%)
Newton	528 (64.1%)	236 (35.9%)
Nodaway	438 (70.5%)	183 (29.5%)
Oregon	324 (89.8%)	37 (10.2%)
Osage	412 (65.3%)	219 (34.7%)
Ozark	49 (49.0%)	51 (51.0%)
Pemiscot	119 (51.7%)	111 (48.3%)
Perry	586 (73.9%)	207 (26.1%)

Pettis	319 (42.5%)	432 (57.5%)
Pike	1,113 (49.6%)	1,131 (50.4%)
Platte	1,263 (54.8%)	1,040 (45.2%)
Polk	662 (61.6%)	412 (38.4%)
Pulaski	268 (79.8%)	68 (20.2%)
Putnam	488 (65.5%)	257 (34.5%)
Ralls	369 (40.9%)	534 (59.1%)
Randolph	595 (49.5%)	606 (50.5%)
Ray	874 (54.0%)	744 (46.0%)
Reynolds	114 (58.2%)	82 (41.8%)
Ripley	306 (88.2%)	41 (11.8%)
St. Charles	772 (57.0%)	583 (43.0%)
St. Clair	347 (62.3%)	210 (37.7%)
St. Francois	541 (57.4%)	401 (42.6%)
Ste. Genevieve	356 (53.6%)	308 (46.4%)
St. Louis	5,530 (44.7%)	6,834 (55.3%)
Saline	599 (41.3%)	853 (58.7%)
Schuyler	472 (62.2%)	287 (37.8%)
Scotland	632 (64.2%)	352 (35.8%)
Scott	222 (39.2%)	345 (60.8%)
Shannon	40 (74.1%)	14 (25.9%)
Shelby	373 (46.3%)	432 (53.7%)
Stoddard	315 (67.6%)	151 (32.4%)
Stone	137 (97.9%)	3 (2.1%)
Sullivan	553 (68.0%)	260 (32.0%)
Taney	388 (91.9%)	34 (8.1%)
Texas	479 (84.0%)	91 (16.0%)
Vernon	302 (63.7%)	172 (36.3%)
Warren	369 (49.4%)	378 (50.6%)
Washington	578 (55.3%)	487 (44.7%)
Wayne	287 (74.2%)	100 (25.8%)
Webster	468 (75.2%)	189 (24.8%)
Wright	267 (80.7%)	64 (19.3%)
Total	**58,360 (54.6%)**	**48,495 (45.4%)**

SOURCE—(Jefferson City) *Jefferson Inquirer*, November 25, 1856; and manuscript returns.

New Hampshire

County	Buchanan (D)	Frémont (R)	Fillmore (A)
Belknap	2,220 (51.6%)	2,062 (47.9%)	21 (0.5%)
Carroll	2,510 (53.3%)	2,185 (46.4%)	17 (0.4%)
Cheshire	2,269 (36.4%)	3,910 (62.7%)	56 (0.9%)
Coos	726 (56.5%)	558 (43.4%)	1 (0.1%)
Grafton	4,551 (47.6%)	4,977 (52.0%)	35 (0.4%)
Hillsborough	5,326 (43.1%)	6,942 (56.2%)	86 (0.7%)
Merrimack	4,730 (48.6%)	4,969 (51.0%)	43 (0.4%)
Rockingham	4,916 (44.9%)	5,915 (54.1%)	112 (1.1%)
Strafford	2,683 (42.8%)	3,566 (56.9%)	20 (0.3%)
Sullivan	1,960 (44.9%)	2,389 (54.7%)	19 (0.4%)
Total	**31,891 (45.7%)**	**37,473 (53.7%)**	**410 (0.6%)**

SOURCE—*New Hampshire Manual, 1889.*

New Jersey

County	Buchanan (D)	Frémont (R)	Fillmore (A&W)
Atlantic	684 (49.2%)	547 (39.3%)	160 (11.5%)
Bergen	1,548 (55.7%)	436 (15.7%)	797 (28.7%)
Burlington	3,682 (43.8%)	3,149 (37.4%)	1,584 (18.8%)
Camden	1,766 (37.8%)	817 (17.5%)	2,088 (44.7%)
Cape May	312 (31.6%)	177 (18.0%)	497 (50.4%)
Cumberland	1,574 (45.7%)	642 (18.6%)	1,231 (35.7%)
Essex	6,845 (42.9%)	4,760 (29.9%)	4,338 (27.2%)
Gloucester	986 (32.8%)	639 (21.3%)	1,380 (45.9%)
Hudson	2,574 (61.9%)	1,702 (41.0%)	1,411 (34.0%)
Hunterdon	3,496 (56.8%)	1,554 (25.2%)	1,106 (18.0%)
Mercer	2,857 (47.0%)	2,155 (35.5%)	1,064 (17.5%)
Middlesex	2,468 (43.6%)	1,209 (21.4%)	1,988 (35.2%)
Monmouth	3,319 (54.1%)	1,003 (16.3%)	1,815 (29.6%)
Morris	3,008 (50.0%)	2,310 (38.4%)	696 (11.6%)
Ocean	660 (35.6%)	892 (48.1%)	304 (16.4%)
Passaic	1,618 (40.5%)	1,422 (35.6%)	954 (23.9%)
Salem	1,769 (47.6%)	432 (11.6%)	1,516 (40.8%)
Somerset	1,846 (47.9%)	1,295 (33.6%)	709 (18.4%)
Sussex	3,054 (65.2%)	1,601 (34.2%)	31 (0.7%)
Warren	2,877 (58.5%)	1,596 (32.4%)	446 (9.1%)
Total	**46,943 (47.2%)**	**28,338 (28.5%)**	**24,115 (24.2%)**
*Stated totals.		*(28,351)	

SOURCE—(Trenton) *New Jersey State Gazette*, November 27, 1856.

New York

County	Frémont (R)	Buchanan (D)	Fillmore (A&W)	Smith (Ab)
Albany	5,016 (27.8%)	7,751 (42.9%)	5,301 (29.3%)	1 (0.01%)
Allegany	6,545 (72.4%)	1,640 (18.1%)	856 (9.5%)	3 (0.03%)
Broome	4,297 (59.7%)	2,106 (29.3%)	791 (11.0%)	2 (0.03%)
Cattaraugus	5,166 (65.2%)	1,773 (22.4%)	978 (12.3%)	5 (0.1%)
Cayuga	7,035 (65.3%)	1,818 (16.9%)	1,924 (17.8%)	3 (0.03%)
Chautauqua	7,037 (64.5%)	1,847 (16.9%)	2,017 (18.5%)	2 (0.02%)
Chemung	2,664 (51.0%)	1,789 (34.3%)	766 (14.7%)	
Chenango	5,458 (61.1%)	2,406 (26.9%)	1,070 (12.0%)	
Clinton	2,659 (43.4%)	2,134 (34.9%)	1,311 (21.4%)	16 (0.3%)
Columbia	3,818 (43.3%)	3,020 (34.2%)	1,981 (22.5%)	
Cortland	3,596 (66.4%)	1,181 (21.8%)	628 (11.6%)	8 (0.1%)
Delaware	4,367 (51.5%)	2,107 (24.8%)	2,009 (23.7%)	
Dutchess	5,512 (47.7%)	4,039 (34.9%)	2,013 (17.4%)	
Erie	6,902 (34.6%)	7,536 (37.8%)	5,521 (27.7%)	
Essex	2,904 (57.7%)	1,173 (23.3%)	956 (19.0%)	1 (0.02%)
Franklin	1,469 (34.9%)	1,600 (38.0%)	1,145 (27.2%)	
Fulton	2,593 (51.8%)	1,374 (27.5%)	1,034 (20.7%)	1 (0.02%)
Genesee	3,620 (58.8%)	1,434 (23.3%)	1,107 (18.0%)	
Greene	2,164 (35.9%)	2,346 (38.9%)	1,533 (25.4%)	
Hamilton	149 (28.9%)	250 (48.4%)	117 (22.7%)	
Herkimer	5,074 (63.8%)	1,650 (20.7%)	1,230 (15.5%)	5 (0.1%)
Jefferson	8,249 (64.4%)	3,496 (27.3%)	1,058 (8.3%)	2 (0.02%)

County	Frémont (R)	Buchanan (D)	Fillmore (A&W)	Smith (Ab)
Kings	7,846 (25.6%)	14,174 (46.2%)	8,647 (28.2%)	4 (0.01%)
Lewis	3,124 (67.1%)	1,114 (23.9%)	418 (9.0%)	3 (0.1%)
Livingston	3,597 (49.7%)	1,652 (22.8%)	1,979 (27.4%)	7 (0.1%)
Madison	6,312 (69.7%)	1,861 (20.6%)	865 (9.6%)	15 (0.2%)
Monroe	7,584 (49.4%)	4,683 (30.5%)	3,069 (20.0%)	4 (0.03%)
Montgomery	3,076 (49.0%)	1,485 (23.7%)	1,713 (27.3%)	
New York	16,469 (21.0%)	41,913 (53.5%)	19,924 (25.4%)	
Niagara	3,906 (50.4%)	1,864 (24.0%)	1,986 (25.6%)	1 (0.01%)
Oneida	11,174 (58.3%)	6,386 (33.3%)	1,612 (8.4%)	10 (0.1%)
Onondaga	10,071 (62.8%)	4,227 (26.4%)	1,724 (10.8%)	7 (0.04%)
Ontario	4,551 (54.2%)	1,642 (19.6%)	2,189 (26.1%)	10 (0.1%)
Orange	4,274 (41.1%)	3,948 (38.0%)	2,172 (20.9%)	
Orleans	3,088 (55.5%)	1,052 (18.9%)	1,425 (25.6%)	
Oswego	8,246 (62.8%)	3,683 (28.1%)	1,175 (9.0%)	19 (0.1%)
Otsego	6,373 (56.9%)	3,595 (32.1%)	1,229 (11.0%)	1 (0.01%)
Putnam	963 (37.9%)	1,096 (43.7%)	479 (18.9%)	
Queens	1,886 (27.7%)	2,394 (35.2%)	2,523 (37.1%)	
Rensselaer	5,153 (36.5%)	4,415 (31.3%)	4,549 (32.2%)	
Richmond	736 (22.8%)	1,550 (47.9%)	947 (29.3%)	
Rockland	668 (21.3%)	1,526 (48.7%)	937 (29.9%)	
St. Lawrence	9,698 (74.7%)	1,950 (15.0%)	1,332 (10.3%)	8 (0.1%)
Saratoga	4,524 (47.4%)	2,446 (25.6%)	2,581 (27.0%)	
Schenectady	1,714 (46.1%)	787 (21.1%)	1,213 (32.7%)	
Schoharie	2,376 (34.7%)	2,837 (41.4%)	1,630 (23.8%)	2 (0.03%)
Schuyler	2,542 (63.8%)	981 (24.6%)	461 (11.6%)	
Seneca	2,163 (42.8%)	1,625 (32.1%)	1,265 (25.0%)	5 (0.1%)
Steuben	7,270 (58.3%)	3,217 (25.8%)	2,034 (16.3%)	
Suffolk	2,393 (37.3%)	2,045 (31.9%)	1,980 (30.8%)	1 (0.02%)
Sullivan	1,690 (31.8%)	1,583 (29.8%)	2,037 (38.4%)	
Tioga	3,331 (56.3%)	2,154 (36.4%)	435 (7.3%)	
Tompkins	4,019 (58.1%)	1,430 (20.7%)	1,470 (21.2%)	
Ulster	2,932 (25.1%)	4,030 (34.5%)	4,703 (40.3%)	
Warren	2,202 (55.8%)	1,006 (25.5%)	735 (18.6%)	
Washington	5,174 (59.7%)	1,632 (18.8%)	1,848 (21.3%)	7 (0.1%)
Wayne	5,776 (62.6%)	1,999 (21.7%)	1,450 (15.7%)	7 (0.1%)
Westchester	4,450 (35.1%)	4,600 (36.2%)	3,641 (28.7%)	
Wyoming	4,066 (62.0%)	1,911 (29.2%)	571 (8.7%)	5 (0.1%)
Yates	2,994 (70.3%)	915 (21.5%)	351 (8.2%)	
Total	**274,705 (46.1%)**	**195,878 (32.9%)**	**124,667 (20.9%)**	**165 (0.03%)**

Source—Manuscript returns.

North Carolina

County	Buchanan (D)	Fillmore (A)
Alamance	717 (61.3%)	452 (38.7%)
Alexander	314 (49.4%)	322 (50.6%)
Anson	311 (30.1%)	723 (69.9%)
Ashe	531 (46.3%)	617 (53.7%)
Beaufort	525 (39.7%)	796 (60.3%)
Bertie	453 (47.0%)	511 (53.0%)
Bladen	463 (55.8%)	367 (44.2%)
Brunswick	364 (48.7%)	384 (51.3%)
Buncombe	778 (51.6%)	731 (48.4%)
Burke	378 (55.0%)	311 (45.0%)
Cabarrus	365 (38.1%)	594 (61.9%)
Caldwell	364 (49.3%)	374 (50.7%)
Camden	89 (15.8%)	474 (84.2%)
Carteret	463 (54.3%)	389 (45.7%)
Caswell	917 (81.2%)	212 (18.8%)
Catawba	653 (79.5%)	168 (20.5%)
Chatham	761 (49.2%)	787 (50.8%)
Cherokee	443 (45.9%)	522 (54.1%)
Chowan	255 (54.6%)	212 (45.4%)
Cleveland	796 (91.8%)	71 (8.2%)
Columbus	527 (71.3%)	212 (28.7%)
Craven	595 (55.6%)	475 (44.4%)
Cumberland	1,257 (62.1%)	767 (37.9%)
Currituck	538 (80.9%)	128 (19.1%)
Davidson	634 (39.7%)	964 (60.3%)
Davie	279 (36.9%)	477 (63.1%)
Duplin	1,173 (90.9%)	117 (9.1%)
Edgecombe	1,581 (91.3%)	151 (8.7%)
Forsyth	1,043 (57.5%)	772 (42.5%)
Franklin	793 (75.7%)	255 (24.3%)
Gaston	597 (91.8%)	53 (8.2%)
Gates	388 (56.0%)	305 (44.0%)
Granville	1,060 (58.4%)	756 (41.6%)
Greene	375 (63.2%)	218 (36.8%)
Guilford	413 (21.4%)	1,515 (78.6%)
Halifax	683 (66.8%)	340 (33.2%)
Haywood	413 (68.5%)	191 (31.5%)
Henderson	434 (51.7%)	406 (48.3%)
Hertford	301 (44.5%)	375 (55.5%)
Hyde	248 (38.4%)	398 (61.6%)
Iredell	302 (19.6%)	1,241 (80.4%)
Jackson	404 (86.1%)	65 (13.9%)
Johnston	958 (60.7%)	619 (39.3%)
Jones	211 (57.3%)	157 (42.7%)
Lenoir	424 (61.6%)	264 (38.4%)
Lincoln	514 (69.5%)	226 (30.5%)
Macon	247 (44.5%)	308 (55.5%)
Madison	460 (71.7%)	182 (28.3%)

Martin	725	(70.0%)	311	(30.0%)
McDowell	380	(58.1%)	274	(41.9%)
Mecklenberg	1,031	(63.6%)	573	(36.4%)
Montgomery	108	(15.7%)	546	(84.3%)
Moore	440	(47.4%)	489	(52.6%)
Nash	1,068	(94.6%)	61	(5.4%)
Northampton	621	(57.1%)	466	(42.9%)
Onslow	683	(82.5%)	145	(17.5%)
Orange	909	(55.0%)	747	(45.0%)
Pasquotank	299	(36.0%)	532	(64.0%)
Perquimans	254	(42.3%)	346	(57.7%)
Person	543	(66.1%)	279	(33.9%)
Pitt	737	(56.1%)	577	(43.9%)
Polk	156	(55.7%)	124	(44.3%)
Randolph	336	(24.7%)	1,025	(75.3%)
Richmond	176	(26.0%)	500	(74.0%)
Robeson	673	(54.3%)	566	(45.7%)
Rockingham	1,001	(73.6%)	359	(26.4%)
Rowan	779	(47.5%)	862	(52.5%)
Rutherford	576	(58.3%)	412	(41.7%)
Sampson	927	(72.1%)	358	(27.9%)
Stanly	108	(12.9%)	731	(87.1%)
Stokes	658	(66.5%)	331	(33.5%)
Surry	706	(66.1%)	362	(33.9%)
Tyrrell	92	(24.9%)	277	(75.1%)
Union	655	(73.5%)	236	(26.5%)
Wake	1,472	(65.1%)	789	(34.9%)
Warren	841	(91.6%)	77	(8.4%)
Washington	226	(38.3%)	364	(61.7%)
Watauga	148	(28.7%)	368	(71.3%)
Wayne	1,172	(84.9%)	208	(15.1%)
Wilkes	380	(27.7%)	992	(72.3%)
Yadkin	483	(41.0%)	694	(59.0%)
Yancey	616	(74.8%)	208	(25.2%)
Total	**46,771**	**(56.4%)**	**36,143**	**(43.6%)**
*New Hanover	1,400	(71.8%)	577	(28.2%)

The vote of New Hanover County was received by the governor after he issued a proclamation of the official returns; therefore, they were not part of these returns.

SOURCE—Manuscript returns.

Ohio

County	Buchanan (D)	Frémont (R)	Fillmore (A)	Smith (Ab)
Adams	1,790 (51.5%)	1,407 (40.5%)	278 (8.0%)	
Allen	1,508 (50.0%)	1,415 (46.9%)	94 (3.1%)	
Ashland	2,089 (51.7%)	1,912 (47.3%)	39 (1.0%)	
Ashtabula	975 (15.4%)	5,108 (80.6%)	252 (4.0%)	
Athens	1,350 (35.5%)	2,299 (60.5%)	154 (4.0%)	
Auglaize	1,604 (61.6%)	912 (35.0%)	88 (3.4%)	
Belmont	2,810 (44.0%)	1,817 (28.5%)	1,753 (27.5%)	
Brown	2,700 (55.0%)	1,785 (36.3%)	428 (8.7%)	
Butler	3,509 (57.5%)	2,301 (37.7%)	296 (4.8%)	
Carroll	1,255 (40.6%)	1,750 (56.6%)	87 (2.8%)	
Champaign	1,711 (42.5%)	1,995 (49.6%)	320 (7.9%)	
Clarke	1,539 (35.4%)	2,641 (60.7%)	168 (3.9%)	
Clermont	2,741 (48.0%)	2,188 (38.3%)	781 (13.7%)	
Clinton	1,170 (33.2%)	2,117 (60.0%)	240 (6.8%)	
Columbiana	2,497 (40.8%)	3,516 (57.5%)	96 (1.6%)	5 (0.1%)
Coshocton	2,281 (50.7%)	2,162 (48.1%)	56 (1.2%)	
Crawford	2,154 (55.6%)	1,685 (43.5%)	32 (0.8%)	
Cuyahoga	4,446 (40.0%)	6,360 (57.3%)	296 (2.7%)	4 (0.04%)
Darke	1,988 (46.4%)	2,086 (48.7%)	209 (4.9%)	
Defiance	895 (51.0%)	821 (46.8%)	38 (2.2%)	2 (0.1%)
Delaware	1,649 (38.8%)	2,367 (55.7%)	230 (5.4%)	4 (0.1%)
Erie	1,377 (37.1%)	2,258 (60.9%)	75 (2.0%)	
Fairfield	3,233 (57.3%)	1,700 (30.1%)	711 (12.6%)	
Fayette	880 (35.7%)	1,209 (49.1%)	373 (15.2%)	
Franklin	3,791 (48.3%)	3,488 (44.4%)	574 (7.3%)	
Fulton	772 (39.9%)	1,098 (56.8%)	64 (0.3%)	
Gallia	1,341 (42.5%)	610 (19.3%)	1,206 (38.2%)	
Geauga	575 (17.3%)	2,694 (81.0%)	58 (1.7%)	
Greene	1,465 (31.1%)	3,032 (64.4%)	214 (4.5%)	
Guernsey	1,932 (42.4%)	2,392 (52.5%)	210 (4.6%)	19 (0.4%)
Hamilton	13,051 (46.5%)	9,345 (33.3%)	5,680 (20.2%)	
Hancock	1,944 (51.8%)	1,773 (47.2%)	37 (1.0%)	
Hardin	882 (42.9%)	1,091 (53.1%)	82 (4.0%)	
Harrison	1,473 (40.4%)	2,060 (56.5%)	110 (3.0%)	
Henry	655 (51.8%)	587 (46.4%)	22 (1.7%)	
Highland	2,140 (44.2%)	1,810 (37.4%)	894 (18.5%)	
Hocking	1,454 (54.6%)	1,092 (41.0%)	115 (4.3%)	
Holmes	2,103 (62.0%)	1,285 (37.9%)	5 (0.1%)	
Huron	1,709 (32.7%)	3,468 (66.3%)	54 (1.0%)	
Jackson	1,383 (50.5%)	938 (34.3%)	416 (15.2%)	
Jefferson	1,991 (42.6%)	2,424 (51.9%)	259 (5.5%)	1 (0.02%)
Knox	2,437 (46.0%)	2,735 (51.6%)	124 (2.3%)	
Lake	628 (20.7%)	2,371 (78.0%)	39 (1.3%)	
Lawrence	1,150 (41.1%)	743 (26.6%)	902 (32.3%)	

County	Buchanan (D)	Frémont (R)	Fillmore (A)	Smith (Ab)
Licking	3,371 (49.5%)	3,027 (44.4%)	417 (6.1%)	
Logan	1,328 (36.0%)	2,093 (56.8%)	267 (7.2%)	
Lorain	1,420 (27.9%)	3,604 (70.7%)	54 (1.1%)	16 (0.3%)
Lucas	1,866 (46.8%)	1,639 (41.1%)	486 (12.2%)	
Madison	656 (30.8%)	997 (46.8%)	475 (22.3%)	
Mahoning	1,937 (45.2%)	2,323 (54.1%)	29 (0.7%)	1 (0.02%)
Marion	1,275 (48.2%)	1,367 (51.7%)	4 (0.2%)	
Medina	1,572 (37.1%)	2,635 (62.2%)	28 (0.7%)	
Meigs	1,603 (40.6%)	1,998 (50.6%)	344 (8.7%)	
Mercer	1,159 (60.9%)	629 (33.1%)	114 (6.0%)	
Miami	1,988 (37.4%)	3,171 (59.6%)	159 (3.0%)	
Monroe	2,812 (66.2%)	1,016 (23.9%)	413 (9.7%)	5 (0.1%)
Montgomery	4,285 (49.2%)	4,038 (46.3%)	391 (4.5%)	
Morgan	1,669 (41.8%)	2,125 (53.2%)	201 (5.0%)	
Morrow	1,667 (43.9%)	2,031 (53.5%)	101 (2.7%)	
Muskingum	3,391 (44.2%)	3,172 (41.4%)	1,092 (14.2%)	12 (0.2%)
Noble	1,337 (43.2%)	1,603 (51.8%)	154 (5.0%)	
Ottawa	477 (51.2%)	454 (48.7%)	1 (0.1%)	
Paulding	170 (25.3%)	497 (74.0%)	5 (0.7%)	
Perry	1,847 (49.6%)	1,385 (37.2%)	492 (13.2%)	
Pickaway	2,066 (49.5%)	1,724 (41.3%)	382 (9.2%)	
Pike	1,175 (56.7%)	523 (25.2%)	375 (18.1%)	
Portage	2,072 (40.6%)	2,983 (58.4%)	6 (0.1%)	43 (0.8%)
Preble	1,561 (38.2%)	2,249 (55.1%)	273 (6.7%)	
Putnam	1,116 (58.4%)	790 (41.4%)	4 (0.2%)	
Richland	2,909 (51.1%)	2,726 (47.9%)	53 (0.9%)	
Ross	2,681 (47.0%)	2,436 (42.7%)	589 (10.3%)	
Sandusky	1,599 (50.1%)	1,548 (48.5%)	45 (1.4%)	
Scioto	1,634 (46.7%)	546 (15.6%)	1,321 (37.7%)	
Seneca	2,605 (49.4%)	2,565 (48.6%)	103 (2.0%)	
Shelby	1,446 (49.4%)	1,356 (46.3%)	127 (4.3%)	
Stark	3,633 (48.8%)	3,770 (50.7%)	29 (0.4%)	9 (0.1%)
Summit	1,746 (34.8%)	3,185 (63.4%)	74 (1.5%)	13 (0.3%)
Trumbull	1,920 (30.2) %	4,049 (69.4%)	18 (0.3%)	6 (0.1%)
Tuscarawas	2,656 (46.8%)	3,007 (52.9%)	18 (0.3%)	
Union	1,055 (38.4%)	1,431 (52.1%)	263 (9.6%)	
Van Wert	789 (50.0%)	758 (48.0%)	32 (2.0%)	
Vinton	1,174 (54.4%)	932 (43.2%)	51 (2.4%)	
Warren	1,776 (36.9%)	2,688 (55.9%)	344 (7.2%)	
Washington	2,251 (42.4%)	2,783 (52.4%)	281 (5.3%)	
Wayne	2,918 (49.6%)	2,904 (49.4%)	47 (0.8%)	15 (0.3%)
Williams	1,022 (42.6%)	1,327 (55.3%)	49 (2.0%)	
Wood	935 (39.0%)	1,319 (55.0%)	143 (6.0%)	
Wyandot	1,278 (48.5%)	1,247 (47.4%)	108 (4.1%)	
Total	**170,874 (44.2%)**	**187,517 (48.5%)**	**28,121 (7.3%)**	**155 (0.04%)**
	*(187,497)		*(28,126)	*(156)

*Stated totals.

SOURCES—Executive Documents, 1865; and (Cleveland) *Morning Leader*, November 27, 1856.

Pennsylvania[10]

County	Buchanan (D)	Union	[Frémont (R) / Fillmore (A)]		Fillmore (StrA)
Adams	2,637 (52.7%)	2,344 (46.8%)	[1,120	1,225]	24 (0.5%)
Allegheny	9,062 (38.0%)	13,907 (58.3%)	[13,671	592]	896 (3.8%)
Armstrong	2,680 (46.9%)	3,076 (53.8%)	[2,963	113]	75 (1.3%)
Beaver	1,905 (39.7%)	2,761 (57.5%)	[2,658	103]	133 (2.8%)
Bedford	2,458 (52.2%)	2,096 (44.5%)	[306	1,784]	152 (3.2%)
Berks	11,272 (70.9%)	4,319 (27.2%)	[1,037	3,282]	304 (1.9%)
Blair	2,069 (41.7%)	2,198 (44.3%)	[445	1,753]	697 (14.0%)
Bradford	2,314 (24.7%)	6,969 (74.5%)	[6,938	30]	71 (0.8%)
Bucks	6,517 (53.0%)	5,465 (44.4%)	[4,682	419]	316 (2.6%)
Butler	2,648 (43.2%)	3,415 (55.7%)	[3,401	14]	67 (1.1%)
Cambria	2,987 (62.8%)	1,665 (35.0%)	[804	861]	107 (2.2%)
Carbon	1,866 (61.7%)	1,000 (33.1%)	[692	309]	156 (5.2%)
Centre	2,895 (55.3%)	1,790 (34.2%)	[390	1,400]	552 (10.5%)
Chester	6,333 (48.4%)	5,928 (45.3%)	[5,308	620]	828 (6.3%)
Clarion	2,760 (61.4%)	1,732 (38.5%)	[788	944]	6 (0.1%)

County	Buchanan (D)	Union	[Frémont (R)/Fillmore (A)]	Fillmore (StrA)
Clearfield	1,978 (58.6%)	1,306 (38.7%)	[718 / 511]	93 (2.8%)
Clinton	1,485 (53.3%)	1,267 (45.5%)	[618 / 648]	34 (1.2%)
Columbia	2,889 (66.0%)	1,486 (33.9%)	[1,239 / 214]	5 (0.1%)
Crawford	3,391 (38.6%)	5,364 (61.0%)	[5,360 / 4]	41 (0.2%)
Cumberland	3,427 (52.9%)	3,032 (46.8%)	[1,472 / 1,565]	14 (0.2%)
Dauphin	3,094 (43.3%)	3,946 (55.2%)	[1,615 / 2,332]	107 (1.5%)
Delaware	2,005 (43.5%)	1,809 (39.3%)	[1,590 / 219]	791 (17.2%)
Elk	575 (63.7%)	320 (35.5%)	[275 / 45]	7 (0.8%)
Erie	2,584 (32.2%)	5,194 (64.7%)	[5,156 / 37]	252 (3.1%)
Fayette	3,554 (52.1%)	3,216 (47.2%)	[2,089 / 1,128]	46 (0.7%)
Franklin	3,469 (48.5%)	3,664 (51.2%)	[2,446 / 1,217]	16 (0.2%)
Fulton	970 (57.8%)	703 (41.8%)	[142 / 561]	5 (0.3%)
Greene	2,747 (62.5%)	1,634 (37.1%)	[1,321 / 272]	14 (0.3%)
Huntingdon	2,164 (45.7%)	1,834 (38.7%)	[926 / 908]	737 (15.6%)
Indiana	1,762 (31.3%)	3,843 (68.2%)	[3,612 / 231]	32 (0.6%)
Jefferson	1,463 (46.6%)	1,646 (52.4%)	[1,063 / 583]	32 (1.0%)
Juniata	1,365 (52.7%)	1,077 (41.6%)	[480 / 597]	150 (5.8%)
Lancaster	8,731 (43.8%)	10,224 (51.3%)	[6,608 / 3,615]	977 (4.9%)
Lawrence	1,220 (27.8%)	3,078 (70.2%)	[3,065 / 11]	85 (1.9%)
Lebanon	2,511 (44.3%)	3,119 (55.0%)	[2,414 / 396]	41 (0.7%)
Lehigh	4,426 (56.9%)	3,319 (42.7%)	[3,237 / 91]	31 (0.4%)
Luzerne	6,775 (54.3%)	5,133 (41.2%)	[4,727 / 305]	562 (4.5%)
Lycoming	3,324 (55.1%)	2,634 (43.7%)	[934 / 1,700]	70 (1.2%)
McKean	526 (38.0%)	819 (59.1%)	[812 / 7]	40 (2.9%)
Mercer	2,699 (41.5%)	3,701 (56.9%)	[3,686 / 15]	103 (1.6%)
Mifflin	1,491 (54.1%)	1,205 (43.7%)	[216 / 989]	61 (2.2%)
Monroe	2,275 (78.3%)	617 (21.2%)	[560 / 57]	12 (0.4%)
Montgomery	7,134 (58.3%)	3,337 (27.3%)	[2,845 / 492]	1,773 (14.5%)
Montour	1,271 (60.9%)	804 (38.5%)	[666 / 138]	11 (0.5%)
Northampton	5,262 (63.6%)	1,813 (21.9%)	[1,168 / 644]	1,194 (14.4%)
Northumberland	3,059 (61.6%)	1,662 (33.5%)	[566 / 1,096]	244 (4.9%)
Perry	2,135 (52.9%)	1,242 (30.8%)	[521 / 750]	657 (16.3%)
Philadelphia	38,222 (54.4%)	20,062 (28.6%)	[7,892 / 12,218]	11,866 (16.9%)
Pike	862 (75.2%)	280 (24.4%)	[270 / 10]	5 (0.4%)
Potter	667 (34.5%)	1,268 (65.4%)	[1,264 / 4]	2 (0.1%)
Schuylkill	7,035 (59.1%)	4,499 (37.8%)	[2,188 / 2,315]	367 (3.1%)
Snyder	1,763 (38.1%)	2,862 (61.9%)	[1,458 / 1,404]	1 (0.02%)
Somerset	1,255 (45.4%)	1,458 (52.8%)	[443 / 1,015]	49 (1.8%)
Sullivan	2,548 (39.4%)	3,871 (59.9%)	[3,861 / 8]	43 (0.7%)
Susquehanna	538 (60.1%)	352 (39.3%)	[309 / 43]	5 (0.6%)
Tioga	1,386 (23.3%)	4,548 (76.4%)	[4,541 / 7]	20 (0.3%)
Union	1,092 (40.3%)	1,600 (59.1%)	[1,429 / 171]	15 (0.6%)
Venango	2,157 (50.5%)	2,106 (49.3%)	[2,041 / 65]	7 (0.2%)
Warren	1,231 (36.5%)	2,093 (62.1%)	[2,091 / 2]	47 (1.4%)
Washington	4,288 (48.8%)	4,371 (49.8%)	[4,237 / 137]	128 (1.5%)
Wayne	2,259 (52.0%)	2,047 (47.1%)	[2,172 / 76]	37 (0.9%)
Westmoreland	5,172 (53.5%)	4,436 (45.9%)	[4,091 / 233]	66 (0.7%)
Wyoming	1,171 (49.1%)	1,156 (48.5%)	[1,138 / 17]	57 (2.4%)
York	6,876 (58.8%)	3,812 (32.6%)	[511 / 3,300]	1,001 (8.6%)
Total	**230,686 (50.1%)**	**203,534 (44.2%)**	*[147,286 (72.5%)/55,852 (27.5%)]*	**26,337 (5.7%)**

SOURCE—(returns) *Legislative Documents of the Commonwealth of Pennsylvania*, Harrisburg, PA: 1857, pp. 670–675.

Rhode Island

County	Buchanan (D)	Frémont (R)	Fillmore (A&W)
Bristol	337 (29.1%)	603 (52.1%)	218 (18.8%)
Kent	566 (30.7%)	1,260 (68.4%)	15 (0.8%)
Newport	750 (28.1%)	1,258 (47.2%)	659 (24.7%)
Providence	4,432 (38.0%)	6,903 (59.2%)	331 (2.8%)
Washington	595 (23.9%)	1,443 (58.0%)	452 (18.2%)
Total	**6,680 (33.7%)**	**11,467 (57.9%)**	**1,675 (8.5%)**

SOURCE—*Providence Journal*, November 7, 1856, and November 6, 1860.

Tennessee

County	Buchanan (D)	Fillmore (A)
Anderson	348 (34.9%)	649 (65.1%)
Bedford	1,378 (47.0%)	1,557 (53.0%)
Benton	632 (58.2%)	453 (41.8%)
Bledsoe	271 (43.4%)	354 (56.6%)
Blount	623 (33.3%)	1,246 (66.7%)
Bradley	1,078 (62.1%)	658 (37.9%)
Campbell	434 (55.7%)	345 (44.3%)
Cannon	809 (65.4%)	428 (34.6%)
Carroll	863 (33.5%)	1,710 (66.5%)
Carter	228 (23.8%)	728 (76.2%)

County	Buchanan (D)		Fillmore (A)	
Cheatham	465	(52.4%)	423	(47.6%)
Claiborne	735	(57.5%)	543	(42.5%)
Cocke	439	(35.6%)	795	(64.4%)
Coffee	990	(76.3%)	307	(23.7%)
Cumberland	261	(51.8%)	243	(48.2%)
Davidson	2,074	(38.9%)	3,259	(61.1%)
Decatur	495	(52.2%)	453	(47.8%)
De Kalb	795	(58.9%)	554	(41.1%)
Dickson	816	(68.1%)	382	(31.9%)
Dyer	599	(47.4%)	666	(52.6%)
Fayette	1,082	(50.05%)	1,080	(49.95%)
Fentress	533	(81.9%)	118	(18.1%)
Franklin	1,427	(81.2%)	331	(18.8%)
Gibson	1,284	(41.2%)	1,832	(58.8%)
Giles	1,584	(56.2%)	1,236	(43.8%)
Grainger	736	(39.7%)	1,117	(60.3%)
Greene	1,852	(67.8%)	880	(32.2%)
Grundy	425	(93.8%)	28	(6.2%)
Hamilton	1,051	(49.7%)	1,064	(50.3%)
Hancock	525	(68.5%)	241	(31.5%)
Hardeman	1,333	(65.9%)	691	(34.1%)
Hardin	905	(54.7%)	748	(45.3%)
Hawkins	1,144	(55.5%)	916	(44.5%)
Haywood	920	(52.2%)	842	(47.8%)
Henderson	805	(38.0%)	1,313	(62.0%)
Henry	1,827	(67.1%)	897	(32.9%)
Hickman	1,086	(82.0%)	238	(18.0%)
Humphreys	695	(71.3%)	280	(28.7%)
Jackson	1,261	(51.7%)	1,180	(48.3%)
Jefferson	567	(26.5%)	1,571	(73.5%)
Johnson	178	(27.9%)	459	(72.1%)
Knox	838	(24.7%)	2,551	(75.3%)
Lauderdale	411	(54.4%)	345	(45.6%)
Lawrence	876	(63.0%)	514	(37.0%)
Lewis	242	(90.6%)	25	(9.4%)
Lincoln	2,670	(86.1%)	431	(13.9%)
Macon	526	(48.5%)	559	(51.5%)
Madison	981	(38.6%)	1,561	(61.4%)
Marion	446	(46.0%)	523	(54.0%)
Marshall	1,278	(66.3%)	649	(33.7%)
Maury	1,823	(58.1%)	1,316	(41.9%)
McMinn	1,059	(52.2%)	970	(47.8%)
McNairy	1,125	(53.7%)	969	(46.3%)
Meigs	635	(83.6%)	125	(16.4%)
Monroe	1,059	(52.2%)	970	(47.8%)
Montgomery	944	(40.8%)	1,368	(59.2%)
Morgan	263	(61.9%)	162	(38.1%)
Obion	533	(64.1%)	950	(35.9%)
Overton	1,505	(82.4%)	322	(17.6%)
Perry	565	(59.2%)	322	(40.8%)
Polk	798	(66.5%)	402	(33.5%)
Rhea	448	(59.0%)	311	(41.0%)
Roane	829	(44.6%)	1,028	(55.4%)
Robertson	928	(46.0%)	1,089	(54.0%)
Rutherford	1,368	(48.2%)	1,469	(51.8%)
Scott	224	(58.9%)	156	(41.1%)
Sevier	164	(15.1%)	921	(84.9%)
Shelby	2,088	(50.8%)	2,016	(49.2%)
Smith	729	(31.4%)	1,596	(68.6%)
Stewart	895	(59.6%)	606	(40.4%)
Sullivan	1,477	(72.9%)	548	(27.1%)
Sumner	1,894	(68.8%)	859	(31.2%)
Tipton	663	(61.0%)	424	(39.0%)
Van Buren	265	(72.0%)	103	(28.0%)
Warren	1,130	(73.3%)	411	(26.7%)
Washington	1,334	(61.7%)	828	(38.3%)
Wayne	563	(44.1%)	714	(55.9%)
Weakley	1,628	(65.5%)	859	(34.5%)
White	740	(47.8%)	808	(52.2%)
Williamson	775	(32.0%)	1,646	(68.0%)
Wilson	1,134	(34.2%)	2,186	(65.8%)
Total	**73,406**	**(52.5%)**	**66,425**	**(47.5%)**

SOURCES—(Nashville) *American*, December 8, 1856; *Tennessee Votes*, p. 39; and W. Dean Burnham, *Presidential Ballots 1836–1892* (reprint edition), New York, NY: Arno Press, 1976, pp. 742–762, 942–3.

Texas

County	Buchanan (D)		Fillmore (A)	
Anderson	612	(65.3%)	325	(34.7%)
Atascosa	87	(60.0%)	58	(40.0%)
Austin	358	(75.0%)	120	(25.0%)
Bandera	9	(42.9%)	12	(57.1%)
Bastrop	403	(63.4%)	233	(36.6%)
Bell	312	(67.4%)	151	(32.6%)
Bexar	747	(70.1%)	318	(29.9%)
Bosque	64	(76.2%)	20	(23.8%)
Bowie	171	(66.0%)	88	(34.0%)
Brazoria	225	(75.3%)	74	(24.7%)
Brazos	56	(43.1%)	74	(56.9%)
Burleson	261	(60.8%)	168	(39.2%)
Burnet	141	(65.0%)	76	(35.0%)
Caldwell	395	(66.9%)	195	(33.1%)
Cameron	492	(80.0%)	123	(20.0%)
Cass	581	(62.3%)	352	(37.7%)
Cherokee	844	(62.2%)	514	(37.8%)
Collin	564	(65.1%)	302	(34.9%)
Colorado	252	(65.5%)	133	(34.5%)
Comal	284	(88.8%)	26	(11.2%)
Comanche	40	(78.4%)	11	(21.6%)
Coryell	118	(63.1%)	69	(36.9%)
Dallas	603	(71.1%)	245	(28.9%)
Denton	308	(70.0%)	132	(30.0%)
De Witt	253	(70.1%)	108	(29.9%)
Ellis	239	(57.6%)	176	(42.4%)
Falls	158	(68.1%)	74	(31.9%)
Fannin	577	(70.8%)	238	(29.2%)
Fayette	567	(58.8%)	398	(41.2%)
Fort Bend	196	(59.0%)	136	(41.0%)
Freestone	341	(100%)	0	
Galveston	431	(57.9%)	314	(42.1%)
Gillespie	115	(82.1%)	25	(17.9%)
Goliad	93	(40.8%)	135	(59.2%)
Gonzales	515	(58.7%)	363	(41.3%)
Grayson	415	(69.5%)	182	(30.5%)
Grimes	323	(55.4%)	260	(44.6%)
Guadalupe	359	(58.5%)	255	(41.5%)
Harris	645	(59.0%)	449	(41.0%)
Harrison	565	(52.8%)	505	(47.2%)
Hays	130	(51.6%)	122	(48.4%)
Henderson	292	(81.1%)	68	(18.9%)
Hill	175	(57.2%)	131	(42.8%)
Hopkins	530	(69.1%)	237	(31.0%)
Houston	400	(69.4%)	176	(69.4%)
Hunt	392	(74.0%)	138	(26.0%)
Jackson	93	(51.4%)	88	(48.6%)
Jasper	185	(65.1%)	99	(34.9%)
Jefferson	109	(69.0%)	49	(31.0%)
Johnson	186	(70.5%)	78	(29.5%)
Karnes	103	(46.4%)	119	(53.6%)
Kaufman	191	(75.2%)	63	(24.8%)
Lamar	555	(70.3%)	235	(29.7%)
Lampasas	77	(55.8%)	61	(44.2%)
Lavaca	360	(75.6%)	116	(24.4%)
Leon	337	(59.8%)	227	(40.9%)
Liberty	180	(63.6%)	103	(36.4%)
Limestone	401	(77.1%)	119	(22.9%)

Llano	55 (70.5%)	23 (29.5%)
Madison	113 (47.5%)	125 (52.5%)
Matagorda	111 (72.1%)	43 (27.9%)
McLennan	293 (59.3%)	201 (40.7%)
Medina	136 (77.7%)	39 (22.3%)
Milam	211 (51.8%)	196 (48.2%)
Montgomery	179 (52.3%)	163 (47.7%)
Nacogdoches	557 (75.4%)	182 (24.6%)
Navarro	300 (58.8%)	210 (41.2%)
Orange	73 (54.9%)	60 (45.1%)
Panola	458 (77.9%)	130 (22.1%)
Polk	285 (80.1%)	71 (19.9%)
Red River	388 (62.3%)	235 (37.7%)
Refugio	82 (68.9%)	37 (31.1%)
Robertson	222 (69.8%)	96 (30.2%)
Rusk	1,154 (63.2%)	669 (36.8%)
Sabine	118 (59.6%)	80 (40.4%)
San Augustine	182 (71.7%)	72 (28.3%)
San Saba	48 (69.6%)	21 (30.4%)
Shelby	308 (80.0%)	77 (20.0%)
Smith	810 (68.6%)	370 (31.4%)
Tarrant	490 (84.2%)	92 (15.8%)
Titus	502 (66.1%)	257 (33.9%)
Travis	551 (54.2%)	466 (45.8%)
Trinity	161 (60.3%)	106 (39.7%)
Upshur	683 (72.8%)	255 (27.2%)
Uvalde	18 (45.0%)	22 (55.0%)
Van Zandt	223 (82.3%)	48 (17.7%)
Victoria	141 (54.7%)	117 (45.3%)
Walker	387 (53.0%)	343 (47.0%)
Washington	653 (57.6%)	481 (42.4%)
Webb	382 (100%)	0
Wharton	76 (65.5%)	40 (34.5%)
Wise	67 (85.9%)	11 (14.1%)
Williamson	307 (56.1%)	240 (43.9%)
Total[11]	**29,139 (65.7%)**	**15,244 (34.3%)**

SOURCES—Manuscript returns; and original county returns.

Vermont

County	Buchanan (D)	Frémont (R)	Fillmore (A&W)
Addison	334 (8.9%)	3,362 (89.3%)	68 (1.8%)
Bennington	785 (26.1%)	2,120 (70.5%)	70 (2.3%)
Caledonia	1,061 (29.3%)	2,540 (70.1%)	23 (0.6%)
Chittenden	688 (19.1%)	2,844 (78.9%)	73 (2.0%)
Essex	274 (30.4%)	622 (69.1%)	4 (0.4%)
Franklin	870 (25.7%)	2,455 (72.4%)	65 (1.9%)
Grand Isle	92 (18.2%)	405 (80.0%)	9 (1.8%)
Lamoille	402 (19.9%)	1,608 (79.5%)	13 (0.6%)
Orange	1,364 (29.4%)	3,207 (69.2%)	61 (1.3%)
Orleans	494 (19.7%)	2,007 (80.1%)	6 (0.2%)
Rutland	839 (14.8%)	4,798 (84.6%)	35 (0.6%)
Washington	1,359 (26.2%)	3,821 (73.7%)	5 (0.1%)
Windham	742 (15.3%)	4,068 (83.8%)	47 (1.0%)
Windsor	1,275 (18.1%)	5,706 (81.0%)	66 (0.9%)
Total	**10,579 (20.9%)**	**39,563 (78.1%)**	**545 (1.1%)**
	*(10,577)		*(546)

*Stated totals.

SOURCE—Manuscript returns.

Virginia

County	Buchanan (D)	Fillmore (A&W)	Frémont (R)
Accomac	821 (49.7%)	830 (50.3%)	
Albemarle	1,092 (42.0%)	1,026 (58.0%)	
Alleghany	383 (67.7%)	183 (32.3%)	
Alexandria	678 (42.0%)	937 (58.0%)	
Amelia	276 (64.8%)	150 (35.2%)	
Amherst	683 (60.3%)	449 (39.7%)	
Appomattox	431 (74.0%)	152 (26.0%)	
Augusta	1,499 (44.7%)	1,904 (55.3%)	
Barbour	938 (74.3%)	325 (25.7%)	
Bath	258 (58.9%)	180 (41.1%)	
Bedford	1,015 (49.3%)	1,044 (50.7%)	
Berkeley	997 (54.1%)	846 (45.9%)	
Boone	273 (70.7%)	113 (29.3%)	
Botetourt	904 (72.6%)	341 (27.4%)	
Braxton	260 (34.5%)	494 (65.5%)	
Brooke	451 (60.0%)	261 (34.7%)	40 (5.3%)
Brunswick	566 (81.2%)	131 (18.8%)	
Buckingham	463 (59.1%)	320 (40.9%)	
Cabell	598 (60.2%)	396 (39.8%)	
Calhoun	335 (93.4%)	23 (6.6%)	
Campbell	896 (45.7%)	1,065 (54.3%)	
Caroline	517 (55.5%)	414 (44.5%)	
Carroll	687 (72.5%)	260 (27.5%)	

County	Buchanan (D)	Fillmore (A&W)	Frémont (R)
Charles City	106 (35.8%)	190 (64.2%)	
Charlotte	463 (65.2%)	247 (34.8%)	
Chesterfield	845 (70.7%)	350 (29.3%)	
Clarke	404 (64.2%)	225 (35.8%)	
Craig	350 (76.4%)	108 (23.6%)	
Culpeper	512 (54.4%)	430 (45.6%)	
Cumberland	274 (59.8%)	184 (40.2%)	
Dinwiddie	351 (71.5%)	140 (28.5%)	
Doddridge	404 (69.4%)	178 (30.6%)	
Elizabeth City	190 (50.8%)	184 (49.2%)	
Essex	298 (46.9%)	338 (53.1%)	
Fairfax	727 (52.8%)	650 (47.2%)	
Fauquier	1,081 (55.0%)	884 (45.0%)	
Fayette	369 (53.7%)	318 (46.3%)	
Floyd	483 (64.1%)	271 (35.9%)	
Fluvanna	309 (53.6%)	268 (46.4%)	
Franklin	1,163 (62.5%)	699 (37.5%)	
Frederick	1,351 (60.1%)	898 (39.9%)	
Giles	439 (61.5%)	275 (38.5%)	
Gilmer	267 (67.8%)	127 (32.2%)	
Gloucester	383 (69.5%)	268 (30.5%)	
Goochland	377 (65.6%)	198 (34.4%)	
Grayson	562 (67.8%)	266 (32.2%)	
Greenbrier	658 (45.4%)	792 (54.6%)	
Greene	472 (89.2%)	57 (10.8%)	
Greensville	207 (79.3%)	54 (20.7%)	
Halifax	1,173 (78.1%)	329 (21.9%)	
Hampshire	1,168 (72.3%)	747 (27.7%)	
Hancock	320 (52.5%)	190 (31.1%)	100 (16.4%)
Hanover	615 (66.1%)	315 (33.9%)	
Hardy	637 (43.1%)	842 (56.9%)	
Harrison	1,221 (59.2%)	840 (40.8%)	
Henrico	709 (48.4%)	755 (51.6%)	
Henry	505 (56.4%)	391 (43.6%)	
Highland	479 (66.9%)	237 (33.1%)	
Isle of Wight	644 (81.9%)	142 (18.1%)	
Jackson	605 (55.4%)	488 (44.6%)	
James City	57 (31.8%)	122 (68.2%)	
Jefferson	946 (52.8%)	845 (47.2%)	
Kanawha	658 (36.4%)	1,149 (63.6%)	
King & Queen	438 (72.3%)	168 (27.7%)	
King George	206 (61.9%)	127 (38.1%)	
King William	274 (79.0%)	73 (21.0%)	
Lancaster	160 (51.6%)	150 (48.4%)	
Lee	916 (70.2%)	388 (29.8%)	
Lewis	712 (70.4%)	299 (29.6%)	
Logan	470 (88.8%)	59 (11.2%)	
Louisa	632 (71.9%)	247 (28.1%)	
Loudoun	858 (30.2%)	1,979 (69.8%)	
Lunenburg	486 (80.6%)	117 (19.4%)	
Madison	750 (92.9%)	57 (7.1%)	
Marion	1,632 (77.6%)	470 (22.4%)	
Marshall	931 (48.2%)	981 (50.8%)	20 (1.0%)
Mason	561 (44.2%)	708 (55.8%)	
Matthews	270 (59.2%)	186 (40.8%)	
Mecklenburg	867 (76.2%)	271 (23.8%)	
Mercer	492 (69.7%)	214 (30.3%)	
Middlesex	249 (66.0%)	128 (34.0%)	
Monongalia	1,447 (70.4%)	609 (29.6%)	
Monroe	747 (50.5%)	731 (49.5%)	
Montgomery	653 (58.3%)	468 (41.7%)	
Morgan	319 (49.2%)	329 (50.8%)	
Nansemond	416 (48.3%)	445 (51.7%)	
Nelson	418 (44.6%)	520 (55.4%)	
New Kent	193 (53.3%)	169 (46.7%)	
Nicholas	298 (44.9%)	366 (55.1%)	
Norfolk	1,230 (55.0%)	1,008 (45.0%)	
Northampton	256 (52.1%)	235 (47.9%)	

County	Buchanan (D)	Fillmore (A&W)	Frémont (R)
Northumberland	340 (58.6%)	240 (41.4%)	
Nottoway	203 (58.2%)	146 (41.8%)	
Ohio	1,632 (50.9%)	1,464 (45.7%)	108 (3.4%)
Orange	437 (60.4%)	287 (39.6%)	
Page	1,034 (94.8%)	57 (5.2%)	
Patrick	594 (60.7%)	385 (39.3%)	
Pendleton	500 (54.1%)	424 (45.9%)	
Pittsylvania	1,355 (52.5%)	1,227 (47.5%)	
Pleasants	303 (63.0%)	178 (37.0%)	
Pocahontas	417 (74.2%)	115 (25.8%)	
Powhatan	244 (72.6%)	92 (27.4%)	
Preston	1,232 (63.1%)	719 (36.9%)	
Prince Edward	429 (66.7%)	214 (33.3%)	
Prince George	306 (80.5%)	74 (19.5%)	
Princess Anne	397 (50.3%)	393 (49.7%)	
Prince William	709 (75.3%)	233 (24.7%)	
Pulaski	331 (62.3%)	200 (37.7%)	
Putnam	396 (50.3%)	391 (49.7%)	
Raleigh	141 (38.2%)	228 (61.8%)	
Randolph	441 (66.9%)	218 (33.1%)	
Rappahannock	492 (58.4%)	351 (41.6%)	
Richmond	225 (43.6%)	291 (56.4%)	
Ritchie	506 (64.6%)	277 (35.4%)	
Roane	212 (45.4%)	255 (54.6%)	
Roanoke	503 (68.8%)	228 (31.2%)	
Rockbridge	1,124 (51.6%)	1,036 (48.4%)	
Rockingham	2,733 (84.3%)	510 (15.7%)	
Russell	755 (66.1%)	388 (33.9%)	
Scott	810 (66.6%)	406 (33.4%)	5 (0.2%)
Shenandoah	2,339 (90.8%)	233 (9.0%)	
Smyth	572 (63.3%)	332 (36.7%)	
Southampton	570 (55.4%)	458 (44.6%)	
Spotsylvania	622 (58.1%)	448 (41.9%)	
Stafford	539 (67.3%)	262 (32.7%)	
Surry	230 (69.3%)	102 (30.7%)	
Sussex	367 (80.7%)	88 (19.3%)	
Taylor	616 (58.8%)	432 (41.2%)	
Tazewell	1,140 (90.5%)	119 (9.5%)	
Tucker	137 (89.5%)	16 (10.5%)	
Tyler	556 (63.1%)	325 (36.9%)	
Upshur	534 (63.6%)	295 (35.2%)	10 (1.2%)
Warren	568 (79.7%)	145 (20.3%)	
Warwick	69 (62.1%)	42 (37.9%)	
Washington	1,115 (63.4%)	644 (36.6%)	
Wayne	362 (57.4%)	269 (42.6%)	
Westmoreland	131 (23.0%)	439 (77.0%)	
Wetzel	704 (89.8%)	80 (10.2%)	
Wirt	322 (62.8%)	191 (37.2%)	
Wise	411 (90.7%)	42 (9.3%)	
Wood	875 (53.7%)	753 (46.3%)	
Wyoming	76 (67.3%)	37 (32.7%)	
Wythe	887 (62.6%)	531 (37.4%)	
York	114 (37.0%)	194 (63.0%)	

Cities & Towns

Norfolk	644 (45.0%)	787 (55.0%)	
Petersburg	836 (55.4%)	672 (44.6%)	
Richmond	1,474 (45.7%)	1,753 (54.3%)	
Williamsburg	57 (50.4%)	56 (49.6%)	
Total	**90,352 (60.0%)**	**60,112 (39.9%)**	**286 (0.2%)**
		*(60,071)	

Stated total. The difference between the stated and added totals is due to a three vote difference in Bedford, and an error in crediting Fillmore with the same total in Doddridge as in Dinwiddie, the county that preceded it in the tally.

Sources—*Richmond Enquirer*, January 2, 1857; and W. Dean Burnham, *Presidential Ballots 1836–1892* (reprint edition), New York, NY: Arno Press, 1976, pp. 816–842, 852–864, 948–51.

Wisconsin

No returns have been located for this election for Chippewa, Door, Douglass and Oconto Counties.

County	Buchanan (D)	Frémont (R)	Fillmore (A&W)
Adams & Juneau	625 (28.1%)	1,591 (71.5%)	9 (0.4%)
Bad Ax	231 (27.2%)	597 (70.3%)	21 (2.5%)
Brown	1,004 (66.8%)	499 (33.2%)	0
Buffalo	163 (70.6%)	68 (29.4%)	0
Calumet	408 (45.6%)	486 (54.3%)	1 (0.1%)
Clark	37 (33.6%)	73 (66.4%)	0
Columbia	1,239 (29.5%)	2,950 (70.3%)	7 (0.2%)
Crawford	429 (45.1%)	521 (54.8%)	1 (0.1%)
Dane	3,443 (46.2%)	3,996 (53.7%)	6 (0.1%)
Dodge	2,784 (44.5%)	3,455 (55.2%)	15 (0.2%)
Dunn	119 (23.4%)	390 (76.6%)	0
Fond du Lac	2,511 (43.1%)	3,292 (56.5%)	25 (0.4%)
Grant	1,419 (32.1%)	2,809 (63.6%)	186 (4.2%)
Green	1,087 (34.8%)	2,004 (64.2%)	32 (1.0%)
Iowa	1,474 (49.2%)	1,497 (49.9%)	27 (0.9%)
Jackson	144 (31.6%)	306 (67.1%)	6 (1.3%)
Jefferson	3,434 (51.0%)	3,290 (48.9%)	6 (0.1%)
Kenosha	831 (35.5%)	1,508 (64.5%)	0
Kewaunee	206 (69.8%)	89 (30.2%)	0
La Crosse	541 (34.8%)	987 (63.6%)	25 (1.6%)
Lafayette	1,722 (54.6%)	1,415 (44.8%)	19 (0.6%)
Manitowoc	1,907 (61.8%)	1,177 (38.2%)	0
Marathon	207 (43.4%)	269 (56.4%)	1 (0.2%)
Marquette	1,032 (28.9%)	2,518 (70.6%)	19 (0.5%)
Milwaukee	7,188 (71.8%)	2,798 (27.9%)	25 (0.2%)
Monroe	254 (25.9%)	722 (72.5%)	6 (0.6%)
Outagamie	753 (55.6%)	602 (44.4%)	1 (0.1%)
Ozaukee	2,032 (84.9%)	360 (15.1%)	0
Pierce	106 (20.0%)	414 (78.0%)	11 (2.1%)
Polk	54 (36.2%)	95 (63.8%)	0
Portage	361 (34.3%)	680 (64.5%)	13 (1.2%)
Racine	1,688 (42.3%)	2,299 (57.6%)	6 (0.1%)
Richland	455 (33.1%)	882 (64.2%)	37 (2.7%)
Rock	1,965 (29.4%)	4,707 (70.4%)	10 (0.2%)
St. Croix	252 (37.7%)	417 (62.3%)	0
Sauk	993 (33.0%)	2,015 (66.9%)	4 (0.1%)
Shawano	21 (23.6%)	68 (76.4%)	0
Sheboygan	1,921 (50.2%)	1,891 (49.4%)	15 (0.4%)
Trempleau	45 (19.1%)	190 (80.9%)	0
Walworth	1,297 (26.9%)	3,518 (73.0%)	4 (0.1%)
Washington	2,641 (76.3%)	813 (23.5%)	7 (0.2%)
Waukesha	2,020 (41.2%)	2,875 (58.6%)	8 (0.2%)
Waupaca	75 (10.5%)	636 (89.4%)	0
Waushara	215 (14.2%)	1,292 (85.4%)	6 (0.4%)
Winnebago	1,415 (33.7%)	2,769 (65.9%)	20 (0.5%)
Wood	95 (26.8%)	260 (73.2%)	0
Total	**52,843 (44.2%)**	**66,090 (55.3%)**	**579 (0.5%)**
*La Pointe	97 (90.7%)	10 (9.3%)	0

Not included in the official returns reported in the (Madison) State Journal, December 9, 1856.

SOURCES—(Madison) *State Journal,* November 29 and December 9, 1856; W. Dean Burnham, *Presidential Ballots 1836–1892* (reprint edition), New York, NY: Arno Press, 1976, pp. 864–880, 952; and James R. Donoghue, *How Wisconsin Voted 1848–1872,* 3rd edition, Madison, WI: Institute of Governmental Affairs, University of Wisconsin, 1974, p. 74.

NOTES

1. The electoral vote for vice president was John Breckinridge (D) 174, William L. Dayton (R) 114 and Andrew J. Donelson (A) 8.

2. Fillmore was initially nominated by a Native American (Know-Nothing) convention. The Whig Party was largely marginalized by this time but held a convention with only 22 states represented (and 69 of 144 delegates from New York) and endorsed Fillmore as their candidate. None of the sources researched gives a breakdown of Fillmore's vote by party; nor is it clear in how many states the Whig Party really functioned. See Michael F. Holt, *The Rise and Fall of the American Whig Party*: Oxford University Press, Chapter 26.

3. Gerrit Smith (Ab) 165.

4. Gerrit Smith (Ab) 155 (156).

5. Millard Fillmore (StrA) 26,337. See note 10 for an explanation of this vote for Fillmore.

6. The national totals for "others" were: Gerrit Smith (Ab) 320 (321) (0.0!%); and Millard Fillmore (StrA) 26,337 (0.65%).

7. The returns from the counties listed below were rejected and not included with the Kentucky returns given here. It is not clear if Frémont received any votes in these counties. The *Politician's Textbook* gives Fremont's total as 314 but Svend Petersen's *A Statistical History of the American Presidential Elections* lists it as 373. In both instances, their totals for the other candidates included the rejected returns. The rejected returns were found in Ruth McQuown and Jasper B. Shannon, *Presidential Politics* in Kentucky 1824–1948, Lexington: Univeristy of Kentucky Press, 1950, pp. 30, 31, citing the *Tribune Almanac 1860*. Burnham, *Presidential Ballots*, p. 915 also citing the *Tribune Almanac* gives the same returns.

County	Buchanan (D)	Fillmore (A)
Bracken	742 (45.9%)	876 (54.1%)
Crittenden	664 (56.8%)	506 (43.2%)
Grant	676 (51.4%)	639 (48.6%)
Harlan	264 (44.4%)	331 (55.6%)
Letcher	287 (78.4%)	79 (21.6%)
Marion	1,154 (73.4%)	418 (26.6%)
Rockcastle	184 (30.6%)	417 (69.4%)
Rowan	237 (69.1%)	106 (30.9%)
Union	925 (58.6%)	653 (41.4%)
Total	*5,133*	*4,025*

8. The votes of the counties listed below were found in the same manuscript collection with the votes of all other Michigan counties. However, *Michigan Manual 1877, 1913, Politicians' Textbook*, and W. Dean Burnham's *Presidential Ballots* citing the *Manual 1913*, state that these counties made no returns. Perhaps they were received too late to be included in the official returns. Both Svend Petersen's *A Statistical History of the American Presidential Elections* and the *Guide* give the same state totals as the above sources.

County	Buchanan (D)	Frémont (R)	Fillmore (A)
Cheboygan	54 (91.5%)	4 (6.8%)	1 (1.7%)
Chippewa	92 (63.4%)	53 (36.6%)	0
Emmet	161 (89.0%)	20 (11.0%)	0
Mackinac	101 (95.3%)	5 (4.7%)	0
Manistee	13 (6.6%)	185 (93.4%)	0
Newaygo	219 (34.0%)	425 (66.0%)	0
Ontonagon	207 (51.0%)	198 (48.8%)	1 (0.2%)
Total	*847*	*890*	*2*

9. There are no returns at the state archives. The above returns are largely based on the (Jackson) *Mississippian*, December 5, 1860, W. Dean Burnham's *Presidential Ballots*, pp. 552–570 citing the *Whig Almanac 1857*, and the *Political Textbook for 1860* whose returns are also from the 1857 *Almanac*. There are minor differences between the *Mississippian's* returns and those of the other sources, except in the case of the Buchanan vote in Tippah County which is listed as 601 in the *Textbook* and *Presidential Ballots*. I believe the larger figure to be correct. The stated totals in the *Textbook* agree with those in the *Mississippian* even though the former lists the Tippah vote for Buchanan as 601. In all other instances, I used the figures from *Presidential Ballots*. (As a point of reference, the Tippah vote for Governor in 1855 totaled 2,671.)

In the case of Greene and Wayne counties, the *Mississippian* gives only a vote for Buchanan: 61 in Greene and 71 in Wayne. The *Textbook* in both instances reports no returns. *Presidential Ballots* reports the above vote for Buchanan in Wayne but no returns in Greene. I believe the above figures may have represented the Buchanan majority in each case. It would seem no vote was ever re-

ported in either county and the alleged Buchanan vote is not included in the returns given here.

10. The term Union was used to identify two almost identical electoral slates made up of supporters of both Frémont and Fillmore. Each slate had the same set of names for 26 of the state's 27 electors. To complete the ticket each party's presidential nominee was also a candidate for elector and their names were listed first on their respective electoral tickets. In fact each party printed their own tickets with this one difference. Furthermore, it was agreed that if this twin slate was victorious, the electoral vote would be cast in the same proportion as the popular vote for Frémont and Fillmore (these are the numbers in the wide brackets — without percentages — next to the Union vote) as electoral candidates. If, however, either candidate could win the election nationally they would receive all the electoral votes.

The combined vote for Frémont and Fillmore differs only slightly from the high Unionist elector: 203,138 as compared to 203,534. The returns as reported did not break down the votes of the other 26 electoral candidates by party.

Additionally there was a separate slate of Fillmore electors (last column). This was largely due to the split within the American Party's ranks primarily over slavery. The group that joined with the Republicans in the Union slate, were often called North Americans and were considered antislavery. They had split from the rest of the American Party following the national convention because of the convention's adoption of a generally proslavery platform. Several sources combine the vote of these two slates to determine Fillmore's total. However, this is incorrect, as the North American electoral slate that was part of the Union ticket was entirely different from the other Fillmore group. This Fillmore group was sometimes referred to as the "straight out Fillmore ticket."

In the national summary, I have used the Frémont and Fillmore votes (as electoral candidates) and placed the "straight out Fillmore ticket" vote in a separate column.

For a discussion of this electoral arrangement, see John F. Coleman, *The Disruption of the Pennsylvania Democracy 1848–1860*, Harrisburg, PA: Pennsylvania Historical and Museum Commission, 1975, Chapter VII.

11. The returns of the counties below "were received after the date fixed for counting the votes" and are listed separately from the accepted tallies in the manuscript returns. The returns for Erath County were found among the original county returns but are not listed in the manuscript returns. The listing for Cass in the late returns was in addition to the returns used here.

County	Buchanan (D)	Fillmore (A)
Angelina	114 (59.7%)	77 (40.3%)
Calhoun	216 (53.2%)	190 (46.8%)
Cass	38 (82.6%)	8 (17.4%)
Cooke	97 (71.3%)	39 (28.7%)
El Paso	1,022 (100%)	0
Erath	26 (66.7%)	13 (33.3%)
Hidalgo	169 (100%)	0
Kerr	16 (64.0%)	9 (36.0%)
Live Oak	19 (54.3%)	16 (45.7%)
Newton	138 (61.1%)	88 (38.9%)
Nueces	128 (100%)	0
Parker	333 (95.7%)	29 (4.3%)
San Patricio	49 (100%)	0
Starr	374 (95.7%)	17 (4.3%)
Tyler	234 (87.6%)	33 (12.4%)
Wood	335 (73.0%)	124 (27.0%)
Young	39 (78.0%)	11 (22.0%)
Total	*3,347*	*654*

1 8 6 0

National Summary[1,2]

(electoral vote in parentheses)

State	Abraham Lincoln (R)	Stephen A. Douglas (ND)	John C. Breckinridge (SD)	John Bell (CU)	*Fusion	Gerrit Smith (U)
Alabama	0	13,618 (15.11%)	48,669 (54.00%) (9)	27,835 (30.89%)		
Arkansas	0	5,390 (9.94%)	28,732 (52.99%) (4)	20,095 (37.06%)		
California	38,734 (32.31%) (4)	38,025 (31.72%)	33,975 (28.34%)	9,136 (7.62%)		
Connecticut	43,486 (53.86%) (6)	17,364 (21.50%)	16,558 (20.51%)	3,337 (4.13%)		
Delaware	3,822 (23.72%)	1,066 (6.62%)	7,339 (45.55%) (3)	3,886 (24.12%)		
Florida	0	221 (1.69%)	8,155 (62.22%) (3)	4,731 (36.10%)		
Georgia	0	11,687 (10.94%)	52,181 (48.85%)(10)[3]	42,954 (40.21%)		
Illinois	171,106 (50.84%) (11)	158,264 (47.03%)	2,291 (0.68%)	4,852 (1.44%)		
Indiana	139,013 (51.14%) (13)	115,166 (42.37%)	12,295 (4.52%)	5,339 (1.96%)		35 (0.01%)
Iowa	70,316 (54.85%) (4)	55,091 (42.97%)	1,038 (0.81%)	1,763 (1.38%)		5 (0.002%)
Kentucky	1,364 (0.93%)	25,641 (17.54%)	53,143 (36.35%)	66,058 (45.18%) (12)		
Louisiana	0	7,625 (15.10%)	22,681 (44.90%) (6)	20,204 (40.00%)		
Maine	62,915 (62.23%) (8)	29,761 (29.44%)	6,377 (6.31%)	2,046 (2.02%)		
Maryland	2,296 (2.48%)	6,080 (6.56%)	42,505 (45.88%) (8)	41,768 (45.08%)		
Massachusetts	106,533 (62.91%) (13)	34,370 (20.30%)	6,105 (3.61%)	22,332 (13.19%)		
Michigan	88,450 (57.23%) (6)	64,889 (41.98%)	805 (0.52%)	415 (0.27%)		
Minnesota	22,076 (63.39%) (4)	11,923 (34.24%)	774 (2.22%)	53 (0.15%)		
Mississippi	0	3,288 (4.76%)	40,797 (59.02%) (7)	25,040 (36.22%)		
Missouri	17,029 (10.30%)	58,804 (35.55%) (9)	31,312 (18.93%)	58,261 (35.22%)		
New Hampshire	37,519 (56.90%) (5)	25,887 (39.26%)	2,125 (3.22%)	412 (0.63%)		
New Jersey	58,344 (48.13%) (4)	(3)			62,869(51.87%)	
New York	353,804 (53.70%) (35)				305,101(46.30%)	
North Carolina	0	2,701 (2.81%)	48,539 (50.44%) (10)	44,990 (46.65%)		
Ohio	231,808 (52.33%) (23)	187,419 (42.31%)	11,404 (2.57%)	12,194 (2.75%)		136 (0.03%)
Oregon	5,344 (36.20%) (3)	4,131 (27.99%)	5,074 (34.37%)	212 (1.44%)		
Pennsylvania	267,242 (55.40%) (27)		16,684 (3.46%)	12,873 (2.67%)	185,600(38.47%)	
Rhode Island	12,244 (61.37%) (4)	7,707 (38.63%)	0	0		
South Carolina	electors chosen by the legislature			(8)		
Tennessee	0	11,384 (7.79%)	65,053 (44.51%)	69,710 (47.70%) (12)		
Texas	0	0	47,639 (75.54%) (4)	15,422 (24.46%)		
Vermont	33,808 (75.90%) (5)	8,649 (19.42%)	1,866 (4.19%)	218 (0.49%)		
Virginia	1,909 (1.14%)	16,183 (9.68%)	74,350 (44.49%)	74,691 (44.69%) (15)		
Wisconsin	86,114 (56.59%) (5)	65,024 (42.73%)	889 (0.58%)	153 (0.10%)		
Total	**1,855,276 (39.67%) (180)**	**1,004,042 (21.47%) (12)**	**672,601 (14.38%) (72)**	**590,980 (12.64%) (39)**	**553,570(11.84%)**	**176 (0.004%)**

For an explanation of these votes and their placement under the Fusion column, see the individual state returns.

Alabama

County	Douglas (ND)	Breckinridge (SD)	Bell (CU)
Autauga	394 (31.2%)	611 (48.5%)	256 (20.3%)
Baldwin	81 (17.7%)	129 (54.1%)	248 (54.1%)
Barbour	9 (3.8%)	1,715 (72.4%)	645 (27.2%)
Bibb	156 (11.5%)	613 (45.4%)	582 (43.0%)
Blount	443 (42.6%)	546 (52.5%)	51 (4.9%)
Butler	111 (5.3%)	918 (43.5%)	1,079 (51.2%)
Calhoun	54 (19.5%)	2,347 (84.9%)	364 (13.2%)
Chambers	157 (7.5%)	1,017 (48.6%)	919 (43.9%)
Cherokee	223 (9.1%)	1,706 (69.5%)	527 (21.5%)
Choctaw	158 (13.5%)	542 (46.2%)	472 (40.3%)
Clarke	77 (6.0%)	952 (74.1%)	255 (19.9%)
Coffee	2 (0.2%)	878 (68.9%)	394 (30.9%)
Conecuh	205 (23.0%)	348 (39.1%)	338 (37.9%)
Coosa	844 (34.0%)	930 (37.5%)	706 (28.5%)
Covington	12 (1.4%)	404 (48.6%)	416 (50.0%)
Dale	5 (0.3%)	1,280 (81.9%)	277 (17.7%)
Dallas	339 (18.9%)	833 (46.5%)	620 (34.6%)
De Kalb	202 (16.1%)	849 (67.6%)	204 (16.3%)
Fayette	37 (2.2%)	1,299 (76.6%)	359 (21.2%)
Franklin	460 (22.1%)	902 (43.4%)	715 (34.4%)
Greene	157 (9.7%)	696 (43.0%)	765 (47.3%)
Henry	0	1,109 (77.8%)	317 (22.2%)
Jackson	565 (23.0%)	1,760 (71.7%)	130 (5.3%)
Jefferson	78 (6.8%)	831 (72.0%)	245 (21.2%)
Lauderdale	790 (40.7%)	706 (36.4%)	444 (22.9%)
Lawrence	576 (39.2%)	370 (35.7%)	525 (35.7%)
Limestone	325 (26.7%)	522 (43.0%)	368 (30.3%)
Lowndes	57 (3.4%)	1,007 (60.8%)	592 (35.7%)
Macon	46 (1.9%)	1,184 (48.5%)	1,210 (49.6%)
Madison	1,300 (56.7%)	591 (25.8%)	400 (17.5%)
Marengo	68 (4.8%)	838 (59.1%)	512 (36.1%)
Marion	62 (5.0%)	986 (79.2%)	197 (7.9%)
Marshall	763 (55.7%)	441 (32.2%)	165 (12.1%)
Mobile	1,823 (36.5%)	1,541 (30.9%)	1,629 (32.6%)
Monroe	222 (18.5%)	530 (44.2%)	447 (37.3%)
Montgomery	133 (4.9%)	1,555 (57.1%)	1,034 (38.0%)
Morgan	545 (44.0%)	549 (44.3%)	144 (11.6%)
Perry	99 (5.3%)	982 (52.4%)	793 (42.3%)
Pickens	16 (0.9%)	1,211 (65.6%)	619 (33.5%)
Pike	84 (2.9%)	1,581 (54.7%)	1,227 (42.4%)

Randolph	343 (13.1%)	1,734 (66.3%)	537 (20.5%)
Russell	53 (2.8%)	993 (52.3%)	854 (44.9%)
St. Clair	240 (17.4%)	963 (69.9%)	174 (12.6%)
Shelby	186 (11.6%)	853 (53.0%)	570 (35.4%)
Sumter	136 (10.5%)	682 (52.8%)	473 (36.6%)
Talladega	74 (3.0%)	1,307 (52.9%)	1,091 (44.1%)
Tallapoosa	298 (9.9%)	1,451 (48.1%)	1,270 (42.1%)
Tuscaloosa	23 (1.0%)	1,219 (53.8%)	1,023 (45.2%)
Walker	303 (35.6%)	446 (12.1%)	103 (12.1%)
Washington	24 (6.8%)	176 (49.6%)	155 (43.7%)
Wilcox	113 (8.7%)	833 (64.0%)	355 (27.3%)
Winston	147 (37.7%)	203 (52.1%)	40 (10.3%)
Total	**13,618 (15.1%)**	**48,669 (54.0%)**	**27,835 (30.9%)**

SOURCE—Manuscript returns.

Arkansas

County	Douglas (ND)	Breckinridge (SD)	Bell (CU)
Arkansas	55 (6.1%)	426 (47.4%)	417 (46.4%)
Ashley	31 (2.9%)	604 (57.1%)	422 (39.9%)
Benton	253 (19.7%)	702 (54.7%)	328 (25.6%)
Bradley	36 (3.2%)	633 (57.1%)	440 (39.7%)
Calhoun	28 (2.2%)	398 (63.2%)	204 (32.4%)
Carroll	26 (2.2%)	791 (66.8%)	368 (31.1%)
Chicot	28 (5.5%)	231 (45.1%)	253 (49.4%)
Clark	32 (2.4%)	804 (60.2%)	500 (37.4%)
Columbia	138 (8.2%)	839 (49.6%)	716 (42.3%)
Conway	52 (5.6%)	549 (59.2%)	326 (35.2%)
Craighead	20 (3.8%)	319 (60.0%)	193 (36.3%)
Crawford	357 (36.7%)	244 (25.0%)	374 (38.4%)
Crittenden	173 (33.4%)	88 (17.0%)	257 (49.6%)
Dallas	55 (5.9%)	513 (54.6%)	371 (39.5%)
Desha	115 (16.1%)	287 (40.2%)	312 (43.7%)
Drew	84 (5.9%)	772 (54.5%)	560 (39.5%)
Franklin	44 (4.4%)	666 (67.1%)	283 (28.5%)
Fulton	56 (16.2%)	252 (72.8%)	38 (11.0%)
Green	48 (11.0%)	328 (75.2%)	60 (13.8%)
Hempstead	208 (12.6%)	762 (46.3%)	675 (41.0%)
Hot Spring	45 (5.5%)	451 (61.5%)	237 (32.3%)
Independence	281 (14.8%)	722 (46.3%)	893 (47.1%)
Izard	128 (13.9%)	524 (56.8%)	271 (29.4%)
Jackson	53 (3.4%)	762 (47.0%)	722 (47.0%)
Jefferson	442 (25.9%)	664 (38.9%)	600 (35.2%)
Johnson	14 (1.4%)	780 (77.1%)	210 (20.9%)
Lafayette	11 (1.4%)	486 (61.8%)	290 (36.8%)
Lawrence	92 (6.3%)	906 (61.5%)	474 (32.2%)
Madison	72 (8.2%)	626 (71.6%)	176 (20.1%)
Marion	64 (7.8%)	527 (64.0%)	232 (28.2%)
Mississippi	90 (25.8%)	83 (23.8%)	176 (50.4%)
Monroe	50 (7.8%)	301 (47.3%)	286 (44.9%)
Montgomery	4 (0.9%)	360 (84.9%)	60 (14.2%)
Newton	19 (4.7%)	315 (78.6%)	67 (16.7%)
Ouachita	82 (4.6%)	929 (51.9%)	779 (43.5%)
Perry	50 (17.8%)	149 (53.0%)	82 (29.2%)
Phillips	62 (4.8%)	619 (48.1%)	606 (47.1%)
Pike	77 (18.2%)	294 (69.7%)	51 (12.1%)
Poinsett	53 (13.0%)	253 (25.0%)	102 (25.0%)
Polk	28 (9.6%)	254 (87.6%)	11 (3.8%)
Pope	12 (1.1%)	663 (61.9%)	396 (37.0%)
Prairie	113 (7.9%)	673 (46.8%)	651 (45.3%)
Pulaski	172 (9.1%)	819 (43.3%)	899 (47.6%)
St. Francis	281 (24.6%)	416 (36.5%)	444 (38.9%)
Saline	48 (6.1%)	556 (59.1%)	337 (35.8%)
Scott	88 (14.4%)	363 (59.5%)	159 (26.1%)
Searcy	117 (19.8%)	276 (46.7%)	198 (33.5%)
Sebastian	319 (22.2%)	575 (40.0%)	545 (37.9%)
Sevier	106 (8.7%)	754 (61.8%)	361 (29.6%)
Union	78 (5.2%)	757 (50.5%)	444 (38.9%)
Van Buren	51 (5.6%)	604 (66.9%)	248 (27.5%)
Washington	244 (11.3%)	1,028 (47.7%)	881 (40.9%)
White	140 (10.6%)	602 (45.5%)	582 (44.0%)
Yell	65 (7.2%)	533 (58.8%)	309 (34.1%)
Total	**5,390 (9.9%)** *(5,227)	**28,732 (53.0%)**	**20,095 (37.1%)** *(20,094)

*Stated totals.

SOURCES—(Little Rock) *Arkansas State Gazette*, December 8, 1860; and W. Dean Burnham, *Presidential Ballots 1836–1892* (reprint edition), New York, NY: Arno Press, 1976, pp. 274–292, 894, citing *Tribune Almanac, 1861*.

California

County	Lincoln (R)	Douglas (ND)	Breckinridge (SD)	Bell (CU)
Alameda	1,033 (49.4%)	513 (24.6%)	481 (23.0%)	62 (3.0%)
Amador	995 (25.0%)	1,866 (46.8%)	945 (23.7%)	178 (4.5%)
Butte	1,437 (32.4%)	1,502 (33.8%)	1,173 (26.4%)	326 (7.4%)
Calaveras	978 (20.3%)	1,885 (39.1%)	1,717 (35.6%)	240 (5.0%)
Colusa	258 (27.1%)	235 (24.7%)	386 (40.5%)	73 (7.7%)
Contra Costa	608 (39.3%)	413 (26.7%)	391 (25.3%)	134 (8.7%)
Del Norte	175 (33.7%)	88 (17.0%)	217 (41.8%)	39 (7.5%)
El Dorado	2,119 (30.1%)	2,695 (38.2%)	1,901 (27.0%)	334 (4.7%)
Fresno	53 (11.3%)	22 (4.7%)	271 (57.8%)	123 (26.2%)
Humboldt	335 (32.5%)	444 (43.1%)	232 (22.5%)	20 (1.9%)
Klamath	92 (13.8%)	377 (56.4%)	163 (24.4%)	36 (5.4%)
Los Angeles	352 (32.5%)	475 (27.7%)	688 (40.1%)	201 (11.7%)
Marin	408 (40.3%)	282 (27.8%)	285 (28.1%)	38 (3.8%)
Mariposa	262 (13.9%)	489 (26.0%)	815 (43.2%)	319 (16.9%)
Mendocino	198 (18.9%)	235 (22.4%)	499 (47.6%)	116 (11.1%)
Merced	42 (10.7%)	52 (13.3%)	233 (59.6%)	64 (16.4%)
Monterey	306 (38.8%)	233 (29.5%)	246 (31.2%)	4 (0.5%)
Napa	441 (24.8%)	518 (29.1%)	679 (38.2%)	141 (7.9%)
Nevada	2,539 (36.5%)	2,373 (34.1%)	1,653 (23.7%)	400 (5.7%)
Placer	1,743 (29.9%)	1,858 (31.9%)	1,448 (24.9%)	775 (13.3%)
Plumas	458 (28.2%)	503 (30.9%)	453 (27.9%)	211 (13.0%)
Sacramento	2,670 (35.4%)	2,836 (37.6%)	1,684 (22.3%)	352 (4.7%)
San Bernardino	305 (37.2%)	224 (27.4%)	192 (23.4%)	98 (12.0%)

County	Lincoln (R)	Douglas (ND)	Breckinridge (SD)	Bell (CU)
San Diego	81 (30.5%)	29 (10.9%)	148 (55.6%)	8 (3.0%)
San Francisco	6,825 (47.5%)	4,035 (28.1%)	2,560 (17.8%)	940 (6.6%)
San Joaquin	1,131 (32.9%)	733 (21.3%)	1,373 (40.0%)	199 (5.8%)
San Luis Obispo	148 (35.0%)	120 (28.4%)	155 (36.6%)	0
San Mateo	389 (35.3%)	543 (49.2%)	130 (11.8%)	41 (3.7%)
Santa Barbara	46 (9.7%)	305 (64.3%)	123 (26.0%)	0
Santa Clara	1,463 (46.1%)	881 (27.7%)	722 (22.7%)	111 (3.5%)
Santa Cruz	670 (47.7%)	286 (20.4%)	319 (22.7%)	129 (9.2%)
Shasta	464 (19.4%)	1,094 (45.7%)	585 (24.4%)	252 (10.5%)
Sierra	1,468 (31.0%)	1,539 (32.4%)	1,347 (28.4%)	389 (8.2%)
Siskiyou	955 (25.6%)	1,503 (40.2%)	760 (20.4%)	516 (13.8%)
Solano	681 (29.3%)	603 (26.0%)	746 (32.1%)	292 (12.6%)
Sonoma	1,236 (32.9%)	611 (16.2%)	1,467 (39.0%)	449 (11.9%)
Stanislaus	167 (18.6%)	232 (25.8%)	433 (48.2%)	67 (7.4%)
Sutter	403 (30.5%)	441 (33.3%)	440 (33.2%)	40 (3.0%)
Tehama	243 (18.6%)	496 (38.1%)	311 (23.8%)	253 (19.4%)
Trinity	593 (27.6%)	885 (41.2%)	516 (24.1%)	153 (7.1%)
Tulare	131 (9.9%)	211 (15.9%)	574 (43.4%)	408 (30.8%)
Tuolumne	1,633 (29.5%)	1,503 (27.1%)	2,034 (36.7%)	372 (6.7%)
Yolo	535 (31.3%)	497 (29.0%)	606 (35.4%)	74 (4.3%)
Yuba	1,665 (32.9%)	1,360 (26.9%)	1,874 (37.1%)	159 (3.1%)
Total	**38,734 (32.3%)**	**38,025 (31.7%)** *(38,023)	**33,975 (28.4%)**	**9,136 (7.6%)**

SOURCES—Manuscript returns; L. P. McCarthy, *The Annual Statistician and Economist 1891*, San Francisco, CA: 1891, pp. 263–4.

Connecticut

County	Lincoln (R)	Douglas (ND)	Breckinridge (SD)	Bell (CU)
Fairfield	7,025 (43.0%)	3,177 (19.4%)	4,097 (25.1%)	2,055 (12.6%)
Hartford	8,519 (64.2%)	3,145 (23.7%)	3,296 (24.9%)	302 (22.8%)
Litchfield	4,812 (59.0%)	1,729 (21.2%)	1,568 (19.2%)	46 (0.6%)
Middlesex	2,883 (52.4%)	1,180 (21.4%)	1,334 (24.2%)	110 (2.0%)
New Haven	8,667 (52.6%)	2,940 (17.9%)	4,282 (26.0%)	575 (3.5%)
New London	5,470 (57.7%)	2,598 (27.4%)	1,199 (12.7%)	211 (2.2%)
Tolland	2,494 (60.4%)	1,139 (27.6%)	479 (11.6%)	18 (0.4%)
Windham	3,616 (67.0%)	1,456 (27.0%)	303 (5.6%)	20 (0.4%)
Total	**43,486 (53.9%)**	**17,364 (21.5%)**	**16,558 (20.5%)**	**3,337 (4.1%)**

SOURCE—*Register, 1889.*

Delaware

County	Lincoln (R)	Douglas (ND)	Breckinridge (SD)	Bell (CU)
Kent	1,075 (26.7%)	143 (3.6%)	2,081 (51.8%)	720 (17.9%)
New Castle	2,073 (28.1%)	719 (9.8%)	3,004 (40.8%)	1,574 (21.4%)
Sussex	674 (14.3%)	204 (4.3%)	2,254 (47.7%)	1,592 (33.7%)
Total	**3,822 (23.7%)**	**1,066 (6.6%)**	**7,339 (45.6%)**	**3,886 (24.1%)**

SOURCE—*Governors' Register*, 1860.

Florida

No returns have been located for this election for Putnam County.

County	Douglas (ND)	Breckinridge (SD)	Bell (CU)
Alachua	5 (0.7%)	527 (72.5%)	195 (26.8%)
Brevard	0	8 (100%)	0
Calhoun	0	57 (86.4%)	9 (13.6%)
Clay	0	57 (33.3%)	114 (66.7%)
Columbia	3 (0.5%)	406 (65.2%)	214 (34.3%)
Dade	0	16 (100%)	0
Duval	51 (8.6%)	346 (58.4%)	195 (33.8%)
Escambia	97 (14.6%)	192 (28.8%)	377 (56.6%)
Franklin	0	284 (82.3%)	61 (17.7%)
Gadsden	0	392 (50.5%)	384 (49.5%)
Hamilton	23 (6.1%)	243 (64.5%)	111 (29.4%)
Hernando	1 (0.6%)	151 (84.4%)	27 (15.1%)
Hillsborough	0	303 (83.5%)	60 (16.5%)
Holmes	0	115 (60.8%)	74 (39.2%)
Jackson	0	512 (52.7%)	462 (47.3%)
Jefferson	0	487 (75.5%)	158 (24.5%)
Lafayette	0	96 (54.5%)	80 (45.5%)
Leon	0	482 (63.1%)	282 (36.9%)
Levy	0	195 (80.6%)	47 (19.4%)
Liberty	0	74 (49.7%)	75 (50.3%)
Madison	0	444 (66.3%)	226 (33.7%)
Marion	1 (0.2%)	510 (83.6%)	99 (16.2%)
Manatee	0	50 (100%)	0

Monroe	0	219 (78.5%)	60 (21.5%)
Nassau	1	291 (77.8%)	82 (21.9%)
New River	7 (1.5%)	278 (59.9%)	179 (38.6%)
Orange	9 (7.4%)	46 (37.7%)	67 (54.9%)
St. Johns	0	211 (74.0%)	74 (26.0%)
Santa Rosa	17 (2.4%)	266 (38.3%)	411 (59.2%)
Sumter	1 (0.6%)	109 (70.8%)	44 (28.6%)
Suwannee	5 (1.4%)	144 (49.1%)	145 (49.5%)
Taylor	0	88 (57.9%)	64 (42.1%)
Volusia	0	69 (80.2%)	17 (19.8%)
Washington	0	151 (71.6%)	61 (28.4%)
Wakulla	1 (0.4%)	175 (62.5%)	104 (37.1%)
Walton	0	161 (48.2%)	173 (51.8%)
Total	**221 (1.7%)**	**8,155 (62.2%)**	**4,731 (36.1%)**

SOURCE—(Tallahassee) *Floridian and Journal*, December 8, 1860.

Georgia

County	Douglas (ND)	Breckinridge (SD)	Bell (CU)
Appling	1 (0.3%)	287 (71.8%)	112 (28.0%)
Baker	2 (0.5%)	259 (69.4%)	112 (30.0%)
Baldwin	95 (10.1%)	440 (47.2%)	397 (42.6%)
Banks	10 (1.8%)	466 (81.8%)	94 (16.5%)
Berrien	1 (0.2%)	316 (59.0%)	219 (40.9%)
Bibb	305 (15.2%)	812 (40.6%)	884 (44.2%)
Brooks	4 (0.6%)	336 (54.1%)	281 (45.2%)
Bryan	1 (0.4%)	198 (71.7%)	75 (27.9%)
Bulloch	1 (0.2%)	67 (96.9%)	7 (1.2%)
Burke	252 (27.4%)	468 (50.1%)	211 (22.6%)
Butts	27 (4.5%)	309 (51.1%)	269 (44.5%)
Calhoun	6 (0.2%)	230 (68.9%)	98 (29.3%)
Camden	0	207 (85.5%)	35 (14.5%)
Campbell	14 (1.2%)	785 (64.8%)	412 (34.0%)
Carroll	29 (1.6%)	1,294 (70.7%)	508 (27.7%)
Cass	328 (16.5%)	1,055 (53.1%)	605 (30.4%)
Catoosa	74 (9.3%)	382 (48.1%)	338 (42.6%)
Charlton	2 (1.1%)	141 (75.8%)	43 (23.1%)
Chatham	320 (11.9%)	1,812 (67.1%)	568 (21.0%)
Chattahouchee	19 (3.5%)	303 (55.3%)	226 (41.2%)
Chattooga	152 (17.4%)	287 (32.8%)	436 (49.8%)
Cherokee	143 (9.9%)	857 (59.3%)	446 (30.8%)
Clarke	57 (4.7%)	452 (37.5%)	695 (57.7%)
Clay	12 (2.2%)	286 (52.6%)	246 (45.2%)
Clayton	103 (16.8%)	197 (32.2%)	311 (50.8%)
Clinch	6 (2.6%)	115 (50.1%)	106 (46.7%)
Cobb	46 (2.3%)	1,368 (67.2%)	623 (35.6%)
Coffee	14 (10.2%)	93 (61.9%)	30 (27.9%)
Columbia	363 (47.4%)	67 (8.7%)	336 (43.9%)
Colquitt	1 (0.5%)	115 (62.8%)	67 (36.6%)
Coweta	55 (3.7%)	896 (60.3%)	536 (36.0%)
Crawford	2 (0.4%)	378 (66.5%)	188 (53.1%)
Dade	23 (5.0%)	259 (56.4%)	177 (38.6%)
Dawson	62 (12.6%)	338 (68.7%)	92 (18.7%)
Decatur	1 (0.1%)	580 (52.7%)	519 (47.2%)
De Kalb	63 (5.7%)	636 (57.0%)	415 (37.2%)
Dooly	28 (4.5%)	348 (55.3%)	253 (40.2%)
Dougherty	26 (3.9%)	372 (55.1%)	277 (41.0%)
Early	1 (0.2%)	294 (70.5%)	122 (29.3%)
Echols	0	87 (77.6%)	25 (22.4%)
Effingham	3 (0.7%)	209 (50.0%)	206 (49.3%)
Elbert	457 (52.6%)	120 (13.8%)	291 (33.5%)
Emanuel	42 (8.5%)	210 (42.5%)	242 (49.0%)
Fannin	92 (11.7%)	545 (69.4%)	148 (18.9%)
Fayette	29 (3.6%)	466 (58.4%)	302 (38.0%)
Floyd	285 (15.1%)	756 (40.0%)	848 (44.9%)
Forsyth	47 (4.5%)	630 (60.5%)	364 (35.0%)
Franklin	3 (0.3%)	726 (83.8%)	137 (65.8%)
Fulton	347 (13.6%)	1,018 (39.8%)	1,195 (46.7%)
Gilmer	33 (3.6%)	755 (83.0%)	122 (13.4%)
Glasscock	173 (70.3%)	58 (23.6%)	15 (6.1%)
Glynn	1 (0.5%)	177 (90.8%)	17 (8.7%)
Greene	151 (17.8%)	114 (13.5%)	581 (68.7%)
Gordon	90 (6.2%)	874 (60.5%)	480 (33.2%)
Gwinnett	234 (14.2%)	643 (38.9%)	774 (46.9%)
Habersham	72 (10.0%)	457 (63.7%)	188 (26.2%)
Hall	83 (7.9%)	467 (44.5%)	500 (47.6%)
Hancock	148 (21.8%)	128 (12.9%)	402 (59.3%)
Haralson	1 (0.2%)	356 (85.0%)	62 (14.8%)
Harris	30 (2.7%)	392 (35.3%)	689 (62.0%)
Hart	90 (12.4%)	482 (66.7%)	151 (20.9%)
Heard	62 (7.0%)	439 (49.8%)	380 (43.1%)
Henry	54 (4.4%)	523 (42.4%)	657 (55.2%)
Houston	31 (3.0%)	555 (48.1%)	569 (49.3%)
Irwin	2 (2.1%)	74 (77.9%)	19 (20.0%)
Jackson	108 (8.1%)	675 (54.2%)	463 (37.2%)
Jasper	173 (21.8%)	251 (31.7%)	368 (46.5%)
Jefferson	326 (13.1%)	67 (8.9%)	363 (45.9%)
Johnson	96 (24.4%)	117 (29.7%)	181 (45.9%)
Jones	14 (3.5%)	235 (50.1%)	214 (46.2%)
Laurens	36 (6.1%)	128 (21.6%)	428 (72.3%)
Lee	17 (3.5%)	240 (50.1%)	222 (46.3%)
Liberty	21 (4.9%)	264 (61.4%)	145 (33.7%)
Lincoln	113 (35.6%)	34 (10.7%)	167 (52.7%)
Lowndes	2 (0.4%)	313 (57.3%)	231 (42.3%)
Lumpkin	30 (4.0%)	393 (53.0%)	319 (43.0%)
Macon	14 (2.0%)	271 (38.5%)	419 (59.5%)
Madison	11 (1.8%)	375 (60.6%)	233 (31.6%)
Marion	41 (6.0%)	321 (47.1%)	321 (47.1%)
McIntosh	0	200 (83.0%)	41 (17.0%)
Meriwether	49 (4.0%)	615 (50.4%)	557 (45.7%)
Miller	0	231 (89.2%)	28 (10.8%)
Milton	25 (3.2%)	417 (53.3%)	340 (43.5%)
Mitchell	28 (5.6%)	327 (65.5%)	144 (28.9%)
Monroe	57 (4.9%)	464 (40.1%)	636 (5.0%)
Montgomery	6 (2.0%)	40 (13.3%)	255 (84.7%)
Morgan	142 (23.5%)	102 (16.9%)	361 (60.0%)
Murray	210 (15.2%)	421 (30.5%)	251 (18.2%)
Muscogee	160 (9.4%)	769 (45.3%)	767 (45.2%)
Newton	351 (23.0%)	364 (23.9%)	810 (53.1%)
Oglethorpe	187 (22.9%)	263 (32.2%)	367 (44.9%)
Paulding	39 (3.8%)	781 (76.7%)	198 (19.4%)
Pickens	45 (7.0%)	452 (69.9%)	150 (23.2%)
Pierce	1 (0.3%)	237 (74.8%)	79 (24.9%)
Pike	15 (1.4%)	596 (57.4%)	425 (41.2%)
Polk	48 (6.7%)	326 (45.3%)	345 (48.0%)
Pulaski	34 (4.3%)	464 (59.2%)	286 (36.5%)
Putnam	157 (25.2%)	176 (28.2%)	291 (46.6%)
Quitman	3 (0.7%)	237 (58.2%)	167 (41.0%)
Rabun	10 (2.6%)	353 (91.9%)	21 (5.5%)
Randolph	57 (5.0%)	587 (51.6%)	494 (43.4%)
Richmond	1,051 (45.7%)	403 (17.5%)	848 (36.8%)
Schley	65 (14.7%)	142 (32.1%)	235 (53.2%)
Screven	34 (6.2%)	343 (62.6%)	171 (31.2%)
Spalding	27 (2.3%)	596 (51.4%)	536 (46.2%)
Stewart	18 (1.7%)	538 (51.7%)	484 (46.5%)
Sumter	131 (10.9%)	380 (31.5%)	694 (57.6%)
Talbot	87 (8.7%)	406 (40.7%)	505 (50.6%)
Taliaferro	220 (54.7%)	9 (2.2%)	173 (43.0%)
Tattnall	4 (0.8%)	312 (60.2%)	202 (39.0%)
Taylor	22 (2.8%)	394 (50.7%)	361 (46.5%)
Telfair	6 (2.6%)	98 (42.4%)	127 (55.0%)
Terrell	69 (10.1%)	227 (33.2%)	387 (56.7%)
Thomas	34 (3.4%)	462 (46.4%)	499 (50.1%)
Towns	94 (24.2%)	192 (49.6%)	101 (26.1%)
Troup	48 (3.4%)	402 (28.3%)	970 (68.0%)
Triggs	6 (1.2%)	320 (63.1%)	181 (35.7%)
Union	11 (1.6%)	474 (67.6%)	216 (30.8%)
Upson	49 (5.3%)	279 (29.9%)	605 (64.8%)

Walker	318	(22.5%)	487	(34.4%)	649 (43.1%)
Walton	183	(13.9%)	555	(42.3%)	574 (43.8%)
Ware	1	(0.4%)	212	(85.8%)	34 (13.8%)
Warren	427	(59.1%)	55	(7.6%)	240 (33.2%)
Washington	282	(23.4%)	313	(26.0%)	608 (50.5%)
Wayne	0		134	(78.4%)	37 (21.6%)
Webster	5	(0.9%)	242	(94.8%)	293 (51.3%)
White	29	(7.3%)	220	(55.0%)	151 (37.8%)
Wilcox	3	(1.7%)	254	(92.0%)	19 (6.9%)

Wilkes	171	(23.1%)	266	(36.0%)	302 (40.9%)
Wilkinson	111	(11.6%)	184	(50.5%)	364 (38.0%)
Whitfield	202	(14.4%)	747	(53.4%)	450 (32.2%)
Worth	3	(0.8%)	263	(67.8%)	122 (31.4%)
Total	**11,687**	**(10.9%)**	**52,181**	**(48.9%)**	**42,954 (40.2%)**

Stated totals.   *(52,210)   *(43,083)

SOURCE—*Executive Council Minutes of Georgia, 1860.*

Illinois

County	Lincoln(R)	Douglas(ND)	Breckinridge(SD)	Bell (CU)	Smith (U)
Adams	3,811 (46.3%)	4,265 (51.9%)	67 (0.8%)	81 (1.0%)	
Alexander	106 (10.1%)	684 (65.3%)	79 (7.5%)	178 (17.0%)	
Bond	987 (49.5%)	981 (49.2%)	2 (0.1%)	25 (1.3%)	
Boone	1,759 (85.0%)	310 (15.0%)	9	0	
Brown	728 (36.6%)	1,202 (60.4%)	26 (1.3%)	33 (1.7%)	
Bureau	3,622 (69.1%)	1,415 (27.0%)	179 (3.4%)	20 (0.4%)	9 (0.2%)
Calhoun	269 (26.8%)	668 (66.6%)	0	66 (6.6%)	
Carroll	1,630 (77.8%)	461 (22.0%)	1 (0.05%)	1 (0.05%)	3 (0.1%)
Cass	1,046 (44.1%)	1,301 (54.9%)	5 (0.2%)	19 (0.8%)	
Champaign	1,793 (58.5%)	1,221 (39.8%)	25 (0.8%)	25 (0.8%)	
Christian	968 (40.2%)	1,408 (58.5%)	9 (0.4%)	20 (0.8%)	
Clark	1,313 (43.1%)	1,724 (56.6%)	0	8 (0.3%)	
Clay	681 (38.2%)	1,070 (60.0%)	2 (0.1%)	30 (1.7%)	
Clinton	748 (35.7%)	1,294 (61.8%)	6 (0.3%)	45 (2.2%)	
Coles	1,495 (49.2%)	1,467 (48.2%)	0	79 (2.6%)	
Cook	14,589 (59.2%)	9,846 (40.0%)	87 (0.4%)	107 (0.4%)	2 (0.01%)
Crawford	931 (39.8%)	1,384 (59.1%)	1 (0.03%)	24 (1.0%)	
Cumberland	629 (40.6%)	909 (58.7%)	2 (0.1%)	9 (0.6%)	
De Kalb	3,049 (75.8%)	965 (24.0%)	1 (0.02%)	8 (0.2%)	
De Witt	1,258 (52.2%)	1,015 (42.2%)	62 (2.6%)	73 (3.0%)	
Douglas	809 (54.5%)	629 (42.4%)	8 (0.5%)	39 (2.6%)	
Du Page	1,790 (68.8%)	803 (30.9%)	2 (0.1%)	3 (0.1%)	4 (0.2%)
Edgar	1,727 (46.3%)	1,923 (51.6%)	11 (0.3%)	66 (1.8%)	
Edwards	580 (60.0%)	370 (38.3%)	0	16 (1.7%)	
Effingham	453 (29.5%)	1,084 (70.5%)	0	0	
Fayette	953 (37.3%)	1,571 (61.5%)	2 (0.1%)	27 (1.1%)	
Ford	235 (61.4%)	148 (38.6%)	0	0	
Franklin	228 (13.4%)	1,391 (81.9%)	5 (0.3%)	75 (4.4%)	
Fulton	3,629 (47.7%)	3,926 (52.2%)	11 (0.1%)	48 (0.6%)	
Gallatin	221 (16.5%)	1,020 (76.0%)	13 (1.0%)	88 (6.6%)	
Greene	979 (30.4%)	2,173 (67.4%)	4 (0.1%)	67 (2.1%)	
Grundy	1,412 (66.4%)	710 (33.4%)	3 (0.1%)	0	
Hamilton	102 (5.8%)	1,553 (88.5%)	0	99 (5.6%)	
Hancock	2,568 (45.3%)	2,960 (52.2%)	31 (0.5%)	115 (2.0%)	
Hardin	107 (16.0%)	499 (74.7%)	0	62 (9.3%)	
Henderson	1,253 (56.5%)	911 (41.1%)	22 (1.0%)	31 (1.4%)	
Henry	3,022 (66.1%)	1,532 (33.5%)	16 (0.3%)	4 (0.1%)	
Iroquois	1,429 (59.7%)	955 (39.9%)	8 (0.3%)	0	
Jackson	315 (15.4%)	1,556 (76.0%)	29 (1.4%)	147 (7.2%)	
Jasper	626 (40.4%)	916 (59.2%)	1 (0.1%)	5 (0.3%)	
Jefferson	459 (18.6%)	1,852 (75.0%)	21 (0.9%)	136 (5.5%)	
Jersey	910 (39.3%)	1,291 (55.7%)	11 (0.5%)	105 (4.5%)	
Jo Daviess	2,782 (59.6%)	1,841 (39.4%)	9 (0.2%)	38 (0.8%)	
Johnson	40 (2.5%)	1,563 (97.0%)	9 (0.6%)	0	
Kane	4,207 (71.6%)	1,651 (28.1%)	12 (0.2%)	8 (0.1%)	
Kankakee	1,977 (70.5%)	803 (28.6%)	16 (0.6%)	9 (0.3%)	
Kendall	1,811 (76.0%)	571 (24.0%)	1 (0.1%)	0	
Knox	3,832 (63.0%)	2,208 (36.3%)	17 (0.3%)	30 (0.5%)	
La Salle	5,342 (55.2%)	4,290 (44.3%)	8 (0.1%)	35 (0.4%)	7 (0.1%)
Lake	2,394 (71.1%)	965 (28.6%)	6 (0.2%)	4 (0.1%)	
Lawrence	764 (43.8%)	970 (55.6%)	0	12 (0.7%)	
Lee	2,420 (67.6%)	1,140 (31.8%)	6 (0.2%)	15 (0.4%)	1 (0.03%)
Livingston	1,474 (57.5%)	1,088 (42.5%)	0	0	
Logan	1,729 (52.7%)	1,521 (46.3%)	4 (0.1%)	28 (0.9%)	
Macon	1,501 (48.0%)	1,541 (49.3%)	29 (0.9%)	56 (1.8%)	
Macoupin	2,192 (42.6%)	2,688 (52.3%)	38 (0.7%)	225 (4.4%)	

County	Lincoln(R)	Douglas(ND)	Breckinridge(SD)	Bell (CU)	Smith (U)
Madison	3,161 (48.9%)	3,100 (48.0%)	21 (0.3%)	178 (2.8%)	
Marion	858 (32.2%)	1,715 (64.3%)	3 (0.1%)	90 (3.4%)	
Marshall	1,630 (53.9%)	1,376 (45.5%)	18 (0.6%)	0	
Mason	1,198 (48.5%)	1,224 (49.5%)	3 (0.1%)	47 (1.9%)	
Massac	121 (11.2%)	873 (81.0%)	0	84 (7.8%)	
McDonough	2,255 (49.1%)	2,266 (49.4%)	6 (0.1%)	62 (1.4%)	
McHenry	3,033 (67.5%)	1,444 (32.1%)	8 (0.2%)	9 (0.2%)	
McLean	3,547 (57.4%)	2,567 (41.5%)	7 (0.1%)	58 (0.9%)	2 (0.03%)
Menard	962 (46.4%)	1,035 (49.9%)	11 (0.5%)	66 (3.2%)	
Mercer	1,808 (59.4%)	1,193 (39.2%)	3 (0.1%)	35 (1.2%)	4 (0.1%)
Montgomery	1,099 (36.5%)	1,401 (61.9%)	0	17 (0.8%)	
Morgan	2,312 (47.8%)	2,419 (50.0%)	14 (0.3%)	94 (1.9%)	
Moultrie	618 (46.2%)	707 (52.9%)	0	12 (0.9%)	
Ogle	3,184 (69.9%)	1,315 (28.9%)	16 (0.4%)	40 (0.9%)	
Peoria	3,539 (48.0%)	3,738 (50.7%)	51 (0.7%)	40 (0.5%)	
Perry	649 (34.4%)	1,101 (58.3%)	1 (0.1%)	138 (7.3%)	
Piatt	782 (54.6%)	599 (41.8%)	0	51 (3.6%)	
Pike	2,553 (45.2%)	3,016 (53.4%)	37 (0.7%)	39 (0.7%)	
Pope	127 (9.0%)	1,202 (85.1%)	1 (0.1%)	83 (5.9%)	
Putnam	751 (63.6%)	366 (31.0%)	64 (5.4%)	0	
Randolph	1,382 (42.2%)	1,815 (55.4%)	8 (0.2%)	71 (2.2%)	
Richland	777 (42.5%)	1,022 (55.9%)	6 (0.3%)	22 (1.2%)	1 (0.03%)
Rock Island	2,088 (57.8%)	1,478 (40.9%)	12 (0.3%)	34 (0.9%)	
St. Clair	3,682 (53.6%)	3,014 (43.9%)	23 (0.3%)	147 (2.1%)	
Saline	100 (6.4%)	1,338 (85.4%)	15 (1.0%)	113 (7.2%)	
Sangamon	3,556 (48.3%)	3,598 (48.9%)	77 (1.0%)	130 (1.8%)	
Schuyler	956 (37.7%)	1,559 (61.4%)	8 (0.3%)	15 (0.6%)	
Scott	832 (42.2%)	1,131 (57.3%)	5 (0.3%)	5 (0.3%)	
Shelby	971 (31.1%)	2,088 (66.9%)	0	61 (2.0%)	
Stark	1,164 (63.1%)	659 (35.7%)	0	23 (1.2%)	
Stephenson	2,670 (59.7%)	1,787 (40.0%)	12 (0.3%)	4 (0.1%)	
Tazewell	2,348 (51.7%)	2,168 (47.7%)	3 (0.1%)	26 (0.6%)	
Union	157 (7.7%)	996 (49.1%)	819 (40.3%)	58 (2.9%)	
Vermilion	2,251 (58.6%)	1,577 (41.1%)	7 (0.2%)	4 (0.1%)	
Wabash	597 (44.9%)	710 (53.4%)	1 (0.1%)	22 (1.7%)	
Warren	2,208 (56.5%)	1,672 (42.8%)	14 (0.4%)	17 (0.4%)	
Washington	793 (32.8%)	1,565 (64.8%)	0	58 (2.4%)	
Wayne	620 (26.7%)	1,645 (71.0%)	5 (0.2%)	48 (2.1%)	
White	756 (32.3%)	1,544 (65.9%)	5 (0.2%)	38 (1.6%)	
Whiteside	2,713 (70.5%)	1,110 (28.8%)	8 (0.2%)	17 (0.4%)	
Will	3,219 (55.9%)	2,515 (43.7%)	12 (0.2%)	12 (0.2%)	1 (0.02%)
Williamson	173 (7.8%)	1,835 (82.9%)	40 (1.8%)	166 (7.5%)	
Winnebago	3,984 (82.8%)	817 (17.0%)	10 (0.2%)	3 (0.1%)	
Woodford	1,238 (45.8%)	1,419 (52.4%)	10 (0.4%)	39 (1.4%)	
Total	**171,106 (50.8%)**	**158,264 (47.0%)**	**2,291 (0.7%)**	**4,852 (1.4%)**	**35 (0.01%)**
*Stated totals.		*(158,254)	*(2,292)	*(4,851)	
*Monroe	845 (37.3%)	1,401 (61.9%)	0	17 (0.8%)	
*Pulaski	220 (25.7%)	550 (64.3%)	40 (4.7%)	45 (5.3%)	

*The returns from Monroe and Pulaski were not included in the official returns "on account of informality."

SOURCE—Adler, Howard and Vincent A. Lacey (ed.), *Illinois Election Returns 1818–1990*, Carbondale, IL: Southern Illinois Univ. Press, 1993, pp. 144–5; and W. Dean Burnham, *Presidential Ballots 1836–1892* (reprint edition), New York, NY: Arno Press, 1976, p. 908.

Indiana

County	Lincoln (R)	Douglas (ND)	Breckinridge (SD)	Bell (CU)	Smith (U)
Adams	632 (40.7%)	887 (57.2%)	22 (1.4%)	11 (0.7%)	
Allen	2,552 (43.6%)	3,224 (55.2%)	42 (0.7%)	32 (0.5%)	
Bartholomew	1,769 (47.6%)	1,846 (49.7%)	66 (1.8%)	34 (0.9%)	
Benton	375 (60.1%)	235 (37.7%)	6 (1.0%)	8 (1.3%)	
Blackford	275 (37.6%)	408 (55.7%)	40 (5.5%)	9 (1.2%)	
Boone	1,699 (50.9%)	941 (28.1%)	649 (19.5%)	47 (1.4%)	
Brown	301 (28.2%)	729 (68.3%)	31 (2.9%)	6 (0.6%)	
Carroll	1,590 (52.0%)	1,446 (47.3%)	5 (0.2%)	14 (0.5%)	
Cass	1,874 (49.8%)	1,727 (45.9%)	130 (3.5%)	34 (0.9%)	
Clinton	1,454 (49.2%)	1,437 (48.6%)	61 (2.1%)	6 (0.2%)	

County	Lincoln (R)	Douglas (ND)	Breckinridge (SD)	Bell (CU)	Smith (U)
Clark	1,369 (36.3%)	1,837 (46.7%)	250 (6.6%)	316 (8.4%)	
Clay	889 (38.6%)	1,316 (57.2%)	47 (2.0%)	50 (2.2%)	
Crawford	778 (46.5%)	844 (50.5%)	8 (0.5%)	42 (2.5%)	
De Kalb	1,500 (52.4%)	1,339 (46.7%)	2 (0.1%)	24 (0.8%)	
Delaware	1,933 (63.0%)	1,029 (33.5%)	98 (3.2%)	10 (0.3%)	
Daviess	934 (39.8%)	749 (31.9%)	529 (22.6%)	133 (5.7%)	
Dearborn	2,004 (44.3%)	2,378 (52.6%)	51 (1.1%)	91 (2.0%)	
Decatur	2,028 (55.0%)	1,546 (41.9%)	93 (2.5%)	20 (0.5%)	
Dubois	301 (18.0%)	1,347 (80.7%)	2 (0.1%)	20 (1.2%)	
Elkhart	2,471 (55.7%)	1,938 (43.7%)	27 (0.6%)	1 (0.02%)	
Fayette	1,343 (58.2%)	917 (39.7%)	39 (1.7%)	9 (0.4%)	
Floyd	1,151 (33.3%)	1,888 (54.6%)	96 (2.8%)	320 (9.3%)	
Fountain	1,656 (50.0%)	1,360 (41.1%)	269 (8.1%)	26 (0.8%)	
Franklin	1,695 (42.1%)	2,272 (56.4%)	49 (1.2%)	9 (0.2%)	
Fulton	1,019 (50.0%)	991 (48.6%)	22 (1.1%)	6 (0.3%)	
Gibson	1,295 (43.1%)	1,565 (52.1%)	29 (1.0%)	112 (3.7%)	
Grant	1,668 (56.2%)	1,223 (41.2%)	33 (1.0%)	46 (1.5%)	
Greene	1,420 (47.9%)	1,316 (44.4%)	204 (6.9%)	20 (0.7%)	5 (0.2%)
Hamilton	2,195 (63.8%)	1,144 (33.2%)	98 (2.8%)	4 (0.1%)	
Hancock	1,201 (46.2%)	1,289 (49.6%)	97 (3.7%)	13 (0.5%)	
Harrison	1,593 (45.6%)	1,848 (52.9%)	36 (1.0%)	17 (0.5%)	
Hendricks	2,050 (60.0%)	1,083 (31.7%)	244 (7.1%)	41 (1.2%)	
Henry	2,926 (69.0%)	1,206 (28.5%)	90 (2.1%)	16 (0.4%)	
Howard	1,589 (63.0%)	875 (34.7%)	34 (1.3%)	25 (1.0%)	
Huntington	1,582 (51.9%)	1,402 (46.0%)	52 (1.7%)	14 (0.5%)	
Jackson	1,185 (38.5%)	1,740 (56.5%)	117 (3.8%)	36 (1.2%)	
Jasper	534 (63.9%)	278 (33.3%)	7 (0.8%)	17 (2.0%)	
Jay	1,135 (50.9%)	1,077 (48.3%)	12 (0.5%)	6 (0.3%)	
Jefferson	2,644 (58.7%)	1,146 (25.4%)	564 (12.5%)	150 (3.3%)	
Jennings	1,649 (51.9%)	830 (29.2%)	326 (11.5%)	42 (1.5%)	
Johnson	1,303 (42.2%)	1,392 (45.0%)	336 (10.9%)	60 (1.9%)	
Knox	1,570 (47.3%)	1,666 (50.2%)	42 (1.3%)	39 (1.2%)	
Kosciusko	2,298 (60.3%)	1,500 (39.4%)	9 (0.2%)	3 (0.1%)	
Lagrange	1,695 (68.6%)	749 (30.3%)	10 (4.0%)	16 (0.6%)	
Lake	1,225 (72.1%)	455 (26.8%)	20 (1.2%)	0	
Laporte	3,167 (61.2%)	1,504 (29.1%)	478 (9.2%)	22 (0.4%)	
Lawrence	1,100 (42.0%)	784 (29.9%)	530 (20.2%)	207 (7.9%)	
Madison	1,709 (46.7%)	1,841 (50.4%)	70 (1.9%)	36 (1.0%)	
Marion	5,024 (51.4%)	3,252 (37.1%)	318 (3.6%)	161 (1.8%)	
Marshall	1,426 (52.3%)	1,273 (46.7%)	24 (0.9%)	2 (0.1%)	
Martin	516 (34.9%)	754 (51.0%)	153 (10.3%)	56 (3.8%)	
Miami	1,835 (52.9%)	1,608 (46.4%)	26 (0.7%)	0	
Monroe	1,198 (50.5%)	716 (30.1%)	395 (16.6%)	64 (2.7%)	
Montgomery	2,366 (49.4%)	2,279 (47.6%)	68 (1.4%)	78 (1.6%)	
Morgan	1,775 (52.7%)	1,516 (45.0%)	65 (1.9%)	15 (0.4%)	
Newton	305 (56.6%)	189 (35.1%)	44 (8.2%)	1 (0.2%)	
Noble	1,742 (56.1%)	1,320 (42.5%)	38 (1.2%)	4 (0.1%)	
Ohio	301 (29.7%)	335 (33.5%)	203 (20.0%)	174 (17.2%)	
Orange	849 (38.2%)	1,114 (50.1%)	176 (7.9%)	85 (3.8%)	
Owen	1,140 (43.2%)	1,293 (49.0%)	88 (3.3%)	118 (4.5%)	
Parke	1,898 (56.5%)	1,321 (39.3%)	55 (1.6%)	84 (2.5%)	
Perry	926 (46.6%)	897 (45.1%)	6 (0.3%)	160 (8.0%)	
Pike	894 (47.7%)	882 (47.1%)	58 (3.1%)	39 (2.1%)	
Porter	1,529 (62.4%)	889 (36.3%)	28 (1.1%)	6 (0.2%)	
Posey	1,055 (36.7%)	1,128 (39.2%)	523 (18.2%)	168 (5.8%)	
Pulaski	571 (45.9%)	663 (53.3%)	4 (0.3%)	7 (0.6%)	
Putnam	1,888 (45.8%)	1,747 (42.4%)	360 (8.7%)	123 (3.0%)	
Randolph	2,295 (64.8%)	1,180 (33.2%)	56 (1.6%)	10 (0.3%)	
Ripley	1,988 (54.4%)	1,458 (39.9%)	174 (4.8%)	37 (1.0%)	
Rush	1,757 (51.9%)	1,119 (33.0%)	476 (14.1%)	35 (1.0%)	
St. Joseph	2,363 (61.0%)	1,489 (38.4%)	23 (0.6%)	0	
Scott	650 (46.1%)	447 (31.7%)	262 (18.6%)	52 (3.7%)	
Shelby	1,900 (47.3%)	2,047 (51.0%)	43 (1.1%)	25 (0.6%)	
Spencer	1,296 (47.1%)	1,108 (40.3%)	172 (6.3%)	175 (6.4%)	
Stark	190 (43.5%)	231 (52.9%)	14 (3.2%)	2 (0.5%)	
Steuben	1,560 (71.0%)	547 (24.9%)	82 (3.7%)	8 (0.4%)	
Sullivan	856 (29.5%)	1,858 (64.1%)	128 (4.4%)	55 (1.9%)	
Switzerland	734 (33.1%)	476 (21.5%)	499 (22.4%)	510 (23.0%)	
Tippecanoe	3,480 (58.9%)	2,276 (38.5%)	117 (2.0%)	34 (0.6%)	

County	Lincoln (R)	Douglas (ND)	Breckinridge (SD)	Bell (CU)	Smith (U)
Tipton	780 (48.0%)	822 (50.6%)	20 (1.2%)	3 (0.2%)	
Union	849 (55.1%)	652 (42.3%)	36 (2.3%)	3 (0.2%)	
Vanderburg	1,867 (47.9%)	1,542 (39.6%)	183 (4.7%)	302 (7.8%)	
Vermillion	1,125 (56.4%)	818 (41.0%)	17 (0.9%)	34 (0.6%)	
Vigo	2,429 (50.5%)	2,127 (44.2%)	44 (0.9%)	211 (4.4%)	
Wabash	2,287 (64.8%)	1,142 (32.4%)	79 (2.2%)	20 (0.6%)	
Warren	1,412 (63.3%)	769 (34.5%)	33 (1.5%)	15 (0.7%)	
Wayne	4,234 (67.3%)	1,784 (28.4%)	164 (2.6%)	108 (1.7%)	
Wells	1,099 (54.5%)	909 (45.1%)	6 (0.3%)	2 (0.1%)	
White	993 (52.8%)	811 (43.1%)	67 (3.6%)	9 (0.5%)	
Whitley	1,133 (50.6%)	1,067 (47.7%)	33 (1.5%)	4 (0.2%)	
Warrick	745 (30.5%)	784 (32.1%)	816 (33.4%)	95 (3.9%)	
Washington	1,378 (40.0%)	1,985 (57.7%)	48 (1.4%)	31 (0.9%)	
Total	**139,013 (51.1%)**	**115,166 (42.4%)**	**12,295 (4.5%)**	**5,339 (2.0%)**	**5 (0.002%)**
	(138,963)	(115,168)	(12,296)	(5,345)	

SOURCES—(Indianapolis) *Indianapolis Daily Sentinel*, November 27, 1860; and W. Dean Burnham, *Presidential Ballots 1836–1892* (reprint edition), New York, NY: Arno Press, 1976, pp. 390–412, 908–909.

Iowa

County	Lincoln (R)	Douglas (ND)	Breckinridge (SD)	Bell (CU)
Adair	42 (47.7%)	44 (50.0%)	1 (1.1%)	1 (1.1%)
Adams	161 (63.6%)	92 (36.4%)	0	0
Allamakee	1,185 (50.4%)	1,151 (49.0%)	5 (0.2%)	9 (0.4%)
Appanoose	853 (39.9%)	1,224 (57.2%)	43 (2.0%)	18 (0.8%)
Audubon	48 (44.9%)	59 (55.1%)	0	0
Benton	1,028 (58.4%)	724 (41.2%)	2 (0.1%)	5 (0.3%)
Black Hawk	1,122 (66.0%)	557 (32.8%)	17 (1.0%)	4 (0.2%)
Boone	365 (45.0%)	446 (54.9%)	0	1 (0.1%)
Bremer	543 (53.5%)	454 (44.7%)	18 (1.8%)	0
Butler	483 (66.2%)	246 (33.7%)	0	1 (0.1%)
Buchanan	962 (60.4%)	621 (39.0%)	10 (0.6%)	1 (0.1%)
Buena Vista	6 (50.0%)	6 (50.0%)	0	0
Calhoun	19 (48.7%)	20 (51.3%)	0	0
Carroll	25 (49.0%)	26 (51.0%)	0	0
Cass	167 (54.2%)	136 (44.2%)	1 (0.3%)	4 (1.3%)
Cedar	1,548 (60.8%)	963 (37.8%)	5 (0.2%)	29 (1.1%)
Cerro Gordo	157 (69.8%)	59 (26.2%)	7 (3.1%)	2 (0.9%)
Cherokee	10 (76.9%)	3 (23.1%)	0	0
Chickasaw	550 (68.2%)	306 (37.9%)	1 (0.1%)	0
Clay	8 (38.1%)	13 (61.9%)	0	0
Clarke	592 (57.1%)	445 (42.9%)	0	0
Clayton	2,089 (56.7%)	1,574 (42.7%)	14 (3.8%)	5 (1.4%)
Clinton	1,974 (55.8%)	1,450 (41.0%)	60 (1.7%)	51 (1.4%)
Crawford	47 (60.2%)	31 (39.8%)	0	0
Dallas	612 (57.9%)	433 (41.0%)	6 (0.6%)	6 (0.6%)
Davis	843 (33.5%)	1,424 (56.5%)	25 (1.0%)	226 (9.0%)
Decatur	680 (42.8%)	898 (56.5%)	0	11 (0.7%)
Delaware	1,268 (61.0%)	789 (37.9%)	3 (0.1%)	20 (1.0%)
Des Moines	1,997 (52.0%)	1,677 (43.7%)	10 (0.3%)	156 (4.1%)
Dickinson	46 (86.8%)	7 (13.2%)	0	0
Dubuque	2,092 (39.7%)	3,059 (58.0%)	56 (1.1%)	63 (1.2%)
Emmett	36 (100%)	0	0	0
Fayette	1,527 (64.5%)	835 (35.2%)	5 (0.2%)	0
Floyd	560 (71.5%)	201 (25.6%)	21 (2.7%)	1 (0.1%)
Franklin	228 (76.8%)	69 (23.2%)	0	0
Fremont	402 (40.9%)	516 (52.4%)	0	66 (6.7%)
Greene	121 (45.5%)	145 (54.5%)	0	0
Grundy	141 (88.1%)	19 (11.9%)	0	0
Guthrie	326 (52.0%)	306 (48.0%)	0	0
Hamilton	224 (66.1%)	100 (29.5%)	13 (3.8%)	2 (0.6%)
Hancock	29 (87.9%)	4 (12.1%)	0	0
Harrison	385 (51.4%)	357 (47.7%)	6 (0.8%)	1 (0.1%)
Hardin	713 (64.8%)	382 (34.7%)	3 (0.3%)	2 (0.2%)
Henry	2,148 (65.5%)	1,066 (32.5%)	0	66 (2.0%)
Howard	386 (58.6%)	273 (41.4%)	0	0

County	Lincoln (R)	Douglas (ND)	Breckinridge (SD)	Bell (CU)
Humboldt	55 (75.3%)	8 (11.0%)	10 (13.7%)	0
Ida	4 (40.0%)	6 (60.0%)	0	0
Iowa	782 (53.0%)	682 (46.2%)	0	11 (0.7%)
Jackson	1,574 (50.2%)	1,505 (48.0%)	18 (0.5%)	40 (1.3%)
Jasper	1,208 (62.9%)	650 (33.8%)	51 (2.7%)	13 (0.7%)
Jefferson	1,463 (53.2%)	1,245 (45.3%)	4 (0.1%)	38 (1.4%)
Johnson	1,804 (53.2%)	1,448 (42.7%)	26 (0.8%)	111 (3.3%)
Jones	1,453 (45.8%)	1,097 (34.6%)	20 (0.4%)	4 (0.1%)
Keokuk	1,330 (52.3%)	1,195 (47.0%)	14 (0.6%)	2 (0.1%)
Kossuth	64 (78.0%)	18 (22.0%)	0	0
Lee	2,617 (48.4%)	2,632 (48.7%)	21 (0.4%)	136 (2.5%)
Linn	2,226 (61.5%)	1,289 (35.6%)	24 (0.7%)	80 (2.2%)
Louisa	586 (54.4%)	483 (44.8%)	14 (0.7%)	26 (1.2%)
Lucas	1,309 (62.4%)	739 (35.2%)	0	8 (0.7%)
Madison	737 (48.5%)	764 (50.3%)	10 (0.7%)	8 (0.5%)
Mahaska	1,639 (54.8%)	1,332 (44.5%)	1 (0.03%)	18 (0.6%)
Marion	1,508 (48.0%)	1,607 (51.2%)	31 (0.7%)	4 (0.1%)
Marshall	854 (67.1%)	403 (31.7%)	0	16 (1.3%)
Mills	441 (55.2%)	327 (41.0%)	16 (2.0%)	14 (1.8%)
Mitchell	594 (76.9%)	172 (22.3%)	5 (0.6%)	1 (0.1%)
Monona	109 (54.5%)	89 (44.5%)	2 (0.1%)	0
Monroe	879 (53.2%)	749 (45.4%)	18 (1.1%)	5 (0.3%)
Montgomery	152 (62.0%)	81 (33.1%)	10 (4.1%)	2 (0.8%)
Muscatine	1,840 (55.4%)	1,285 (38.7%)	85 (2.6%)	109 (3.3%)
O'Brien	8 (38.1%)	10 (47.6%)	0	3 (14.3%)
Page	469 (59.3%)	290 (36.7%)	22 (2.8%)	10 (1.3%)
Palo Alto	4 (12.1%)	29 (87.9%)	0	0
Plymouth	32 (84.2%)	6 (15.8%)	0	0
Pocahontas	31 (67.7%)	10 (32.3%)	0	0
Polk	1,303 (53.4%)	1,074 (44.1%)	22 (0.9%)	37 (1.5%)
Pottawattamie	413 (46.8%)	410 (46.4%)	32 (0.4%)	28 (0.3%)
Poweshuck	721 (59.7%)	484 (40.1%)	0	2 (0.2%)
Ringgold	348 (65.2%)	182 (34.1%)	0	3 (0.6%)
Sac	15 (27.8%)	39 (72.2%)	0	0
Scott	2,739 (63.5%)	1,377 (31.9%)	79 (1.8%)	115 (2.7%)
Shelby	100 (61.0%)	64 (39.0%)	0	0
Sioux	3 (20.0%)	10 (66.7%)	0	2 (13.3%)
Story	418 (55.7%)	333 (44.3%)	0	0
Tama	775 (65.0%)	413 (34.6%)	0	5 (0.4%)
Taylor	353 (58.1%)	248 (40.8%)	0	7 (1.2%)
Union	198 (48.8%)	208 (51.2%)	0	0
Van Buren	1,667 (50.6%)	1,552 (47.1%)	57 (1.7%)	19 (0.6%)
Wapello	1,399 (44.5%)	1,686 (53.6%)	38 (1.2%)	22 (0.7%)
Warren	1,152 (57.9%)	795 (40.0%)	2 (0.1%)	40 (2.0%)
Washington	1,721 (60.3%)	1,052 (36.9%)	20 (0.7%)	60 (2.1%)
Wayne	579 (46.8%)	648 (52.4%)	3 (0.2%)	7 (0.6%)
Webster	253 (49.2%)	207 (40.3%)	53 (10.3%)	1 (0.2%)
Winneshick	1,382 (63.9%)	780 (36.1%)	0	0
Winnebago	24 (53.3%)	21 (46.7%)	0	0
Woodbury	129 (49.8%)	117 (45.2%)	8 (0.3%)	5 (1.9%)
Worth	109 (78.4%)	30 (21.6%)	0	0
Total	**70,316 (54.9%)**	**55,091 (43.0%)**	**1,038 (0.8%)** *(1,035)	**1,763 (1.4%)**
*Wright	90 (70.9%)	23 (18.1%)	14 (11.0%)	0

*No vote for Wright County in the manuscript returns. These returns were located in W. Dean Burnham's Presidential Ballots.

SOURCES—Manuscript returns; and W. Dean Burnham, *Presidential Ballots 1836–1892* (reprint edition), New York, NY: Arno Press, 1976, pp. 412–434, 909–911.

Kentucky

County	Lincoln (R)	Douglas (ND)	Breckinridge (SD)	Bell (CU)
Adair	1 (0.1%)	355 (32.1%)	348 (31.4%)	403 (36.4%)
Allen	0	404 (35.4%)	229 (20.1%)	507 (44.5%)
Anderson	0	132 (12.0%)	670 (61.0%)	296 (27.0%)
Ballard	1 (0.1%)	271 (22.5%)	452 (37.5%)	481 (39.9%)
Barren	14 (0.7%)	492 (26.2%)	289 (15.4%)	1,086 (57.7%)

County	Lincoln (R)	Douglas (ND)	Breckinridge (SD)	Bell (CU)
Bath	0	143 (8.3%)	878 (51.2%)	694 (40.5%)
Boone	1 (0.1%)	228 (12.3%)	739 (40.0%)	881 (47.6%)
Bourbon	3 (0.2%)	29 (1.6%)	755 (43.1%)	966 (55.1%)
Boyd	18 (2.2%)	115 (14.2%)	191 (23.5%)	488 (60.1%)
Boyle	3 (0.2%)	52 (4.8%)	331 (30.6%)	697 (64.4%)
Bracken	4 (0.2%)	246 (13.9%)	644 (36.3%)	881 (49.6%)
Breathitt	0	1 (0.2%)	459 (80.1%)	113 (19.7%)
Breckinridge	3 (0.2%)	382 (23.6%)	281 (17.3%)	956 (58.9%)
Bullitt	2 (0.2%)	444 (44.7%)	96 (9.7%)	451 (45.4%)
Butler	5 (0.5%)	321 (34.0%)	119 (12.6%)	500 (52.9%)
Caldwell	3 (0.3%)	48 (4.3%)	618 (55.4%)	446 (40.0%)
Calloway	0	118 (9.1%)	904 (69.8%)	274 (21.1%)
Campbell	314 (11.9%)	960 (36.2%)	520 (19.6%)	854 (32.3%)
Carroll	0	70 (6.5%)	572 (53.1%)	436 (40.4%)
Carter	1 (0.1%)	146 (13.7%)	616 (57.9%)	301 (28.3%)
Casey	8 (0.8%)	202 (21.8%)	176 (19.0%)	541 (58.4%)
Christian	1 (0.1%)	467 (25.5%)	411 (22.4%)	954 (52.0%)
Clark	1 (0.1%)	60 (4.2%)	391 (27.7%)	959 (68.0%)
Clay	4 (0.5%)	108 (13.4%)	353 (43.8%)	341 (42.3%)
Clinton	3 (0.4%)	255 (35.9%)	192 (27.0%)	261 (36.7%)
Crittenden	1 (0.1%)	67 (5.3%)	630 (50.4%)	553 (44.2%)
Cumberland	7 (0.8%)	192 (22.2%)	82 (9.5%)	584 (67.5%)
Daviess	7 (0.3%)	530 (23.4%)	654 (28.9%)	1,074 (47.4%)
Edmonson	15 (2.9%)	137 (26.6%)	179 (34.7%)	185 (35.8%)
Estill	56 (5.5%)	19 (1.9%)	512 (50.2%)	433 (42.4%)
Fayette	5 (0.1%)	99 (3.9%)	1,051 (41.0%)	1,411 (55.0%)
Fleming	2 (0.1%)	100 (5.5%)	827 (45.0%)	907 (49.4%)
Floyd	0	0	609 (90.5%)	64 (9.5%)
Franklin	0	37 (2.1%)	907 (52.3%)	790 (45.6%)
Fulton	0	107 (15.0%)	307 (43.0%)	300 (42.0%)
Gallatin	0	34 (4.1%)	420 (50.2%)	383 (45.7%)
Garrard	21 (1.9%)	145 (13.3%)	195 (17.9%)	730 (66.9%)
Grant	0	112 (7.5%)	709 (47.3%)	677 (45.2%)
Graves	0	140 (6.9%)	1,225 (60.5%)	660 (32.6%)
Grayson	8 (0.7%)	219 (19.7%)	387 (34.9%)	497 (44.7%)
Green	2 (0.2%)	188 (19.2%)	367 (37.6%)	420 (43.0%)
Greenup	4 (0.3%)	89 (7.2%)	350 (28.3%)	795 (64.2%)
Hancock	3 (0.3%)	65 (7.3%)	427 (47.9%)	397 (44.5%)
Hardin	6 (0.3%)	912 (43.6%)	144 (6.9%)	1,029 (49.2%)
Harlan	2 (0.3%)	4 (0.7%)	264 (44.1%)	329 (54.9%)
Harrison	0	98 (4.2%)	1,272 (54.6%)	960 (41.2%)
Hart	1 (0.1%)	751 (52.2%)	153 (10.6%)	535 (37.1%)
Henderson	5 (0.3%)	211 (13.5%)	498 (31.9%)	846 (54.3%)
Henry	2 (0.1%)	390 (21.2%)	773 (42.1%)	672 (36.6%)
Hickman	1 (0.1%)	66 (6.8%)	618 (63.8%)	284 (29.3%)
Hopkins	2 (0.1%)	171 (10.9%)	666 (42.4%)	731 (46.6%)
Jackson	101 (25.9%)	13 (3.3%)	136 (34.9%)	140 (35.9%)
Jefferson	106 (1.1%)	3,441 (36.0%)	1,122 (11.7%)	4,896 (51.2%)
Jessamine	3 (0.2%)	37 (3.1%)	559 (46.5%)	603 (50.2%)
Johnson	0	26 (3.9%)	618 (92.8%)	22 (3.3%)
Kenton	267 (7.5%)	1,312 (36.9%)	650 (18.3%)	1,327 (37.3%)
Knox	11 (1.2%)	76 (8.7%)	211 (24.1%)	579 (60.0%)
Larue	3 (0.3%)	450 (50.8%)	32 (3.6%)	401 (45.3%)
Laurel	10 (1.3%)	8 (1.0%)	370 (47.9%)	385 (49.8%)
Lawrence	0	10 (1.0%)	515 (53.8%)	433 (45.2%)
Letcher	0	1 (0.3%)	281 (75.3%)	91 (24.4%)
Lewis	31 (2.8%)	73 (6.6%)	501 (45.1%)	506 (45.5%)
Lincoln	4 (0.3%)	72 (6.0%)	380 (31.7%)	743 (62.0%)
Livingston	0	96 (10.6%)	350 (38.6%)	460 (50.8%)
Logan	3 (0.1%)	342 (17.1%)	169 (8.4%)	1,490 (74.4%)
Lyon	0	11 (1.5%)	431 (57.8%)	304 (40.7%)
Madison	85 (4.1%)	56 (2.6%)	914 (43.7%)	1,038 (49.6%)
Magoffin	0	4 (0.8%)	311 (63.7%)	173 (35.5%)
Marion	0	904 (54.5%)	281 (16.9%)	475 (28.6%)
Marshall	0	107 (9.9%)	797 (73.8%)	176 (16.3%)
Mason	26 (1.1%)	247 (10.4%)	799 (33.6%)	1,305 (54.9%)
Mc Cracken	8 (0.6%)	280 (22.5%)	244 (19.7%)	710 (57.2%)
Mc Lean	0	162 (30.2%)	132 (24.6%)	242 (45.2%)
Meade	1 (0.1%)	305 (27.2%)	152 (13.5%)	664 (59.2%)

County	Lincoln (R)		Douglas (ND)		Breckinridge (SD)		Bell (CU)	
Mercer	2	(0.1%)	224	(12.3%)	992	(54.3%)	608	(33.3%)
Metcalfe	3	(0.4%)	237	(29.6%)	34	(4.2%)	527	(65.8%)
Monroe	3	(0.3%)	142	(14.8%)	324	(33.6%)	494	(51.3%)
Montgomery	0		49	(4.5%)	489	(45.4%)	540	(50.1%)
Morgan	0		0		776	(80.4%)	189	(19.6%)
Muhlenberg	4	(0.2%)	557	(41.2%)	51	(3.8%)	741	(54.8%)
Nelson	0		641	(40.5%)	333	(21.0%)	609	(38.5%)
Nicholas	1	(0.1%)	26	(1.4%)	988	(58.0%)	690	(40.5%)
Ohio	2	(0.1%)	582	(39.8%)	201	(13.8%)	677	(46.3%)
Oldham	2	(0.2%)	263	(28.2%)	299	(31.9%)	372	(39.7%)
Owen	0		43	(1.8%)	1,760	(75.2%)	539	(23.0%)
Owsley	1	(0.1%)	5	(0.8%)	370	(52.4%)	330	(46.7%)
Pendleton	2	(0.1%)	231	(12.8%)	807	(44.9%)	758	(42.2%)
Perry	1	(0.2%)	3	(0.7%)	293	(68.9%)	128	(30.2%)
Pike	1	(0.1%)	1	(0.1%)	726	(90.6%)	73	(9.1%)
Powell	0		4	(1.2%)	184	(52.7%)	161	(46.1%)
Pulaski	55	(2.6%)	56	(2.7%)	1,098	(52.6%)	877	(42.1%)
Rockcastle	64	(9.1%)	9	(1.3%)	257	(36.5%)	374	(53.1%)
Rowan	0		23	(6.9%)	189	(56.8%)	121	(36.3%)
Russell	1	(0.1%)	48	(6.2%)	299	(38.6%)	427	(55.1%)
Scott	0		44	(2.3%)	1,176	(60.2%)	734	(37.5%)
Shelby	0		228	(11.4%)	594	(29.7%)	1,176	(58.9%)
Simpson	0		194	(21.1%)	319	(34.8%)	404	(44.1%)
Spencer	0		304	(41.6%)	94	(12.8%)	334	(45.6%)
Taylor	1	(0.1%)	457	(49.6%)	151	(16.4%)	312	(33.9%)
Todd	4	(0.4%)	147	(13.7%)	274	(25.7%)	642	(60.2%)
Trigg	1	(0.1%)	177	(12.2%)	646	(44.6%)	623	(43.1%)
Trimble	1	(0.1%)	84	(9.1%)	581	(62.9%)	258	(27.9%)
Union	0		459	(29.1%)	464	(29.5%)	651	(41.4%)
Warren	3	(0.2%)	615	(31.9%)	182	(9.4%)	1,126	(58.5%)
Washington	1	(0.1%)	610	(50.0%)	290	(23.8%)	318	(26.1%)
Wayne	5	(0.4%)	7	(0.6%)	695	(53.0%)	603	(46.0%)
Webster	0		176	(18.4%)	575	(60.2%)	205	(21.4%)
Whitley	7	(0.8%)	14	(1.6%)	318	(37.1%)	519	(60.5%)
Wolfe	0		0		352	(76.4%)	109	(23.6%)
Woodford	0		16	(1.3%)	547	(45.8%)	633	(52.9%)
Total	**1,364**	**(0.9%)**	**25,641**	**(17.5%)**	**53,143**	**(36.4%)**	**66,058**	**(45.2%)**
			*(25,652)					

*Stated total.

SOURCES—(Frankfort) *Tri-Weekly Commonwealth*, December 5, 1860; Ruth McQuown and Jasper B. Shannon, *Presidential Politics in Kentucky 1824–1948*, Lexington, KY: University of Kentucky Press, 1950, pp. 35–6, citing manuscript returns; *Tribune Almanac 1860*; and (Lexington) *Kentucky Statesman*, December 4, 1860.

Louisiana

Parish	Douglas (ND)		Breckinridge (SD)		Bell (CU)	
Ascension	356	(45.7%)	144	(18.5%)	279	(35.8%)
Assumption	478	(46.4%)	311	(30.4%)	233	(22.8%)
Avoyelles	7	(0.7%)	750	(71.6%)	290	(27.7%)
Bienville	134	(12.1%)	682	(61.5%)	293	(26.4%)
Bossier	55	(7.0%)	489	(61.4%)	253	(31.7%)
Caddo	37	(3.0%)	648	(52.7%)	545	(44.3%)
Calcasieu	0		396	(94.3%)	24	(5.7%)
Caldwell	51	(10.0%)	325	(63.4%)	136	(26.6%)
Carroll	58	(5.9%)	530	(53.8%)	398	(40.4%)
Catahoula	20	(1.8%)	676	(59.6%)	439	(38.7%)
Claiborne	166	(9.3%)	896	(50.2%)	720	(40.4%)
Concordia	5	(1.5%)	175	(52.7%)	152	(45.8%)
De Soto	2	(0.2%)	634	(63.4%)	364	(36.4%)
East Baton Rouge	136	(11.4%)	490	(41.0%)	569	(47.6%)
East Feliciana	131	(16.7%)	377	(48.0%)	277	(35.3%)
Franklin	40	(6.4%)	342	(55.0%)	240	(38.6%)
Iberville	101	(11.7%)	535	(62.1%)	229	(26.6%)
Jackson	109	(11.2%)	527	(54.2%)	337	(34.6%)
Jefferson	406	(25.6%)	198	(12.5%)	984	(62.0%)
Lafayette	1	(0.2%)	468	(86.7%)	71	(13.1%)

Parish	Douglas (ND)	Breckinridge (SD)	Bell (CU)
Lafourche Interior	509 (48.6%)	214 (20.4%)	324 (30.9%)
Livingston	117 (14.8%)	425 (53.7%)	249 (31.5%)
Madison	92 (17.7%)	172 (33.1%)	255 (49.1%)
Morehouse	47 (6.1%)	381 (49.2%)	347 (44.8%)
Natchitouches	106 (7.6%)	754 (54.1%)	534 (38.3%)
Orleans	2,998 (27.6%)	2,645 (24.4%)	5,215 (48.0%)
Ouachita	148 (18.5%)	312 (39.0%)	340 (42.5%)
Plaquemines	127 (28.3%)	267 (60.0%)	54 (12.1%)
Point Coupee	71 (8.0%)	626 (70.3%)	193 (21.7%)
Rapides	98 (5.6%)	1,036 (59.1%)	620 (35.3%)
Sabine	45 (6.5%)	420 (60.7%)	227 (32.8%)
St. Bernard	39 (13.9%)	186 (66.2%)	56 (19.9%)
St. Charles	16 (9.8%)	79 (48.5%)	68 (41.7%)
St. Helena	18 (2.8%)	331 (51.6%)	292 (45.6%)
Saint. James	108 (19.3%)	160 (28.6%)	292 (52.1%)
St. John the Baptist	87 (2.2%)	129 (32.9%)	176 (44.9%)
St. Landry	21 (1.1%)	961 (51.5%)	884 (47.4%)
St. Martin	49 (4.1%)	572 (48.1%)	567 (42.7%)
St. Mary	88 (9.3%)	462 (49.0%)	392 (41.6%)
St. Tammany	132 (21.5%)	164 (30.4%)	243 (45.1%)
Tensas	3 (0.8%)	254 (65.0%)	134 (34.3%)
Terrebone	84 (8.7%)	441 (45.7%)	440 (45.6%)
Union	22 (1.7%)	726 (55.8%)	552 (42.5%)
Vermillon	1 (0.3%)	211 (59.6%)	142 (40.1%)
Washington	5 (1.0%)	387 (76.8%)	112 (22.2%)
West Baton Rouge	27 (6.9%)	147 (37.5%)	218 (55.6%)
West Feliciana	33 (6.1%)	272 (55.2%)	188 (38.1%)
Winn	241 (28.3%)	354 (41.5%)	257 (30.2%)
Total	**7,625 (15.1%)**	**22,681 (44.9%)**	**20,204 (40.0%)**

SOURCES—*New Orleans Bee*, December 3, 1860; and W. Dean Burnham, *Presidential Ballots 1836–1892* (reprint edition), New York, NY: Arno Press, 1976, pp. 486–500, 915, citing *Tribune Almanac, 1861.*

Maine

County	Lincoln (R)	Douglas (ND)	Breckinridge (SD)	Bell (CU)
Androscoggin	3,526 (64.4%)	1,838 (33.5%)	65 (1.2%)	50 (0.9%)
Aroostook	1,176 (66.1%)	428 (24.0%)	169 (9.5%)	7 (0.4%)
Cumberland	7,934 (59.0%)	4,815 (35.8%)	345 (2.6%)	345 (2.6%)
Franklin	2,281 (61.7%)	1,358 (36.7%)	56 (1.5%)	3 (0.1%)
Hancock	3,322 (60.3%)	932 (16.9%)	1,062 (19.3%)	189 (3.4%)
Kennebec	6,599 (70.9%)	2,353 (25.3%)	156 (1.7%)	200 (2.1%)
Knox	2,518 (54.8%)	1,825 (39.7%)	183 (4.0%)	68 (1.5%)
Lincoln	2,510 (61.8%)	1,073 (26.4%)	210 (5.2%)	267 (6.6%)
Oxford	4,244 (60.8%)	2,523 (36.1%)	199 (2.9%)	16 (0.2%)
Penobscot	6,997 (65.1%)	1,555 (14.5%)	2,018 (18.8%)	185 (1.7%)
Piscataquis	1,656 (67.7%)	401 (16.4%)	374 (15.3%)	14 (0.6%)
Sagadahoc	2,257 (68.3%)	630 (19.1%)	142 (4.3%)	276 (8.4%)
Somerset	4,048 (64.6%)	1,833 (29.2%)	212 (3.4%)	174 (2.8%)
Waldo	3,800 (64.9%)	1,434 (24.5%)	537 (9.2%)	84 (1.4%)
Washington	3,515 (56.1%)	2,320 (37.1%)	348 (5.6%)	75 (1.2%)
York	6,532 (57.5%)	4,443 (39.1%)	301 (2.6%)	93 (0.8%)
Total	**62,915 (62.2%)**	**29,761 (29.4%)**	**6,377 (6.3%)**	**2,046 (2.0%)**

SOURCES—*Rockland Democrat*, December 19, 1860; and *Maine Legislative Documents, 1861.*

Maryland

County	Lincoln (R)	Douglas (ND)	Breckinridge (SD)	Bell (CU)
Allegany	520 (12.3%)	1,202 (28.5%)	979 (23.2%)	1,521 (36.0%)
Anne Arundel	3 (0.1%)	98 (4.5%)	1,017 (47.1%)	1,041 (48.2%)
Baltimore	37 (0.5%)	449 (6.3%)	3,305 (46.0%)	3,388 (47.2%)
Calvert	1 (0.1%)	43 (5.2%)	387 (46.6%)	399 (48.1%)
Caroline	12 (0.8%)	100 (6.9%)	616 (42.8%)	712 (49.4%)
Carroll	59 (1.3%)	334 (7.4%)	1,799 (40.1%)	2,294 (51.1%)
Cecil	158 (4.1%)	393 (10.2%)	1,506 (39.1%)	1,792 (46.6%)

County	Lincoln (R)	Douglas (ND)	Breckinridge (SD)	Bell (CU)
Charles	6 (0.5%)	38 (3.2%)	723 (60.4%)	430 (35.9%)
Dorchester	35 (1.4%)	31 (3.2%)	1,176 (47.0%)	1,262 (50.4%)
Frederick	103 (1.4%)	437 (6.0%)	3,176 (43.3%)	3,617 (49.3%)
Harford	81 (2.3%)	82 (2.3%)	1,528 (43.0%)	1,862 (52.4%)
Howard	1 (0.1%)	189 (12.2%)	530 (34.2%)	830 (53.5%)
Kent	42 (2.5%)	74 (4.5%)	694 (41.8%)	852 (51.3%)
Montgomery	50 (2.1%)	99 (4.1%)	1,125 (46.7%)	1,155 (48.0%)
Prince George's	1 (0.1%)	43 (2.2%)	1,048 (53.0%)	885 (44.8%)
Queen Anne's	0	87 (4.6%)	879 (46.9%)	908 (48.5%)
St. Mary's	1 (0.1%)	190 (13.8%)	920 (67.1%)	261 (19.0%)
Somerset	2 (0.1%)	96 (3.2%)	1,338 (45.0%)	1,536 (51.7%)
Talbot	2 (0.1%)	98 (5.5%)	898 (50.1%)	793 (44.3%)
Washington	95 (1.8%)	282 (5.2%)	2,479 (45.7%)	2,567 (47.3%)
Worcester	0	212 (7.9%)	1,425 (52.9%)	1,059 (39.3%)
Baltimore (city)	1,087 (3.6%)	1,503 (5.0%)	14,957 (49.6%)	12,604 (41.8%)
Total	**2,296 (2.5%)**	**6,080 (6.6%)**	**42,505 (45.9%)**	**41,768 (45.1%)**

SOURCE—Manuscript returns.

Massachusetts

County	Lincoln (R)	Douglas (ND)	Breckinridge (SD)	Bell (CU)
Barnstable	2,371 (75.3%)	133 (4.2%)	360 (11.4%)	283 (9.0%)
Berkshire	5,202 (61.2%)	2,865 (33.7%)	199 (2.3%)	238 (2.8%)
Bristol	7,980 (73.8%)	1,713 (15.8%)	483 (4.5%)	640 (5.9%)
Dukes	338 (59.7%)	116 (20.5%)	64 (11.3%)	58 (10.2%)
Essex	14,832 (65.6%)	3,778 (16.7%)	829 (3.7%)	3,186 (14.1%)
Franklin	3,994 (74.3%)	917 (17.1%)	331 (6.2%)	135 (2.5%)
Hampden	5,184 (64.3%)	1,993 (24.7%)	595 (7.4%)	295 (3.7%)
Hampshire	4,597 (81.8%)	608 (10.8%)	230 (4.1%)	182 (3.2%)
Middlesex	17,806 (58.1%)	7,069 (23.1%)	921 (3.0%)	4,850 (15.8%)
Nantucket	420 (78.2%)	32 (6.0%)	9 (1.7%)	76 (14.2%)
Norfolk	8,860 (55.8%)	3,589 (22.6%)	450 (2.8%)	2,987 (18.8%)
Plymouth	6,703 (65.2%)	1,423 (13.8%)	288 (2.8%)	1,872 (18.2%)
Suffolk	10,974 (48.8%)	4,891 (21.8%)	964 (4.3%)	5,640 (25.1%)
Worcester	17,272 (69.7%)	5,243 (21.2%)	382 (1.5%)	1,890 (7.6%)
Total	**106,533 (62.9%)**	**34,370 (20.3%)**	**6,105 (3.6%)**	**22,332 (13.2%)**

SOURCE—Manuscript returns.

Michigan

County	Lincoln (R)	Douglas (ND)	Breckinridge (SD)	Bell (CU)
Allegan	1,896 (54.9%)	1,544 (44.7%)	11 (0.3%)	1 (0.03%)
Alpena	82 (74.5%)	28 (25.5%)		
Barry	1,901 (64.2%)	1,038 (35.0%)	23 (0.8%)	
Bay	311 (48.8%)	324 (50.9%)		2 (0.3%)
Berrien	2,620 (52.3%)	2,337 (46.6%)	52 (1.0%)	24 (0.5%)
Branch	3,074 (66.1%)	1,558 (33.5%)	19 (0.4%)	1 (0.02%)
Calhoun	4,072 (61.7%)	2,449 (37.1%)	45 (0.7%)	38 (0.6%)
Cass	2,068 (55.4%)	1,624 (43.5%)	34 (1.0%)	4 (0.1%)
Cheboygan	20 (21.3%)	74 (78.7%)		
Chippewa	64 (41.8%)	89 (58.2%)		
Clinton	1,569 (55.2%)	1,273 (44.8%)		
Eaton	2,135 (61.5%)	1,328 (38.3%)	6 (0.2%)	
Genesee	2,832 (59.3%)	1,920 (40.2%)		22 (0.5%)
Grand Traverse	407 (67.3%)	198 (32.7%)		
Gratiot	496 (61.2%)	314 (38.8%)		
Hillsdale	3,749 (68.1%)	1,719 (31.2%)	25 (0.5%)	12 (0.2%)
Huron	299 (58.9%)	209 (41.1%)		
Ingham	2,181 (54.2%)	1,838 (45.7%)	3 (0.7%)	
Ionia	2,231 (63.1%)	1,294 (36.6%)	6 (0.2%)	3 (0.1%)
Iosco	20 (32.8%)	41 (67.2%)		
Isabella	123 (48.5%)	131 (51.5%)		
Jackson	3,396 (56.2%)	2,596 (43.0%)	46 (0.8%)	3 (0.05%)
Kalamazoo	3,230 (60.9%)	2,031 (38.3%)	4 (0.1%)	38 (0.7%)

County	Lincoln (R)	Douglas (ND)	Breckinridge (SD)	Bell (CU)
Kent	3,647 (58.0%)	2,540 (40.4%)	87 (1.4%)	7 (0.1%)
Lapeer	1,762 (58.8%)	1,222 (40.8%)	8 (0.3%)	5 (0.2%)
Lenawee	5,080 (58.6%)	3,510 (40.5%)	57 (0.7%)	23 (0.3%)
Livingston	2,075 (50.8%)	2,003 (49.1%)	4 (0.1%)	
Mackinac	41 (31.5%)	89 (68.5%)		
Macomb	2,533 (53.6%)	2,166 (45.8%)	15 (0.3%)	15 (0.3%)
Manistee	126 (68.5%)	58 (31.5%)		
Manitou	56 (45.5%)	67 (54.5%)		
Mason	89 (64.5%)	49 (35.5%)		
Mecosta	109 (66.5%)	55 (33.5%)		
Midland	157 (78.5%)	43 (21.5%)		
Monroe	2,282 (51.2%)	2,165 (48.6%)	10 (0.2%)	
Montcalm	565 (61.0%)	361 (39.0%)		
Muskegon	502 (67.5%)	241 (32.4%)	1 (0.1%)	
Newaygo	364 (63.7%)	207 (36.3%)		
Oakland	4,411 (53.3%)	3,768 (45.5%)	83 (1.0%)	19 (0.2%)
Oceana	192 (54.9%)	158 (45.1%)		
Ontonagon	331 (52.5%)	300 (47.5%)		
Ottawa	1,414 (53.7%)	1,217 (46.3%)		
St. Clair	2,589 (56.3%)	1,955 (42.5%)	37 (0.8%)	19 (0.4%)
St. Joseph	2,832 (58.6%)	1,980 (41.0%)	21 (0.4%)	
Saginaw	1,479 (54.8%)	1,206 (44.7%)	8 (0.3%)	8 (0.3%)
Sanilac	899 (68.9%)	396 (30.4%)	9 (0.7%)	
Shiawassee	1,606 (56.5%)	1,221 (43.0%)	7 (0.2%)	7 (0.2%)
Tuscola	747 (68.1%)	350 (31.9%)		
Van Buren	2,175 (62.6%)	1,274 (36.7%)	26 (0.7%)	
Washtenaw	4,286 (53.6%)	3,630 (45.4%)	56 (0.7%)	25 (0.3%)
Wayne	7,325 (51.3%)	6,701 (47.0%)	102 (0.7%)	139 (1.0%)
Total[4]	**88,450 (57.2%)**	**64,889 (42.0%)**	**805 (0.5%)**	**415 (0.3%)**

SOURCES—Manuscript returns; *Michigan Manual, 1913*; and W. Dean Burnham, *Presidential Ballots 1836–1892* (reprint edition), New York, NY: Arno Press, 1976.

Minnesota

No returns have been located for this election for Benton, Crow Wing, Jackson, Pine and Todd Counties.

County	Lincoln (R)	Douglas (ND)	Breckinridge (SD)	Bell (CU)
Anoka	277 (63.5%)	150 (34.4%)	9 (2.1%)	
Blue Earth	677 (63.0%)	374 (34.8%)	24 (2.2%)	
Brown	409 (80.2%)	91 (17.8%)	10 (2.0%)	
Carver	505 (60.8%)	324 (39.0%)	1 (0.1%)	
Chisago	379 (81.2%)	64 (13.7%)	24 (5.1%)	
Dakota	1,023 (53.1%)	882 (45.8%)	22 (11.4%)	
Dodge	581 (69.2%)	206 (24.5%)	53 (6.3%)	
Fairbault	270 (80.4%)	63 (18.8%)	3 (0.9%)	
Fillmore	1,610 (65.9%)	809 (33.1%)	24 (1.0%)	
Freeborn	595 (75.8%)	188 (23.9%)	2 (0.3%)	
Goodhue	1,352 (75.2%)	429 (23.9%)	17 (0.9%)	
Hennepin	1,770 (70.1%)	705 (27.9%)	47 (1.9%)	4 (0.2%)
Houston	594 (48.7%)	622 (51.0%)	3 (0.2%)	
Isanti	41 (85.4%)	7 (14.6%)	0	
Kanabec	15 (100%)	0	0	
Kandiyohi	13 (81.3%)	3 (18.7%)	0	
Le Sueur	566 (50.0%)	555 (49.1%)	9 (0.8%)	1 (0.1%)
Martin	40 (87.0%)	6 (13.0%)	0	
McLeod	240 (74.8%)	81 (25.2%)	0	
Meeker	166 (63.6%)	83 (31.8%)	11 (4.2%)	1 (0.4%)
Mille Lacs	18 (94.7%)	1 (5.3%)	0	
Monongalia	42 (71.2%)	17 (28.8%)	0	
Morrison	53 (35.3%)	93 (62.0%)	4 (2.7%)	
Mower	501 (72.1%)	194 (27.9%)	0	
Nicollet	461 (59.1%)	291 (37.3%)	25 (3.2%)	3 (0.4%)
Olmsted	1,348 (75.9%)	404 (22.7%)	24 (1.4%)	
Otter Tail	5 (45.5%)	6 (54.5%)	0	
Ramsey	1,234 (49.4%)	1,107 (44.3%)	143 (5.7%)	16 (0.6%)
Renville	89 (60.5%)	41 (27.9%)	15 (10.2%)	2 (1.4%)
Rice	996 (66.1%)	503 (33.4%)	8 (0.5%)	

County	Lincoln (R)	Douglas (ND)	Breckinridge (SD)	Bell (CU)
St. Louis	40 (58.8%)	22 (32.4%)	6 (8.8%)	
Scott	529 (43.7%)	643 (53.1%)	38 (3.1%)	
Sherburne	120 (66.7%)	58 (32.2%)	2 (1.1%)	
Sibley	398 (49.8%)	384 (48.0%)	18 (2.3%)	
Stearns	439 (47.1%)	482 (51.7%)	12 (1.3%)	
Steele	523 (76.0%)	157 (22.8%)	8 (1.2%)	
Toombs	7 (70.0%)	3 (30.0%)	0	
Wabasha	1,231 (63.3%)	550 (28.3%)	150 (7.7%)	14 (0.7%)
Waseca	304 (68.0%)	143 (32.0%)	0	
Washington	752 (62.4%)	423 (35.1%)	19 (1.6%)	12 (1.0%)
Winona	1,291 (67.9%)	571 (30.0%)	39 (2.1%)	
Wright	572 (74.9%)	188 (24.6%)	4 (0.4%)	
Total	**22,076 (63.4%)** *(11,922)	**11,923 (34.2%)**	**774 (2.2%)**	**53 (0.2%)**

Stated total.

SOURCE—Bruce M. White, *Minnesota Votes*, St. Paul, MN: Minnesota Historical Society, 1977, p.11.

Mississippi

County	Douglas (ND)	Breckinridge (SD)	Bell (CU)
Adams	158 (16.1%)	376 (38.3%)	448 (45.6%)
Amite	3 (0.4%)	427 (52.5%)	383 (47.1%)
Attala	5 (0.3%)	1,030 (66.0%)	525 (33.7%)
Bolivar	18 (0.4%)	218 (42.5%)	277 (54.0%)
Calhoun	54 (4.5%)	791 (65.9%)	355 (29.6%)
Carroll	11 (0.6%)	1,188 (59.8%)	788 (39.7%)
Choctaw	25 (1.3%)	1,336 (66.7%)	642 (32.1%)
Chickasaw	33 (2.0%)	1,070 (65.2%)	538 (32.8%)
Claiborne	26 (3.7%)	421 (59.3%)	263 (37.0%)
Clark	76 (5.7%)	904 (68.3%)	343 (25.9%)
Coahoma	41 (10.0%)	157 (38.2%)	213 (51.8%)
Copiah	14 (0.9%)	1,052 (65.6%)	538 (33.5%)
Covington	8 (1.6%)	391 (77.4%)	106 (21.0%)
De Soto	401 (20.1%)	745 (37.4%)	845 (42.4%)
Franklin	3 (0.6%)	335 (67.8%)	156 (31.6%)
Greene	0	200 (81.6%)	45 (18.4%)
Hancock	0	257 (84.5%)	47 (15.5%)
Harrison	0	460 (83.9%)	88 (16.1%)
Hinds	40 (1.9%)	1,015 (47.0%)	1,103 (51.1%)
Holmes	9 (0.6%)	784 (55.1%)	629 (44.2%)
Issaquena	6 (2.5%)	104 (42.8%)	133 (54.7%)
Itawamba	63 (2.5%)	1,684 (68.1%)	727 (27.4%)
Jackson	17 (4.7%)	316 (88.3%)	25 (7.0%)
Jasper	18 (1.6%)	712 (65.3%)	361 (33.0%)
Jefferson	49 (7.6%)	333 (51.4%)	266 (44.0%)
Jones	0	263 (73.3%)	96 (26.7%)
Kemper	69 (5.5%)	689 (54.8%)	499 (39.7%)
Lafayette	144 (7.7%)	1,034 (55.5%)	686 (36.8%)
Lauderdale	142 (9.8%)	951 (65.8%)	353 (24.4%)
Lawrence	5 (0.5%)	839 (84.7%)	146 (14.7%)
Leake	2 (0.2%)	690 (65.1%)	368 (34.7%)
Lowndes	36 (0.2%)	929 (56.6%)	676 (41.2%)
Madison	17 (1.5%)	627 (53.7%)	524 (44.9%)
Marion	2 (0.6%)	298 (89.0%)	35 (10.4%)
Marshall	269 (10.7%)	1,149 (45.7%)	1,098 (43.6%)
Monroe	49 (2.5%)	1,273 (65.8%)	612 (31.6%)
Neshoba	10 (1.1%)	732 (81.0%)	162 (17.9%)
Newton	29 (3.1%)	684 (73.5%)	217 (23.3%)
Noxubee[5]	57 (4.8%)	701 (58.4%)	442 (36.8%)
Oktibbeha	20 (2.0%)	746 (72.8%)	259 (25.3%)
Panola	186 (12.9%)	551 (38.3%)	700 (48.7%)
Perry	6 (1.9%)	201 (64.4%)	105 (33.7%)
Pike	0	831 (79.0%)	221 (21.0%)
Pontotoc	339 (12.5%)	1,512 (56.1%)	845 (37.3%)
Rankin	11 (0.9%)	676 (56.7%)	505 (42.4%)
Scott	8 (0.8%)	693 (69.3%)	299 (29.9%)
Simpson	3 (0.6%)	370 (72.7%)	136 (26.7%)

County	Douglas (ND)	Breckinridge (SD)	Bell (CU)
Smith	5 (0.7%)	517 (68.4%)	234 (31.0%)
Sunflower	1 (0.3%)	173 (55.4%)	138 (44.2%)
Tallahatchie	35 (6.0%)	285 (48.6%)	266 (45.4%)
Tippah	254 (10.0%)	1,456 (57.4%)	826 (32.6%)
Tishomingo	303 (8.7%)	1,748 (50.5%)	1,412 (40.8%)
Tunica	9 (3.3%)	122 (45.0%)	140 (51.7%)
Warren	83 (5.6%)	580 (39.2%)	816 (55.2%)
Washington	0	180 (47.1%)	201 (52.9%)
Wayne	0	180 (62.1%)	110 (37.9%)
Wilkinson	34 (4.5%)	404 (53.0%)	324 (42.5%)
Winston	2 (0.2%)	800 (72.7%)	299 (27.2%)
Yalobusha	76 (4.5%)	919 (54.0%)	707 (41.5%)
Yazoo	4 (0.3%)	688 (48.1%)	739 (51.6%)
Total	**3,288 (4.8%)**	**40,797 (59.0%)**	**25,040 (36.2%)** *(25,040)

*Stated total.

SOURCES—(Jackson) *Mississippian*, December 5, 1860; W. Dean Burnham, *Presidential Ballots 1836–1892* (reprint edition), New York, NY: Arno Press, 1976; and manuscript returns.

Missouri

County	Lincoln (R)	Douglas (ND)	Breckinridge (SD)	Bell (CU)
Adair	185 (12.9%)	616 (43.0%)	339 (23.7%)	293 (20.4%)
Andrew	97 (5.1%)	819 (42.8%)	319 (16.7%)	677 (35.4%)
Atchison	68 (7.2%)	645 (68.5%)	63 (6.7%)	165 (17.5%)
Audrain	1 (0.1%)	289 (26.9%)	206 (19.1%)	580 (53.9%)
Barry	1 (0.1%)	257 (29.3%)	286 (32.6%)	333 (37.9%)
Barton	28 (9.2%)	107 (35.2%)	93 (30.6%)	76 (25.0%)
Bates	30 (2.4%)	511 (40.1%)	348 (27.3%)	386 (30.3%)
Benton	74 (7.0%)	574 (54.5%)	100 (9.5%)	306 (29.0%)
Bollinger	23 (4.3%)	250 (46.3%)	99 (18.3%)	166 (30.7%)
Boone	12 (0.4%)	578 (19.8%)	652 (22.4%)	1,671 (57.4%)
Buchanan	452 (11.4%)	1,626 (40.9%)	614 (15.4%)	1,287 (32.3%)
Butler	1 (0.3%)	235 (68.9%)	17 (5.0%)	88 (25.8%)
Caldwell	43 (5.0%)	263 (30.6%)	186 (21.7%)	367 (42.7%)
Callaway	15 (0.6%)	839 (31.9%)	472 (17.9%)	1,306 (49.6%)
Camden	6 (1.0%)	269 (42.6%)	132 (20.9%)	224 (35.5%)
Cape Girardeau	175 (10.3%)	543 (32.1%)	325 (19.2%)	651 (38.4%)
Carroll	3 (0.2%)	752 (47.5%)	276 (17.4%)	552 (34.9%)
Carter	0	4 (3.9%)	83 (80.6%)	16 (15.5%)
Cass	23 (1.4%)	242 (15.2%)	607 (38.2%)	715 (45.1%)
Cedar	4 (0.5%)	324 (37.2%)	277 (31.8%)	266 (30.5%)
Chariton	1 (0.1%)	692 (43.4%)	295 (18.5%)	608 (38.1%)
Christian	0	120 (15.6%)	308 (40.0%)	342 (44.4%)
Clark	277 (13.4%)	542 (26.2%)	497 (24.0%)	752 (36.4%)
Clay	0	528 (28.1%)	305 (16.2%)	1,045 (55.6%)
Clinton	11 (0.8%)	368 (26.9%)	314 (23.0%)	674 (49.3%)
Cole	114 (9.1%)	430 (34.2%)	487 (38.7%)	226 (18.0%)
Cooper	20 (0.9%)	988 (44.1%)	281 (12.5%)	952 (42.5%)
Crawford	35 (5.5%)	169 (26.4%)	192 (30.0%)	243 (38.0%)
Dade	8 (0.8%)	282 (28.2%)	305 (30.5%)	406 (40.6%)
Dallas	20 (2.8%)	225 (31.9%)	172 (24.4%)	288 (40.9%)
Daviess	33 (2.1%)	692 (45.1%)	265 (17.3%)	545 (35.5%)
De Kalb	7 (1.0%)	239 (34.0%)	213 (30.3%)	243 (34.6%)
Dent	7 (0.9%)	207 (26.0%)	338 (42.5%)	243 (30.6%)
Dunklin	0	150 (34.2%)	79 (18.0%)	209 (47.7%)
Franklin	494 (23.9%)	888 (43.0%)	108 (5.2%)	577 (27.9%)
Gasconade	433 (52.2%)	188 (22.7%)	51 (6.2%)	157 (18.9%)
Gentry	201 (10.9%)	873 (47.2%)	259 (14.0%)	517 (27.9%)
Greene	42 (2.4%)	298 (17.1%)	414 (23.8%)	986 (56.7%)
Grundy	129 (10.4%)	416 (33.5%)	190 (15.3%)	507 (40.8%)
Harrison	297 (18.8%)	910 (57.7%)	50 (3.2%)	319 (20.2%)
Henry	16 (1.0%)	623 (39.6%)	232 (14.7%)	703 (44.7%)
Hickory	15 (0.3%)	298 (45.6%)	143 (21.9%)	197 (30.2%)
Holt	202 (17.2%)	453 (38.6%)	171 (14.6%)	348 (29.6%)
Howard	1 (0.05%)	939 (44.6%)	247 (11.7%)	920 (43.7%)
Howell	0	136 (33.7%)	91 (22.6%)	176 (43.7%)

County	Lincoln (R)	Douglas (ND)	Breckinridge (SD)	Bell (CU)
Iron	109 (15.8%)	349 (50.7%)	36 (5.2%)	194 (28.2%)
Jackson	191 (5.2%)	1,095 (29.6%)	943 (25.5%)	1,473 (39.8%)
Jasper	38 (3.6%)	407 (38.4%)	192 (18.1%)	424 (40.0%)
Jefferson	142 (11.8%)	490 (40.7%)	155 (12.9%)	416 (34.6%)
Johnson	18 (0.8%)	617 (25.9%)	527 (22.1%)	1,224 (51.3%)
Knox	161 (9.6%)	687 (41.2%)	301 (18.0%)	520 (31.2%)
Laclede	6 (0.7%)	189 (23.4%)	276 (34.2%)	335 (41.6%)
Lafayette	24 (0.9%)	774 (28.2%)	371 (13.5%)	1,577 (57.4%)
Lawrence	59 (5.1%)	138 (11.9%)	516 (44.6%)	445 (38.4%)
Lewis	43 (2.2%)	468 (24.1%)	597 (30.8%)	833 (42.9%)
Lincoln	3 (1.6%)	805 (42.0%)	395 (20.6%)	725 (37.8%)
Linn	105 (7.5%)	521 (37.5%)	219 (15.7%)	546 (39.3%)
Livingston	20 (1.4%)	401 (27.3%)	470 (32.0%)	578 (39.3%)
Macon	134 (5.6%)	1,176 (49.4%)	414 (17.4%)	655 (27.5%)
Madison	9 (1.4%)	305 (47.8%)	98 (15.4%)	226 (35.4%)
Maries	7 (1.4%)	98 (19.3%)	309 (60.7%)	95 (18.7%)
Marion	235 (7.1%)	1,240 (37.7%)	432 (13.1%)	1,385 (42.1%)
McDonald	3 (0.6%)	206 (38.0%)	195 (36.0%)	138 (25.5%)
Mercer	80 (5.6%)	682 (48.0%)	169 (11.9%)	491 (34.5%)
Miller	23 (2.9%)	94 (11.7%)	495 (61.5%)	193 (24.0%)
Mississippi	1 (0.1%)	233 (32.2%)	185 (25.6%)	305 (42.1%)
Moniteau	87 (6.0%)	476 (33.0%)	332 (23.0%)	546 (37.9%)
Monroe	8 (0.4%)	680 (31.2%)	408 (18.7%)	1,086 (49.8%)
Montgomery	45 (3.2%)	612 (43.8%)	83 (5.9%)	658 (47.1%)
Morgan	18 (1.6%)	550 (50.3%)	204 (18.7%)	321 (29.4%)
New Madrid	0	117 (23.4%)	160 (32.0%)	223 (44.6%)
Newton	22 (1.6%)	654 (48.9%)	255 (19.1%)	406 (30.4%)
Nodaway	147 (11.9%)	546 (44.3%)	274 (22.2%)	265 (21.5%)
Oregon	2 (5.5%)	66 (18.4%)	245 (68.4%)	45 (12.6%)
Osage	258 (26.0%)	235 (23.7%)	308 (31.1%)	190 (19.2%)
Ozark & Douglas	0	81 (26.6%)	155 (50.8%)	69 (22.6%)
Pemiscot	0	118 (34.5%)	70 (20.5%)	154 (45.0%)
Perry	139 (15.7%)	467 (52.7%)	63 (7.1%)	217 (24.5%)
Pettis	9 (0.7%)	369 (30.6%)	211 (17.5%)	615 (51.1%)
Phelps	37 (4.0%)	254 (27.6%)	430 (46.7%)	199 (21.6%)
Pike	15 (0.5%)	1,117 (39.2%)	420 (14.7%)	1,300 (45.6%)
Platte	6 (0.2%)	845 (28.8%)	877 (29.9%)	1,208 (41.1%)
Polk	4 (0.3%)	125 (9.4%)	477 (35.7%)	730 (54.6%)
Pulaski	7 (1.5%)	107 (23.4%)	281 (61.4%)	62 (13.6%)
Putnam	111 (8.4%)	590 (44.8%)	246 (18.7%)	369 (28.0%)
Ralls	1 (0.1%)	391 (34.7%)	149 (13.2%)	585 (52.0%)
Randolph	0	360 (21.2%)	520 (30.6%)	821 (48.3%)
Ray	9 (0.4%)	881 (41.4%)	233 (10.9%)	1,006 (47.3%)
Reynolds	4 (1.6%)	123 (49.2%)	85 (34.0%)	38 (15.2%)
Ripley	0	78 (27.5%)	232 (81.7%)	74 (26.1%)
St. Charles	534 (26.1%)	831 (40.6%)	64 (3.1%)	619 (30.2%)
St. Clair	1 (0.1%)	344 (36.9%)	249 (26.7%)	338 (36.3%)
St. Francois	19 (1.6%)	592 (50.5%)	141 (12.0%)	421 (35.9%)
Ste. Genevieve	48 (6.9%)	357 (51.4%)	72 (10.4%)	217 (31.3%)
St. Louis	9,945 (40.2%)	9,264 (37.4%)	610 (2.5%)	4,931 (19.9%)
Saline	0	563 (28.7%)	366 (18.6%)	1,035 (52.7%)
Schuyler	14 (1.4%)	455 (46.1%)	251 (25.4%)	267 (27.1%)
Scotland	197 (12.6%)	741 (47.5%)	187 (12.0%)	436 (27.9%)
Scott	6 (0.9%)	215 (32.8%)	192 (29.3%)	243 (37.0%)
Shannon	2 (1.1%)	27 (14.2%)	123 (64.7%)	38 (20.0%)
Shelby	90 (5.9%)	476 (31.1%)	293 (19.1%)	702 (45.9%)
Stoddard	0	230 (28.3%)	198 (24.4%)	385 (47.4%)
Stone	0	83 (36.7%)	112 (49.6%)	31 (13.7%)
Sullivan	83 (5.2%)	557 (35.1%)	575 (36.2%)	373 (23.5%)
Taney	0	97 (22.7%)	287 (67.2%)	43 (10.1%)
Texas	6 (0.8%)	61 (7.9%)	511 (66.2%)	194 (25.1%)
Vernon	0	151 (20.5%)	380 (51.5%)	207 (28.0%)
Warren	95 (9.5%)	510 (50.9%)	89 (8.9%)	307 (30.7%)
Washington	28 (2.3%)	635 (52.1%)	62 (5.1%)	493 (40.5%)
Wayne	3 (0.4%)	185 (25.6%)	291 (40.2%)	245 (33.8%)
Webster	7 (0.8%)	172 (19.3%)	376 (42.2%)	335 (37.6%)
Wright	0	44 (8.1%)	369 (68.2%)	128 (23.7%)
Total	**17,029 (10.3%)**	**58,804 (35.6%)**	**31,312 (18.9%)**	**58,261 (35.2%)**

SOURCES—Manuscript returns except for Butler, Dade, Jasper, McDonald and Newton Counties (not in file). These returns were taken from the *Jefferson Inquirer*, December 1, 1860. The returns with one vote discrepancies in Dade (Douglas) and McDonald (Breckinridge) were also found in W. Dean Burnham, *Presidential Ballots 1836–1892* (reprint edition), New York, NY: Arno Press, 1976, citing the *Tribune Almanac, 1861*. The *Inquirer's* figures were used, as they are listed as official.

New Hampshire

County	Lincoln (R)	Douglas (ND)	Breckinridge (SD)	Bell (CU)
Belknap	1,981 (51.9%)	1,786 (46.8%)	48 (1.3%)	5 (0.1%)
Carroll	2,148 (51.3%)	1,993 (47.6%)	42 (1.0%)	8 (0.2%)
Cheshire	3,843 (64.7%)	1,912 (32.2%)	166 (2.8%)	21 (0.4%)
Coos	1,349 (49.5%)	1,330 (48.8%)	43 (1.6%)	2 (0.1%)
Grafton	4,823 (55.4%)	3,505 (40.2%)	343 (3.9%)	42 (0.5%)
Hillsborough	6,888 (58.6%)	4,558 (38.8%)	221 (1.9%)	88 (0.7%)
Merrimack	4,794 (53.6%)	3,817 (42.7%)	276 (3.1%)	56 (0.6%)
Rockingham	5,720 (59.0%)	3,228 (33.3%)	631 (6.5%)	117 (1.2%)
Strafford	3,536 (60.6%)	1,995 (34.2%)	258 (4.4%)	43 (0.7%)
Sullivan	2,437 (56.3%)	1,763 (40.7%)	97 (2.2%)	30 (0.7%)
Total	**37,519 (56.9%)**	**25,887 (39.3%)**	**2,125 (3.2%)**	**412 (0.6%)**
		*(25,883)		

*Stated total.

SOURCE—*New Hampshire Manual, 1889.*

New Jersey

County	Fusion[6]	Lincoln (R)
Atlantic	794 (41.7%)	1,109 (58.3%)
Bergen	2,092 (59.0%)	1,453 (41.0%)
Burlington	4,036 (43.4%)	5,269 (56.6%)
Camden	2,643 (51.6%)	2,483 (48.4%)
Cape May	520 (43.3%)	680 (56.7%)
Cumberland	1,630 (41.4%)	2,305 (58.6%)
Essex	9,711 (52.4%)	8,812 (47.6%)
Gloucester	1,476 (43.0%)	1,953 (57.0%)
Hudson	5,150 (59.6%)	3,491 (40.4%)
Hunterdon	3,934 (58.2%)	2,827 (41.8%)
Mercer	3,423 (48.2%)	3,675 (51.8%)
Middlesex	3,605 (55.2%)	2,924 (44.8%)
Monmouth	3,312 (48.7%)	3,484 (51.3%)
Morris	4,089 (56.9%)	3,096 (43.1%)
Ocean	701 (33.4%)	1,398 (66.6%)
Passaic	2,415 (46.2%)	2,814 (53.8%)
Salem	1,973 (47.0%)	2,226 (53.0%)
Somerset	2,297 (53.7%)	1,979 (46.3%)
Sussex	3,087 (63.6%)	1,768 (36.4%)
Union	2,756 (55.6%)	2,197 (44.4%)
Warren	3,225 (57.3%)	2,401 (42.7%)
Total	**62,869 (51.9%)**	**58,344 (48.1%)**
		*(58,346)

*Stated total.

SOURCES—(Trenton) *New Jersey State Gazette*, November 15, 1860; and manuscript returns.

New York

County	Lincoln (R)	Fusion[7]
Albany	9,835 (46.8%)	11,158 (53.2%)
Allegany	6,443 (71.8%)	2,535 (28.2%)
Broome	4,554 (61.3%)	2,874 (38.7%)
Cattaraugus	5,955 (63.5%)	3,420 (36.5%)
Cayuga	7,922 (66.7%)	3,956 (33.3%)
Chautauqua	8,481 (69.8%)	3,670 (30.2%)
Chemung	2,949 (54.3%)	2,477 (45.7%)
Chenango	5,685 (60.6%)	3,691 (39.4%)
Clinton	3,961 (54.8%)	3,272 (45.2%)
Columbia	5,108 (52.0%)	4,720 (48.0%)
Cortland	3,893 (69.5%)	1,712 (30.5%)
Delaware	5,001 (59.8%)	3,358 (40.2%)
Dutchess	6,763 (52.6%)	6,086 (47.4%)
Erie	12,430 (53.3%)	10,897 (46.7%)
Essex	3,454 (65.8%)	1,795 (34.2%)
Franklin	3,103 (55.9%)	2,440 (44.1%)
*Fulton	2,977 (55.1%)	2,429 (44.9%)
Genesee	4,464 (64.5%)	2,456 (35.5%)
Greene	3,137 (47.0%)	3,537 (53.0%)
*Hamilton	134 (22.3%)	467 (77.7%)
Herkimer	5,302 (61.2%)	3,366 (38.8%)
Jefferson	8,796 (61.3%)	5,542 (38.7%)
Kings	15,883 (43.5%)	20,599 (56.5%)
Lewis	3,257 (58.8%)	2,278 (41.2%)
Livingston	5,178 (61.3%)	3,264 (38.7%)
Madison	6,289 (66.2%)	3,218 (33.8%)
Monroe	10,808 (59.7%)	7,300 (40.3%)
Montgomery	3,528 (52.0%)	3,253 (48.0%)
New York	33,290 (34.8%)	62,482 (65.2%)
Niagara	4,992 (57.2%)	3,748 (42.8%)
Oneida	12,508 (58.1%)	9,031 (41.9%)
Onondaga	11,243 (60.8%)	7,259 (39.2%)
Ontario	5,764 (61.3%)	3,643 (38.7%)
Orleans	3,859 (63.2%)	2,247 (36.8%)
Oswego	9,076 (62.6%)	5,418 (37.4%)
Otsego	6,543 (56.3%)	5,082 (43.7%)
Putnam	1,243 (48.3%)	1,329 (51.7%)
Queens	3,749 (46.1%)	4,391 (53.9%)
Rensselaer	8,464 (49.9%)	8,492 (50.1%)
Richmond	1,408 (37.3%)	2,370 (62.7%)
Rockland	1,410 (37.3%)	2,368 (62.7%)
St. Lawrence	11,324 (73.7%)	4,049 (26.3%)
Saratoga	5,900 (56.4%)	4,557 (43.6%)
Schenectady	2,154 (51.9%)	1,997 (48.1%)
Schoharie	3,279 (43.8%)	4,212 (56.2%)
Schuyler	2,551 (60.0%)	1,709 (40.0%)
Seneca	3,025 (50.2%)	2,997 (49.8%)
Steuben	8,250 (62.2%)	5,023 (37.8%)
Suffolk	3,756 (51.6%)	3,521 (48.4%)
Tioga	3,760 (57.8%)	2,745 (42.2%)
Tompkins	4,348 (59.0%)	3,027 (41.0%)
Ulster	6,775 (52.0%)	6,242 (48.0%)
Warren	2,719 (58.0%)	1,972 (42.0%)
Washington	6,173 (64.6%)	3,486 (35.4%)

Wayne	6,668	(62.8%)	3,942	(37.2%)
Westchester	6,771	(45.4%)	8,126	(54.6%)
Wyoming	4,498	(65.3%)	2,393	(34.7%)
Yates	3,014	(67.2%)	1,473	(32.8%)
Total[8]	**353,804**	**(53.7%)**	**305,101**	**(46.3%)**

In the manuscript returns, Fulton and Hamilton Counties were reported as one, but the Tribune Almanac, 1861 gives the vote for each county, and those numbers are used here. The total for the two counties separately is the same as the total found in the manuscript returns.

SOURCES—Manuscript returns; and *Tribune Almanac, 1861.*

North Carolina[9]

County	Douglas (ND)		Breckinridge (SD)		Bell (CU)	
*Alamance	36	(2.9%)	536	(43.5%)	661	(53.6%)
*Alexander	2	(0.2%)	403	(46.0%)	471	(53.8%)
*Anson	7	(0.6%)	245	(21.8%)	872	(77.6%)
*Ashe	1	(0.1%)	229	(24.2%)	717	(75.7%)
*Beaufort	42	(2.5%)	549	(32.8%)	1,082	(64.7%)
*Bertie	17	(1.7%)	399	(39.4%)	597	(58.9%)
Brunswick	1	(0.1%)	326	(45.7%)	386	(54.1%)
Buncombe	49	(3.5%)	662	(46.8%)	705	(49.8%)
Burke	4	(0.4%)	470	(51.0%)	447	(48.5%)
Cabarrus	18	(1.4%)	445	(35.0%)	810	(63.6%)
Caldwell	9	(1.2%)	229	(31.1%)	499	(67.7%)
Camden	8	(1.3%)	83	(14.0%)	503	(84.7%)
Carteret	42	(4.9%)	370	(43.4%)	441	(51.7%)
Caswell	13	(1.0%)	994	(79.9%)	237	(19.1%)
Catawba	3	(0.3%)	878	(74.2%)	302	(25.5%)
Chatham	194	(11.0%)	604	(34.2%)	970	(54.9%)
Cherokee	15	(1.3%)	459	(39.9%)	677	(58.8%)
Chowan	38	(8.1%)	194	(41.2%)	239	(50.7%)
Cleveland	0		1,091	(84.8%)	196	(15.2%)
Columbus	6	(0.6%)	723	(68.8%)	322	(30.6%)
Craven	122	(9.3%)	492	(37.6%)	693	(53.0%)
Cumberland	35	(2.2%)	879	(55.5%)	670	(42.3%)
Currituck	0		595	(89.7%)	68	(10.3%)
Davidson	15	(0.8%)	728	(37.7%)	1,186	(61.5%)
Davie	31	(3.1%)	329	(32.9%)	641	(64.0%)
Duplin	3	(0.2%)	1,380	(90.1%)	149	(9.7%)
Edgecombe	17	(0.9%)	1,789	(89.4%)	196	(9.8%)
Forsyth	70	(3.8%)	825	(44.4%)	965	(51.9%)
Franklin	14	(1.3%)	759	(69.6%)	318	(29.1%)
Gaston	56	(5.5%)	826	(81.5%)	131	(12.9%)
Gates	12	(1.6%)	338	(45.4%)	394	(53.0%)
Granville	83	(4.6%)	870	(47.8%)	868	(47.7%)
Greene	0		381	(53.9%)	326	(46.1%)
Guilford	118	(5.2%)	304	(13.5%)	1,838	(81.3%)
Halifax	22	(1.7%)	757	(57.1%)	546	(41.2%)
Harnett	78	(10.3%)	543	(71.5%)	138	(18.2%)
Haywood	13	(2.1%)	367	(58.4%)	248	(39.5%)
Henderson	4	(0.4%)	435	(46.5%)	496	(53.0%)
Hertford	20	(0.4%)	246	(36.0%)	418	(61.1%)
Hyde	3	(0.4%)	395	(46.1%)	459	(53.6%)
Iredell	31	(1.6%)	328	(16.5%)	1,625	(81.9%)
Jackson	0		403	(73.9%)	142	(26.1%)
Johnston	40	(2.4%)	974	(59.2%)	630	(38.3%)
Jones	10	(2.7%)	197	(53.0%)	165	(44.4%)
Lenoir	21	(2.4%)	533	(61.2%)	317	(36.4%)
Lincoln	5	(0.7%)	473	(65.6%)	243	(33.7%)
Macon	13	(1.8%)	221	(31.4%)	469	(66.7%)
Martin	22	(2.0%)	751	(67.9%)	333	(30.1%)
McDowell	1	(0.2%)	276	(44.2%)	347	(55.6%)
Mecklenburg	135	(6.5%)	1,101	(53.4%)	826	(40.1%)
Montgomery	3	(0.4%)	102	(12.3%)	725	(87.3%)
Moore	179	(16.8%)	299	(28.0%)	588	(55.2%)
Nash	4	(0.3%)	1,323	(95.1%)	64	(4.6%)
New Hanover	5	(0.2%)	1,617	(71.4%)	644	(28.4%)
Northampton	43	(3.6%)	654	(54.4%)	506	(42.1%)
Onslow	24	(2.5%)	781	(81.5%)	153	(16.0%)
Orange	72	(4.0%)	787	(43.4%)	956	(52.7%)
Pasquotank	55	(7.1%)	239	(31.0%)	477	(61.9%)
*Perquimans	4	(0.7%)	234	(40.4%)	341	(58.9%)

County	Douglas (ND)	Breckinridge (SD)	Bell (CU)
*Person	9 (1.0%)	420 (46.1%)	483 (53.0%)
Pitt	8 (0.6%)	731 (50.4%)	710 (49.0%)
Polk	1 (0.3%)	270 (69.4%)	118 (30.3%)
Randolph	44 (2.8%)	321 (20.2%)	1,224 (77.0%)
Richmond	4 (0.5%)	269 (32.9%)	544 (66.6%)
Robeson	134 (8.9%)	720 (47.9%)	648 (43.1%)
Rockingham	162 (9.7%)	1,017 (61.1%)	485 (29.1%)
Rowan	13 (0.6%)	1,026 (49.8%)	1,023 (49.6%)
Rutherford	3 (0.3%)	695 (58.3%)	495 (41.5%)
Sampson	6 (0.4%)	977 (65.0%)	520 (34.6%)
Stanly	9 (0.9%)	53 (5.3%)	934 (93.8%)
Stokes	5 (0.4%)	745 (63.0%)	432 (36.5%)
*Surry	28 (2.1%)	811 (60.5%)	502 (37.4%)
Tyrrell	22 (5.5%)	77 (19.3%)	300 (75.2%)
Union	0	858 (69.4%)	379 (30.6%)
Wake	276 (10.5%)	1,216 (46.4%)	1,130 (43.1%)
Warren	6 (0.6%)	890 (86.1%)	138 (13.3%)
Washington	44 (7.1%)	159 (25.8%)	413 (67.0%)
Watauga	0	147 (31.3%)	322 (68.7%)
Wayne	11 (0.7%)	1,359 (84.5%)	239 (14.9%)
Wilkes	3 (0.2%)	363 (21.5%)	1,323 (78.3%)
Yadkin	23 (1.7%)	495 (36.4%)	842 (61.9%)
Yancey	4 (0.5%)	500 (64.2%)	275 (35.3%)
Total	**2,703 (2.8%)	**48,539 (50.5%)	**44,912 (46.7%)
	2,701 (2.8%)	**48,539 (50.4%)**	**44,990 (46.7%)**
*Bladen	3 (0.3%)	601 (56.3%)	463 (43.4%)
Madison	34 (5.9%)	323 (56.2%)	218 (37.9%)

*Not included in manuscript returns. (See also note 9.)
**Added totals. (See also note 9.)

Ohio

County	Lincoln (R)	Douglas (ND)	Breckinridge (SD)	Bell (CU)	Smith (U)
Adams	1,667 (43.3%)	2,010 (52.2%)	39 (1.0%)	131 (3.4%)	
Allen	1,796 (48.2%)	1,882 (50.5%)	29 (7.8%)	21 (5.6%)	
Ashland	2,166 (49.0%)	1,720 (38.9%)	496 (11.2%)	34 (7.7%)	
Ashtabula	5,566 (81.1%)	860 (12.5%)	342 (5.0%)	77 (1.1%)	14 (0.2%)
Athens	2,526 (61.6%)	1,494 (36.4%)	43 (10.5%)	36 (8.8%)	1 (0.02%)
Auglaize	1,088 (36.1%)	1,836 (60.9%)	69 (2.3%)	22 (0.7%)	
Belmont	2,675 (41.0%)	1,456 (22.3%)	1,289 (19.7%)	1,111 (17.0%)	
Brown	2,105 (38.7%)	3,006 (55.3%)	90 (1.7%)	238 (4.4%)	
Butler	2,867 (39.2%)	4,109 (56.2%)	156 (2.1%)	184 (2.5%)	
Carroll	1,767 (59.3%)	1,043 (35.0%)	143 (4.8%)	28 (0.9%)	
Champaign	2,325 (52.1%)	1,810 (40.6%)	62 (1.4%)	264 (5.9%)	
Clark	3,017 (60.1%)	1,730 (34.5%)	104 (2.1%)	165 (3.3%)	
Clermont	2,965 (46.1%)	3,206 (49.8%)	57 (0.9%)	209 (3.2%)	
Clinton	2,483 (61.6%)	1,464 (36.3%)	15 (0.4%)	70 (1.7%)	
Columbiana	3,864 (60.4%)	2,130 (33.3%)	306 (4.8%)	96 (1.5%)	5 (0.1%)
Coshocton	2,106 (47.6%)	2,099 (47.4%)	217 (4.9%)	2 (0.1%)	
Crawford	2,064 (41.7%)	2,752 (55.6%)	117 (2.4%)	18 (0.4%)	
Cuyahoga	8,686 (62.5%)	4,814 (34.6%)	333 (2.4%)	75 (0.5%)	
Darke	2,460 (49.2%)	2,479 (49.6%)	16 (0.3%)	42 (0.8%)	
Defiance	1,038 (43.9%)	1,304 (55.1%)	14 (0.6%)	8 (0.3%)	2 (0.1%)
Delaware	2,699 (56.9%)	1,967 (41.5%)	46 (1.0%)	28 (0.6%)	
Erie	2,886 (63.6%)	1,538 (33.9%)	88 (1.9%)	28 (0.6%)	
Fairfield	2,178 (37.7%)	3,249 (56.2%)	201 (3.5%)	155 (2.7%)	
Fayette	1,458 (50.6%)	1,122 (38.9%)	46 (1.6%)	257 (0.9%)	
Franklin	4,295 (46.0%)	4,848 (51.9%)	78 (0.8%)	119 (0.8%)	
Fulton	1,629 (61.6%)	984 (37.2%)	26 (1.0%)	3 (0.1%)	1 (0.04%)
Gallia	1,887 (52.6%)	1,472 (41.0%)	37 (1.0%)	190 (5.3%)	
Geauga	2,877 (79.7%)	677 (18.8%)	33 (0.9%)	17 (0.5%)	6 (0.2%)
Greene	3,260 (63.1%)	1,751 (33.9%)	35 (0.7%)	124 (2.4%)	
Guernsey	2,510 (55.2%)	1,933 (42.5%)	34 (0.7%)	55 (1.2%)	17 (0.4%)
Hamilton	16,282 (45.4%)	15,531 (43.3%)	366 (1.0%)	3,685 (10.3%)	
Hancock	2,135 (47.6%)	2,307 (51.5%)	24 (0.5%)	16 (0.4%)	
Hardin	1,432 (52.7%)	1,198 (44.1%)	32 (1.2%)	54 (2.0%)	

County	Lincoln (R)	Douglas (ND)	Breckinridge (SD)	Bell (CU)	Smith (U)
Harrison	2,175 (60.1%)	759 (21.0%)	637 (17.6%)	45 (1.2%)	9 (0.2%)
Henry	808 (43.6%)	1,039 (56.1%)	3 (0.2%)	3 (0.2%)	
Highland	2,409 (45.3%)	2,272 (42.8%)	157 (3.0%)	475 (8.9%)	
Hocking	1,329 (42.4%)	1,784 (56.9%)	7 (0.2%)	12 (0.4%)	1 (0.03%)
Holmes	1,392 (37.3%)	2,287 (61.4%)	45 (1.2%)	3 (0.1%)	
Huron	4,107 (65.3%)	2,083 (33.1%)	52 (0.8%)	37 (0.6%)	2 (0.03%)
Jackson	1,738 (53.2%)	1,436 (43.9%)	15 (0.5%)	80 (2.4%)	
Jefferson	2,682 (57.9%)	1,163 (25.1%)	703 (15.2%)	79 (1.7%)	
Knox	2,860 (51.5%)	2,060 (37.1%)	524 (9.4%)	98 (1.8%)	14 (0.3%)
Lake	2,524 (77.8%)	622 (19.2%)	87 (2.7%)	13 (0.4%)	
Lawrence	1,813 (56.1%)	1,147 (35.5%)	76 (2.4%)	198 (6.1%)	
Licking	3,502 (47.1%)	3,154 (42.4%)	634 (8.5%)	151 (2.0%)	1 (0.1%)
Logan	2,415 (59.3%)	1,542 (37.8%)	17 (0.4%)	100 (2.5%)	
Lorain	4,045 (66.9%)	1,766 (29.2%)	168 (2.8%)	47 (0.8%)	21 (0.3%)
Lucas	2,899 (58.7%)	1,840 (37.3%)	79 (1.6%)	121 (2.4%)	
Madison	1,417 (53.0%)	1,016 (38.0%)	68 (2.5%)	171 (6.4%)	
Mahoning	2,907 (57.4%)	1,999 (39.5%)	132 (2.6%)	26 (0.5%)	
Marion	1,595 (49.0%)	1,640 (50.4%)	13 (0.4%)	4 (0.1%)	1 (0.03%)
Medina	3,068 (62.6%)	1,765 (36.0%)	58 (1.2%)	5 (1.0%)	2 (0.04%)
Meigs	2,689 (58.3%)	1,699 (36.8%)	7 (0.2%)	215 (4.7%)	2 (0.04%)
Mercer	838 (34.2%)	1,606 (65.5%)	6 (0.2%)	2 (0.2%)	
Miami	3,437 (58.7%)	2,337 (39.9%)	39 (6.7%)	39 (6.7%)	
Monroe	1,335 (28.6%)	3,147 (67.4%)	47 (1.0%)	142 (3.0%)	1 (0.02%)
Montgomery	4,994 (50.1%)	4,720 (47.4%)	72 (0.7%)	179 (1.8%)	
Morgan	2,445 (57.0%)	1,757 (41.0%)	65 (1.5%)	20 (0.5%)	
Morrow	2,260 (53.2%)	1,928 (45.4%)	38 (0.9%)	22 (0.5%)	2 (0.05%)
Muskingum	4,004 (49.4%)	3,550 (43.8%)	157 (1.9%)	396 (4.9%)	
Noble	1,944 (52.0%)	1,647 (44.1%)	91 (2.4%)	52 (1.4%)	3 (0.1%)
Ottawa	579 (44.7%)	692 (54.3%)	23 (1.8%)	1 (0.1%)	
Paulding	554 (58.1%)	391 (41.0%)	9 (0.9%)	0	
Perry	1,605 (43.5%)	1,950 (52.9%)	23 (0.6%)	111 (3.0%)	
Pickaway	2,002 (42.7%)	2,425 (51.7%)	50 (1.1%)	211 (4.5%)	
Pike	958 (38.4%)	1,397 (56.1%)	10 (0.4%)	127 (5.1%)	
Portage	3,065 (59.3%)	1,970 (38.1%)	117 (2.3%)	7 (0.1%)	6 (0.1%)
Preble	2,596 (59.3%)	1,733 (39.6%)	20 (0.5%)	32 (0.7%)	
Putnam	1,016 (40.6%)	1,478 (59.0%)	3 (0.1%)	4 (0.2%)	
Richland	3,023 (47.6%)	3,135 (49.4%)	115 (1.8%)	77 (1.2%)	1 (0.02%)
Ross	3,043 (47.3%)	2,806 (43.7%)	273 (4.2%)	305 (4.7%)	
Sandusky	1,938 (45.3%)	2,319 (54.2%)	13 (0.3%)	10 (0.2%)	
Scioto	2,186 (50.4%)	1,756 (40.5%)	40 (0.9%)	352 (8.1%)	
Seneca	3,052 (48.1%)	3,175 (50.1%)	70 (1.1%)	43 (0.7%)	
Shelby	1,599 (48.4%)	1,669 (50.5%)	17 (0.5%)	24 (0.7%)	
Stark	4,064 (52.9%)	2,826 (36.8%)	774 (10.1%)	13 (0.2%)	
Summit	3,607 (65.5%)	1,785 (32.4%)	97 (1.8%)	11 (0.2%)	5 (0.1%)
Trumbull	4,349 (69.2%)	1,672 (26.6%)	245 (3.9%)	17 (0.3%)	4 (0.1%)
Tuscarawas	3,136 (51.7%)	2,846 (46.9%)	74 (1.2%)	8 (0.1%)	
Union	1,792 (55.5%)	1,145 (35.5%)	136 (4.2%)	153 (4.7%)	
Van Wert	1,015 (50.9%)	959 (48.1%)	15 (0.8%)	4 (0.2%)	
Vinton	1,246 (49.3%)	1,237 (48.9%)	23 (0.9%)	23 (0.9%)	
Warren	3,326 (60.7%)	2,011 (36.7%)	21 (0.4%)	122 (2.2%)	
Washington	3,169 (49.4%)	3,060 (47.7%)	13 (0.2%)	175 (2.7%)	
Wayne	3,204 (48.7%)	3,250 (49.4%)	115 (1.7%)	6 (0.1%)	
Williams	1,713 (56.4%)	1,186 (39.1%)	94 (3.1%)	29 (0.1%)	15 (0.05%)
Wood	2,014 (59.9%)	1,330 (39.5%)	14 (0.4%)	5 (0.1%)	
Wyandot	1,567 (47.7%)	1,670 (50.9%)	20 (0.6%)	27 (0.8%)	
Total	**231,808 (52.3%)** (231,809)	**187,419 (42.3%)** (187,421)	**11,404 (2.6%)** (11,403)	**12,194 (2.8%)** (12,193)	**136 (0.03%)**

SOURCE—*Executive Documents*, Columbus, OH: 1865.

Oregon

County	Lincoln (R)	Douglas (ND)	Breckinridge (SD)	Bell (CU)
Benton	202 (27.8%)	140 (19.3%)	381 (52.5%)	3 (0.4%)
Clackamas	409 (45.0%)	173 (19.0%)	324 (35.6%)	3 (0.3%)
Clatsop	68 (50.4%)	38 (28.2%)	29 (21.5%)	0
Columbia	59 (43.4%)	41 (30.2%)	36 (26.5%)	0

County	Lincoln (R)	Douglas (ND)	Breckinridge (SD)	Bell (CU)
Coos	71 (38.2%)	90 (48.4%)	22 (11.8%)	3 (1.6%)
Curry	42 (24.7%)	69 (40.6%)	53 (31.2%)	6 (3.5%)
Douglas	321 (28.3%)	288 (25.4%)	502 (44.3%)	23 (2.0%)
Jackson	394 (25.2%)	407 (26.0%)	675 (43.2%)	88 (5.6%)
Josephine	261 (29.5%)	221 (25.0%)	371 (41.9%)	32 (3.6%)
Lane	492 (40.3%)	167 (13.7%)	555 (45.4%)	8 (0.7%)
Linn	580 (37.0%)	312 (19.9%)	671 (42.8%)	5 (0.3%)
Marion	598 (33.9%)	865 (49.0%)	286 (16.2%)	17 (1.0%)
Multnomah	571 (47.5%)	364 (30.3%)	261 (21.7%)	5 (0.4%)
Polk	180 (22.8%)	391 (49.4%)	215 (27.2%)	5 (0.6%)
Tillamook	11 (34.3%)	8 (25.0%)	13 (40.6%)	0
Umpqua	151 (50.2%)	72 (23.9%)	75 (24.9%)	3 (0.1%)
Wasco	168 (29.3%)	148 (25.8%)	258 (45.0%)	0
Washington	360 (56.4%)	135 (21.2%)	140 (21.9%)	3 (0.5%)
Yamhill	420 (49.0%)	214 (25.0%)	216 (25.2%)	7 (0.8%)
Total	**5,344 (36.2%)**	**4,131 (28.0%)**	**5,074 (34.4%)**	**212 (1.4%)**

SOURCE—Burton W. Onstine, *Oregon Votes: 1858–1972*, Salem, OR: Oregon Historical Society, 1973, n.p.

Pennsylvania[10]

County	Lincoln (R)	(D Fus)	Douglas (ND)	Bell (CU)
Adams	2,724 (50.1%)	2,644 (48.6%)	36 (0.7%)	38 (0.7%)
Allegheny	16,725 (68.1%)	6,725 (27.4%)	523 (2.1%)	570 (2.3%)
Armstrong	3,355 (60.8%)	2,108 (38.2%)	5 (0.1%)	50 (1.0%)
Beaver	2,824 (62.7%)	1,621 (36.0%)	4 (0.1%)	58 (1.3%)
Bedford	2,505 (51.9%)	2,224 (46.1%)	14 (0.3%)	86 (1.8%)
Berks	6,709 (41.7%)	8,846 (54.9%)	420 (2.6%)	130 (0.8%)
Blair	3,050 (61.5%)	1,275 (25.7%)	239 (4.8%)	397 (8.0%)
Bradford	7,091 (76.2%)	2,188 (23.5%)	9 (0.1%)	22 (0.2%)
Bucks	6,443 (52.8%)	5,174 (42.4%)	487 (4.0%)	95 (0.8%)
Butler	3,640 (60.6%)	2,332 (38.8%)	13 (0.2%)	22 (0.4%)
Cambria	2,277 (54.8%)	1,643 (39.6%)	110 (2.6%)	124 (3.0%)
Carbon	1,758 (51.0%)	1,301 (37.7%)	369 (10.7%)	21 (0.6%)
Centre	3,021 (55.1%)	2,423 (44.2%)	26 (0.5%)	16 (0.3%)
Chester	7,771 (58.7%)	5,008 (37.8%)	263 (2.0%)	202 (1.5%)
Clarion	1,829 (46.7%)	2,078 (53.0%)	0	12 (0.3%)
Clearfield	1,702 (47.8%)	1,836 (51.6%)	0	23 (0.6%)
Clinton	1,736 (56.9%)	1,244 (40.8%)	72 (2.3%)	0
Columbia	1,873 (43.2%)	2,366 (54.5%)	86 (2.0%)	14 (0.3%)
Crawford	5,779 (65.5%)	2,961 (33.6%)	62 (0.7%)	22 (0.2%)
Cumberland	3,593 (51.7%)	3,183 (45.8%)	26 (0.4%)	147 (2.1%)
Dauphin	4,531 (62.2%)	2,392 (32.8%)	195 (2.7%)	169 (2.3%)
Delaware	3,181 (62.1%)	1,500 (29.3%)	152 (3.0%)	288 (5.6%)
Elk	407 (43.8%)	523 (56.2%)	0	0
Erie	6,160 (70.0%)	2,531 (28.8%)	17 (0.2%)	90 (1.0%)
Fayette	3,454 (49.8%)	3,308 (47.7%)	24 (0.3%)	147 (2.1%)
Forest	107 (69.5%)	47 (30.5%)	0	0
Franklin	4,151 (56.4%)	2,515 (34.2%)	622 (8.4%)	76 (1.0%)
Fulton	788 (45.1%)	911 (52.1%)	1 (0.1%)	49 (2.8%)
Greene	1,614 (37.3%)	2,665 (61.7%)	26 (0.6%)	17 (0.4%)
Huntingdon	3,089 (64.5%)	1,622 (33.9%)	55 (1.1%)	22 (0.5%)
Indiana	3,910 (74.1%)	1,347 (25.5%)	0	22 (0.4%)
Jefferson	1,704 (59.8%)	1,134 (39.8%)	6 (0.2%)	5 (0.2%)
Juniata	1,494 (55.2%)	1,147 (42.4%)	2 (0.1%)	62 (2.3%)
Lancaster	13,352 (67.9%)	5,135 (26.1%)	728 (3.7%)	441 (2.2%)
Lawrence	2,937 (77.9%)	788 (20.9%)	16 (0.4%)	31 (0.8%)
Lebanon	3,868 (65.6%)	1,917 (32.5%)	10 (0.2%)	103 (1.7%)
Lehigh	4,170 (49.3%)	4,094 (48.4%)	145 (1.7%)	52 (0.6%)
Luzerne	7,300 (51.8%)	6,803 (48.2%)	0	0
Lycoming	3,494 (56.6%)	2,402 (38.9%)	187 (3.0%)	91 (1.5%)
McKean	1,077 (64.5%)	591 (35.4%)	0	2 (0.1%)
Mercer	3,855 (59.7%)	2,546 (39.5%)	2 (0.03%)	49 (0.8%)
Mifflin	1,701 (56.5%)	1,189 (39.5%)	83 (2.8%)	36 (1.2%)
Monroe	844 (35.2%)	1,262 (52.6%)	291 (12.1%)	0
Montgomery	5,826 (46.2%)	5,590 (44.3%)	509 (4.0%)	690 (5.5%)
Montour	1,043 (48.6%)	786 (36.7%)	311 (14.5%)	4 (0.2%)

County	Lincoln (R)	(D Fus)	Douglas (ND)	Bell (CU)
Northampton	3,839 (44.0%)	4,597 (52.7%)	115 (1.3%)	171 (2.0%)
Northumberland	2,422 (49.5%)	2,306 (47.1%)	97 (2.0%)	72 (1.5%)
Perry	2,371 (57.0%)	1,743 (41.9%)	8 (0.2%)	38 (0.9%)
Philadelphia	39,223 (50.8%)	21,619 (28.0%)	9,274 (12.0%)	7,131 (9.2%)
Pike	381 (31.4%)	831 (68.5%)	0	1 (0.1%)
Potter	1,545 (74.8%)	521 (25.2%)	0	0
Schuylkill	7,568 (57.8%)	4,968 (37.9%)	422 (3.2%)	139 (1.1%)
Snyder	1,678 (63.2%)	910 (34.3%)	60 (2.3%)	5 (0.2%)
Somerset	3,218 (73.1%)	1,175 (26.7%)	1 (0.02%)	10 (0.2%)
Sullivan	429 (46.3%)	497 (53.6%)	0	1 (0.1%)
Susquehanna	4,470 (63.6%)	2,548 (36.3%)	2 (0.03%)	6 (0.1%)
Tioga	4,754 (78.6%)	1,277 (21.1%)	11 (0.2%)	9 (0.1%)
Union	1,824 (68.3%)	812 (30.4%)	28 (1.0%)	6 (0.2%)
Venango	2,680 (58.0%)	1,932 (41.8%)	6 (0.1%)	6 (0.1%)
Warren	2,284 (67.7%)	1,087 (32.2%)	4 (0.1%)	0
Washington	4,724 (53.7%)	3,975 (45.2%)	8 (0.1%)	91 (1.0%)
Wayne	2,857 (52.2%)	2,618 (47.8%)	0	2 (0.04%)
Westmoreland	4,887 (50.3%)	4,796 (49.4%)	13 (1.3%)	13 (1.3%)
Wyoming	1,286 (50.8%)	1,237 (48.9%)	8 (0.3%)	0
York	5,128 (43.6%)	5,497 (46.7%)	562 (4.8%)	574 (4.9%)
Total	**268,030 (56.3%)**	**178,871 (37.5%)**	**16,765 (3.5%)**	**12,770 (2.7%)**

SOURCES—(Harrisburg) *Patriot & Union*; and (Philadelphia) *Press,* November, December, 1860.

Rhode Island

County	Lincoln (R)	Douglas[11] (ND)
Bristol	667 (59.1%)	462 (40.9%)
Kent	1,246 (65.5%)	657 (34.5%)
Newport	1,610 (64.9%)	879 (35.1%)
Providence	7,202 (59.6%)	4,875 (40.4%)
Washington	1,519 (64.6%)	834 (35.4%)
Total	**12,244 (61.4%)**	**7,707 (38.6%)**

SOURCES—*Providence Journal*, November 9, 1860; and W. Dean Burnham, *Presidential Ballots 1836–1892* (reprint edition), New York, NY: Arno Press, 1976, p. 940.

Tennessee

County	Douglas (ND)	Breckinridge (SD)	Bell (CU)
Anderson	30 (3.1%)	339 (34.5%)	614 (62.5%)
Bedford	35 (1.2%)	1,389 (47.4%)	1,506 (51.4%)
Benton	5 (0.4%)	713 (60.9%)	452 (38.6%)
Bledsoe	38 (6.6%)	177 (36.7%)	361 (62.7%)
Blount	47 (2.5%)	586 (30.9%)	1,261 (66.6%)
Bradley	301 (17.0%)	759 (42.9%)	710 (40.1%)
Campbell	20 (3.1%)	271 (42.6%)	345 (54.2%)
Cannon	20 (1.4%)	922 (66.5%)	445 (32.1%)
Carroll	129 (5.3%)	737 (30.3%)	1,570 (64.4%)
Carter	15 (1.4%)	205 (19.0%)	859 (79.6%)
Claiborne	10 (0.7%)	718 (53.5%)	614 (45.8%)
Cocke	14 (1.0%)	473 (33.3%)	933 (65.7%)
Coffee	7 (0.5%)	1,101 (74.9%)	361 (24.6%)
Cumberland	4 (0.8%)	236 (47.1%)	261 (52.1%)
*Davidson	383 (5.7%)	2,432 (36.5%)	3,850 (57.8%)
Decatur	81 (8.9%)	362 (39.6%)	473 (51.6%)
De Kalb	13 (0.8%)	882 (56.1%)	677 (43.1%)
Dickson	86 (0.7%)	768 (60.0%)	427 (33.3%)
Dyer	154 (11.0%)	450 (32.1%)	798 (56.9%)
Fayette	583 (30.7%)	364 (19.2%)	953 (50.2%)
Fentress	16 (2.6%)	468 (75.6%)	135 (21.8%)
Franklin	26 (1.3%)	1,526 (78.7%)	388 (20.0%)
Gibson	241 (7.6%)	1,039 (32.6%)	1,909 (59.9%)
Giles	86 (3.0%)	1,511 (51.9%)	1,313 (45.1%)
Grainger	17 (1.0%)	667 (38.5%)	1,047 (60.5%)
Greene	38 (1.2%)	2,054 (65.4%)	1,048 (33.4%)
Grundy	0	431 (85.3%)	74 (14.7%)
Hamilton	165 (8.0%)	820 (39.8%)	1,074 (52.2%)
Hancock	18 (2.2%)	493 (60.1%)	309 (37.7%)
Haywood	458 (26.9%)	358 (21.0%)	885 (52.0%)
Hardeman	754 (36.3%)	555 (26.7%)	767 (36.9%)

County	Douglas (ND)	Breckinridge (SD)	Bell (CU)
Hawkins	84 (3.6%)	1,155 (50.1%)	1,067 (46.3%)
Hardin	142 (9.3%)	718 (46.9%)	671 (43.8%)
Henderson	74 (3.8%)	611 (31.6%)	1,246 (64.5%)
Henry	24 (3.8%)	1,808 (66.5%)	888 (32.6%)
Hickman	16 (1.2%)	1,067 (78.7%)	273 (20.1%)
Humphreys	14 (1.4%)	654 (64.2%)	350 (34.4%)
Jackson	33 (1.5%)	1,050 (46.4%)	1,182 (52.2%)
Jefferson	35 (1.5%)	681 (29.1%)	1,625 (69.4%)
Johnson	4 (0.6%)	140 (21.5%)	508 (77.9%)
Knox	128 (3.7%)	859 (24.8%)	2,471 (71.5%)
Lauderdale	270 (28.9%)	172 (18.4%)	493 (52.7%)
Lawrence	58 (4.8%)	690 (50.7%)	470 (38.6%)
Lewis	8 (2.6%)	255 (84.2%)	40 (13.2%)
Lincoln	293 (9.0%)	2,442 (75.1%)	517 (15.9%)
Macon	27 (2.6%)	430 (42.2%)	563 (55.2%)
Madison	429 (18.4%)	460 (19.7%)	1,441 (61.8%)
Marion	56 (6.2%)	347 (38.5%)	498 (55.3%)
Marshall	43 (2.1%)	1,326 (65.3%)	662 (32.6%)
Maury	63 (2.0%)	1,731 (53.6%)	1,434 (44.4%)
McMinn	141 (6.7%)	978 (46.5%)	986 (46.8%)
McNairy	514 (24.8%)	493 (23.8%)	1,064 (51.4%)
Meigs	88 (11.6%)	521 (68.6%)	150 (19.8%)
Monroe	52 (2.5%)	1,099 (53.2%)	915 (44.3%)
*Montgomery	95 (3.7%)	1,042 (40.7%)	1,426 (55.6%)
Morgan	46 (10.6%)	218 (50.5%)	168 (38.9%)
Obion	165 (9.5%)	885 (51.0%)	686 (39.5%)
Overton	40 (2.2%)	1,417 (76.6%)	394 (21.3%)
Perry	19 (2.0%)	520 (55.9%)	391 (42.0%)
Polk	63 (4.9%)	825 (64.2%)	396 (30.8%)
Rhea	24 (3.4%)	386 (55.2%)	289 (41.3%)
Roane	43 (2.2%)	839 (42.2%)	1,105 (55.6%)
*Robertson	79 (3.4%)	930 (40.1%)	1,309 (56.5%)
Rutherford	21 (0.7%)	1,505 (49.1%)	1,540 (50.2%)
Scott	1 (0.1%)	154 (37.8%)	252 (61.9%)
Sequatchie	28 (9.1%)	104 (33.9%)	175 (57.0%)
Sevier	7 (0.6%)	188 (15.3%)	1,035 (84.1%)
Shelby	2,959 (43.8%)	744 (11.0%)	3,048 (45.1%)
Smith	60 (2.8%)	618 (28.7%)	1,475 (68.5%)
Stewart	144 (9.3%)	786 (51.0%)	612 (39.7%)
Sullivan	69 (3.2%)	1,517 (71.4%)	538 (25.3%)
Sumner	153 (5.6%)	1,677 (61.8%)	883 (32.5%)
Tipton	563 (52.4%)	91 (8.5%)	420 (39.1%)
Van Buren	12 (3.8%)	187 (59.4%)	116 (36.8%)
Warren	14 (0.9%)	1,220 (75.7%)	378 (23.4%)
Washington	67 (2.8%)	1,331 (56.3%)	967 (40.9%)
Wayne	73 (6.3%)	392 (33.6%)	701 (60.1%)
Weakley	126 (5.3%)	1,335 (56.5%)	900 (38.1%)
White	28 (1.9%)	686 (46.9%)	763 (51.7%)
Williamson	32 (1.3%)	797 (33.0%)	1,587 (65.7%)
Wilson	63 (1.8%)	1,166 (33.8%)	2,223 (64.4%)
Total	**11,384 (7.8%)**	**65,053 (44.5%)**	**69,710 (47.7%)**

Vote of Cheatham County included in Davidson, Montgomery and Robertson Counties.

Sources—(Nashville) *American*, November 27, 1860; and W. Dean Burnham, *Presidential Ballots 1836–1892* (reprint edition), New York, NY: Arno Press, 1976.

Texas

No returns have been located for this election for Clay County.

County	Breckinridge (SD)	Bell (CU)
Anderson	853 (88.3%)	113 (11.7%)
Angelina	213 (63.6%)	122 (36.4%)
Atascosa	194 (90.2%)	21 (9.8%)
Austin	395 (74.5%)	135 (25.5%)
Bandera	6 (15.8%)	32 (84.2%)
Bastrop	433 (70.2%)	184 (29.8%)
Bee	121 (83.4%)	24 (16.6%)
Bell	486 (71.7%)	192 (28.3%)
Bexar	986 (77.1%)	293 (22.9%)
Blanco	136 (82.9%)	28 (17.1%)
Bosque	218 (82.6%)	46 (17.4%)
Bowie	324 (72.0%)	126 (28.0%)
Brazoria	390 (85.7%)	65 (14.3%)
Brazos	253 (95.1%)	13 (4.9%)
Brown	39 (81.3%)	9 (18.7%)
Burleson	506 (82.1%)	110 (17.9%)

Burnet	148	(52.1%)	136	(47.9%)	
Caldwell	423	(77.2%)	128	(22.8%)	
Calhoun	350	(74.2%)	122	(25.8%)	
Cameron	335	(80.3%)	82	(19.7%)	
Cass	536	(69.6%)	234	(30.4%)	
Chambers	106	(84.8%)	19	(15.2%)	
Cherokee	905	(85.1%)	158	(14.9%)	
Collin	667	(62.4%)	402	(37.6%)	
Colorado	569	(59.1%)	393	(40.9%)	
Comal	201	(91.0%)	20	(9.0%)	
Cook	264	(66.0%)	136	(34.0%)	
Coryell	249	(77.6%)	72	(22.4%)	
Dallas	868	(75.8%)	277	(24.2%)	
Denton	586	(75.6%)	189	(24.4%)	
De Witt	490	(85.5%)	83	(14.5%)	
Ellis	416	(66.9%)	206	(33.1%)	
El Paso	1,042	(99.0%)	11	(1.0%)	
Erath	214	(91.8%)	19	(8.2%)	
Falls	161	(65.4%)	85	(34.6%)	
Fannin	778	(67.4%)	377	(32.6%)	
Fayette	744	(62.8%)	441	(37.2%)	
Fort Bend	362	(92.1%)	31	(7.9%)	
Freestone	569	(89.2%)	69	(10.8%)	
Galveston	730	(72.1%)	283	(27.9%)	
Gillespie	66	(48.5%)	70	(51.5%)	
Goliad	243	(64.1%)	136	(35.9%)	
Gonzalez	646	(75.1%)	214	(24.9%)	
Grayson	776	(63.8%)	441	(36.2%)	
Grimes	604	(74.8%)	203	(25.2%)	
Guadalupe	244	(63.5%)	140	(36.5%)	
Hamilton	108	(93.1%)	8	(6.9%)	
Hardin	231	(93.5%)	16	(6.5%)	
Harris	990	(72.2%)	382	(27.8%)	
Harrison	681	(63.7%)	388	(36.3%)	
Hays	164	(55.4%)	132	(44.6%)	
Henderson	464	(79.5%)	120	(20.5%)	
Hill	389	(75.0%)	130	(25.0%)	
Hopkins	812	(75.0%)	271	(25.0%)	
Houston	431	(77.1%)	128	(22.9%)	
Hunt	712	(75.2%)	235	(24.8%)	
Jack	100	(74.1%)	35	(25.9%)	
Jackson	181	(61.1%)	115	(38.9%)	
Jasper	268	(75.7%)	88	(24.3%)	
Jefferson	257	(75.1%)	85	(24.9%)	
Johnson	446	(88.3%)	59	(11.7%)	
Karnes	160	(71.7%)	63	(28.3%)	
Kaufman	663	(79.7%)	169	(20.3%)	
Kerr	86	(73.5%)	31	(26.5%)	
Lamar	791	(70.4%)	332	(29.6%)	
Lampasas	80	(52.6%)	72	(47.4%)	
Lavaca	596	(84.4%)	110	(15.6%)	
Leon	576	(81.8%)	138	(18.2%)	
Liberty	345	(98.3%)	6	(1.7%)	
Limestone	482	(92.3%)	40	(7.7%)	
Live Oak	133	(92.4%)	11	(7.6%)	
Llano	153	(76.1%)	48	(23.9%)	
Madison	232	(89.9%)	26	(10.1%)	

Marion	446	(70.8%)	184	(29.2%)
Mason	17	(94.4%)	1	(5.6%)
Matagorda	195	(96.1%)	8	(3.9%)
McLennan	524	(72.2%)	202	(27.8%)
Medina	146	(80.2%)	36	(19.8%)
Milam	474	(73.1%)	174	(26.9%)
Montague	120	(78.9%)	32	(21.1%)
Montgomery	263	(69.9%)	113	(30.1%)
Nacogdoches	381	(66.6%)	191	(33.4%)
Navarro	491	(74.2%)	171	(25.8%)
Nueces	128	(74.0%)	44	(26.0%)
Orange	129	(95.6%)	6	(4.4%)
Palo Pinto	152	(96.2%)	6	(3.8%)
Panola	518	(79.9%)	130	(20.1%)
Parker	775	(82.4%)	166	(17.6%)
Polk	562	(90.1%)	62	(9.9%)
Red River	514	(62.3%)	311	(37.7%)
Refugio	155	(81.2%)	36	(18.8%)
Robertson	341	(78.0%)	96	(22.0%)
Rusk	1,149	(68.9%)	518	(31.1%)
Sabine	232	(95.5%)	11	(4.5%)
San Augustine	219	(86.6%)	34	(13.4%)
San Patricio	64	(95.5%)	3	(4.5%)
San Saba	115	(74.7%)	39	(25.3%)
Shelby	425	(84.5%)	78	(15.5%)
Smith	1,155	(76.8%)	348	(23.2%)
Starr	40	(27.4%)	106	(72.6%)
Tarrant	618	(74.8%)	208	(25.2%)
Titus	884	(76.1%)	278	(23.9%)
Travis	556	(58.2%)	421	(41.8%)
Trinity	218	(89.0%)	27	(11.0%)
Tyler	496	(98.4%)	8	(1.6%)
Upshur	945	(73.9%)	334	(26.1%)
Uvalde	81	(80.2%)	20	(19.8%)
Van Zandt	335	(92.0%)	29	(8.0%)
Victoria	235	(71.6%)	93	(28.4%)
Walker	499	(75.6%)	161	(24.4%)
Washington	908	(84.2%)	170	(15.8%)
Webb	76	(98.7%)	1	(1.3%)
Wharton	215	(91.1%)	21	(8.9%)
Williamson	487	(68.4%)	225	(31.6%)
Wilson	47	(54.0%)	40	(46.0%)
Wise	169	(65.5%)	89	(34.5%)
Wood	515	(67.1%)	252	(32.9%)
Young	98	(89.9%)	11	(10.1%)
Zapata	151	(100%)	0	
Total	**47,639**	**(75.5%)**	**15,422**	**(24.5%)**
*Stated totals.	*(47,640)		*(15,523)	
*Comanche	104	(92.0%)	9	(8.0%)
*Hidalgo	64	(100%)	0	
*Newton	100	(89.3%)	12	(10.7%)

*Not included in the official returns as they arrived after the deadline.

SOURCES—Manuscript returns; and W. Dean Burnham, *Presidential Ballots 1836–1892* (reprint edition), New York, NY: Arno Press, 1976.

Vermont

County	Lincoln (R)		Douglas (ND)		Breckinridge (SD)		Bell (CU)	
Addison	2,626	(86.6%)	344	(11.3%)	47	(1.5%)	17	(0.6%)
Bennington	1,937	(70.4%)	710	(25.8%)	94	(3.4%)	12	(0.4%)
Caledonia	2,139	(73.0%)	581	(19.8%)	189	(6.5%)	20	(0.7%)
Chittenden	2,241	(77.8%)	545	(18.9%)	69	(2.4%)	25	(0.9%)
Essex	646	(66.7%)	312	(32.2%)	10	(1.0%)	1	(0.1%)
Franklin	1,979	(74.7%)	538	(20.3%)	127	(4.8%)	20	(0.8%)
Grand Isle	333	(71.0%)	89	(19.0%)	41	(8.7%)	6	(1.3%)
Lamoille	1,280	(78.4%)	312	(19.1%)	37	(2.3%)	3	(0.2%)

County	Lincoln (R)	Douglas (ND)	Breckinridge (SD)	Bell (CU)
Orange	2,714 (68.9%)	973 (24.7%)	212 (5.4%)	38 (1.0%)
Orleans	1,749 (80.7%)	293 (13.5%)	120 (5.5%)	6 (0.3%)
Rutland	4,178 (73.8%)	1,348 (23.8%)	116 (2.0%)	23 (0.4%)
Washington	2,941 (70.1%)	1,209 (28.8%)	43 (1.0%)	4 (0.1%)
Windham	3,732 (79.7%)	461 (9.9%)	470 (10.0%)	17 (0.4%)
Windsor	5,313 (80.9%)	934 (14.2%)	291 (4.4%)	26 (0.4%)
Total	**33,808 (75.9%)**	**8,649 (19.4%)**	**1,866 (4.2%)**	**218 (0.5%)**
	*(33,888)			*(217)

*Stated totals.

SOURCE—Manuscript returns.

Virginia

County	Lincoln (R)	Douglas (ND)	Breckinridge (SD)	Bell (CU)
Accomac		80 (5.2%)	737 (47.5%)	736 (47.4%)
Albemarle		97 (3.9%)	1,056 (42.8%)	1,317 (53.3%)
Alexandria	14 (8.5%)	3 (0.8%)	46 (28.0%)	101 (61.6%)
Alleghany		37 (5.9%)	344 (54.5%)	250 (39.6%)
Amelia		32 (5.6%)	259 (45.2%)	282 (49.2%)
Amherst		26 (1.8%)	808 (55.5%)	622 (42.7%)
Appomattox		10 (1.3%)	563 (70.9%)	221 (27.8%)
Augusta		1,094 (28.3%)	218 (5.6%)	2,553 (66.1%)
Barbour	3 (0.2%)	39 (0.2%)	910 (66.2%)	422 (30.7%)
Bath		22 (5.4%)	163 (40.2%)	220 (54.3%)
Bedford		91 (3.5%)	1,037 (39.9%)	1,468 (56.5%)
Berkeley		106 (5.7%)	830 (44.9%)	913 (49.4%)
Boone		24 (6.9%)	204 (58.5%)	121 (34.7%)
Botetourt		174 (12.9%)	589 (43.5%)	590 (43.6%)
Braxton		46 (8.4%)	227 (41.5%)	274 (50.1%)
Brooke	178 (20.3%)	76 (8.7%)	450 (51.3%)	173 (19.7%)
Brunswick		137 (15.4%)	444 (49.9%)	308 (34.6%)
Buchanan		19 (11.4%)	134 (80.2%)	14 (8.4%)
Buckingham		22 (2.0%)	523 (48.0%)	545 (50.0%)
Cabell	4 (0.5%)	407 (45.8%)	161 (18.1%)	316 (35.6%)
Calhoun		1 (0.3%)	285 (93.4%)	19 (6.2%)
Campbell		146 (5.1%)	1,208 (42.0%)	1,521 (52.9%)
Caroline		18 (1.3%)	772 (57.1%)	561 (41.5%)
Carroll		11 (1.0%)	729 (69.1%)	315 (29.9%)
Charles City		9 (2.6%)	111 (32.3%)	224 (65.1%)
Charlotte		25 (2.8%)	465 (51.2%)	418 (46.0%)
Chesterfield		588 (34.5%)	328 (19.2%)	788 (46.2%)
Clarke		49 (7.3%)	335 (49.9%)	288 (42.9%)
Clay		0	37 (23.7%)	119 (76.3%)
Craig		2 (0.5%)	322 (73.9%)	112 (25.7%)
Culpeper		19 (1.8%)	525 (49.1%)	526 (49.2%)
Cumberland		37 (6.3%)	276 (46.7%)	278 (47.0%)
Dinwiddie	1 (0.1%)	183 (22.1%)	254 (30.7%)	389 (47.0%)
Doddridge		91 (15.4%)	356 (60.2%)	143 (24.2%)
Elizabeth City		24 (5.5%)	164 (37.6%)	248 (56.9%)
Essex		4 (0.7%)	308 (52.1%)	279 (47.2%)
Fairfax		91 (6.2%)	685 (46.7%)	691 (47.1%)
Fauquier		39 (1.9%)	1,027 (50.0%)	989 (48.1%)
Fayette		65 (9.5%)	241 (35.1%)	381 (55.5%)
Floyd		36 (4.4%)	400 (48.8%)	384 (46.8%)
Fluvanna		7 (0.7%)	443 (47.3%)	487 (52.0%)
Franklin		133 (6.4%)	1,076 (51.9%)	863 (41.7%)
Frederick		66 (2.8%)	1,315 (56.1%)	963 (41.1%)
Giles		63 (9.4%)	244 (36.3%)	366 (54.4%)
Gilmer		27 (6.6%)	268 (65.0%)	117 (28.4%)
Gloucester		0	460 (60.4%)	301 (39.6%)
Goochland		37 (5.2%)	428 (60.4%)	244 (34.4%)
Grayson		16 (2.1%)	447 (57.5%)	315 (40.5%)
Greenbrier		133 (8.2%)	505 (31.0%)	993 (60.9%)
Greene		10 (1.7%)	521 (86.1%)	74 (12.2%)
Greensville		41 (12.4%)	151 (45.6%)	139 (42.0%)
Halifax		138 (6.9%)	1,312 (65.2%)	563 (28.0%)
Hampshire	1 (0.05%)	75 (3.7%)	1,054 (52.5%)	878 (43.7%)
Hancock	254 (40.1%)	85 (13.4%)	262 (41.3%)	33 (5.2%)

County	Lincoln (R)	Douglas (ND)	Breckinridge (SD)	Bell (CU)
Hanover		27 (6.6%)	749 (55.4%)	575 (42.6%)
Hardy		74 (5.6%)	355 (26.8%)	894 (67.6%)
Harrison	22 (1.0%)	107 (4.8%)	1,191 (52.9%)	931 (41.4%)
Henrico		189 (8.5%)	641 (28.7%)	1,403 (62.8%)
Henry		59 (5.6%)	444 (42.4%)	543 (51.9%)
Highland		255 (39.8%)	170 (26.6%)	215 (33.6%)
Isle of Wight		19 (2.1%)	757 (82.0%)	147 (15.9%)
Jackson	21 (2.2%)	64 (6.6%)	500 (51.4%)	388 (39.9%)
James City		5 (2.3%)	60 (28.2%)	148 (69.5%)
Jefferson		440 (23.7%)	458 (24.7%)	959 (51.6%)
Kanawha		52 (3.0%)	513 (29.5%)	1,176 (67.5%)
King George		37 (8.3%)	223 (50.2%)	184 (41.4%)
King William		8 (1.7%)	315 (67.7%)	142 (30.5%)
King & Queen		2 (0.3%)	510 (66.5%)	255 (33.2%)
Lancaster		12 (3.3%)	142 (39.1%)	209 (57.6%)
Lee		10 (0.7%)	894 (65.4%)	462 (33.8%)
Lewis		247 (20.9%)	604 (51.1%)	332 (28.1%)
Logan		6 (1.6%)	271 (71.9%)	100 (26.5%)
Loudoun	11 (0.4%)	120 (4.1%)	778 (26.4%)	2,033 (69.1%)
Louisa		2 (0.2%)	754 (60.1%)	498 (39.7%)
Lunenburg		32 (4.0%)	527 (65.1%)	251 (31.0%)
Madison		20 (2.2%)	834 (89.9%)	74 (8.0%)
Marion	1 (0.05%)	137 (6.7%)	1,337 (65.4%)	569 (27.8%)
Marshall	195 (9.6%)	108 (5.3%)	809 (39.7%)	928 (45.5%)
Mason	59 (3.9%)	297 (19.7%)	439 (29.1%)	716 (49.4%)
Matthews		0	306 (54.9%)	251 (45.1%)
McDowell		0	37 (51.4%)	35 (48.6%)
Mecklenburg		63 (4.5%)	901 (64.6%)	430 (30.8%)
Mercer		13 (1.5%)	432 (48.6%)	443 (49.9%)
Middlesex		0	241 (61.5%)	151 (38.5%)
Monongalia	77 (3.7%)	757 (36.4%)	601 (28.9%)	622 (29.9%)
Monroe		83 (6.4%)	520 (40.1%)	693 (53.5%)
Montgomery		74 (6.1%)	425 (35.1%)	712 (58.8%)
Morgan		20 (2.2%)	254 (43.6%)	308 (52.9%)
Nansemond		1 (0.1%)	429 (47.3%)	477 (52.6%)
Nelson		112 (9.0%)	390 (31.5%)	733 (59.5%)
New Kent		2 (0.5%)	172 (39.3%)	264 (60.3%)
Nicholas		48 (8.8%)	152 (27.9%)	345 (65.3%)
Norfolk		52 (4.3%)	447 (37.2%)	704 (58.5%)
Northampton		6 (1.3%)	214 (47.1%)	234 (51.5%)
Northumberland		1 (0.2%)	350 (55.8%)	276 (41.0%)
Nottoway		28 (6.4%)	179 (40.8%)	232 (52.8%)
Ohio	771 (21.4%)	716 (19.9%)	915 (25.4%)	1,202 (33.4%)
Orange		12 (1.3%)	475 (52.0%)	427 (46.7%)
Page		75 (6.5%)	937 (81.3%)	141 (12.2%)
Patrick		70 (7.5%)	432 (46.2%)	433 (46.3%)
Pendleton		133 (17.7%)	217 (28.9%)	400 (53.3%)
Pittsylvania		177 (6.0%)	1,057 (36.0%)	1,702 (58.0%)
Pleasants		119 (28.0%)	166 (39.1%)	140 (32.9%)
Pocahontas		30 (5.7%)	333 (63.3%)	163 (31.0%)
Powhatan		120 (25.4%)	127 (26.9%)	225 (47.7%)
Preston	110 (5.9%)	239 (12.9%)	942 (50.8%)	562 (30.3%)
Prince Edward		65 (7.5%)	423 (49.1%)	374 (43.4%)
Prince George		126 (22.5%)	191 (34.1%)	243 (43.4%)
Princess Anne		16 (1.9%)	379 (44.8%)	451 (53.3%)
Prince William	55 (5.3%)	26 (2.5%)	718 (68.9%)	243 (23.3%)
Pulaski		5 (0.9%)	250 (42.6%)	332 (56.6%)
Putnam		38 (5.0%)	327 (42.7%)	400 (52.3%)
Raleigh		14 (4.5%)	69 (22.0%)	230 (73.5%)
Randolph		143 (22.2%)	243 (37.7%)	259 (40.2%)
Rappahannock		29 (3.1%)	409 (44.0%)	491 (52.9%)
Richmond		6 (1.1%)	185 (34.0%)	353 (64.9%)
Ritchie	12 (1.4%)	73 (8.6%)	544 (63.8%)	224 (26.3%)
Roane		16 (3.1%)	264 (51.1%)	237 (45.8%)
Roanoke		52 (7.2%)	373 (51.9%)	293 (40.8%)
Rockbridge		641 (28.7%)	361 (16.2%)	1,231 (55.1%)
Rockingham		1,354 (46.5%)	676 (23.2%)	883 (30.3%)
Russell		0	526 (52.7%)	473 (47.3%)
Scott		91 (7.7%)	594 (50.5%)	491 (41.8%)

County	Lincoln (R)	Douglas (ND)	Breckinridge (SD)	Bell (CU)
Shenandoah	13 (0.5%)	170 (6.8%)	1,883 (75.5%)	427 (17.1%)
Smyth		49 (4.9%)	496 (50.1%)	446 (45.0%)
Southampton		9 (0.8%)	563 (50.4%)	545 (48.8%)
Spotsylvania		257 (18.7%)	516 (37.6%)	599 (43.7%)
Stafford		165 (17.0%)	402 (41.4%)	404 (41.6%)
Surry		55 (15.0%)	115 (31.3%)	197 (53.7%)
Sussex		96 (16.9%)	294 (51.9%)	177 (31.2%)
Taylor	4 (0.3%)	26 (2.1%)	575 (45.9%)	647 (51.7%)
Tazewell		0	934 (75.3%)	306 (24.7%)
Tucker		23 (16.0%)	99 (68.8%)	22 (15.3%)
Tyler		197 (21.1%)	423 (45.2%)	315 (33.7%)
Upshur		54 (5.5%)	589 (60.5%)	381 (39.1%)
Warren		12 (1.6%)	462 (61.6%)	276 (36.8%)
Warwick		0	32 (30.8%)	72 (69.2%)
Washington		56 (2.6%)	1,178 (54.5%)	916 (42.6%)
Wayne	10 (1.7%)	82 (14.0%)	166 (28.4%)	326 (55.8%)
Webster		9 (4.7%)	96 (50.3%)	86 (45.0%)
Westmoreland		4 (0.7%)	160 (26.6%)	438 (72.8%)
Wetzel	6 (0.7%)	153 (17.9%)	607 (70.9%)	90 (10.5%)
Wirt		16 (3.8%)	255 (60.6%)	150 (35.6%)
Wise		8 (1.7%)	363 (76.7%)	102 (21.6%)
Wood	81 (4.5%)	56 (3.1%)	832 (46.2%)	832 (46.2%)
Wythe		22 (1.5%)	795 (55.4%)	617 (43.0%)
York		3 (0.9%)	90 (28.1%)	227 (70.9%)
Cities & Towns				
Alexandria	2 (0.1%)	138 (8.8%)	519 (33.1%)	911 (58.0%)
Norfolk		233 (14.1%)	439 (26.5%)	983 (59.4%)
Petersburg		613 (33.9%)	223 (12.3%)	970 (53.7%)
Portsmouth	4 (0.3%)	214 (14.7%)	559 (38.4%)	678 (46.6%)
Richmond		753 (17.4%)	1,167 (37.7%)	2,402 (55.6%)
Williamsburg		24 (20.7%)	43 (37.1%)	49 (42.2%)
Total[12]	**1,909 (1.1%)**	**16,183 (9.7%)**	**74,350 (44.5%)**	**74,691 (44.7%)**
*Stated totals.	*(1,929)			*(74,641)
*Wyoming		9 (9.2%)	29 (29.6%)	60 (61.2%)

*Vote of the county received too late and not included in the official returns.

Sources—*Richmond Enquirer*, December 4, 7 and 25, 1860; and W. Dean Burnham, *Presidential Ballots*.

Wisconsin

County	Lincoln (R)	Douglas (ND)	Breckinridge (SD)	Bell (CU)
Adams	844 (73.7%)	296 (25.9%)	5 (0.4%)	0
Ashland	35 (52.2%)	32 (47.8%)	0	0
Bad Ax	1,145 (70.2%)	465 (28.5%)	22 (1.3%)	0
Brown	873 (41.3%)	1,239 (58.7%)	0	0
Buffalo	459 (70.6%)	189 (29.1%)	1 (0.2%)	1 (0.2%)
Calumet	706 (53.9%)	605 (46.1%)	0	0
Chippewa	256 (51.5%)	241 (48.5%)	0	0
Clark	152 (62.6%)	89 (36.6%)	2 (0.8%)	0
Columbia	3,386 (67.6%)	1,614 (32.2%)	4 (0.1%)	3 (0.1%)
Crawford	828 (49.7%)	832 (49.9%)	6 (0.4%)	0
Dane	4,798 (53.2%)	4,174 (46.3%)	40 (0.4%)	3 (0.03%)
Dodge	4,398 (49.4%)	4,456 (50.1%)	43 (0.5%)	2 (0.02%)
Door	250 (67.0%)	123 (33.0%)	0	0
Douglas	70 (45.8%)	66 (43.1%)	15 (9.9%)	2 (0.1%)
Dunn	564 (65.7%)	341 (32.3%)	9 (1.0%)	0
Eau Claire	490 (57.5%)	342 (40.1%)	19 (2.2%)	1 (0.1%)
Fond du Lac	4,106 (51.7%)	3,001 (42.1%)	3 (0.4%)	12 (1.7%)
Grant	3,579 (64.7%)	1,922 (34.7%)	33 (0.6%)	0
Green	2,372 (64.0%)	1,324 (35.7%)	10 (0.3%)	0
Green Lake	1,957 (73.0%)	708 (26.4%)	17 (0.6%)	0
Iowa	1,909 (54.0%)	1,581 (44.7%)	46 (1.3%)	2 (0.1%)
Jackson	654 (76.0%)	207 (24.0%)	0	0
Jefferson	3,077 (52.4%)	2,794 (47.5%)	4 (0.1%)	1 (0.02%)
Juneau	1,033 (57.9%)	737 (41.3%)	9 (0.5%)	5 (0.3%)
Kenosha	1,637 (63.9%)	920 (35.9%)	4 (0.2%)	0

County	Lincoln (R)	Douglas (ND)	Breckinridge (SD)	Bell (CU)
Kewaunee	326 (32.1%)	688 (67.9%)	0	0
Lafayette	1,737 (47.1%)	1,898 (51.4%)	47 (1.3%)	9 (0.2%)
La Crosse	1,477 (63.5%)	765 (32.9%)	65 (2.8%)	18 (0.8%)
La Pointe	43 (58.9%)	4 (5.5%)	26 (35.6%)	0
Manitowoc	2,041 (51.1%)	1,947 (48.7%)	9 (2.3%)	0
Marathon	219 (31.1%)	481 (68.2%)	4 (0.6%)	1 (0.1%)
Marquette	782 (46.8%)	883 (52.8%)	6 (0.4%)	0
Milwaukee	4,831 (41.5%)	6,726 (57.8%)	39 (0.3%)	37 (0.3%)
Monroe	1,229 (65.8%)	631 (33.8%)	2 (0.1%)	8 (0.4%)
Oconto	598 (67.5%)	287 (32.4%)	1 (0.1%)	0
Outgamie	832 (43.0%)	1,082 (55.9%)	20 (1.0%)	0
Ozaukee	627 (25.5%)	1,823 (74.2%)	8 (0.3%)	0
Pepin	326 (73.8%)	105 (23.8%)	11 (2.5%)	0
Pierce	637 (60.7%)	411 (39.1%)	2 (0.2%)	0
Polk	199 (59.6%)	122 (36.5%)	12 (3.6%)	1 (0.3%)
Portage	944 (64.1%)	471 (32.0%)	58 (3.9%)	0
Racine	2,635 (61.1%)	1,659 (38.5%)	8 (0.2%)	8 (0.2%)
Richland	1,168 (59.1%)	777 (39.3%)	28 (1.4%)	3 (0.2%)
Rock	5,198 (72.3%)	1,916 (26.7%)	64 (0.9%)	10 (0.1%)
St. Croix	664 (52.5%)	597 (47.2%)	3 (0.2%)	0
Sauk	2,309 (69.3%)	985 (29.6%)	37 (1.1%)	2 (0.1%)
Sheboygan	2,731 (55.5%)	2,179 (44.3%)	7 (0.1%)	0
Shawano	163 (58.8%)	114 (41.2%)	0	0
Trempealeau	490 (78.5%)	134 (21.5%)	0	0
Walworth	3,910 (70.8%)	1,591 (28.8%)	15 (0.3%)	3 (0.1%)
Waukesha	3,020 (53.8%)	2,563 (45.7%)	10 (0.8%)	19 (0.4%)
Washington	939 (25.5%)	2,747 (74.5%)	1 (0.03%)	0
Waupeca	1,340 (69.4%)	575 (29.8%)	16 (0.8%)	0
Waushara	1,534 (78.2%)	405 (20.6%)	24 (1.2%)	0
Winnebago	3,225 (63.2%)	1,859 (36.4%)	16 (0.3%)	2 (0.04%)
Wood	362 (50.2%)	301 (41.7%)	58 (8.0%)	0
Total	**86,114 (56.6%)**	**65,024 (42.7%)**	**889 (0.6%)**	**153 (0.1%)**

Source — *The Legislative Manual of the State of Wisconsin, 1863*, pp. 157–166.

NOTES

1. The electoral vote for vice president was Hannibal Hamlin (R) 180, Joseph Lane (SD) 72, Edward Everett (CU) 39, and Herschel V. Johnson (ND) 12.

2. The Democratic Party split over issue of slavery. The first national convention meeting at Charleston, SC, adjourned without making a nomination. A reconvened convention meeting in Baltimore, lacking many southern delegates (they had walked out of the original convention), nominated Senator Douglas. The other segment of the party reconvened, again in Charleston, and nominated vice president Breckinridge. The Constitutional Union Party, which to some degree represented remnants of the American and Whig parties, formed primarily as a response to the growing sectional split in the nation, adopted a union preservation platform and nominated former senator and congressman, John Bell.

One of the myths about Lincoln's victory is that it was due to the split in the opposition vote. Notwithstanding his share of the popular vote, the lowest percentage of any candidate to achieve an electoral college majority, Lincoln carried all but two of the states he won with a majority of the popular vote. Thus, the combined popular vote of all his opponents in all the states would not have changed the result of the election.

3. The legislature cast the electoral vote because no candidate received a majority of the popular vote.

4. The counties below are listed as having made no returns, according to the *Michigan Manual, 1913* and W. Dean Burnham's *Presidential Ballots*. However, the manuscript returns contain them, as well as the accepted returns given here. No summary sheet was found or any explanation about why these returns were apparently excluded from the official returns.

County	Lincoln (R)	Douglas (ND)	Bell (CU)
Emmett	30 (15.2%)	168 (84.8%)	
Houghton	621 (43.9%)	794 (56.1%)	
Marquette	264 (58.5%)	180 (39.9%)	7 (1.6%)

5. In the manuscript returns, none are listed for Noxubee County, "not having being received by the Secretary." However, in the *Mississippian*, whose returns are listed as official, the Noxubee returns were included. W. Dean Burnham's *Presidential Ballots*, citing "Manuscript Records of the Secretary of State," also lists the same returns that are included here.

6. The Fusion slate consisted of three electors pledged to Douglas, and two each to Breckinridge and Bell. Nonetheless, different electors appeared in some counties for Breckinridge and Bell, resulting in lower totals for them and a split electoral outcome. The three Douglas electors were elected and four of those pledged to Lincoln. The Breckinridge and Bell electors finished behind all other candidates. The Fusion vote used here is the vote for the high elector on the slate, who was pledged to Douglas.

7. The slate of electors were pledged to three different candidates: 18 to Douglas, ten to Bell, and seven to Breckinridge.

8. The State Board of Canvassers did not include the vote of Orange and Sullivan Counties in the official returns, apparently because they were received too late. However, the returns from these two counties were included in all other elections. The vote of the counties is listed below and was taken from Svend Petersen's *A Statistical History of the American Presidential Elections*, W. Dean Burnham's *Presidential Ballots*, *The Tribune Almanac 1861* and the *Evening Journal Almanac 1861*. All presented the same figures.

County	Lincoln (R)	Fusion
Orange	5,898 (49.5%)	6,011 (50.5%)
Sullivan	2,944 (48.2%)	3,170 (51.8%)

9. For the official returns, only statewide totals were published in the (Raleigh) *Weekly Standard*, November 21, 1860. Most of the county returns were taken from the manuscript returns, but these returns are incomplete. The missing county returns, those preceded by an asterisk (*), were taken from W. Dean Burnham, *Presidential Ballots 1836–1892* (reprint edition), New York, NY: Arno Press, 1976, citing the *Tribune Almanac 1861*. The votes of Bladen and Madison Counties were not included in the official return totals. The added totals are those immediately below the county returns in lightface type. The official statewide totals, used in the national summary, are below the added totals in bold.

10. The Democratic Party chose its slate of electors before the National Convention. The electoral candidates agreed in advance to support the eventual nominee of the convention. However, the convention, meeting in Charleston, SC, adjourned without selecting a candidate, after several southern delegates left. A convention reassembled in Baltimore with more than a third of the delegates absent and nominated Douglas. Another convention assembled again in Charleston, with many of the delegates who left the original convention present, along with other delegates, and nominated Breckinridge. Both candidates' supporters claimed the right for their man to be considered the party candidate and the support of the electoral slate. Eventually, the state party worked out an agreement: if either candidate could win the national election with Pennsylvania's electoral vote, then all her electoral votes would go to that candidate. Of the 27 electoral candidates, 15 were Breckinridge supporters; the remaining 12 were for Douglas. This was often referred to as the Reading electoral slate, because it was in that city that the state party chose it. However, not all of the Douglas supporters agreed to this deal and established a separate Douglas only ticket. This slate comprised the 12 Douglas electoral candidates on the Reading ticket, and 15 additional Douglas supporters. This ticket was usually referred to as the Straight Douglas ticket. Thus 12 electoral candidates appeared on two tickets, Reading and Straight Douglas.

In listing the vote, the original or Reading slate is called Democratic-Fusion. In the national summary, this vote is listed under the Fusion column, not the Breckinridge column as many other sources do, because this ticket was pledged to either of two candidates based on the national result. Additionally, the slate was almost equally divided between supporters of Breckinridge and Douglas. For a discussion of these events, see John F. Coleman, *The Disruption of the Pennsylvania Democracy 1848–1860,* Harrisburg, PA: Pennsylvania Historical and Museum Commission, 1975, Chapter IX.

The county vote as reported here for the Democratic-Fusion slate is for one of the Breckinridge electors (John Ahl). Neither the state nor the county votes for any of the Douglas electors on the Fusion slate is known because their votes were always given as the combined vote of the Straight Douglas and Fusion slates. The high vote for an elector on both tickets was 194,834 (Joseph Laubach). Therefore, the vote reported under the Douglas column is for a Straight Douglas elector who was not on the Fusion ticket. I could not find a county by county vote for each elector or, as indicated, a breakdown by ticket for Douglas.

Complicating this matter further was the fact that the secretary of state, after initially reporting the official returns in late November, revised them in early December. The late November returns are used here because none of the sources researched gave the county returns for an elector who was only on the Reading slate. For purposes of the national summary, the December returns are used. The differences were minor: Lincoln lost 788, Douglas lost 81, and Bell gained 103.

11. The Douglas ticket in Rhode Island was supported by Breckinridge and Bell supporters.

12. The statewide vote for each electoral candidate was printed on the December 4, 1860, in the *Enquirer* without county returns. On December 25, 1860, the *Enquirer* printed the official returns by county. However, the state totals given in the later issue differ slightly from the December 4 totals for all the candidates but Lincoln. In the case of Breckinridge and Bell, the December 25 totals were greater than those of the high electors in the earlier issue: Breckinridge 74,350 (Dec. 25) and 74,306 (Dec. 4), Bell 74,691 compared to 74,534. In the case of Douglas, his total of 16,183 compared to the high elector's 16,251, but no elector in the December 4 issue received that total. I have not found any explanation for these differences. Unfortunately the manuscript returns are incomplete, with 33 counties missing.

Additionally, the electoral vote was split: nine Bell and six Breckinridge electors were elected, but the entire electoral vote was cast for Bell. Five of the six Breckinridge electors had resigned and one was too ill to attend the voting ceremony. Six other individuals replaced the resignees, but the above electoral vote still resulted. The reasons for these unusual events are discussed in detail in the *Enquirer*, December 7, 1860.

MAPS

Listed below are state and county maps that show the boundaries of presidential elector districts in those instances where a state was divided into two or more such districts. The state maps, in addition to the elector district boundaries, show the counties of the state. County maps are shown when counties were divided between districts. In the case of Maine and Massachusetts's county maps, the subdivisions shown are the towns and cities. The list below indicates the election or elections each map covered, as well as the order in which they appear.

Map	Election(s)
Delaware	1789
Massachusetts	1789
Virginia	1789
Kentucky	1792 & 1796
Massachusetts	1792
North Carolina	1792–1800
Virginia	1792 & 1796
Maryland	1796 & 1800
Massachusetts	1796
Bristol and Plymouth Counties	1796
Essex, Middlesex, Norfolk and	
Suffolk Counties	1796
Hampshire County	1796
Worcester County	1796
District of Maine	1796
Lincoln County	1796
Kentucky	1800
Kentucky	1804
Maryland	1804–1824
Dorchester County	1804–1828
Montgomery and Prince	
George's Counties	1804–1824
North Carolina	1804 & 1808
Tennessee	1804
Kentucky	1808

Map	Election(s)
Tennessee	1808
Kentucky	1812–1820
Massachusetts	1812
District of Maine	1812
Tennessee	1812 & 1816
Illinois	1820
Maine	1820
Cumberland County	1820
Kennebec County	1820
Lincoln County and part of	
Hancock County	1820
York County	1820
Tennessee	1820
Illinois	1824
Kentucky	1824
Maine	1824
Cumberland County	1824
Kennebec County	1824
Lincoln	1824
Missouri	1824
Tennessee	1824
Maryland	1828
New York	1828
Tennessee	1828
Maryland	1832

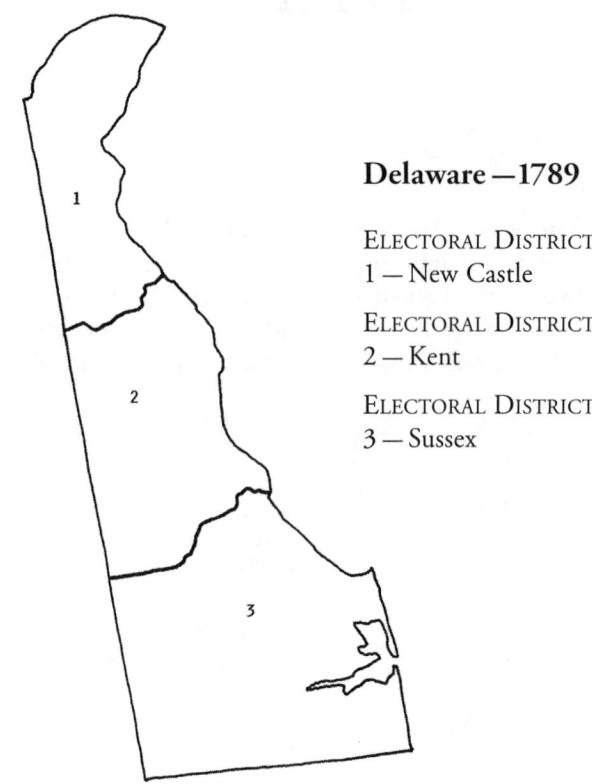

Delaware—1789

ELECTORAL DISTRICT
1 — New Castle

ELECTORAL DISTRICT
2 — Kent

ELECTORAL DISTRICT
3 — Sussex

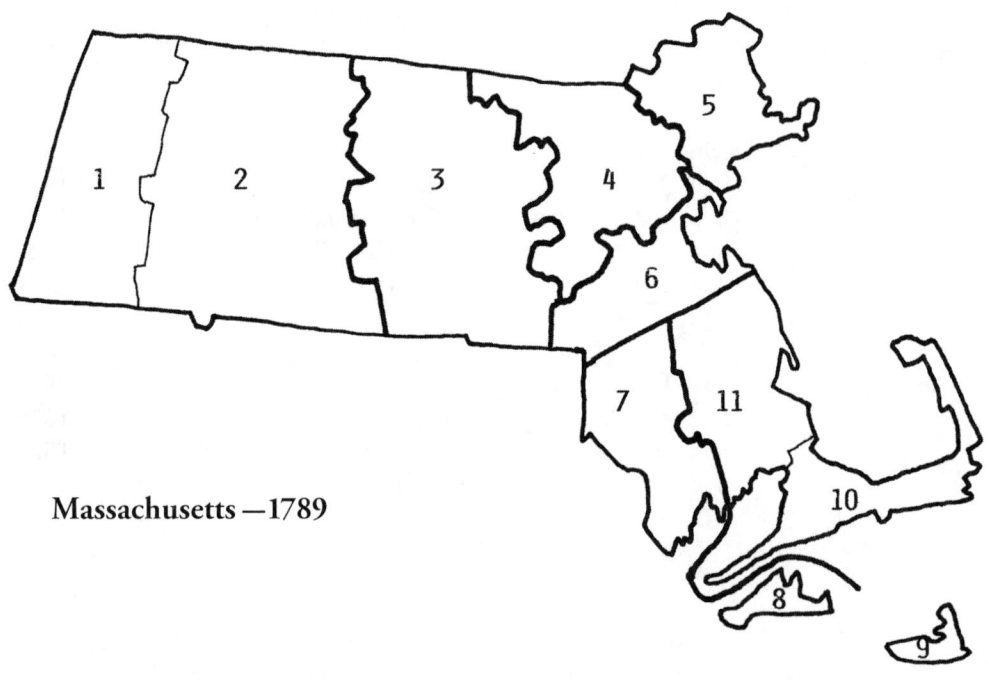

Massachusetts—1789

ELECTORAL DISTRICT
  1 — Berkshire
  2 — Hampshire

ELECTORAL DISTRICT
  3 — Worcester

ELECTORAL DISTRICT
  4 — Middlesex

ELECTORAL DISTRICT
  5 — Essex

ELECTORAL DISTRICT
  6 — Suffolk

ELECTORAL DISTRICT
  7 — Bristol
  8 — Dukes
  9 — Nantucket

ELECTORAL DISTRICT
  10 — Barnstable
  11 — Plymouth

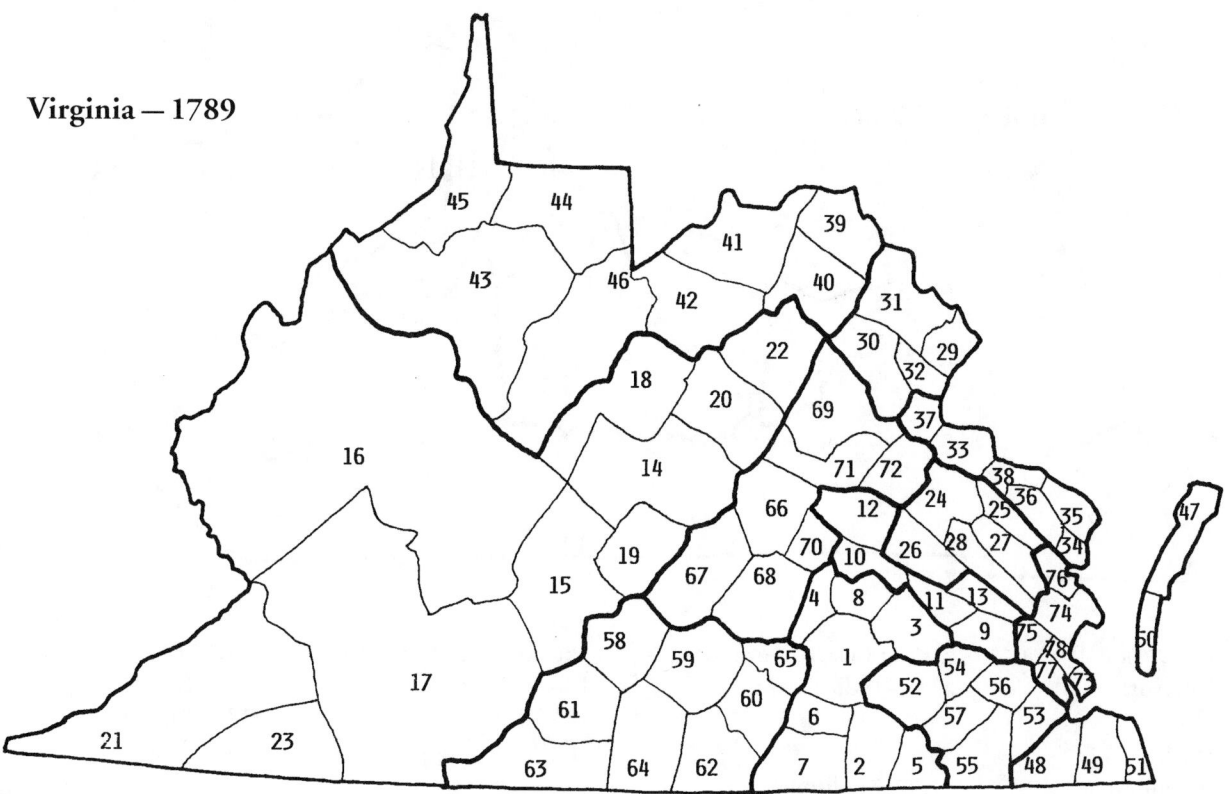

Virginia — 1789

1ST ELECTORAL DISTRICT
1 — Amelia
2 — Brunswick
3 — Chestefield
4 — Cumberland
5 — Greensville
6 — Lunenburg
7 — Mecklenburg
8 — Powhatan

2ND ELECTORAL DISTRICT
9 — Charles City
10 — Goochland
11 — Henrico
12 — Louisa
13 — New Kent

***3RD ELECTORAL DISTRICT**
14 — Augusta
15 — Botetourt
16 — Greenbrier
17 — Montgomery
18 — Pendleton
19 — Rockbridge
20 — Rockingham
21 — Russell
22 — Shenandoah
23 — Washington

4TH ELECTORAL DISTRICT
24 — Caroline
25 — Essex
26 — Hanover
27 — King & Queen
28 — King William

5TH ELECTORAL DISTRICT
29 — Fairfax
30 — Fauquier
31 — Loudoun
32 — Prince William

6TH ELECTORAL DISTRICT
33 — King George
34 — Lancaster
35 — Northumberland
36 — Richmond
37 — Stafford
38 — Westmoreland

7TH ELECTORAL DISTRICT
39 — Berkeley
40 — Frederick
41 — Hampshire
42 — Hardy
43 — Harrison
44 — Monongalia
45 — Ohio
46 — Randolph

8TH ELECTORAL DISTRICT
47 — Accomack
48 — Nansemond
49 — Norfolk
50 — Northampton
51 — Princess Anne

9TH ELECTORAL DISTRICT
52 — Dinwiddie
53 — Isle of Wight
54 — Prince George
55 — Southampton
56 — Surry
57 — Sussex

10TH ELECTORAL DISTRICT
58 — Bedford
59 — Campbell
60 — Charlotte
61 — Franklin
62 — Halifax
63 — Henry
64 — Pittsylvania
65 — Prince Edward

11TH ELECTORAL DISTRICT
66 — Albemarle
67 — Amherst
68 — Buckingham
69 — Culpeper
70 — Fluvanna
71 — Orange
72 — Spottsylvania

12TH ELECTORAL DISTRICT
73 — Elizabeth City
74 — Gloucester
75 — James City
76 — Middlesex
77 — Warwick
78 — York

District extended westward to include the District (present state of) Kentucky.

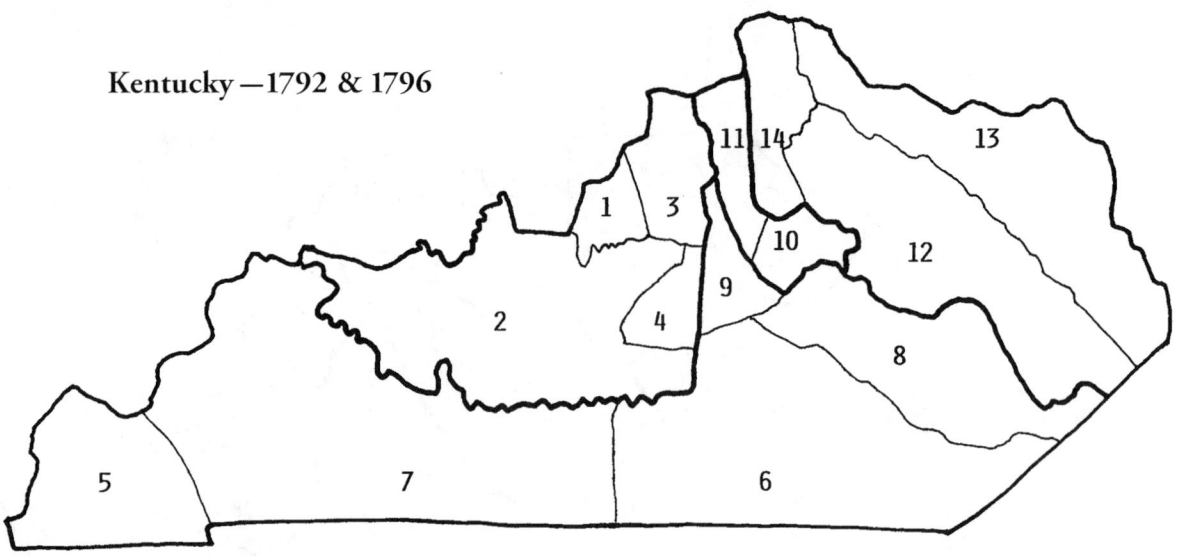

Kentucky — 1792 & 1796

1ST ELECTORAL DISTRICT
1 — Jefferson
2 — Nelson
3 — Shelby
4 — Washington

2ND ELECTORAL DISTRICT
5 — Indian Lands
6 — Lincoln
7 — Logan
8 — Madison
9 — Mercer

3RD ELECTORAL DISTRICT
10 — Fayette
11 — Woodford

4TH ELECTORAL DISTRICT
12 — Bourbon
13 — Mason
14 — Scott

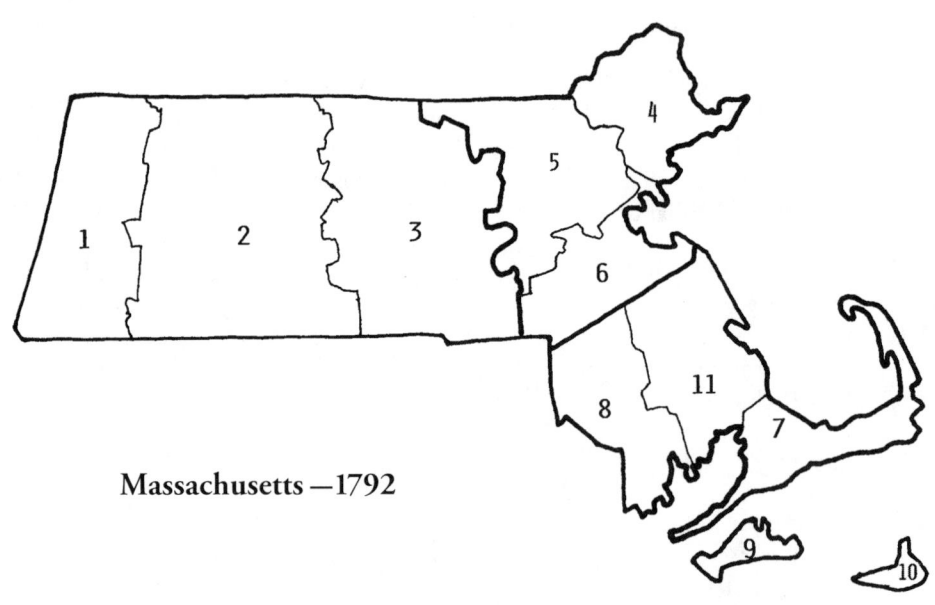

Massachusetts — 1792

ELECTORAL DISTRICT (five elected)
1 — Berkshire
2 — Hampshire
3 — Worcester

ELECTORAL DISTRICT (five elected)
4 — Essex
5 — Middlesex
6 — Suffolk

ELECTORAL DISTRICT (three elected)
7 — Barnstable
8 — Bristol
9 — Dukes
10 — Nantucket
11 — Plymouth

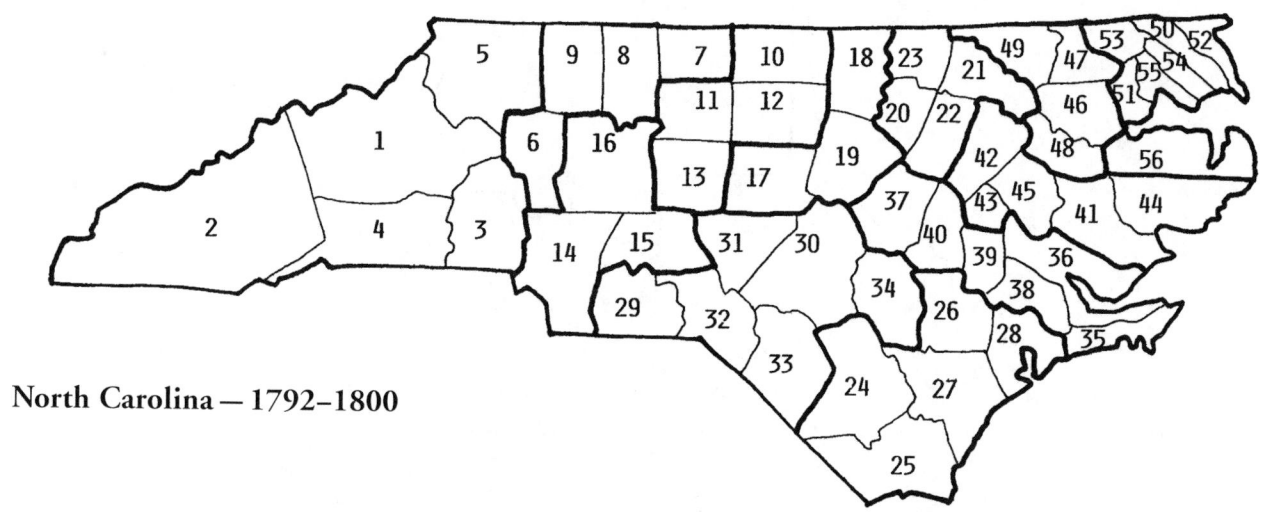

North Carolina — 1792–1800

1ST ELECTORAL DISTRICT
1 — Burke
2 — Indian Lands
3 — Lincoln
4 — Rutherford
5 — Wilkes

2ND ELECTORAL DISATRICT
6 — Iredell
7 — Rockingham
8 — Stokes
9 — Surry

3RD ELECTORAL DISTRICT
10 — Casewell
11 — Guilford
12 — Orange
13 — Randolph

4TH ELECTORAL DISTRICT
14 — Mecklenburg
15 — Montgomery
16 — Rowan

5TH ELECTORAL DISTRICT
17 — Chatham
18 — Granville
19 — Wake

6TH ELECTORAL DISTRICT
20 — Franklin
21 — Halifax
22 — Nash
23 — Warren

7TH ELECTORAL DISTRICT
24 — Bladen
25 — Brunswick
26 — Duplin
27 — New Hanover
28 — Onslow

8TH ELECTORAL DISTRICT
29 — Anson
30 — Cumberland
31 — Moore
32 — Richmond
33 — Robeson
34 — Sampson

9TH ELECTORAL DISTRICT
35 — Carteret
36 — Craven
37 — Johnston
38 — Jones
39 — Lenoir
40 — Wayne

10TH ELECTORAL DISTRICT
41 — Beaufort
42 — Edgecomb
43 — Glasgow
44 — Hyde
45 — Pitt

11TH ELECTORAL DISTRICT
46 — Bertie
47 — Hertford
48 — Martin
49 — Northampton

12TH ELECTORAL DISTRICT
50 — Camden
51 — Chowan
52 — Currituck
53 — Gates
54 — Pasquotank
55 — Perquimans
56 — Tyrrell

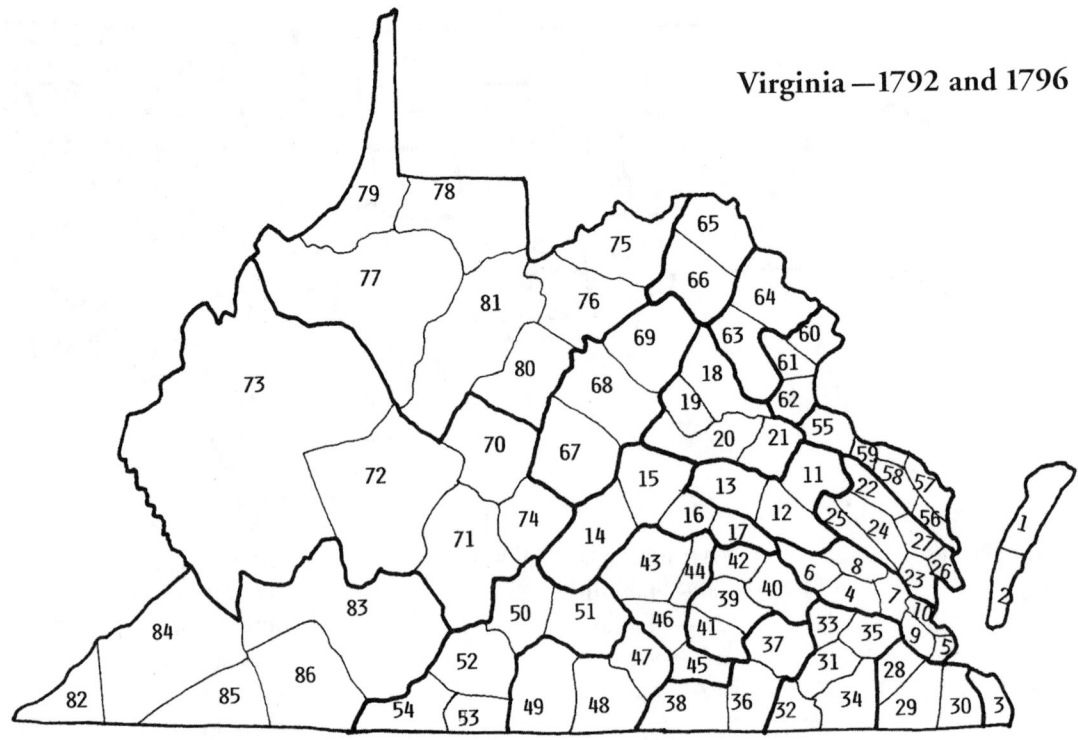

Virginia—1792 and 1796

1ST ELECTORAL DISTRICT
1 — Accomack
2 — Northampton
3 — Princess Anne

2ND ELECTORAL DISTRICT
4 — Charles City
5 — Elizabeth City
6 — Henrico
7 — James City
8 — New Kent
9 — Warwick
10 — York

3RD ELECTORAL DISTRICT
11 — Caroline
12 — Hanover
13 — Louisa

4TH ELECTORAL DISTRICT
14 — Amherst
15 — Albemarle
16 — Fluvanna
17 — Goochland

5TH ELECTORAL DISTRICT
18 — Culpeper
19 — Madison
20 — Orange
21 — Spotsylvania

6TH ELECTORAL DISTRICT
22 — Essex
23 — Gloucester
24 — King & Queen
25 — King William
26 — Mathews
27 — Middlesex

7TH ELECTORAL DISTRICT
28 — Isle of Wight
29 — Nansemond
30 — Norfolk

8TH ELECTORAL DISTRICT
31 — Sussex
32 — Greensville
33 — Prince George
34 — Southampton
35 — Surry

9TH ELECTORAL DISTRICT
36 — Brunswick
37 — Dinwiddie
38 — Mecklenburg

10TH ELECTORAL DISTRICT
39 — Amelia
40 — Chesterfield
41 — Nottoway
42 — Powhatan

11TH ELECTORAL DISTRICT
43 — Buckingham
44 — Cumberland
45 — Lunenburg
46 — Prince Edward

12TH ELECTORAL DISTRICT
47 — Charlotte
48 — Halifax
49 — Pittsylvania

13TH ELECTORAL DISTRICT
50 — Bedford
51 — Campbell
52 — Franklin
53 — Henry
54 — Patrick

14TH ELECTORAL DISTRICT
55 — King George
56 — Lancaster
57 — Northumberland
58 — Richmond
59 — Westmoreland

15TH ELECTORAL DISTRICT
60 — Fairfax
61 — Prince William
62 — Stafford

16TH ELECTORAL DISTRICT
63 — Fauquier
64 — Loudoun

17TH ELECTORAL DISTRICT
65 — Berkeley
66 — Frederick

18TH ELECTORAL DISTRICT
67 — Augusta
68 — Rockingham
69 — Shenadoah

19TH ELECTORAL DISTRICT
70 — Bath
71 — Botetourt
72 — Greenbrier
73 — Kanawha
74 — Rockbridge

20TH ELECTORAL DISTRICT
75 — Hampshire
76 — Hardy
77 — Harrison
78 — Monongalia
79 — Ohio
80 — Pendleton
81 — Randolph

21ST ELECTORAL DISTRICT
82 — Lee
83 — Montgomery
84 — Russell
85 — Washington
86 — Wythe

1ST ELECTORAL DISTRICT
1 — Calvert
2 — Charles
3 — St. Mary's

2ND ELECTORAL DISTRICT
4 — Montgomery
5 — Prince George's

3RD ELECTORAL DISTRICT
6 — Frederick

4TH ELECTORAL DISTRICT
7 — Allegany
8 — Washington

5TH ELECTORAL DISTRICT
9 — Anne Arundel
10 — City of Baltimore

6TH ELECTORAL DISTRICT
11 — Baltimore
12 — Harford

7TH ELECTORAL DISTRICT
13 — Cecil
14 — Kent

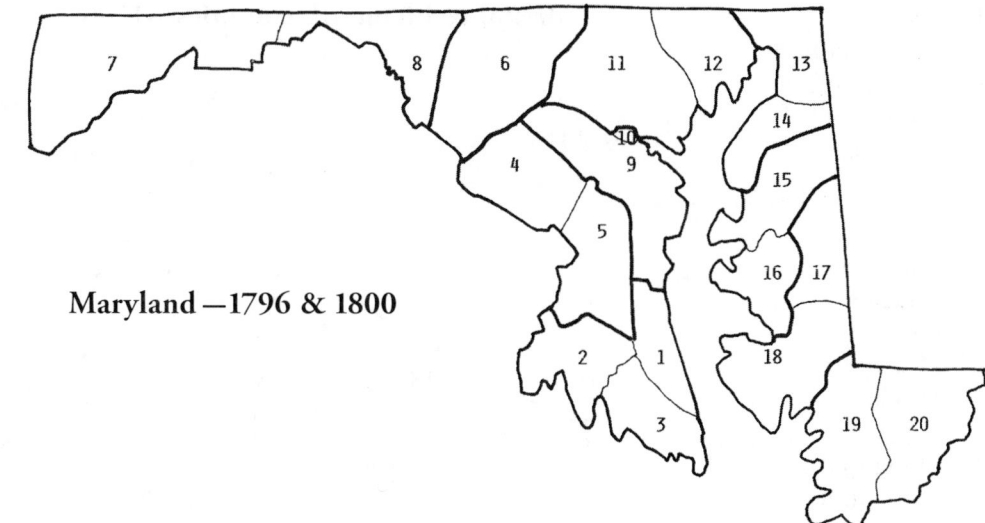

Maryland — 1796 & 1800

8TH ELECTORAL DISTRICT
15 — Queen Anne's
16 — Talbot

9TH ELECTORAL DISTRICT
17 — Caroline
18 — Dorchester

10TH ELECTORAL DISTRICT
19 — Somerset
20 — Worcester

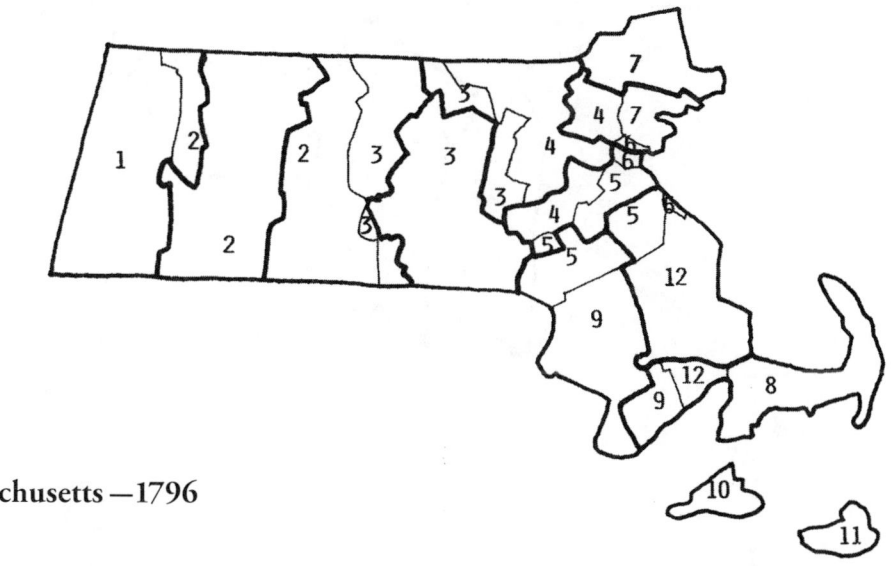

Massachusetts — 1796

1ST WESTERN DISTRICT
1 — Berkshire
2 — Hampshire (part)

2ND WESTERN DISTRICT
2 — Hampshire (part)

3RD WESTERN DISTRICT
2 — Hampshire (part)
3 — Worcester (part)

4TH WESTERN DISTRICT
3 — Worcester (part)

1ST MIDDLE DISTRICT
4 — Middlesex (part)
5 — Norfolk (part)

2ND MIDDLE DISTRICT
3 — Worcester (part)
4 — Middlesex (part)

3RD MIDDLE DISTRICT
4 — Middlesex (part)
6 — Suffolk (part)
7 — Essex (part)

4TH MIDDLE DISTRICT
7 — Essex (part)

1ST SOUTHERN DISTRICT
8 — Barnstable
9 — Bristol (part)
10 — Dukes
11 — Nantucket
12 — Plymouth (part)

2ND SOUTHERN DISTRICT
5 — Norfolk (part)
12 — Plymouth (part)
6 — Suffolk (part)

3RD SOUTHERN DISTRICT
9 — Bristol (part)
5 — Norfolk (part)

1ST SOUTHERN DISTRICT (PART)
(Bristol County)
1 — Bedford
2 — Darthmouth
(Norfolk County)
3 — Rochester
4 — Wareham

2ND SOUTHERN DISTRICT (PART)
(Norfolk County)
5 — Abington
6 — Bridgwater
7 — Carver
8 — Duxbury
9 — Halifax
10— Hanover
11 — Kingston
12 — Marshfield
13 — Middleborough
14 — Pembroke
15 — Plymouth
16 — Plympton
17 — Scituate

3RD SOUTHERN DISTRICT (PART)
(Plymouth County)
18 — Attleboro
19 — Berkley
20 — Dighton
21 — Easton
22 — Freetown
23 — Mansfield
24 — Norton
25 — Raynham
26 — Rehoboth
27 — Somerset
28 — Swansea
29 — Taunton
30— Westport

Bristol & Plymouth Counties — 1796

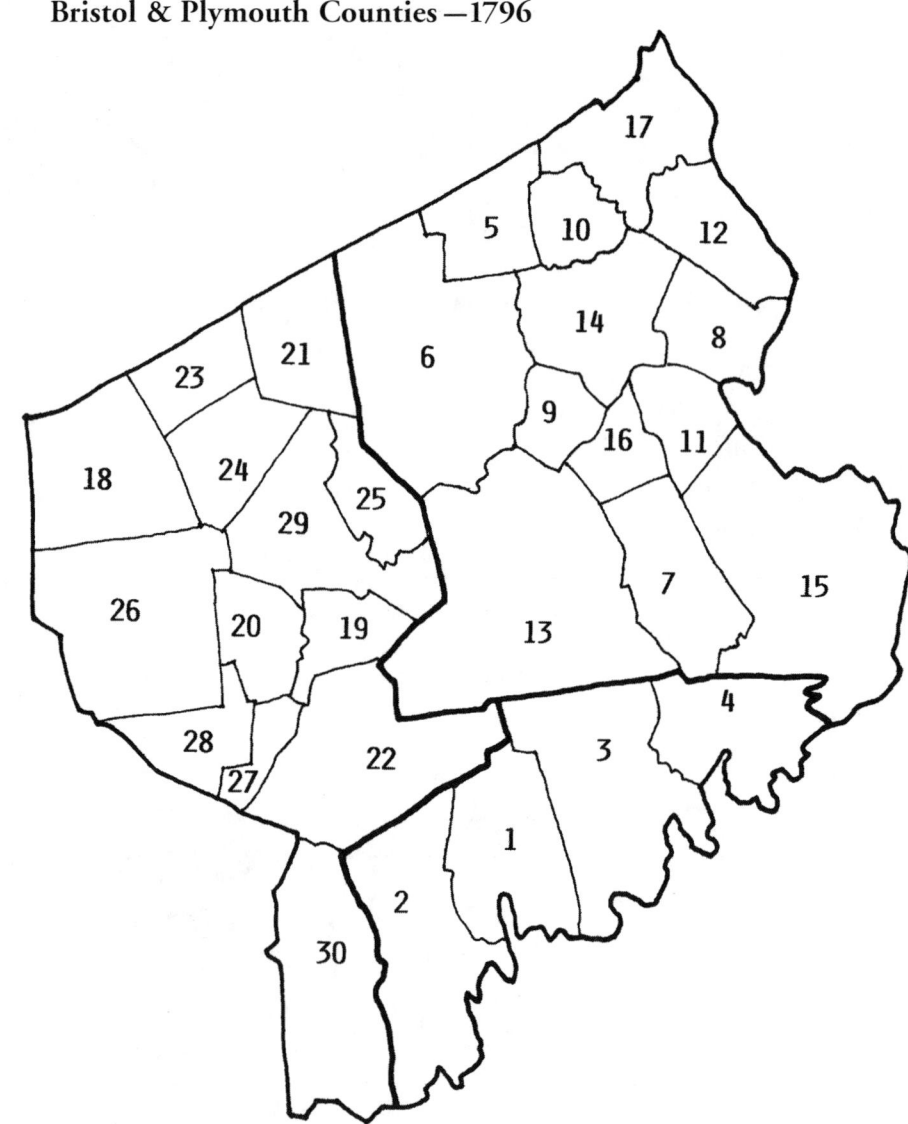

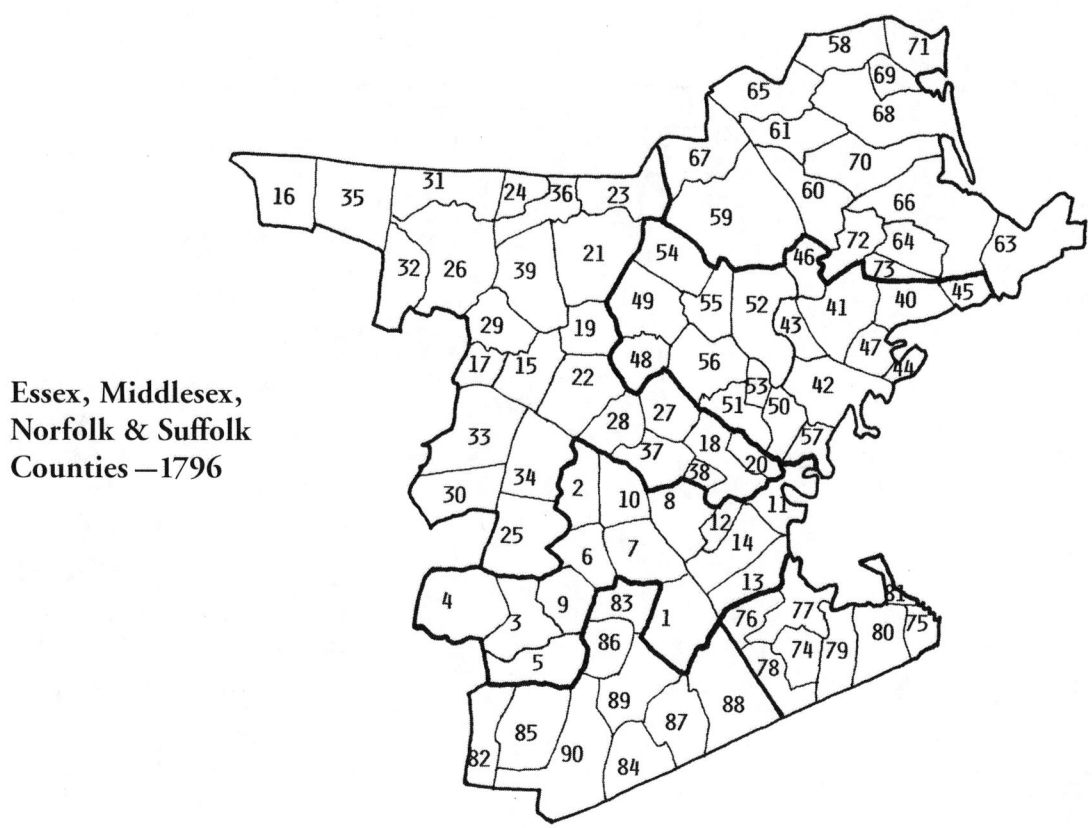

Essex, Middlesex, Norfolk & Suffolk Counties — 1796

1ST MIDDLE DISTRICT
(Middlesex County)
1 — Dedham
2 — East Sudbury
3 — Holliston
4 — Hopkinton
5 — Medway
6 — Natick
7 — Needham
8 — Newton
9 — Sherborn
10 — Weston
(Suffolk County)
11 — Boston
(Norfolk County)
12 — Brookline
13 — Dorchester
14 — Roxbury

2ND MIDDLE DISTRICT (PART)
(Middlesex County)
15 — Acton
16 — Ashby
17 — Boxborough
18 — Cambridge
19 — Carlisle
20 — Charlestown
21 — Chelmsford
22 — Concord
23 — Dracut
24 — Dunstable
25 — Framingham
26 — Groton
27 — Lexington
28 — Lincoln
29 — Littleton
30 — Marlborough
31 — Pepperell
32 — Shirley
33 — Stow
34 — Sudbury
35 — Townsend
36 — Tynsborough
37 — Waltham
38 — Watertown
39 — Westford

3RD MIDDLE DISTRICT
(Essex County)
40 — Beverly
41 — Danvers
42 — Lynn
43 — Lynnfield
44 — Marblehead
45 — Manchester
46 — Middleton
47 — Salem
(Middlesex County)
48 — Bedford
49 — Billerica
50 — Malden
51 — Medford
52 — Reading
53 — Stoneham
54 — Tewksbury
55 — Wilmington
56 — Woburn
(Suffolk County)
57 — Chelsea

4TH MIDDLE DISTRICT
(Essex County)
58 — Amesbury
59 — Andover
60 — Boxford
61 — Bradford
63 — Gloucester
64 — Hamilton
65 — Haverhill
66 — Ipswich
67 — Methuen
68 — Newbury
69 — Newburyport
70 — Rowley
71 — Salisbury
72 — Topsfield
73 — Wenham

2ND SOUTHERN DISTRICT (PART)
(Norfolk County)
74 — Braintree
75 — Cohasset
76 — Milton
77 — Quincy
78 — Randolph
79 — Weymouth
(Plymouth County)
80 — Hingham
(Suffolk County)
81 — Hull

3RD SOUTHERN DISTRICT (PART)
(Norfolk County)
82 — Bellingham
83 — Dover
84 — Foxborough
85 — Franklin
86 — Medfield
87 — Sharon
88 — Stoughton
89 — Walpole
90 — Wrentham

Hampshire County —1796

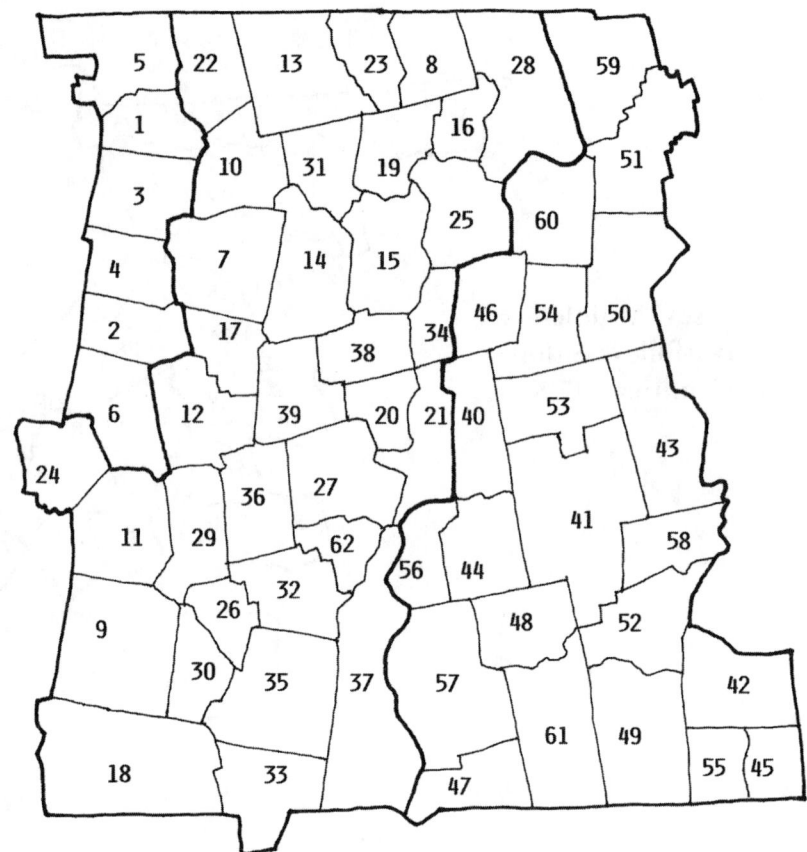

Worcester County — 1796

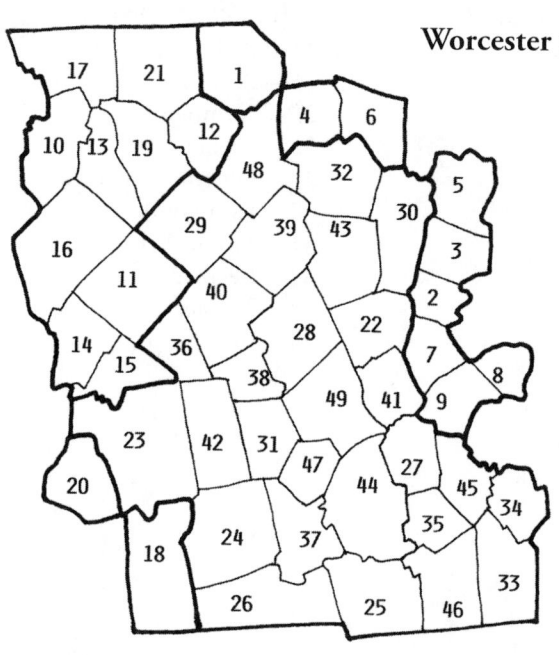

2ND MIDDLE DISTRICT (PART)
1 — Ashburnham
2 — Berlin
3 — Bolton
4 — Fitchburg
5 — Harvard
6 — Lunenburg
7 — Northborough
8 — Southborough
9 — Westborough

3RD WESTERN DISTRICT (PART)
10 — Athol
11 — Barre
12 — Gardner
13 — Gerry
14 — Hardwick
15 — New Braintree
16 — Petersham
17 — Royalston
18 — Sturbridge
19 — Templeton
20 — Western
21 — Winchedon

4TH WESTERN DISTRICT
22 — Boylston
23 — Brookfield
24 — Charlton
25 — Douglas
26 — Dudley
27 — Grafton
28 — Holden
29 — Hubbardton
30 — Lancaster
31 — Leicester
32 — Leominster
33 — Mendon
34 — Milford
35 — Northbridge
36 — Oakham
37 — Oxford
38 — Paxton
39 — Princeton
40 — Rutland
41 — Shrewsbury
42 — Spencer
43 — Sterling
44 — Sutton
45 — Upton
46 — Uxbridge
47 — Ward
48 — Westminster
49 — Worcester

**District of Maine —
1796**

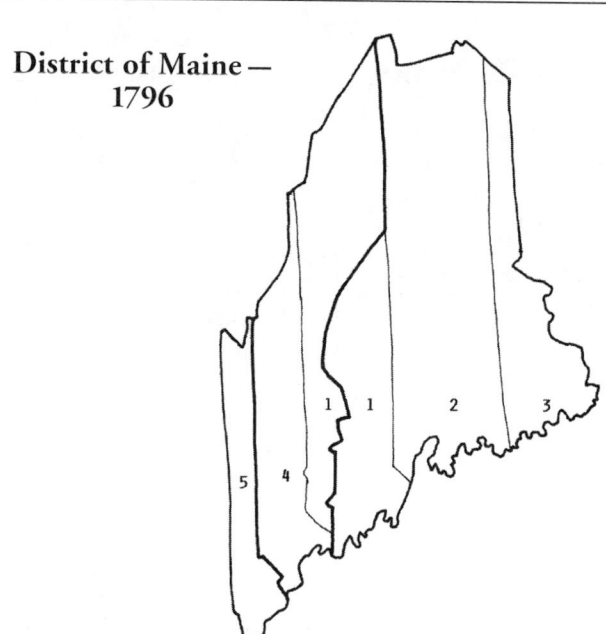

1ST EASTERN DISTRICT
1 — Lincoln (part)
2 — Hancock
3 — Washington

2ND EASTERN DISTRICT
1 — Lincoln (part)
4 — Cumberland (part)

3RD EASTERN DISTRICT
4 — Cumberland (part)
5 — York

Lincoln County—1796

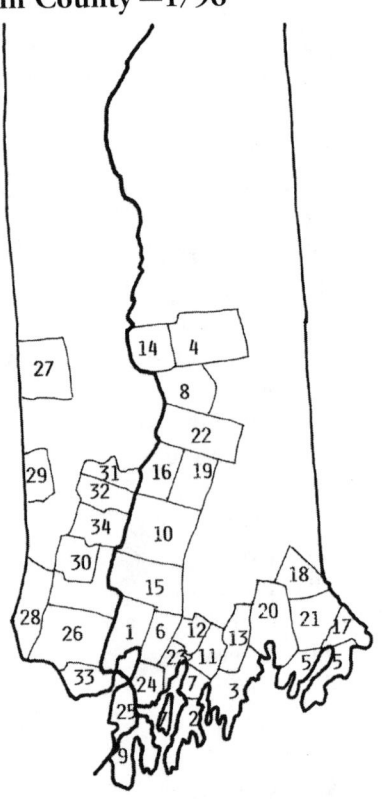

1ST EASTERN DISTRICT
1 — Bowdoiham
2 — Boothbay
3 — Bristol
4 — Canaan
5 — Cushing
6 — Dresden
7 — Edgecomb
8 — Fairfield
9 — Georgetown
10 — Hallowell
11 — Newcastle
12 — New Milford
13 — Nobleboro
14 — Norridgewick
15 — Pittstown
16 — Sidney
17 — Thomaston
18 — Union
19 — Vasalboro
20 — Waldboro
21 — Warren
22 — Winslow
23 — Wiscasset
24 — Woolwich

2ND EASTERN DISTRICT
25 — Bath
26 — Bowdoin
27 — Farmington
28 — Greene
29 — Livermore (part)
30 — Monmouth
31 — Mount Vernon
32 — Readfield
33 — Topsham
34 — Winthrop

1ST ELECTORAL DISTRICT
1 — Bullitt
2 — Breckinridge
3 — Cumberland
4 — Green
5 — Hardin
6 — Henry
7 — Jefferson
8 — Nelson
9 — Shelby
10 — Washington

2ND ELECTORAL DISTRICT
11 — Barren
12 — Christian
13 — Garrard
14 — Henderson
15 — Indian Lands
16 — Knox
17 — Lincoln
18 — Livingston
19 — Logan
20 — Madison
21 — Mercer
22 — Muhlenberg
23 — Ohio
24 — Pulaski
25 — Warren

Kentucky—1800

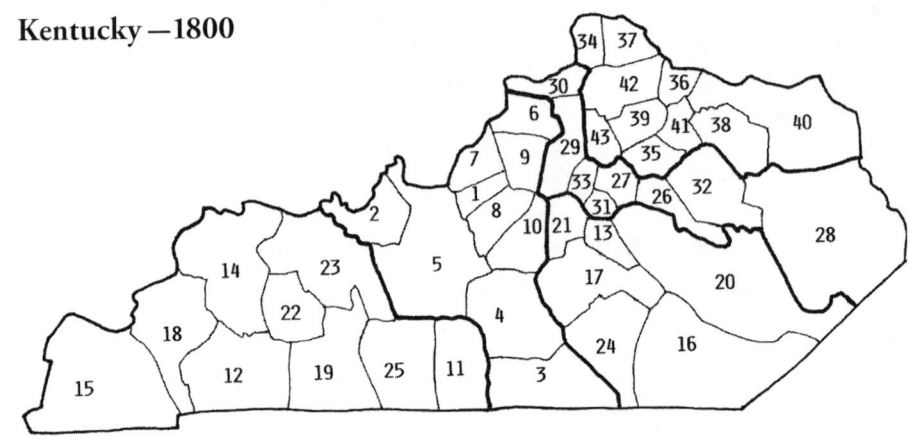

3RD ELECTORAL DISTRICT
26 — Clark
27 — Fayette
28 — Floyd
29 — Franklin
30 — Gallatin
31 — Jessamine
32 — Montgomery
33 — Woodford

4TH ELECTORAL DISTRICT
34 — Boone
35 — Bourbon
36 — Bracken
37 — Campbell
38 — Fleming
39 — Harrison
40 — Mason
41 — Nicholas
42 — Pendleton
43 — Scott

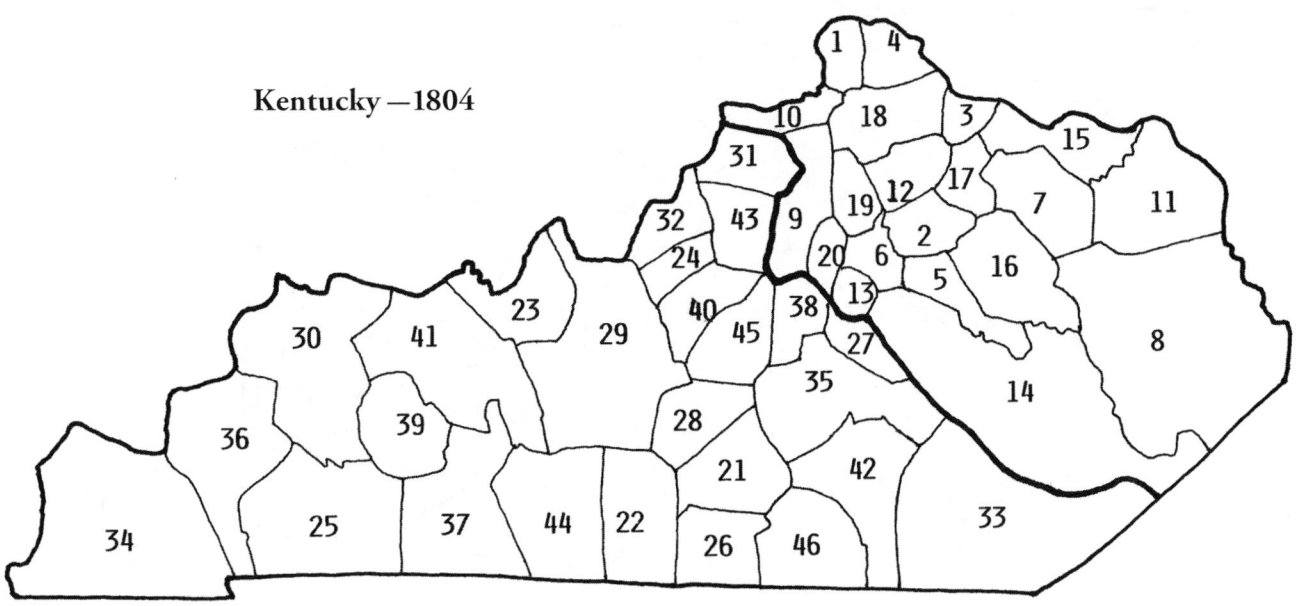

Kentucky —1804

NORTHERN ELECTORAL DISTRICT (FOUR ELECTED)

1 — Boone
2 — Bourbon
3 — Bracken
4 — Campbell
5 — Clark
6 — Fayette
7 — Fleming
8 — Floyd
9 — Franklin
10 — Gallatin
11 — Greenup
12 — Harrison
13 — Jessamine
14 — Madison
15 — Mason
16 — Montgomery
17 — Nicholas
18 — Pendleton
19 — Scott
20 — Woodford

SOUTHERN ELECTORAL DISTRICT (FOUR ELECTED)

21 — Adair
22 — Barren
23 — Breckinridge
24 — Bullitt
25 — Christian
26 — Cumberland
27 — Garrard
28 — Green
29 — Hardin
30 — Henderson
31 — Henry
32 — Jefferson
33 — Knox
34 — Indian Lands
35 — Lincoln
36 — Livingston
37 — Logan
38 — Mercer
39 — Muhlenberg
40 — Nelson
41 — Ohio
42 — Pulaski
43 — Shelby
44 — Warren
45 — Washington
46 — Wayne

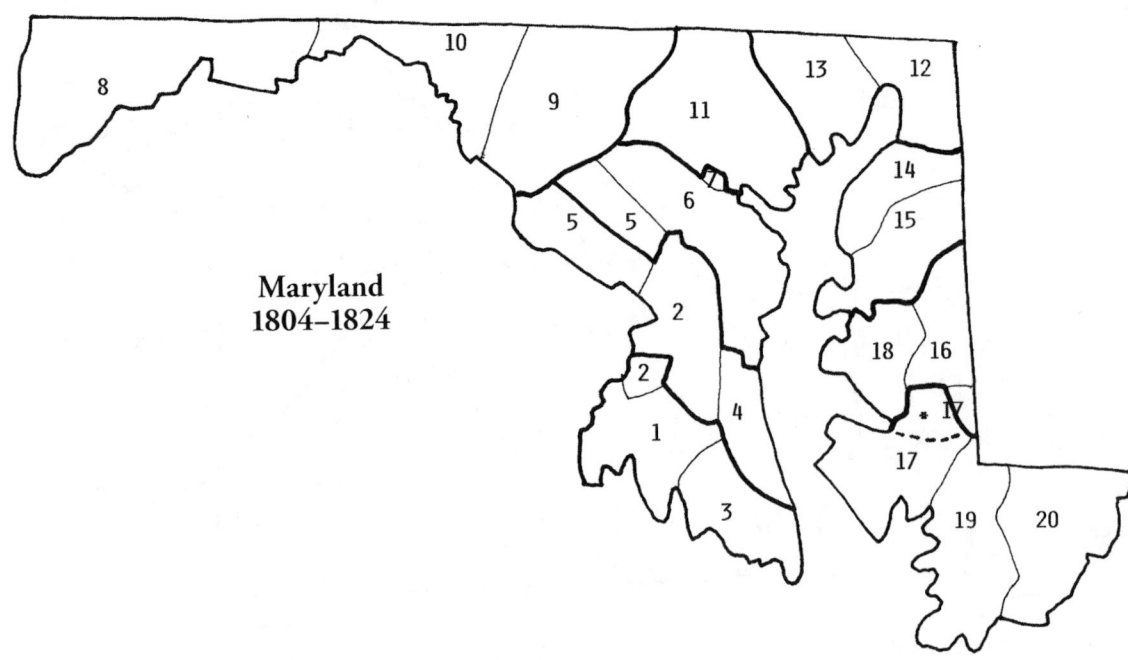

**Maryland
1804–1824**

1ST ELECTORAL DISTRICT
1 — Charles
2 — Prince George's (part)
3 — St. Mary's

2ND ELECTORAL DISTRICT
4 — Calvert
5 — Montgomery (part)
2 — Prince George's (part)

3RD ELECTORAL DISTRICT (TWO
  ELECTED)
6 — Anne Arundel
7 — city of Baltimore
5 — Montgomery (part)

4TH ELECTORAL DISTRICT (TWO
  ELECTED)
8 — Allegany
9 — Frederick
10 — Washington

5TH ELECTORAL DISTRICT
11 — Baltimore

6TH ELECTORAL DISTRICT
12 — Cecil
13 — Harford

7TH ELECTORAL DISTRICT
14 — Kent
15 — Queen Anne's

8TH ELECTORAL DISTRICT
16 — Caroline
17 — Dorchester (part)
18 — Talbot

9TH ELECTORAL DISTRICT
17 — Dorchester (part)
19 — Somerset
20 — Worcester

*See Dorchester County map for
explanation of the broken line.*

**Dorchester County
1804–1828**

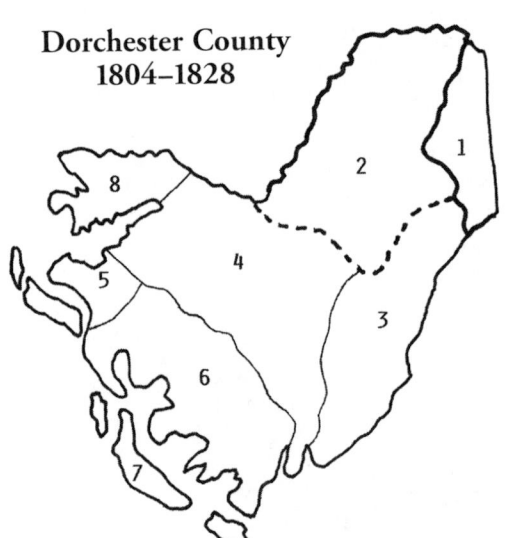

8TH ELECTORAL DISTRICT (PART)
1st Election District, 1804–1828
2nd Election District, elections of 1820–1828

9TH ELECTORAL DISTRICT (PART)
2nd Election District through election of 1816
3rd–8th Election Districts, 1804–1828

*The heavy broken line indicates boundary for elections
1820–1828.*

The numbers on this map refer to election districts.

Montgomery & Prince George's Counties —1804–1824

1ST ELECTORAL DISTRICT (PART)
(Prince George's County)
  5th Election District

2ND ELECTORAL DISTRICT
(Montgomery County)
  3rd & 4th Election Districts
(Prince George's County)
  1st–4th and 6th Election Districts

3RD ELECTORAL DISTRICT (PART)
(Montgomery County)
  1st and 2nd Election Districts

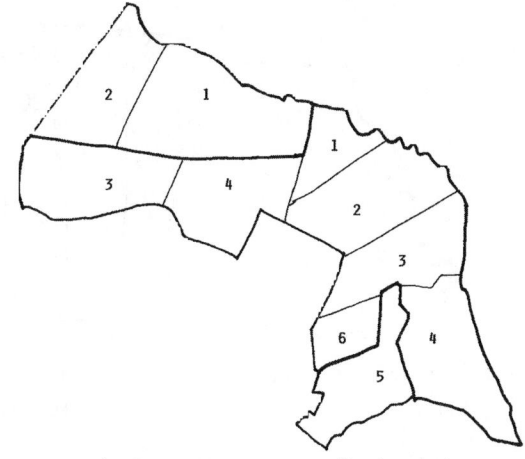

NOTE: The law dividing Montgomery County into election districts and the apportionment law creating the above districts both speak of five districts. However the census of 1820 (the first to give data by such districts) and an early map of the county indicate only four districts as indicated above.

Prince George's County was originally divided into five election districts with only the Fifth District placed in the 1st Electoral District. The Sixth Election District was created in 1816 from the 3rd and 5th Districts and placed in the 2nd Electoral District. The map reflects this change and differs slightly from the original.

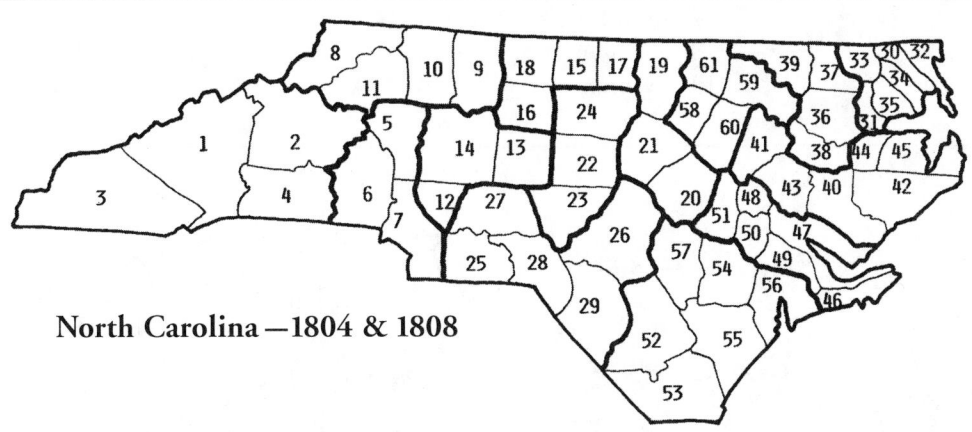

North Carolina —1804 & 1808

1ST ELECTORAL DISTRICT
1 — Buncombe
2 — Burke
3 — Indian Lands
4 — Rutherford

2ND ELECTORAL DISTRICT
5 — Iredell
6 — Lincoln
7 — Mecklenberg

3RD ELECTORAL DISTRICT
8 — Ashe
9 — Stokes
10 — Surry
11 — Wilkes

4TH ELECTORAL DISTRICT
12 — Cabarrus
13 — Randolph
14 — Rowan

5TH ELECTORAL DISTRICT
15 — Caswell
16 — Guilford
17 — Person
18 — Rockingham

6TH ELECTORAL DISTRICT
19 — Granville
20 — Johnston
21 — Wake

7TH ELECTORAL DISTRICT
22 — Chatham
23 — Moore
24 — Orange

8TH ELECTORAL DISTRICT
25 — Anson
26 — Cumberland
27 — Montgomery
28 — Richmond
29 — Robeson

9TH ELECTORAL DISTRICT
30 — Camden
31 — Chowan
32 — Currituck
33 — Gates
34 — Pasquotank
35 — Perquimans

10TH ELECTORAL DISTRICT
36 — Bertie
37 — Hertford
38 — Martin
39 — Northampton

11TH ELECTORAL DISTRICT
40 — Beaufort
41 — Edgecombe
42 — Hyde
43 — Pitt
44 — Washington
45 — Tyrrell

12TH ELECTORAL DISTRICT
46 — Carteret
47 — Craven
48 — Greene
49 — Jones
50 — Lenoir
51 — Wayne

13TH ELECTORAL DISTRICT
52 — Bladen
53 — Brunswick
54 — Duplin
55 — New Hanover
56 — Onslow
57 — Sampson

14TH ELECTORAL DISTRICT
58 — Franklin
59 — Halifax
60 — Nash
61 — Warren

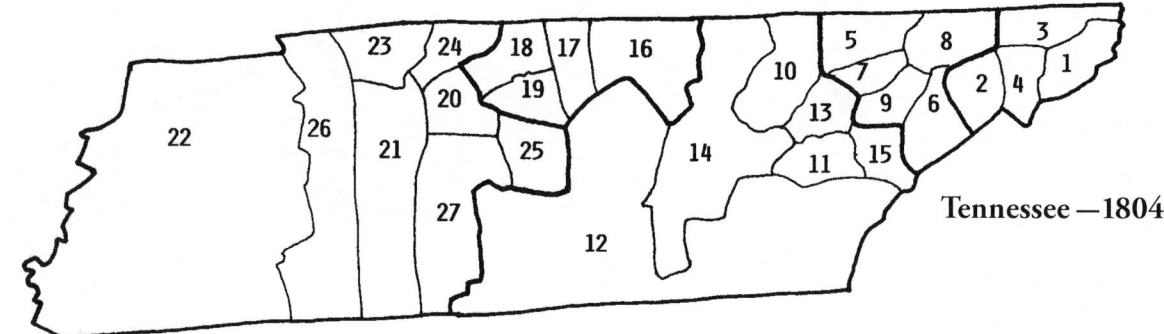

Tennessee — 1804

1st Electoral District
1 — Carter
2 — Greene
3 — Sullivan
4 — Washington

2nd Electoral District
5 — Claiborne
6 — Cocke
7 — Grainger
8 — Hawkins
9 — Jefferson

3rd Electoral District
10 — Anderson
11 — Blount
12 — Indian Lands
13 — Knox
14 — Roane
15 — Sevier

4th Electoral District
16 — Jackson
17 — Smith
18 — Sumner
19 — Wilson

5th Electoral District
20 — Davidson
21 — Dickson
22 — Indian Lands
23 — Montgomery
24 — Robertson
25 — Rutherford
26 — Stewart
27 — Williamson

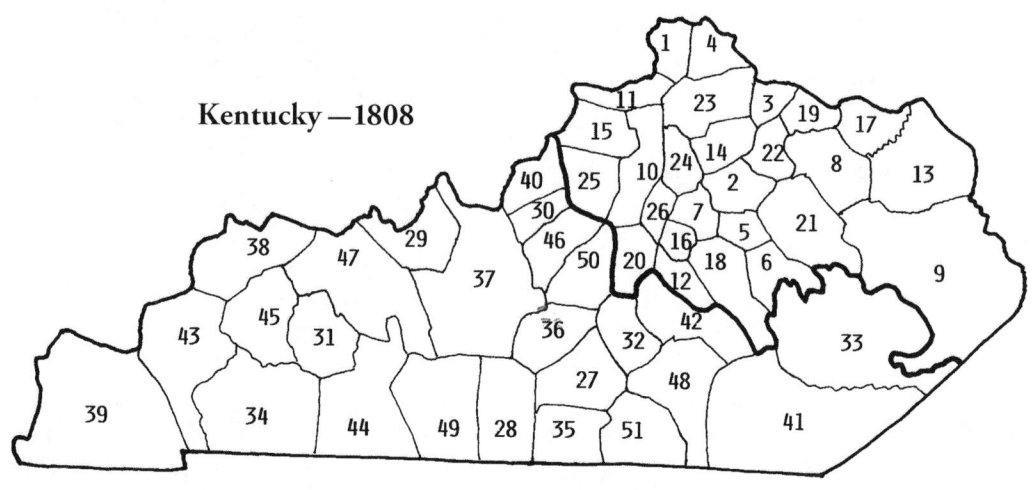

Kentucky — 1808

Northern Electoral District
1 — Boone
2 — Bourbon
3 — Bracken
4 — Campbell
5 — Clark
6 — Estill
7 — Fayette
8 — Fleming
9 — Floyd
10 — Franklin
11 — Gallatin
12 — Garrard
13 — Greenup
14 — Harrison
15 — Henry
16 — Jessamine
17 — Lewis
18 — Madison
19 — Mason
20 — Mercer
21 — Montgomery
22 — Nicholas
23 — Pendleton
24 — Scott
25 — Shelby
26 — Woodford

Southern Electoral District
27 — Adair
28 — Barren
29 — Breckinridge
30 — Bullitt
31 — Butler
32 — Casey
33 — Clay
34 — Christian
35 — Cumberland
36 — Green
37 — Hardin
38 — Henderson
39 — Indian Lands
40 — Jefferson
41 — Knox
42 — Lincoln
43 — Livingston
44 — Logan
45 — Muhlenberg
46 — Nelson
47 — Ohio
48 — Pulaski
49 — Warren
50 — Washington
51 — Wayne

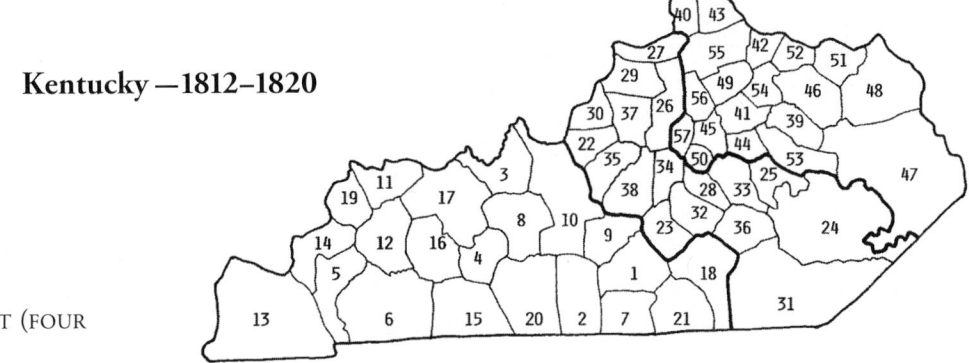

1ST ELECTORAL DISTRICT
1 — Carter
2 — Greene
3 — Hawkins
4 — Sullivan
5 — Washington

2ND ELECTORAL DISTRICT
6 — Claiborne
7 — Cocke
8 — Grainger
9 — Jefferson
10 — Sevier

3RD ELECTORAL DISTRICT
11 — Anderson
12 — Bledsoe
13 — Blount
14 — Indian Lands
15 — Knox
16 — Rhea
17 — Roane

4TH ELECTORAL DISTRICT
18 — Franklin
19 — Jackson
20 — Overton
21 — Smith
22 — Sumner
23 — Warren
24 — White
25 — Wilson

5TH ELECTORAL DISTRICT
26 — Bedford
27 — Davidson
28 — Dickson
29 — Hickman
30 — Indian Lands
31 — Maury
32 — Montgomery
33 — Robertson
34 — Rutherford
35 — Stewart
36 — Williamson

Tennessee — 1808

Kentucky — 1812–1820

1ST ELECTORAL DISTRICT (FOUR ELECTED)
1 — Adair
2 — Barren
3 — Breckinridge
4 — Butler
5 — Caldwell
6 — Christian
7 — Cumberland
8 — Grayson
9 — Green
10 — Hardin
11 — Henderson
12 — Hopkins
13 — Indian Lands
14 — Livingston
15 — Logan
16 — Muhlenberg
17 — Ohio
18 — Pulaski
19 — Union
20 — Warren
21 — Wayne

2ND ELECTORAL DISTRICT (FOUR ELECTED)
22 — Bullitt
23 — Casey
24 — Clay
25 — Estill
26 — Franklin
27 — Gallatin
28 — Garrard
29 — Henry
30 — Jefferson
31 — Knox
32 — Lincoln
33 — Madison
34 — Mercer
35 — Nelson
36 — Rockcastle
37 — Shelby
38 — Washington

3RD ELECTORAL DISTRICT (FOUR ELECTED)
39 — Bath
40 — Boone
41 — Bourbon
42 — Bracken
43 — Campbell
44 — Clark
45 — Fayette
46 — Fleming
47 — Floyd
48 — Greenup
49 — Harrison
50 — Jessamine
51 — Lewis
52 — Mason
53 — Montgomery
54 — Nicholas
55 — Pendleton
56 — Scott
57 — Woodford

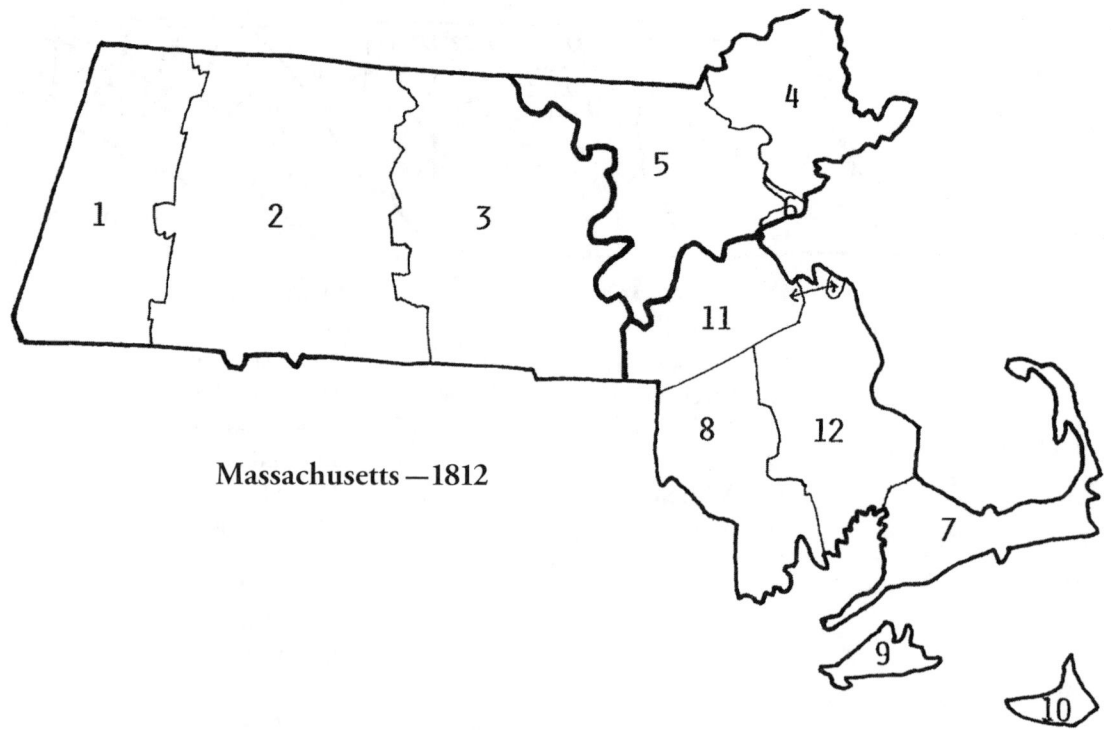

Massachusetts—1812

ELECTORAL DISTRICT (SIX ELECTED)
1 — Berkshire
2 — Hampshire
3 — Worcester

ELECTORAL DISTRICT (FIVE ELECTED)
4 — Essex
5 — Middlesex
6 — Suffolk

ELECTORAL DISTRICT (FOUR ELECTED)
 7 — Barnstable
 8 — Bristol
 9 — Dukes
10 — Nantucket
11 — Norfolk
12 — Plymouth

District of Maine—1812

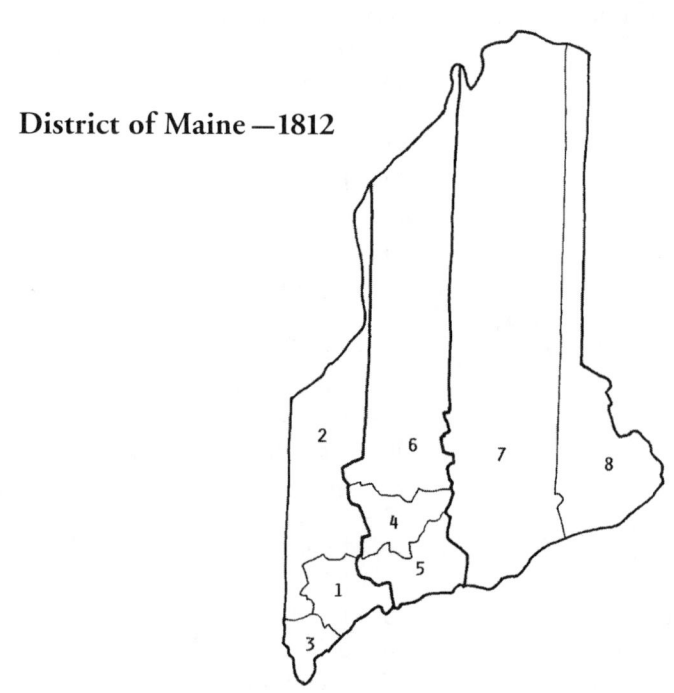

ELECTORAL DISTRICT (THREE ELECTED)
1 — Cumberland
2 — Oxford
3 — York

ELECTORAL DISTRICT (THREE ELECTED)
4 — Kennebec
5 — Lincoln
6 — Somerset

ELECTORAL DISTRICT (ONE ELECTED)
7 — Hancock
8 — Washington

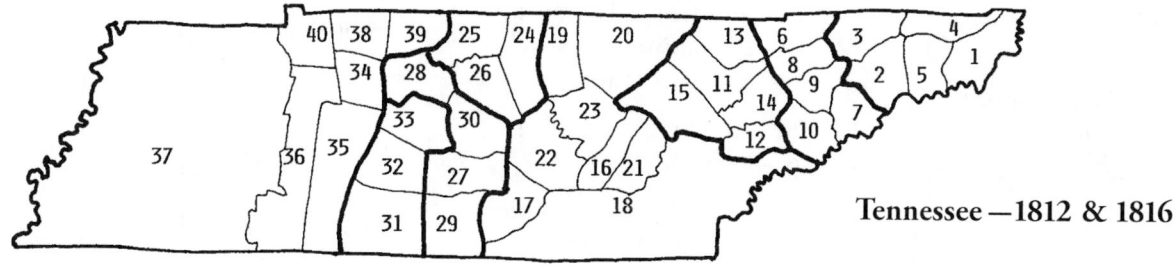

Tennessee — 1812 & 1816

1ST ELECTORAL DISTRICT
1 — Carter
2 — Greene
3 — Hawkins
4 — Sullivan
5 — Washington

2ND ELECTORAL DISTRICT
6 — Claiborne
7 — Cocke
8 — Grainger
9 — Jefferson
10 — Sevier

3RD ELECTORAL DISTRICT
11 — Anderson
12 — Blount
13 — Campbell
14 — Knox
15 — Roane

4TH ELECTORAL DISTRICT
16 — Bledsoe
17 — Franklin
18 — Indian Lands
19 — Jackson
20 — Overton
21 — Rhea
22 — Warren
23 — White

5TH ELECTORAL DISTRICT
24 — Smith
25 — Sumner
26 — Wilson

6TH ELECTORAL DISTRICT
27 — Bedford
28 — Davidson
29 — Lincoln
30 — Rutherford

7TH ELECTORAL DISTRICT
31 — Giles
32 — Maury
33 — Williamson

8TH ELECTORAL DISTRICT
34 — Dickson
35 — Hickman
36 — Humphreys
37 — Indian Lands
38 — Montgomery
39 — Robertson
40 — Stewart

Illinois — 1820

1ST ELECTORAL DISTRICT
1 — Bond
2 — Madison
3 — Monroe
4 — Saint Clair

2ND ELECTORAL DISTRICT
5 — Alexander
6 — Franklin
7 — Jackson
8 — Johnson
9 — Pope
10 — Randolph
11 — Union
12 — Washington

3RD ELECTORAL DISTRICT
13 — Clark
14 — Crawford
15 — Edwards
16 — Gallatin
17 — Jefferson
18 — Wayne
19 — White

1ST ELECTORAL DISTRICT
1 — York (part)

2ND ELECTORAL DISTRICT
2 — Cumberland (part)

3RD ELECTORAL DISTRICT
4 — Hancock (part)
3 — Lincoln (part)

4TH ELECTORAL DISTRICT
4 — Hancock (part)
5 — Washington

5TH ELECTORAL DISTRICT
3 — Lincon (part)
6 — Kennebec (Part)

6TH ELECTORAL DISTRICT
6 — Kennebec (part)
7 — Somerset

7TH ELECTORAL DISTRICT
8 — Oxford
2 — Cumberland (part)
1 — York (part)

Maine —1820

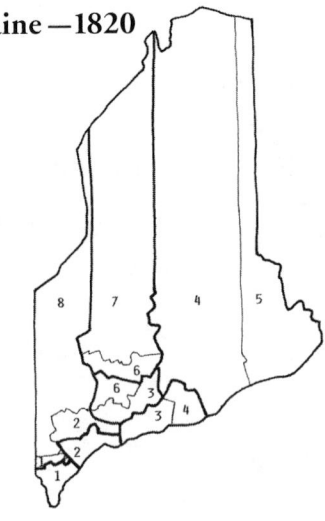

Cumberland County —1820

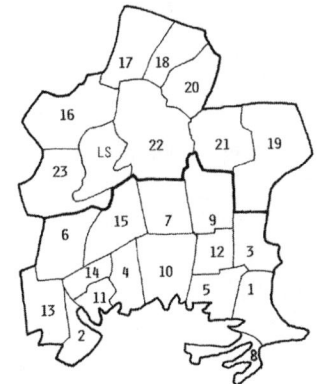

2ND ELECTORAL DISTRICT
1 — Brunswick
2 — Cape Elizabeth
3 — Durham
4 — Falmouth
5 — Freeport
6 — Gorham
7 — Gray
8 — Harpswell
9 — New Gloucester
10 — North Yarmouth
11 — Portland
12 — Pownal
13 — Scarborough
14 — Westbrook
15 — Windham

7TH ELECTORAL DISTRICT (PART)
16 — Baldwin
17 — Bridgton
18 — Harrison
19 — Minot
20 — Otisfield
21 — Poland
22 — Raymond
23 — Standish
LS — Lake Sebago

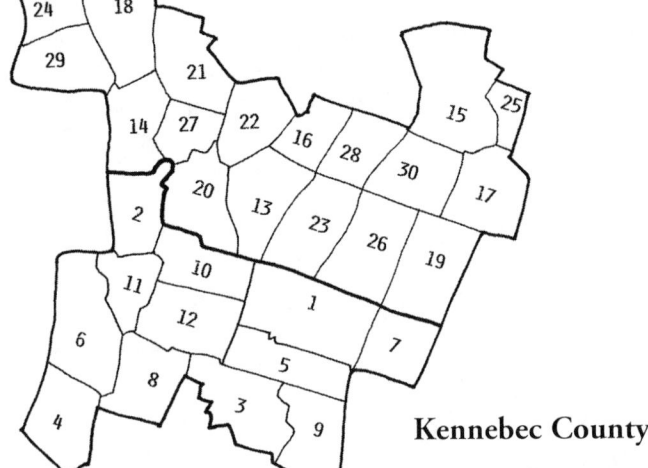

Kennebec County —1820

5TH ELECTORAL DISTRICT (PART)
1 — Augusta
2 — Fayette
3 — Gardiner
4 — Greene
5 — Hallowell
6 — Leeds
7 — Malta
8 — Monmouth
9 — Pittstown
10 — Readfield
11 — Wayne
12 — Winthrop

6TH ELECTORAL DISTRICT (PART)
13 — Belgrade
14 — Chesterville
15 — Clinton
16 — Dearborn
17 — Fairfax
18 — Farmington
19 — Harlem
20 — Mount Vernon
21 — New Sharon
22 — Rome
23 — Sidney
24 — Temple
25 — Unity Plantation
26 — Vasalborough
27 — Vienna
28 — Waterville
29 — Wilton
30 — Winslow

Lincoln County and part of Hancock County —1820

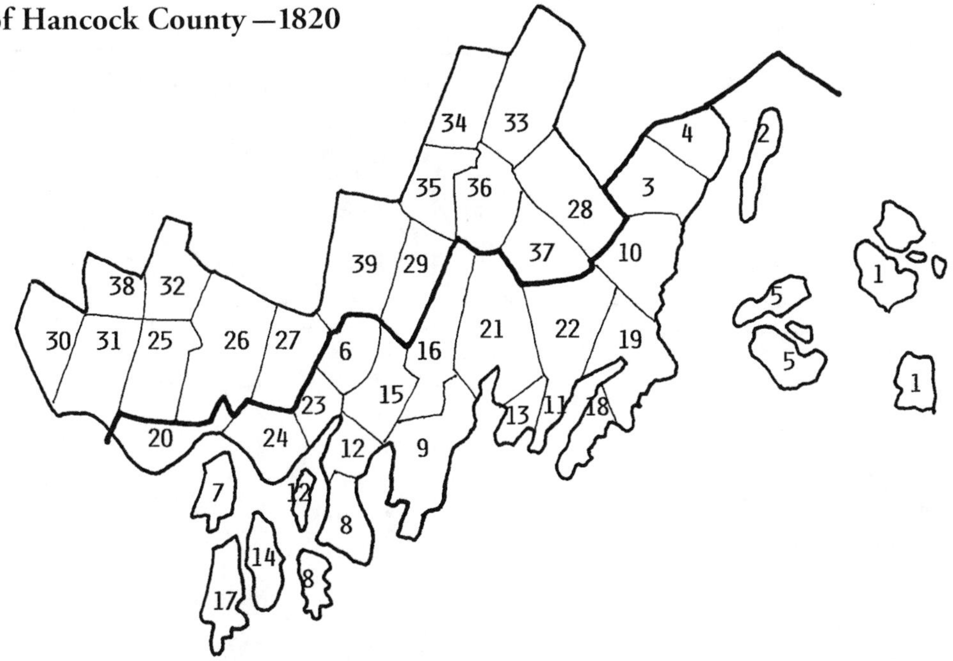

3RD ELECTORAL DISTRICT
(Hancock County part)

1 — Deer Isle
2 — Isleboro
3 — Lincolnville
4 — Northport
5 — Vinalhaven

(Lincoln County part)

6 — Alna
7 — Bath
8 — Boothbay
9 — Bristol
10 — Camden
11 — Cushing
12 — Edgecomb
13 — Friendship
14 — Georgetown
15 — Newcastle
16 — Nobleboro
17 — Philippsburg
18 — St. George
19 — Thomaston
20 — Topsham
21 — Waldboro
22 — Warren
23 — Wiscasset
24 — Woolwich

5TH ELECTORAL DISTRICT (PART)
(Lincoln County part)

25 — Bowdoin
26 — Bowdoinham
27 — Dresden
28 — Hope
29 — Jefferson
30 — Lewiston
31 — Lisbon

32 — Litchfield
33 — Montville
34 — Palermo
35 — Patricktown Plantation
36 — Putnam
37 — Union
38 — Wales
39 — Whitefield

York County —1820

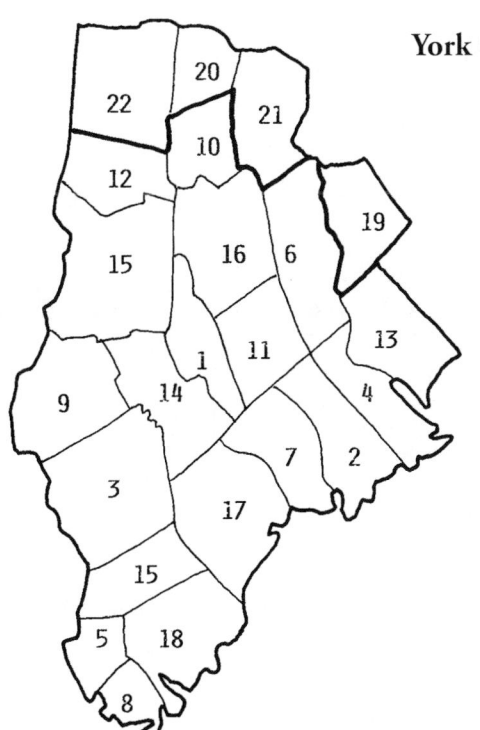

1ST ELECTORAL DISTRICT

1 — Alfred
2 — Arundel
3 — Berwick
4 — Biddeford
5 — Eliot
6 — Hollis
7 — Kennebunk
8 — Kittery
9 — Lebanon
10 — Limerick
11 — Lynn
12 — Newfield
13 — Saco
14 — Sanford
15 — Shapleigh
16 — Waterboro
17 — Wells
18 — York

7TH ELECTORAL DISTRICT
(PART)

19 — Buxton
20 — Cornish
21 — Limington
22 — Parsonsfield

Tennessee — 1820

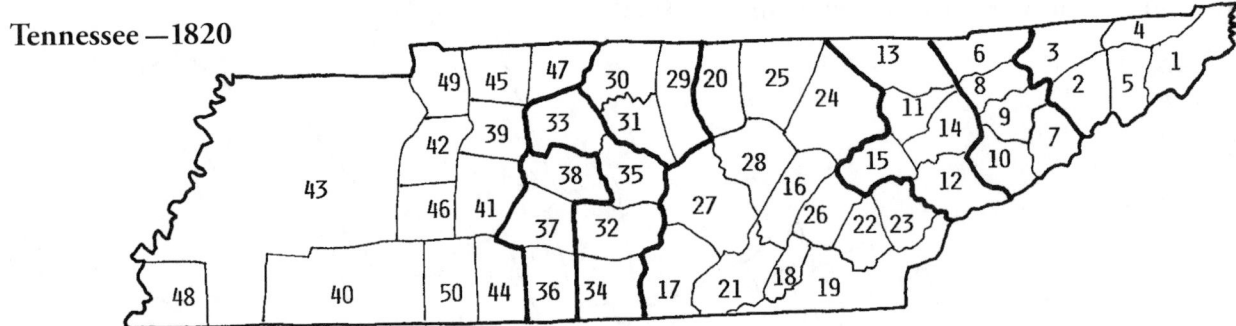

1ST ELECTORAL DISTRICT
1 — Carter
2 — Greene
3 — Hawkins
4 — Sullivan
5 — Washington

2ND ELECTORAL DISTRICT
6 — Claiborne
7 — Cocke
8 — Grainger
9 — Jefferson
10 — Sevier

3RD ELECTORAL DISTRICT
11 — Anderson
12 — Blount
13 — Campbell
14 — Knox
15 — Roane

4TH ELECTORAL DISTRICT
16 — Bledsoe
17 — Franklin
18 — Hamilton
19 — Indian Lands
20 — Jackson
21 — Marion
22 — McMinn
23 — Monroe
24 — Morgan
25 — Overton
26 — Rhea
27 — Warren
28 — White

5TH ELECTORAL DISTRICT
29 — Smith
30 — Sumner
31 — Wilson

6TH ELECTORAL DISTRICT
32 — Bedford
33 — Davidson
34 — Lincoln
35 — Rutherford

7TH ELECTORAL DISTRICT
36 — Giles
37 — Maury
38 — Williamson

8TH ELECTORAL DISTRICT
39 — Dickinson
40 — Hardin
41 — Hickman
42 — Humphreys
43 — Indian Lands
44 — Lawrence
45 — Montgomery
46 — Perry
47 — Robertson
48 — Shelby
49 — Stewart
50 — Wayne

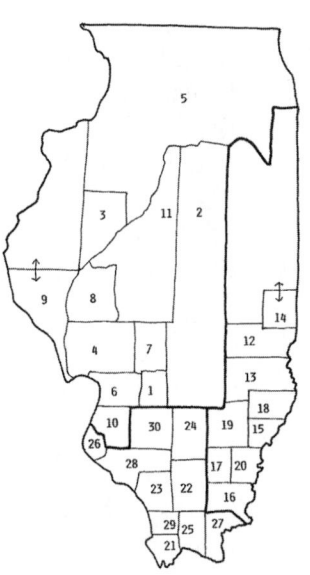

Illinois — 1824

1ST ELECTORAL DISTRICT
1 — Bond
2 — Fayette
3 — Fulton
4 — Greene
5 — Indian Lands
6 — Madison
7 — Montgomery
8 — Morgan
9 — Pike
10 — St. Clair
11 — Sangamon

2ND ELECTORAL DISTRICT
12 — Clark
13 — Crawford
14 — Edgar
15 — Edwards
16 — Gallatin
17 — Hamilton
18 — Lawrence
19 — Wayne
20 — White

3RD ELECTORAL DISTRICT
21 — Alexander
22 — Franklin
23 — Jackson
24 — Jefferson
25 — Johnson
26 — Monroe
27 — Pope
28 — Randolph
29 — Union
30 — Washington

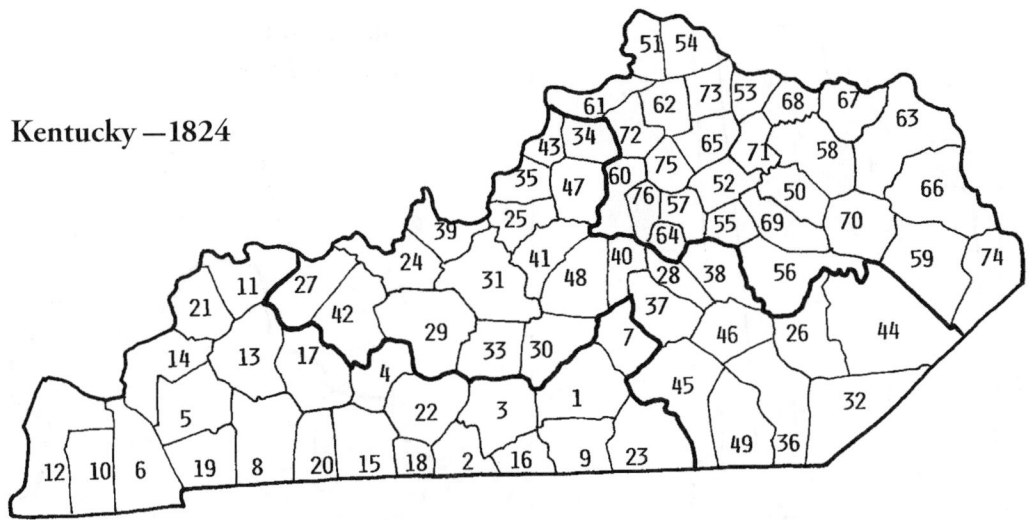

Kentucky —1824

1ST ELECTORAL DISTRICT
(FOUR ELECTED)
1 — Adair
2 — Allen
3 — Barren
4 — Butler
5 — Caldwell
6 — Calloway
7 — Casey
8 — Christian
9 — Cumberland
10 — Graves
11 — Henderson
12 — Hickman
13 — Hopkins
14 — Livingston
15 — Logan
16 — Monroe
17 — Muhlenberg
18 — Simpson
19 — Trigg
20 — Todd
21 — Union
22 — Warren
23 — Wayne

2ND ELECTORAL DISTRICT
(FIVE ELECTED)
24 — Breckinridge
25 — Bullitt
26 — Clay
27 — Daviess
28 — Garrard
29 — Grayson
30 — Green
31 — Hardin
32 — Harlan
33 — Hart
34 — Henry
35 — Jefferson
36 — Knox
37 — Lincoln
38 — Madison
39 — Meade
40 — Mercer
41 — Nelson
42 — Ohio
43 — Oldham
44 — Perry
45 — Pulaski
46 — Rockcastle
47 — Shelby
48 — Washington
49 — Whitley

3RD ELECTORAL DISTRICT
(FIVE ELECTED)
50 — Bath
51 — Boone
52 — Bourbon
53 — Bracken
54 — Campbell
55 — Clark
56 — Estill
57 — Fayette
58 — Fleming
59 — Floyd
60 — Franklin
61 — Gallatin
62 — Grant
63 — Greenup
64 — Jessamine
65 — Harrison
66 — Lawrence
67 — Lewis
68 — Mason
69 — Montgomery
70 — Morgan
71 — Nicholas
72 — Owen
73 — Pendleton
74 — Pike
75 — Scott
76 — Woodford

Maine — 1824

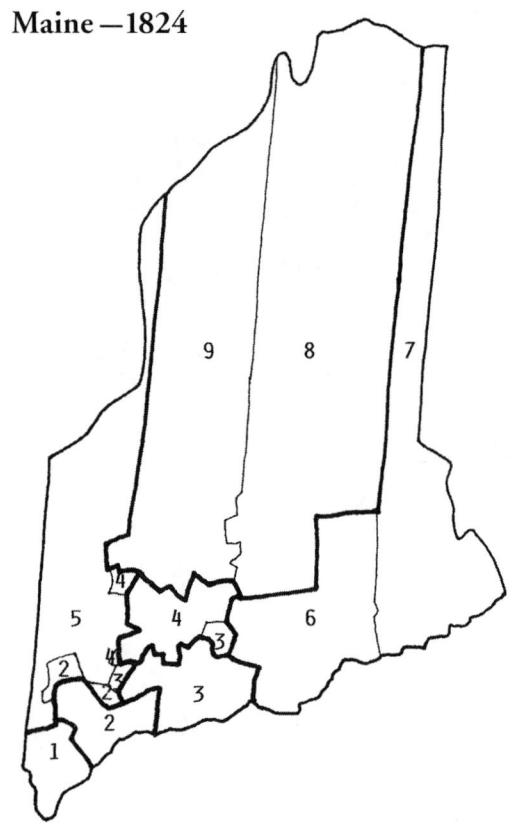

Cumberland County — 1824

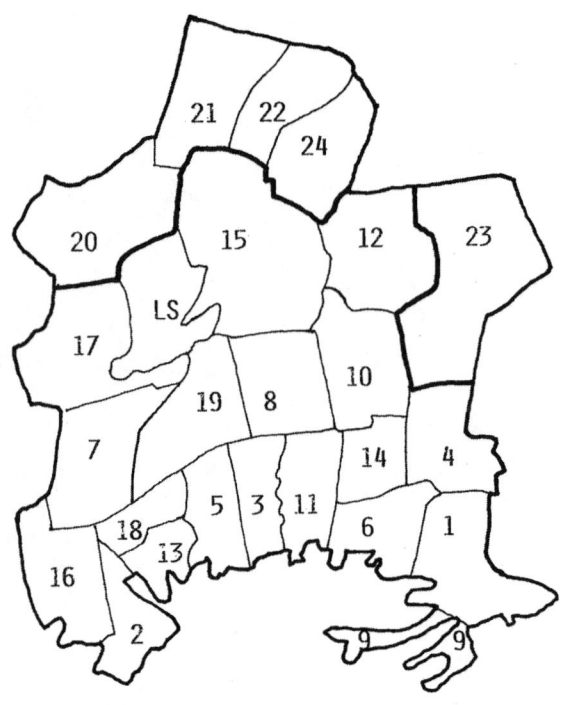

1ST ELECTORAL DISTRICT
1 — York

2ND ELECTORAL DISTRICT
2 — Cumberland (part)

3RD ELECTORAL DISTRICT
3 — Lincoln (part)

4TH ELECTORAL DISTRICT
4 — Kennebec (part)
3 — Lincoln (part)

5TH ELECTORAL DISTRICT
2 — Cumberland (part)
3 — Lincoln (parrt)
4 — Kennebec (part)
5 — Oxford

6TH ELECTORAL DISTRICT
6 — Hancock
7 — Washington

7TH ELECTORAL DISTRICT
8 — Penobscot
9 — Somerset

2ND ELECTORAL DISTRICT
1 — Brunswick
2 — Cape Elizabeth
3 — Cumberland
4 — Durham
5 — Falmouth
6 — Freeport
7 — Gorham
8 — Gray
9 — Harpswell
10 — New Gloucester
11 — North Yarmouth
12 — Poland
13 — Portland
14 — Pownal
15 — Raymond
16 — Scarborough
17 — Standish
18 — Westbrook
19 — Windham
LS- Lake Sebago

5TH ELECTORAL DISTRICT (PART)
20 — Baldwin
21 — Bridgton
22 — Harrison
23 — Minot
24 — Otisfield

Kennebec County — 1824

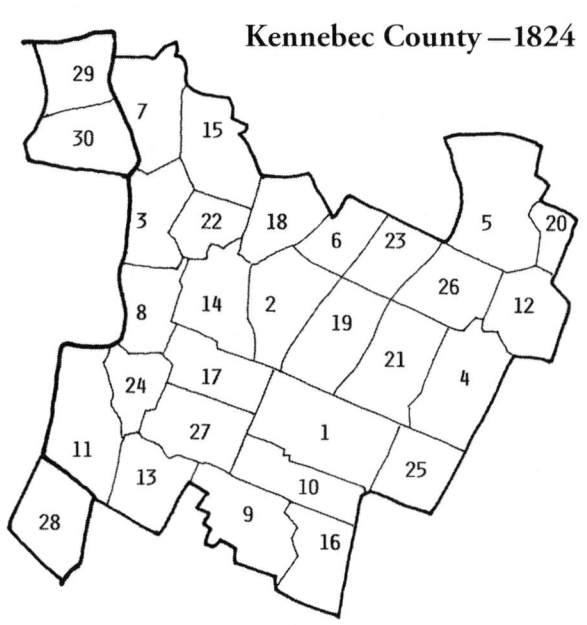

4TH ELECTORAL DISTRICT (PART)
1 — Augusta
2 — Belgrade
3 — Chesterville
4 — China
5 — Clinton
6 — Dearborn
7 — Farmington
8 — Fayette
9 — Gardiner
10 — Hallowell
11 — Leeds
12 — Lygonia
13 — Monmouth
14 — Mount Vernon
15 — New Sharon
16 — Pittstown
17 — Readfield
18 — Rome
19 — Sidney
20 — Unity Plantation
21 — Vasalborough
22 — Vienna
23 — Waterville
24 — Wayne
25 — Windsor
26 — Winslow
27 — Winthrop

5TH ELECTORAL DISTRICT (PART)
28 — Greene
29 — Temple
30 — Wilton

Lincoln County — 1824

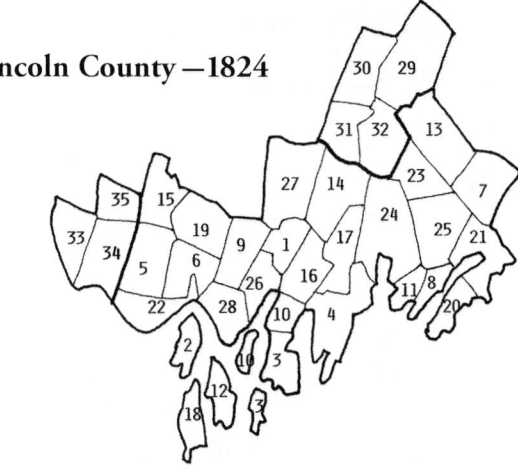

3RD ELECTORAL DISTRICT
1 — Alna
2 — Bath
3 — Boothbay
4 — Bristol
5 — Bowdoin
6 — Bowdoinham
7 — Camden
8 — Cushing
9 — Dresden
10 — Edgecomb
11 — Frienship
12 — Georgetown
13 — Hope
14 — Jefferson
15 — Litchfield
16 — Newcastle
17 — Nobleboro
18 — Phippsburg
19 — Richmond
20 — St. George
21 — Thomaston
22 — Topsham
23 — Union
24 — Waldboro
25 — Warren
26 — Wiscasset
27 — Whitefield
28 — Woolwich

4TH ELECTORAL DISTRICT (PART)
29 — Montville
30 — Palermo
31 — Patricktown Plantation
32 — Washington

5TH ELECTORAL DISTRICT (PART)
33 — Lewiston
34 — Lisbon
35 — Wales

Missouri —1824

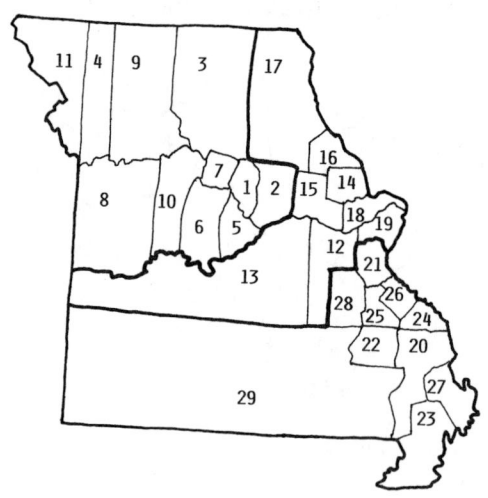

Tennessee —1824

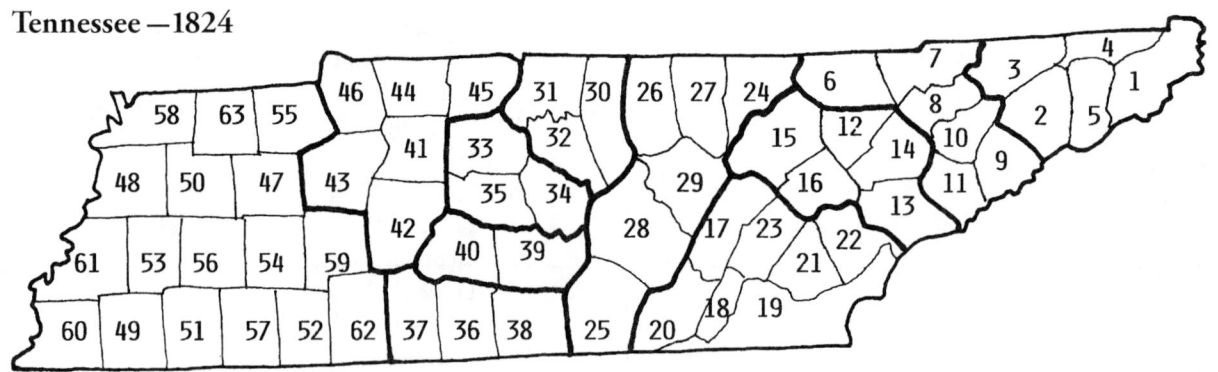

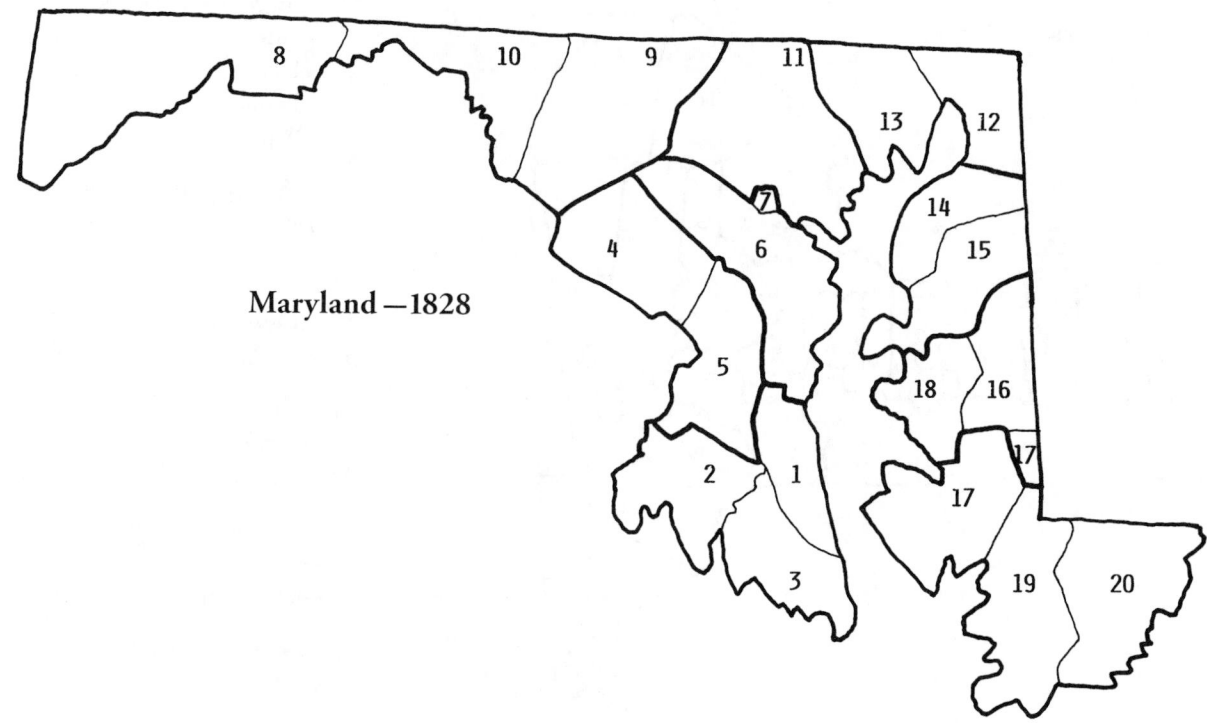

Maryland — 1828

1ST ELECTORAL DISTRICT
  1 — Calvert
  2 — Charles
  3 — St. Mary's

2ND ELECTORAL DISTRICT
  4 — Montgomery
  5 — Prince George's

3RD ELECTORAL DISTRICT (TWO
  ELECTED)
  6 — Anne Arundel
  7 — City of Baltimore

4TH ELECTORAL DISTRICT (TWO
  ELECTED)
  8 — Allegany
  9 — Frederick
  10 — Washington

5TH ELECTORAL DISTRICT
  11 — Baltimore

6TH ELECTORAL DISTRICT
  12 — Cecil
  13 — Harford

7TH ELECTORAL DISTRICT
  14 — Kent
  15 — Queen Anne's

8TH ELECTORAL DISTRICT
  16 — Caroline
  17 — Dorchester (part)
  18 — Talbot

9TH ELECTORAL DISTRICT
  17 — Dorchester (part)
  19 — Somerset
  20 — Worcester

New York — 1828

19TH ELECTORAL DISTRICT
27 — Clinton
28 — Essex
29 — Franklin
30 — Warren

20TH ELECTORAL DISTRICT (TWO ELECTED)
31 — Jefferson
32 — Lewis
33 — Oswego
34 — St. Lawrence

21ST ELECTORAL DISTRICT
35 — Broome
36 — Chenango

22ND ELECTORAL DISTRICT
37 — Cortland
38 — Madison

23RD ELECTORAL DISTRICT
39 — Onondaga

24TH ELECTORAL DISTRICT
40 — Cayuga

25TH ELECTORAL DISTRICT
41 — Tioga
42 — Tompkins

26TH ELECTORAL DISTRICT (TWO ELECTED)
43 — Ontario
44 — Seneca
45 — Wayne
46 — Yates

27TH ELECTORAL DISTRICT
47 — Livingston
48 — Monroe

28TH ELECTORAL DISTRICT
49 — Allegany
50 — Cattaraugus
51 — Steuben

29TH ELECTORAL DISTRICT
52 — Genesee
53 — Orleans

30TH ELECTORAL DISTRICT
54 — Chautauqua
55 — Erie
56 — Niagara

1ST ELECTORAL DISTRICT
1 — Queens
2 — Suffolk

2ND ELECTORAL DISTRICT
3 — King
4 — Richmond
5 — Rockland

3RD ELECTORAL DISTRICT (THREE ELECTED)
6 — New York

4TH ELECTORAL DISTRICT
7 — Putnam
8 — Westchester

5TH ELECTORAL DISTRICT
9 — Dutchess

6TH ELECTORAL DISTRICT
10 — Orange

7TH ELECTORAL DISTRICT
11 — Sullivan
12 — Ulster

8TH ELECTORAL DISTRICT
13 — Columbia

9TH ELECTORAL DISTRICT
14 — Rensselaer

10TH ELECTORAL DISTRICT
15 — Albany

11TH ELECTORAL DISTRICT
16 — Delaware
17 — Greene

12TH ELECTORAL DISTRICT
18 — Schenectady
19 — Schoharie

13TH ELECTORAL DISTRICT
20 — Otsego

14TH ELECTORAL DISTRICT
21 — Oneida

15TH ELECTORAL DISTRICT
22 — Herkimer

16TH ELECTORAL DISTRICT
23 — Hamilton
24 — Montgomery

17TH ELECTORAL DISTRICT
25 — Saratoga
18th Electoral District
26 — Washington

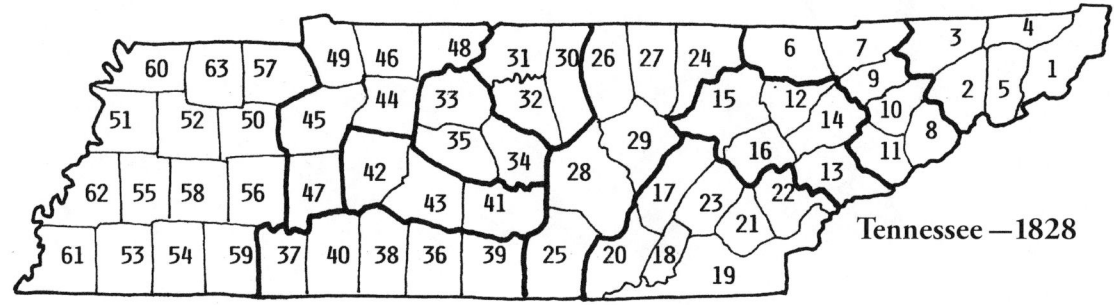

Tennessee—1828

1ST ELECTORAL DISTRICT
1 — Carter
2 — Greene
3 — Hawkins
4 — Sullivan
5 — Washington

2ND ELECTORAL DISTRICT
6 — Campbell
7 — Claiborne
8 — Cocke
9 — Grainger
10 — Jefferson
11 — Sevier

3RD ELECTORAL DISTRICT
12 — Anderson
13 — Blount
14 — Knox
15 — Morgan
16 — Roane

4TH ELECTORAL DISTRICT
17 — Bledsoe
18 — Hamilton
19 — Indian Lands
20 — Marion
21 — McMinn
22 — Monroe
23 — Rhea

5TH ELECTORAL DISTRICT
24 — Fentress
25 — Franklin
26 — Jackson
27 — Overton
28 — Warren
29 — White

6TH ELECTORAL DISTRICT
30 — Smith
31 — Sumner
32 — Wilson

7TH ELECTORAL DISTRICT
33 — Davidson
34 — Rutherford
35 — Williamson

8TH ELECTORAL DISTRICT
36 — Giles
37 — Hardin
38 — Wayne
39 — Lincoln
40 — Wayne

9TH ELECTORAL DISTRICT
41 — Bedford
42 — Hickman
43 — Maury

10TH ELECTORAL DISTRICT
44 — Dickson
45 — Humphreys
46 — Montgomery
47 — Perry
48 — Robertson
49 — Stewart

11TH ELECTORAL DISTRICT
50 — Carroll
51 — Dyer
52 — Gibson
53 — Fayette
54 — Hardeman
55 — Haywood
56 — Henderson
57 — Henry
58 — Madison
59 — Mc Nairy
60 — Obion
61 — Shelby
62 — Tipton
63 — Weakley

1ST ELECTORAL DISTRICT
(FOUR ELECTED)
1 — Allegany
2 — Anne Arundel
3 — Calvert
4 — Charles
5 — Frederick
6 — Montgomery
7 — Prince George's
8 — St. Mary's
9 — Washington

2ND ELECTORAL DISTRICT
(TWO ELECTED)
10 — City of Baltimore

3RD ELECTORAL DISTRICT
11 — Baltimore

4TH ELECTORAL DISTRICT
(THREE ELECTED)
12 — Caroline
13 — Cecil
14 — Dorcester
15 — Harford
16 — Kent
17 — Queen Anne's
18 — Somerset
19 — Talbot
20 — Worcester

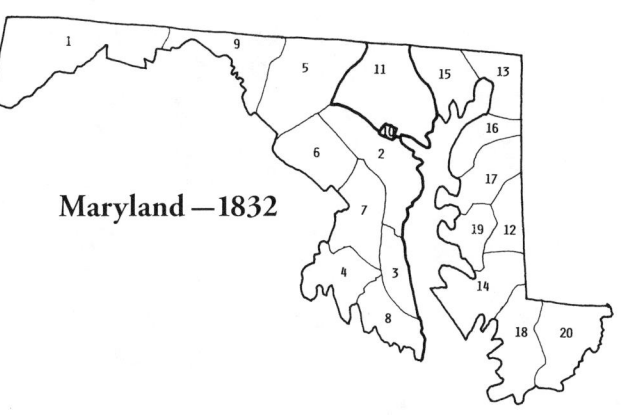

Maryland—1832

BIBLIOGRAPHY

Books and Government Documents

Adler, Howard, and Vincent A. Lacey, *Illinois Election Returns 1818–1990*. Carbondale: Southern Illinois University Press, 1993.

Atkins, Jonathan M. *Parties, Politics, and the Sectional Conflict in Tennessee 1832–1861*. Knoxville: University of Tennessee Press, 1997.

Bouton, Nathaniel, et al. *Documents and Records Relating to New Hampshire*, Vol. 21.

Burnham, W. Dean. *Presidential Ballots 1836–1892*. New York: Arno Press, 1976 (reprint edition).

Coleman, John F. *The Disruption of the Pennsylvania Democracy 1848–1860*. Harrisburg: Pennsylvania Historical and Museum Commission, 1975.

(Delaware) *Governor's Register, 1810–1851*.

Delaware History, April 1970.

Diamond, Robert A. (ed.) *Guide to U. S. Elections*, 1st ed. Washington, D.C.: Congressional Quarterly, 1975.

Donoghue, James R. *How Wisconsin Voted 1848–1872*, 3d ed. Madison: Institute of Governmental Affairs, University of Wisconsin, 1974.

Eure, Thad (Secretary of State). *North Carolina Government 1585–1979*. Raleigh: 1979.

Everton, George B. *The Handy Book for Genealogists*, 6th ed. Logan, Utah: Everton Publishers, 1971.

(Georgia) *Executive Council Minutes of Georgia*.

____. *History of Erie County, Pennsylvania*. Chicago: Worcester Beers & Co., 1884.

Havel, James T. *U. S. Presidential Candidates and the Elections,* Vol. 2. New York: Prentice-Hall, 1996.

Higginbotham, Sanford W. *The Keystone in the Democratic Arch: Pennsylvania Politics 1800–1816*. Harrisburg: Pennsylvania Historical and Museum Commission, 1952.

Holt, Michael F. *The Rise and Fall of the American Whig Party*. New York: Oxford University Press, 1999.

Jensen, Merrill, and Robert Becker (eds.). *Documentary History of the First Federal Elections 1788–1790*, Vol. 1. Madison: University of Wisconsin Press, 1976.

Maine Legislative Documents, Augusta, ME.

Matthias, Benjamin. *Politician's Register*. Philadelphia: 1835.

McCarthy, L. P. *The Annual Statistician and Economist, 1891*. San Francisco: 1891.

McCormick, Richard. *The Second American Party System*. Chapel Hill: University of North Carolina Press, 1966.

McQuown, Ruth, and Jasper B. Shannon. *Presidential Politics in Kentucky 1824–1948*. Lexington: University of Kentucky Press, 1950.

Michigan Manual, 1877, 1913.

Murray, Paul. *The Whig Party in Georgia, 1825–1853*. Chapel Hill: University of North Carolina Press, 1948.

New Hampshire Manual, 1889, 1917 (Secretary of State, Concord).

Ohio Election Statistics 1985–6. (Secretary of State, Columbus)

(Ohio) Executive Documents 1865, Columbus: 1866.

Onstine, Burton W. *Oregon Votes: 1858–1972*. Salem: Oregon Historical Society, 1973.

Pease, Theodore (ed.). *Illinois Election Returns 1818–1848*. Springfield: Illinois State Historical Society Library, 1923.

(Pennsylvania) *Journal of the Senate of the Commonwealth of Pennsylvania*, Harrisburg: 1849.

(Pennsylvania) *Legislative Documents of the Commonwealth of Pennsylvania*, Harrisburg: 1857.

Petersen, Svend. *A Statistical History of the American Presidential Elections*. New York: Frederick Ungar Publishing Co., 1963.

____. *Political Textbook for 1860*. Tribune Association, New York: 1860.

(Rhode Island) *Acts and Resolves of the General Assembly, 1801–4*. Providence.

Riker, Dorothy F., and Gayle Thornbrough (eds.). *Indiana Election Returns 1816–1851*. Indianapolis: Indiana Historical Bureau, 1960.

Storey, Henry W. *History of Cambria County* [Pennsylvania], Vol. 1.

(Texas) *Governor's Register*.

Tinckom, Harry M. *The Republicans and Federalists in Pennsylvania 1790–1801*. Harrisburg: Pennsylvania Historical and Museum Commission, 1950.

Whig/Tribune Almanac 1844–1860. Tribune Association, New York.

White Bruce M. *Minnesota Votes*. St. Paul: Minnesota Historical Society, 1977.

Willis, John T. *Presidential Elections in Maryland*. Mount Airy, MD: Lomond Publications, 1984.

Newspapers (by State)

Arkansas
Little Rock   *Arkansas Gazette*

California
San Francisco   *Daily Alta*

Delaware
Wilmington   *Delaware Gazette*

Florida
Tallahassee   *The Floridian*

Georgia
Augusta   *Augusta Chronicle*
                 Constitutionalist
Milledgeville   *Journal*
                 Southern Journal
                 Southern Recorder
Savannah   *Daily Republican*

Indiana
Indianapolis   *Indiana Daily Sentinel*

Iowa
Iowa City   *Iowa Capitol Reporter*
                 Iowa Republican

Kentucky
Bardstown   *Western American*
Frankfort   *Argus*
                 Argus of Western America
                 Commonwealth
                 Palladium
                 Tri-Weekly Commonwealth
                 Western Argus
Lancaster   *Intelligencer & Weekly Advertiser*
                 Political Theatre
Lexington   *Kentucky Gazette*
                 Kentucky Statesman
                 Observer & Reporter
                 Reporter
                 Western Monitor
Louisville   *Daily Journal*
                 Daily Louisville Public Advertiser

Louisiana
New Orleans   *Daily Picayune*
                 Louisiana Courier
                 New Orleans Bee

Maine
Augusta   *Kennebec Journal*
Portland   *Eastern Argus*
Rockland   *Rockland Democrat*

Mississippi
Jackson   *Mississippian*
Natchez   *Statesman & Gazette*
Vicksburg   *Advocate & Register*

Missouri
Columbia   *Missouri Intelligencer*
Jefferson City   *Jeffersonian*
                 Jefferson Enquirer
St. Louis   *Missouri Republican*

New Hampshire
Concord   *Courier of New Hampshire*
Portsmouth   *Portsmouth Phoenix*

New Jersey
Newark   *Sentinel of Freedom*
Trenton   *New Jersey State Gazette*
                 True American

New York
Albany   *Albany Argus*
Norwich   *Norwch Journal*
Plattsburgh   *Plattsburgh Republican*

North Carolina
New Bern   *Morning Herald*
Raleigh   *Minerva*
                 Raleigh Register
Washington   *Washington Gazette & Weekly Advertiser*

Ohio
Columbus   *Ohio State Journal*
Sandusky   *The Clarion*

Pennsylvania
Harrisburg   *Democratic Union*
                 Intelligencer
                 Patriot & Union
                 Pennsylvania Reporter & State Journal
                 Pennsylvania Republican
                 Reporter & Democratic Herald Telegraph
Lancaster   *Intelligencer*
                 Journal
Philadelphia   *Aurora*
                 Democratic Press

	General Advertiser	Knoxville	*Knoxville Enquirer*
	Press	Nashville	*American*
Troy	*Democratic Analyzer*		*Daily Union*
Uniontown	*Genius of Liberty*		*Nashville Gazette*
			National Banner & Nashville Whig
Rhode Island			*Republican*
Newport	*Newport Mercury*		*True Whig*
	Rhode Island Republican		*Whig*
Providence	*Columbian Phenix*	Sparta	*The Review*
	Providence Daily Partiot		
	Impartial Observer	**Virginia**	
	Providence Journal	Richmond	*Enquirer*
			Richmond Examiner
Tennessee			
Clarksville	*Clarksville Gazette*	**Wisconsin**	
Fayetteville	*Village Messenger*	Madison	*State Journal*
Jackson	*Jackson Gazette*		

ELECTORAL CANDIDATES INDEX

This index lists those who were candidates for presidential elector followed by the state they sought election from and the year of their candidacy.

Adair, Alexander (KY) 1816
Adams, Samuel (MA) 1796
Alexander, James (KY) 1820
Allen, James (KY) 1804
Allen, Joseph (MA) 1796
Anderson, William E. (TN) 1824
Avery, Isaac (VA) 1788/9

Bacon, Ebenezer (MA) 1796
Badger, Joseph (NH) 1796
Baker, Abner (KY) 1820
Baker, Samuel (MA) 1792
Baldwin, Loammi (MA) 1796
Banning, John D. (D) 1788/9
Bartlett, Bailey (MA) 1796
Bartlett, Josiah (NH) 1792
Baylor, Walker (KY) 1816
Beatte, Adam (KY) 1820
Bedford, George (D) 1788/9
Bellows, Benjamin (NH) 1792, 1796
Bellows, Thomas (NH) 1796
Benton, Jesse (TN) 1824
Berryman, Josiah (KY) 1820
Bibb, Richard (KY) 1804
Bigelow, Daniel (MA) 1796
Bishop, Phanuel (MA) 1792
Blackburn, Thomas (VA) 1792
Bland, Theodorick (VA) 1792
Bledsoe, Jesse (KY) 1820
Bount, Willie (TN) 1824
Bodley, Thomas (KY) 1804, 1808, 1816, 1820
Brooks, Eleazur, (MA) 1788/9
Brooks, John (MA) 1788/9
Broole, Charles (P) 1796
Brown, Elias (MD) 1832
Brown, Joseph, (TN) 1824
Brown, Richard C. (TN) 1824
Burdett, Giles (TN) 1824

Cabell, William (VA) 1788/9
Cabot, George (MA) 1788/9
Caldwell, David (KY) 1808, 1816, 1820
Campbell, Charles (IL) 1820
Campbell, William (IL) 1820
Carr, Walter (KY) 1808
Carrington, Edward (VA) 1788/9
Chambers, James (KY) 1820
Chapline, Abraham (KY) 1820
Cilley, Joseph (NH) 1788/9, 1892
Clark, Spencer (TN) 1824

Clay, Thomas (KY) 1808
Coburn, John (KY) 1804
Coffey, Richard N. (KY) 1820
Cogswell, Thomas (NH) 1792
Colb, David (MA) 1788/9
Coleman, Robert (P) 1796
Coney, Daniel (MA) 1788/9, 1792, 1796
Cosby, Fortonatus (KY) 1804
Crosby, Dabney C. (KY) 1820
Crutcher, James (KY) 1806, 1816, 1820
Cushing, Nathaniel (MA) 1788/9
Cutts, Edward (MA) 1792

Dana, Francis (MA) 1788/9, 1792
Darke, William (VA) 1788/9
Davidge, Henry (KY) 1804
Davies, Thomas (MA) 1788/9, 1792, 1796
Daviess, Joseph H. (KY) 1804
Davis, Caleb (MA) 1788/9
Devins, Richard (MA) 1792
Dickson, Joseph (TN) 1820
Dixon, Tilman (TN) 1824
Dougherty, Michael (KY) 1820
Dudley, John (NH) 1788/9
Dupont, Charles H. (F) 1848
Dwight, Elijah (MA) 1788/9, 1792
Dyer, Robert H. (TN) 1824

Edgar, John (IL) 1820
Edwards, Ninian (KY) 1804
Ely, Justin (MA) 1796
Ewing, Ephraim M. (KY) 1820
Ewing, Robert (KY) 1804, 1808, 1816

Farrar, Timothy (NH) 1792, 1796
Fillmore, Millard (P) 1856
Fitzhugh, William (VA) 1788
Folsom, Nathaniel (NH) 1788/9
Foster, Dwight (MA) 1792
Foster, Jabez (MA) 1788/9
Fowler, Samuel (MA) 1788/9
Freeman, Jonathan (NH) 1792
Freeman, Solomon (NH) 1792, 1796
Frémont, John (P) 1856

Garrard, James (KY) 1804
Gerry, Elbridge (MA) 1796
Gilchrist, Robert (VA) 1788/9
Gill, Moses (MA) 1788/9, 1792, 1796
Gilman, Benjamin (NH) 1788/9

Gilman, John T. (NH) 1792, 1796
Goodhue, Benjamin (MA) 1788/9
Goodhue, Nathaniel (MA) 1788/9
Goodwin, Ichabad (MA) 1796
Graham, John (TN) 1824
Grayson, Robert H. (KY) 1804, 1808
Green, Willis (KY) 1804, 1812
Greenup, Christopher (KY) 1804, 1808
Guy, Henry (VA) 1788/9

Hall, Benjamin (MA) 1788/9
Hall, John (KY) 1804, 1808
Hall, Josiah, (TN) 1824
Hardin, Martin D. (IL) 1820
Harle, Baldwin (TN) 1824
Harwie, John (VA) 1788/9
Hastings, John (MA) 1788/9
Henry, Patrick (VA) 1788/9
Henry, William (P) 1792
Henshaw, Samuel (MS) 1788/9
Henshawing, Samuel (MA) 1792
Hogg, Samuel (TN) 1824
Holten, Samuel (MA) 1788/9, 1792
Hopkins, Samuel (KY) 1808
Howard, Cornelius, (MD) 1832
Howard, Tilghman (TN) 1824
Hubbard, Adolphus F. (KY) 1820
Hunt, Ebenezer, (MA) 1788/9, 1796

Irwin, Thomas (KY) 1804
Irvine, William (KY) 1804, 1808, 1812, 1816

Jarvis, Charles (MA) 1792
Johnson, James (KY) 1820
Johnston, Zachariah (VA) 1788/9
Jones, Joseph (VA) 1788/9
Jones, Michael (KY) 1820
Jovitt, John (KY) 1816

Kello, Samuel (VA) 1788/9
Kimmel, Peter (IL) 1820
King, John E. (KY) 1820
Kinney, William (IL) 1820
Kinsley, Martin (MA) 1792
Kinstry, Martin (MA) 1788/9

Larned, Simon (MA) 1796
Leathers, Benjamin W. (KY) 1820
Lee, Willis A. (KY) 1816
Leonard, Zephaniah (MA) 1796

PRESIDENTIAL AND VICE PRESIDENTIAL CANDIDATES INDEX

This index is list of all presidential and vice presidential candidates including the years of their candidacy. All candidates are considered presidential candidates through 1800. Vice presidential candidates are separately identified, beginning with 1804, by the italicization of the years in which they ran for the office.